Richard Waymire,

Program Manager, SQL Server Development,
Microsoft Corporation

Rick Sawtell,

MCT, MCSD

Teach Yourself

Microsoft® SQL
Server™ 7.0
in 21 Days

SAMS

A Division of Macmillan Computer Publishing
201 West 103rd St., Indianapolis, Indiana, 46290 USA

Sams Teach Yourself Microsoft® SQL Server™ 7.0 in 21 Days

Copyright © 1999 by Sams Publishing

International Standard Book Number: 0-672-31290-5

Library of Congress Catalog Card Number: 98-84447

Printed in the United States of America

First Printing: December 1998

00 99 98   4 3 2 1

Trademarks

All terms mentioned in this book that are known to be trademarks or service marks have been appropriately capitalized. Sams Publishing cannot attest to the accuracy of this information. Use of a term in this book should not be regarded as affecting the validity of any trademark or service mark. Microsoft is a registered trademark of Microsoft Corporation. SQL Server is a trademark of Microsoft Corporation.

Warning and Disclaimer

Every effort has been made to make this book as complete and as accurate as possible, but no warranty or fitness is implied. The information provided is on an "as is" basis. The authors and the publisher shall have neither liability nor responsibility to any person or entity with respect to any loss or damages arising from the information contained in this book.

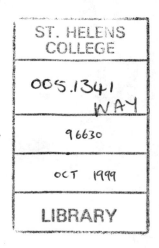
EXECUTIVE EDITOR
Rosemarie Graham

ACQUISITIONS EDITOR
Rosemarie Graham

DEVELOPMENT EDITOR
Marla Reece-Hall

MANAGING EDITOR
Jodi Jensen

PROJECT EDITOR
Tonya Simpson

COPY EDITOR
Sarah Burkhart

INDEXER
Bruce Clingaman

PROOFREADER
Mona Brown

TECHNICAL EDITOR
Matt Larson

TEAM COORDINATOR
Carol Ackerman

INTERIOR DESIGN
Gary Adair

COVER DESIGN
Aren Howell

LAYOUT TECHNICIANS
Ayanna Lacey
Heather Hiatt Miller
Amy Parker

What's New in *Sams Teach Yourself Microsoft SQL Server 7.0 in 21 Days*

With Microsoft's newest version of its enterprise-level relational database management system, SQL Server 7.0, come many new features and improvements, including new administrative tools and a desktop installation. Throughout the step-by-step guides in this book, you'll leverage new wizards and graphical dialog boxes to create database objects, set permissions, and manage your database—along with traditional coding methods. The following are some of the features and new tools you'll learn to use.

On Day 1, "Introduction to SQL Server 7.0 and Relational Databases," you'll learn the behind-the-scenes changes in the structure and architecture of this release. On Day 2, "Installing SQL Server 7.0," you'll learn important information and the steps to install SQL Server with both Windows NT and the Windows 95/98 platforms.

Day 3, "Using the SQL Server 7.0 Tools and Utilities," outlines the features of such tools as the Query Analyzer and the improvements to SQL Server Enterprise Manager.

Day 4, "Using SQL Server 7.0 Data Transformation Services," shows you how to use this utility to move, update, and alter data for importing or exporting.

Although SQL Server 7.0 offers wizards and improved graphical tools to help make replication easier, many DBAs still find this process difficult to manage. Days 17, "Understanding Replication Design and Methodologies," and 18, "Implementing Replication Methodologies," offer expanded coverage to help make the planning phase and the process easier to follow.

Day 19, "Using the SQL Server Agent," helps you take advantage of this powerful management tool to automate your administration tasks with scheduling and mail messaging.

On Day 20, "Configuring and Monitoring SQL Server 7.0, you'll use the SQL Server Profiler and the Index Tuning Wizard to monitor, tune, and optimize your database's performance.

Contents at a Glance

Contents

About the Authors

RICHARD WAYMIRE is a program manager with the SQL Server development team at Microsoft. He is also a Microsoft Certified Trainer, Solution Developer, and Systems Engineer + Internet. He is the immediate past president of the Pacific NorthWest SQL Server User's Group. Richard was a SQL Server trainer before joining Microsoft, although he has also focused on training and consulting on Windows NT and other BackOffice and development technologies. He is still a database administrator at heart. Richard can be reached at rwaymir@ibm.net.

RICK SAWTELL is both a Microsoft Certified Solutions Developer and a Microsoft Certified Trainer. He owns his own consulting firm based in the southwestern United States and currently consults, trains, and writes computer books on several Microsoft products. He has over 13 years of experience in the consulting and programming arena, with an emphasis on database front-end and back-end development. Rick can be reached at Quickening@email.msn.com.

Dedication

This book is dedicated to SQL Server professionals—both the experienced and the newly ordained. SQL Server 7.0 is a FANTASTIC database, and you will never regret learning about it with this book.

Acknowledgments

I would like to thank Rick for all his hard work. Writing a book is truly a labor of love—and just a few late-night phone calls to your coauthor. I also think Marla, Tonya, and Rosemarie did a great job, especially in light of the fact that this book was written during the beta, with everything changing while we wrote.

I'd also like to thank all the wonderful folks on the SQL Server team at Microsoft, who have patiently put up with my questions, bug reports, and queries (pardon the pun) while writing this book.

This project (like any extracurricular project) has been hardest on my family. My wife, Tracy, and two children (including the one added while writing this book) have been extremely patient and understanding. I couldn't have done it without their love and understanding. I dedicate this book to my daughter, Kathryn—Daddy is done now, and now I can go push you on the swing. Thanks for understanding, even though you were too young for me to expect that of you! And Rick is right—no dedication is complete without thanking your parents… Mom, thanks for everything! You KNOW I couldn't have done it without you.

—Richard

I would like to thank Richard for doing such a wonderful job with this book. I would also like to thank the staff at Sams Publishing for keeping everything together. When you have 25 or so elements of a book running around, along with hundreds of screen shots, it can get crazy. Marla and Rosemarie, you did a fantastic job.

I've got to say thanks to my wonderful wife, Melissa. I thought being a computer geek was hard, but I can't imagine trying to be married to one! You are absolutely fantastic.

Of course, no acknowledgment would be complete without thanking my parents. You did an excellent job!

—Rick

Tell Us What You Think!

As the reader of this book, *you* are our most important critic and commentator. We value your opinion and want to know what we're doing right, what we could do better, what areas you'd like to see us publish in, and any other words of wisdom you're willing to pass our way.

As the Executive Editor for the Database Team at Macmillan Computer Publishing, I welcome your comments. You can fax, email, or write me directly to let me know what you did or didn't like about this book—as well as what we can do to make our books stronger.

Please note that I cannot help you with technical problems related to the topic of this book, and that due to the high volume of mail I receive, I might not be able to reply to every message.

When you write, please be sure to include this book's title and author as well as your name and phone or fax number. I will carefully review your comments and share them with the author and editors who worked on the book.

Fax:	317-817-7070
Email:	databases@mcp.com
Mail:	Rosemarie Graham
	Executive Editor
	Database Team
	Macmillan Computer Publishing
	201 West 103rd Street
	Indianapolis, IN 46290 USA

Introduction

Welcome to *Sams Teach Yourself Microsoft SQL Server 7.0 in 21 Days*. We hope this book will help not only teach you about SQL Server but also prove valuable for everyday work involving SQL Server. We have worked hard to see that the skills you learn from this book will easily translate into real-world methods and solutions.

There are certain skills you need to successfully install, administer, troubleshoot, and configure SQL Server. The kinds of skills you must know can be divided into two general categories:

- SQL Server programmer
- SQL Server administrator

 Note   In a small company, the developer, programmer, and administrator might be the same person; large companies usually have the functions separate.

A SQL Server developer is generally responsible for designing, programming, and populating the database. *Sams Teach Yourself Transact-SQL in 21 Days* is a great place to start for beginning SQL programmers. After the database has been created, responsibility for the database is often turned over to an administrator, who takes care of the ongoing maintenance.

A SQL Server administrator is usually responsible for the day-to-day administration of the database. This book is designed more for administrators, although many lessons apply to programmers as well. Although some administrators might never have to do any SQL programming, we have these lessons in enough detail so that administrators can begin to pick up on SQL programming if they want to. Programming tasks covered here relate to skills administrators might be called on to perform—such as creating tables, creating indexes, and writing complex queries.

About This Book

This book is designed to teach you to become a SQL Server administrator. It has been divided into 21 lessons, which you can do in 21 days. Although some lessons are longer than others, no lesson should take more than four hours—the average is about two hours.

This book starts with the basics of SQL Server and progresses through various skills and techniques a SQL Server administrator needs to perform his or her job. We wrote this book with the beginner in mind—we have tried very hard to explain not only what to do, but also why it should be done.

This book includes 21 lessons designed to teach you the skills necessary to become proficient in SQL Server. The lessons are composed of roughly 21 equal days of instruction. Because the lessons build on each other, it is important that you go through them in order, or at least understand what is in a given day's lesson if you skip over it. The following section discusses the lessons contained in this book and the skills you will learn.

Week 1's Lessons

Week 1's lessons are about SQL Server and building databases. It is a week of fundamentals, when you will lay the groundwork for the more detailed discussions found in Week 2 and Week 3.

During Week 1, the actual days' lessons, and the skills you will learn, are as follows:

- Day 1, "Introduction to SQL Server 7.0 and Relational Databases"—You learn about SQL Server and what makes up a relational database. You also learn about the history of SQL Server.

- Day 2, "Installing SQL Server 7.0"—You learn the requirements for SQL Server, how to install it, and some simple configuration settings for both Windows 9x and a Windows NT installation.

- Day 3, "Using the SQL Server 7.0 Tools and Utilities"—You learn about the tools and utilities that ship with SQL Server and when to best use them.

- Day 4, "Creating and Implementing Databases, Files, and Filegroups"—You learn details about how SQL Server stores databases and how to create, edit, and delete databases and database files. Filegroups are beyond the scope of this book, but you learn a brief explanation of their use and utility.

- Day 5, "Using SQL Server Login and User Security"—You learn how to add login accounts to SQL Server and how to create users and roles for each database.

- Day 6, "Working with Permissions"—You learn how to assign permissions to users and roles inside SQL Server. You also learn what permissions the default system and database roles contain.

- Day 7, "Implementing Backups in SQL Server 7.0"—In this chapter, you learn how to handle one of the most important tasks in SQL Server—creating and saving backups of your databases and transaction logs.

Week 2's Lessons

The second week expands on the foundation of skills and understanding you built in the first seven days of this book. This week is geared toward retrieving and manipulating your data. Here are details on individual lessons.

- Day 8, "Restoring SQL Server Databases"—In this chapter you learn how to recover and restore your databases in SQL Server. You also learn some strategies to keep in mind when you are developing your emergency procedures.

- Day 9, "Creating Tables"—On this day you learn about the different data types that make up the fields in a table. You then learn how to combine those data types to create new tables in your databases.

- Day 10, "Using SQL Server 7.0 Data Transformation Services"—In this chapter you learn how to move data into and out of SQL Server and other OLE DB data sources.

- Day 11, "Retrieving Data with Queries"—On this day you learn the ins and outs of using SELECT statements to gather data and manipulate your data. You also learn some more advanced queries using data aggregation as well as correlated sub-queries.

- Day 12, "Data Modification with Queries"—In this chapter, you learn how to modify data using the INSERT, UPDATE, and DELETE statements.

- Day 13, "Enhancing Performance with Indexing"—You learn how to plan and build indexes so that queries run more efficiently.

- Day 14, "Ensuring Data Integrity"—You learn techniques to ensure that your data stays reliable, accurate, and consistent. The concepts presented in this lesson are often referred to as DRI (declarative referential integrity).

Week 3's Lessons

The third week contains various advanced topics dealing with SQL Server.

- Day 15, "Working with Views, Stored Procedures, and Triggers"—You learn the uses of and how to create views, stored procedures, and triggers.

- Day 16, "Programming SQL Server 7.0"—You learn how to use the programming features of SQL Server. This lesson is an excellent introduction to the programming concepts related to SQL Server 7.0.

- Day 17, "Understanding Replication Design and Methodologies"—In this lesson you learn the concepts of replication, the terminology, and the various styles and methods you can use to set up replication.

- Day 18, "Implementing Replication Methodologies"—In this lesson you learn how to implement replication from both a publisher and a subscriber.
- Day 19, "Using the SQL Server Agent"—You can use the SQL Server Agent to automate many of the tasks in SQL Server.
- Day 20, "Configuring and Monitoring SQL Server 7.0"—Although SQL Server is said to be self-tuning, it is still good to understand what the different configuration options actually accomplish in your SQL Server database.
- Day 21, "Integrating SQL Server and the World Wide Web"—You learn various methods to integrate SQL Server with the Internet.

Who Should Read This Book?

This book assumes no prior SQL Server knowledge. If you have already had some exposure to SQL Server, you will only be the better for it.

Windows NT experience, although not required, is useful when dealing with SQL Server because many of the optional features of SQL Server require interaction with Windows NT. If you find your Windows NT experience lacking, try reading *Sams Teach Yourself NT in 14 days*, also by Sams Publishing.

Conventions Used in This Book

Although SQL Server is not case sensitive, we have put commands in the format shown as follows. Also note that most Transact-SQL (the language of SQL Server) is shown in all capital letters. We did this to show you which words are Transact-SQL reserved words and which words are parameters.

CREATE DATABASE

Occasionally, we show you output or code generated by SQL Server. This code might not follow the same capitalization that our code does, but you should be able to recognize the same keywords.

 You'll find new terms marked with this icon for quick reference—especially if you're looking for the definition as a reference from the page number in the index.

Look for the Input and Output icons to practice using examples of code. Also notice that we use a code continuation character ➥ to denote that a line had to be broken to fit the width of the printed page. Just treat such instances as you would one long line as you type.

 The Analysis icon denotes the explanation of code.

Note You'll find helpful information set off in boxes like this one. Watch for helpful pointers (tips), and pay particular attention to the cautions.

WEEK 1

At a Glance

In this first week, you are going to learn enough information on Microsoft SQL Server 7.0 to enable you to do some light database administration and some initial database design.

Day 1 introduces you to SQL Server and gives you some background information on relational database and design. On Day 2 you actually install SQL Server and examine several setup options.

Day 3 covers the tools and utilities that come packaged with SQL Server. These tools are used extensively for the rest of your career with SQL Server.

Day 4 covers storage. You'll learn about databases, files, and filegroups. On Day 5 you learn how to examine the process of securing your SQL Server system, including creating logins and database users.

Day 6 discusses the creation and management of database roles and the permissions that can be granted to these database users and roles.

Day 7 begins one of the most important aspects of working with any database, backups. We authors have often been called paranoid due to the amount of importance we place on database backups (and restorations). Then again, we have never been released from a company because our database was unrecoverable. This chapter outlines the database backup process and some tips for keeping your job.

1

2

3

4

5

6

7

This might seem a little overwhelming at first, but relax. This book was intended for you. You will take each new concept from a solid fundamental principle and then add new concepts to it each day. For this reason, it is important that you do all the exercises at the end of each day. This will reinforce the fundamentals and give you a good foundation on which to build the other two weeks.

DAY 1

Introduction to SQL Server 7.0 and Relational Databases

Today's lesson starts with background material on SQL Server and Windows (both Windows 9x and Windows NT). You then look at databases and what makes up a client/server environment. Databases and their contents are the next subject. Finally, you end the lesson with a look at designing databases. Your exercise for this day is to go through a simulated interview with a client and look at a design for a simple database.

SQL Server Is Hot!

SQL Server 7.0 is Microsoft's flagship database engine product. It is generating huge amounts of interest and excitement in the market. Microsoft is committed to investing large amounts of money in support and marketing of the product and is counting on SQL Server 7.0 to become the premier database engine in the computing industry for the Windows NT platform.

Microsoft has entered the database market with a very strong product in SQL Server 7.0. SQL Server can run on either Windows NT (4.0 or later) or Windows 95/98. SQL Server's price/performance records have allowed many companies to have the power of an RDBMS (Relational Database Management System) for a fraction of the cost of just a few years ago. Microsoft continues to develop and market SQL Server, which should continue this trend for many years.

Microsoft's SQL Server has sold millions of copies since it was first introduced. The current version is 7.0, which was released in late 1998. Before taking a closer look at SQL Server 7.0 and learning how to use it, you'll find that the history of SQL Server is worth looking at.

Tip

The location of up-to-the minute news and support for SQL Server is `http://www.microsoft.com/sql/`.

The History of SQL Server

IBM invented a computer language back in the 1970s designed specifically for database queries called SEQUEL, which stood for Structured English Query Language. Over time the language has been added to, so that it is not just a language for queries but can also be used to build databases and manage security of the database engine. IBM released SEQUEL into the public domain, where it became known as SQL. Because of this heritage you can pronounce it as "sequel" or spell it out as "S-Q-L" when talking about it. Various versions of SQL are used in today's database engines. Microsoft SQL Server uses a version called Transact-SQL. Although you will use Transact-SQL in this book and learn the basics of the language, the emphasis in this book is on installing, maintaining, and connecting to SQL Server. Sams Publishing also has a book titled *Teach Yourself Transact-SQL in 21 Days*, which has more details on the language and its usage.

Microsoft initially developed SQL Server (a database product that understands the SQL language) with Sybase Corporation for use on the IBM OS/2 platform. Oh what a tangled web we weave! When Microsoft and IBM split, Microsoft abandoned OS/2 in favor of its new network operating system, Windows NT Advanced Server. At that point, Microsoft decided to further develop the SQL Server engine for Windows NT by itself. The resulting product was Microsoft SQL Server 4.2, which was updated to 4.21. After Microsoft and Sybase parted ways, Sybase further developed its database engine to run on Windows NT (Sybase System 10 and now System 11), and Microsoft developed SQL Server 6.0—then SQL Server 6.5, which also ran on top of Windows NT. SQL Server 7.0 now runs on Windows NT as well as on Windows 95 and Windows 98.

1

> **Note**
>
> Although you can run SQL Server 7.0 on a Windows 9x system, you do not get all the functionality of SQL Server. When running it on the Windows 9x platform, you lose the capability to use multiple processors, Windows NT security, NTFS (New Technology File System) volumes, and much more. We strongly urge you to use SQL Server 7.0 on Windows NT rather than on Windows 9x. Windows NT has other advantages as well. The NT platform is designed to support multiple users. Windows 9x is not designed this way, and your SQL Server performance degrades rapidly as you add more users.

SQL Server 7.0 is implemented as a service on either NT Workstation or NT Server (which makes it run on the server side of Windows NT) and as an application on Windows 95/98. The included utilities, such as the SQL Server Enterprise Manager, operate from the client side of Windows NT Server or NT Workstation. Of course, just like all other applications on Windows 9x, the tools run as applications.

NEW TERM A *service* is an application NT can start when booting up that adds functionality to the server side of NT. Services also have a generic application programming interface (API) that can be controlled programmatically. Threads originating from a service are automatically given a higher priority than threads originating from an application.

What Is a Database?

SQL Server uses a type of database called a relational database.

NEW TERM *Relational databases* are databases in which data is organized into tables. Tables are organized by grouping data about the same subject and contain columns and rows of information. The tables are then related back to each other by the database engine when requested.

A database can generally be thought of as a collection of related data. In earlier database products a database was usually just a file—something like employee.dbf, which contained a single table of data. Inside the employee.dbf file were columns relating to employee data such as salary, hire date, name, Social Security number, and so on. There was a row for each person in the company, with corresponding values in the appropriate columns. Indexes, used to speed data access, were in a separate file, as was any security-related item.

In SQL Server, a database is not necessarily tied to a file—it is more of a logical concept based on a collection of related objects. For example, a database in SQL Server contains not only the raw data, it also contains the structure of the database, any indexes, the security of the database, and perhaps other objects such as views or stored procedures related to that particular database.

Relational Database Objects

As you just saw, a relational database is composed of different types of objects. These objects are all described in more detail in the particular day's lesson that applies to them.

NEW TERM   The following are some of the more common objects:

• Tables—These are the objects that contain the data types and actual raw data. Tables are the focus of Day 9, "Creating Tables."

• Columns—These are the parts of the table holding the data. Columns must be assigned a data type and unique name.

• Data types—There are various data types to choose from, such as character, numeric, or date. A single data type is assigned to a column within a table.

• Stored procedures—These are like macros in that Transact-SQL code can be written and stored under a name. By executing the stored procedure, you actually run the Transact-SQL code within the procedure. One use would be to take the Transact-SQL code that runs a weekly report, save it as a stored procedure, and from then on just run the stored procedure to generate the report. Stored procedures can also be used as security mechanisms.

• Triggers—Triggers are stored procedures that activate when data is added, modified, or deleted from the database. They are used to ensure that business rules or other data integrity rules are enforced in the database. For example, a trigger can ensure that every book in a bookstore has a valid publisher assigned to it.

• Rules—Rules are assigned to columns so that data being entered must conform to standards you set. For example, rules can be used to make sure that a person's phone number contains only numbers.

• Primary keys—Although not objects per se, keys are essential to relational databases. Primary keys enforce uniqueness among rows, providing a way to uniquely identify every item you want to store.

• Foreign keys—Again, not objects per se, foreign keys are columns that reference the primary keys or unique constraints of other tables. SQL Server uses primary and foreign keys to relate the data back together from separate tables when queries are performed.

• Constraints—Constraints are server-based, system-implemented data-integrity enforcement mechanisms.

- Defaults—Defaults can be set on fields so that if no data is entered during an INSERT operation, default values will be used. An example is setting the area code for the area where most of your customers come from, which saves you from entering the area code for local customers.

- Views—Views are basically queries stored in the database that can reference one or many tables. You can create and save them so you can use them easily in the future. Views usually either exclude certain columns from a table or link two or more tables together. You can also use them as security mechanisms.

- Indexes—Indexes can help organize data so that queries run faster. Day 13, "Enhancing Performance with Indexing," covers indexes in detail.

Designing Relational Databases

The following section on designing relational databases is important for two reasons:

- You might be called on to design a relational database.

- You might have been given a relational database, but you want to understand why certain design decisions were made.

As a SQL Server administrator, you will likely be given a relational database that has been designed by someone else—this doesn't mean you can be clueless when it comes to designing a relational database. Knowing some do's and don'ts about designing databases and knowing about normalization can only help you in your job.

Although the process of designing a good relational database could fill a book by itself, here are some basic steps to consider:

- Analyze the situation to gather information about the proposed database.

- Decide on columns, data types, and lengths of data.

- Normalize the data into tables.

- Create the database and tables.

When you take related data and organize it into related tables, you are following normalization rules, which you will learn about shortly.

The design process should start with a good look at the business situation and what the customer is trying to accomplish. Brainstorming about different variables and how they all fit together into tables is the next step. The process then moves to designing reports and queries that will benefit the users, as well as other pieces of the design, including access to World Wide Web pages.

The following list of do's and don'ts will help you during the design process.

Do	Don't
DO ask the users what they need.	**DON'T** ignore the users.
DO create a list of objects.	**DON'T** create objects you will never use.
DO keep object names short yet descriptive.	**DON'T** use complex names, names with spaces, or names with unusual characters because they are harder to type.
DO organize properties of objects into correct groupings.	**DON'T** have a column that contains more than one value.
DO create the identically named columns in different tables to relate them back together. These columns become your primary and foreign keys.	**DON'T** create tables with a huge number of columns.
DO test your design with some sample data.	**DON'T** assume that because your design works well with 5 rows that it will perform well with 500,000 rows.
DO create at least one index for tables that will be queried.	**DON'T** create a lot of indexes (over five) per table.
DO design your tables with security in mind.	**DON'T** forget to set security on your data.
DO document table names, column names, and primary and foreign keys.	**DON'T** lose your documentation.
DO follow a standardized naming convention for your database objects. This can greatly simplify working with your objects. We like to use prefixes. For example, use `tblEmployees` for a table object named Employees and `idxLastName` for an index based on last name.	

The exercise at the end of this chapter goes through a simulated interview with a customer and proceeds into design of a relational database.

Interview with the Customer

A good database design starts with a thorough understanding of the situation and desired outcome of the customer. That's why the people who design new systems are called analysts—they analyze the problem in detail and try to think of ways to solve the problem.

Sometimes an old-fashioned interview is the best way to find out exactly what the customer wants, especially if you don't fully understand what the current situation is and what the goal is.

Use questions like these to probe for your customer's needs:

- What is working for you now?
- What parts of the current system would you most like to replace?
- Are there additional reports you would like to be able to generate?
- What items would you most like to keep track of?
- Is the data private or public?
- Who needs access to the data and what kind of access should each user or group have?
- Would you like the data posted on the Internet?
- Would you like the public to be able to look up things via the Internet?
- Do you have sufficient hardware in place to run both the database server and client software?
- If money and technology were no object, what would you like to incorporate into the new system?

By asking these kinds of questions you can quickly build a sense of why a database is needed. Although you might not be able to provide everything (given the limitations of the assigned budget, time frame, and hardware allowances), you will have the start of a long-term plan for growth and expansion of the database.

Organizing the Objects

After the interview (you did take good notes didn't you?) it is best to brainstorm about possible objects, including their names, types, and lengths. After the objects have been decided on, you can group them into related tables.

SQL Server supports several different data types, including those for characters, numbers, dates, and money. More detail on data types is provided on Day 9, "Creating Tables." After you have decided on your tables, specify the properties (columns) within these tables. Keep column names simple yet descriptive.

Column lengths should satisfy all but the most extreme cases. When dealing with names, your limitation might be how many characters can fit onto a mailing label—not how many to store.

Normalizing the Data

Now that you have decided on the columns, you must organize the data into related tables, which is referred to as normalizing the data.

NEW TERM *Normalization* is the process of organizing data into related tables. By normalizing the data you are attempting to eliminate redundant data. For example, suppose the same customer buys two cars. In a single-table database his information would have to be entered twice. What's worse, if the customer happens to move, you will have to change his address in both places or your data will not be internally consistent. By entering his information once in a customer table and linking his record to any car purchase, you have not only eliminated redundant (and sometimes conflicting) data, you now must change his record in only one spot. Figure 1.1 shows an example of how these tables might look. Notice that separate tables for customers and cars have been created. In the Cars table, the SoldTo field represents a single Customer ID. As you can see, Suzanne got the Jimmy, Mary got the Corvette, Joe got the Blazer, and Larry got the Mustang.

FIGURE 1.1

Organizing variables into a relational database.

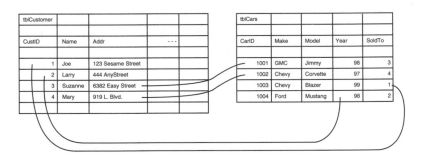

The First Three Normalization Forms

There are rules established for the normalization of data. These rules are known as

- First Normal Form (FNF)—This rule states that a column cannot contain multiple values. For example, a person's name must be broken down into last name, middle name, and first name to follow FNF.

- Second Normal Form (SNF)—This rule states that every nonkey column must depend on the entire key and not just a part of the primary key. For example, if you are using a customer ID and part number for a key, all the columns in that table must apply only to a particular customer and part number together. So, a part_description would not belong in this table. A table must also comply with first normal form to be in second normal form.

- Third Normal Form (TNF)—This rule is much like the previous one and states that all nonkey columns must not depend on any other nonkey columns. For example, if you have a table that has addresses in it, the zip code must not depend on another nonkey field like state. It should depend on the entire primary key. Of course, the table must also comply with second normal form. The TNF is often violated for convenience sake.

Creating the Database and Tables

Because tables are the building blocks of databases, it is apparent that well-designed tables (and thus the columns within the tables) are critical to the success of databases.

As with most things, planning and designing is the hard part; actually creating the database and tables is the easy part. A table is composed of columns that store the properties of a table.

Day 4, "Creating Databases, Files, and Filegroups," covers databases and their creation in more detail, and Day 9 covers tables in greater detail.

SQL Server and the Client/Server Model

Microsoft's SQL Server is a client/server database engine, so it is important for you to understand the client/server model.

NEW TERM A *client/server* application can be defined as one that is split into two parts: One part runs on a server, and the other part runs on workstations. The server side of the application provides security, fault tolerance, performance, concurrency, and reliable backups. The client side provides the user interface and can contain empty reports, queries, and forms. The idea is to have the best of both worlds by taking advantage of both and pairing them together.

SQL Server is the server part of the equation; various clients to choose from can connect to SQL Server, including the utilities that come with SQL Server, such as the SQL Server Query Analyzer.

SQL Server provides the following advantages for both clients and servers. Client advantages:

- Easy to use
- Supports multiple hardware platforms
- Supports multiple software applications
- Familiar to the user

Server advantages:

- Reliable
- Concurrent
- Sophisticated locking
- Fault tolerant
- High-performance hardware
- Centralized control

In client/server computing, when a query is run, the server searches the database and sends only the rows that are a match to the client. This not only saves bandwidth, but it can be faster than having the workstations perform the query, as long as the server is a powerful enough machine.

Summary

The material presented in today's lesson introduces you to this book, as well as to basic concepts of relational databases (including SQL Server). Microsoft's SQL Server is capturing more and more market share and is a client/server-based relational database management system. SQL Server 7.0 uses Transact-SQL as its dialect of the SQL language.

SQL Server developers are responsible for designing and implementing the database, while the SQL Server administrators are responsible for the day-to-day management tasks. However, these tasks are becoming less distinct as SQL Server becomes more widely deployed. This book is targeted to both sets of database users.

A relational database is composed of tables, which contain columns and rows of data. The process of breaking a database into related tables is called normalization.

Designing a good database starts with understanding the client's requirements for the database. The data can then be grouped into tables.

Q&A

Q Do I need to know all of this Transact-SQL stuff?

A If you are a developer, you should know it. If you plan mostly to administer existing databases, then SQL Enterprise Manager provides a graphical interface you can use to do most things. Familiarity with Transact-SQL can only help you because there are commands you must enter as Transact-SQL code, and everything in SQL Server Enterprise Manager is actually entering Transact-SQL commands.

1

Q How similar is this to Sybase, Oracle, or Access?

A Earlier versions of SQL Server (4.x) closely resembled Sybase. Since Microsoft and Sybase went their separate ways, each of their products has become more unique. SQL Server least resembles Oracle, although administrators coming from an Oracle background tend to pick up SQL Server quickly because the concepts of relational databases are similar. Access is a single-computer database, although it can act as a server for small implementations (fewer than 20 users or performance really suffers). Access makes a great front end to SQL Server, but the JET engine that supports earlier versions of Access just isn't as powerful a database engine as SQL Server. Note that Access 2000 includes the Microsoft Data Engine (MSDE), the core technology of SQL Server 7.0.

Workshop

The Workshop provides quiz questions to help you solidify your understanding of the concepts presented in this chapter. In addition to the quiz questions, exercises are provided to let you practice what you have learned in this chapter. Try to understand the quiz and exercise answers before continuing to the next day's lesson. Answers are provided in Appendix A, "Answers."

Quiz

1. What is the building block of a relational database?
2. What are some of the objects held in a database?
3. Who is responsible for backing up SQL Server databases?

Exercises

1. Try to design a database on your own. You will go through a simulated interview and then try to make some sense out of the interview by creating variables and organizing them into tables. You can also see one way of doing it. Remember, in this case there isn't just one right answer—just different ways of doing the same thing.

2. Imagine that your Uncle Joel has had a used car lot for practically as long as you can remember. You have helped him set up his computers and network, and now he calls you into his office.

   Joel: Glad you could come by. My lot has grown so big I'm having a hard time keeping track of everything. Sue almost sold a car I don't have, and Larry practically gave one away because he wrote down the wrong price. I need to get organized.

You: Have you considered some sort of database?

Joel: You're the computer expert—just design me something I can use to keep track of my cars. I'm also having a hard time keeping track of my salespeople and how much they have sold. It wasn't that hard when I had a small lot, but now it takes too much of my time.

You: Would you want the database to print reports based on monthly activity by salesperson and other such reports?

Joel: That would help a lot.

You: Do you want the database to have pictures with it?

Joel: Can you do that? That would be really neat. I've also been reading about this Internet stuff, and I think it would be great if I could have my cars on it.

You: Just what were you thinking?

Joel: I don't know—you're the computer expert.

You: Do you want people to be able to look at your cars and prices on the Internet?

Joel: Can you do that? That would be neat. Can we show color pictures, too?

You: Yes, we can put pictures and prices and features on the Web page. What exact information do you want to put in the database?

Joel: I would want the year, make, model, color, mileage, and features such as air conditioning, four-wheel-drive, CD player, blue-book price, and retail price for everyone to see. I'd also want people to see a picture of the car and be able to compare the different cars I have. I'd want additional stuff that only my salespeople would see, such as the actual cost and any notes about the car, such as how anxious we are to get rid of it and when the car came on the lot.

You: That should be enough to start with. Do you have a budget in mind?

Joel: Well, I can't blow the whole budget on it, but I've got to get something or my salespeople will be losing money on deals if I'm not careful.

You: I'll come up with some ideas and get back to you.

Summary of the Interview

What you got out of the interview is that not only does Joel need a database that will keep track of cost and sales information, but the database should link to a Web page so that anyone can access public data about the various cars available for sale.

DAY 2

Installing SQL Server 7.0

In yesterday's lesson, you learned a little bit about SQL Server 7.0 and relational databases in general. Microsoft SQL Server is a mature product, but the 7.0 release consists of a dramatic set of new functionality. You also looked at why a typical developer or database administrator might need a relational database—customers demand it. They need to keep track of objects and properties that translate rather nicely to tables with rows of data, divided into columns.

Today's lesson examines how to install SQL Server 7.0. Although running the setup program isn't very difficult, you will make critical decisions that affect your entire development, and undoing any mistakes can be quite time consuming later. You also must understand issues such as hardware and software prerequisites so you can choose the best environment for SQL Server.

What Kinds of SQL Servers Are There?

A great first question to ask yourself is "Which SQL Server do I need?" Microsoft is simultaneously releasing four editions of SQL Server 7.0. After you examine their requirements/needs, it should be obvious which one you will use. However, the most important thing to remember is that regardless of the edition of SQL Server you choose, they are all built on a common code base, so the same rules, conditions, and administration apply.

Standard Edition

The Standard Edition is what most people mean when they refer to SQL Server 7.0. This is the version of the product that supplies full functionality and is intended to run on a Windows NT Server 4.0 or later computer. This book was developed using beta copies of the Standard Edition of SQL Server 7.0. However, the material also applies to the other versions of the product, as noted earlier. This version will support up to four central processing units (CPUs) and up to 2GB of random access memory (RAM).

Enterprise Edition

The Enterprise Edition of SQL Server 7.0 is for very high-end installations. It runs on Windows NT Server 4.0 Enterprise Edition (or later) and provides features such as large memory support (greater than 2GB of RAM), Microsoft Clustering support (high-availability support), and support for up to 32 CPUs.

Small Business Server Edition

The Small Business Server (SBS) edition of SQL Server 7.0 is just what it sounds like— a solution for small businesses (generally fewer than 50 users). It supports up to four processors and up to 2GB of RAM, but it is limited to 50 users, and a database cannot exceed 10GB in size. If you need databases larger than this, you should use the Standard (or Enterprise) Edition of SQL Server.

Desktop Edition

You won't find a "Desktop" Edition for sale; you get the right to install SQL Server 7.0's Desktop Edition for each license you buy for a Standard or Enterprise Edition product. However, the Desktop Edition is one of the most exciting aspects of the SQL Server 7.0 product release.

The Desktop Edition runs on Windows 95 and Windows 98 (Windows 9x henceforth) and Windows NT Workstation 4.0 or later. It is meant as a development and remote SQL Server installation to support a central server. It can support several users simultaneously (Microsoft didn't hard code a limit), but it is typically meant for fewer than 10 users. There's no limit on database size, but Windows NT Workstation supports only two processors and Windows 9x supports only one processor.

The Desktop Edition supports most of the features of SQL Server, but it doesn't allow you to publish in transactional replication (you'll examine replication on Day 17,

"Understanding Replication Design and Methodologies"). There are several additional restrictions when running on the Windows 9x platform, and these are detailed later in today's lesson. However, most of these aren't visible to a database developer, so you can develop with the Desktop Edition and then deploy to the Standard or Enterprise Edition and know that your code is 100 percent compatible.

SQL Server Requirements

It is critical that you understand the prerequisites before you begin the installation of SQL Server 7.0. There are physical requirements (hardware and software) as well as licensing requirements that must be met. In addition, when running SQL Server on Windows NT computers, there are a couple of additional considerations such as hardware and software options, Windows NT options, and licensing options.

Hardware and Software Options

Perhaps the first thing to consider is whether your computer can even run SQL Server 7.0. As with most new Microsoft software releases, SQL Server 7.0 requires more horsepower than previous releases. In general, the more powerful your computer, the happier you will be with the performance of SQL Server 7.0.

Supported Hardware

The lowest-powered CPUs supported are Pentium 166 processors and DEC Alpha processors. Pentium, Pentium Pro, and Pentium II computers are available at the time this chapter is being written. Of course, Pentium instruction-set–compatible systems are also supported. You will need at least 32MB of RAM, although the Enterprise Edition requires 64MB of RAM.

Note

> Although a Pentium 166 is the lowest-powered configuration supported, SQL Server 7.0 will probably work (albeit run slower) on any Pentium-based computer. It will not run on a 486.

The amount of disk space required varies, based on which software components you choose to install. A minimal install will require at least 65MB of space on your hard drive, and a full install will require about 180MB of hard drive space. Any additional SQL Server components, such as Microsoft English Query (examined shortly) will require more space in addition to the numbers mentioned here. English Query requires 12MB, and Microsoft SQL Server OLAP (OnLine Analytical Processing) Services can require up to 50MB of disk space.

A CD-ROM installation (a local CD-ROM drive) is recommended; however, if you have access to a network, you can install a copy of SQL Server 7.0 from a network share that was copied from a CD-ROM. This could be a very practical setup method if you want to perform automated unattended installations of SQL Server components.

Supported Operating System Choices

When you have the supported hardware, you must select or consider which operating systems are supported. SQL Server 7.0 will run on a Windows NT computer (version 4.0 or later with Service Pack 4 or later), any version (Workstation, Server, Small Business Server, or Server Enterprise Edition). SQL Server will also run on a Windows 9x computer. There are some restrictions to consider for the Windows platforms.

Windows 9x Restrictions

The client components of SQL Server run unchanged on the Windows 9x platform. However, the Desktop Edition of SQL Server will behave differently on the Windows platform due to restrictions built into the operating system:

- Named Pipes, Banyon VINES, and AppleTalk network libraries are not supported.
- Windows NT Authentication Mode (also known as integrated security) is not available.
- Server-side multiprotocol encryption is not supported.
- Asynchronous input/output (I/O) and scatter-gather I/O are not available.
- SQL Server components don't run as services because Windows doesn't support services. They run as applications—just like any other program you can run.
- Performance monitor and event viewer are not available.
- Memory tuning is optimized for minimal memory usage.

Some of these terms might not mean much now, but before your 21 days are up you will understand all these restrictions and their implementation details. However, you will not notice most of them.

Windows NT Options

Now that you have examined some issues with the Windows 9x platform, it's time to examine some of the Windows NT-specific features. As a historical note, this is the first release of SQL Server that supports Windows 9x. Therefore, if you've used SQL Server 6.5 or earlier releases, most of these features will not be new to you. Windows NT is definitely the recommended platform because all features are available.

The most important Windows NT options are security and the NTFS file system. Therefore, you will examine each of these briefly here. However, there are several other reasons to choose Windows NT. This book assumes that all features are available on most platforms but highlights features available only on Windows NT.

Security Options

Perhaps the most important option available with Windows NT is security. Windows NT is a secure operating system, allowing you to restrict who can do what to files as well as control access rights with Windows NT accounts. This is known as Windows NT Authentication Mode or integrated security. This feature allows you to use Windows NT user and group accounts directly in SQL Server. You examine this feature in great detail on Day 5, "Using SQL Server Login and User Security."

The other security-related issue is whether to install SQL Server 7.0 on a domain controller. From a SQL Server perspective, it's best to isolate SQL Server on its own computer, so you'll see better performance by keeping SQL Server on a member (or standalone) server. Do note that to take advantage of SQL Server's integrated security with Windows NT, you must install SQL Server on a computer that has access to accounts in your domain. This means (for Windows NT 4.0 networks) that you should install SQL Server on a computer that is a member of a domain that trusts your master account domains. If you don't understand this paragraph, please refer to your Windows NT documentation or find your network administrator. They will be able to help you place SQL Server on the right computer in your network.

File System Options

You can use the file allocation table (FAT), FAT32 (NT 5.0), or NTFS file systems with SQL Server 7.0. I strongly recommend using the NTFS file system, both for security and for reliability. You should secure your database files after you have created them, and the only way to do so is with NTFS. NTFS is also much faster in terms of new database creation. There are several new features planned for the NTFS file system of Windows NT 5.0 that will make it an even better choice.

Licensing Options

Three types of licenses are available in SQL Server 7.0: per-seat licensing, per-server licensing, and Internet Connector licensing. Per-seat licensing requires you to purchase a license for each computer that will access a SQL server. However, after you have purchased a per-seat license, you can connect to any number of SQL servers in your network. You also get the right to install a local Desktop Edition of SQL Server for each per-seat license.

Per-server licensing licenses a concurrent number of computer connections to a single SQL Server instance. Therefore, if you have two copies of SQL Server running, each with per-server licensing, and you wanted to access both of them, you need two licenses. Another example might be when there is a single SQL Server. If there are 200 computers in the office, but only 50 users at any time are connected to your SQL Server, you can purchase 50 licenses instead of 200.

Caution | The right to install the Desktop Edition of SQL Server 7.0 is only given to users who have a per-seat client access license. Therefore, don't choose the per-server license if you want to install the Desktop Edition of SQL Server.

The Internet Connector License

The Internet connector license is for SQL servers being accessed from the Internet. You must pay a fee for each processor on your server that is connected to the Internet. This is true even if you are connecting through an Internet Information Server (IIS) or via Microsoft Transaction Server. After you have paid the fixed fee, you can have an unlimited number of users access SQL Server. Note that this license does not apply to intranets (those that are private to you, your company, or others associated with your company). For intranets, you must purchase either per-seat or per-server licenses.

One final note on licensing: Neither of us authors is a lawyer, and neither of us plays one on TV: Please rely on your legal counsel for advice on licensing SQL Server properly. The outline in this book is just for informational purposes. Licenses might be subject to change or subject to special conditions your company has negotiated. Okay, it's a relief to get rid of that paranoia.

Installing SQL Server 7.0

Now that you've got your licenses figured out and your platform (hardware and operating system choices) selected, it's time to begin the installation process. This book was written on Windows NT Server 4.0 Service Pack 4 on a Pentium II—400 with 128MB of RAM. SQL Server 6.5 (with Service Pack 4) is also installed so you can see all possible menu choices in the screen shots. All the screen shots you will see are from this system. Again, platform-specific issues will be pointed out as they come up later.

Beginning the Installation Process

To begin the installation, insert the CD-ROM into your CD-ROM drive. You are presented with the autoplay dialog box if that feature is enabled on your system (see Figure 2.1). If Figure 2.1 (or something similar) is not presented when you insert your CD, use Windows Explorer to locate your CD-ROM drive and run the autorun.exe program in the root directory.

FIGURE 2.1

The Microsoft SQL Server automenu.

The Autoplay Menu

There are several choices for you to make right away on the automenu. Your best first step is to click ReadMe.txt. This will start Notepad and allow you to view the last-minute information that didn't make it into the manuals. There might be quite a bit of information in the readme file, but focus on just the relevant parts for installation before continuing. By its very nature, we won't know what's in the readme.txt file until after SQL Server ships. Therefore, it's a wise precaution to review this file just in case.

NEW TERM If you want to browse the online manuals (from here on referred to as *Books Online*), you must first have Internet Explorer 4.01 installed to be able to view them. This allows you to read the installation manual if you don't have a paper copy before you install SQL Server. However, this chapter covers anything you need to know to install SQL Server 7.0. There's also a shortcut to the Microsoft SQL Server Web site (http://www.microsoft.com/sql) where you can get additional information and utilities for SQL Server 7.0. The second line down refers to SQL Server 7.0's prerequisites.

Prerequisites Based on Operating System

The prerequisites depend on the operating system on which you are installing SQL Server. For Windows 95 and Windows NT 4.0, you are required to install Internet Explorer 4.01 Service Pack 1 (or a later release). This requirement won't stop you from using another Web browser (such as Netscape Navigator), but you must install the Internet Explorer minimal install before you can continue. Windows 98 and Windows NT 5.0 already have this technology integrated. Internet Explorer 4.01 Service Pack 1 is on the SQL Server 7.0 CD-ROM.

For Windows NT 4.0 computers, you must have Service Pack 4 installed as well. Service Pack 4 is included with SQL Server 7.0 on a separate CD-ROM. Windows NT 5 is in beta test while this book is being written, but SQL Server 7.0 does run on Beta2 (or later) releases.

Both of these components (Internet Explorer and the NT Service Pack) must be in place before you can begin installing SQL Server.

Installing the Prerequisites

To install either of these prerequisites, select Install SQL Server 7.0 Prerequisites from the menu by highlighting these words and clicking. You will then be requested to identify which operating system you need the prerequisites for—Windows 95 or Windows NT 4.0. Note that Windows 98 and Windows NT 5.0 (beta 2 or later) have no prerequisites. Click the appropriate operating system, and you will see the prerequisite screen (Figure 2.2 shows this screen for Windows NT 4.0).

The screen is a little misleading here. To actually install Service Pack 4 for Windows NT, you will need to insert your Service Pack 4 CD-ROM separately. From there, an autoplay menu will guide you to installing the service pack. However, the Internet Explorer options are indeed on the SQL Server CD-ROM.

You can choose to perform a minimum install if you want to have only the components required to support the SQL Server utilities (such as the Books Online and SQL Server Enterprise Manager). Otherwise, if you would like to install the full Web browser and additional components, you can choose Launch Setup Wizard. This will launch the Internet Explorer 4.01 Service Pack 1 Setup Wizard, which will guide you through installing the necessary software (and allow you to select additional components).

FIGURE 2.2

The SQL Server 7.0 Prerequisites menu.

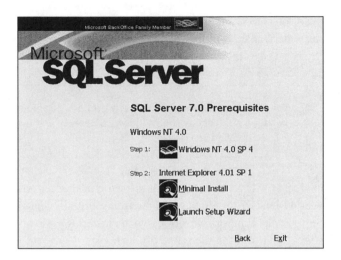

If you install Service Pack 4 for Windows NT, you will be required to reboot your computer before you can continue. The same is true for an Internet Explorer install. Therefore, you will need to remove and reinsert the CD after the reboot to see the autoplay menu again.

Installing SQL Server 7.0 (Full Product)

After you have installed the prerequisite software (or if you didn't need to), you can begin installing SQL Server 7.0. From the main autoplay menu, select the option to Install SQL Server 7.0 Components (see Figure 2.3).

FIGURE 2.3

Installation of SQL Server 7.0 components.

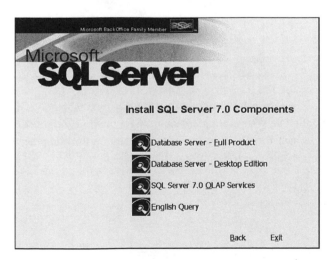

Here you can select to install the Standard Edition of SQL Server (noted as Full Product in the menu), the Desktop Edition, or additional SQL Server services (OLAP Services or English Query). You examine both of these options later in today's lesson.

> **Tip**
>
> The Desktop Edition can run on any supported computer—Windows 9x, Windows NT Workstation, Windows NT Server, and even the Enterprise Edition of Windows NT Server.

This setup chapter will walk you through the setup of the full product (the Standard Edition of SQL Server 7.0). However, the setup is virtually identical for the Desktop Edition. Setup of the Enterprise Edition, when clustering is involved, has many special considerations and is beyond the scope of this book.

1. Click Full Product to begin the SQL Server setup. You will first be presented with the option of installing SQL Server either on a remote computer or on your local computer (see Figure 2.4). Accept the default of installing on your local computer and click Next.

FIGURE 2.4

Local or remote setup?

2. Setup will search your computer to determine whether SQL Server was previously installed on your computer (including a previous release), and after it has determined whether SQL Server 7.0 is already on the computer (assuming it isn't), you are presented with Figure 2.5, the welcome screen.

FIGURE 2.5

Welcome to SQL Server 7.0 setup.

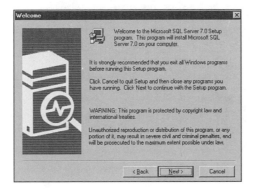

2

> **Note**
>
> Follow the advice on the screen and make sure all programs and services that aren't necessary are not running. In particular, make sure that any service on Windows NT that might be using ODBC (Open Database Connectivity) components is stopped.

3. Click Next, and you will see the license agreement (see Figure 2.6). You should read the license agreement, and if you don't like what you see and click No (that you don't agree), setup terminates and you should return SQL Server to wherever you purchased it. Because, of course, you won't do that, simply click Yes, you agree, and move to the User Information screen (see Figure 2.7).

FIGURE 2.6

The SQL Server 7.0 license agreement.

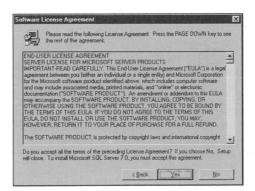

FIGURE 2.7

Gathering user information.

4. After you have entered your name and company name, click Next and you will be presented with Figure 2.8. Here you must enter the 10-digit CD Key. It should be on the yellow sticker of your CD liner notes or sleeve. If you do not have a valid SQL Server product identification number, you will not be able to continue with setup.

   After you have entered the proper product ID, click OK. You will see a confirmation screen showing you the full product ID. You should write this number down so you can provide it if you ever need to call for product support from Microsoft.

FIGURE 2.8

Specify your CD Key.

Note

For Windows NT computers only, if you have SQL Server 6.x installed on your computer, you will be presented with Figure 2.9. You can request that the SQL Server Upgrade Wizard run at the end of setup, allowing you to upgrade your SQL Server 6.x (6.0 or 6.5) databases to SQL Server 7.0. Upgrading from previous releases is beyond the scope of this book. If you want to have a go at it, click the box next to Yes, Run the SQL Server Upgrade Wizard. It's a very safe process (I even wrote some of the code that is run during upgrade; search the files for my name, you'll find it :)) and should be straightforward if you know the previous release of SQL Server from which you are upgrading.

This option won't be presented if you are installing on a Windows 9x platform because SQL Server 6.0 and 6.5 never ran on those platforms.

FIGURE 2.9

Upgrading your SQL Server 6.x installation.

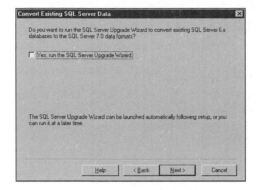

5. For the purposes of this setup chapter, do not check the upgrade box; just click Next. You will then see the Setup Type dialog (see Figure 2.10).

FIGURE 2.10

Select the setup type.

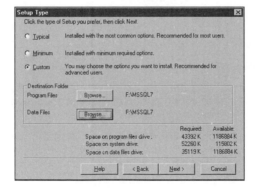

If you select Typical, all the default options are taken, and setup will jump to Figure 2.16. All components except the development tools and the full-text search service will be installed. Selecting a Minimum install will follow the same path in terms of the screens you will see, but will install only the client access components (ODBC, and so on) and the SQL Server core services. It will not install any management tools or the Books Online.

As you can see in Figure 2.10, I have selected a custom setup. This will allow you to see each setup option and select it for yourself. I will also identify which components on each screen are installed by default during a typical or minimum installation.

6. After selecting the setup type, you can change the setup location for SQL Server's program files (the programs needed to run SQL Server) and SQL Server's data files (the system databases, explained shortly, and the default location for your

databases). The space requirements are listed at the bottom of the dialog box. I
don't have enough room to install on my C drive, so I will install SQL Server on
the F drive of my computer. Most people choose to accept the default drive of C.

Tip

> I recommend that you leave the directory as the default of \mssql7, even if
> you choose a different hard drive. This default is well understood to be a
> SQL Server directory, and should make people think before they start
> deleting files later.

Navigating the Custom Setup

When you click Next, you will then have the option of selecting the components you
want to install for SQL Server 7.0. The amount of disk space you use will depend greatly
on which components you choose to install. Your choices here will also affect what you
are able to do with your SQL Server installation down the road.

Select Components

Your first step is to select the components you want to install (see Figure 2.11). There are
several key decisions to be made here, as well as the possibility of performing a client-
tools-only installation. Each selection possibility is described next.

FIGURE 2.11

Select the server com-
ponents to install.

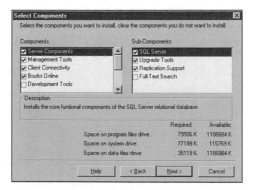

Tip

> For the purposes of going through this book, please select all available
> options.

Server Components

Under Server Components, the following options are available:

- SQL Server—This is the core database engine (known as MSSQLServer and explained shortly) and the management support service (known as SQL Server Agent and also examined shortly). This option is enabled by default.

- Upgrade Tools—This is the database upgrade support so you can run the Version Upgrade Wizard to upgrade a SQL Server 6.x installation. Note that you don't have to have SQL Server 6.x installed on the same computer as SQL Server 7.0 to be able to migrate data to the server, but the computer must be running the Windows NT operating system. This option is enabled by default.

- Replication Support—If you plan to use replication, you should leave this option enabled (as is the default).

- Full-Text Search—An exciting feature of SQL Server 7.0 is the capability to use technology from Microsoft Index Server to build indexes on textual data. This option is examined further on Day 13, "Enhancing Performance with Indexing." However, this option is not installed by default. It is also available only on Windows NT Server and Windows NT Server, Enterprise Edition (without clustering).

Management Tools

Under Management Tools, the following options are available (see Figure 2.12):

FIGURE 2.12

Select the management tools to install.

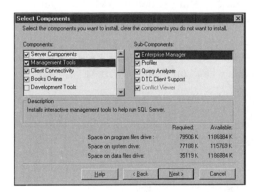

- Enterprise Manager—This is the graphical management interface for both development and administration of SQL Server. This option is enabled by default.

- Profiler—The SQL Server Profiler is a great tool for monitoring SQL Server activities. This includes queries and how these queries are run and provides performance measurements. This option is enabled by default.

- Query Analyzer—This is the tool to use to enter and run Transact-SQL statements. You can also view how SQL Server will optimize and run your queries. Experienced Transact-SQL developers tend to use this tool. This option is enabled by default.

- DTC Client Support—This is the DTC (distributed transaction coordinator) Management console and is examined more tomorrow. This option is enabled by default

- Conflict Viewer—This is the conflict resolution wizard for merge replication. This option is enabled by default.

Client Connectivity

Client connectivity is the set of components that allows you to talk to SQL Server. This includes Open Database Connectivity (ODBC) components, Object Linking and Embedding Database (OLE DB) components, and DB-Library components. Each of these libraries allows you to write programs or use programs that connect to SQL Server. Without these you can't do much of anything, so as you'd expect, they're enabled by default.

Books Online

Here you have the choice of installing the Books Online onto the local hard drive, to add shortcuts in Windows to your SQL Server CD-ROM for the Books Online, or to not install them. I strongly recommend you always install Books Online at every instance of SQL Server. There's nothing more frustrating than working on a server and not being able to view the manuals when you need them most.

Development Tools

None of the development tools are installed by default. However, you have the following options (see Figure 2.13):

- Headers and Libraries—These are the include and library files for C/C++ that you need to develop SQL Server programs.

- Backup/Restore API—This option includes a sample program, necessary C/C++ files, and documentation on how to build backup and restore programs.

- Debugger Interface—This option installs the components necessary to allow Microsoft Visual Studio components the capability to debug stored procedures.

FIGURE 2.13

Select the development tools to install.

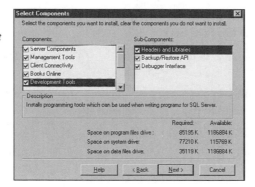

Code Samples

None of the code samples are installed by default. However, you have the following options (see Figure 2.14):

FIGURE 2.14

Select the code samples to install.

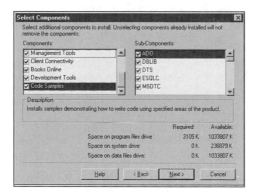

- ADO—This includes programming examples for ActiveX Data Objects (ADO).

- DBLIB—Includes programming examples for the DB-Library API. DB-Library was the native Database Application Programming Interface (API) of SQL Server in earlier releases, and is supported in SQL Server 7.0 for backward compatibility only.

- DTS—Includes programming examples for data transformation services (DTS). DTS is a way to move data from one source to another.

- ESQLC—Includes the programming examples for Embedded SQL for the C programming language.

- MSDTC—Includes the programming examples for the Microsoft Distributed Transaction Coordinator (MS DTC).

- ODBC—Includes the programming examples for the open database connectivity programming API in SQL Server.

- ODS—Includes the programming examples for the open data services (ODS) API for SQL Server.

- OLE Automation—Includes the programming examples to support OLE Automation for SQL Server.

- Replication—Includes the programming examples for SQL Server replication.

- SQLDMO—Includes programming examples for the SQL-Distributed Management Objects administrative programming interface.

- SQLNS—Includes programming examples for the SQL NameSpace administrative programming interface.

A Client-Tools-Only Installation

One other option (although it's not necessarily obvious from your menu choices) is to install only the client tools for SQL Server. You can do this by unchecking the Server Components option. You can then select only the tools you want installed on your computer (or Books Online, Development Libraries, and so on) and then have those installed. Unfortunately, Microsoft did not provide a simple or obvious way to perform a client-tools-only installation, but when you know how to do it, it's not too bad. Note that the only way to do this, however, is to perform a custom installation, and you must meet the operating system prerequisites first.

Character Set/Sort Order/Unicode Collation

After you have selected all available options, click Next to continue to the Character Set/Sort Order/Unicode Collation dialog. It is here that you make another critical decision about your SQL Server installation. You must choose in what character set non-Unicode data is to be stored, how it will be sorted when returned from SQL Server, and the Unicode Collation (how Unicode data will be sorted and returned to the user).

 Caution

If you want to change your character set, sort order, or Unicode Collation after you have installed SQL Server 7.0, you will have to reload your data and rebuild your indexes. This is a time-consuming task and makes it imperative that you make the correct choices now.

You should first choose a character set, then a sort order, and then your Unicode Collation. Choosing a character set determines which sort orders are available for that character set. When a character set and sort order are selected, together they determine the default Unicode Collation.

> **Note**
>
> What is Unicode? That's a great question. Traditional computer storage has allowed one byte of storage for each character you see on the screen. However, this only works out to allowing 256 choices of characters. The first 128 characters are typically the same, and the last 128 characters vary, based on the character set (also known as the code page) you select.
>
> If you take a global perspective, there are not nearly enough characters to represent all the languages on the planet. Unicode is a way to allow a computer to keep 2 bytes per character. Although you've doubled your storage space requirements, you can now keep data in any language in your server, and it will never need to be translated—it's always stored correctly. For any kind of international effort when multiple languages are involved, Unicode solves a very difficult problem—letting Germans store their data in German, Chinese speakers store data in Chinese, and so on, but all within a single column in your database.

The default character set is a 1252/ISO (International Standards Organization) Character Set. This character set represents U.S. English and most Western European languages well. You should select this character set unless you have a compelling reason not to do so (for example, you're in China and you want the Chinese default character set). You might also choose an alternative character set to maintain backward compatibility with previous installations of SQL Server that used a different character set.

After you've selected your character set, select your sort order. The default sort order for the ISO character set is Dictionary Order, Case Insensitive. This means that if you ask SQL Server to sort a list of names for you, the results will be returned in the same order as they appear in the dictionary and will not be sorted by case—meaning that "s" and "S" are equivalent. Again, I strongly recommend that you adopt this default sort order.

However, there are some good reasons to change the sort order. Many application vendors use the binary sort order (meaning, results return in their ASCII sequence). Then the application assumes the responsibility of sorting. Another option is to use a case-sensitive server, so that "S" and "s" are sorted in different groups. You can then choose whether upper- or lowercase letters come first. However, this has a profound side effect. In SQL Server, if you create a table called "Sales," it is not the same table as "SALES." You've therefore forced your users (and yourself) to be very precise. Additionally, a search for my last name, Waymire, would fail unless the first letter was capitalized. So if you enter "waymire," you won't find that information.

Finally, select the default Unicode Collation. Unless you are outside the United States and Canada, don't touch that dial. Otherwise, you can select a Unicode Collation that matches the preferences for your country. The Unicode Collations available are based on operating system support. See your Windows NT documentation for full details of the implementation of Unicode. They don't affect sorting only; they also affect comparison checks. There are also several check boxes exposed, including the following:

- Case insensitive—If checked (the default), you get the same case-insensitive behavior described for sort order.
- Accent insensitive—If checked (not checked is the default), comparisons of e and é are treated as equal.
- Width insensitive—If checked (the default), differences in width for East Asian languages are ignored.
- Kana insensitive—If checked (the default), differences in Kana sensitivity are ignored.

Note SQL Server exports the Unicode features to the Windows 9x platform, even though you don't usually have Unicode support in these operating systems.

Network Libraries

Click Next after accepting your localized settings (this book used all the defaults), and you are presented with the Network Libraries screen (see Figure 2.15).

Here you will need to choose the available network libraries to support for SQL Server. These are the network libraries that client computers will be able to use to talk to your copy of SQL Server. The default for Windows NT computers is to install Named Pipes, Multiprotocol, and Transmission Control Protocol/Internet Protocol (TCP/IP) Sockets. For Windows 9x computers, only Multiprotocol and TCP/IP Sockets are installed.

It's a good idea to have a brief understanding of each network library.

Named Pipes

Named Pipes is actually a file-system approach to network communications. When you connect to a file share, you specify a Universal Naming Convention (UNC) path to a file server: \\FILESERVER\Sharename. To connect to a named pipe, you connect to a share that is of the form \\COMPUTER\pipe\sql\query. You can change the named pipe on which you want SQL Server to listen, but you shouldn't do so unless you are an advanced SQL Server administrator and understand the implications.

Named Pipes is required for Windows NT systems and cannot be removed. This has been the traditional network library for the last several releases of SQL Server—so if you have SQL Server 6.x clients on your network, they will most likely be using Named Pipes when they try to connect to your server.

Named Pipes is not available (on the server side) for Windows 9x systems. You can use it to connect to a server, but the server part of Named Pipes is not available, so the option is not available during a desktop SQL Server installation on the Windows 9x environments.

FIGURE 2.15

Select the network libraries to install.

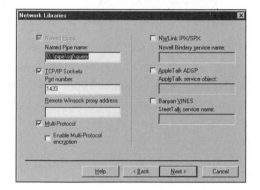

TCP/IP Sockets

TCP/IP Sockets connect to SQL Server using TCP/IP's sockets network capabilities. The default assigned socket for SQL Server is 1433. You use sockets every day (using socket 80 for World Wide Web browsing). This protocol is available and supported on all operating systems and is the default network library on the Windows 9x platforms.

Multiprotocol

Multiprotocol, as it sounds, supports any available communications method between computers using Remote Procedure Calls (RPCs). The key advantage to the multiprotocol network library is the option to enable encryption of all traffic over the network. For any kind of secure environment (banks, government, and so on), this is a great option to use to protect your data while it crosses the network. Multiprotocol is installed on all operating systems by default. Multiprotocol encryption is not available for SQL Servers running on Windows 9x.

NWLink IPX/SPX

NWLink IPX/SPX is used to support legacy Novell environments. Do not use this option unless you are still using IPX/SPX only to connect using Novell client software.

AppleTalk ADSP

AppleTalk (as the name implies) is used to support communications over Macintosh- and Apple-computer–based networks. You must also install the services for Macintosh software for Windows NT before this network library will function.

Banyon VINES

Banyon VINES is used (surprisingly enough) in a Banyon VINES network environment. If you are on a Banyon StreetTalk network, select this option. Again, additional software components are necessary for Windows NT to enable this functionality.

The Services Accounts

Make any changes you need to the network libraries and click Next to see the Services Accounts dialog (see Figure 2.16). This option will appear on Windows NT computers only. Windows 9x doesn't support the concept of services, so SQL Server on Windows will always run in the context of the logged-in user. However, SQL Server on Windows NT runs as a background service. This means that it doesn't require anyone to log in to the computer to enable SQL Server services. However, even services must log in to the operating system to function.

FIGURE 2.16

Select the services accounts.

The Local System account is a special account in Windows NT that is generally understood to mean the operating system itself. Selecting the Local System account will always work. However, this special account has no network access rights. Therefore, if you want to integrate more than one SQL Server on your network or to integrate SQL Server with other BackOffice services such as Microsoft Exchange Server, you should run the SQL Server services under a user account.

Setup selects the account of the user running setup by default. This is rarely the correct choice. You should create a special user account to use for the SQL Server services. After you have created the account, you should make the account a member of the local administrator's group on the computer. Although making this account a member of the administrator's group is not mandatory, it makes life much simpler.

The other choice here is to use the same account for both default SQL Server services (they are explained later in today's lesson). You can use separate accounts for each service, but it's much easier to accept the default configuration. If this is your own personal SQL Server, use the administrator's account or create a custom account (as shown in Figure 2.16) with User Manager or User Manager for Domains. If you are on an organized corporate network, have an appropriate account created for your use.

Make sure the account you use has the following characteristics in addition to being for an administrator:

- User cannot change password
- Password never expires
- All logon hours allowed

Finishing Setup

After you have selected the needed service accounts, click Next and you will get to Figure 2.17, showing you that setup is ready to begin copying files. This is the dialog box you see after selecting a typical or minimum setup option.

When you are ready to continue, click Next and you are presented with the licensing mode dialog for SQL Server. You can choose per-seat or per-server licensing for your SQL Server. You looked at licensing at the beginning of today's lesson. After you have selected the type of licensing you want to use, click Continue and a confirmation dialog will appear. You must check the I Agree box to confirm that you accept the licensing conditions; then click OK to begin copying data files.

After the files are copied onto your computer, SQL Server setup installs the components you selected. It first installs the client connectivity components, referred to as Microsoft Data Access Components (MDAC). Then it installs the Microsoft Management Console (MMC)—this is the shell that contains SQL Server Enterprise Manager. MSDTC (explained shortly) is then installed, followed by the Hypertext Markup Language (HTML) help engine. The Full-Text Search engine is then installed (if requested), and then SQL Server is configured by running several Transact-SQL scripts.

When setup is complete, you might be prompted to restart your computer; you will get such a request if this is the first time you have installed the MDAC components. If requested to do so, restart your computer.

FIGURE 2.17

Setup is ready to begin copying files.

Other SQL Server Optional Components

After you have installed SQL Server 7.0, you can install three additional services: the Microsoft Search Service, the Microsoft SQL Server OLAP Services, and Microsoft English Query. Although you can install the Microsoft Search Service (full-text indexing) during the default setup of SQL Server, you can also install the two other services after the initial setup is complete. You can also install these other two services independently of SQL Server if you want.

Microsoft Search Service (Full-Text Indexing)

The Microsoft Search Service is the combination of SQL Server and Microsoft Index Server technologies that allows you to index data in text columns in SQL Server 7.0. This service is optional—you don't get it by default, but it's an exciting new technology that will be examined on Day 13, "Enhancing Performance with Indexing."

Microsoft SQL Server OLAP Services

Microsoft SQL Server OLAP Services (code named Plato while under development) is a set of technologies to extend data warehousing into SQL Server. The OLAP Services help you build OLAP (OnLine Analytical Processing) data to perform detailed trend analysis in many ways. The service provides the capability to build and control these cubes, and a user interface to build, administer, and query these cubes is also installed. The server side installs only on Windows NT 4.0. The client components and user interface are also available in Windows 9x. Because the OLAP services merit an entire book on their own, they are not examined further.

Microsoft English Query

Microsoft English Query allows an administrator to configure a database schema and allows end users to run their database queries in English instead of Transact-SQL. This is particularly beneficial for Internet-based applications that don't want to force users to run SQL statements. For example, you can say "Show me the number of books sold for each author this year" instead of a complicated SQL statement. English Query can be installed on any supported platform for SQL Server 7.0.

Postinstallation: What Did You Get?

So now that you've installed SQL Server 7.0, what did you get for your time? You have a set of services (or applications, if you look at them on Windows 9x), a set of tools, and a set of manuals. You also have several files installed on your computer, and modifications have been made to your Windows registry. Several default SQL Server databases were also installed, and the default security configuration was set up.

The SQL Server Services

The following is the complete list of SQL Server services that might have been installed:

- MSSQLServer—The service that is the actual database server. When you stop or start SQL Server, it typically means you have stopped the MSSQLServer service.

- SQL Server Agent—The service that provides support for scheduled jobs, alerts, event management, and replication. You examine this further on Day 19, "Using the SQL Server Agent."

- MSDTC—The service that supports distributed transactions across multiple servers. You examine distributed transactions on Day 16, "Programming SQL Server 7.0."

- Microsoft Search—The service to support indexing of text fields in SQL Server.

- DSS Analysis Server—The supporting service for Microsoft SQL Server OLAP Services, as described earlier in today's lesson.

Tip   DSS stands for Decision Support Services. At one point Microsoft was going to use that name instead of OLAP Services, so the service still uses that name even though the "official" product name is SQL Server OLAP Services.

Each of these services can potentially be controlled in several different ways. By far the easiest is to use the Service Manager utility or the SQL Server Enterprise Manager. You will learn how to use both of these in tomorrow's lesson when you examine the SQL Server tools and utilities. You can also use a variety of Windows NT tools, such as Control Panel—services in Windows NT 4.0 or the Server Manager utility. However, my favorite method is still the good old command prompt.

The NET START and NET STOP commands can stop or start any service, but I use them most frequently for the SQL Server services. Open a command prompt (Start, Programs, Command Prompt) and type NET START to see the list of running services (see Figure 2.18).

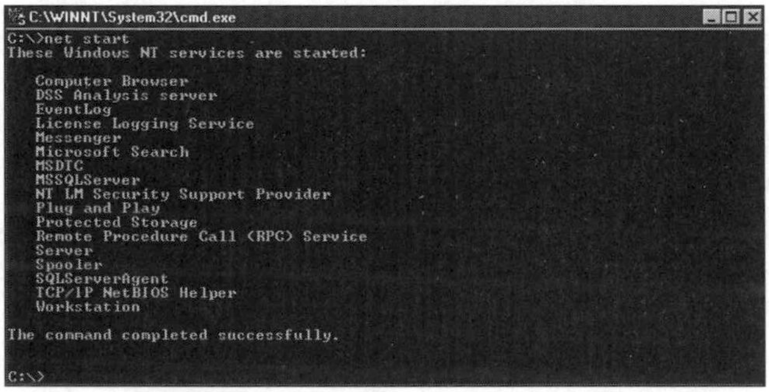

FIGURE 2.18

The list of services showing all SQL Server services.

In this list, to stop the SQL Server Agent service, you type Net Stop SQLServerAgent and the service will stop. To start the service, type Net Start SQLServerAgent. You start the other services in a similar fashion.

Installation Folders

Table 2.1 shows the folders that are created on your system and what is installed in each:

TABLE 2.1   SQL SERVER'S FOLDERS

File Location	Components Installed
\MSSQL7	The default folder holding all other MSSQLServer and SQL Server Agent service support files, as well as the uninstall support files.
\MSSQL7\Backup	The default location for SQL Server backups. The folder is empty by default.
\MSSQL7\Binn	The location of all SQL Server program files and supporting DLLs.
\MSSQL7\Books	The location of Books Online compiled HTML files.
\MSSQL7\Data	The default location for SQL Server data files (the system databases, as well as your databases).

File Location	Components Installed
\MSSQL7\DevTools	The location of the developer support tools (C Header files, for example).
\MSSQL7\FTData	The location for storing Microsoft Search Service indexes.
\MSSQL7\Html	All HTML files related to SQL Server, including those used by the MMC.
\MSSQL7\Install	The location of the SQL Scripts, which are run during setup, as well as the .OUT files reporting their success or failure.
\MSSQL7\Jobs	When jobs need to save data to a temporary location, this is the folder they use. It is empty by default.
\MSSQL7\Log	This folder contains the SQL Server error logs.
\MSSQL7\ReplData	This folder is used extensively during replication but is empty until replication is used.
\MSSQL7\Upgrade	This folder contains all programs and files needed to upgrade from a previous release of SQL Server to SQL Server 7.0.
\Program Files\OLAP Services	The default folder location for the OLAP services components.
\Program Files\Microsoft Query	The default location for Microsoft English English Query components.

Windows Registry Entries

Your registry was modified in quite a few places to install the SQL Server services; to register with the Windows NT performance monitor, event viewer, and license manager applications; and to support the needed startup locations for the services. The most important location for you to know about is the key HKEY_LOCAL_MACHINE\Software\Microsoft\MSSQLServer. If you start up regedit.exe (or regedt32.exe on Windows NT computers, although regedit.exe works), you can navigate to this key. Figure 2.19 shows my registry keys.

I hope you will never have need to change anything here, but it's a good idea to know where these entries are, just in case. You will also find registry configuration options stored in HKEY_CURRENT_USER\Software\Microsoft\MSSQLServer for your individual user preferences for the client utilities as well.

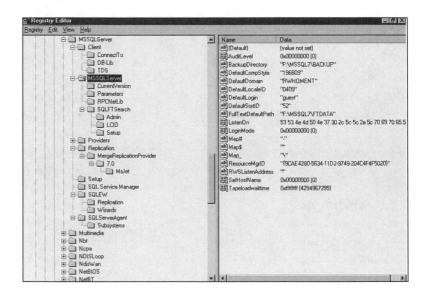

FIGURE 2.19

The SQL Server registry keys.

Services are stored under HKEY_LOCAL_MACHINE\System\CurrentControlSet\ Services\<servicename>.

The SQL Server Default Databases

After you have installed SQL Server 7.0, the databases discussed in the following sections (master, model, tempdb, MSDB, pubs, and Northwind) will be installed. You can add your own later, but these are guaranteed to be there. Some of these (master, model, tempdb, and MSDB) are system databases—you cannot drop one of these databases without causing serious harm to SQL Server. The other two, the pubs and Northwind databases, are simply samples to assist you in learning SQL Server. You can safely drop these on your production SQL Servers.

The Master Database

As just mentioned, the master database is the key database for running SQL Server. It contains a pointer to the primary data file for every other database installed on your system, as well as key serverwide information. This serverwide information includes such items as systemwide error messages, login information, system stored procedures, and connected or linked servers. The master database can be recovered only in the event of a disaster with special techniques examined on Day 8, "Restoring SQL Server Databases." It is about 9MB after installation.

The Model Database

The model database is best thought of as a template database. Each time you create a new database, the model database is actually copied, and then the size and other changes you requested for your new database are applied. Therefore, any object that exists in the model database will be copied to the new database as it is created. For example, you can place a table or a username in this database right after you install SQL Server. Each time a database is created after that, the table and your username appear in every database. The model database is about 1.5MB after installation. Because the model is copied to create each new database, no database can be smaller than the model.

The Tempdb Database

The tempdb database is where sorts, joins, and other activities that require temporary space are performed. It is approximately 2.5MB after installation, but as is the case with all databases in SQL Server 7.0 by default, it can grow as you need more space. The tempdb database is reinitialized each time SQL Server (the MSSQLServer service) is restarted.

The MSDB Database

The MSDB database supports the SQL Server Agent service, including storing information about jobs, alerts, events, and replication. A history of all backup and restore activity is also kept in this database. The MSDB database is about 8.5MB by default.

The Pubs Database

The pubs database is meant to be a learning tool. It contains a sample database about a publisher, including authors, books, and sales. Most of the examples in the SQL Server Books Online (and this book) are based on the pubs database. Most database features are highlighted via their implementation in the pubs database. Pubs is just under 2MB in size after installation.

The Northwind Database

The Northwind database is an alternative learning database to the pubs database. Northwind has been the sample database supplied with Microsoft Access for some time now. Because more and more Microsoft Access users are migrating to SQL Server, the Northwind database was brought over to assist them in learning the features of the product with a familiar database. Northwind is about 4MB by default.

SQL Server Default Login IDs

Strangely enough, one of the first things you'll want to do after you've installed SQL Server is to log in. The default login for SQL Server is sa (lowercase on case-sensitive sort-order servers). The letters "sa" stand for system administrator. In addition, SQL Server 7.0 introduces the concept of roles for SQL Server. Think of SQL Server roles as similar to Windows NT groups. You explore security in great detail on Day 5, "Using SQL Server Login and User Security."

sa

The sa login is a member of the sysadmin fixed server role. As a member of this role, sa can do anything in SQL Server. The sa account always exists and cannot be dropped. The password for sa is blank right after installation. You will want to change that. For now, the easiest way to do this is to click Start, Programs, Microsoft SQL Server 7.0, Query Analyzer. Change the server name to your computer name, and check the box to Start SQL Server if stopped. Select to use SQL Server authentication, enter a Login Name of sa, and leave the password blank (Figure 2.20).

FIGURE 2.20

Connecting to SQL Server.

After you have completed the dialog, click OK. You will be logged in, and SQL Server will be started if it wasn't already running. Now, run the following query (type it exactly as you see here), except replace *<newpass>* with your own new password. Make sure you use a password you will remember because if you forget it, you might have to reinstall SQL Server.

```
Exec sp_password NULL,<newpass>
```

Your new password doesn't need to be in quotation marks or anything; simply type whatever you want. After you've typed the statement, select Query, Execute from the menu to run the query. Figure 2.21 shows an example of a completed query.

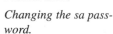

FIGURE 2.21

Changing the sa password.

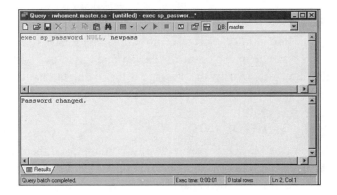

2

After this is complete, whenever you try to log in as sa you must use the password you just added.

Windows NT Local Administrators Group

If you are on a Windows NT computer and are a member of the local administrators group, you don't have to use SQL Server authentication. You can simply make sure to select Use Windows NT authentication in Figure 2.20. During setup, SQL Server 7.0 adds members of the local Windows NT Administrators group to the sysadmin role, just as sa was added. On Windows 9x computers, there is no Windows NT authentication, so you must use sa. Password control is not necessary in SQL Server when using Windows NT authentication; SQL Server simply uses your Windows NT login credentials.

Troubleshooting Your Installation

Setup of SQL Server is a relatively straightforward adventure. However, in the unlikely event something goes wrong, you will want to gather information on what failed so you can take corrective action. Installation failures have been extremely rare with SQL Server 7.0, so I hope you'll never need to use the following information.

sqlstp.log

Located in your windows directory (c:\winnt on my system), you will find the sqlstp.log file. This is the output log from the setup program. Any problems that occur should be logged to this file. If you encounter a problem, search this file for a report of what failed. Typically you would find the failure information close to the bottom of the report.

*.OUT Files

In the \mssql7\install folder, several setup scripts might have been run. If the sqlstp.log file indicates a failure in one of them, you can find the results of the run in the .OUT files in this directory. Usually the message will be straightforward—such as "Failed to create xxx."

SQL Server Error Log

If SQL Server (the MSSQLServer service) was started, and there was some kind of failure, it's likely you'll find something useful in the SQL Server error log. These files are located in the \MSSQL7\Log directory and are numbered from newest to oldest. The current error log is a file called Errorlog. (with no extension). The next oldest is Errorlog.1, then Errorlog.2, and so on.

NT Application Event Log

If you are running Windows NT, you might want to also check your error logs in the Windows NT Event Viewer. Select Start, Programs, Administrative Tools, Event Viewer. There are three different logs in the event viewer application: the system error log, the security error log, and the application error log. Switch to the application error log by selecting Log, Application from the menu. Look for any errors with a red stop sign next to them. If you see any, examine these for additional troubleshooting information.

Removing SQL Server

If, for some reason, you need to remove SQL Server, it's very easy. Select Control Panel, Add/Remove Programs; and SQL Server 7.0 will be in the list of programs—just like any other application on your computer. You can also use the uninstall shortcut in the SQL Server 7.0 program group to remove SQL Server 7.0. This will remove all files and registry keys related to SQL Server but won't remove shared components that were installed, such as the MDAC components.

There is one important issue to deal with if you upgrade to SQL Server 7.0 on a computer that has SQL Server 6.x installed. When you are sure that you no longer want to use SQL Server 6.x, do not run the 6.x setup program to remove the previous release of SQL Server. It can damage your SQL Server 7.0 installation. Microsoft wrote a special uninstall program for SQL Server 6.x and placed a shortcut to it in your Microsoft SQL Server Switch menu. It's called, surprisingly enough, Uninstall SQL Server 6.x.

Summary

SQL Server 7.0 is very easy to install. The hard part is making the correct decisions during setup because you have to live with them for the rest of the time you are using the product. Setup starts the automenu program when you insert the CD and then helps you install the prerequisite software if needed. Remember, this is Windows NT 4.0 Service Pack 4 (for Windows NT 4.0) and Internet Explorer 4.01 Service Pack 1 on Windows 95 and Windows NT 4.0. Windows NT 5.0 and Windows 98 have no prerequisites.

You must select which of the versions of SQL Server 7.0 you want to install. You can select the Standard Edition if running Windows NT Server. The Enterprise Edition is the proper choice for Windows NT Server, Enterprise Edition. SQL Server 7.0 is also available with the Small Business Server package but has restrictions on the maximum database size. Finally, the Desktop Edition runs on Windows 95, Windows 98, and Windows NT Workstation (4.0 or later).

After you have completed the prerequisites, you can begin the setup of SQL Server. If you are willing to accept the defaults (now that you know them), perform a typical installation. The rest is basically automatic. Do remember to create and use a service account if you are installing on Windows NT, if you ever intend to link your SQL Server with other SQL Servers or with other Microsoft BackOffice components.

Your most critical choice during setup is in the Character Set, Sort Order, and Unicode Collation. If you change your mind, you will have to basically copy all of your data out of SQL Server, essentially reinstall the product, and recreate all objects and reload your data. It's not pretty, so you'll want to get this one right the first time.

Although they're not examined in further detail in this book, remember that SQL Server 7.0 also includes the OLAP Services and English Query tools to extend the functionality of SQL Server in new and exciting ways.

Now, let's test your knowledge with a few warm-up questions and then a quiz.

Q&A

Q Which setup option will take the least amount of space on your hard drive?

A A minimal setup.

Q How do I perform a client-tools–only installation?

A Perform a custom setup and then uncheck the server components.

Q Which Network Libraries are installed by default on Windows NT?

A Named Pipes, Multiprotocol, and TCP/IP Sockets.

Q Which file should I review before I begin setup?

A The readme.txt file—a shortcut appears on the SQL Server automenu.

Workshop

The Workshop provides quiz questions to help you solidify your understanding of the concepts presented in this chapter. In addition to the quiz questions, exercises are provided to let you practice what you have learned in this chapter. Try to understand the quiz and exercise answers before continuing to the next day's lesson. Answers are provided in Appendix A, "Answers."

Quiz

1. What sort order should you use if you want data returned in ASCII order?
2. What does the Unicode Collation affect?
3. What component installs the OLE DB and ODBC drivers?
4. Which account should I use to control my SQL Server services?
5. How can I start SQL Server if it isn't running?
6. Which file system is recommended for SQL Server when running on Windows NT?
7. How do I get the Microsoft Search service installed?

Exercises

1. Set up SQL Server 7.0 if you haven't already done so. Select a custom setup and install as many components as your version allows.
2. Look at your error log and the sqlstp.log file in your Windows directory. Also examine the .out files in your \mssql7\install directory to look for any problems.
3. Install Microsoft SQL Server OLAP Services. Although not discussed in detail in this book, you might find the product quite useful.
4. Verify the SQL Server registry keys so you know where they are in case you need to use them.

DAY **3**

Using the SQL Server 7.0 Tools and Utilities

Yesterday you learned how to install SQL Server 7.0. As you quickly discovered, running the setup program isn't very difficult (in fact, it's almost trivial). It's understanding the critical selections you are making that requires effort. Once selected, changing your sort order, character set, or Unicode collation is a significant effort.

Today's lesson focuses on the tools and utilities you installed (assuming you installed all of them). You will examine not just the utilities that appear in your Start menu, but the command-line utilities and utilities that simply don't have Start menu shortcuts. These utilities might be a bit hidden, but don't underestimate their value.

The Microsoft SQL Server 7.0 Program Group

The best place to start when examining the available tools is the SQL Server 7.0 program group in your Start menu. Click Start, Programs, Microsoft SQL Server 7.0 to see Figure 3.1.

FIGURE 3.1

The Microsoft SQL Server 7.0 program group.

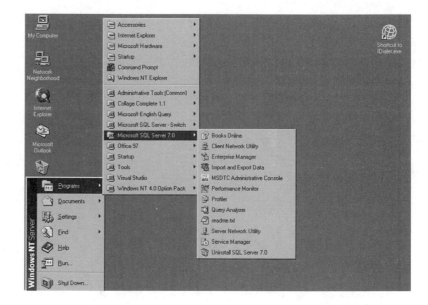

This is the main group of tools you will work with when building SQL Server database applications or when administering SQL Server. You must be familiar with each tool in this program group because you will almost certainly end up using every one of them before your 21-day adventure into SQL Server is over. Today's lesson examines them in the order you will probably want to look at them—not in the order they appear in your Start menu.

The readme.txt File

A great place to start is with the readme.txt file. The readme.txt file contains important information you should read before you install, as well as information that didn't quite make it into the manuals before the product shipped. You will want to review this file once to make sure there's nothing you must do or change before moving on with SQL Server 7.0. Of course, you did this yesterday before you installed the product.

Books Online

The SQL Server Books Online is your primary reference source for information (except, of course, for this book!). When you have a question about SQL Server, you can go to the Books Online. The Books Online is shipped in lieu of actual paper manuals, although you can order hard copies from Microsoft. The books ship as a compiled set of HTML pages, so you can view them within the context of Microsoft Internet Explorer 4.01 (service pack 1) or later. Figure 3.2 shows the SQL Server Books Online utility.

FIGURE 3.2

The SQL Server 7.0 Books Online.

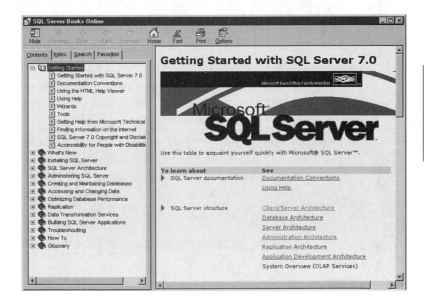

3

Books Online gives you the functionality you would expect from a set of manuals—the ability to view information, search for that information, and print paper copies. To print any topic, simply right-click the topic and select Print. You will be prompted to print either the single page you are looking at or the page and all subpages.

Tip

Unless you want to kill lots of trees, be careful not to print from the top-level books.

The left pane of the Books Online is broken into four tabs by default:

- Contents—The Contents tab shows every SQL Server Book as if you had paper copies of the manual. If you know what book a topic is in, simply expand the book (by clicking on the plus (+) sign) to view the contents. Most books have several levels you will need to drill down into to find a particular topic of interest.

- Index—The Index is a sorted list of just about every keyword in the Books, arranged in alphabetical order. Simply type in the name of the word you are looking for, and the index will scroll to the closest index entry. To then display the contents (or, if there are multiple entries for a keyword, an option to select which entry to go to), double-click on the entry in the index.

- Search—The Search tab is where you will usually end up. Simply type in the concept, command, or option you want to know more about and click List Topics. The results of your search will be displayed. Again, simply double-click an entry to have the entry displayed on the right half of your screen.

- Favorites—Just as you can in Internet Explorer, you can keep a list of favorites in the Books and simply click on the entries here rather than search for items over and over. When you are viewing a topic, click on the Add button (Figure 3.3). When you want to go back to that topic, simply double-click the entry in your favorites list.

FIGURE 3.3

The Books Online Favorites option.

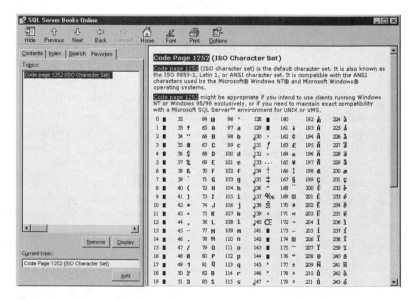

The SQL Server Books Online is further broken into several "Books", which you see on the Contents tab. Each of these books is explained in the following sections.

Getting Started

The Getting Started book provides links to the rest of the books; documentation conventions (so you can understand the syntax statements and other formatting options); a list of the tools, wizards, and other features of SQL Server; and information on contacting SQL Server Technical Support. Additionally, information for people with disabilities and on backward compatibility is included in this section. Everyone should read this section.

What's New

The What's New book includes a brief overview of features of the product that are new to people who have used previous releases of SQL Server. If you have used earlier versions of SQL Server, you should review this section to see what's changed.

Installing SQL Server

The Installing SQL Server book includes detailed information about setting up a new instance of SQL Server 7.0. Because you have already read the lesson for Day 2, "Installing SQL Server 7.0," you don't need to read this book.

SQL Server Architecture

The SQL Server Architecture book gives a detailed look at the architecture of SQL Server 7.0. It provides many details on how SQL Server works and how everything fits together. You will encounter most of the information in the Architecture book on your 21-day adventure, but a great section to look at is the "Technical Specifications." Here you will find all the limits in SQL Server documented. This includes information like how big a database can be, how many tables can be in a database, and other detailed information.

Administering SQL Server

This book documents how to administer SQL Server. *Sams Teach Yourself SQL Server 7.0 in 21 Days* teaches you everything you need to know to perform the basics (and some advanced options) of SQL Server administration. Therefore, you will have little need to review this book of the Books Online.

Creating and Maintaining Databases

This book documents how to create databases and all the objects to be contained in your databases. Again, *Sams Teach Yourself SQL Server 7.0 in 21 Days* teaches you everything you need to know on a day-to-day basis, so reading *Creating and Maintaining Databases* is also unnecessary.

3

Accessing and Changing Data

Accessing and Changing Data explains how to query and modify data in SQL Server. As with the other topics, *Sams Teach Yourself SQL Server 7.0 in 21 Days* has everything you need, and you don't need to review this book either.

Optimizing Database Performance

This book presents performance tuning information for SQL Server. Day 20, "Configuring and Monitoring SQL Server 7.0," will help you with some performance tuning and monitoring basics, and you will encounter additional performance tuning information throughout your 21-day odyssey. However, performance tuning is a huge topic, so you might want to read this section of the Books Online (when you've completed this book). I also recommend the *Microsoft SQL Server 7 Unleashed* book from Sams Publishing for additional performance tuning information.

Replication

This book explains SQL Server 7.0 replication. Day 17, "Implementing Standard Replication," and Day 18, "Implementing Merge Replication," fully cover SQL Server replication. So again, no need to review this part of the Books Online. See what a bargain this book is?

Data Transformation Services

Data Transformation Services (DTS) is explained in this book of the Books Online. Day 10, "Using SQL Server 7.0 Data Transformation Services," covers the majority of what you need to use DTS. However, DTS is a very sophisticated tool and could be an entire 21-day book by itself. Therefore, for advanced transformations you might choose to reference this book.

Building SQL Server Applications

Building SQL Server Applications is *huge*! It contains the Transact-SQL reference (the syntax and explanations for all commands in SQL Server), as well as programming references for a variety of client and server technologies. The good news is that what you need to know about SQL Server commands is interspersed throughout the *Sams Teach Yourself* book. This book does not attempt to be a client programming reference, so some topics in this section of the Books Online are useful—particularly if you are writing client programs using open database connectivity (ODBC), object linking and embedding database (OLE DB), or ActiveX Data Objects (ADO). SQL Distributed Management Objects (SQL-DMO) is the programmatic administrative interface for SQL Server, and is also documented here.

Troubleshooting

The Troubleshooting book explains the most common problems and how to resolve them. After your 21 days, you should understand and be able to resolve most problems without ever referring to the Books Online. But this section is available just in case.

How To

The How To book explains how to perform specific actions using Transact-SQL, SQL Server tools and utilities, and other programming interfaces. You won't typically go directly to this book—there are hyperlinks (jumps) throughout the other books that take you to the appropriate How To topic.

Glossary

The Glossary is an explanation of terms used throughout the SQL Server Books Online.

Service Manager

The SQL Server Service Manager utility enables you to control the SQL Server-related services on your computer (or any SQL Server computer on your network). When you start this utility, you see something similar to Figure 3.4.

FIGURE 3.4

The SQL Server Service Manager utility.

The Server field contains the name of the server you are monitoring. The Services box shows which service you are examining, and there is a graphical representation of the state of the service. When a service is running, the green light will show. This indicates that, in this case, the MSSQLServer service is currently running. As you learned on Day 2, this is the main service that runs SQL Server.

You can also stop or pause a service. Some services do not support being paused, and those that do vary in their behavior. For example, the MSSQLServer service will continue to function when paused, but new connections will not be allowed.

Note There is also an option to auto-start each service when the operating system starts. This option is especially handy on Windows 9x computers because they don't have services that can be configured to start automatically. Simply make sure the check box next to the Auto-Start Service When OS Starts is checked for each service you want to have started automatically.

The Services drop-down list shows which services can be controlled from this utility. This includes the MSSQLServer service, the SQLServerAgent service, the MSDTC service, and (if installed) the Microsoft Search service. You can use the server drop-down list to select another server. The list can be somewhat unreliable, and the utility is flexible enough to allow you to simply type the name of the server you'd like to examine. After you've typed a server name, click the drop-down list for Services. The service manager will then attempt to connect to the remote server.

Note that all the functionality of this application is also available from SQL Server Enterprise Manager. However, the Service Manager runs from your taskbar and can be very convenient to access.

Note Note that at this point your security will be checked. You must be a Windows NT administrator or a server operator on the server you are connecting to in order to control services (if the remote computer is a Windows NT computer). SQL Server permissions have no effect on your Windows NT permissions, so even if you are a SQL Server administrator, that doesn't guarantee you can control SQL Server services.

The SQL Service Manager utility has a somewhat hidden functionality. Click the icon in the upper-left corner of the application, and the normal application menu shows up with a couple of additions (see Figure 3.5). Notice that two additional menu choices are available: Connect and Options.

FIGURE 3.5

The additional features of the SQL Server Service Manager utility.

Connect

If you have typed or selected a remote computer name under the Server list box, you can connect from the menu rather than click the Services list box. They perform the same action—attempting to connect to the remote computer to determine the state of the SQL Server services.

Options

When you click the Options tab you will see Figure 3.6.

FIGURE 3.6

The SQL Server Service Manager Options dialog box.

Verifying Your Service Control Actions

The Verify Service Control Action option is enabled by default. When you click the appropriate icon, the action you've requested is taken, but only after you are prompted with an Are you sure? dialog box (see Figure 3.7). To turn off this verification and simply have services stopped and started when you double-click the appropriate graphic, uncheck the check box here in the options dialog box.

FIGURE 3.7

The SQL Server Service Manager Are you sure? dialog box.

Setting the Polling Interval

The polling interval determines how often the Service Manager utility checks for the state of the services you are monitoring. The default interval is five seconds. This means that every five seconds the utility will query the server for the state of all SQL Server-related services.

Client Network Utility

The Client Network utility is not a difficult tool to use, but it has a tremendous impact on the connectivity of your client computers to your SQL Server. When you start the utility, you will see a screen that looks like Figure 3.8.

FIGURE 3.8

The SQL Server Client Configuration utility.

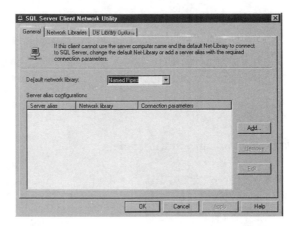

This screen tells you which network library you will use by default when you try to connect to any SQL Server using SQL Server client software. Think of it as a language. If your server speaks only English and French and you attempt to speak German, the server won't understand you and cannot respond. On Windows NT computers, the default is to use the Named Pipes network library. On Windows 9x computers, the default is to use the TCP/IP (Transmission Control Protocol/Internet Protocol) Sockets network library.

Yesterday's lesson discussed each of these network libraries during installation. Simply select the one that makes the most sense for your environment. The "universal" network library is TCP/IP sockets, so switching to that should allow you to connect to any SQL Server, regardless of which Windows operating system it's running on. Do note, however, that you do not have to install TCP/IP sockets. Named Pipes is required on Windows NT, so you know it will work.

Tip

> One convenient tip here. When connecting with a server name of (local) or . (a single dot), you bypass the default network library. On Windows NT, you use what's known as a local named pipe. On Windows 9x, you use the shared memory network library. These libraries are much faster because you don't need to go across the network to view your local SQL Server. Note that the shared memory network library is not available on Windows NT, and Named Pipes is not available on Windows 9x systems.

If you select a network library that is not supported by a server, your connection attempt will result in the error Specified SQL Server Not Found. This could mean that the MSSQLServer service isn't running on the remote computer, but it could also mean that the server doesn't support the network library with which you are attempting to connect.

You can also override the default settings and connect to a named server with a specific network protocol. For example, if you have a server named Sales, and the server's copy of SQL Server supports only the Multiprotocol Net Library but the rest of your servers use Named Pipes, you can add an entry on this screen. Click Add and you will see something like Figure 3.9. Select Multiprotocol (or whatever network library you want to use), type the name of the server (in this case, SALES), and configure any additional fields provided. Each network library supports different configuration options. Click OK, and you've added the server with the selected protocol. After you've done this, whenever you type SALES as a server name in any SQL Server application or utility from this computer, you will use the Multiprotocol Net Library.

FIGURE 3.9

The Add New Network Library Configuration dialog box.

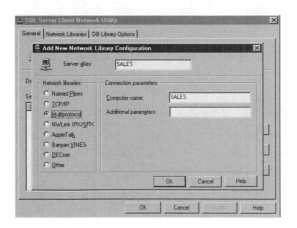

The Network Libraries Tab

The Network Libraries tab shows you each network library installed on your computer, along with the filename, version, file date, and file size. This information is most useful when you are looking for support. The versions will tell your support vendor which service packs and which releases of the network libraries you are using. All network libraries are installed on your computer by default.

The DB Library Options Tab

When you click the DB Library Options tab, you will see Figure 3.10. Several options are exposed here, which you will learn about. However, note that DB Library is supported in SQL Server 7.0 for backward compatibility only. ODBC and OLE DB technologies are the preferred mechanisms to connect to SQL Server 7.0. All the client utilities that ship with SQL Server 7.0 (except isql.exe) use ODBC. Isql.exe still uses DB Library, and older user-written applications might still use this network library.

FIGURE 3.10

*The DB Library
Options tab.*

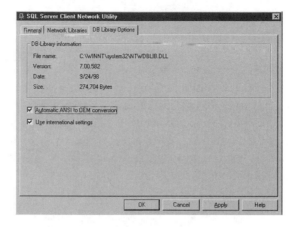

This screen tells you which version of the DB Library dynamic link library (DLL) you are using on your system. It indicates where the file is physically located, the date and size of the DLL, and the name of the DLL. You also have two options available: Use International Settings and Automatic ANSI to OEM Conversion.

International Settings uses certain settings, such as date and time formats, from Windows 9x and Windows NT. For example, if you're using Windows NT and have enabled a non-United States setting, your local settings will be used in favor of the settings on SQL Server. The ANSI to OEM conversion translates data coming back from SQL Server into the local code page used by your client. Generally, you should not disable either of these options.

Server Network Utility

The Server Network utility looks and feels like the Client Configuration utility. They are, as you might guess, closely related. Unlike the Client Configuration utility, which controls how your applications will connect to SQL Server, the Server Network utility reflects which network libraries SQL Server 7.0 is listening on (see Figure 3.11). Using the language comparison already described, this utility presents the list of languages your server knows how to speak. If you attempt to connect using any other network library, your SQL Server will not hear you.

Just as with the Client Configuration utility, simply click the Add button to list additional network libraries. To reconfigure a network library, click the Edit button; to remove a network library, highlight the library and click Remove. The changes you make will take effect the next time the MSSQLServer service is restarted.

FIGURE 3.11

The Server Network utility.

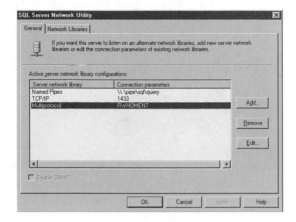

The Network Libraries tab is exactly the same as the Network Libraries tab of the Client Configuration utility.

Query Analyzer

The SQL Server Query Analyzer is your primary interface for running Transact-SQL queries or stored procedures. You will be using this utility throughout the rest of your 21 days, and it's a good idea to get comfortable with several options available to you. This said, it's worth noting that many of the features of this application are somewhat sophisticated, and you will explore them as you progress through this book.

Because you will use this application frequently, you might choose to simply click Start, Run, and type the application name. For historical reasons, this application's name is ISQLW.exe. So click Start, Run, isqlw and the Query Analyzer starts.

As you will learn on Day 5, "Using SQL Server Login and User Security," every operation in SQL Server is a secure operation. Therefore, you must first log in and identify yourself to any SQL Server to which you want to connect (see Figure 3.12). As mentioned in the discussion of the Client Configuration utility, you can enter (local) or . to connect to your local copy of SQL Server. You can also leave the server name blank. The Query Analyzer will figure out what you mean and connect to your SQL Server. If you are at the computer running the SQL Server to which you want to connect, the default local network connection is used (again, local Named Pipes for Windows NT and shared memory for Windows 9x). Otherwise, whatever client network library you have configured will be used.

FIGURE 3.12

The Connect to SQL Server dialog box of the SQL Server Query Analyzer.

If you like, you can have SQL Server automatically start if you attempt to connect and the MSSQLServer service is not running. This option is fine for local or Windows 9x computers, but make sure you think it through when connecting to production servers. Why is the server down? Is it for maintenance, which you will harm if you restart the MSSQLServer service prematurely?

You'll also need to provide login information. If you are on a Windows 9x computer, you will only be able to use the Use SQL Server authentication option. Use a login name of sa and no password. On case-sensitive servers, the login is also case sensitive, so make sure you enter it in lowercase. If you are on a Windows NT computer or connecting to a copy of SQL Server running on Windows NT, select the Use Windows NT authentication option to log in using your Windows NT security credentials. If you can do so, using Windows NT authentication is much simpler. By default, members of the Windows NT local administrator's group can log in to SQL Server. In either case, you are logging in as a system administrator or superuser to SQL Server. There is nothing you can't do.

After you've clicked OK or pressed Enter, you will be logged in to the appropriate instance of SQL Server (assuming you've typed valid login ID and password information or your Windows NT credentials allow you to connect). You will then see a screen that looks like Figure 3.13.

FIGURE 3.13

The SQL Server Query Analyzer.

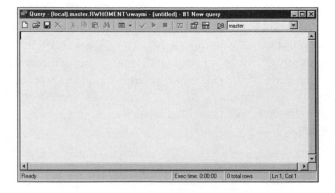

If your login doesn't go smoothly, you might see a screen similar to Figure 3.14. Usually you will see this screen if you've mistyped your password. Simply try again. You should also verify that you've typed your login name properly. If you have changed the sa password, make sure you type in the newest one in Figure 3.12.

FIGURE 3.14

Login Failed window.

Figure 3.15 shows another error you might get. If you receive this error, there are several things to look for. First, verify that the MSSQLServer service is running on the computer you are trying to log in to. If it is, then the problem might be with your client configuration. See the Client Configuration utility discussion earlier in today's lesson. Otherwise, make sure you typed the server name correctly. To see a list of servers on the network, instead of typing a server name, click the three dots next to the SQL Server name box to see a list of the active SQL Server machines on your network. I have had mixed success with this list. Don't be alarmed if your server does not show up here; you can still connect to a server that isn't visible by typing its computer name here.

FIGURE 3.15

Network connectivity problems.

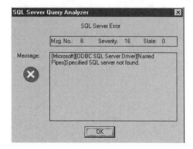

Figure 3.16 shows another blank query analyzer, but there are a couple of things worth noticing. There are actually two separate connections open here. The query analyzer can have up to 32 separate connections open at any one time. Each connection has a title bar that identifies the following:

- Which computer you are logged in to
- Which database you are currently using
- Which login you used to connect
- The title of any query you have opened (examined shortly)
- Which window number is being displayed

As you might guess, having this information in the title bar when you have 32 connections open can be extremely handy. So in Figure 3.16, you see one connection as the user sa and one using my Windows NT security credentials RWHOMENT\rwaymi. Both are connected to my computer, RWHOMENT, in the master database.

FIGURE 3.16

Multiple connections in a single instance of the Query Analyzer.

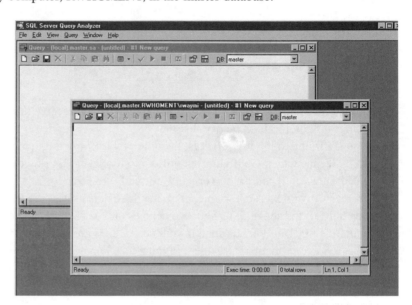

The Query Toolbar

After you have successfully logged in, you can start running Transact-SQL queries (you will learn how to program these queries starting on Day 11, "Retrieving Data with Queries"). You can open multiple windows inside the Query Analyzer by selecting the New Query button (the leftmost button on the toolbar). Note that this is not the same as having multiple connections because each of those could have been to a different computer. Each new query window you open is a separate connection to SQL Server; so if you open too many, you might be wasting resources on your SQL Server.

If you select the second button (which looks like a standard windows File Open button), it will open a standard dialog box to find Transact-SQL scripts (which by default have a .SQL extension). The next button, the Save Query/Result button, will either save the text in your query window to a file or, if you have run a query and selected (or clicked in) the Results window, save the results of a query you have run. The next button (with the red x) clears your query window of any text so you can start with a clean slate. The next several buttons are the Windows standard Cut, Copy, Paste, and Find buttons. They become enabled when appropriate (see Figure 3.17).

FIGURE 3.17

The Query Analyzer toolbar.

The next button gives you the option of determining where your results will appear when you run a query. The default is to simply display whatever text is returned from SQL Server (lined up under any titles for columns of data that are returned). However, as you can see in Figure 3.18, you can also choose to receive the results of your query into a grid. The Grid option works very nicely because many names in SQL Server 7.0 can be 128 Unicode characters in length. The default of displaying the text will usually pad out all 128 characters with spaces if the names are not fully used. The Grid option typically leaves enough space only for the widest data column to be displayed.

FIGURE 3.18

Query mode selection.

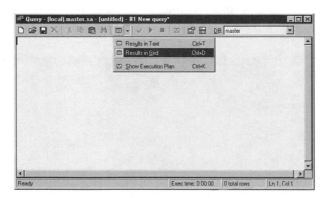

The last option on the pull-down menu in Figure 3.18 is Show Execution Plan. This option shows you the methods and indexes SQL Server will use to find the data you request with your queries. Unlike the Text or Grid options, where you either have one or the other turned on, the Show Execution option is either on or off, regardless of the grid or text options.

The easiest way to understand these options is with an example. Type the following text in your query window:

```
Use Pubs
Select * from authors
```

This query is straightforward when you understand what these commands mean. The first statement, Use Pubs, instructs the server to switch to the pubs database. The pubs database is a sample database installed on all SQL Servers. The second statement, Select * from authors, requests that SQL Server return all rows and all columns of data from a table or view named authors (and, because you switched to the pubs database, you know it's in pubs).

So, in English, these statements mean

```
Switch to the pubs database
Return all data about authors
```

After you have typed the two preceding commands, you can verify that they have been entered correctly. Notice that several options on the toolbar are now available. Click the blue check mark on the toolbar to verify that you have typed everything correctly. SQL Server will parse your query—meaning it will check that it's syntactically correct. If it works okay, you will get back

```
The command(s) completed successfully.
```

Now, to actually run the query, click the next button over—the play button. You can also select Query, Execute from the menu, type F5 on your keyboard, or (my favorite) Alt+x. After you run the query, the results pane appears with all information about authors in the pubs database (see Figure 3.19).

FIGURE 3.19

Your query results.

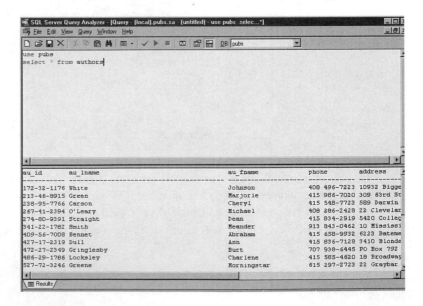

Notice that while your query was executing, the Stop option on the toolbar became available. You can cancel a query while it is still running. Your queries should run so fast that you'll never get a chance to cancel them.

Now, back to the Text versus Grid option. Click the current mode button on the toolbar, and switch to Results in Grid. You can also type Ctrl+D to set this option. Now rerun the query and examine your results pane. It will look like Figure 3.20.

FIGURE 3.20

Your query results in a grid.

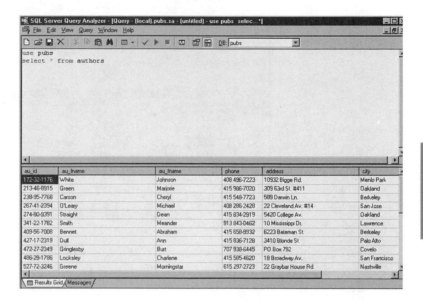

To take it a step further, add another line of code so that your query pane contains the following Transact-SQL commands:

```
Use Pubs
Select * from authors
Select * from titles
```

Run these queries again (using one of the methods examined earlier), and notice that now SQL Server Query Analyzer's results are in three tabs (see Figure 3.21). If you look at the bottom of the screen, you will see Results Grid #1, Results Grid #2, and Messages. The results of your first query are shown on Grid #1, the second on Grid #2, and any nondata messages (either informational or error messages) on the Messages tab.

FIGURE 3.21

Your query results in multiple grids.

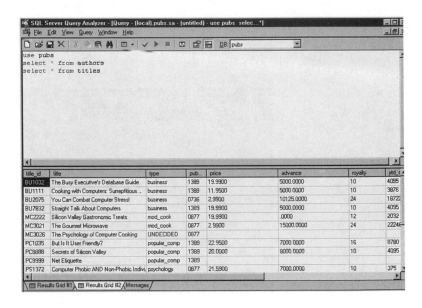

Moving on to the rest of the toolbar, the next option will show you how SQL Server will run your queries internally. You look at this feature in more detail on Day 13, "Enhancing Performance with Indexing."

Skip over the next button or two for a moment. The drop-down box next to the button labeled DB: provides a list of the installed databases on the server to which you are connected. If you change the value here, the SQL script you run will use this database unless you specify a different database in the SQL script itself. When you do specify a different database in your script, when the script is finished running the changed database will be reflected in this list box.

Configuring SQL Server Query Analyzer Options

The button with a hand holding a piece of paper (the one you skipped over a minute ago) displays the Query Analyzer Connection Options dialog box when pressed (see Figure 3.22). You can see the same dialog box by selecting Query, Connection options from the menu.

FIGURE 3.22

The query Connection Options dialog box.

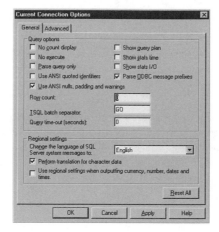

A significant number of options are exposed here. The help file explains each of them in detail, but you won't set most of them until you become a much more advanced SQL Server programmer/administrator. You configure how long the Query Analyzer will wait when attempting to log in to SQL Server. You can also configure how long to wait for long-running queries (0 means wait forever; any other value is a number of seconds), as well as set language and other international settings.

If you examine the Advanced tab, you will notice that you can configure items such as how to align the results of your queries and the maximum number of characters that can be returned for a single column of data. If you are having problems with the Query Analyzer, however, you might want to enable the ODBC tracing options for your support personnel. SQL Server Query Analyzer uses ODBC exclusively to connect to SQL Server 7.0.

Choose these options carefully—they can really change your output and you might easily forget you have set any options here.

NEW TERM I mentioned that you are running a script. A Transact-SQL *script* is any set of SQL commands that are stored and executed together. In fact, the File, Open and File, Save options allow you to save a query (or set of queries) and then run them again later. By default, scripts have the file extension .SQL.

Help Options

The last option to examine here is Help. If you can't remember the syntax of a command (the right way to type a command or a list of options), highlight a keyword with your mouse and type Shift+F1. Help for the command should pop up in a window. Help is built in for just about every Transact-SQL command.

Another really useful option is Alt+F1. If you highlight the name of a SQL Server object, such as a table, the default help will be provided in the Results window. The exact type of help you receive will depend on the type of object you're asking for help with, but will typically show you useful properties about an object.

> **Tip**
>
> There's one thing to note before moving on. If you highlight a command in the Query window, and then execute the query, just the highlighted text will be run. So you don't have to execute every statement in a window.

Enterprise Manager

SQL Server Enterprise Manager is the primary graphical administrative and development interface for SQL Server. There is very little SQL Server Enterprise Manager can do that you can't accomplish from a Transact-SQL command. However, using the Enterprise Manager is sometimes more convenient (especially when you are new to SQL Server).

SQL Server Enterprise manager is what's known as an MMC snap-in. MMC stands for the Microsoft Management Console. The MMC is a common utility that Microsoft and third-party vendors can use as the common administrative interface to their respective products. All BackOffice products use the MMC as their primary administrative interfaces.

Registering a Server

When you start SQL Server Enterprise Manager, you might need to register a server. If you are sitting at a computer that has SQL Server installed, your local SQL Server will be registered for you during setup. If you have a previous release of SQL Server installed on the Windows NT computer on which you installed SQL Server 7.0, you might also see a SQL Server 6.x group. To register a server, select Action, New SQL Server Registration from the menu bar. The Register SQL Server Wizard appears (see Figure 3.23).

I recommend you check the box to not use the wizard in the future because registering a SQL server is one of the easier tasks you can perform. Click Next, and you will be presented with the default dialog box to register a SQL server (see Figure 3.24).

FIGURE 3.23

The Register SQL Server Wizard.

FIGURE 3.24

The Registered SQL Server Properties dialog box.

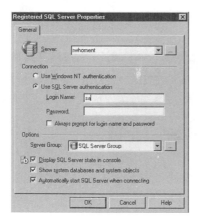

Enter your computer name as I have done in Figure 3.24, and then select the security mode you want to use. You can use either Windows NT security mode (if the SQL Server is running on Windows NT), or you can specify a SQL Server security login (which works on Windows 9x and Windows NT by default). Select the SQL Server login option, and complete your SQL Server login credentials if you select to use SQL Server Authentication. Just as in Figure 3.24, use sa (lowercase) with no password. The sa login is installed on all SQL Servers with a blank password by the setup program.

Notice that you can also choose to be prompted for your login and password every time you try to connect. Use this option on a Windows 9x computer to protect your security. If you are concerned about security, you should probably be using Windows NT, which is much more secure than the Windows 9x operating systems.

Notice that you can select to add this server under the default grouping of servers or create a new grouping in the server group text box at the bottom of the dialog box. This grouping is used strictly as an organization tool for your desktop. The SQL Server computers on your network have no knowledge of this grouping. You can also change several options such as to automatically start SQL Server when you use SQL Server Enterprise Manager and attempt to connect to the server and view the system databases. For this book, please make sure that you check all available options. Now click OK—that's it! You've configured your first registration for Enterprise Manager.

Examining How Enterprise Manager Works

Close this dialog by clicking the Close button, and you will see your server now in the left pane of Enterprise Manager (see Figure 3.25). In the figure, I have clicked on the plus sign in front of my server to connect to the server. You can tell when you are connected by the presence of the red lightning bolt through your server icon.

FIGURE 3.25

Enterprise Manager with your server registered.

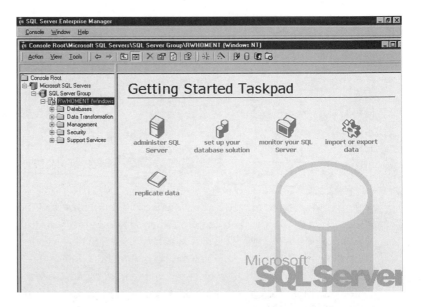

The Databases folder contains a list of the databases installed on your server. The Data Transformation Services (DTS) folder shows you any DTS "packages" that you have set up. The Management folder shows you administrative management features of SQL Server. The Security folder allows you to configure security in SQL Server. Finally, the Support Services folder enables you to control other SQL Server-related services on your computer, such as MSDTC. An expanded view of each folder is shown in Figure 3.26.

FIGURE 3.26

The left pane of Enterprise Manager with expanded folders.

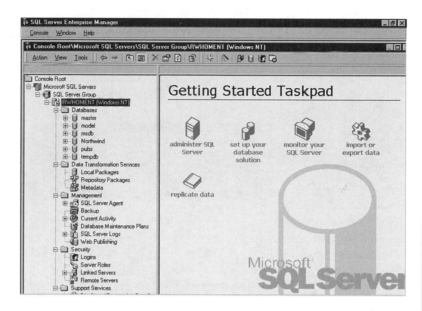

Now expand the pubs database folder, and then highlight the pubs database in the left pane. Notice how a Web page then displays in the right pane (see Figure 3.27). This is how Enterprise Manager works: Container objects are typically shown on the left side of the pane and the contents of the container objects, or other information, are displayed in the right pane.

FIGURE 3.27

The pubs database.

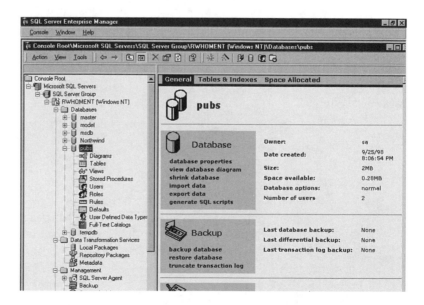

Some dialog boxes also open separate windows or dialog boxes for you to work with. For example, right-click the pubs database folder in the left pane and select Properties from the pop-up menu. Notice that you are presented with a new dialog on top of Enterprise Manager (see Figure 3.28). Property sheets (dialogs with the descriptions of properties of an object) often appear in these separate dialogs.

FIGURE 3.28

The properties of the pubs database.

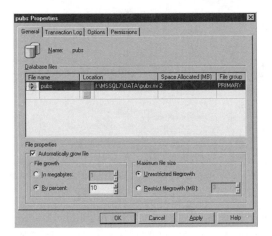

Click Cancel to dismiss the properties of the pubs database without making any changes. Another feature that's worth examining is the menu options. The options available will change depending on what you have highlighted. For example, you will see Figure 3.29 if you click the Tools menu with the pubs database highlighted. Don't be intimidated; you will learn what every option here does as you progress through the rest of your 21-day journey into SQL Server 7.0.

FIGURE 3.29

Menu options in SQL Server Enterprise Manager.

Explanations of Enterprise Manager could literally fill another 20 to 30 pages. However, you should know enough now to begin using the tool as you move on. You will use Enterprise Manager every single day, so by Day 21 you will be an Enterprise Manager expert!

Import and Export Data

The import and export data menu choice starts the DTS Wizard. You will examine DTS in great detail on Day 10.

MSDTC Administrative Console

The MSDTC administrative console lets you control and monitor distributed transactions. Distributed transactions are an advanced topic, and you will examine this (and normal transactions) on Day 16, "Programming SQL Server 7.0." However, you do not need to use this utility.

3

Performance Monitor

This menu option starts the Windows NT performance monitor utility with a preconfigured performance monitor chart (.PMC) file named sqlctrs.pmc. This chart shows you the top counters that the SQL Server development team thought you would be monitoring. You can change this .PMC file and have more or fewer counters displayed by default. You would primarily use this utility to monitor SQL Server's performance, which you will do on Day 20.

Profiler

The SQL Server Profiler utility enables you to monitor all activity on your SQL Server. You can also use the profiler to perform performance tuning activities, such as examining the execution plan that SQL Server will use to run your queries. The profiler has sophisticated filtering mechanisms to let you keep track only of specific users, applications, or types of commands. There are close to 100 different events you can monitor from SQL Server 7.0. You examine the profiler on Day 20.

Uninstall SQL Server 7.0

This utility does as you would expect. It uninstalls SQL Server, including the MSSQLServer, sqlserveragent, MSDTC, and Microsoft Search services. All programs and utilities also are removed. You must therefore stop all SQL Server services and close all SQL Server tools on the server (including the SQL Server Service Manager in your taskbar) before running the uninstall program.

The Microsoft SQL Server—Switch Program Group

The second program group contains two possible entries. Note that this program group will appear only on Windows NT installations of SQL Server 7.0. These entries are the SQL Server Version Upgrade Wizard and possibly a SQL Server 6.x switch. The following sections examine each entry.

SQL Server Version Upgrade Wizard

You examined the Version Upgrade Wizard yesterday when you learned about installing SQL Server 7.0. SQL Server Version Upgrade on Windows NT computers enables you to upgrade either SQL Server 6.0 or SQL Server 6.5 databases and server properties. You can upgrade a single database, multiple databases, or server and scheduled job properties from a previous release of SQL Server.

SQL Server 6.0 and SQL Server 6.5 are the only releases supported for upgrade. No other previous releases are supported. You will find the version upgrade utility only on Windows NT systems because previous releases of SQL Server ran only on Windows NT.

The version upgrade process leaves your SQL Server 6.x database files in place. When you upgrade, the data is exported from SQL Server 6.x into SQL Server 7.0, and new databases and files are created in SQL Server 7.0. You can either upgrade your previous installation of SQL Server on the same computer or you can install SQL Server 7.0 on a second computer and then upgrade into the new SQL Server 7.0 computer.

Microsoft SQL Server 6.x Switch

This program group entry is present only on systems that had a previous release of SQL Server installed. When you click this option, you switch back to your previous release of SQL Server. Your start menu is changed to reflect the SQL Server 6.x utilities, and the previous release of SQL Server is available to run. When running SQL Server 6.x, the entry in the Start menu is renamed to Microsoft SQL Server 7.0. When you select it again, you are returned to SQL Server 7.0, and your start menu entries are restored.

Uninstall SQL Server 6.x

This program group entry is present only on systems that had a previous release of SQL Server installed. When you click this option, you uninstall your previous release of SQL Server. This is a custom uninstall program that will safely remove your previous release of SQL Server.

Caution

Do not run setup to remove your old release of SQL Server 6.x. The custom uninstaller that is installed with SQL Server 7.0 is the only safe way to remove the previous release without potentially damaging your SQL Server 7.0 installation.

Other SQL Server Tools/Utilities

Several utilities that don't have shortcuts on your start menu are available. These utilities, however, can be very useful. They are grouped into connectivity tools, server diagnostics, and maintenance utilities.

Connectivity Tools

Connectivity tools are the command-line utilities that provide a query interface or are network testing utilities. The first two tools you examine, OSQL and ISQL, allow you to connect to SQL Server and run Transact-SQL commands. These are the command-line equivalents of the SQL Server Query Analyzer. The second two sets of utilities, makepipe/readpipe and ODBCPing, let you test the network connectivity to your SQL Server.

OSQL

The OSQL.exe utility provides an ODBC-based query interface to SQL Server. The OSQL.exe utility uses ODBC to connect to SQL Server. You can use this utility to run batch queries to support production tasks. You can also easily script Windows command files to run OSQL and run Transact-SQL commands to add new data, change data, or remove data from your databases. You can also create scripts (as you saw for the SQL Server Query Analyzer) and then run them without having to use a graphical interface.

```
osql -U login_id [-P password] [-S server_name] [-E] [-e] [-p] [-n]
[-d db_name] [-q "query"] [-Q "query"] [-c cmd_end] [-h headers]
[-w column_width] [-s col_separator] [-t time_out] [-m error_level]
[-L] [-?]  [-r {0 ¦ 1}] [-H wksta_name] [-R] [-i input_file]
[-o output_file] [-u] [-a packet_size] [-b] [-O] [-l time_out]
```

▼ SYNTAX

where

- -U is your SQL Server login ID.

- -P is the SQL Server login password. If you don't enter it, OSQL will prompt you to enter it when the program is running.

- -E requests a Windows NT Authentication Mode connection, so you don't need to specify the -U or -P parameters.

▼

- -S tells OSQL which server to connect to. If not specified, OSQL will connect to the local server.
- -e echoes each statement you run in the output from that statement.
- -p will print out performance information for your queries.
- -n removes the numbers and the > prompt that OSQL normally includes in each row when you enter a set of commands.
- -d specifies which database to switch to when you connect.
- -q tells OSQL to run the query you surround in quotes when it starts. OSQL continues to run after running the query. If you must specify quotes, use double quotes around the query and single quotes in your query.
- -Q tells OSQL to run the query you surround in quotes when it starts, and then quit osql.exe.
- -c—In SQL Server scripts, the word GO tells SQL Server to submit your queries to SQL Server. However, you can override this and use your own indicator to OSQL to submit your queries to SQL Server. You shouldn't override this option.
- -h indicates to OSQL how many rows to print between your column headings and your query results. If you specify -h-1, no headings are produced for your queries.
- -w allows you to override the width of your output from the default of 80 characters.
- -s allows you to override the default column separator of a blank space.
- -t tells OSQL how long to wait before it considers your connection to the server to be a failure.
- -m changes error message reporting. The syntax is -m ##, where the number is the severity level of errors. Day 20 explains error severity.
- -L shows a list of all SQL Servers found on the network.
- -? is the standard request for this syntax list.
- -r indicates that error messages should go to the stderr device. If 0, only severity 17 or higher messages are sent to the stderr device. 1 indicates that all messages go to the stderr device.
- -H is your computer name if you want to send it to SQL Server.
- -R allows client-side conversion when converting money and date time values from SQL Server.
- -i is the pathname and filename of the Transact-SQL script you want run.
- -o is the file you want your results from your script to be stored in. The output file will be in Unicode if your input file was in Unicode.

▼
- -u tells OSQL that the results of your query in your output file should be in Unicode.

- -a indicates the packet size to use on the network.

- -b tells OSQL to set the DOS error level when an error occurs. OSQL returns 1 when an error message with a severity level higher than 10 occurs.

- -O tells OSQL to emulate ISQL for backward compatibility.

- -l tells OSQL the login timeout (how long before it's assumed that your server isn't running).

▲ To run the commands you ran earlier for the SQL Server Query Analyzer, you would see the following in your command prompt:

```
C:\>osql /Usa
Password:
1> use pubs
2> select * from authors
3> go
```

and then you would see your query results displayed, ending in

```
893-72-1158 McBadden                              Heather
        707 448-4982 301 Putnam
        Vacaville            CA      95688         0
 899-46-2035 Ringer                               Anne
        801 826-0752 67 Seventh Av.
        Salt Lake City       UT      84152         1
 998-72-3567 Ringer                               Albert
        801 826-0752 67 Seventh Av.
        Salt Lake City       UT      84152         1

(23 rows affected)
1>
```

ANALYSIS The GO keyword is the signal to OSQL to begin running the command or commands you have specified. The 1> at the end is your indicator that OSQL is ready to accept a new Transact-SQL command. Two other commands worth noting are Reset and Exit.

- Reset stops any command and returns you to the 1> prompt.

- Exit leaves OSQL.

A batch file might look like this:

```
Osql -E -iC:\mssql7\runquery.sql -oc:\mssql7\results.txt
```

3

The input file would contain your queries and the results would show up in the results.txt file. This command would make a Windows NT authenticated connection to SQL Server. You could then run this batch file any time and even schedule this batch file to run at some scheduled time.

ISQL

ISQL.exe is the command-line query tool from previous releases of SQL Server. It uses the DB-Library network library to connect to SQL Server. Because it is based on DB-Library, it won't understand or be able to work with the new features of SQL Server, including Unicode. For this reason, you should discontinue using this utility if you have batch jobs already set up and definitely not start using this tool now.

```
isql -U login_id [-e] [-E] [-p] [-n] [-d db_name] [-q "query"]
[-Q "query"] [-c cmd_end] [-h headers] [-w column_width]
[-s col_separator] [-t time_out] [-m error_level] [-L] [-?]
[-r {0 ¦ 1}] [-H wksta_name] [-P password] [-S server_name]
[-i input_file] [-o output_file] [-a packet_size]
[-b] [-O] [-l time_out] [-x max_text_size]
```

Many of these parameters are similar to OSQL.exe, but you really shouldn't use this utility in SQL Server 7.0 except to support jobs that ran in previous releases.

Makepipe/Readpipe

You use these utilities to verify the integrity of the Named Pipes file system. You looked at them on Day 2, and they will not be discussed further here.

ODBCPing

ODBCPing enables you to verify that ODBC is working successfully from a client to a connection to SQL Server.

```
odbcping   [-?] ¦ [{-Sserver ¦ -Ddatasource} [-Ulogin] [-Ppassword]]
```

where

- -S is the server to which you want to connect.
- -D is the name of an ODBC data source.
- -U is the login ID you're using to connect to SQL Server.

- -P is the password for the login ID you've chosen.

When you installed SQL Server 7.0, ODBC version 3.7 was also installed. Try the following to test that connection.

Go to a command prompt and enter the following to connect to your copy of SQL Server. Specify your server name instead of mine (RWHOMENT):

```
odbcping -Srwhoment -Usa -P
```

The server should respond with something similar to this:

```
CONNECTED TO SQL SERVER
ODBC SQL Server Driver Version: 03.70.0554
SQL Server Version: Microsoft SQL Server  7.00 - 7.00.554 (Intel X86)
        Aug 14 1998 03:25:07
        Copyright  1988-1998 Microsoft Corporation
        Standard Edition on Windows NT 4.0 (Build 1381: Service Pack 4,
        ➥RC 1.99)
```

This means that ODBC is working fine. You can also connect to an ODBC DSN (Data Source Name), which is a preset configuration to a server you configure with the ODBC applet in your Windows Control Panel.

Server Diagnostics/Maintenance Utilities

The Server Diagnostic/Maintenance utilities are a set of utilities and tools you use at various times after you have installed SQL Server 7.0.

SQLServr.exe

SQLServr.exe is the actual program that runs SQL Server (normally, the MSSQLServer service). However, if you want to, you can run SQL Server from a command prompt. You would usually do this if you had to start SQL Server in what's known as single-user mode. You examine how to do this in more detail on Day 8, "Restoring SQL Server Databases," because that's when you typically must run SQL Server in single-user mode.

▼ **SYNTAX**

sqlservr [**-c**] [**-f**] [**-d**master_path] [**-l**master_log_path] [**-m**] [**-n**]
[**-e**error_log_path] [**-p**precision_level] [**-s**registry_key] [**-T**trace#]
[**-v**] [**-x**]

where

- -c indicates that SQL Server should run as a program and not as a Windows NT service. This makes SQL Server start faster in a command window.

- -f indicates that SQL Server should start in a "minimal" configuration. You would specify this option when you manually set a configuration setting that prevents SQL Server from starting normally. It's an emergency mode meant to allow you to fix any mistakes you make.

- -d indicates the pathname and filename of your master database file. If you don't specify this option, the default you set during setup is found in your Registry and used. The default location is c:\mssql7\data\master.mdf (or whatever drive on which you chose to install SQL Server).

▼

▼
- -l indicates the pathname and filename of your master database transaction log file. If you don't specify this option, the default you set during setup is found in your Registry and used. The default location is c:\mssql7\data\master.ldf (or whatever drive on which you chose to install SQL Server).

- -m indicates that SQL Server will start in single-user mode, and only one user is allowed to connect to SQL Server at any time with a single connection. This method is set during recovery situations after losing critical data files (such as recovering your master database from a backup).

- -n turns off logging of errors to the Windows NT Event Log (not recommended).

- -e is the pathname and filename of the SQL Server Errorlog. This defaults to c:\mssql7\log\errorlog (or whatever drive on which you chose to install SQL Server).

- -p is the maximum precision to allow for the decimal and numeric data types. By default, SQL Server allows these data types to hold up to 28 digits of precision. However, you can change this by specifying a number here, from 1 to 38. Specify this option if you plan to hold really big numbers in SQL Server.

- -s is used to specify a different Registry key to start SQL Server with. This is an advanced configuration option.

- -T specifies a trace flag to use in SQL Server. A trace flag is a numeric switch that tells SQL Server to enable special (nonstandard) behavior. You would typically only use these when directed to do so by SQL Server product support. To specify more than one, use multiple -T options.

- -v displays the version number of sqlservr.exe.

▲
- -x turns off SQL Server performance statistics (not recommended).

For example, stop SQL Server with the SQL Service Control Manager or SQL Server Enterprise Manager, and then open a command prompt. Type the following:

```
C:\>sqlservr.exe -c
```

SQL Server will run in that command window and will look like Figure 3.30 when it's ready for you to begin logging in with a query tool.

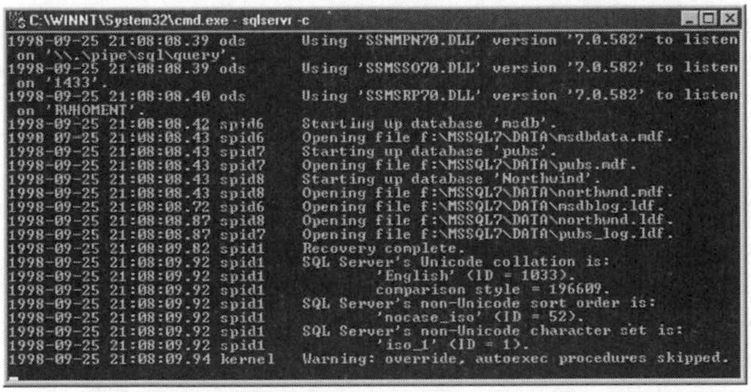

FIGURE 3.30

SQL Server when running in a command window.

To stop SQL Server, type Ctrl+c with the command window selected, and you will be prompted with

```
Do you wish to Shutdown SQL Server (Y/N)?
```

Type Y, and SQL Server stops. You can then restart SQL Server as a service.

The Rebuild Master Utility (rebuildm.exe)

The Rebuild Master utility rebuilds your master database, as well as the msdb, model, tempdb, pubs, and Northwind databases. You would run this utility for the following reasons:

- You lose a hard drive and don't have any backups.
- You want to change the sort order or character set.
- You want to change the Unicode collation sequence.

When you run the Rebuild Master utility, new copies of each of these databases are made from your SQL Server 7.0 CD, and then the sort order, character set, and Unicode collation choices you have made are applied. Any databases (in addition to those just mentioned) that were defined in your previously running SQL Server will no longer be defined, and you will need to re-create all your databases, or "reattach" the databases to your SQL Server. Note that if you change the sort order, character set, or Unicode collation, you will not be able to simply reattach any previous databases.

Rebuilding master is typically done in a disaster recovery scenario, which is where you will examine the utility further on Day 8.

The Registry Rebuild Utility (regrebld.exe)

The Registry Rebuild utility can be used when your Windows NT registry becomes corrupted for some reason or when you are instructed to do so by Microsoft SQL Server product support. Regrebld.exe simply re-creates all the registry keys that were built during setup.

SYNTAX

```
regrebld [-Backup ¦ -Restore ]
```

where

- `-Backup` saves a backup copy of your registry in the \mssql7\binn directory.
- `-Restore` restores your registry from the backup in the \mssql7\binn directory.

When SQL Server 7.0 setup completes, `regrebld -Backup` is run to prepare you in the event of a needed restore.

SQLMaint.exe

This command supports routine system maintenance, including backup, consistency checking, and index maintenance. There's a wizard in SQL Server Enterprise Manager called the Database Maintenance Plan Wizard. It helps you configure maintenance plans and backups for your databases without having to know a lot about what's going on behind the scenes. What the wizard is actually doing is configuring automated jobs to call this utility. There are many options here—most of which won't make much sense now. However, by Day 19, "Using the SQL Server Agent," when you learn to configure the SQL Server Agent, including setting up scheduled jobs, you should review this syntax and look at how to use this program to automate much of your server database maintenance. The basic syntax is examined here, but as you can see by the number of parameters, manual configuration of sqlmaint.exe can be a little tricky.

▼ SYNTAX

```
sqlmaint [-?] ¦
[ [-S server] [-U login_ID [-P password]]

{ [ -D database_name ¦ -PlanName name ¦ -PlanID guid ]

[-Rpt report_file [-DelTxtRpt <time_period>] ] [-To operator_name]

[-HtmlRpt report_file [-DelHtmlRpt <time_period>] ]

[-RmUnusedSpace threshold_percent free_percent]

[-CkDB ¦ -CkDBNoIdx] [-CkAl ¦ -CkAlNoIdx] [-CkTxtAl] [-CkCat]

[-UpdSts] [-UpdOptiStats sample_percent]

[-RebldIdx free_space] [-WriteHistory]

[ {-BkUpDB [backup_path] ¦ -BkUpLog [backup_path] }

{-BkUpMedia  {DISK [ [-DelBkUps <time_period>]

[-CrBkSubDir ] [ -UseDefDir ]]

¦ TAPE }}
```

▼ `[-BkUpOnlyIfClean]`

`[-VrfyBackup] ] } ]`

```
<time_period> ::=
number[minutes ¦ hours ¦ days ¦ weeks ¦ months]
```

where

- `-S`, as with the other utilities, is the name of the server you're running against.
- `-U` is the login name you're using to run the utility.
- `-P` is the password for the login name you just specified.
- `-D` specifies the name of the database you are maintaining.
- `-Rpt` is the parameter that identifies where to put such information as the output file reporting errors from running this utility. It should be a full pathname and filename.
- `-To` is the name of an email account you'd like to have a copy of the report sent to. You will examine email integration (called SQLMAIL) on Day 19.
- `-HTMLRpt` is the parameter that identifies where to put such information as the output file (in the form of a Web page) reporting errors from running this utility. It should be a full pathname and filename.
- `-RmUnusedSpace` is the parameter that tells sqlmaint.exe to remove any free space on databases larger than the `threshold_percent` parameter if the database is set to grow automatically (the default). The database will be shrunk, leaving some percentage of free space, specified in the `free_percent` parameter. Therefore, if you had a 100MB database, but only 50MB was used, and you had a `free_percent` of 10, the database would only shrink to 55MB (because 10% of the 50MB used is 5MB, the database would have 5MB of free space remaining).
- `-CkDB ¦ -CkDBNoIdx` parameters run the DBCC `Checkdb` command. This command is examined further on Day 7, "Implementing Backups in SQL Server 7.0."
- `-CkAI ¦ -CkAlNoIdx` parameters run the DBCC `Checkalloc` command. See Day 7 for more details.
- `-CkTxtAl` is the DBCC `Textall` command. Again, see Day 7.
- `-CkCat` is the DBCC `CHECKCATALOG` command. Is this getting familiar?
- `-UpdSts` runs the `Update Statistics` command. You'll examine statistics on Day 13.
- `-UpdOptiSts` runs the Update Statistics command with an optional parameter. You'll examine statistics on Day 13.

▼

3

- -Rebldldx runs the DBCC DBREINDEX command to re-establish your fillfactors on your indexes—again, Day 13.

- -WriteHistory records that the maintenance plan was run in a system table in the MSDB database (the sysdbmaintplan_history table).

- -BkUpDB ¦ -BkUpLog is where your backups will be placed. You can back up either the full database or just the transaction log. Backups are examined on Day 7.

- -BkUpMedia indicates you're backing up to either disk or tape.

- -DelBkUps indicates how long you want to keep your backups if you save them to disk.

- -BkUpOnlyIfClean indicates that the database should be backed up only if it's not corrupt. This is the most powerful feature of this utility and is discussed further on Day 7.

- -VrfyBackup verifies that the backup is readable after it has been made. Again, this is examined on Day 7.

Note

We're not trying to hide anything; it's just that most of these options will mean a lot more to you when you're finished reading the book than they do right now. That's why we keep saying "You'll learn more about this on Day x."

SQLDiag.exe

The SQLDiag utility is used to prepare for a call to SQL Server Product Support. SQLDiag captures the last 100 queries that were run on your SQL Server. It also gathers your error logs, your server configuration information, and the version of SQL Server you are using (including any service packs that have been applied), operating system information, computer system information, and other useful troubleshooting information, and places it all into a single file. This file is named SQLDIAG.txt and is placed in your \mssql7\binn directory by default. When you run the utility, you will see output as shown in Figure 3.31.

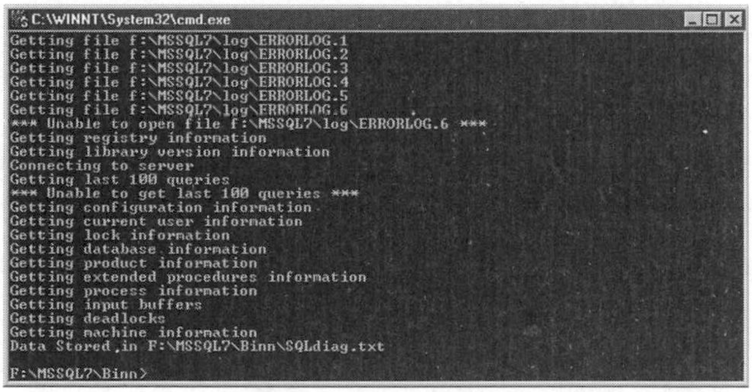

FIGURE 3.31

The results of SQL-DIAG.exe.

Print out this text file (or copy it to somewhere safe) because it contains so much valuable information about your system. Running this utility and having the information available to Microsoft's product support team will speed up any support call you make.

BCP—In a Class by Itself

BCP stands for the Bulk Copy Program. This utility loads data from a file into SQL Server or exports data from SQL Server to a file. You learn the details of this utility, including its syntax, on Day 10.

Summary

SQL Server 7.0 ships with the best toolset yet from Microsoft. You can easily administer your entire organization from a single graphical management console. You have tools to run queries, examine performance information, and monitor your SQL Server services. You can configure your network connectivity and even have network connectivity troubleshooting tools already installed on your system. Some tools are available via your Start menu, while others are available only from the command prompt in your mssql7\binn directory. Either way, you will end up using all these tools and utilities at one time or another—most likely in the remaining 18 days of this book.

Q&A

Q Which SQL Server utilities can I use to control the SQL Server-related services on my server?

A The SQL Server Service Manager and SQL Server Enterprise Manager.

Q Which utilities allow me to run queries against SQL Server 7.0?

A SQL Server Query Analyzer, osql.exe, and isql.exe.

Q **Which tool provides most of the functionality you will need to support SQL Server as an administrator (or a developer, for that matter)?**

A SQL Server Enterprise Manager.

Q **Which tool contains syntax help for you if you can't remember the exact way to type a command?**

A SQL Server Books Online or Help in the SQL Server Query Analyzer.

Workshop

The Workshop provides quiz questions to help you solidify your understanding of the concepts presented in this chapter. In addition to the quiz questions, exercises are provided to let you practice what you have learned in this chapter. Try to understand the quiz and exercise answers before continuing to the next day's lesson. Answers are provided in Appendix A, "Answers."

Quiz

1. How do you prevent someone from logging into SQL Server using your security credentials in Enterprise Manager?

2. Where would you set the default network library for your client computer?

3. Where would you add the NWLink IPX/SPX Network Library for your server?

4. Which utilities would you use to gather performance information about SQL Server 7.0?

5. Which utility would you run before calling Microsoft Product Support?

Exercises

1. Explore Books Online, looking for additional information about the utilities you examined today.

2. Change your client network utility default setting to a setting not supported by your server, and attempt to connect using the SQL Server Query Analyzer.

3. Explore Enterprise Manager, examining what happens when you click some objects and seeing what menu options are available. Try to get accustomed to right-clicking an object and exploring the pop-up menus and the options that are available. The more comfortable you are with Enterprise Manager, the easier the rest of your time with SQL Server will be.

DAY 4

Creating and Implementing Databases, Files, and Filegroups

On Day 3, "Using the SQL Server 7.0 Tools and Utilities," you learned about the different tools and utilities that come bundled with SQL Server 7.0. You learned about the SQL Server Enterprise Manager, which is a utility within the Microsoft Management Console (MMC). You will use the SQL Server Enterprise Manager and the SQL Server Query Analyzer utilities to do much of the work described today.

This chapter shows you how to create, alter, and drop a database. When you create a database, the database is stored in at least two separate files. One file contains the data, system tables, and other database objects; the other file stores the transaction log. In SQL Server 7.0 you can have your database dynamically grow by specifying database or transaction log file growth options.

Filegroups are a tricky subject, and you will learn the basics of their use in this chapter as well. Essentially, a filegroup enables you to explicitly place database objects like tables and indexes onto a specific database file (or group of files). This can have advantages for both the administration and maintenance of the database, as well as potentially improving performance for larger instances of SQL Server.

You will also look at the different database configuration options and how they affect your databases.

Creating a Database

To create a new database in SQL Server 7.0, you can use one of three methods:

- The Database Creation Wizard
- The SQL Server Enterprise Manager
- The CREATE DATABASE statement

When you create a new database, you are really just making a copy of the model database. Remember that everything in the model database will show up in any new databases you create. After you create the database by copying the model database, it expands to whatever size you have requested.

Databases need files to physically store their data on disk. When you create a new database, you must specify at least one file to store data and system tables as well as a separate file to hold your transaction log. Your database and transaction log can span multiple files as shown in Figure 4.1.

FIGURE 4.1

A database and transaction log can span multiple database files.

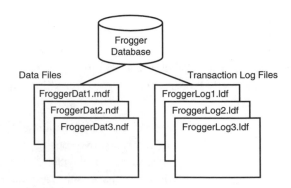

Note

The database files you create cannot be shared by any other database or transaction log.

In this section, you will break down the CREATE DATABASE statement and learn what each of the different parameters mean. When you understand what is being accomplished, you will see how to create a database using the SQL Server Enterprise Manager.

▼ SYNTAX

Here is the CREATE DATABASE statement:

```
CREATE DATABASE database_name
[ON {[PRIMARY]
(NAME = logical_name,
FILENAME ='physical_name'
[,SIZE = size]
[,MAXSIZE = max_size ¦ UNLIMITED]
[,FILEGROWTH = growth_increment])
}[,...n]]
[LOG ON
{(NAME = logical _name,
FILENAME = 'physical_name'
[,SIZE=size ¦ UNLIMITED]
[,MAXSIZE = max_size ¦ UNLIMITED]
[,FILEGROWTH = growth_increment])}
[,...n]]
[FOR LOAD ¦ FOR ATTACH]
```

▲

As you can see from the preceding syntax, the items necessary to create a database are the database name, the logical name of the primary database file, the physical name of the database's primary file, and the transaction log's logical and physical filenames. The following list describes the different CREATE DATABASE parameters:

- *database_name*—This parameter refers to the database as a whole.

- ON PRIMARY—This parameter specifies to which filegroup this database file is a member. The default filegroup is Primary. Filegroups are discussed later today.

- NAME—This parameter specifies the logical name you will use within SQL Server to refer to the physical database file on the hard disk.

- FILENAME—This parameter is the pathname and filename pertaining to where the data will be stored on hard disk.

- SIZE—This parameter specifies how big the database file should be. This value can be expressed in either megabytes or kilobytes. The default size is the size of the Model file. To specify megabytes or kilobytes, attach the MB or KB suffix to your size parameter. For example, 10MB would create a 10 megabyte file.

- MAXSIZE—This parameter specifies the maximum size to which the database can dynamically grow. If you do not specify a size here and the autogrowth option is turned on, your database could grow to fill your entire hard disk. This parameter is also expressed in either megabytes or kilobytes.

4

- FILEGROWTH—This parameter specifies which increments are used for the auto-growth of this database file. It can be expressed as either a number of megabytes, kilobytes, or as a percentage of the size of the file at the time of the growth. The default, if not specified, is 1MB.

- LOG ON—Describes where the transaction log files are located and what size they are.

- FOR LOAD—This parameter marks the database for dbo use only. The option is provided for backward compatibility only, and it should not be used in SQL Server 7.0.

- FOR ATTACH—This parameter reattaches a set of files that make up a database. The files for the database must have been previously created and then detached from SQL Server 7.0. You will examine this option later in this lesson.

Here are some examples of creating a database using the SQL Server Query Analyzer utility.

Listing 4.1 shows the code necessary for creating a database that starts out reserving 25MB—20MB are reserved for the data portion of the file and 5MB are reserved for the log portion of the file. The files could grow to a total of 100MB for data and 15MB for the transaction log, for a total of 115MB of disk space used.

INPUT   **LISTING 4.1   CREATING A DATABASE RESERVING 25MB**

```
USE master
GO
CREATE DATABASE Frogger ON PRIMARY
( NAME = FroggerData,
  FILENAME = 'C:\MSSQL7\DATA\FroggerData.mdf',
  SIZE = 20MB,
  MAXSIZE = 100MB,
  FILEGROWTH = 10MB   )
LOG ON
( NAME = FroggerLog,
  FILENAME = 'C:\MSSQL7\DATA\FroggerLog.ldf',
  SIZE = 5MB,
  MAXSIZE = 15MB,
  FILEGROWTH = 1MB )
GO
```

OUTPUT
```
The CREATE DATABASE process is allocating 20.00 MB on disk
'FroggerData'.
The CREATE DATABASE process is allocating 5.00 MB on disk
'FroggerLog'.
```

Tip

With SQL Server 7.0, it might be better for you to specify the amount of space needed right now to store your data and logs, rather than reserving the total amount of disk space you might need in the future. You can then take advantage of the FILEGROWTH and MAXSIZE parameters to let the database grow as needed and conserve hard disk space now.

Caution

You should specify a maximum size for your database and transaction log. If you do not specify a maximum size and you didn't specifically restrict auto-growth, your database could fill the entire hard disk. When a hard disk partition in Windows becomes full, Windows will generate errors and might not continue to operate until you have released space on the affected partition.

Listing 4.2 is an example of how to create a database that spans multiple files for both the data and the log. Notice that the logs and data files use the suggested Microsoft extensions. The first data file should have an extension of .MDF, and subsequent data files have the .NDF extension. Log files should use the .LDF extension.

INPUT   LISTING 4.2   CREATING A DATABASE THAT SPANS MULTIPLE FILES

```
USE master
GO
CREATE DATABASE Leap ON PRIMARY
( NAME = LeapData1,
  FILENAME = 'C:\MSSQL7\DATA\LeapData1.mdf',
  SIZE = 5,
  MAXSIZE = 20,
  FILEGROWTH = 1 ),
( NAME = LeapData2,
  FILENAME = 'C:\MSSQL7\DATA\LeapData2.ndf',
  SIZE = 5,
  MAXSIZE = 20,
  FILEGROWTH = 5 )
LOG ON
( NAME = LeapLog1,
  FILENAME = 'C:\MSSQL7\DATA\LeapLog1.ldf',
  SIZE = 2,
  MAXSIZE = 20,
  FILEGROWTH = 1 ),
( NAME = LeapLog2,
  FILENAME = 'C:\MSSQL7\DATA\LeapLog2.ldf',
  SIZE = 2,
  MAXSIZE = 10,
  FILEGROWTH = 2 )
GO
```

4

OUTPUT The CREATE DATABASE process is allocating 5.00 MB on disk
'LeapData1'.
The CREATE DATABASE process is allocating 5.00 MB on disk
'LeapData2'.
The CREATE DATABASE process is allocating 2.00 MB on disk
'LeapLog1'.
The CREATE DATABASE process is allocating 2.00 MB on disk
'LeapLog2'.

When you specify the use of multiple data files, SQL Server will automatically stripe information across all the data files specified. This can help reduce database contention and hotspots in your data. Note that SQL Server never stripes log files. The files will fill up with information sequentially, and when one log file is full, the data will move on to the next transaction log file.

Tip

If you are not using RAID 5 or higher, it is strongly suggested that you to place your transaction logs on separate physical hard disks. This will allow for greater recoverability in the event of a hard disk failure. An additional benefit is that writes to the transaction log will not interfere with writes to the data files.

You can also use the SQL Server Enterprise Manager to create a new database. Follow the steps outlined here to create a new database:

1. Start the SQL Server Enterprise Manager by selecting the Start button, Programs, Microsoft SQL Server 7.0, Enterprise Manager.

2. Connect to your SQL Server.

3. Expand your Databases folder as shown in Figure 4.2.

4. Right-click on either the Databases folder or in the whitespace in the right pane, and choose New Database from the context menu.

5. You should now be on the General tab of the Database Properties dialog box (see Figure 4.3).

6. Specify a database name. I will use Croak. Notice that the Database Files panel begins to change. You should see a new database file named Croak_Data with an initial size of 2MB in your default MSSQL7\data folder. If you look at File Properties at the bottom of the dialog, you will note that the Automatically Grow File option is turned on and that File Growth properties have been set. In addition to this, the maximum file size is set to Unrestricted Filegrowth.

FIGURE 4.2

The right pane of the SQL Server Enterprise Manager shows the databases, and the pop-up menu lets you arrange icons or perform tasks.

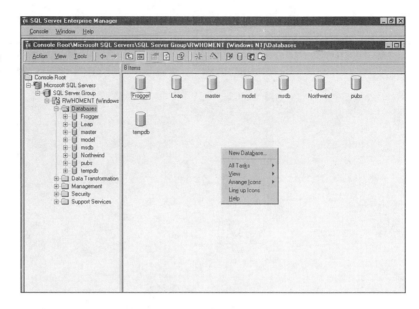

FIGURE 4.3

Use this tab to see the properties of a database such as the name, size, and filegroup.

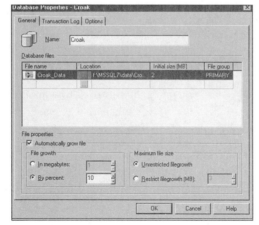

7. To change the properties of the database files, simply click in the appropriate box and make your modifications. I chose the defaults for this screen. Note that you can add additional database files if you simply go to the next box and add additional file properties.

8. Click the Transaction Log tab. You will notice that it has a default name of Croak_Log and is 1MB.

9. You will find out more about the Options tab a little later in this lesson. Click OK when you are finished. You should now have a screen similar to Figure 4.4. If you

don't see your Frogger, Leap, or Croak databases, right-click the Databases folder
and choose Refresh from the pop-up menu.

FIGURE 4.4

*The two new databases
have been added.*

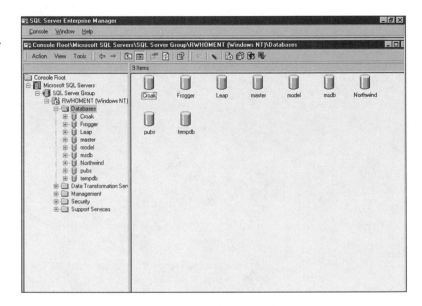

Gathering Database Information

As you might have suspected, you can gather information about your databases in
several ways. You can use the SQL Server Enterprise Manager, or you can use the SQL
Server Query Analyzer utility and run some system stored procedures.

You can use the sp_helpdb system stored procedure to examine an individual database
or gather summary information on all databases in SQL Server. If you run sp_helpdb
without specifying a database, you will get summary information on all databases in
SQL Server. For example:

**INPUT/
OUTPUT**

```
EXEC sp_helpdb

name      db_size    owner          dbid  Created    status
--------  ---------  ---------      ----  ---------  -----------
Croak     3.00 MB    RIBBIT\Admin... 8    Apr 14 1998 no options
set
Frogger   25.00 MB   sa             6     Apr 14 1998 no options set
Leap      14.00 MB   Sa             7     Apr 14 1998 no options set
master    7.31 MB    Sa             1     Mar 23 1998 trunc. log on
                                                      ➥chkpt.
```

```
model     1.19 MB   Sa            3    Apr 13 1998 no options set
msdb      3.75 MB   Sa            4    Apr 13 1998 trunc. log on -
                                                   ➥chkpt.
pubs      2.00 MB   Sa            5    Apr 13 1998 no options set
tempdb    8.75 MB   Sa            2    Mar 23 1998 select
                                                   ➥into/bulkcopy

(8 Row(s) affected)
```

As you can see, sp_helpdb gives you summary information about the databases in SQL Server. For example, the Frogger database is 25MB and is owned by the sa login, and it doesn't have any database options set. To gather more information about a single database, specify it in the sp_helpdb statement as follows:

EXEC sp_helpdb Croak

```
name    Db_size   Owner                dbid  Created     status
-----   --------  ----------           ----  ----------  ------
Croak   3.00 MB   RIBBIT\Administrator  8    Apr 14 1998 no options
                                                         ➥set

(1 row(s) affected)

Name         Fileid   Filename                   ...   Usage
----------------------------------------------------------------------

Croak_Data    1       F:\mssql7\data\Croak_Data.mdf  ...  Data only
Croak_Log     2       F:\mssql7\data\Croak_Log.ldf   ...  Log only

(2 row(s) affected)
```

In addition to what you get for the Frogger row shown previously, you will also get information about the files and how they are allocated. For example, the output from the previous statement shows the file Croak_Data is 2MB and is used for data only. Croak_Log is also 1MB and is used for the transaction log only.

You can also use the SQL Server Enterprise Manager to gather information about your databases. Open the SQL Server Enterprise Manager and expand the Databases folder. In the right pane, double-click on a database; this will bring up the editing screens shown earlier. You can also gather information by drilling down through the Databases folder and then highlighting an individual database, as shown in Figure 4.5. Figure 4.5 shows general information on the Leap database. You can select other options to see how space is allocated and how much space is being used. For example, Figure 4.6 shows how the space is allocated and used for the Leap database.

4

FIGURE 4.5

*General information on
the Leap database.*

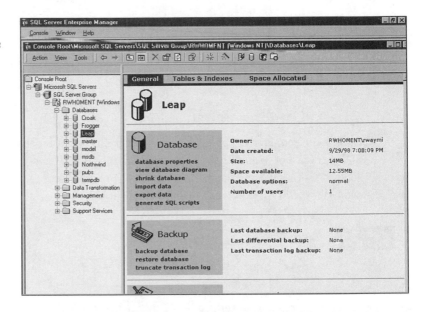

FIGURE 4.6

*File space and usage
information for the
Leap database.*

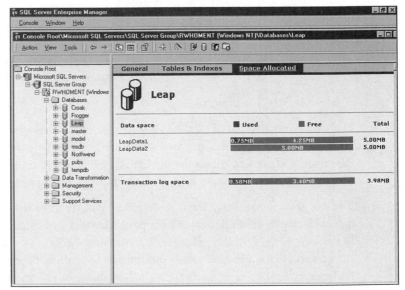

Setting Database Options

Now you will learn a little bit more about the database options that can be applied to your
databases. As usual, you can modify database options with stored procedures in the SQL
Server Query Analyzer or through the SQL Server Enterprise Manager.

To view and modify database options using the SQL Server Enterprise Manager, simply drill down until you find the database with which you want to work (pubs in this example). After you have located the database, you can either double-click the database in the right panel or right-click the database and choose Properties from the context menu. This will bring up the pubs Properties screen. Click the Options tab to view the database options as shown in Figure 4.7.

FIGURE 4.7

The Options tab of the pubs Properties dialog.

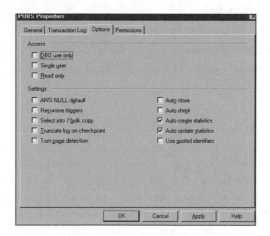

As you can see, the database options are broken into two categories: Access and Settings. Here's what each of these settings means:

- DBO Use Only—Specifies that only members of the db_owner fixed database role can use the database. This option is often set when a database administrator is performing maintenance and doesn't want ordinary users working in a database.

- Single User—Specifies that only one user at a time can access this database. Note that this actually allows only a single user connection to the database, even if each user has been issued a USE <dbname> statement.

- Read Only—Marks the database as read only, and no changes will be allowed.

- ANSI NULL Default—When selected, this option defines new table columns as null by default (or not). You will learn more about tables and columns on Day 9, "Creating Tables."

- Recursive Triggers—A recursive trigger occurs when a data modification on one table (I will call it TableA) fires a trigger on another Table (TableB). TableB then fires a trigger on the original TableA.

- Select Into/Bulk Copy—Allows nonlogged operations to be performed. This includes statements that use the SELECT INTO keywords. Because these operations

4

are not written to the transaction log, you should back up your database after performing them.

- Truncate Log On Checkpoint—Checkpoints are used to write used data pages and log records from random access memory (RAM) to your hard disks. When the system runs a checkpoint, this option removes the committed transactions from the transaction log. This is useful in a development environment where database recoverability is not an issue.

- Torn Page Detection—Detects when a partial page write has occurred to disk (a form of corruption of your data). I recommend that you turn this option on.

- Auto Close—The database will automatically close when the last user has exited from it. This option conserves resources on your server for a database that isn't used frequently.

- Auto Shrink—When this option is set, both data and log files will automatically shrink. Log files will automatically shrink after a backup of the log has been performed. The database files will shrink when a periodic check on the database finds that the database has more than 25 percent of its assigned space unused. The autoshrink process will shrink your database to a size that that has 25 percent of the space unused. Note that the autoshrink process will not shrink a database to a size smaller than its original size.

- Auto create statistics—Automatically generates statistics on the distribution of values in a column of data. This is used by the SQL Server query optimizer to generate a query plan based on the cost of using different columns.

- Auto update statistics—This option works in conjunction with the auto create statistics database option. Over time, the information in your columns will change; however, the statistics on those columns will not. To alleviate this problem, you must occasionally update your statistics. The auto update statistics option does this for you automatically.

- Use quoted identifiers—This option enables you to use double quotation marks as part of a SQL Server identifier. An identifier is the name of an object. This can be a variable, table, or something else. Quoted identifiers are useful when you have an identifier that also happens to be a SQL reserved word.

You can also accomplish these same tasks using the SQL Server Query Analyzer utility and the sp_dboption system stored procedure. For example, to mark the pubs database as DBO Use Only, you would run the code shown in Figure 4.8 from the SQL Server Query Analyzer utility. The code is

```
EXEC sp_dboption pubs, 'DBO Use Only', True
```

FIGURE 4.8

The code to mark the pubs database as DBO use only.

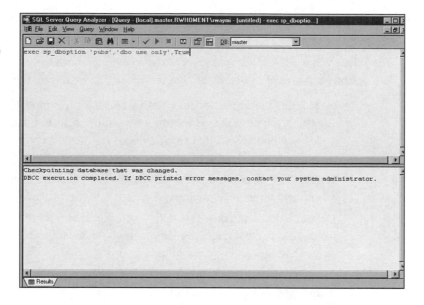

After running the preceding command, you can check to see whether it was really applied by running the sp_helpdb pubs system stored procedure, as shown in Figure 4.9. Notice the status section in the resultset; it shows dbo use only. The trunc. Log on Checkpt. option is also set (which is the system default after installation).

FIGURE 4.9

The Results Grid shows the change and status.

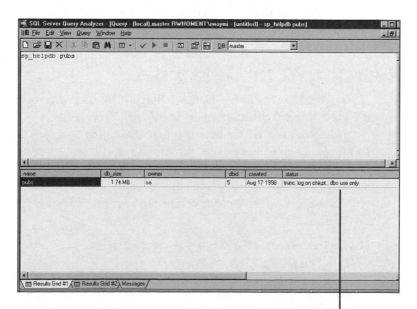

Status shows restriction

To turn off the DBO Use Only status, simply rerun the following code: `sp_dboption pubs, 'DBO Use Only', False` and the option is no longer set.

When you use the `sp_dboption` stored procedure, you can use an additional seven options that are not available through the Enterprise Manager. These are listed here:

- Concat null yields null—This option works a lot like multiplying by zero. Anything you do where you multiply by zero results in a zero. The concat null yields null option says that anything you concatenate a `null` with will result in a `null`. For example, `'Hello World' + null = null`.

- Cursor close on commit—This option specifies that any open cursors are closed when the transaction completes. A cursor is the resultset from a query.

- Default to local cursor—This option specifies that when a cursor is created without the `GLOBAL` keyword, it is available only to the local batch, trigger, stored procedure, and so on, that generated the cursor.

- Merge publish—This option enables the database to be used as a publisher in a merge replication scenario. Replication scenarios are covered on Day 17, "Understanding Replication Design and Methodologies."

- Offline—This option closes and shuts down the database. After a database has been taken offline, it can be moved to removable media and distributed.

- Published—This option allows a database to publish articles for replication.

- Subscribed—This option specifies that this database is the recipient of published data.

Resizing Your Database

If you would like to change the file definitions and size settings for a database, you can use the `ALTER DATABASE` statement or the SQL Server Enterprise Manager. To shrink a database, you must use the `DBCC SHRINKDATABASE` or `DBCC SHRINKFILE` commands. To add filegroups to your database, you can use the `ALTER DATABASE` statement. In this section, you will first examine the `ALTER DATABASE` statement and make some modifications to the databases already created in this lesson; you then will see how to shrink a database with the `DBCC SHRINKDATABASE` command. You will finish this section with a short lesson on filegroups.

Here is the syntax for the `ALTER DATABASE` statement:

▼ SYNTAX

```
ALTER DATABASE database
{
  ADD FILE <File specification> [,...n] [TO FILEGROUP filegroup_name]
¦ ADD LOG FILE <File specification> [,...n]
```

```
▼ ¦ REMOVE FILE logical_name
  ¦ ADD FILEGROUP filegroup_name
  ¦ REMOVE FILEGROUP filegroup_name
  ¦ MODIFY FILE <File specification>
  ¦ MODIFY FILEGROUP filegroup_name, filegroup_property
  }


  <File specification>
  (NAME = logical_name,
  FILENAME ='physical_name'
  [,SIZE = size]
  [,MAXSIZE = max_size ¦UNLIMITED]
▲ [,FILEGROWTH = growth_increment])
```

Here is the breakdown of the different elements listed in the syntax box:

- *database*—The name of the database to be altered.

- ADD FILE—Specifies a file be added.

- File specification—These are the same specifications listed earlier in the CRE-
  ATE DATABASE examples.

- TO FILEGROUP—Specifies the filegroup to add this file to. If none is specified, the
  file will be added to the default filegroup (PRIMARY).

- ADD LOGFILE—Adds a new log file to the database.

- REMOVE FILE—Removes a file from the database. The file must be empty before
  removal. You can use the DBCC SHRINKFILE statement to empty a file. This is covered later in this lesson.

- ADD FILEGROUP—Adds a new filegroup—you must also specify the new filegroup
  name.

- REMOVE FILEGROUP—Removes a filegroup. This will also delete all files that are
  members of the filegroup. The files in the filegroup must be empty. You can use the
  DBCC SHRINKFILE statement to empty files. This is covered later in this lesson.

- MODIFY FILE—Allows you to modify the properties of a file, including its physi-
  cal_name, filegrowth, and maxsize options. If you modify the size parameter, the
  new size must be larger than the current size. You can change the FILENAME parameter only for files that reside in tempdb; this change doesn't take effect until you
  restart SQL Server.

- MODIFY FILEGROUP—Allows you to change filegroup properties—this includes the
  READONLY, READWRITE, and DEFAULT properties.

4

> **Note**
> You must have CREATE DATABASE permissions in order to use the ALTER DATABASE statements.

Now take a look at expanding your database with the ALTER DATABASE command.

Expanding Your Database

You can expand your databases by adding additional files for growth. You can add files to the data portion as well as the log portion of the database. Unless you specifically turned off the autogrow features in your database, the database files will automatically grow until you run out of disk space. Remember that data stored across multiple files in a database will automatically stripe the information across those multiple files. You might be asking yourself, "If the database file automatically grows as needed, why in the world would I want to create multiple files for my data to live on? This would appear to make the maintenance of my database more cumbersome." The answer is yes, it would make the maintenance a little bit more cumbersome, but there are advantages as well. Multiple database files have the following benefits:

- You can place files on separate physical hard disks.
- You can improve performance because reads and writes to the database have a better chance of going to separate disk controllers.
- Database files can be backed up independently of each other.
- If you use filegroups, specific portions of your data can be placed in specific files. For example, the payroll table could be placed in its own filegroup in its own file.

In Listing 4.3, you will add a new data file to the Croak database from the SQL Server Query Analyzer.

INPUT   **LISTING 4.3**   ADDING A NEW DATA FILE TO THE CROAK DATABASE

```
ALTER DATABASE croak
ADD FILE
( NAME = CroakData2,
  FILENAME = 'C:\MSSQL7\DATA\CroakData2.ndf',
  SIZE = 2,
  MAXSIZE = 10,
  FILEGROWTH = 2)
```

OUTPUT   Extending database by 2.00 MB on disk 'CroakData2'.

You can now run the following sp_helpdb system stored procedure to verify that your database was successfully enlarged:

sp_helpdb croak

Your database should be 4MB with files of Croak_Data, Croak_Log, and CroakData2.

Now you can extend the database log file:

INPUT/
OUTPUT
```
ALTER DATABASE croak
ADD LOG FILE
( NAME = CroakLog2,
  FILENAME = 'C:\MSSQL7\DATA\CroakLog2.ndf',
  SIZE = 2,
  MAXSIZE = 10,
  FILEGROWTH = 2)
```

```
Extending database by 2.00 MB on disk 'CroakLog2'.
```

Verify your results by running the sp_helpdb Croak procedure now. Your database should now be 6MB.

You can accomplish much the same thing using the SQL Server Enterprise Manager. Follow these steps to modify the Frogger database created earlier:

1. Start SQL Server Enterprise Manager.
2. Expand your Databases folder and open the properties dialog for the Frogger database. (You can do this by right-clicking the Frogger database and choosing Properties from the context menu.)
3. In the General tab under the Database files dialog, click the empty box under FroggerData and add FroggerData2, as shown in Figure 4.10.
4. In the Location box, specify the new filename F:\MSSQL7\DATA\FroggerData2.NDF, or you can take the default value of FroggerData2_data.ndf. Note that your drive letter might be different.
5. In the Space Allocated (MB) box, add the number 2.
6. Leave the Filegroup as PRIMARY.
7. In the File Properties section, make sure that Automatically Grow File is checked.
8. Set the File Growth option to In Megabytes, and set it to 2.
9. In the Maximum File Size section, set the Restrict Filegrowth (MB) option to 4.
10. Now that you have added a data file, extend the transaction log as well. Instead of adding a new log file, just change the space allocated from 5MB to 10MB.

4

FIGURE **4.10**

Adding FroggerData2 *in the Database files with a space alloca-tion of 2.*

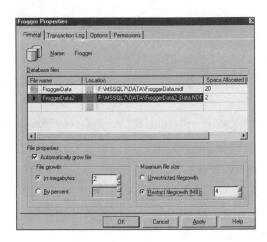

> **Note**
>
> Although you can specify a size less than the current size of the file, you cannot shrink a file from here. You must use either the DBCC SHRINKDATA-BASE or DBCC SHRINKFILE command.

11. Click OK when you are finished.

12. To verify that Frogger was modified, you can click the Frogger database in the left panel under the Databases folder. In the right panel, choose the Space Allocated option shown in Figure 4.11.

FIGURE **4.11**

Verifying that the database has the space you allocated.

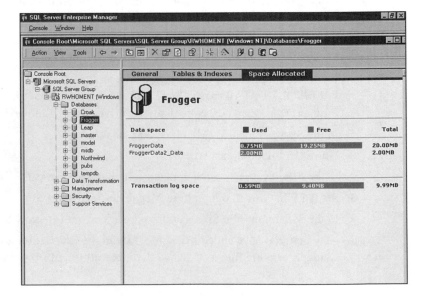

Shrinking Your Database

To shrink an entire database, you can use the DBCC SHRINKDATABASE command. Here is the syntax:

SYNTAX

```
DBCC SHRINKDATABASE {
(database_name
[, target_percent]
[,{NOTRUNCATE ¦ TRUNCATEONLY}])
}
```

Here are the arguments:

- *database_name*—The name of the database to be shrunk.

- *target_percent*—The percentage of free space left in the database after you have shrunk it.

- NOTRUNCATE—Forces freed file space to be retained in the database files. The default is to release the freed space back to the operating system.

- TRUNCATEONLY—Forces unused space in the data files to be released to the operating system. Note that when you choose TRUNCATEONLY, the *target_percent* parameter is ignored and all free space is released back to the system.

What exactly does this do? How does all this work, and what is really going on?

Here's the skinny on how this statement works. Essentially, the SHRINKDATABASE statement attempts to shrink all data files in the database to your new target percentage. Used pages at the end of your data files are relocated below your percentage threshold. For example, if you have a 5MB database and you shrink it to 80 percent, all rows located in the last 1MB (80 percent of 5MB is 4MB leaving 1MB) are moved to the lower 4MB area and the last 1MB is released back to the system. Note that you cannot shrink your database smaller than what is needed to store your data; nor can you shrink your database smaller than the model database. For example, if your database was already using 85percent of the data pages available, and you tried to shrink it to 80 percent, it would just move the used pages around to free up space at the end of the file. The amount of freed space would be 15 percent rather than 20 percent. The last 15 percent would then be released to the operating system.

If you choose the NOTRUNCATE option, data is relocated to free up space at the end of the file, but the newly freed space is retained by the database rather than released to the operating system.

The TRUNCATEONLY option frees up all unallocated space without moving any data around. If there happen to be empty pages at the end of a file, those will be released back to the system.

4

You can shrink individual files within your database using the DBCC SHRINKFILE statement. DBCC SHRINKFILE can be used to modify individual files rather than all files in a database as the DBCC SHRINKDATABASE does. Here is the syntax for the DBCC SHRINKFILE statement:

SYNTAX

```
DBCC SHRINKFILE {
(file_name ¦ file_id }
[, target_size]
[, {EMPTYFILE ¦ NOTRUNCATE ¦ TRUNCATEONLY}])
}
```

When you use the DBCC SHRINKFILE statement, you must specify either a database filename or its file_id. You can find the file_id by running the sp_helpdb system stored procedure, as you saw earlier in this lesson.

The target_size is used in the same manner as it was used for the SHRINKDATABASE statements earlier. The TRUNCATEONLY and NOTRUNCATE statements are also the same as described earlier. The EMPTYFILE parameter is interesting in that it will relocate any used data pages in the current database file to other database files in the filegroup. After all pages have been moved, the database file is marked as empty and you won't be allowed to store any data there. This can be useful if you want to use the REMOVE FILE or REMOVE FILEGROUP parameter in the ALTER DATABASE statement because it requires the file to be empty.

Here are some examples of using these statements:

Listing 4.4 empties the FroggerData2 file and uses the REMOVE FILE option to remove it from the Frogger database.

INPUT   **LISTING 4.4**   EMPTYING THE FILE AND USING REMOVE FILE

```
USE frogger
GO
DBCC SHRINKFILE (FroggerData2,EMPTYFILE)
GO
ALTER DATABASE Frogger REMOVE FILE FroggerData2
```

OUTPUT

DbId	FileId	CurrentSize	MinimumSize	UsedPages	EstimatedPages
7	3	256	256	0	0

(1 row(s) affected)

DBCC execution completed. If DBCC printed error messages, contact
➥your system administrator.
The file 'FroggerData2' has been removed.

As you can see, FroggerData2 was first emptied using the EMPTY FILE option. You then ran the second half of the batch statement where you altered the database and dropped the file. To verify that the file has been dropped, you can run EXEC sp_helpdb Frogger:

EXEC sp_helpdb Frogger

```
name      Db_size   Owner                dbid  Created       status
-------   --------- --------             ----- -----------   ----------
Frogger   30.00 MB  RIBBIT\Administrator 8     Apr 14 1998   no options set

(1 row(s) affected)

Name         Fileid  Filename                         Filegroup .../
-----------  ------- ------------------------------   ----------.../
FroggerData  1       F:\mssql7\data\FroggerData.mdf   PRIMARY    .../
FroggerLog   2       F:\mssql7\data\FroggerLog.ldf    NULL       .../

/...size           maxsize      growth      Usage
/...-----          ---------    -------     -----
/...20480 KB       102400 KB    10240 KB    Data only
/...10240 KB       15360 KB     1024 KB     Log only

(2 row(s) affected)
```

Notice that there is no more FroggerData2 associated with the Frogger database. If you use Explorer and navigate to your \MSSQL7\DATA folder, you will find that the FroggerData2.ndf file has also been removed from your system.

Renaming a Database

There might be times when you would like to rename a database. This could be due to an organizational change, such as merging the accounting and finance departments, or you might be moving a development database into the production environment. For whatever reason you want to change your database name, doing so is a relatively straightforward task.

To rename a database, you must execute the sp_renamedb system stored procedure. Keep these restrictions in mind when you rename a database:

- You must be a member of the sysadmin fixed server role to rename a database.
- Some SQL scripts might depend on the database name in order to run correctly. You might want to check your database for these.
- The database must be in single-user mode.
- The database files and filegroups are not affected by a name change.
- You must be in the master database to execute the sp_renamedb system stored procedure.

```
sp_renamedb 'old_name, 'new_name'
```

In this example, you will rename the Frogger database to TsingWa (Tsing Wa is Chinese for little frog):

```
USE master
GO
EXEC sp_dboption Frogger, 'Single User', True
EXEC sp_renamedb 'Frogger', 'TsingWa'
EXEC sp_dboption TsingWa, 'Single User', False
GO

DBCC execution completed. If DBCC printed error messages, contact
➥your system administrator.
The database is now single user.

(1 row(s) affected)

DBCC execution completed. If DBCC printed error messages, contact
➥your system administrator.
The database is renamed and in single user mode.
A member of the sysadmin role must reset the database to multiuser
➥mode with sp_dboption.
DBCC execution completed. If DBCC printed error messages, contact
➥your system administrator.
The database is now multiuser.
```

To verify that the name was changed, run sp_helpdb:

```
EXEC sp_helpdb

name      db_size  Owner                 dbid  created     status
-------   -------  --------------------- ----- --------    -------------
Croak     6.00 MB  Ribbit\Administrator  8     Apr 14 1998 no options set
Leap      14.00 MB Sa                    7     Apr 14 1998 no options set
master    7.31 MB  Sa                    1     Mar 23 1998 trunc. Log ...
model     1.19 MB  Sa                    3     Apr 13 1998 no options set
msdb      3.75 MB  Sa                    4     Apr 13 1998 trunc. Log ...
pubs      2.00 MB  Sa                    5     Apr 13 1998 dbo use only
tempdb    8.50 MB  Sa                    2     Mar 23 1998 select into/...
TsingWa   32.00 MB Sa                    6     Apr 14 1998 no options set

(8 row(s) affected)
```

Working with Database Filegroups

Filegroups enable you to explicitly place database objects like tables and indexes onto a specific set of database files. It can be useful for administration as well as performance. For example, if you are not using RAID 5 (redundant array of inexpensive disks) technology, you can place files in a filegroup onto separate physical disk drives and then place specific tables, indexes, and other database objects onto the files that are members of that filegroup. This can improve performance because reads and writes to the database can be running on separate physical disk drives at the same time. An administrative advantage is that you can back up and restore individual files in a filegroup.

There are two types of filegroups in SQL Server: the PRIMARY filegroup and user-defined filegroups. The PRIMARY filegroup is also the default filegroup. It must contain the primary data file and any other files that are not in another filegroup. You create user-defined filegroups when you alter your database and add files to a specific filegroup.

There are a few rules you should keep in mind when working with filegroups:

- A file cannot be a member of more than one filegroup.
- The primary data file must reside in the PRIMARY filegroup.
- You can allocate tables, indexes, text, ntext, and image data to a filegroup.
- All system files must reside in the PRIMARY filegroup on the primary file.
- If the PRIMARY filegroup runs out of space, new data pages will not automatically be allocated to the user-defined filegroups.

In the following examples you will create a new filegroup and then add a data file to it. You will then alter your database again and modify the filegroup property and make it part of the default filegroup. The default filegroup is PRIMARY and is created when you create your database. Only one filegroup can be the default in your database. When you mark a new filegroup as the default filegroup, new files that are added to the database will be placed here if you do not specify PRIMARY. You will finish the examples by removing the filegroup.

To create a new filegroup, run the following:

```
ALTER DATABASE Leap
ADD FILEGROUP LeapGroup1
GO
```

```
The command(s) completed successfully
```

To verify that the filegroup is part of the Leap database, you can run the following procedure:

```
use Leap
GO
EXEC sp_helpfilegroup
```

```
Groupname          Groupid      Filecount
-----------        -------      ---------
PRIMARY            1                2
```

```
LeapGroup1          2              0
```

```
(2 row(s) affected)
```

Now alter the database and add a new file to the filegroup:

```
ALTER DATABASE Leap
ADD FILE
(Name = LeapDataG1,
 FILENAME = 'C:\MSSQL7\DATA\LeapDataG1.ndf',
 SIZE = 2)
TO FILEGROUP LeapGroup1
GO
```

```
Extending database by 2.00 MB on disk 'LeapDataG1'.
```

Rerun the sp_helpfilegroup stored procedure again. You should have something similar to this:

```
USE Leap
GO
EXEC sp_helpfilegroup
```

Groupname	Groupid	Filecount
PRIMARY	1	2
LeapGroup1	2	1

```
(2 row(s) affected)
```

You can make the user-defined filegroup LeapGroup1 part of the default filegroup by modifying its filegroup property. You can also mark the filegroup as READONLY or READ-WRITE. See the SQL Server Books Online for more information on READONLY and READ-WRITE options.

To mark your new filegroup as the default filegroup, run the following:

```
USE Leap
GO
ALTER DATABASE Leap
MODIFY FILEGROUP LeapGroup1 DEFAULT
```

```
The filegroup property 'DEFAULT' has been set.
```

To test your new default filegroup, you can add a new data file without specifying a filegroup:

```
USE pubs
GO
ALTER DATABASE Leap
ADD FILE
(NAME = LeapDataTest,
```

```
  FILENAME = 'C:\MSSQL7\DATA\LeapDataTest.ndf',
  SIZE = 2)
GO
```

```
Extending database by 2.00 MB on disk 'LeapDataTest'.
```

To view which files reside in which groups, you can run the `sp_helpfile` stored procedure.

To remove a filegroup, you first must make the default filegroup the PRIMARY filegroup. Then empty the files in the old filegroup. After you have emptied the files, you can safely remove the files and then the filegroup. Here is an example:

```
USE Leap
GO

ALTER DATABASE Leap
ALTER FILEGROUP [PRIMARY] DEFAULT
GO

ALTER DATABASE Leap
REMOVE FILE LeapDataG1
Go

ALTER DATABASE Leap
REMOVE FILE LeapDataTest
GO

ALTER DATABASE Leap
REMOVE FILEGROUP LeapGroup1
GO
```

You should see messages to the effect that your filegroup LeapDataG1 and the files contained in that filegroup are also deleted.

You can run `sp_helpfile` again to verify that the filegroup and the files have been successfully removed.

You can also accomplish this through the SQL Server Enterprise Manager in much the same way that you created files. Follow these steps to create a new database file and add it to a new filegroup:

1. Drill down to the Croak database and open its property sheet.
2. To create a filegroup and add a file to it, click in the empty box below CroakData2 and add CroakDataG1.
3. Fill in the location as C:\Mssql7\Data\CroakDataG1.ndf.
4. In the space allocated field type 1.

4

5. In the File group box, add CroakGroup1, as shown in Figure 4.12.

6. Click OK when you are finished.

FIGURE 4.12

Select the filegroup in the Properties for the database.

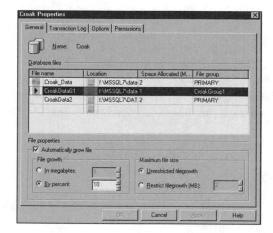

This section provides just an overview of what filegroups are and how they are created. Filegroups can be very complex and are not covered further in this book. For more information on filegroups, please take a look at the SQL Server Books Online or *SQL Server 7.0 Unleashed*, which is published by Sams Publishing and available in bookstores and libraries near you. After you have completed study with this 21-day book, your skills should be somewhere between intermediate and advanced intermediate with SQL Server 7.0. To take your SQL Server education further, I strongly suggest that you pick up a copy of the *Unleashed* book.

Removing a Database

At times it might be necessary to remove a database from your system. Perhaps you no longer need the database, or the database has been corrupted and must be rebuilt and reloaded. In any event, removing a database from SQL Server is relatively straightforward. As you might have already guessed, you can do this from both the SQL Server Enterprise Manager and through Transact-SQL.

Before you actually drop a database, there are a few things you should keep in mind:

- Dropping a database removes the database information from the system tables and removes the data file from the system.

- A dropped database can be re-created only by restoring it with a backup.

- There can be no users in the database at the time you drop it.
- You must be a member of the db_owner database role (or the sysadmin server role) to drop your database.
- You must be in the master database when you issue the DROP DATABASE statement.

Here is the DROP DATABASE syntax and an example:

```
DROP DATABASE database_name, database_name2...
```

The DROP DATABASE statement enables you to drop multiple databases at one time. In this example, you will drop both the TsingWa (formerly Frogger) and the Croak databases. Run this code from the SQL Server Query Analyzer:

```
USE MASTER
GO
DROP DATABASE TsingWa, Croak
GO
```

```
Deleting database file 'C:\mssql7\data\Croak_Data.MDF'.
Deleting database file 'C:\mssql7\data\Croak_Log.LDF'.
Deleting database file 'C:\mssql7\data\CroakData2.ndf'.
Deleting database file 'C:\mssql7\data\CroakLog2.ldf'.
Deleting database file 'C:\mssql7\data\CroakDataG1.NDF'.
Deleting database file 'C:\mssql7\data\froggerdata.mdf'.
Deleting database file 'C:\mssql7\data\froggerlog.ldf'.
Deleting database file 'C:\mssql7\data\Froggerdata2.ndf'.
```

As you can see, all the data files associated with these two databases were deleted and the databases were removed from the system. To verify, you could run sp_helpdb.

You can also use the SQL Server Enterprise Manager to drop a database. Follow these steps:

1. Start the SQL Server Enterprise Manager and drill down to the Databases folder.
2. Right-click the Leap database and choose Delete from the context menu.
3. You will get a Delete Database confirmation box. Click Yes.
4. That's all there is to it. The database is no longer part of your system. The database files have also been deleted.

Summary

Today you learned how to create, alter, and drop a database as well as how to set different database options. When you create a database, the database is stored in at least two separate files. One file contains the data, system tables, and other database objects, and the other file stores the transaction log. In SQL Server 7.0, you can have your database dynamically grow by specifying database or transaction log filegrowth options. You also learned a little bit about filegroups and how they can be used for administration and performance benefits. The chapter ended with a discussion on dropping a database.

To create a database, you can use the SQL Server Enterprise Manager or the CREATE DATABASE statement. When you create a database, you must specify a logical name as well as a physical filename. You must include the logical and physical names of the transaction log associated with that database. You also learned about filegrowth options that enable you to specify how a file can be automatically made larger when it runs out of space, how much larger it will grow, as well as a maximum size that it can be grown.

You then learned how to add additional files to your database and transaction log. Included in this was the capability to modify the parameters of existing files. You used the ALTER DATABASE statements to accomplish this.

Database options determine how a particular database behaves, whether it is marked for single-user access, or whether it is marked for read-only access. To set these options, you can use the Database Property sheet in Enterprise Manager or the sp_dboption stored procedure.

You rename a database by using the sp_renamedb stored procedure. Remember that when you rename a database, you must be in the sysadmin user role and the database must be in single-user mode.

You create filegroups either through the SQL Enterprise Manager in the Database Properties dialog or through the ALTER DATABASE statements. With a filegroup, you can add data files that can have tables and indexes explicitly placed into them. This can benefit performance and administration.

The lesson concluded with a look at removing a database from the SQL Server. To accomplish this task you can use the SQL Server Enterprise Manager, right-click on the database you want to drop, and choose the Delete context menu item. From the SQL Server Query Analyzer, you must make sure that you are in the master database. When you get there, you can issue the DROP DATABASE statements to remove the database information from the system tables and delete the database files from the operating system.

Q&A

Q Will I create a lot of databases in the real world?

A That depends on what type of business you are running. In my consulting business, I have found that I don't create a lot of databases. The databases I do create tend to be development databases where I can store test data and do development work.

When that database is ready, I'll re-create it in the production environment and let it run.

Q Should I use the SQL Server Enterprise Manager or the SQL Server Query Analyzer to create and modify my databases?

A Excellent question. If the database is going into the production environment, or if the database might need to be re-created several times, I tend to use the Query Analyzer. This is an advantage for me because the Query Analyzer enables me to save my script files for easy reuse. If the database I'm working with is for development and I can quickly and easily re-create it, then I will most likely use the Enterprise Manager in those instances.

Q How big should I make my database and transaction logs?

A The initial size of your database should be large enough to hold all the data you are planning to place in it. This includes the amount of data in each row and the number of rows that will fit on a single data page. Don't forget that indexes can take up a lot of data space as well. You will learn more about database size on Day 9, "Creating Tables," where you will learn how much space different data types require and how they are stored. The transaction log size is dependent on how much change is going to take place in your database. If your database is read-only, then your transaction log can be very small—perhaps 5 percent of the size of your data files. If your database will be undergoing lots of updates, deletes, and inserts, then you might want to make a larger transaction log. I would suggest a log in the vicinity of 25 percent to 30 percent of the total size of your data files. For normal database usage, I recommend a log size somewhere between 10 percent and 15 percent of data file size.

Q Should I have a bunch of small data files in my database or just a few large ones?

A That is really up to you. More data files means more complex administration. With complexity, you do gain certain advantages. For example, instead of backing up one huge data file, you can back up several smaller data files. It is really up to you.

Q Which database options are changed the most often?

A That depends on what you are doing with your database. For example, I have several databases that are loaded with data from a text file generated by an AS400 every night. The quickest way to get those files into the database tables is to set the Select Into/Bulk Copy parameter to True and then run a bulk copy script. There are times when you will use the DBO Use Only option as well. Throughout this book, you will see examples of when these different options are required.

Q How important are filegroups?

A Filegroups are mainly an optimization tool. Most databases will run just as well without any additional user-defined filegroups being added.

Q Why would you want to remove a database and how often does that occur?

A You can probably think of many reasons to drop a database from the system. There are all kinds of scenarios. The two most common reasons I have removed databases are to get rid of test/development databases and when a database is corrupted, so I can re-create it.

Q Should I use the autogrowth feature or disable it?

A The autogrowth feature is one of SQL Server 7.0's greatest strengths. It allows for dynamic sizing of your database with very little overhead. If you decide to use autogrowth, I suggest that you also specify the maximum size to which your database can grow.

Workshop

The Workshop provides quiz questions to help you solidify your understanding of the concepts presented in this chapter. In addition to the quiz questions, exercises are provided to let you practice what you have learned in this chapter. Try to understand the quiz and exercise answers before continuing to the next day's lesson. Answers are provided in Appendix A, "Answers."

Quiz

1. What is the SQL code needed to create the following database?

   Database: Accounting

   FileSize: 20MB with a maximum of 40MB growing by 2MB

   LogSize: 5MB with a maximum of 10MB growing by 1MB

2. What does the following code do?
   ```
   ALTER DATABASE Test
   ADD FILE
   (NAME = TestData2,
    FILENAME = 'C:\mssql7\data\TestData2.ndf',
   SIZE = 10)
   ```

3. What is the code used to drop the following four databases: Von, Ron, Don, and Christina?

Exercises

This exercise is only one question long with several different pieces. The next piece of the exercise requires that you successfully complete the previous pieces. Please read the entire set of instructions for each step before attempting the step.

1. Create a new database called Frog with the following characteristics:

   - Two data files named FrogData1 and FrogData2.

   - The data files should be 3MB at initial creation.

   - The data files should be able to grow to a maximum size of 20MB, each growing 2MB each time.

   - Add two log files called FrogLog1 and FrogLog2.

   - The log files should be 1MB each at initial creation.

   - The maximum size the log files should be is 5MB each.

   - Use the default growth increment.

2. Add an additional data file named FrogData3 with default properties for all other values.

3. Shrink the database by 20 percent.

4. Empty the FrogLog2 log file.

5. Remove the FrogLog2 file.

6. Rename the database to TreeFrog.

7. Drop the database.

4

WEEK 1

DAY 5

Using SQL Server Login and User Security

Yesterday you examined how to create databases, along with their files. You also learned how and when to use file groups with SQL Server 7.0. You will rarely need to use file groups, but it's good to understand the basics of their operation. Everything you do in SQL Server is authenticated, including when you created the databases and files yesterday. Understanding SQL Server security is critical to the successful operation of your SQL Server. In today's lesson you examine how SQL Server authenticates connections to the SQL Server and to individual databases, and you learn how Windows NT authentication works. The Windows 95/98 platform doesn't have all the security mechanisms available to Windows NT users, so a brief examination of the differences is provided. Permissions on individual objects within each database are examined on Day 6, "Working with Permissions."

The SQL Server Security Access Model

Connecting to SQL Server 7.0 so far has been a relatively easy thing to do. You've been using SQL Server Mixed Mode Security (the default security mode), logging in with the SQL Server sa login. As you connect, several things are happening that might not be obvious at first.

When you are running SQL Server under Windows NT, there are three different places that security is checked as you attempt to connect to SQL Server 7.0 (see Figure 5.1). You might be validated by Windows NT, SQL Server itself (in the form of a SQL Server login) and then at the individual database level (in the form of a database username). Note that having a login doesn't say anything about which databases you can access; only a database username sets that policy. Also note that you haven't actually attempted to access any database objects yet; that requires permissions, which are examined in tomorrow's lesson.

FIGURE 5.1

Network and SQL Server security authentication layers.

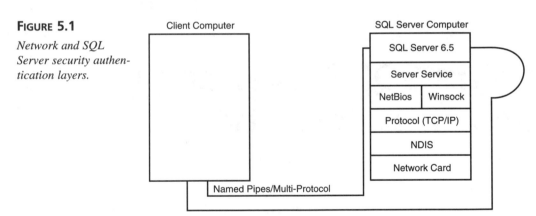

Windows NT Authentication

When you connect from your client computer to a Windows NT computer running SQL Server 7.0, Windows NT might require validation of your network connection. This depends on your SQL Server network library. If you are using Named Pipes or Multiprotocol as your SQL Server network library, you must be validated as an authorized Windows NT connection before you will be allowed to talk to SQL Server.

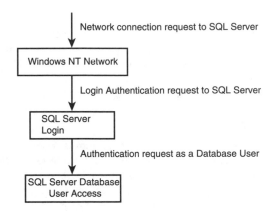

FIGURE 5.2

SQL Server network communications.

As you can see in Figure 5.2, both Named Pipes and Multiprotocol pass through the Windows NT Server service, which performs network validation of a user's connection request. Hence, you must have a valid set of Windows NT security credentials to connect to the Windows NT server computer. Because the Transmission Control Protocol/Internet Protocol (TCP/IP) Sockets network library doesn't go through the Server service, you would not need a valid Windows NT account to connect to SQL Server 7.0.

> **Note**
>
> Windows 9x doesn't authenticate network connections in the same way as Windows NT, so security checks start out at the SQL Server login stage for SQL Servers running on a Windows 9x computer. Also, Windows 9x doesn't support running Named Pipes for server applications, so you can't connect to a Windows 9x server with that protocol. The default protocol for Windows 9x, as mentioned on Day 2, "Installing SQL Server 7.0," is TCP/IP sockets.

> **Note**
>
> As a troubleshooting tool, understanding this security architecture can be useful. If you get the infamous Specified SQL Server Not Found message, it could be that you are being denied permission to connect to the Windows NT computer on which SQL Server is installed. To see whether this is the problem, create a share on the SQL Server computer and attempt to connect to the server (or attempt to connect to an existing share if one exists). If you are unable to connect, or are prompted for a user ID/password, you won't be able to connect to SQL Server. To verify for certain that this is the problem, finish the connection to the aforementioned share and then try to connect again to SQL Server.
>
> If you are then able to connect, you must modify the security settings on your Windows NT computer. You can do this in one of three ways:

5

- Enable the guest account (not recommended). If you enable the guest account you have compromised Windows NT security to some extent. To keep your system secure, create an individual account for every user.

- Create a local NT account with User Manager for Domains with the same password as the account you are currently logged in with (a last resort).

- Have your server join a domain that is either a member of or trusts the domain where your network account resides (a better option). This option is the best option available to you. If it's possible on your network, you should use this option. Consult with your network administrator or a book on Windows NT security to examine Windows NT domains and security in more detail.

SQL Server Login Authentication

You must provide a valid SQL Server login name and password to connect to SQL Server (or have a valid Windows NT Integrated connection). You will see the details on how to do this shortly. If your login credentials are valid, you will be connected to SQL Server. If your credentials are not valid, you will be denied access—even if Windows NT network authentication (your network connection to the Windows NT computer) succeeded.

SQL Server Database Username

To use each database on your system, you must explicitly be allowed to enter each database. There are a variety of ways to get access to a database, all of which are discussed later in today's lesson. If you don't have a database username, you will be denied access to the database you are attempting to connect to.

Permissions

The final layer of security is permissions. After you've successfully logged into SQL Server and switched to a database, you must then be given the explicit right to access database objects (either for read-only or modification). Tomorrow's lesson examines permissions in great detail.

The Security Modes of SQL Server (Including Logins)

SQL Server 7.0 provides two different security modes: Windows NT Integrated Mode and Mixed Mode (both Windows NT Integrated and SQL Server authentication). The security mode determines whether Windows NT or both Windows NT and SQL Server are responsible for validating SQL Server connection requests. This validation is completely independent of the Windows NT network connection authentication that you examined previously. It is critical that you understand the differences so you can properly implement SQL Server security.

Mixed Mode Security

In SQL Server 7.0 Mixed Mode security, a user can connect to SQL Server using either Windows NT Integrated Mode or SQL Server Authentication Mode. This mode is the best selection for backward compatibility, and it provides the greatest amount of connectivity with non-Windows–networked computers like Novell NetWare users. To understand both of these authentication modes, you must examine them closely. It's easiest to start with an understanding of SQL Server Authentication Mode, which for historical reasons has been the way SQL Server connectivity was provided.

SQL Server Authentication Mode

SQL Server Authentication Mode is the mode in which SQL Server accepts a login ID and password from a user and validates whether the credentials are valid, without any help from Windows NT. This is the method that will always be used on a Windows 9x computer and is optional on a Windows NT computer. Information about logins is kept inside SQL Server (in the master database, in the sysxlogins system table). In all previous releases of SQL Server, there is a mode of SQL Server authentication called Standard Security, which is equivalent to SQL Server Authentication Mode. So if you see any documentation that uses the old term, don't be confused—just map it to the new terminology.

When you've connected using the login sa, you've been using SQL Server Authentication Mode. Therefore, there's an entry in the sysxlogins system table for the sa login ID, as well as a password if you've assigned one (by default, the sa password is NULL). After installing SQL Server 7.0, only the sa login exists. On a Windows NT computer, the local Administrators group will also have been added as the equivalent of sa (as members of the sysadmin security role).

5

Passwords

SQL Server Authentication Mode login passwords are kept in the password column of the sysxlogins table in the master database. To look at the entries in the sysxlogins table, start the SQL Server Query Analyzer and run this query (you must be logged in as sa (or a member of the sysadmin role, explained later, to run this):

INPUT

```
SELECT  substring(name,1,25) AS name,
        substring(password,1,20) as password, language
        FROM sysxlogins
```

OUTPUT

```
name                       password                          language
------------------------   ------------------------------    -------------
BUILTIN\Administrators     NULL                              us_english
sa                         NULL                              us_english
RWHOMENT\SQLService        NULL                              us_english
NULL                       NULL                                    NULL

(4 row(s) affected)
```

Note The row in the preceding result set for the BUILTIN\Administrators NT group, as well as the SQL Server service account (SQLService), won't be present on a Windows 9x SQL Server installation, as mentioned earlier.

The first row in the preceding output represents the local Windows NT Administrators group, and you'll examine NT Integrated security in the following text. The sa login ID is installed with a null password. All logins and passwords will be kept here. If the password is null, you will see the NULL keyword in the password column. If a password is anything other than null, it will be stored as encrypted text, and you will see a hex representation of the encrypted text. For the purposes of comparison, it's safe to think of null as blank in the context of security logins.

Passwords that are viewable with a query might seem a bit disconcerting at first. There are a few things to consider, however, before you worry too much. First, only the sa login (or a member of the sysadmin role) can view the password column. No other login/user can view this unless you explicitly give them the right to do so (which you'll learn how to do on Day 6, "Working with Permissions"). Secondly, the encryption algorithm is a one-way algorithm. When a password is encrypted, it cannot be decrypted. When you log in, the password you provide is encrypted and then compared to the encrypted password in the sysxlogins table. If they match, access is granted to the server. If they don't match, you will get the Login Failed error message and will be unable to connect.

Tip

> If you are concerned about security, particularly with passwords, the best solution is to use Windows NT Authentication.

Administering SQL Server Authentication Mode Logins

The first step in setting up your server for access is to create logins. You can add logins with the sp_addlogin system stored procedure or through the SQL Server Enterprise Manager. Note again that if you're using Windows NT, Windows NT Integrated Mode is the preferred method of security administration and is examined later in today's lesson.

```
sp_addlogin [@loginame =] 'login' [,[@passwd =] 'password'
[,[@defdb =] 'database' [,[@deflanguage =] 'language'
[,[@sid =] 'sid' [,[@encryptopt =] 'encryption_option']]]]]
```

where

- *login* is the name you want the user to use when logging in. This name must be a valid SQL Server identifier (begins with a letter or the following characters: #, @, or _, and the rest of the characters can be these characters or letters plus numbers—up to 128 Unicode characters).

- *passwd* is the password for this login. The password will be null if you do not choose one at this time.

- *defdb* is the default database you would like the user to be put into when he or she logs in. If you do not specify this parameter, the default database will be set to master.

- *deflanguage* is the default language to be used for this user when he or she logs in. The default language will be US_English if you do not specify this parameter.

- *sid* is where you can specify a security identifier for a user (this option is not recommended).

- *encryptopt* is the option you can use to turn off the encryption of passwords (mentioned earlier). Again, it's recommended that you do not use this feature but accept the default (an encrypted password). To turn off encryption, use the literal string skip_encryption here.

To add a login to your server, open the SQL Server Query Analyzer and log in as sa. Run the following Transact-SQL command:

```
Exec sp_addlogin 'yourname', 'yourpassword'
```

 Note I ran `sp_addlogin 'richard', 'password'`. If you want to follow along with exactly what's in this book, you should use this login name and password. Otherwise, whenever you see `richard` for a login, substitute your name.

If you run the query you ran earlier against the sysxlogins table again, you will see a new row with your name and an encrypted password. If you create a new connection to SQL Server, you will be able to log in with the name and password you have just added.

The next thing you might want to do is change your password. You can accomplish this either through the SQL Server Enterprise Manager or use the sp_password system stored procedure.

▼ SYNTAX

```
sp_password [[@old =] 'old',] {[@new =] 'new'}
[,[@loginame =] 'login']
```

where

- *old* is your old password.
- *new* is your new password.
- *login*: If you are logged in as sa (or a member of the sysadmin role), you can change anyone's password. In fact, you do not need to know a person's old password. You can simply script the old password as null.

▲

An example of the sp_password system stored procedure looks like this:

```
Exec sp_password NULL, 'newpass', 'richard'
```

Although you don't know Richard's old password, you can change it because you're the system administrator. Ordinary users are unable to do this and must know their old password to change it.

Change your passwords regularly. Unfortunately, SQL Server 7.0 does not have any way to enforce password restrictions and other security precautions. This is one reason why you might choose to implement integrated security. Windows NT has the capability to specify minimum password lengths, frequency of change, and minimal password complexity rules.

Another thing you might like to change is the default database or the default language that a user is logged in with. This can be done from the SQL Server Enterprise Manager or with the `sp_defaultdb` and `sp_defaultlanguage` system stored procedures.

SYNTAX

```
sp_defaultdb loginname, defdb
sp_defaultlanguage loginname [, language]
```

The parameters are the same as discussed previously. These options simply allow you to change various fields in the sysxlogins table (the default database or the default language).

Two additional system stored procedures can be used to manage logins. These are the `sp_helplogins` and `sp_droplogin` system stored procedures. The system stored procedure `sp_helplogins` enables you to get a report on the logins that have been created on your server. Figure 5.3 shows a sample run of this stored procedure.

FIGURE 5.3

The results of
sp_helplogins.

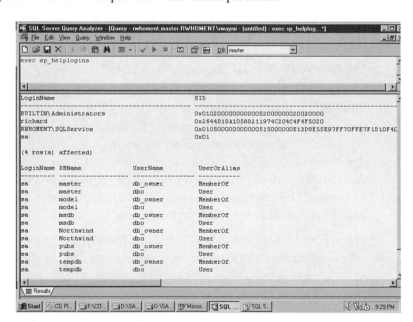

5

The system stored procedure `sp_droplogin` removes the login entry from the sysxlogins table. After an entry is deleted, the user can no longer log in to SQL Server.

```
sp_droplogin login
```

where

- *login* has the same meaning as it does for each of these stored procedures.

You have learned how to accomplish SQL Server Authentication Mode login management using the various system stored procedures. You will look at how to manage security with the SQL Server Enterprise Manager later in today's lesson.

Windows NT Authentication Mode

NEW TERM   Windows NT Authentication Mode is the other option in Mixed Mode security, but you will examine it later in the "Windows NT Integrated Mode" section because they are identical in functionality and administration. One terminology note is in order before you examine Windows NT connections. A connection made via Windows NT authentication is said to be a *trusted connection*. So when you see the term *trusted connection*, think of it as a Windows NT authenticated connection.

Windows NT Integrated Mode

In Windows NT Integrated Mode security, after you've gotten to SQL Server over the network, you must present SQL Server with your Windows NT Security credentials (known as your access token). You build these credentials in the process of logging into a Windows NT network. These security credentials are silently passed for you, so you don't need to do anything special to have your security passed. Unlike SQL Server Authentication Mode, Windows NT integrated logins are kept track of via SIDs (Security Identifiers). You can grant access to SQL Server via Windows NT security accounts directly, or indirectly via Windows NT groups.

The best part about Windows NT Integrated Mode is that users don't have to worry about logging in separately to SQL Server. This complies with the concept that users should have to log in to the network only once and remember only a single password. Not only that, but you can take advantage of the fact that it's likely most of your users already have Windows NT accounts, thus reducing the administrative overhead of managing login accounts for your SQL Server.

Setting Up Windows NT Groups and Users

The first step to configuring Windows NT Integrated Mode security isn't a SQL Server step at all—it's a visit to the User Manager for Domains utility (or User Manager on Windows NT Workstation). You should first create Windows NT groups for users, then create the users (if they don't already exist) and add them to the new groups you just created, and then assign them permissions to log in to SQL Server. To do this, select Start, Programs, Administrative Tools, User Manager for Domains. This starts the User Manager for Domains program shown in Figure 5.4.

FIGURE 5.4

*User Manager for
Domains.*

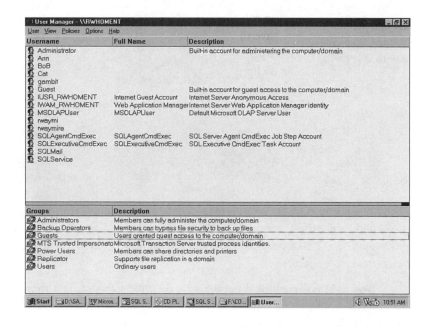

> **Note**
>
> Of course this tool doesn't apply to Windows 9x installations. Also, on Windows NT Workstation computers, the application is named User Manager, not User Manager for Domains.

You must add new local groups to the Windows NT security accounts manager (SAM) database of the machine on which SQL Server is running. Microsoft has also named this database the directory database in preparation for Windows NT 5.0 and the active directory. Note that this is a Windows NT internal database—not a SQL Server database. The title bar of User Manager for Domains will tell you which domain's (or computer's) security database you are viewing. You must view the security database of the computer where SQL Server is installed. Just to be sure you are looking at the right security database, select User, Select Domain from the menu. Enter two backslashes, followed by the name of your computer as shown in Figure 5.5. If your computer is a primary or backup domain controller, the name of the domain is appropriate because the domain database is the local security database. For most servers, the computer name is correct.

5

FIGURE 5.5

Set the proper security database.

When you click OK after typing your computer name, you will see the list of accounts and local groups for the SQL Server computer. If you get an error about security, you must log in to the computer running SQL Server as a Windows NT administrator and then start again.

Now that you are looking at the right security database, you should create three new local groups to use with SQL Server. One group will contain users who can log in as SQL Server administrators (those Windows NT users who can fully administer SQL Server), another group for Sales people, and another for Marketing users. You can then assign users to each group as you want. You'll be able to determine what the users can do after they're logged in when you examine this topic later in today's lesson and on Day 6.

The first group will be for administrative access to SQL Server. Select User, New Local Group from the menu in User Manager for Domains. Fill in the Group Name field as in Figure 5.6. Then type a description explaining the purpose of the group. You'll notice that the Administrator has been added to your group. This does not mean that the Administrator must exist in every group; instead, it simply means you had that user highlighted when you requested User Manager for Domains to create a new group. You can highlight Administrator and click the Remove button to remove that account from your group. This would mean you don't want the Windows NT administrative user to be able to log into your SQL Server as the system administrator.

Now put your account into the group as shown in Figure 5.7. Click the Add button next to the Members button, and you will see a list of accounts you can add. The list is made up of the global groups and accounts from your default domain, or just the accounts if your SQL Server computer is not a member of a domain.

FIGURE 5.6

Adding a new local group for Windows NT security.

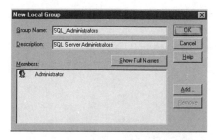

FIGURE 5.7

The Add Users and Groups dialog box.

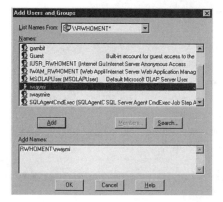

If you do not see your computer name in the List Names From: pane, select it from the drop-down list. You will see your computer name, your default domain, and any trusted domains in the dialog box. Note that if you are using a domain, you should select your domain account to add to the list rather than create and add a duplicate Windows NT account. Now that you're looking at the right list, add your username to the group by selecting your account name, clicking Add, and then clicking OK.

Note

You should also add the account you used for the SQLServerAgent service during setup (SQLService if you followed the setup on Day 2). The SQLServerAgent service requires that it make a trusted connection to SQL Server to function properly. If you don't add the account, and the SQLServerAgent can't make a trusted connection to SQL Server, all functionality provided by that service will fail. This includes tasks, alerts, email integration, and replication.

If you did not use an account for the service (you selected the LocalSystem account option), you do not need to do anything special for that account here. You also don't need to do anything special if you choose to keep Windows NT administrators as SQL Server Administrators (the default configuration).

5

The completed group should look something like Figure 5.8.

FIGURE 5.8

*The completed New
Local Group dialog
box.*

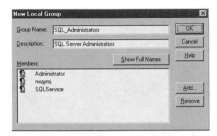

Click OK and then repeat the process and create a group called Sales, and then do it
again to create the group Marketing. This time, however, add a different user or set of
users. On my system I set up three extra users: Ann, Bob, and Cat, for this purpose. I put
Ann and Bob in Sales, and I put Bob and Cat in Marketing. It's intentional that Bob is in
both groups. If you've never added a user to an NT security database before, select User,
New User to access the Add User dialog box. Make sure to uncheck the User Must
Change Password at Next Login option.

Giving Windows NT Accounts Permission to Log In to SQL Server

After you've set up the users and groups, it's time to grant those groups access to SQL
Server. You can accomplish this using the system stored procedures `sp_grantlogin`,
`sp_revokelogin`, and `sp_denylogin`. These will function very much like `sp_addlogin`
and `sp_droplogin`, which you examined along with SQL Server Authentication Mode.

Give permission for logins to Windows NT groups first and then only as needed to individual users. This method of granting logins will allow you to run the fewest commands
and have the lowest administrative overhead, while still allowing individual control of
login privileges. To grant permissions to log in, use the `sp_grantlogin` system stored
procedure.

```
sp_grantlogin [@loginame =] 'login'
```

where

- *login* is the name of the Windows NT group or user to whom you will grant the
  right to log in to SQL Server. The login should be in the form of
  SECURITY_DATABASE\Username—for example, MYDOMAIN\Richard.

For example, to grant the Sales group permissions to log in to SQL Server, you could run

```
Exec sp_grantlogin 'RWHOMENT\Sales'
```

replacing RWHOMENT with your computer name (or domain name if running SQL Server on a domain controller). You should receive a message similar to this:

```
Granted login access to 'RWHOMENT\Sales'.
```

Now any Windows NT user who is a member of the Sales group can log into SQL Server. You can test this by logging into Windows NT as either Ann or Bob, starting up the SQL Server Query Analyzer, and selecting the Use Windows NT Authentication button to force a trusted connection to SQL Server 7.0. In the title bar of the query connection you will see your Windows NT username. Notice that you are connected as yourself in Windows NT, even though the Sales group was the entity that was actually granted login rights to SQL Server.

Note

If you find you can't log in as Ann or Bob, and you get the message The Local Policy Of This System Does Not Permit You To Log On Interactively, don't panic. Log in as an administrator on your computer, and start User Manager for Domains (as described earlier). Select Policies, User Rights from the menu. Select Log on Locally, click Add, and select Everyone. You should see something like Figure 5.9.

Click OK, and all users will be able to log on locally to your computer.

FIGURE 5.9

The completed Log On Locally User Rights Policy dialog box.

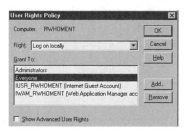

5

You can also take away a Windows NT user's or groups' right to log in to SQL Server. You would do this using the sp_revokelogin system stored procedure.

SYNTAX

```
sp_revokelogin [@loginame =] 'login'
```

where

- *login* is the name of the Windows NT group or user from which you want to remove the right to log into SQL Server.

Note that all sp_revokelogin does is remove a previously granted login right. So the following will remove the ability of anyone in the Sales group to log in to SQL Server because the Sales group had previously been given this right:

```
Exec Sp_revokelogin 'RWHOMENT\Sales'
```

However, the following will have no effect because Marketing had not previously been granted login rights to SQL Server:

```
Exec sp_revokelogin 'RWHOMENT\Marketing'
```

Also note that, although you can revoke Ann's right to log in, such as the following, this will not affect any rights she receives from groups:

```
Exec sp_revokelogin 'RWHOMENT\Ann'
```

Therefore, if the Sales group has the right to log in, and you've run the preceding statement, it will not change Ann's ability to log in to SQL Server.

If you want to specify that anyone in the Sales group can log in except Ann, you must use the `sp_denylogin` system stored procedure.

SYNTAX

```
sp_denylogin [@loginame =] 'login'
```

where

- *login* is the name of the Windows NT group or user from which you want to deny the right to log into SQL Server.

Try this code as an example (again substituting the correct security database name in place of RWHOMENT):

```
Exec sp_grantlogin 'RWHOMENT\Sales'
Exec sp_denylogin 'RWHOMENT\Ann'
```

Now log in to your Windows NT system as Ann, and attempt to connect to SQL Server. You will be denied login permissions. Log in to Windows NT as Bob, and connect to SQL Server, and it will work just fine. Ann has been denied permissions, but Bob, as a member of Sales, has been given permission to log in. Deny rights always supersede any other granted rights.

Setting the Security Mode

So far, you've learned how to add SQL Server Authentication Mode users and Windows NT users and groups to SQL Server. However, you must know which security mode to use. To establish which security mode your server is currently using, start the SQL Server Enterprise Manager and right-click your server in the left pane of the tool. Select Properties from the pop-up menu and click the Security tab.

If you are on a Windows NT computer, you will see the dialog box shown in Figure 5.10, and you can select either Windows NT Only or SQL Server and Windows NT (the default). On a Windows 9x computer, most of this dialog box will be grayed out because there is no Windows NT authentication on those systems. To change the security setting, simply click the option you'd like. The change won't take effect until the SQL Server service (MSSQLServer) is restarted.

FIGURE 5.10

The security configura-tion dialog box.

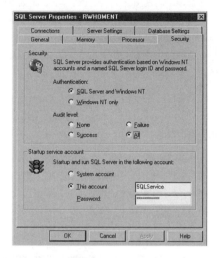

> **Tip**
>
> You will want to enable auditing for your server. No auditing is turned on by default. You can audit Failure (failed logins to SQL Server), Success (logins to SQL Server that go through), or both. I recommend both, as you see in Figure 5.10. You can view these audits in both the SQL Server error log and the Windows NT Event Viewer application. You must stop and restart the MSSQLServer service for auditing to begin.

5

Finally, the Startup Service Account frame allows you to change the account that SQL Server is using to run the MSSQLServer service. This option was addressed on Day 2.

After you've made any changes in this dialog box, you must stop and restart SQL Server (the MSSQLServer service) for the changes to take effect. Because it's unlikely you'll make this kind of change more than once, this shouldn't be too big a problem.

Graphically Managed Logins

Now is a great time to take a moment and examine what you've learned so far today. There are two kinds of logins to SQL Server:

- Windows NT logins, either via groups or individual user IDs
- SQL Server logins, stored in the sysxlogins system table in the master database

Each has its advantages. SQL Server logins can be used on the Windows 9x platform and don't require you to have organized Windows NT domains on Windows NT systems. Windows NT logins, however, are preferred if you are already on a properly configured Windows NT network because they've already been created and uniquely identify each user in your organization. You've learned how to create each of them and how to allow logins to SQL Server. You did this through the use of system stored procedures like `sp_addlogin`, `sp_password`, and so on. However, there's an easier way: SQL Server Enterprise Manager.

I didn't hold out on showing you SQL Server Enterprise Manager to be mean. It's just that you can create both types of logins easily from a single graphical interface, so it's best to understand them both before examining this interface.

Figure 5.11 shows what my system looks like after running the code from earlier in today's lesson. I've granted permissions for the Windows NT Sales group to log in to SQL Server and explicitly denied the Windows NT user Ann from logging in. The BUILTIN\Administrators Windows NT group is added during setup, and the sa login is also created during setup. I've added myself as a standard (SQL Server) login.

FIGURE 5.11

The logins information in SQL Server Enterprise Manager.

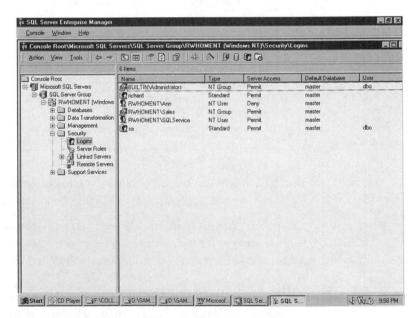

To add the Marketing group as a valid login, right-click anywhere in the right panel of the Enterprise Manager window and select New Login from the pop-up dialog box. You are presented with Figure 5.12. Complete the dialog box as shown in the figure to add the Marketing group.

FIGURE 5.12

Adding a Windows NT login via Enterprise Manager.

Click OK to finish adding the login, and then do the same to add an account for Bob. Notice that you don't really need to add an account for Bob because Bob has been able to log in from either the Sales or Marketing groups. Add a SQL Server login named Don, with a password of password. Figure 5.13 shows the configuration dialog box. When you click OK, you will have to confirm the password you've entered.

FIGURE 5.13

Adding a SQL Server login via Enterprise Manager.

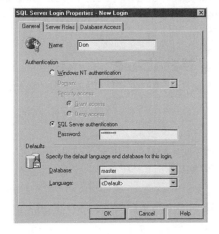

Notice that all you must do to deny someone access is to click the Deny Access button. This only makes sense for Windows NT logins. To deny access to a SQL Server login, simply don't create it.

To edit an existing login, right-click the login in the right panel, with the Logins folder highlighted, and select Properties from the pop-up menu. You have noticed by now that there are two other tabs in the dialog box you've been working with: Server Roles and Database Access. These are the next two topics you'll examine.

Database Users

After you have configured login security and have established your logins, you can begin to configure access to databases. Having a login to SQL Server does not give you access to any databases in the server. For that you must have a database username.

Each database has a separate access path, which is stored in the sysusers system table in each database. Logins are essentially mapped to a username in each database the user needs to access. You can create that mapping or create a database user in a database using the sp_grantdbaccess system stored procedure or with the SQL Server Enterprise Manager.

> **Note**
>
> You might also find several system stored procedures to perform similar tasks. These include sp_adduser, sp_dropuser, sp_addgroup, sp_drop-group, and sp_changegroup. These are legacy system stored procedures that are used in previous releases. Although they still work to control SQL Server Authentication Mode login to username mappings, they won't function properly to control Windows NT Authentication Mode usernames and group names. Therefore, you should not use them unless you have a server that has been upgraded and was using them before. However, even in this instance, you should change over to the new system stored procedures at your earliest convenience.

Adding a User to a Database

▼ SYNTAX

```
sp_grantdbaccess [@loginame =] 'login' [,[@name_in_db =]
➥'name_in_db']
```

where

- *login* is the login name you added earlier (either as a SQL Server login or a Windows NT login or group).

- *name_in_db* is the name you want an individual to have while he or she is in this database (the username). If you don't specify a name, it is set to the same as the login name.

▲

I recommend that you set the username to the login name at every opportunity so it is easier to follow security from logins to users in each database. You don't have to, but isn't it a bit confusing to log in as Richard, but have a username of Bill in the sales database and Johnny in the pubs database? Keeping the names the same eliminates confusion (which is in everyone's best interest in a complex product like SQL Server).

So if you want Bob to be able to access the pubs database on your server, run

Use pubs
```
Exec sp_grantdbaccess 'RWHOMENT\Bob'
```

and you should get

```
Granted database access to 'RWHOMENT\Bob'.
```

You can do the same thing with an NT group:

```
Exec sp_grantdbaccess 'RWHOMENT\Marketing'
```

and, again, you should receive a success message.

To remove someone's database access, you would run the sp_revokedbaccess system stored procedure.

SYNTAX

```
sp_revokedbaccess [@name_in_db =] 'name_in_db']
```

where

- *name_in_db* is the name of the database user to remove.

Only members of the dbaccessadmin and dbowner roles (or the sysadmin fixed server role) can run either of these system stored procedures. You examine roles later in today's lesson.

To see which users are in your database and which login they belong to, you can run the sp_helpuser system stored procedure.

SYNTAX

```
sp_helpuser [[@name_in_db =] 'username']
```

where

- *username* is optional and is either a username or role name.

If you don't specify a username, a report of all users and roles will be produced. Otherwise you get a report for a specific user or role.

When you create a database, two users are already there. One of these users is named dbo (for DataBase Owner). The dbo user is mapped to the sa login by default. When you install SQL Server, the sa login is considered the owner of all databases. If another login were to create a database, that login would be the owner of the database. Within a database, there is nothing the dbo user cannot do. It is as powerful as the sa login within each database. However, only the sa login (or members of system roles, discussed later) have certain systemwide privileges.

5

The other user that exists by default is known as INFORMATION_SCHEMA. This username exists as the owner of several views used to provide system catalog information compliant with the American National Standards Institute (ANSI) specification. Although you will not examine these ANSI views further in this book, you will examine views in detail on Day 15, "Working with Views, Stored Procedures, and Triggers."

Now try to create a user in the pubs database. If you've been following along, you should have a login named Don in your SQL Server. You created this user as a SQL Server login earlier in today's lesson. Start up the SQL Server Query Analyzer and run the following T-SQL (Transact-SQL) statements:

```
USE pubs
EXEC sp_grantdbaccess Don
```

This will add the new user Don to the pubs database, mapped back to the login ID of Don in the sysxlogins table in the master database. You can verify this by running sp_helpuser in the pubs database (see Figure 5.14).

FIGURE 5.14

The results of sp_helpuser.

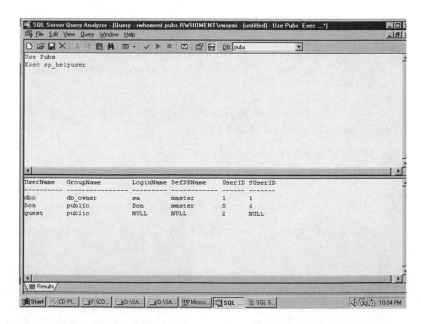

You can see that Don has been added as a user to the database, with a login name of Don. You can probably see why it would be confusing to use different names here. You can also see that the grants you ran earlier for Windows NT users and groups are also there, along with dbo and INFORMATION_SCHEMA.

I said a while back that a login does not allow you to access any databases, and yet when you log in you can access all the system databases as well as the sample pubs and Northwind databases. How is this possible? It's because of the guest username.

If you run sp_grantdbaccess guest in a database, it adds a special user account to the database known as guest. If you look in the results of the sp_helpuser system stored procedure in Figure 5.14, you will notice this guest account. You will also see that it is not mapped back to a login; it is mapped to a null login. It is a special user and not subject to normal rules. When a guest user account exists in a database, any login that requests access to the database and does not have a username specifically created in the database (either via group membership or an individual account) will be allowed in as guest. Hence, during setup there is a guest account built into each of the default databases on your server.

> **Note**   You cannot remove the guest username from the master or the tempdb databases. If you did, where would a user go when he or she had a login but no specific database access?

The Guest Username

If you log in with a login for which you have not created a specific username in the pubs database, you will be accessing the database as the guest username. If you try to access a database in which you don't have a username, and there is no guest username, you will get an error message. For example, if you try to use the Northwind database (either by selecting it in the Database: text box in the SQL Server Query Analyzer or running the Transact-SQL command use Northwind) after you've removed the guest username (with sp_revokedbaccess), you will receive a message similar to this:

```
Msg 916, Level 14, State 1
[Microsoft][ODBC SQL Server Driver][SQL Server]Server user
'Don' is not a valid user in database 'Northwind'.
```

The error reports that your login is not properly mapped to a user in the Northwind database and implies that there is also no guest account. To fix this problem, either add the guest account by running the following, or, more likely, add an appropriate login mapping to the database:

```
Use Northwind
Exec sp_grantdbaccess 'guest'
```

> **Note**
>
> SQL Server 7.0 includes a guest account in every database (except Model) by default, so there's no need to explicitly add the guest user here. However, after you remove it, you can reproduce this issue. If the guest user is in the model database, every new database you create will have a guest user.

So far you have discovered two ways to access a database: by being mapped as a user from a login or by using the guest username. You can also be the dbo, meaning you're the login who actually created the database. Or you might be aliased to another user for historical reasons.

> **Caution**
>
> The following section on aliasing is provided strictly for backward compatibility. You should not use aliases in SQL Server 7.0. Roles provide a much cleaner solution, as you will see shortly.

Adding an Alias

You can add what's known as a database username alias with the `sp_addalias` system stored procedure. This allows a login to impersonate another database user, instead of mapping his or her login to his or her own username or NT group name.

`sp_addalias` *login_name, username*

where

- *login_name* is the login name of the user you want to map.
- *username* is the database user you would like to impersonate.

Aliasing was created to help streamline security in a database. You can alias as many logins as you'd like to a single username in a database. If a login already has a username mapped in the database, that login cannot also be aliased to a user. Again, roles provide a much cleaner and better security model.

This database access option is typically used to map logins to the dbo user in a database. However, there can be only one "real" database owner at any time. Because most companies have more than one administrator, they might want more than one user to act as owner of the database. Roles will take care of this problem.

If you should change your mind and decide to drop the alias, you can do so with the `sp_dropalias` system stored procedure.

Syntax

```
sp_dropalias login_name
```

where

- *login_name* is the login name of the user.

Aliases should exist only in a database that was upgraded from SQL Server 6.0 or 6.5 to SQL Server 7.0 and should be removed as time and testing permit because they will likely not be supported in future releases of Microsoft SQL Server.

Changing the Database Owner

You might want to change the owner of an existing database to assign responsibility for a database to a particular database administrator (DBA). To do this, the login must not exist in the database as a username.

To change the owner, run the sp_changedbowner system stored procedure.

▼ Syntax

```
sp_changedbowner [@loginame =] 'login' [,[@map =] drop_alias_flag]
```

where

- *login* is the SQL Server login ID to be mapped.
- *drop_alias_flag* is an optional parameter, which, if you do not provide it, will cause all users aliased as dbo to be dropped when you change the database owner. If you specify the TRUE parameter, all those who are currently aliased to the old dbo will now be aliased to the new dbo.

▲

You have examined four distinct ways to access a database after you have successfully logged into SQL Server. They are checked in the following order:

5

- sa—The sa (or any member of the sysadmin server role) will always be able to access a database and will always appear to be dbo, even when you've assigned database ownership to another login with sp_changedbowner.
- Database username—The "normal" way to access a database is with a username mapped to a SQL Server login ID (either a Windows NT username or group name). This includes Windows NT groups that you might be mapped into.
- Alias—You can be aliased to a valid database user. Inside the database you will emulate the other user in terms of permissions and privileges.
- Guest—If all other checks fail, SQL Server will see whether a guest account exists in the sysusers database system table. If one exists, access will be granted as guest. Otherwise, access will be denied.

> **Note**
>
> You might find that Windows NT accounts are not mapped back to logins. If an NT user gets login and database access via membership in a Windows NT group, further mappings with an individual login would be redundant. You won't typically create this situation, but SQL Server might. For example, suppose you add a Windows NT group to a database, and then a user creates a table. To keep track of who owns the table, SQL Server creates a new user for the Windows NT user.

Roles

I've put off talking about roles until now because they tie everything else together in SQL Server 7.0. You can think of roles as SQL Server groups. We don't use the term *groups* so we won't confuse these options in SQL Server with Windows NT groups.

SQL Server roles allow you to combine database usernames into groupings. It doesn't matter whether the database usernames were derived from Windows NT groups, Windows NT users, or SQL Server logins. Roles can even contain other roles as members.

The Public Role

SQL Server 7.0 contains one built-in role in each database named public. All users, groups, and roles are members of the public role and can't be removed. Think of the public role as similar to the Everyone group from Windows NT. It's a convenient shortcut to refer to all users without having to explicitly name them. You'll see this used on Day 6's discussion of permissions. Back in Figure 5.14 you saw the group name of public displayed for most users.

Server-Wide Roles

Something that keeps coming up in today's lesson is that the sa login is all-powerful and can do anything he or she wants on an instance of SQL Server. Although this is true, it's really because the sa login is a member of the server-wide role named sysadmin. SQL Server has seven server-wide roles. You can make a login a member of one or more of these server-wide roles at any time. You cannot, however, remove or add to the list of available server-wide roles. You cannot remove sa from the sysadmin server-wide role.

Available Server-Wide Roles

The following list is the complete set of available server-wide roles. Study them carefully so you know when to use them.

- sysadmin—Members of the sysadmin role can do anything to the SQL Server. They appear to be the dbo of every database (even if they're not). They essentially override the permissions and security systems.

- serveradmin—Members of the serveradmin role can set configuration options with the sp_configure system stored procedure and can shut down the server. Server operators are good candidates to be members of this role. Note that members of this role can only issue the Transact-SQL SHUTDOWN command to shut down the server. Their permissions to control services are Windows NT rights—not SQL Server rights.

- setupadmin—Members of the setupadmin role can install and configure linked servers and mark a stored procedure to run on startup.

- securityadmin—Members of the securityadmin role can create and control server logins as well as permissions to create databases and can read the SQL Server error log. Again, operators are candidates for this role, and most likely your help desk personnel would be members of this role.

- processadmin—Members of the processadmin role can control processes running on the database server. This typically involves "killing" runaway queries, and help desk personnel might need this right.

- dbcreator—Members of the dbcreator role can create and alter databases on your server. DBAs are good candidates for this role (if you don't want your DBA to be a member of the sysadmin role).

- diskadmin—Members of the diskadmin role can manage files and file growth on the server. DBAs are good candidates for this role (if you don't want your DBA to be a member of the sysadmin role).

Assigning a Login to a Server Role

To assign a login to a specific server role, use either the SQL Server Enterprise Manager or the sp_addsrvrolemember system stored procedure.

```
sp_addsrvrolemember [@loginame =] 'login' ,[@rolename =] 'role'
```

where

- *login* is the SQL Server login ID to add to the role.
- *role* is the server role name you want to have the login assigned to.

A single login can belong to zero, one, or many roles. However, the sysadmin role encompasses all other roles—both serverwide and database-specific—so there's no need to assign any other role if you select the sysadmin role. To remove a login from a server-wide role, use the sp_dropsrvrolemember system stored procedure.

SYNTAX

```
sp_dropsrvrolemember [@loginame =] 'login' ,[@rolename =] 'role'
```

where

- *login* is the SQL Server login ID removed from the role.
- *role* is the server role name you want to have the login removed from.

As an example, to make RWHOMENT\Bob a member of the server role securityadmin, you could run the following:

```
Exec sp_addsrvrolemember 'RWHOMENT\Bob','securityadmin'
```

and you would see the following output:

```
'RWHOMENT\Bob' added to role 'securityadmin'.
```

To remove Bob from this role, you could then run

```
Exec sp_dropsrvrolemember 'RWHOMENT\Bob','securityadmin'
```

and receive this success message:

```
'RWHOMENT\Bob' dropped from role 'securityadmin'.
```

To accomplish the same changes with the SQL Server Enterprise Manager, expand your server, expand the security folder, and then highlight the Server Roles menu item (the icon with the key next to it). In the right pane you will see the seven serverwide roles. Double-click the Security Administrators to see the Server Role Properties dialog box. Click Add, and you will be presented with a list of valid logins. Select RWHOMENT\Bob (or the equivalent on your server) and click OK, and you should see something similar to Figure 5.15. After you click OK again, you will have essentially run the sp_addsrvrolemember system stored procedure, except you've used the graphical interface.

FIGURE 5.15

The Server Role Properties for the Security Administrator role.

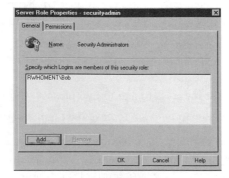

Database Roles

Each database can contain roles. Some of these roles are fixed, and you also have the ability to add your own roles (unlike serverwide roles). One thing to keep in mind is that database roles are database specific, so you can't have roles that affect more than a single database at any time. However, you can create the same roles in each database.

Database-Specific Fixed Roles

Each database also has a set of fixed database roles a username can be assigned to. There are nine by default, and these nine will always exist (you can't delete any of them). Each database role, just like each server role mentioned earlier, will assign users specific permissions and capabilities. You'll learn more about permissions in tomorrow's lesson.

- db_owner—Members of the db_owner role can do anything they want—but only within their database. Being a member of the db_owner role gives a user all the same rights and permissions as the dbo user of a database (the owner).

- db_accessadmin—Members of the db_accessadmin role can add or remove users' access to the database (running the sp_grantdbaccess system stored procedure, for example).

- db_securityadmin—Members of the db_securityadmin role can control all permissions, roles, role membership, and owners of objects in the database.

- db_ddladmin—Members of the db_ddladmin role can create, modify, and drop all database objects, but they can't issue security-related commands (grant, revoke, deny). You'll learn more about these commands in tomorrow's lesson.

- db_dumpoperator—Members of the db_dumpoperator role can issue the dbcc, checkpoint, and backup commands.

- db_datareader—Members of the db_datareader role have the select permission on any table or view in the database.

- db_datawriter—Members of the db_datawriter role have insert, update, and delete rights on any table or view in the database.

- db_denydatareader—Members of the db_denydatareader role cannot select data from any table or view in the database.

- db_denydatawriter—Members of the db_denydatawriter role cannot modify any data in the database with the insert, update, or delete statements on any table or view in the database.

5

User-Defined Database Roles

In addition to the fixed database roles available, you can create roles yourself and then assign users or roles to these newly created roles. You would create roles in a SQL Server database for the same reasons you would create a Windows NT group—to conveniently group users together who perform similar functions. You should create as many roles as make sense. There is no restriction on how many roles a user can be a member of, and roles can be members of other roles.

To create a role, you can start with the sp_addrole system stored procedure.

```
sp_addrole [@rolename =] 'role' [,[@ownername =] 'owner']
```

where

- *role* is the name you want to have for the new role.
- *owner* is the SQL Server username you want to own the role (each user can own his or her own roles). The default value is dbo, and it's likely that that's exactly what you want to happen.

Only members of the sysadmin server-wide role or db_owner or db_securityadmin roles can add a new role to a server. This holds true for dropping roles as well. One oddity about roles: Although you can specify the owner name, the role name must still be unique in the database. Hence, you don't need to know the owner when you drop a role because the name is unique in a database.

Speaking of dropping roles, run the sp_droprole system stored procedure to drop a role from a database.

SYNTAX

```
sp_droprole [@rolename =] 'role'
```

where

- *role* is the name of the user-created role you want to delete.

You cannot delete a role if there are any users or other roles as members of the role. You also can't delete the role if it owns any objects. You'll learn more about object ownership in tomorrow's lesson. This brings up another interesting question: How do I add users to a role?

SYNTAX

```
sp_addrolemember [@rolename =] 'role', [@membername =]
➥'security_account'
```

where

- *role* is the name of the role you want to add a user to.
- *security_account* is the username or role name you want to add to this role.

This stored procedure can be used to add users to either user-defined roles or fixed database roles. To remove a member from a role, run sp_droprolemember.

▼ Syntax

▲

```
sp_droprolemember [@rolename =] 'role', [@membername =]
➥'security_account'
```

where

- *role* is the name of the role you want to remove a user from.
- *security_account* is the username or role name you want to remove from this role.

Here's some code to show how these stored procedures might be used. To add a new role in our pubs database and then assign a user to it, run this code:

```
Use pubs
Exec sp_addrole 'Management'
Exec sp_addrole 'Operations'
Exec sp_addrolemember 'Management','Don'
Exec sp_addrolemember 'Operations','RWHOMENT\Marketing'
```

and you should see this:

```
New role added.
New role added.
'Don' added to role 'Management'.
'RWHOMENT\Marketing' added to role 'Operations'.
```

Notice that if you try to drop a role with members, you get an error:

```
Exec sp_droprole 'Operations'
```

resulting in

```
Server: Msg 15144, Level 16, State 1
The role has members.
It must be empty before it can be dropped.
name
------------------------------------------------------------------
RWHOMENT\Marketing

(1 row(s) affected)
```

SQL Server is even nice enough to tell you which members remain in the role. To clean this up, run the following:

```
Exec sp_droprolemember 'Operations','RWHOMENT\Marketing'
Exec sp_droprole 'Operations'
```

and get success!

```
'RWHOMENT\Marketing' dropped from role 'Operations'.
Role dropped.
```

5

Membership in each role is stored in a combination of the sysusers system table and the sysmembers system table. You can examine which roles exist by running the `sp_helpro`-`le` system stored procedure or the `sp_helprolemember` system stored procedure. Both stored procedures take a single parameter—the role name in quotation marks. You can achieve the same results with SQL Server Enterprise Manager. Go back to the Logins folder for your server and either double-click a login or right-click and select Properties from the pop-up menu. I've selected RWHOMENT\Bob for the following example. You will see that server roles can be configured here as well on the Server Roles tab. However, for now focus on the last tab, Database Access. Highlight the pubs database, and you should see a list of roles appear in the Database roles window. It should look like Figure 5.16.

FIGURE 5.16

The SQL Server Login Properties showing the database access.

Not only do all the fixed database roles appear, but your user-created roles do, as well. Scroll to the bottom of the list, and Management should be there. To make this database user a member of a role, simply check the box next to the role name. To remove it from the role, uncheck the box. It's that simple!

To create a new role with SQL Server Enterprise Manager, expand the databases folder, and then expand the database you're interested in working with. For the example, expand the pubs database. Then highlight the Roles folder, and the list of roles appears in the right pane. To add a new role, right-click in the whitespace in the right pane, and select New Database Role from the pop-up menu. Add a new role named Finance, with Don as a member of the role. When completed, the dialog box should look like Figure 5.17. Click OK to finish creating the role. You'll learn more about the application role option in the next section.

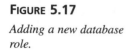

FIGURE 5.17

Adding a new database role.

Application Roles

Application roles are a very exciting new feature of SQL Server 7.0. Although you can think of application roles as similar to other roles you've examined, they perform a function that is different from other roles.

An application role serves some of the same purposes roles do—they are a wonderful way to group users so that permissions can be applied at a higher level than maintaining them on a user-by-user basis. However, they are different in that application roles can be "turned on" by an application. After an application has enabled an application role, all the permissions of the user are suspended, and only the permissions of the role are enforced. Of course, the role requires a password to be successfully enabled (unless you don't want a password).

Imagine a payroll application as a great example of their use. Although all the administrators in the payroll department must update employee salary and bonus information periodically, you'd rather have them use your application than directly query the SQL Server database themselves (with potentially disastrous consequences). When the application starts, you can have the user log in to SQL Server as themselves (either with a SQL Server login or preferably with their Windows NT credentials so they don't even know it's happening). Then run the appropriate code (the sp_setapprole system stored procedure) to turn on the payroll application role. From that moment on, until the application terminates its connection to the database, the permissions of the role are enforced and the permissions of the user are turned off. Therefore, if the payroll role has permissions to modify the payroll tables, but the payroll administrators don't, you can still have them run the application. Better yet, they can't knowingly (or unknowingly) go around any security or controls you've put in place with your application. The best part is that all activity is still audited with the user's login information.

Application roles tell a compelling story. Now examine how to implement them. I think you'll agree that they're relatively simple, given how powerful they are. You'll learn how to assign permissions to roles in tomorrow's lesson.

First, create an application role. Do this with the sp_addapprole system stored procedure.

SYNTAX

```
sp_addapprole [@rolename =] 'role', [@password =] 'password'
```

where

- *role* is the name of the role you want to create.
- *password* is the password the application must pass to enable the role.

To drop an application role, run the sp_dropapprole system stored procedure.

SYNTAX

```
sp_dropapprole [@rolename =] 'role'
```

where

- *role* is the name of the role you want to remove.

To then use the role in your application, you would execute the sp_setapprole system stored procedure.

▼ SYNTAX

```
sp_setapprole [@rolename =] 'role' ,
[@password =] {Encrypt N 'password'} ¦ 'password'
[,[@encrypt =] 'encrypt_style']
```

where

- *role* is the name of the role you want to enable.
- *password* is the password specified in the sp_addapprole execution.
- *Encrypt N 'password'* requests that the password be encrypted when sent over the network (if you just specify the password, it's sent over the network without encryption).
- *encrypt_style* specifies the type of encryption to use. Currently there are two available values: none and odbc. Open database connectivity (ODBC) is specified when you are using an ODBC-based client and means that the ODBC canonical encrypt function will be used to encrypt the password before it's sent over the network. Note that if you are using an object linking and embedding database (OLE DB) client, this function is still available. Simply specify odbc and the same type of encryption will take place.

▲

To create and then use an application role, you can run the following script within the SQL Server Query Analyzer (an ODBC-based tool):

```
Use pubs
Exec sp_addapprole 'Payroll','password'
Go
Exec sp_setapprole 'Payroll', {Encrypt N 'password'},'odbc'
```

You receive the following success messages:

```
New application role added.
The application role 'Payroll' is now active.
```

From this point on, all permissions for this connection to SQL Server will use the permissions of the application role. Auditing of activity performed will still show up with an individual user's login information—not the application role. So, you can still tell what an individual is doing, even when he or she has enabled this group functionality.

Summary

To access SQL Server data, you must pass through several layers of security. If using Named Pipes or Multiprotocol for your SQL Server network library, Windows NT will validate your connection request at the network level, regardless of the security mode. If you are in Mixed Security Mode, either SQL Server or Windows NT will validate your login. The sysxlogins system table in the master database will be used if you request a SQL Server authenticated connection. If you are in Windows NT Authentication Security Mode, or when requesting Windows NT validation in Mixed Mode, Windows NT will be called to validate your login request and allow you access to SQL Server. Remember that connections that have been validated by Windows NT are sometimes referred to as "trusted connections."

After you're logged in, you still need database access for each database you'd like to use. You must be a member of a Windows NT group that's been added to a database, have a username created for your login in a database, have an alias in a database, or have a guest username before you are allowed access to that database. This has nothing at all to do with the rights (or permissions) you will have when you are in the database. Rights and permissions are the subject of tomorrow's lesson.

You should use SQL Server roles when Windows NT groups aren't available or are otherwise inconvenient. Roles are database specific, so they contain users, not logins. You should use the fixed database roles whenever possible. Server-wide roles are available for permissions that cross multiple databases. Application roles are a way to have an application provide database functionality that individual users don't have with their own security accounts.

5

Q&A

Q **What is the difference between integrated and mixed security?**

A Integrated security allows only trusted connections, whereas mixed security will also allow SQL Server-authenticated connections if you request them.

Q **What security mode is appropriate if you have mostly Windows NT clients but also a few UNIX computers that need access to SQL Server?**

A Mixed security because UNIX computers probably won't be logged into your Windows NT domain.

Q **What stored procedure activates application roles?**

A The sp_setapprole system stored procedure.

Q **If you have a login but not a username, why can you use the pubs database?**

A Because the guest username exists in the pubs database.

Workshop

The Workshop provides quiz questions to help you solidify your understanding of the concepts presented in this chapter. In addition to the quiz questions, exercises are provided to let you practice what you have learned in this chapter. Try to understand the quiz and exercise answers before continuing to the next day's lesson. Answers are provided in Appendix A, "Answers."

Quiz

1. How would you revoke the right of Windows NT administrators to log into SQL Server as system administrators (sa)?

2. If you wanted someone to have all the rights of the owner of a database, but someone else was already the dbo, what would you do?

3. When would you need to create an individual SQL Server login for a Windows NT user instead of using a Windows NT group?

Exercises

1. Create the following logins in SQL Server. Also, add each login to a user-defined database on your server.

   George

   Henry

   Ida

   John

2. Now make John the dbo of the database you just referenced. Fix any errors you receive to make this change possible.

5

DAY 6

Working with Permissions

Yesterday you examined SQL Server 7.0's security model. SQL Server has two different security modes: Windows NT Integrated and the default Mixed Mode security. You can use either your Windows NT user/group account or a SQL Server security mode login to connect to SQL Server. Although this allows you to log in to SQL Server, you must have a user account to connect to and use a database. A user account in a database can be an NT group, NT user, or SQL Server user, and all of these can be grouped with SQL Server roles. Application roles are also available and provide a powerful feature to help secure your database applications.

When you are in a database, however, you must have permissions to actually do anything. SQL Server is an inherently secure system. If you want to perform some action, you must have been given permission to do so. In today's lesson you will examine how permissions work, the difference between statement and object permissions, and how permissions are combined between roles and user accounts. You also examine ownership chains, exploring what they are and why you must understand them.

Why Use Permissions?

Up until now you have done all your work in SQL Server using either the sa (system administrator) login or your Windows NT account, which is a member of the local administrator's group and hence a member of the sysadmin fixed server role. The sa login is also a member of that role, as you learned on Day 5, "Using SQL Server Login and User Security." Therefore, when you examine the sysadmin fixed server role, you are also examining what the sa login can do. Members of the sysadmin fixed server role have no restrictions on what they can do in SQL Server, which is not only convenient but necessary for many of the administrative tasks you might have to perform in SQL Server. Ordinary users, however, should not be connecting to SQL Server using either the sa login or as members of the sysadmin fixed server role because they would have all permissions to the SQL Server—enough to delete all the databases and shut the server down!

By designing and implementing a good security plan for SQL Server, you can eliminate many problems before they happen, instead of spending your time trying to figure out how your data (or SQL Server) became damaged. You can successfully restrict what data modifications can be made as well as what data a user is allowed to see. You can also restrict whether a user can back up a database, back up the transaction log for a database, or create and manipulate objects in a database.

Another benefit of enabling multiple logins, users, and permissions is that you can track what individual users are allowed to do and audit their activity. This is critical if you want to have any hope of determining what happened when something magically "disappears" from your database.

Implementing Database Permissions

One critical point must be clear up front: All permissions in SQL Server are given to database users. So when you examine permissions, you are always looking at a database user's permissions, not the permissions for a login. This means that permissions are database specific.

Note

For every rule there's an exception. Fixed server roles are granted to logins, not to database users. This makes sense, however, because being a member of one of these fixed server roles gives you permissions across the entire server.

For example, Sue has all permissions to the library database (she is a senior librarian). Sue might have SELECT (read) permissions on tables in the purchasing database (she can see books on order, but only her supervisors can order new books). Finally, Sue might have no permissions in the accounting database (only the accountants have permissions in the accounting database).

In this example, Sue must connect to SQL Server with either a SQL Server authentication mode login or use her Windows NT account credentials. Within each database she will have a separate user account (or use her Windows NT group) to gain access. As you saw in yesterday's lesson, she might also use guest permissions, for example, in the accounting database (if a guest username exists). For each user in each database, there are separate permissions.

> **Note**
>
> The sysprotects and syspermissions database system tables track security within a database. That's why security is database specific. This is also true for the master database. These two tables can be found in every database in SQL Server.

Types of Permissions

SQL Server 7.0 uses three terms to indicate what action you are taking in reference to permissions. These are the GRANT, REVOKE, and DENY statements. You will examine these statements in detail later, but it's useful to begin with a brief example of the terminology.

To let a user perform an action, you must grant the user some kind of permission. To prevent a user from performing an action, you deny the user the right to perform an action. To remove a previously granted permission, you revoke the permission.

There are two types of permissions: statement level and object level. Statement-level permissions enable a user to run a particular Transact-SQL command, whereas object-level permissions allow a user to perform some operation: SELECT data (read), INSERT data, UPDATE data, or DELETE data.

Permissions Precedence

Understanding how permissions are applied is critical to understanding when a particular permission will be in effect. All permissions in SQL Server are cumulative, except for the DENY permission, which overrides other permissions.

6

If you have the SELECT permission from your membership in role1 and the INSERT permission from your membership in role2, you effectively have the SELECT and INSERT permissions. If you then were to be denied SELECT permissions within either of these roles or within your individual account, you would no longer have the SELECT permission. DENY always overrides any other permission.

SQL Server's Special Permissions

SQL Server 7.0 has several different levels of permissions. Most of these permissions are database specific. However, as mentioned earlier, fixed server roles are tied to logins, not database users. As you saw on Day 5, each role implies a specific set of permissions. In addition, sa implies its own particular set of permissions.

Within each database are also fixed database roles, each of which is associated with a particular set of permissions. There is also a special user in each database known as dbo (the database owner). Although you never will see information directly in SQL Server about it, there is a concept of a database object owner. There are special permissions inherent for anyone who is in this conceptual role as well.

Later in today's lesson you will examine the public role and what permissions are implied with it. In this next section, you will learn more about the fixed server roles and their permissions.

Fixed Server Role Permissions

Each role has implicit permissions associated with it, and you can view these by running the system stored procedure sp_srvrolepermission.

SYNTAX

```
sp_srvrolepermission [[@srvrolename =] 'role']
```

where

- *role* is the name of the fixed server role for which you would like to see the permissions

Here are the results of running this system stored procedure. For example, if you ran

```
sp_srvrolepermission 'dbcreator'
```

You would see the following:

```
ServerRole                              Permission
--------------------------------------  ----------------------------------
dbcreator                               Add member to dbcreator
dbcreator                               ALTER DATABASE
dbcreator                               CREATE DATABASE
```

```
dbcreator                               Extend database
dbcreator                               sp_renamedb
```

(5 row(s) affected)

Each of these permissions and server roles are explained in the following sections.

sysadmin

Members of the sysadmin server role can do anything they want to SQL Server (literally). Members of this fixed server role are granted an extremely powerful set of permissions and should be considered carefully. The sa login is always a member of this role and cannot be removed from the sysadmin role. Members of the sysadmin fixed server role are always considered to be the DBO of every database they use. Members of the sysadmin role cannot be prevented from accessing any database on SQL Server.

There is no list of rights given for sysadmin members—there's nothing they can't do. Keep this in mind when deciding whether to give someone membership in this role. Am I starting to sound paranoid yet?

serveradmin

Server administrators who won't otherwise be administering databases or other objects are best suited to be members of the serveradmin role. Members of this role can perform the following operations:

- Add another login to the serveradmin fixed server role
- Run the DBCC PINTABLE command
- Drop extended stored procedures
- Run the sp_configure system stored procedure to change system options
- Run the RECONFIGURE command to install changes made with sp_configure
- Run the sp_tableoption system stored procedure for any table in any database
- Run the SHUTDOWN command to shut down SQL Server

setupadmin

Members of the setupadmin role are typically administrators who are configuring remote servers. Members of this role can perform the following operations:

- Add another login to the setupadmin fixed server role
- Add, drop, or configure linked servers
- Mark a stored procedure as startup

6

securityadmin

Members of the securityadmin role can perform any operation related to security in SQL Server. Help desk personnel (individuals who set up new accounts) are great candidates for membership in this role. Members of this role can perform the following operations:

- Add members to the securityadmin fixed server role
- Grant, revoke, or deny the CREATE DATABASE statement permission
- Read the SQL Server error log
- Run security-related system stored procedures, including

  sp_addlogin

  sp_droplogin

  sp_defaultdb

  sp_defaultlanguage

  sp_addlinkedsrvlogin

  sp_droplinkedsrvlogin

  sp_grantlogin

  sp_revokelogin

  sp_denylogin

  sp_grantdbaccess

  sp_helplogins

  sp_remoteoption

Note Being a securityadmin member doesn't give you access to every database. Therefore, some stored procedures, such as sp_helpdb or sp_droplogin, might return an error if you try to access a database that you don't have permissions to see. The information you are allowed to see will still be displayed, and in the case of sp_droplogin logins will still be dropped.

processadmin

Members of the processadmin role can control processes running on the database server. This typically involves "killing" runaway queries, and help desk personnel might need this right. The following operations are allowed:

- Add members to the processadmin fixed server role
- Run the KILL command to end a SQL Server process

dbcreator

Members of the dbcreator fixed server role can perform operations relating to creating and modifying databases, which most likely includes senior database administrators. The permissions of this role include the following operations:

- Add members to the dbcreator fixed database role
- Run the sp_renamedb system stored procedure
- Run the CREATE DATABASE and ALTER DATABASE commands

diskadmin

Members of the diskadmin fixed server role can manage files. This role is mostly for backward compatibility. In general, most database administrators are better served with the dbcreator fixed server role. Members of the diskadmin fixed server role can perform the following operations:

- Add members to the diskadmin fixed server role
- Run the following DISK commands (for backward compatibility):

  DISK INIT

  DISK REINIT

  DISK REFIT

  DISK MIRROR

  DISK REMIRROR

- Run the following system stored procedures:

  sp_diskdefault

  sp_dropdevice

- Run the sp_addumpdevice system stored procedure to add backup devices

sa

The sa login is worth separate mention here. In previous releases of SQL Server, all permissions for serverwide administration were associated with the sa SQL Server Authenticated login. There were no separate roles breaking up these permissions. Sa is still included for backward compatibility and still has all the permissions it had in previous releases. However, this is because of the login's membership in the sysadmin fixed server role. You cannot remove sa from this role.

The sa login (and all members of the sysadmin fixed server role) always emulates being the dbo user in each database. You cannot change this. This is not the same thing as being a member of the db_owner fixed database role.

6

Fixed Database Roles

Members of fixed database roles are given specific permissions within each database. Unlike fixed server roles, however, they are specific to each database. Being a member of a fixed database role in one database has no effect on permissions in any other database. Now examine each of the nine fixed database roles. You can view these roles by running the sp_dbfixedrolepermission system stored procedure.

SYNTAX

```
sp_dbfixedrolepermission [[@rolename =] 'role']
```

where

- *role* is the name of the fixed database role for which you would like to see permissions

The results of running this system stored procedure are described in the following sections.

db_owner

Members of the db_owner fixed database role are the "owners" of a database. They have very broad permissions within a database and can do almost everything the actual database owner can do. Members of the db_owner fixed database role can perform the following operations within their databases:

- Add members to or remove members from any fixed database role except for db_owner
- Run any data definition language (DDL) statement
- Run the BACKUP DATABASE and BACKUP LOG statements
- Run the RESTORE DATABASE and RESTORE LOG statements
- Issue a CHECKPOINT in a database
- Run the following Database Consistency Checker (DBCC) commands:

  ```
  dbcc checkalloc
  dbcc checkcatalog
  dbcc checkdb
  dbcc textall
  dbcc textalloc
  dbcc updateusage
  ```

- Grant, revoke, or deny the SELECT, INSERT, UPDATE, DELETE, REFERENCES, or EXECUTE permissions on every object (as appropriate for each object type)

- Add users, groups, roles, or aliases to a database with the following system stored procedures:

  sp_addalias

  sp_addapprole

  sp_addrole

  sp_addrolemember

  sp_adduser

  sp_approlepassword

  sp_change_users_login

  sp_dropalias

  sp_dropapprole

  sp_droprole

  sp_droprolemember

  sp_dropuser

  sp_grantdbaccess

  sp_revokedbaccess

- Modify stored procedures with the following system stored procedures:

  sp_procoption

  sp_recompile

- Rename any object with the sp_rename system stored procedure.
- Modify some table-specific options with the sp_tableoption system stored procedure.
- Change the owner of any object with the sp_changeobjectowner system stored procedure.

Note

The db_owner fixed database role permissions specify that members of the role can "run any data definition language (DDL) statement except for GRANT, REVOKE, and DENY." This deserves a little explanation. By default, members of the db_owner role can grant, revoke, or deny permissions to any object in the database. However, the database object owner (DBOO), examined later in today's lesson, can take away the abilities of the dbo and members of the db_owner fixed database role.

6

db_accessadmin

Members of the db_accessadmin fixed database role manage which logins can access a database. As with the securityadmin role, your help desk staff might be the best candidates for membership in this role. Members can perform the following operations:

- Run the following system stored procedures:

```
sp_addalias
sp_adduser
sp_dropalias
sp_dropuser
sp_grantdbaccess
sp_revokedbaccess
```

db_securityadmin

Members of the db_securityadmin fixed database role can administer security within a database, and their abilities include performing the following operations:

- Running the GRANT, REVOKE, or DENY statements
- Running the following system stored procedures:

```
sp_addapprole
sp_addrole
sp_addrolemember
sp_approlepassword
sp_changeobjectowner
sp_dropapprole
sp_droprole
sp_droprolemember
```

db_ddladmin

Members of the db_ddladmin fixed database role can perform the following operations:

- Run any DDL command except for GRANT, REVOKE, and DENY
- Grant the REFERENCES permission on any table
- Modify stored procedures with the following system stored procedures:

```
sp_procoption
sp_recompile
```

- Rename any object with the sp_rename system stored procedure

- Modify some table-specific options with the sp_tableoption system stored procedure
- Change the owner of any object with the sp_changeobjectowner system stored procedure

db_backupoperator

Members of the db_backupoperator fixed database role can perform all operations related to backing up a database, including the following:

- Run the BACKUP DATABASE and BACKUP LOG statements
- Issue a CHECKPOINT in a database
- Run the following DBCC commands:

```
dbcc checkalloc
dbcc checkcatalog
dbcc checkdb
dbcc textall
dbcc textalloc
dbcc updateusage
```

Note The DBCC commands just listed are discussed in more detail on Day 7, "Implementing Backups in SQL Server 7.0."

db_datareader

Members of the db_datareader fixed database role have the SELECT permission on any table or view in a database. They cannot grant permission to or revoke it from anyone else.

db_datawriter

Members of the db_datawriter fixed database role have the INSERT, UPDATE, and DELETE permissions on all tables or views in a database. They cannot grant permission to or revoke it from anyone else.

db_denydatareader

Members of the db_denydatareader fixed database role cannot run the SELECT statement on any table or view in the database. This option is useful if you want your database administrator (DBA) to set up your objects (as a member of the db_ddladmin fixed database role) but not be able to read any sensitive data in the database.

6

db denydatawriter

Members of the db_denydatawriter fixed database role cannot run the INSERT, UPDATE, or DELETE statement on any table or view in the database.

The Database Owner (dbo)

The dbo user has all the rights that members of the db_owner role have. There can be only one dbo for each database. The dbo is the only database user who can add a user to the db_owner fixed database role.

In addition, if a user is the dbo, when he or she creates an object, the owner of the object will be dbo of that object, as you'd expect. This is not true for members of the db_owner fixed database role (or any other user of the database). Unless they qualify their object names with the dbo owner name, the owner's name will be his or her username.

You are considered the dbo of a database in any of the following four situations:

- You are the creator of a database. The login that created a database is the dbo. By default, the sa SQL Server login is the owner of every database when you install SQL Server 7.0.

- You are assigned as the database owner. The owner of a database can later be assigned using the sp_changedbowner system stored procedure. You examined sp_changedbowner yesterday.

- You connect to SQL Server as any member of the sysadmin fixed server role. If you connect to SQL Server using either the sa login or any other member of the sysadmin fixed server role, you have all permissions in all databases because you emulate the dbo in each database.

- You connect to a database with a login aliased to the dbo of a database. Only a single user can be the dbo at any given time. In previous releases of SQL Server, you could alias a login to another user in a database. This technique is obsolete in SQL Server 7.0; however, aliases are supported for backward compatibility. You should not use them. If you have upgraded from a previous release and had logins aliased to dbo, they will emulate being the dbo for your database. You should add users to the db_owner role in SQL Server 7.0 instead of using aliases.

Database Object Owner (DBOO) Permissions

A user who creates a database object is the DBOO of that object. By default, a user who creates an object is the owner of the object. Members of the db_owner and db_ddladmin fixed database roles can create objects as themselves or can qualify the object name as owned by the dbo. So if I issue the following create statement while logged in as Joe, with a database username of Joe, the owner is Joe:

```
Create table mytable (c1 int NOT NULL)
GO
```

To check the ownership of this object, you can run the following code:

```
Execute sp_help mytable
```

And you will see

```
Name              Owner     Type              Created_datetime
----------------  --------  ----------------  ---------------------
mytable           joe       user table        1998-08-16 22:50:34.007

(1 row(s) affected)

...

The object does not have any indexes.

No constraints have been defined for this object.

No foreign keys reference this table.
```

Notice the owner is Joe.

However, if I have membership in the db_owner or db_ddladmin roles, I can run the following:

```
Create table dbo.mytable (c1 int)
GO
EXEC sp_help mytable
```

and the output will look like this:

```
Name              Owner     Type              Created_datetime
----------------  --------  ----------------  ---------------------
mytable           dbo       user table        1998-08-16 22:51:30.016

(1 row(s) affected)

...

The object does not have any indexes.

No constraints have been defined for this object.

No foreign keys reference this table.
```

Notice that the object is no longer owned by Joe but by dbo when you run the sp_help mytable command (as expected).

6

It's a good idea to use objects only in production databases owned by the dbo user. You will examine why when you look at ownership chains later in today's lesson. If the owner is specified as dbo, the dbo user is the owner of the object—not the user who actually created the object. Hence, the user who creates an object with the owner qualified is not the DBOO of that object.

A user who owns a database object is automatically granted all permissions to that object. The appropriate permissions for each type of object are granted to the owner. For example, when a user creates a table, he or she will be granted the SELECT, INSERT, UPDATE, DELETE, REFERENCES, and BACKUP permissions on that table. Ownership of an object can be changed with the sp_changeobjectowner system stored procedure.

▼ SYNTAX

```
sp_changeobjectowner [@objname =] 'object', [@newowner =] 'owner'
```

where

- *object* is the name of a database object (table, view, or stored procedure). The object can be qualified with the owner name if necessary (and it's a good idea to always do so).

- *owner* is the username, role name, or Windows NT user or group you want to own the object you specified with the object parameter.

▲

So to change the ownership of Joe's table to Ann (assuming Ann exists in the same database), run the following:

```
Exec sp_changeobjectowner 'joe.mytable', 'Ann'
```

User Permissions

Most people who use your database will be ordinary users. The database user has no inherent rights or permissions (other than those given to the public role, examined in the next section). All rights must be explicitly granted or assigned to the user, the user's roles, or the public role.

Permissions granted to users can be categorized into statement and object permissions:

NEW TERM   *Statement* permissions allow users to create new databases, create new objects within an existing database, or back up the database or transaction log. Statement permissions give you the ability to run particular commands instead of operating on particular objects.

NEW TERM   *Object* permissions enable users to perform actions on individual objects. For example, users might have the ability to read (select) data from a table, execute a stored procedure, or modify data in a table or view (with INSERT, UPDATE, and DELETE permissions). Details for both types of permissions, as well as how to grant them, are discussed in the following section.

The PUBLIC Role

The PUBLIC role exists in each database and cannot be removed. It's mentioned here because it's extremely useful, but you must understand how to use it.

Every database user, role, Windows NT user, and Windows NT group within a database are members of the PUBLIC role, and cannot be removed from it. Therefore, PUBLIC is a great role to use when you want everyone to have a permission.

An example of this use is already present on your SQL Server system. SELECT permission, as well as the execute permission on many system stored procedures, is granted to PUBLIC on all system tables in each database. This is required for successful operation of SQL Server and should not be changed.

 Caution Be careful when granting permissions to the PUBLIC role. Remember, this means that everyone, including users who are added to the database later, will have these permissions.

Statement Permissions

Statement permissions allow a database user, database role, or Windows NT user or group to perform various tasks such as creating databases, creating objects, or backing up the database. Statement permissions allow a user to run a particular command (or set of commands) rather than merely manipulate a particular object.

Granting a user or role permissions to create an object should be considered carefully. When a user creates an object he or she becomes the owner of that object (unless the creator specifies the owner as dbo when he or she creates it) and have all the permissions associated with database object ownership. Later, you will see that having objects owned by different owners can create some difficult permissions situations.

Statement permissions should be granted only when explicitly needed. The haphazard granting of statement permissions can leave a database with unnecessary and even unusable objects.

You can grant statement permissions to individual database users, Windows NT users/groups, or database roles, including the PUBLIC role. The statement permissions that can be granted, revoked, or denied include

- CREATE DATABASE
- CREATE TABLE
- CREATE PROCEDURE

6

- CREATE DEFAULT
- CREATE RULE
- CREATE VIEW
- BACKUP DATABASE
- BACKUP LOG

These permissions can be granted individually or all at once (using the keyword ALL). Each of these commands has implications that must be considered before you use it.

The CREATE DATABASE Permission

The CREATE DATABASE permission enables users to create their own databases and thus become the dbos of those databases. Database ownership can later be changed with the sp_changedbowner system stored procedure. Only members of the SYSADMIN or DBCREATOR fixed server role are allowed to grant a user the CREATE DATABASE permissions. Because permissions are always granted to users (and never to logins), you must grant this permission in the master database only. This statement permission does not exist in any other database. The CREATE DATABASE permission also grants you rights to use the ALTER DATABASE command. In other words, you cannot use the ALTER DATABASE statement unless you have the CREATE DATABASE permission.

Tip

> It's much better to use the DBCREATOR fixed server role than grant the CREATE DATABASE statement permission. You will usually need the other rights granted by the DBCREATOR fixed server role anyway, and it's easier to figure out who has what rights when you take advantage of SQL Server roles.

The CREATE TABLE, VIEW, PROCEDURE, DEFAULT, and RULE Permissions

CREATE TABLE, VIEW, PROCEDURE, DEFAULT, and RULE permissions enable users to run the referenced statement to create objects in the database where the permissions were given. Programmers will frequently be given these permissions to allow them to create the resources they need in a database during development.

Caution   All CREATE permissions include the right to alter or drop any objects created by a user. This can cause serious problems in your database because a user can drop objects he or she is finished with, only to find that others were using the object. A user might also alter an object and make it unusable to some other user in the database. To check for these types of dependencies, you can run the sp_depends system stored procedure.

The BACKUP DATABASE and BACKUP LOG Statement Permissions

BACKUP DATABASE and BACKUP LOG permissions can also be assigned to individual users, Windows NT users/groups, and roles. Although backing up the database and transaction logs is usually an automated process carried out by scheduled jobs created by the system administrator, some environments require that individual users be given the ability to perform these backups.

Tip   Again, it's much better to use the db_backupoperator fixed database role than grant the BACKUP DATABASE and BACKUP LOG statement permissions. You will usually need the other rights granted by the role membership anyway, and it's easier to figure out who has what rights when you take advantage of SQL Server roles.

Assigning Statement Permissions

You can use Transact-SQL or SQL Server Enterprise Manager to grant, revoke, and deny statement permissions.

The GRANT Statement Permission Command

The GRANT command is used to give an account statement permissions.

```
GRANT {ALL ¦ statement_list} TO {account}
```

where

- *ALL* stands for all possible statement permissions.
- *statement_list* is an enumerated list of the statement permissions you would like to give to an account.
- *account* is the name of a database user, a database role, a Windows NT user, or a Windows NT group.

▼ SYNTAX

6

The REVOKE Statement Permission Command

The REVOKE command is used to take away statement permissions already granted.

REVOKE {ALL | statement_list} TO {account}

where

- ALL stands for all possible statement permissions.
- statement_list is an enumerated list of the statement permissions you would like to take away.
- account is the name of a database user, a database role, a Windows NT user, or a Windows NT group.

The DENY Statement Permission Command

Unlike a REVOKE command, DENY is used to explicitly take away a statement permission. The permission does not have to first be granted to a user. For example, if Joe is a member of a database role, and that role has the CREATE TABLE statement permission, Joe can also create tables. However, if you don't want Joe to be able to create tables, even though he is a member of a role that has the permission, you can deny the statement permission from Joe. Therefore, Joe will not be able to run the CREATE TABLE statement, even though his role would normally give him the right to do so.

DENY {ALL | statement_list} TO {account}

where

- ALL stands for all possible statement permissions.
- statement_list is an enumerated list of the statement permissions you would like to deny from an account.
- account is the name of a database user, a database role, a Windows NT user, or a Windows NT group.

Transact-SQL Permissions Examples

Working through a few examples is the easiest way to understand how to use these commands.

To grant a user named Joe permission to create a view in a database, you can run

```
GRANT CREATE VIEW TO JOE
```

To revoke the permission to create views and tables from Joe and Mary you can run

```
REVOKE CREATE TABLE, CREATE VIEW FROM MARY, JOE
```

To grant Joe all permissions in a database you run

```
GRANT ALL TO JOE
```

Note If the GRANT ALL command is executed in the master database, the user specified is given all permissions in that database. If executed in any other database, the user is given all permissions except CREATE DATABASE because that particular permission can be granted only in the master database.

Assuming that user Bob is a member of Role1 and Role2, what would the permissions be at the end of this set of statements?

```
GRANT CREATE TABLE TO Role1
GRANT CREATE VIEW to Role2
GRANT CREATE DEFAULT to Bob
REVOKE ALL FROM Role1
DENY CREATE VIEW to Bob
```

ANALYSIS At this point, Bob can create a default, and that's all. His CREATE TABLE permissions (given to Role1) were later taken away by the REVOKE ALL FROM Role1 command. The CREATE VIEW permissions gained from Bob's membership in Role2 were lost when Bob was denied CREATE VIEW permission. Therefore, the only permission still in effect is the CREATE DEFAULT permission.

Administering Statement Permissions Using SQL Server Enterprise Manager

SQL Server Enterprise Manager provides a graphical interface for implementing statement permissions. To view or edit statement permissions in SQL Server Enterprise Manager, open the databases folder for your SQL Server. Right-click the database you want to view or modify, and select Properties. Click the Permissions tab to view the Statement Permissions dialog box for your database. You should see something similar to Figure 6.1, which is a view of the Pubs database.

As you grant and revoke permissions, the boxes will contain one of three indicators:

- Check mark—A statement permission that has been granted
- Red X—A deny statement permission
- Blank—No explicit permission assigned

6

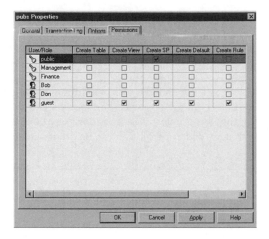

FIGURE 6.1

The statement Permissions tab for pubs.

To grant a permission, check the appropriate box for an account. To deny a permission, click the box twice (to make the red X appear). If a permission has been previously granted, clicking the box once makes the red X appear. Remember that this is a deny permission. You must click again to clear the check box if you want SQL Server Enterprise Manager to send a REVOKE command to your server. Click the OK or Apply buttons to make your changes permanent.

Note that if you look at statement permissions on any database other than the master database, the CREATE DB permission is not present because that right is assignable only from the master database. Figure 6.2 shows the statement Permissions tab for the master database.

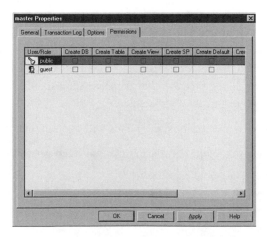

FIGURE 6.2

The master database statement Permissions dialog.

Caution

> The ability to create objects in a database is a serious matter. Do not grant permissions to do so unless it is necessary for a user to perform his or her job.

Object Permissions

Object permissions allow a user, role, or Windows NT user or group to perform actions against a particular object in a database. The permissions apply only to the specific object named when granting the permission and not to all the objects contained in the entire database. Object permissions enable users to give individual user accounts the rights to run specific Transact-SQL statements on an object. Object permissions are the most common types of permissions granted.

Here is a list of available object permissions:

- SELECT—View data in a table, view, or column.
- INSERT—Add data to a table or a view.
- UPDATE—Modify existing data in a table, view, or column.
- DELETE—Remove data from a table or view.
- EXECUTE—Run a stored procedure.
- REFERENCE—Refer to a table with foreign keys (see Day 14, "Ensuring Data Integrity").

Note

> The reference permission (abbreviated to DRI, which means Declarative Referential Integrity in SQL Server Enterprise Manager) allows users (or applications) to compare a value against values in another table without being able to actually see the data in the other table. For example, this permission can be used to let an application find a matching Social Security number without giving enough rights for the application to see the other Social Security numbers.

6

Assigning Object Permissions

You can use Transact-SQL or SQL Server Enterprise Manager to grant, revoke, and deny object permissions.

Granting Object Permissions Using Transact-SQL

The GRANT command gives someone one or more object permissions. This will also remove a DENY permission.

```
GRANT {ALL [PRIVILEGES] ¦ permission_list [,…n]}
{
[(column[,…n])] ON {table ¦ view}
¦ ON {table ¦ view}[(column[,…n])]
¦ ON {stored_procedure ¦ extended_stored_procedure}
}
TO account[,…n]
[WITH GRANT OPTION]
[AS {group ¦ role}]
```

where

- ALL stands for all possible object permissions that apply to a particular object type.

- permission_list is an enumerated list of the object permissions you would like to give to an account.

- column is the level down to which object permissions can be granted (only for SELECT or UPDATE).

- account is the name of a database user, a database role, a Windows NT user, or a Windows NT group.

- WITH GRANT OPTION allows the user who is the recipient of the grant to also give away the permission he or she has been granted to other users.

- AS {group ¦ role} If you have multiple roles or Windows NT groups that might have conflicting permissions, you should specify which group or role you are using for a particular grant.

The REVOKE Object Permission Command

The REVOKE command is used to take away one or more object permissions that has already been granted. You will not receive an error message if you revoke a command that hasn't previously been granted. It just won't have any effect.

```
REVOKE [GRANT OPTION FOR]
{ALL [PRIVILEGES] ¦ [,…permission_list n]}
{
[(column[,…n])] ON {table ¦ view}
¦ ON {table ¦ view}[(column[,…n])]
¦ {stored_procedure ¦ extended_stored_procedure}
}
FROM account[,…n]
[CASCADE]
[AS {group ¦ role}]
```

▼ where

- ALL stands for all possible object permissions that apply to a particular object type.

- permission_list is an enumerated list of the object permissions you would like to take away from an account.

- *column* stands for the column or columns you want to revoke permissions from. Object permissions at the column level apply only to the SELECT or UPDATE commands.

- ACCOUNT is the name of a database user, a database role, a Windows NT user, or a Windows NT group.

- CASCADE is used when you want to revoke permissions that were granted by a user who was previously given the WITH GRANT OPTION grant.

- AS {*group* | *role*} If you have multiple roles or Windows NT groups that might have conflicting permissions, you should specify which group or role you are using
▲ for a particular revoke.

The DENY Object Permission Command

Unlike a REVOKE command, DENY is used to explicitly take away an object permission. The permission does not have to first be granted to a user. For example, if Joe is a member of a database role and that role has the SELECT permission on the authors table, Joe can read data in the authors table. However, if you don't want Joe to be able to read data from the authors table, even though he is a member of a role that has the permission, you can deny Joe the permission. Therefore, Joe will be able to select data from the authors table, even though his role would normally give him the right to do so.

```
DENY
{ALL [PRIVILEGES] | permission_list [,…n]}
{
[(column[,…n])] ON {table | view}
| ON {table | view}[(column[,…n])]
| ON {stored_procedure | extended_stored_procedure}
}
TO account[,…n]
[CASCADE]
```

where

- ALL stands for all possible object permissions that apply to a particular object type.

- permission_list is an enumerated list of the object permissions you would like to deny for an account.

- *column* is the column or columns you want to deny access to. Object permissions
▼ at the column level only apply to the SELECT or UPDATE commands.

6

▼   • *account* is the name of a database user, a database role, a Windows NT user, or a Windows NT group.

   • CASCADE is used when you want to deny permissions to an account as well as deny permissions to any account that has been previously granted the permission from a
▲   user who had the WITH GRANT OPTION grant.

Transact-SQL Permissions Examples

Working through a few examples is the easiest way to understand how to use these commands.

To grant a user named Joe permission to select data from the sales table in the pubs database, run

```
GRANT SELECT ON SALES TO JOE
```

To revoke Joe and Mary's permission to select data from and insert data into the authors table, run the following:

```
REVOKE SELECT, INSERT ON AUTHORS FROM MARY, JOE
```

To grant Joe column-level permissions to select data from the au_fname and au_lname columns in the authors table from the pubs database run

```
GRANT SELECT ON AUTHORS (AU_FNAME, AU_LNAME) TO JOE
```

Note that this is the same as

```
GRANT SELECT (AU_FNAME, AU_LNAME) on AUTHORS TO JOE
```

> **Tip**
>
> Although you can grant permissions to accounts at the column level, it is a better idea to restrict access to tables by creating a view and then granting permissions on that view. A view is a predefined Transact-SQL statement or group of statements that can return data. For the previous example, you can create a view called viewAuthorName, which selects the au_fname and au_lname fields from the authors table. You can then grant Joe permissions on that view. (You learn more about views on Day 15, "Working with Views, Stored Procedures, and Triggers.")
>
> The reason this is more efficient is that any user who references that table will have to be checked for his or her column-level permissions. If you create a view instead of using column-level permissions, permissions will need to be checked only once on the view rather than on each column.

To grant Ann the right to select and update the publishers table and give others the right to read and update the publishers table, run the following:

```
GRANT SELECT, INSERT ON PUBLISHERS TO ANN WITH GRANT OPTION
```

To then take the permissions away from Ann, and from anyone Ann has given the permissions to, run

```
REVOKE SELECT, INSERT ON PUBLISHERS FROM ANN CASCADE
```

Granting Object Permissions Using SQL Server Enterprise Manager

Object permissions are part of system administration. Granting and revoking these permissions is a very common event that you will be performing on a day-to-day basis.

SQL Server Enterprise Manager provides a fast, easy, and visual way to control object permissions. Permissions can be viewed based on objects or users. The ability to view the information in two different ways can make tracking down errors much easier.

Viewing Permissions for an Object

To view or modify object permissions in SQL Server Enterprise Manager, follow these steps:

1. Expand a database folder for a database you want to view or modify, and then highlight the icon for the object type you would like to control.
2. Right-click the object, and select Properties from the pop-up menu.
3. Click the Permissions button. Figure 6.3 shows this dialog for the authors table in the Pubs database.

FIGURE 6.3

The Object Properties dialog showing permissions for a table.

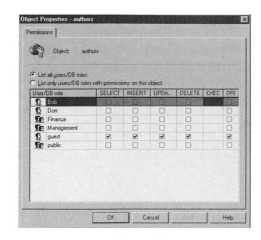

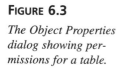

6

You can control whether you see all users, groups, and Windows NT users or groups available in the database as opposed to just a list of accounts that have already been given permissions on the object you are viewing. Note that implied permissions are not shown here. This means two different things:

- DBOO permissions are not shown. So if Joe creates a table, SQL Server Enterprise Manager (and the Transact-SQL help commands) will not show Joe's SELECT, INSERT, UPDATE, DELETE, and REFERENCES permissions, even though they are in place. Again, this is because they are implied by Joe's object ownership.

- If Ann is a member of the accounting role and the accounting role has INSERT permissions for a table, the permissions will not show up for Ann because, again, the permissions are implied by her role membership. However, if you explicitly grant Ann permissions, they will show up here.

The object permissions dialog works just like the statement permissions dialog. To grant a permission, check a box. To deny a permission, place a red X in the box. To revoke a permission, clear the appropriate box. After you have made the changes you would like, click Apply or OK to make your changes take effect.

Notice that SQL Server Enterprise Manager is smart enough to present you with only the appropriate permissions options depending on the type of object you have selected.

Note

Unfortunately, you cannot set column-level permissions with the SQL Server Enterprise Manager. You must use Transact-SQL statements to accomplish this. Again, Microsoft recommends you avoid column-level permissions because they can complicate your permissions administration.

Viewing Permissions for a User or Database Role

You can also choose to view permissions for a user or role. To view or modify permissions in SQL Server Enterprise Manager on a user or role basis, follow these steps:

1. Expand a database folder for a database you want to view or modify; then highlight the icon for either Database Users or Database Roles.

2. Right-click the user or role and select Properties from the pop-up menu.

3. Click the Permissions button. Figure 6.4 shows the dialog box for the database user Bob in the pubs database.

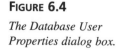

*The Database User
Properties dialog box.*

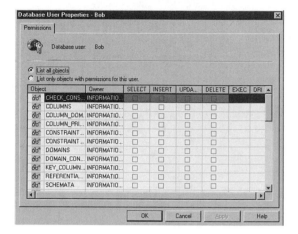

Click the appropriate boxes to grant or revoke object permissions. When you are finished setting your permissions, click Apply or OK to make your changes permanent.

Permissions on Views and Stored Procedures

Both views and stored procedures can help you administer permissions by allowing you to grant fewer permissions directly to the tables that hold your data. They can also help you avoid using column-level permissions because column-level permissions can overly complicate your security administration model. Although you will not necessarily under-stand all the details about views and stored procedures (at least until Day 15), you will be able to see how they can help you restrict permissions.

Permissions on Views

The easiest way to think of a view is as a stored query that appears as a table to users. The stored query appears as a SELECT statement. In order to restrict certain users from accessing particular columns or rows, you can create a view that refers only to selected columns of a table. Permissions can then be assigned to the view for those users, and they won't have any rights to see the underlying table. They will only be able to view data from the table through the view. Figure 6.5 illustrates this point. In Figure 6.5 there is a table called Employees, with columns for first name, last name, address, and salary. Even if Mary is assigned the task of updating everyone's address, she will not have (and shouldn't have) permissions to the salary column. You have two choices on how to accomplish this: You can assign Mary permissions on a column-by-column basis (an awkward solution) or create a view based on only those columns you want her to be able to see and update (View_1, as shown in Figure 6.5).

FIGURE 6.5

Using a view to provide column-level security.

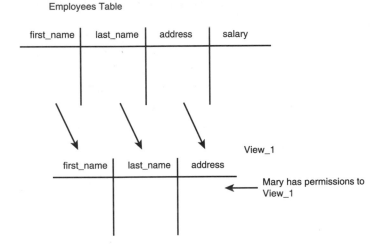

> **Note**
>
> Although a view can reference two or more tables, you cannot insert, update, or delete data through a view that references more than one table. For more information about this and additional restrictions on views, refer to Day 15.

Permissions on Stored Procedures

Very much like permissions on views, permissions on stored procedures enable you to abstract users from the tables and not grant permissions directly on your tables. Unlike views, however, stored procedures can contain many statements and operations. In fact, in some ways stored procedures are miniprograms. They can view or modify data in many tables or views and can gather data from other databases. In SQL Server 7.0, they can even get data from other data sources. Therefore, they make nice containers in which to put many operations together. As you saw earlier in today's lesson, a user needs only a single permission—EXECUTE—to run a stored procedure. It does not matter what the stored procedure does—users still need only that single permission. This is one of many reasons why people use stored procedures extensively in SQL Server. You will examine stored procedures in great detail on Day 15.

Ownership Chains

Every object in SQL Server will have an owner assigned to it. Although it is best if only the dbo user owns all the database objects, ordinary users can own objects in your database if you permit it. The ramifications of dbo ownership versus user ownership are discussed in the following paragraphs.

NEW TERM For example, a user can create a view based on another user's tables and views. Users can also create stored procedures that use another user's tables, views, and stored procedures. These types of objects are called *dependent objects*. In a large database, there can be a long series of dependencies and owners. This series is the chain of ownership.

Consider this example. The dbo owns a table and gives Mary the right to select from his table. Mary creates a view based on the original table and gives Paul permission to select from her view. When Paul attempts to select information from Mary's view, the data is actually coming from the original (owned by the dbo) table. Did the dbo ever give Paul permission to select from the original table? Should Paul be allowed to view this data?

SQL Server handles these cases by looking at the ownership chain of objects and where permissions have been assigned.

There are two distinct types of ownership chains: the single-owner chain and the broken ownership chain, where more than one user owns objects in a dependency chain.

Single-Owner Chain

A single-owner chain is created when the same user owns all the dependent objects within a chain. In this case, SQL Server will only check permissions on the first object in the chain being accessed, and will not check permissions on objects later in the chain.

For example, in Figure 6.6 the dbo owns all the objects in the chain. The dbo creates View1 based on the two tables (which are also owned by the dbo) and then creates a second view (View2) based on View1 (which is based on the tables). If the dbo gives Melissa permission to SELECT from View2, permissions would be checked only once—when Melissa attempts to SELECT on View2. SQL Server 7.0 doesn't bother to check objects at a higher level because the owner (dbo in this instance) is the same. SQL Server assumes that if the owner is the same, then the original owner would have granted permissions had SQL Server required it.

6

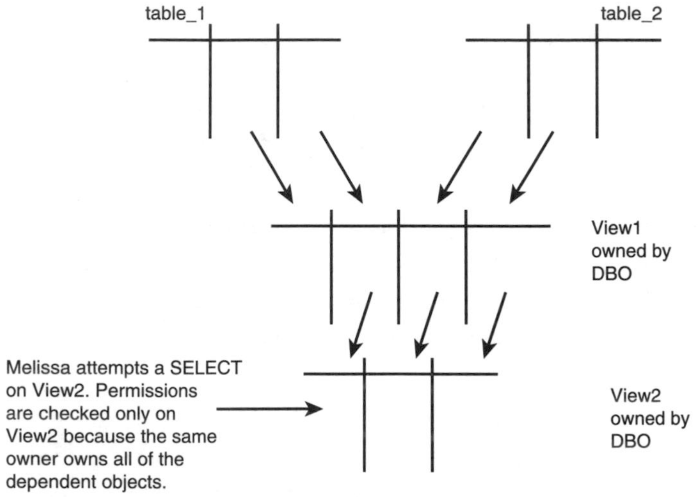

FIGURE 6.6

Example of a single-user ownership chain.

table_1   table_2

View1
owned by
DBO

Melissa attempts a SELECT
on View2. Permissions
are checked only on
View2 because the same
owner owns all of the
dependent objects.

View2
owned by
DBO

Broken Ownership Chains

When an object is dependent on other objects owned by different users, there is a broken ownership chain. Permissions are checked on the first object and every object where there is a change of ownership. In Figure 6.7, Melissa has created a view (View2) based on the dbo's View1. If Melissa gives Scott permission to select from her View2, permissions for Scott will be checked on Melissa's View2 and then again on the dbo's View1. If Scott does not have permissions to select from the dbo's View1, he cannot use the SELECT command on Melissa's view.

FIGURE 6.7

Example of a broken ownership chain.

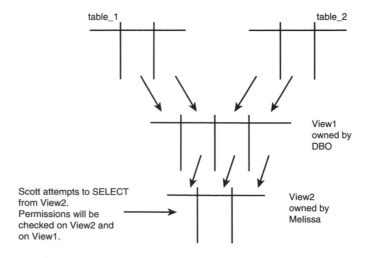

table_1   table_2

View1
owned by
DBO

Scott attempts to SELECT
from View2.
Permissions will be
checked on View2 and
on View1.

View2
owned by
Melissa

> **Caution**   Broken ownerships can become very complex very quickly. If you let users create objects, your database security will soon resemble a bowl of spaghetti. For this reason, all objects should be created by the dbo or users who are members of the db_owner or db_ddladmin role who have specifically set the object owner to dbo in their CREATE statements. Note that this applies to production servers and might not apply to development servers (if you're not concerned about ownership chains).

Now imagine a chain of 10 or more objects. Trying to figure out which permissions are needed rapidly becomes a nightmare. Stick to single-owner chains whenever possible.

Designing a Permissions Strategy

Up until now, today's lesson has focused on how to implement security. The next section discusses why and when to implement a permissions scenario, as well as presents a list of do's and don'ts.

Best Practices

SQL Server allows very flexible security, which can present a problem when trying to find the best way to secure your system. There are several rules you should follow, as well as general guidelines for assigning permissions. However, as usual in the computer industry, your situation might be different enough that the rules won't apply exactly.

If one person is in charge of the entire SQL Server, that person will need to connect as a member of the sysadmin fixed server role or as the sa login. If a user is in charge of a single database, that user should be assigned as the dbo of that particular database (or a member of the db_owner role). If a user doesn't need special permissions in order to do his or her job, that user should be treated as a normal database user and get permissions from the public role, one or more roles of which the user is a member, or from permissions directly assigned to him or her.

When assigning permissions, it is easiest to maintain and document your security implementation if you

- Assign permissions that all users need to the public role
- Assign permissions that all members of a group of people need to that particular Windows NT group, or create a role and grant permissions to the role
- Assign individual permissions to users only if the permissions they need cannot be assigned to a role or Windows NT group

6

Do's and Don'ts

Here are some general guidelines in the form of a Do/Don't list that will help you better manage your security. Most of these guidelines have to deal with the fact that users should only have permissions they really need.

Do	Don't
DO grant users the permissions they need to do their jobs. For example, if all the users need to see the data, be sure to grant SELECT permissions—probably to the public role. Don't grant permissions unless necessary. Users like to have permissions even when they don't need them. For example, if a certain user needs only SELECT permissions, grant only that permission, even though the user might request all permissions. **DO** keep track of the permissions you have granted. Keep a log of what you do to your SQL Server. Another option is to generate scripts that document all the objects and permissions contained in the database. You learn how to generate scripts a little later in today's lesson. **DO** assign a user to be the dbo of a database if the user is responsible for that database. If other users need permissions associated with being the dbo user, you will need to assign other users membership in the db_owner role because there can be only one person assigned as the dbo.	**DON'T** grant users all permissions to fix a problem. Take the time to find out exactly which permissions they really need, and grant only those permissions. For example, solving issues caused by lack of permissions can easily be accomplished by making the user a member of the sysadmin or db_owner roles. Although this will fix the original security problem, it introduces new, more critical problems in that the user has too many permissions and can easily damage the database (or the entire server). **DON'T** allow ordinary users to create databases or create objects within databases. If you allow users to make databases and objects, you not only lose control over what SQL Server contains and where databases and objects reside, you also must deal with broken ownership chains. All objects within a database should be created by the dbo (or members of the db_owner or db_ddladmin roles specifying the object owner as dbo) and be documented.

Another problem with granting users excessive permissions is that it is often difficult to take those permissions away later.

In a perfect world, all users could log in as members of the sysadmin role and they would make changes only to the database to which they are supposed to make changes. Of course, because this isn't a perfect world, having everyone with sysadmin permissions is just asking for trouble sooner or later (usually sooner). Believe it or not, there are actually some systems out there in which everyone does indeed connect with the sa login.

In cases where excessive permissions exist, everything might be fine until one of the following occurs:

- Accidental user destruction of records
- Intentional user destruction of records
- Malfunctioning program destruction of records

A wise administrator will guard against these situations through the judicious use of permissions.

Generating Scripts for Security

SQL Server has the capability to "reverse engineer" database objects and security, and can generate a script that can be run at a later time to reconstruct objects and security. To access the scripting function from SQL Server Enterprise Manager, right-click a database and choose Task, Generate SQL Scripts, or highlight the database and select Generate SQL Scripts in the right pane, and you will see Figure 6.8.

FIGURE 6.8

Selecting to generate SQL scripts.

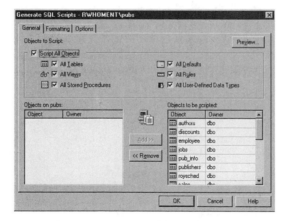

When you are in the Generate SQL Script dialog box, you have a choice as to what kind of script to generate. The General tab contains the objects you are going to script. If you click the Formatting tab, note that the default is to generate a script that will drop and create objects. Uncheck both of these options and any other option that is set on the Formatting dialog box. Click the Options tab, and click the appropriate security scripting options (see Figure 6.9).

6

FIGURE **6.9**

Selecting options to generate a script to re-create the security of a database.

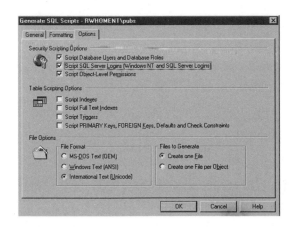

To do the actual scripting you can click OK, which will prompt you for a filename and location for the script, or you can select the Preview button on the General tab, which will cause the scripts to be generated in a preview window. If you choose Preview, you can save the script after you look at it by clicking the Save As button, or you can copy the entire script into the Windows Clipboard by selecting the Copy button (see Figure 6.10).

FIGURE **6.10**

A preview of a script.

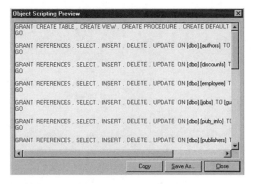

Note that you can select different options from the main Generate SQL Scripts screen depending on your desired outcome.

Summary

SQL Server provides a secure environment through the use of permissions. A user connected to SQL might have certain rights based on the type of user he or she is. Security in SQL Server is hierarchical, with the sa account having all permissions, the dbo account having all permissions in its particular database, and the DBOO having all permissions to the individual object it owns. Database users have no inherent permissions; they have only those they have been granted.

The combination of statement and object permissions enables a system administrator to control exactly what occurs on the SQL Server. Statement permissions allow you to create objects and back up databases and transaction logs. Object permissions allow you to specify who can do what with the data contained in the objects. Common object permissions include SELECT, INSERT, UPDATE, and DELETE commands.

You can assign or revoke permissions using Transact-SQL commands or by using the SQL Server Enterprise Manager.

Ownership chains demonstrate some of the challenges that can occur by allowing different users to create objects within a database.

Permissions must be implemented correctly and thoroughly to ensure the security and usability of your data.

SQL Server can reverse engineer objects and permissions so you can save scripts that can easily and quickly reconstruct the security of a database.

Q&A

Q This seems like a lot of work. Are permissions really that important?

A It depends. The more secure you want to keep your database, the more control and maintenance you will have to perform using the permissions hierarchy.

Q Should I use roles, or should I just assign permissions to users directly?

A Roles and Windows NT groups are much easier to administer because you can manage the permissions for hundreds or even thousands of users with a single command or click of a check box.

Q Must I use the built-in roles, or can I assign permissions without them?

A You do not have to use roles, but you are only hurting yourself by not using them. They provide convenient groupings of permissions for common administrative tasks.

6

Workshop

The Workshop provides quiz questions to help you solidify your understanding of the concepts presented in this chapter. In addition to the quiz questions, exercises are provided to let you practice what you have learned in this chapter. Try to understand the quiz and exercise answers before continuing to the next day's lesson. Answers are provided in Appendix A, "Answers,"

Quiz

1. How would you grant user Mary permission to read data from the table MyTable?

2. Mary created a table called MaryTable and gave Joe SELECT permissions on it. Joe created a view called JoeView. Joe wants Paul to have permission to SELECT from his view. Assuming that the users created their objects using their own owner IDs (not dbo), what permissions are necessary?

3. Joe is granted permission to SELECT on dbo.MYTABLE. PUBLIC is denied SELECT on MYTABLE. What are the effective permissions?

4. Joe is granted permission to SELECT on dbo.MYTABLE. PUBLIC is revoked SELECT on MYTABLE. What are the effective permissions?

5. What is the preferred way to prevent broken ownership chains?

6. You are the owner of a database. You want all users to be able to query the table MYTABLE. What command would you execute?

7. You execute the command GRANT ALL TO JOE in a user database. What permissions does Joe have?

Exercises

1. Create the following logins in SQL Server. Also, add each login to a user-defined database on your server:

   George

   Henry

   Ida

   John

2. Now make John the dbo of the database you just referenced. Fix any errors you receive to make this change possible.

DAY 7

Implementing Backups in SQL Server 7.0

In yesterday's lesson you examined permissions and how to set them to secure your database. SQL Server 7.0 is an inherently secure system; users can't do anything unless you explicitly grant them permissions to perform a particular action. It's very easy to give someone permissions and easy to revoke any given permissions. Permissions are cumulative, so you should add up the permissions the user has, as well as any Windows NT groups and SQL Server roles of which the user is a member. If a deny permission is in effect, it overrides any other permissions.

Today and tomorrow you will turn to what is perhaps the most important but least glamorous aspect of supporting a relational database: backup and recovery. No matter how much work you do to make your database secure and your data available, data protection is the most critical aspect of your job. If your server crashes and all your data is lost, it's likely you've lost something else as well—your job! In today's lesson you will examine the backup process and the types of backup SQL Server supports. To lead off your examination of backup, you will look at the protection you can provide so you don't lose disks and your SQL Server stays up and running.

Protecting Data with Mirroring, Duplexing, and Striping

To begin, you will examine fault-tolerance protection for disks on your server, look at SQL Server mirroring, and then examine backup and recovery. Backup and recovery is all about preventing data loss; implementing fault tolerance for disks and devices also guards against data loss. Implementing fault tolerance does not imply that you don't need to back up your databases.

NEW TERM It's best to start by defining some key terms. Two disks are said to be *mirrored* if they contain exactly the same data. When one disk is modified, the other is also modified (see Figure 7.1). *Duplexing* implies that the disks are mirrored, but a separate disk controller device (like small computer system interface [SCSI] cards) controls each disk (as shown in Figure 7.2). This is different from mirroring because mirrored disks are assumed to be using the same disk controller, as Figure 7.1 illustrates. *Striped* disks implies that the data is distributed evenly across multiple disks, with part of each logical piece of data on each disk in the striped set of disks as shown in Figure 7.3.

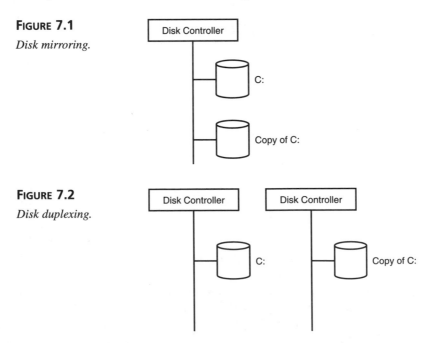

FIGURE 7.1

Disk mirroring.

FIGURE 7.2

Disk duplexing.

FIGURE 7.3

Disk striping.

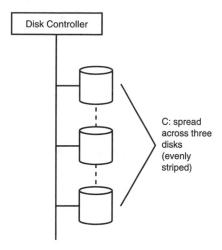

This discussion assumes that you are using SCSI disks. Although they are not required (in fact, the servers we're using to write this book are using standard Integrated Development Environment [IDE] hard drives), SCSI disks generally provide superior performance and reliability when compared to non-SCSI disks.

RAID

Mirroring, duplexing, and striping all fit into a scheme known as RAID (Redundant Array of Inexpensive Disks). You configure disks into these RAID arrays to protect data on the disks and to provide high availability. If you can prevent your data from becoming unavailable, then you can insulate your users from most hardware failures. There are six commonly accepted RAID levels: 0 through 5.

- RAID 0—Striped sets without parity information
- RAID 1—Disk mirroring or duplexing
- RAID 2, 3, 4—Iterations leading to RAID 5 (rarely implemented)
- RAID 5—Striped sets with parity information evenly distributed within the stripe
- RAID 10—Striped sets with parity mirrored across two controllers

Note

RAID 10 is becoming more widely deployed, but it is not typically included in a list of RAID options in most texts. It is included here because you will most likely run into this term when working with hardware vendors.

RAID 10 is not in wide use right now because it requires twice as much storage space as a RAID 5 system. Remember that RAID 10 not only stripes information, it also mirrors those stripe sets across multiple controllers.

7

RAID 0 provides no fault tolerance by itself, which means it isn't useful for fault tolerance. However, it can benefit performance. RAID 10 is a better option for fault tolerance while still providing superior performance.

RAID 1 is either mirroring or duplexing of data. With mirroring, however, if you lose the SCSI card controlling your mirrored disks, the data on those disks becomes unavailable. But you can still lose one of the disks and continue to access the data. If you duplex your disks, you can lose either a single disk or a disk controller card and still access your data. Therefore, duplexing is a superior fault-tolerance mechanism (but it costs more because you need the additional disk controller card).

RAID levels 2, 3, and 4 were iterations of striping with parity that were functionally replaced with RAID 5.

RAID 5 is a set of three or more disks logically grouped together. Each disk will contain either a "stripe" or section of data or parity information. In RAID 5, the parity information for each stripe is distributed evenly throughout the set of disks. For example, if your RAID stripe set includes three disks, it might look like Figure 7.4.

FIGURE 7.4

RAID 5 striping of data with parity.

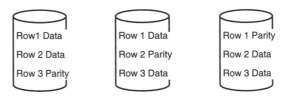

Parity information is a computed set of values that can be used to recalculate missing data. Current parity values are accurate to 1 in 2 billion. If you have lost a single data disk and still have the rest of the data disks, as well as the parity disk, you can rebuild the missing data disk using the parity information. If you lose the disk with the parity information on it, you still have all the data. Either way, you don't lose any data when using RAID with parity.

In row 1, half the data is on disk 1, the other half is on disk 2, and parity information (which, when combined with either of the disks, is enough information to rebuild the missing data) is on disk 3. Row 2 has half the data on disk 1, half on disk 3, and parity information on disk 2. Row 3 is similarly distributed. As you add additional disks to the set, it becomes more efficient in terms of overhead, with a higher risk of having more than one disk become unavailable at the same time (because the disk failure rate is theoretically constant for each disk). Although the example here shows three disks, you can have as many disks as your hardware or software allows.

RAID 5 is generally accepted as the most inexpensive option because it has the least overhead—especially as you increase the number of disks. RAID 10 is generally considered the best solution for high-end installations of SQL Server. Mirroring or duplexing is considered to be fairly expensive because it requires you to use double the amount of disk space to hold a given amount of information.

In the sample case here, you should have 27GB of data space available for your database server. You choose to implement a RAID 5 array using 9GB SCSI disks (the current industry standard as of this writing). You would need at least four disks. This is because you are effectively losing one disk total for parity, leaving three disks available for data storage, and three disks × 9GB = 27GB. To implement the same amount of storage with mirroring, you would need six 9GB disks (and a much bigger wallet, typically).

Hardware-Level RAID

Many computer companies implement hardware RAID solutions. These solutions tend to provide superior performance when compared with your other choice, Windows NT software RAID (examined next). Typically, hardware RAID is implemented with special controller cards and also might use external disk cabinets (either standalone or mounted on server "racks"). The downside of using hardware RAID is that these special controller cards (at least the good ones) are very expensive. You can buy a bunch of disks for the same price as one of these cards. Most people still buy these cards, however, so there must be a really good reason.

Software RAID with Windows NT Server

If you are running SQL Server 7.0 on Windows NT Server (or Windows NT Server Enterprise Edition), you can take advantage of the built-in features of the operating system to implement RAID across ordinary disks. RAID levels 0, 1, and 5 are implemented on Windows NT's server products.

Other Supported Windows Platforms and RAID

Windows 95/98 and Windows NT Workstation don't support these software features, but will generally run just fine on hardware RAID implementations (because the operating system isn't aware that RAID has been implemented).

File System Choices

One other consideration when using RAID and disks in general is which file system to use for SQL Server. There are currently three supported file systems for the supported windows operating systems (Windows 9x, Windows NT Workstation, Windows NT Server):

7

- FAT—Also known as FAT16, this is the file system that's been around since early versions of MS-DOS. This file system has no security for files and doesn't support advanced options such as encryption. It is generally not recommended to hold SQL Server files.

- FAT32—FAT32 is the newer implementation of the FAT16 file system. It implements much more efficient storage of data on disk but has the same limitations as FAT in terms of security and encryption. FAT32 is implemented on later versions of Windows 95 (OSR2) and is fully supported on Windows 98 and Windows NT 5.0. Note that FAT32 isn't supported on Windows NT 4.0.

- NTFS—NTFS (the NT File System) supports many advanced features, including compression and encryption (in Windows NT 5.0), neither of which should be used in most OLTP (Online Transaction Processing) environments. More importantly, NTFS supports permissions on individual directories and files. This allows you to secure access to the SQL Server data files to only the SQL Server service accounts (and Windows NT administrators).

How Backup Works

SQL Server 7.0 backs up data *dynamically*. This means that you do not have to stop using a database to back it up. As always, it's a good idea to run your backups at a time of relative inactivity because it takes some resources to run a backup. However, benchmarks have shown that the backup process has very little impact on the overall throughput of SQL Server's real work, your data queries, and modifications.

SQL Server database backups are consistent at the point of the completion of a database backup. Therefore, if your backup finishes at 6 p.m., you know that you have an image of all your data as of that time.

 Note

In all previous releases of SQL Server, the backup was consistent with the beginning of the backup. This might be an insignificant change, or it might affect any previously designed backup strategies you have. Either way, it's worth noting.

You can store database and transaction log backups in files dynamically, or you can pre-allocate storage locations on what are known as backup devices. A backup device can be a physical disk file, a tape, a remote physical disk file, or a named pipe. Named pipes are typically used with third-party backup solutions. You will most likely back up your databases to disk or to tape.

A member of the sysadmin fixed server role or the db_owner or db_backupoperator database roles can back up a database or transaction log. As you saw on Day 6, "Working with Permissions," you can grant others permissions to back up a database and a transaction log.

| Caution | SQL Server 7.0 backups are not compatible with any previous release of SQL Server. SQL Server 7.0 can't read backups taken with earlier versions of SQL Server. This is mostly an upgrade consideration but something you'll want to be aware of if you are administering SQL Server. The only way to read a SQL Server backup from earlier releases is to install the earlier release and use the SQL Server Version Upgrade Wizard against the database. |

Backup Types

There are several kinds of backups you can perform in SQL Server 7.0. You will examine full database backups, differential database backups, file and file group backups, and transaction log backups. For the context of the discussion here, all backups except transaction log backups are going to be referred to as *database backups*.

| Tip | For historical reasons, backups are sometimes referred to as *dumps* or *database dumps*. |

Here is an overview of the different types of backups:

- Database backup—Backs up an entire database, including all tables, indexes, system tables, and database objects (which are contained in those system tables). A database backup also backs up transaction log records. A database backup does not store empty pages, and it does not remove any transaction log records from a database.

- Differential database backup—Backs up all the data pages modified since the last full database backup. The reason you might want to use differential backups is that restoring them is faster than restoring transaction log backups. You examine the restoration process in tomorrow's lesson.

- File and/or File group backup—This type of backup involves backing up only selected files or file groups rather than the entire database. If you were to place one or more tables or indexes on separate file groups rather than leaving all data and indexes on the default file group, you could independently back up that data.

7

The advantage here is that if an individual disk failed and you had a backup of just the files from the failed disk, you could restore the affected files without recovering the entire database. This should be faster than a full database backup. However, this is getting beyond what the average SQL Server administrator is likely to do This advanced backup mechanism is discussed in more detail in *SQL Server 7.0 Unleashed* by Sams Publishing.

- Transaction log backup—This type of backup contains a copy of the records of each change made to your database over time. This includes statements run by users, as well as background system activity, such as allocating space within your database. The log can then be "replayed" to restore all the activity (transactions) that have been recorded in the transaction log. Another nice feature of the transaction log is that you can replay your transactions to a specific point in time. You learn more about this on Day 8, "Restoring SQL Server Databases."

Transactions and Checkpoints

Transactions (which are discussed in depth on Day 16, "Programming SQL Server 7.0") are a logical set of operations that either all complete successfully or all fail. Each data modification statement you run against a database is (by default) a transaction and is recorded in the transaction log (a set of records in a separate database file) for each database. You can also explicitly request a transaction so that multiple statements complete or fail as if they were a single operation.

The information recorded in the transaction log can be used to recover changes to your database to a point in time other than when you have taken a full database backup. Other tasks, such as space allocation, are also written to the transaction log. Over time, the transaction log will fill up if you do not back it up or erase it (or it will fill the disk that the log file is on if you haven't disabled the autogrow feature of the file). Autogrowth options are discussed on Day 4, "Creating Databases, Files, and Filegroups." Cleaning out completed transactions from the transaction log file is accomplished with the BACKUP LOG statement, examined later in today's lesson. When a transaction is completed (all modifications to the data completed successfully), the transaction log records are written to disk immediately. This is part of what guarantees that your database can be recovered in the event of a failure. However, what writes the data pages to disk? The answer is the checkpoint process.

Checkpoints

NEW TERM   Day 16 has a full explanation of the checkpoint process, but a cursory examination is necessary here. A *checkpoint* is a periodic operation that copies out to disk data pages that have been modified in memory. Many events can also cause data pages and log records to be written to disk. However, checkpoints are the primary mechanism of synchronizing a database between what has occurred in memory and what has physically been written to your disks. The checkpoint itself is also a *logged transaction*. This means that the checkpoint itself is also written to the transaction log and saved to disk.

Alternative Backup Strategies

Some administrators believe that an alternative way to back up SQL Server is to stop the MSSQLServer service and then back up all files associated with SQL Server (in particular, the files from your MSSQL7\DATA folder). However, this is not as fully functional as it sounds because it might not allow you to recover databases individually and won't provide the ability to perform a point-in-time recovery. Therefore, it is strongly recommended that you use SQL Server backups and not back up the files directly. You should also note that "normal" Windows NT backups will not back up the device files for SQL Server while it is running because the files are open when SQL Server is running.

Backup Terminology

NEW TERM SQL Server 7.0 introduces some new terms used during backups. A *backup set* is what you have after you have run a single backup command. It is the database backup that resides on a backup device (your backup media—examined later in today's lesson). When you create a backup, you are also creating a *media set*. A media set is one or more backup devices used during a backup or set of backups. This is particularly handy when you look at SQL Server 7.0's capability to back up to multiple devices. This feature is known as "parallel striped backup" and is examined later in today's lesson as well.

NEW TERM The other term to know is *media family*. Media family refers to all the tapes used for a single backup device. So if you perform a backup and it takes five tapes, those five tapes together are the media family for that backup. In that case, it's basically the same as a backup set. If you perform a parallel striped backup, each set of tapes from each tape drive involved in the backup is known as a media family.

 Tip

> Sound confusing? Maybe, but these terms are sprinkled throughout the Microsoft documentation on backups and restoring databases. The good news is you can run plenty of backups and never use these terms. The bad news is, you might see them periodically, and it's good to have some idea what the documentation is talking about.

7

Backup Considerations

There are many things to consider when performing backups. How often should you back up your databases? Which databases should you back up? Where should you back them up to? How long should your backups be kept? Who is responsible for the backups, and how will you verify that they are good backups? Now examine these questions one at a time, starting with who is responsible.

Who Is Responsible for the Backups?

I like to say, "If it's not someone's problem, it won't get done." When it comes to talking about backups, this is especially true. Backups are, well, boring. When it comes to glamour, this isn't it. It takes a lot of work to properly set up backups and test them on a regular basis. Backup responsibility might very well fall on the database administrator or the system administrator. It is also entirely possible that the network administrator will want to help perform backups. Ultimately, however, the important thing is that they be someone's responsibility and that they are performed.

How Will You Verify That the Backups Are Good?

If a database becomes corrupt, you might still be able to back it up. However, you might not. There might not even be a warning message about the corruption. There are some checks you should run before the backup begins (you'll see these shortly), and SQL Server runs many checks internally to detect corruption (and possibly even fix it). But if you don't run the consistency checks, or don't check the results first, you will not be able to tell that your backups are good until you attempt to restore them. It's a really good idea to periodically test your backups by restoring one to a test server and ensuring that everything is working as expected. This will let you know whether your backups are good and will help you to periodically test your restoration process. SQL Server 7.0 includes the capability to verify the integrity of the backup after it has been taken. Besides, who's ever heard of database administrators being fired because they were paranoid with their backup and recovery planning?

Which Databases Should You Back Up?

This might sound obvious, but you should back up all your user-defined databases. If it was important enough to create the database and put it on a server, it's important enough to back up. So what about system databases? You should back up master and msdb. Having a backup of the model database might be useful, but tempdb doesn't need to be backed up. If you are using replication, you should also back up your distribution database at regular intervals. I recommend you treat it like any other frequently modified user database.

Where Should You Back Them Up To?

As mentioned previously, you can back up your databases to disk, tape, a network drive, or a named pipe. Tape is most people's preferred media but has some significant limitations, not the least of which is speed. Backups to disk are usually the fastest. An alternative is to back up your database to another server's disk over the network. You should back up your disk backups to tape, whether those disk backups are to a local disk or to another server's disk. A typical scenario might be to back up to a network server over a fast network connection (100MB Ethernet, ATM, and so on), and then use Windows NT's built-in backup program to back up the backup devices or files. An alternative to all these is to purchase a third-party backup utility (which might or might not use the named pipe option). Most major brands of backup utilities include an add-in to back up SQL Server databases.

As tape speeds increase, they become the preferred media for backups. The limitation for SQL Server backups (in terms of speed) is typically the speed of the tape drives, not the speed of SQL Server.

How Often Should You Back Up Your Databases?

The answer to this question depends on the size of your database and how quickly you want the recovery process to run. For databases smaller than a few gigabytes in size, the answer is usually a full database backup daily, with transaction log backups at some point during the day. At a minimum, you should back up your databases weekly, with at least daily transaction log backups. There are special considerations for the system databases, and you'll examine them shortly.

As a database grows significantly larger, you might not have enough time to fully back it up every day. However, as tape drives become faster (or you take advantage of parallel backups), this limitation might disappear. Again, the SQL Server 7.0 software is typically not the limitation on the speed of your backups.

How Long Should Your Backups Be Kept?

Some backups might not be needed as soon as the next one is taken. It's usually a good idea, however, to have a few around in case one of the previous backups is found to be corrupt. Many sites choose to maintain the last two weeks of backups as an arbitrary retention period. There might also be legal requirements to maintain data, such as tax data needing several years of backups. You should investigate these requirements before determining your backup retention policies. The last thing in the world you want is to be criminally culpable for not storing backups long enough.

7

How Long Will It Take to Recover a Backup?

There's nothing worse than having a server crash, except possibly when your boss approaches you and asks, "So, how long will it take to recover the server?" and you have absolutely no idea. Therefore, regular testing of recovery of your backups will help you avoid embarrassment in a difficult situation and help you understand your recovery process better. The recovery process is examined in tomorrow's lesson.

Do You Have a Disaster Recovery Plan?

One of the best things ever done in the mainframe era involved having a disaster recovery plan and occasionally running disaster "drills." I was once involved in such a drill. We grabbed our tapes, jumped on a plane, and flew to a backup site and got our mainframe up and running, as well as our databases. If you'd like to test a backup plan and verify that everything you need is being backed up, run one of these drills. It's amazing how many things you forget. Interesting problems might arise, such as does your backup site have the same brand/model of tape drive available? Did you remember to get the software you need in your backups?

Some typical items to consider including are the following:

- Windows NT on CD.
- The latest service pack for Windows NT.
- A SQL Server 7.0 CD, along with the latest service pack.
- Any application-specific software or external .DLLs (extended stored procedures) you've incorporated into SQL Server. This includes third-party backup and recovery software (if used).
- YOUR BACKUPS!

You don't necessarily have to jump on a plane if you have the discipline to make sure no one cheats and grabs that last file you need off the network or sneaks back to his or her desk. Here are some other questions to ask yourself:

- Do you know on what drive SQL Server is installed?
- Do you know what character set and sort order were used?
- Which network libraries are installed?
- Do you know the network account SQL Server was using?
- What drives and filenames are used for each database?
- What mail profile was used to automate email with SQL Server?

You get the idea. If you have more than one SQL Server, the problem can quickly become unmanageable without a plan. Perhaps this plan requires some serious thought before a disaster occurs. Remember that disasters can happen at any time. Floods, fire, ice storms, tornadoes, hurricanes, earthquakes, volcanoes, sabotage, and self-inflicted problems (a poorly written transaction, for example) are all real problems in various parts of the world (perhaps even in your area).

Where Do You Keep Your Backup Tapes?

Do you keep your backup tapes in your desk? On top of the server? In the tape drive on the server? I've heard all these before. If an earthquake has just leveled your building (and perhaps all the buildings around yours as well), can you still get to your building, let alone your backup tapes? You should invest in an off-site storage location for your tapes. Some companies simply have an employee rotate them to his or her house. A better solution for databases that are relatively small is to look into a safe deposit box at your bank. For larger backups, tape vault companies specialize in safe, secure offsite storage. Most reputable tape vault companies will deliver and pick up tapes, and should even pick them out and bring them to you in an emergency (for a nominal fee). You will want to inspect the vault and verify that the company has taken adequate precautions (and security has been addressed) to protect one of your company's most valuable assets—its data!

Miscellaneous Tape Considerations

If you choose to back up to tapes, you should be aware of the following:

- SQL Server writes to tape using American National Standards Institute (ANSI) tape headers. This means that SQL Server can share tapes with Windows NT backups.

- SQL Server will use the console program to notify an operator when a tape needs to be changed (if the program is running).

- As you might expect, you can store more than one backup on a single tape.

- Make sure that if you are going to take advantage of any special features of a particular model of tape drive, such as hardware compression, the same model will be available when you need to recover using the tape. This is particularly true if you plan to keep the tapes around for a long time. Are you sure that you'll still have that brand of tape drive available in five years?

7

Backing Up User Databases

As just stated, user-created databases should be backed up regularly. At a minimum, this means weekly for full database backups and daily for transaction log backups. Daily database backups are preferred, with periodic transaction log backups. Remember that a full database backup does not empty transactions from the transaction log of a database. A differential backup also does not remove entries from the transaction log.

There are some reasons not to back up a database on a regular basis:

- If the data is read-only, a single (verified) backup is probably sufficient
- It's a test database, and the data is not significant or can be easily re-created
- The data can be re-created quickly from an alternative source

However, you should focus on when you need to back up your databases. If you have a large database (bigger than a few gigabytes), you might want to back it up immediately after you create it. It's entirely possible that it's faster to re-create the database with the FOR LOAD option mentioned on Day 4 and then restore the database backup.

Nonlogged Operations and Backups

There is one other time (beyond the obvious scheduled backups) that you would want to back up your database—after a nonlogged operation. Nonlogged operations are a bit of a misnomer. It's extremely unlikely that an operation will be truly nonlogged. When you've enabled the Select Into/Bulkcopy database option, operations such as the Select Into statement (discussed further on Day 11, "Retrieving Data with Queries"), and a fast bulk copy (discussed further on Day 10, "Using SQL Server 7.0 Data Transformation Services") are allowed. You can also use certain statements with text or image data types that are not logged. Each of these operations runs faster than other operations of a similar nature by bypassing the transaction log. Earlier I said that normal changes to a database are first written to a transaction log and then to the table or index as appropriate. With these operations, that logging does not occur. This means that the database is at least partially unrecoverable.

> **Note**   The allocation of physical storage space is always recorded in the transaction log, even during a nonlogged operation.

Because the transaction log is no longer useful for recovery, a full database backup is the only way to guarantee recoverability of your database. After you've completed the database backup, you should clear out the transaction log with the BACKUP LOG statement, using either the NO_LOG or TRUNCATE_ONLY options (discussed later in today's lesson). In short, these options erase the transaction log without actually backing it up.

Even in the previous cases when backups might not be necessary, you might want to perform them anyhow. Sometimes building a test database with a good set of sample data can be very useful to have around. You could back up this "pure" environment, and then restore it as needed during a development process. Even if a database can be restored quickly from an alternative source, recovering from a SQL Server database backup might be faster than recovering from that alternative source and reloading all the data.

Backing Up System Databases

Next you examine the system databases and how often you should back them up. System databases include master, model, msdb, and tempdb. Their backup strategy will be different than the backup strategy you use for databases you create.

The Master Database

The master database is a special system database. If you lose the master database for some reason, SQL Server 7.0 is unable to function. Therefore, how and when you back up this database is critical.

Note   Unlike all previous releases of SQL Server, the master database is now kept on its own set of files, with the transaction log as a separate file. If you are upgrading from a previous release, note the changes here carefully.

Microsoft recommends that you back up the master database each time you modify it. As a practical matter, however, this is not really possible in most environments. Consider the items found in the master database: databases, logins, system and user error messages, and more. Logins, for example, include passwords. It's not always practical to back up the master database each time someone changes his or her password. I recommend that you back up the master database daily. This means that any passwords that were changed after the last backup you've recovered will not be set properly. However, this only applies to logins created with SQL Server Authentication Mode security.

7

It's also critical to back up the master database after any significant changes are made to your server, such as configuration changes; creating, changing, or dropping databases; adding remote or linked servers; or enabling replication.

> **Caution**
>
> By default, the Truncate Log On Checkpoint database option is enabled for the master database. You should probably leave this option on because you can perform full database backups of the master database only. Differential, file, file group, and transaction log backups are not available for the master database.

The MSDB Database

The msdb database contains the support information for the SQLServerAgent service, as well as for replication operations. It also contains support for the SQL Server Web Assistant, which is discussed on Day 21, "Integrating SQL Server and the World Wide Web." If you choose to take advantage of the SQLServerAgent service (and I suspect you will), you'll need to take regular backups of this database.

As a rule, msdb should be backed up at least weekly, with log backups daily. Just like user databases, more frequent backups might be justified. You might want to synchronize your backups with the master database. If you must rebuild the master database (likely in the event of a significant media failure), your msdb database will be reinitialized and will therefore need to be restored from backup as well.

The Model Database

The model database probably won't be changing often. After you add custom tables, views, security, and stored procedures to the model database, they tend to remain there with few modifications over time. However, because paranoia in an administrator can be a very good thing, it's good to have a backup. If you should have to rebuild your master database, the model database will also be reset.

The Tempdb Database

The tempdb database is reset after each restart of the MSSQLServer service. Therefore, there is no need to back up the tempdb database. You should leave the Truncate Log On Checkpoint database option set so the transaction log won't fill up.

The Distribution Database

If you're using replication, the distribution database stores replicated transactions. You examine replication in more detail on Day 17, "Implementing Standard Replication." You should treat the distribution database like any important user database; daily backups and occasional transaction log backups are recommended. Perform more frequent backups as time and maintenance overhead allow.

Preparing to Implement Backups

Now that you have gone over much of the theory and ideas of database backups, you can focus on the physical implementation of backups. You examine full database backups, differential backups, as well as file and file group backups. You will also look at transaction log backups. Finally, you'll wrap up the section by examining a real-world server configuration and setting up a backup plan for the server.

Along the way there are a few topics of interest thrown in that you need to know. You must store your backups somewhere, and you must verify the integrity of your backups and your databases. Does all this sound like fun? Good! Start with an examination of a backup device.

Creating a Backup Device

The first step in preparing to back up your databases is to create a backup device. Although not technically necessary when performing backups, having predeclared backup devices can make your backup command syntax easier, as well as help out the poor administrator who must work on the system when you're finished with it.

A backup device is simply a pointer in the SQL Server system catalog (sysdevices system table in the master database) that contains a logical name and a physical path to a local hard disk file, a local tape drive, or a remote file on another computer. Backups can't be performed using remote tape drives. When you specify the BACKUP command, you can reference this logical name rather than specifying the full path and filename each time. This helps reduce the overhead of you typing all that information in repeatedly and is less error-prone.

When you first install SQL Server 7.0, no backup devices are defined on your system. One of your first steps will be to create them. If you want to back up to a tape device, you typically create only a single backup device pointing to the tape drive. You might still create multiple "logical" devices, each one pointing back to the same tape drive.

7

For disk (or network) backup devices, you would typically create one backup device for each database. A good place to start is to define backup devices for your system databases that exist on your server.

Controlling Backup Devices with Transact-SQL

You create the backup devices with the sp_addumpdevice system-stored procedure.

```
sp_addumpdevice [@devtype=] 'device_type', [@logicalname =]
➥'logical_name',
[@physicalname =] 'physical_name' [, {[@cntrltype =] cntrltype ¦
➥[@devstatus =]
'device_status'}]
```

where

- *device_type* is the type of device you want the backup device to point to. It is one of the following:

   Disk—A pointer to a physical file on a local hard disk

   Tape—A pointer to a local tape drive

   Pipe—A pointer to a named pipe

- *logical_name* is the name you want to use in your backup and restore commands when referencing this physical backup location.

- *physical_name* is the physical location of the backup device. For disks, this would be the path and filename. For a tape, it's the pointer to the tape drive. And, finally, for a named pipe, it's the network address of the named pipe.

- *cntrltype* is an obsolete parameter provided for backward compatibility.

- *device_status* determines whether the ANSI tape headers are ignored when writing to this backup device. If you specify a device_type of Tape, SQL Server will assume you mean NoSkip here. This means that if a tape has header information about a previous backup on the tape, SQL Server will not automatically ignore it and reinitialize the tape. If this is the behavior you want (automatically initializing the tape even if it contains data), you can specify Skip here.

ANALYSIS A quick mention of some details for the *physical_name* parameter in the syntax is necessary here. If you specify a local path, it must be fully qualified. An example might be

```
f:\mssql7\backup\master_backup.bak
```

A network file must be in the form of a UNC (Universal Naming Convention) path, such as

```
\\remoteserver\backups\sql7\master_backup.bak.
```

Finally, tape units are specified using the convention

```
\\.\tape#
```

starting at 0 for the first tape drive on your system. So if you have a single tape unit, you would refer to it as

```
\\.\tape0"
```

> **Note**
>
> The term *dump device* is a throwback to earlier releases of SQL Server. It is still used here for backward compatibility with SQL Server 6.x.

Here is an example of creating a dump device that can be used for the master database:

```
exec sp_addumpdevice 'disk', 'master_backup',
➥'f:\mssql7\backup\master_backup.dat'
```

This command adds a new disk backup device called master_backup in the appropriate physical location.

To drop a backup device, you run the sp_dropdevice system-stored procedure.

▼ SYNTAX

sp_dropdevice [@logicalname =] '*logical_name*', [@delfile =] '*delfile*'

where

- *logical_name* is the name you want to use in your backup and restore commands when referencing this physical backup location.

- *delfile*, if included, specifies that the physical backup file (if on disk) should be deleted.

▲

So if you want to drop the pubs_backup backup device, run

```
exec sp_dropdevice 'pubs_backup'
```

To get rid of the backup file at the same time (assuming you're backing pubs up to disk), run the following:

```
exec sp_dropdevice 'pubs_backup','delfile'
```

You should receive output similar to this:

```
File 'f:\MSSQL7\BACKUP\pubs_backup.BAK' closed.
Device dropped.
DBCC execution completed. If DBCC printed error messages,
➥ contact your system administrator.
```

To view a list of all devices on your system, run the sp_helpdevice system-stored procedure.

7

sp_helpdevice [[@devname =] '*logical_name*']

where

- *logical_name* is the name you want to use in your backup and restore commands when referencing this physical backup location.

For example, if you run

```
exec sp_helpdevice
```

you will see the following output, which is broken here to fit the page:

```
Master        f:\MSSQL7\DATA\MASTER.MDF            ...
Master_backup f:\MSSQL7\BACKUP\master_backup.BAK  ...
Mastlog       f:\MSSQL7\DATA\MASTLOG.LDF           ...
Modeldev      f:\MSSQL7\DATA\MODEL.MDF             ...
Modellog      f:\MSSQL7\DATA\MODELLOG.LDF          ...
tempdev       f:\MSSQL7\DATA\TEMPDB.MDF            ...
templog       f:\MSSQL7\DATA\TEMPLOG.LDF           ...
```

```
➡      special, physical disk,   4 MB    2  0  512
➡      disk, backup device                16 2  0
➡      special, physical disk,   0.8 MB  2  0  96
➡      special, physical disk,   0.6 MB  2  0  80
➡      special, physical disk,   0.8 MB  2  0  96
➡      special, physical disk,   2 MB    2  0  256
➡      special, physical disk,   0.5 MB  2  0  64
```

Notice that several are reported as special, physical disk. However, one is reported as disk, backup device. This is your backup device. You will need to sift through the results of sp_helpdevice to find your backup devices.

Controlling Backup Devices with SQL Server Enterprise Manager

SQL Server Enterprise Manager can also be used to create or remove a backup device. Expand your server and highlight the Backup Devices folder. Right-click the folder (or anywhere on the right side of the Enterprise Manager window), and select New Backup Device from the pop-up menu. You will be presented with a dialog that looks like Figure 7.5. Notice again that there are no backup devices defined when you first install SQL Server 7.0 (notice however, that the master_backup device added with Transact-SQL above is present).

FIGURE 7.5

The Backup Device Properties dialog.

Just as you did before, you can create a backup device here to hold your database backups. I have created a backup device here named msdb_backup as a container to hold the msdb database. Note that SQL Server Enterprise Manager fills in the filename for you when you type the device name and defaults to keeping the same name as the logical name of the device. It's an exceptionally good idea to keep the device logical and physical names the same.

After you've filled out the dialog, click OK to finish creating the device. If you want to change a device to point to a network location, enter the UNC path to that remote server in the Name text box. Never use mapped drive letters because getting them working is very complicated. Remember that when you create the backup device, you are simply creating a pointer in the system tables. No actual data is written to the device yet.

To remove a backup device with SQL Server Enterprise Manager, simply right-click the device in the Backup Devices folder and select Delete from the pop-up menu. Confirm the deletion, and the device is removed from the SQL Server system tables. If the physical file has been created, your removal of the backup device in SQL Server Enterprise Manager will not delete it.

Verifying Database Consistency

When you have a backup device available, you are almost ready to begin backing up your databases. There's an important step that might be necessary before you can start, however. As just mentioned, a corrupt database backup is worthless. Therefore, you must verify that your backup is good. Microsoft provides two options for you to verify the integrity of your database and your backups. The backup command has an option to validate the backup after it's complete. There is also a set of commands that provide the capability to verify your database's integrity.

For now, focus on the consistency checking capabilities you have within your SQL Server database. If your database is okay before the backup, it's very likely that your backup itself will also be okay. To verify the consistency of your database, use

7

extensions of the DBCC (DataBase Consistency Checker) utility. There are several different DBCC utilities that check various aspects of database integrity. The one you're most likely to run is the DBCC CHECKDB command.

```
DBCC CHECKDB ( 'database_name' [, Noindex ¦
{ Repair_Allow_Data_Loss ¦ Repair_Fast¦ Repair_Rebuild }] )
[With {ALL_ERRORMSGS ¦ NO_INFOMSGS}]
```

where

- *database_name* is the name of the database for which you want to check integrity.

- Noindex specifies that you don't want the utility to check the integrity of your non-clustered indexes. (You examine indexes on Day 13, "Enhancing Performance with Indexing.")

- Repair_Fast modifies corrupted indexes if it is safe to do so (no data can be lost using this option). It will also only make repairs that are quick and easy (such as corrupted index keys). The database must be in single-user mode to specify this option.

- Repair_Rebuild fixes corrupted indexes just like the Repair_Fast option, but will perform more time-consuming fixes such as re-creating corrupted indexes. The database must be in single-user mode to specify this option.

- Repair_Allow_Data_Loss specifies that all repairs that would have been performed by the Repair_Rebuild option will be done and "cleans up" broken pages and text/image pages, regardless of whether this will cause data loss. The database must be in single-user mode to specify this option.

- ALL_ERRORMSGS returns all messages from the command. By default, SQL Server will stop returning error messages after you receive 200 messages. I hope you never need this option.

- NO_INFOMSGS specifies that only significant error messages will be reported; no informational messages will be reported. This is the option you'll want to use most of the time.

SQL Server 7.0 has introduced not just the capability to check your database for integrity, but the capability to repair consistency problems. You'll examine the Repair options on Day 8. For now, here's a code sample of the command to check your database's consistency and integrity:

INPUT/OUTPUT

```
DBCC CHECKDB ('pubs') With NO_INFOMSGS
```

which returns (I hope)

```
DBCC execution completed. If DBCC printed error messages,
➥ contact your system administrator.
```

ANALYSIS If you leave off the With NO_INFOMSGS from the command, you will see many rows (two for each table in your database) similar to this:

```
DBCC results for 'pubs'.
DBCC results for 'sysobjects'.
There are 112 rows in 3 pages for object 'sysobjects'.
DBCC results for 'sysindexes'.
There are 50 rows in 2 pages for object 'sysindexes'.
...
DBCC results for 'dtproperties'.
There are 7 rows in 1 pages for object 'dtproperties'.
CHECKDB found 0 allocation errors and 0 consistency errors in
➥database 'pubs'.
DBCC execution completed. If DBCC printed error messages,
➥ contact your system administrator.
```

It's considerably easier to interpret the results of your command if you use the NO_INFOMSGS option. Unless you're looking for a report on the number of rows and pages, there's no point in leaving the NO_INFOMSGS option off.

If you do get some other kind of message, your database likely has some form of corruption. Troubleshooting errors from the DBCC CHECK* commands is outside the scope of this book, but you can find additional information in Microsoft's knowledge base (http://support.microsoft.com). If you are unable to repair any damage to your databases, you will most likely need to restore from your last backup. You'll examine how to perform recovery on Day 8.

The DBCC CHECKDB consistency check will be more than adequate 90% of the time. In fact, with SQL Server 7.0 it probably won't be necessary to run DBCC commands. However, because paranoia is a good thing when your company's data is involved, a daily DBCC check is probably a good idea. Unless your database is very large (tens or hundreds of gigabytes), you shouldn't encounter any problems with how long it takes to check the integrity of your databases. Only members of the sysadmin server role or db_owner database role can run the DBCC CHECKDB command.

Other Consistency Checks

Some other consistency checks are useful to run from time to time. The first of these, DBCC CHECKCATALOG, checks the referential integrity of the system tables. You learn more about referential integrity on Day 14, "Ensuring Data Integrity."

7

```
DBCC CHECKCATALOG ( 'database_name' ) [WITH NO_INFOMSGS]
```

where

- *database_name* is the name of the database for which you want to check integrity.

- NO_INFOMSGS specifies that only significant error messages will be reported. No informational messages will be reported. This is the option you'll want to use most of the time.

```
DBCC CHECKCATALOG('Pubs')
```

Results in

```
DBCC results for 'pubs'.
DBCC execution completed. If DBCC printed error messages,
➥ contact your system administrator.
```

ANALYSIS Notice that there are only two lines of output. For this DBCC command, the NO_INFOMSGS option only eliminates the first line.

```
DBCC Results for 'databasename'.
```

Only members of the sysadmin server role or db_owner database role can run the DBCC CHECKCATALOG command.

The next two commands, DBCC CHECKALLOC and DBCC CHECKTABLE, are subsets of DBCC CHECKDB. They are run when you run a DBCC CHECKDB, so there's no need to run them if you can use DBCC CHECKDB. You would use these commands together if your database were so large (hundreds of gigabytes or larger) that you couldn't afford to run DBCC CHECKDB and have it complete in a reasonable amount of time. They are included here for the sake of providing you with complete information.

```
DBCC CHECKALLOC ( 'database_name' [, NOINDEX ¦
{ REPAIR_ALLOW_DATA_LOSS ¦ REPAIR_FAST
¦ REPAIR_REBUILD }]
) [WITH {ALL_ERRORMSGS ¦ NO_INFOMSGS}]
```

where

- *database_name* is the name of the database for which you want to check integrity.

- NOINDEX specifies that you don't want the utility to check the integrity of your non-clustered indexes. (You examine indexes on Day 13.)

- REPAIR_FAST modifies corrupted indexes if it is safe to do so (no data can be lost using this option). It will also only make repairs that are quick and easy (such as corrupted index keys). The database must be in single-user mode to specify this option.

▼
- REPAIR_REBUILD fixes corrupted indexes just like the REPAIR_FAST option, but will perform more time-consuming fixes such as re-creating corrupted indexes. The database must be in single-user mode to specify this option.

- REPAIR_ALLOW_DATA_LOSS specifies that all repairs that would have been performed by the REPAIR_REBUILD option will be done, as well as "cleans up" broken pages and text/image pages, regardless of whether this will cause data loss. The database must be in single-user mode to specify this option.

- ALL_ERRORMSGS returns all messages from the command. By default, SQL Server will stop returning error messages after you receive 200 messages. Hopefully you will never need this option.

- NO_INFOMSGS specifies that only significant error messages will be reported. No informational messages will be reported. This is the option you'll want to use most
▲   of the time.

SYNTAX

```
DBCC CHECKTABLE ( 'table_name' [, NOINDEX ¦ index_id
¦ { REPAIR_ALLOW_DATA_LOSS ¦ REPAIR_FAST ¦ REPAIR_REBUILD }]
) [WITH {ALL_ERRORMSGS ¦ NO_INFOMSGS}]
```

▼

where

- *table_name* is the name of the table for which you want to check integrity.

- NOINDEX specifies that you don't want the utility to check the integrity of your non-clustered indexes. (You examine indexes on Day 13.)

- *index_id* specifies that you would like to check the integrity of a particular index. (You examine index IDs on Day 13.)

- REPAIR_FAST modifies corrupted indexes if it is safe to do so (no data can be lost using this option). It will also only make repairs that are quick and easy (such as corrupted index keys). The database must be in single-user mode to specify this option.

- REPAIR_REBUILD fixes corrupted indexes just like the REPAIR_FAST option, but will perform more time-consuming fixes such as re-creating corrupted indexes. The database must be in single-user mode to specify this option.

- REPAIR_ALLOW_DATA_LOSS specifies that all repairs that would have been performed by the REPAIR_REBUILD option will be done, as well as "cleans up" broken pages and text/image pages, regardless of whether this will cause data loss. The database must be in single-user mode to specify this option.

- ALL_ERRORMSGS returns all messages from the command. By default, SQL Server will stop returning error messages after you receive 200 messages. Hopefully you
▼   never will need this option.

7

▼
▲
- NO_INFOMSGS specifies that only significant error messages will be reported. No informational messages will be reported. This is the option you'll want to use most of the time.

Both DBCC CHECKTABLE and DBCC CHECKALLOC require that you be a member of the sysadmin server role or the db_owner database role. The same cautions and usage of DBCC CHECKDB apply to these commands because the commands are a subset of the DBCC CHECKDB command.

Backing Up a Database

Wow, can you believe you've made it to the actual backup commands? There's a lot to do before you back up your databases. It's never a trivial pursuit, even on a small system. When you've got your backup devices and verified that your databases are not corrupt, it's time to back up each database. The first step to examine is which backup devices you want to use and how you will use those backup devices.

Backup Device Options

You can back up to a single backup device or to multiple devices; or you can put multiple backups on a single device. Everywhere that you can specify a backup device, you can also specify a filename instead in the BACKUP command. Take a look at each of the options.

Single-Device Backups

A single-device backup is the default and the most often recommended way to perform a backup. If each database has a corresponding backup device, you can perform a one-to-one backup strategy. If you are backing up to disk backup devices, this is recommended. If you lose a file for some reason, you would lose only a single backup of a single database, instead of losing multiple backups contained in a single file. If you are backing up to tape, it's much more acceptable (and cost effective) to back up multiple databases to a single tape (backup device).

Parallel Striped Backups

A parallel striped backup allows you to back up a single database to multiple backup devices. You simply enumerate more than one backup device in the backup command, which you will learn about shortly. SQL Server 7.0 initiates a thread for each device you choose to use in your parallel striped backup, with up to 32 devices (and hence threads) possible.

The big advantage with parallel striped backups is with tape backups. You can attach multiple tape drives to a single server and back up a database to multiple tapes at the same time. If you have a single database that takes three hours to back up and you purchase two additional tape drives (for a total of three) you can quite possibly finish your backup of that database in one hour. The news gets better: You don't need to have the same number of tape drives available when it comes to restoring from the backup.

> **Tip**
>
> This is particularly important for disaster recovery. There's no guarantee you'll get the same number of tape drives in your recovery server. Also note that you still need all the tapes to recover your database.

> **Caution**
>
> After you use a tape in a parallel striped backup, you can't use it for anything but another parallel striped backup with the same number of tape drives until you reformat the tape.

Multiple Backups on a Single Device

You can also put multiple backups on a single backup device. If you think about it, this is the default configuration you want for a tape backup. It's likely that you'll want to put as many database backups on a single tape as possible. You can also do that with disk devices; however, I don't recommend this for disk devices because if the single file becomes corrupt or lost, all database backups on that device are lost.

The BACKUP DATABASE Command (for Entire Databases)

Backing up the database is the next logical step (finally). You do this using the BACKUP command.

▲ **SYNTAX**

```
BACKUP DATABASE {database_name ¦ @database_var}
TO <backup_device> [, …n]
[WITH [BLOCKSIZE = {blocksize ¦ @blocksize_variable}]
[[,] DESCRIPTION = {text ¦ @text_variable}]
[[,] DIFFERENTIAL]
[[,] EXPIREDATE = {date ¦ @date_var}
¦ RETAINDAYS = {days ¦ @days_var}]
[[,] FORMAT ¦ NOFORMAT]
[[,] {INIT ¦ NOINIT}]
[[,] MEDIADESCRIPTION = {text ¦ @text_variable}]
[[,] MEDIANAME = {media_name ¦ @media_name_variable}]
[[,] [NAME = {backup_set_name ¦ @backup_set_name_var}]
[[,] {NOSKIP ¦ SKIP}]
▼ [[,] {NOUNLOAD ¦ UNLOAD}]
```

7

```
[[,] [RESTART
[[,] STATS [= porcentage]]
]
Where:
<backup_device> :: =
{
{backup_device_name ¦ @backup_device_name_var}
¦
{DISK ¦ TAPE ¦ PIPE} =
{'temp_backup_device' ¦ @temp_backup_device_var}
}
```

Here's what the myriad of options mean. They won't be repeated unless they're specific to one of the other backup commands when you see them later, so you might need to refer to this description for the BACKUP LOG and BACKUP FILE/FILEGROUP options.

- database_name is the name of the database you want to back up.

- @database_var is the name of the database you want to back up—only it's expressed as a variable.

- backup_device is either the name of a backup device or a variable placeholder for the backup device. You can also specify just the name of the file, tape, or named pipe you want to use for the backup. Again, you can also specify this as a variable.

- blocksize is where you specify the block size you'd like to use if you are using a tape or named pipe. See your Windows NT documentation or tape drive hardware manual for recommended block sizes.

- description is up to 255 characters describing this backup. Again, you can specify a variable for this parameter.

- differential deserves its own section for a complete description. See the following section.

- EXPIREDATE is the date that the tape can be overwritten. If you attempt to write to a tape before the EXPIREDATE for a backup has passed, you will be unable to do so without specific override parameters.

- RETAINDAYS has the same effect as EXPIREDATE, except that you specify the number of days rather than a specific date.

- Format/noformat allows you to request that your tape be reformatted. Any password protection or existing data is ignored. This is the equivalent of specifying both the INIT and SKIP options.

- INIT/NOINIT specifies whether to initialize your backup device before writing this backup. NOINIT is the default, meaning that if your backup device already has another backup of some kind on it, the current backup request will be appended to

▼

the tape or disk file. If there is no backup on the device, it is initialized and then written to. INIT will overwrite the existing content of the tape or disk file. For tapes, if the retention date has not expired or the backup MediaName doesn't match, the tape is not initialized. You must specify the SKIP option if that is your intention (and if that's what you want, you might as well use the Format option).

- MediaDescription is another comment field for the backup, up to 255 characters long.

- MediaName is a description of the backup set—up to 128 characters. This is the name used for overwrite comparisons. If you plan to use a single tape to hold both Windows NT and SQL Server backups, you must specify a MediaName.

- Name is yet another name for the backup set. Again, it can also be specified as a variable.

- Skip/Noskip specifies whether to skip reading the tape header when writing to a tape. If Noskip is specified (the default), the tape header is read and the expiration date and MediaName are checked to prevent accidentally overwriting a tape.

- Nounload/Unload specifies that the tape is ejected when the backup is complete (or not).

- restart lets you restart a backup if it was interrupted and you want to continue from wherever it left off. When you do, you must specify the restart parameter. This parameter is valid only when making a multitape backup.

- Stats=percentage specifies how frequently you will be notified of progress in your backup. The default is 10, meaning that each time 10% of your backup completes, SQL Server will return a message telling you of its progress.

▲

The BACKUP command can look very intimidating, so how about a sample? Sometimes there's nothing like a little code to clear things up. The following script creates a new backup device for the pubs database, checks the integrity of the database, and then backs up the database.

**INPUT/
OUTPUT**

```
exec sp_addumpdevice 'disk',
'pubs_backup',
'f:\mssql7\backup\pubs_backup.dat'
go

use pubs
go

dbcc checkdb ('pubs') With NO_INFOMSGS
go

BACKUP DATABASE pubs to pubs_backup WITH INIT
go
```

7

See, that wasn't nearly as scary as it sounded. This code segment backs up the pubs database, but this time you'll specify the local tape drive. You won't be able to run this unless you have a tape drive installed on the computer that is running SQL Server 7.0. This time, you're specifying that the tape will expire in 30 days, the tape should be formatted before it's written, and the block size for the tape is 8192 bytes. The name of the backup will be Pubs Backup Tape.

INPUT/ OUTPUT

```
exec sp_addumpdevice 'tape',
'pubs_tape_backup', '\\.\tape0'
go

use pubs
go

dbcc checkdb ('pubs') With NO_INFOMSGS
go

BACKUP DATABASE pubs to pubs_backup WITH FORMAT,
Retain_days = 30,
MediaName='Pubs Backup Tape',
Blocksize=8192
go
```

The DIFFERENTIAL BACKUP DATABASE Command

As you discovered earlier in today's lesson, the differential backup copies all the modified pages in the database—this means all pages that have changed since the last full backup. If a differential backup is taken, and then another differential backup is taken, the second differential backup contains everything that was on the first one plus all changed pages that happened after that first backup. Do note, however, that a differential backup only makes sense as a follow-up to a full database backup.

Now make a differential backup of the pubs database. First, you'll create a table and add one row to it (so there's something new to back up). You won't make a new backup device, but you will append the differential backup onto the same device that contained the database backup. You might want to specify NOINIT (as I have done) just to be clear, even though it's the default.

INPUT/ OUTPUT

```
use pubs
go

Create table backuptest (col1 int not null)
go

Insert backuptest values (1)
go
```

```
BACKUP DATABASE pubs to pubs_backup WITH differential, NOINIT
Go
```

You will receive output looking like this:

```
(1 row(s) affected)

Processed 168 pages for database 'pubs', file 'pubs' on file 2.
Processed 1 pages for database 'pubs', file 'pubs_log' on file 2.
Backup or restore operation successfully processed
➥ 169 pages in 1.056 seconds (1.304 MB/sec).
```

You will need a lot of information to use differential backups properly. However, that's best left to Day 8.

Note

The restart option is exciting if you have large database backups. If the backup fails for some reason, you don't have to start from the beginning; you can start where you left off and continue the backup. Note, however, that if you have only a single tape or are still on the first tape, you will start over from the beginning regardless of whether you specify the restart parameter or not.

Setting the Media Retention for Tape Backups

If you don't pass either the `expire_date` or `retain_days` options to a tape backup, the retention date for the tape will be set to the default `media retention` server configuration option. You can set this option like you would any other server configuration option with the `sp_configure` system-stored procedure. For example, to set the default retention of tapes to 30 days, you can run the following code:

```
exec sp_configure 'media retention',30
GO

RECONFIGURE WITH OVERRIDE
GO
```

You must stop and restart SQL Server 7.0 to make this change take effect. The default configuration of the media retention is 0 days (no retention period).

The BACKUP DATABASE Command (for Files and File Groups)

The syntax for backing up files or file groups is shown here for the sake of completeness. However, you should back up files or file groups only if you can't accomplish a full database backup (or a combination of full and differential backups) in a reasonable

7

amount of time. There are other valid reasons why you might want to use file group backups in particular, but that's an advanced topic and beyond the scope of this book.

Essentially what this command allows you to do is back up an individual file or set of files known as a file group (described on Day 4). You still need a transaction log backup if you want to use a file or file group backup to restore your database.

▼ SYNTAX

```
BACKUP DATABASE {database_name ¦ @database_name_var}
<file_or_filegroup> [, …m]
TO <backup_device> [, …n]
[WITH
[BLOCKSIZE = {blocksize ¦ @blocksize_variable}]
[[,] DESCRIPTION = {text ¦ @text_variable}]
[[,] EXPIREDATE = {date ¦ @date_var}
¦ RETAINDAYS = {days ¦ @days_var}]
[[,] FORMAT ¦ NOFORMAT]
[[,] {INIT ¦ NOINIT}]
[[,] MEDIADESCRIPTION = {text ¦ @text_variable}]
[[,] MEDIANAME = {media_name ¦ @media_name_variable}]
[[,] [NAME = {backup_set_name ¦ @backup_set_name_var}]
[[,] {NOSKIP ¦ SKIP}]
[[,] {NOUNLOAD ¦ UNLOAD}]
[[,] [RESTART]
[[, ] STATS [= percentage]]
]
```

where

```
<file_or_filegroup> ::· =
{
FILE = {logical_file_name ¦ @logical_file_name_var}
¦
FILEGROUP = {logical_filegroup_name ¦ @logical_filegroup_name_var}
}
```

where most options have been covered except

- FILE specifies the name of the single file (or a variable listing a single file path and name) that you want to back up.
- FILEGROUP specifies the logical name of the file group you want to back up. All files within the file group will be backed up.

▲

The BACKUP LOG Command

You can also back up just the transaction log for a database. You can accomplish this using the BACKUP LOG command.

▼ SYNTAX

```
BACKUP LOG {database_name ¦ @database_name_var}
{[WITH  { NO_LOG ¦ TRUNCATE_ONLY }] }
¦
{TO <backup_device> [, …n]
[WITH
[BLOCKSIZE = {blocksize ¦ @blocksize_variable}]
[[,] DESCRIPTION = {text ¦ @text_variable}]
[[,] EXPIREDATE = {date ¦ @date_var}
¦ RETAINDAYS = {days ¦ @days_var}]
[[,] FORMAT ¦ NOFORMAT]
[[,] {INIT ¦ NOINIT}]
[[,] MEDIADESCRIPTION = {text ¦ @text_variable}]
[[,] MEDIANAME = {media_name ¦ @media_name_variable}]
[[,] [NAME = {backup_set_name ¦ @backup_set_name_var}]
[[,] NO_TRUNCATE]
[[,] {NOSKIP ¦ SKIP}]
[[,] {NOUNLOAD ¦ UNLOAD}]
[[,] [RESTART]
[[,] STATS [= percentage]]
]
}
```

Most of these options have been covered except the following:

- TRUNCATE_ONLY removes committed transactions from the log but does not actually back up the entries. For example, after backing up a database that has had non-logged operations run against it, the transaction log is no longer useful. You might want to issue a BACKUP LOG WITH TRUNCATE_ONLY followed by a full database backup. The fact that the log is truncated is in itself a logged operation. You should also note that this option does not actually perform a backup—hence the name of a backup device is unnecessary.

- NO_LOG is used under nearly the same circumstances as the TRUNCATE_ONLY option. However, it does not record the fact that the transaction log was truncated. If your transaction log fills up completely, you will not be able to back up the transaction log. Because a transaction log backup is itself a logged operation, as long as the log is full you can't back it up. Therefore, Microsoft made a special option that truncates the log in this special circumstance. It will work just like a TRUNCATE_ONLY when the log is not full and when it is full. This is yet another reason to let your transaction logs autogrow.

- The NO_TRUNCATE option makes a backup of the transaction log (just like a BACKUP LOG without any special options). However, it does something that an ordinary back-up can't; it can back up the transaction log even if a database is not available. For example, assume that you have a database where the data file is on one physical

7

▼

▼

▲

disk and the transaction log is on a separate disk. If the data file is lost for some reason, you can run the BACKUP LOG statement with NO_TRUNCATE to capture all transactions that have occurred since the last backup of the transaction log. This allows you to recover your database right up to the point of failure of the disk.

You can back up the transaction log for a database only if you've previously made a full database backup. You cannot make a transaction log backup if either of the Truncate Log On Checkpoint or Select Into/Bulkcopy Database options has been set.

Transaction log backups are a sequence of backups. Unlike differential backups, there is no duplication between one transaction log backup and the next. When you must restore the transaction logs, you'll need every single one you've made since your last full database backup. Tomorrow's lesson goes into greater detail on how to restore your database using transaction logs.

How often should you back up your transaction log? A typical scenario might look something like this (for a database used primarily during business hours):

6:00 a.m.	Daily full database backup with FORMAT
6:05 a.m.	Back up the transaction log with FORMAT
10:00 a.m.	Back up the transaction log again (NOINIT)
12:00 p.m.	Differential database backup (NOINIT)
2:00 p.m.	Back up the transaction log again (NOINIT)
6:00 p.m.	Back up the transaction log again (NOINIT)
8:00 p.m.	Differential database backup (NOINIT)
10:00 p.m.	Back up the transaction log (last time)

The script would look something like Listing 7.1 for the pubs database.

Tip

The pubs database has the Truncate Log on Checkpoint option set by default. When this option is set, you won't be able to back up the transaction log. So if you want to run the code in Listing 7.1, you must turn off this option with SQL Server Enterprise Manager or run

```
Exec sp_dboption 'pubs','Trunc. Log on Chkpt','False'
```

```
--SCRIPT BEGINS AT 6:00 AM
use pubs
go
dbcc checkdb ('pubs') With NO_INFOMSGS
go
BACKUP DATABASE pubs to pubs_backup WITH FORMAT,
Retain_days = 30,
MediaName='Pubs Backup Tape',
Blocksize=8192
Go

-- 6:05 AM
BACKUP LOG pubs to pubs_log_backup WITH INIT
Go
-- 10:00 AM
BACKUP LOG pubs to pubs_log_backup
Go
-- 12:00 PM
BACKUP DATABASE pubs to pubs_backup WITH DIFFERENTIAL,
NOINIT,
NOSKIP,
Retain_days = 30,
MediaName='Pubs Backup Tape',
Blocksize=8192
Go

-- 2:00 PM
BACKUP LOG pubs to pubs_log_backup
Go

-- 6:00 PM
BACKUP LOG pubs to pubs_log_backup
Go

-- 8:00 PM
BACKUP DATABASE pubs to pubs_backup WITH DIFFERENTIAL,
NOINIT,
NOSKIP,
Retain_days = 30,
MediaName='Pubs Backup Tape',
Blocksize=8192
Go

-- 10:00 PM
BACKUP LOG pubs to pubs_log_backup
Go
```

7

This allows you to recover your database and not lose transactions (as long as you don't lose the backup devices). This example assumes two tape drives—one for the full/differential database backups and one for the transaction log backups.

Using SQL Server Enterprise Manager for Backups

As you would expect, SQL Server Enterprise Manager is fully functional in the area of backups.

To begin, create two more backup devices: one for the pubs database (called pubs_backup) and another for the Northwind database (called northwind_backup). Turn off the Truncate Log on Checkpoint option for both of these databases.

Now expand the Databases folder, right-click the database you want to back up, and select All Tasks, Backup Database, or highlight the database and click the words Backup Database. Figure 7.6 shows the resulting SQL Server Backup dialog.

FIGURE 7.6

The SQL Server Backup—pubs dialog.

Now that you've examined all the Transact-SQL backup syntax options, this dialog should be a piece of cake. Fill in the appropriate details for the description of the backup (if you want), and select the backup type. Remember, if you want to back up the transaction log you must have first made a full database backup, and the Select Into/Bulkcopy and the Truncate Log On Checkpoint database options must not be enabled.

Under Destination, click Add to be presented with the Choose Backup Destination dialog (see Figure 7.7). Here you select a file location, a tape drive, a network location, a named pipe, or (the easy choice) a backup device. Select the backup device option, and then pick the pubs_backup backup device from the list, as shown in Figure 7.7.

FIGURE 7.7

The Choose Backup Destination dialog.

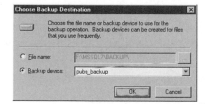

Click OK to finish selecting the backup device, and move on to the Overwrite section of the dialog. The default (as described earlier) is to append your backup to any previous backups that might exist on a particular backup device or backup file. Choose the Overwrite Existing Media option if you want to wipe out the contents of the backup device before writing the current backup.

The Schedule check box gives you an interface into the scheduling engine for SQL Server, which is provided by the SQLServerAgent service. Check this box if you want SQL Server to perform regular backups as scheduled jobs on whatever time basis you'd like. This is most likely what you'd do: go through this user interface, set your backup the way you'd like it, and then check the Schedule button and configure the schedule. Because scheduling backups is just one use (a very important one) of the scheduling features of SQL Server, these features are treated in depth on Day 19, "Using the SQL Server Agent." This allows for a thorough discussion of your scheduling options.

Now click the Options tab to get Figure 7.8. Notice that the Verify Backup Upon Completion option is checked. This verifies that your backup is intact and doesn't appear to be corrupted.

FIGURE 7.8

The SQL Server Backup Options tab.

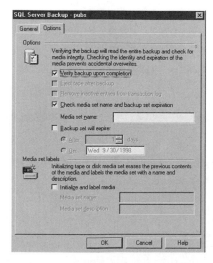

7

Caution   The Verify option is not the same as a DBCC CHECKDB. It does not check the integrity within the database; it just checks that the backup media itself is not corrupted.

Each option that is grayed out is simply unavailable for the type of backup you have selected—in this case, a full database backup to disk. If this were a transaction log backup, you'd have available the option Remove Inactive Entries From Transaction Log. This specifies the default behavior of a log backup. If you want the equivalent of the NO_TRUNCATE option for the log backup, uncheck this option.

The rest of the options on this tab are specific to tape drives and are self-explanatory. To begin your backup, click OK. You will see something like Figure 7.9, showing you the progress of your backup.

FIGURE 7.9

The Backup option in progress.

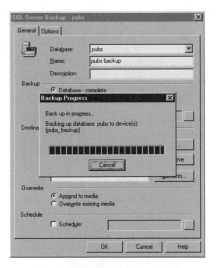

If you selected the Verify option, you will also see the dialog in Figure 7.10 if the verification is successful.

FIGURE 7.10

SQL Server verifies the backup's success.

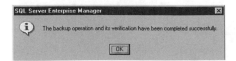

Now, here's the best part about using backup devices instead of files directly. Expand the Management folder, click the Backup icon, and double-click the pubs_backup backup device. Click the now active View Contents button, and you will be presented with a list of all the backups that are stored on that backup device—the type of backup and when it was completed (see Figure 7.11). This is very handy information to keep around. Notice in Figure 7.11 that there is both a full database backup and a transaction log backup on the backup device.

FIGURE 7.11

The View Backup Media Contents dialog.

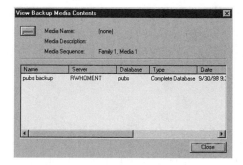

That's it! Backing up your databases and transaction logs with SQL Server Enterprise Manager is that simple. Of course, understanding what you are doing and what all the options mean has been a little bit of work, but I hope you agree that it was worth it.

Summary

Backing up and restoring are probably the most important parts of maintaining your SQL Server system. Backing up a database requires careful planning. You must determine which kinds of backups you will need (full database backups, differential backups, log backups, and file/file group backups), and there is no right answer. It depends on the size of your database and your restore requirements. Only through careful planning and then the implementation of those plans will you know whether you have the right set of backups. Don't forget to plan for things like major disasters, as well as the "accidental" deletion of data that always seems to happen right before a holiday. Protect your servers with RAID so you have less need to use your backups. You will most likely want to schedule your backups rather than run them interactively. Scheduling backups (and any other command) is examined on Day 19.

Q&A

Q Can you back up a database to a new file dynamically?

A Yes. Simply specify the device as a file instead of the name of a backup device.

Q Which command is used to create a backup device?

A sp_addumpdevice (or SQL Server Enterprise Manager).

7

Q Does RAID level 0 protect your data when a disk is lost?

A No. RAID level 0 is just striping of data and doesn't provide any fault tolerance.

Q When would you not be able to back up your transaction log?

A When the Select Into/Bulkcopy or Truncate Log On Checkpoint database options have been set or a full database backup has not been made first.

Q Can you back up the transaction log of the master database?

A No. You can only perform a full database backup of the master database.

Workshop

The Workshop provides quiz questions to help you solidify your understanding of the concepts presented in this chapter. In addition to the quiz questions, exercises are provided to let you practice what you have learned in this chapter. Try to understand the quiz and exercise answers before continuing to the next day's lesson. Answers are provided in Appendix A, "Answers."

Quiz

1. Which RAID option would be preferred for holding transaction logs?

2. Can you back up to a device whose physical location is \\myserver\sqlbackups\master_backup.dat?

3. In the Database Backup dialog, the transaction log backup option is unavailable. Can you explain why this might be the case?

4. Where should you keep your backup tapes?

5. Will a checkpoint interfere with your transaction log backups?

Exercises

1. Create backup devices for each of your databases and perform backups for each database. Examine the database options that are set so you can see which databases can have their transaction logs backed up.

2. Perform a differential database backup of your pubs and Northwind database.

3. Back up the transaction log of the pubs database.

WEEK 1

In Review

Let's take a quick refresher on what you covered this first week.

You were introduced to SQL Server 7.0 on Day 1. You learned about relational databases, data warehousing, and some history of SQL Server and relational database design. If you did the exercises, you participated in an interview with a client and designed the tables for a simple database.

On Day 2 you went through the installation process and examined various components you can install with SQL Server.

On Day 3 you learned about the tools and utilities that come packaged with SQL Server. You examined when and how you will use each of these tools.

On Day 4 you examined how storage is handled in SQL Server. More specifically, you developed an understanding of the relationship between databases and files. You also learned how to create, edit, and delete databases and database files.

By Day 5 you had installed the server and created databases and files. In order for anyone to be able to have access to your newly created databases, you needed to create some login IDs and user accounts. This gave you access to the SQL Server and the databases, but it did not allow you to do much of anything inside a database.

You might have created user accounts, logins, and roles, but your users will have some difficulty accessing data. Day 6 covered how to assign rights and database roles to your users so that they have permission to access your database objects.

Day 7 was the first of two presentations into the realm of the paranoid database adminis-trator. On Day 7 you learned how to protect your job and your data by implementing var-ious types of database and transaction log backups.

WEEK 2

At a Glance

During your second week, you are going to learn how to recover your databases, create tables, import and export information, retrieve and modify data, index, and ensure the integrity of your data.

Day 8 completes your trip to the realm of the paranoid administrator. You learn how to recover and restore the databases that you backed up on Day 7. Although this process is not difficult, knowing when to back up your data and how to restore your data can be crucial.

On Day 9 you learn what different data types are available in SQL Server 7.0. You also learn how to create your own user-defined data types. Now that you have data types, you can combine them into a table definition.

On Day 10 you learn how to import and export information from other SQL servers, databases, and flat files. You learn to use both the bcp (bulk copy) utility and the Data Transformation Services wizards included with SQL Server 7.0.

Day 11 covers the fundamentals of data retrieval. You learn about the SELECT statement and its syntax and use. Be sure you understand this new construct because the second half of Day 11 builds upon it. You learn how to use more powerful statements to gather just the data you want, work with subqueries, aggregate functions, and many system functions. This is a long chapter, but it is an excellent overview of a large piece of the Transact-SQL language.

8

9

10

11

12

13

14

After completing Day 12, you will be able to modify existing data in your database both one record at a time or an entire set of records. You will be able to add (insert), remove (delete), or modify (update) data.

All this data retrieval and modification that you have learned can be optimized through the use of indexing. Day 13 covers indexing in detail, focusing on both clustered and non-clustered indexes. You also are introduced to full-text indexing.

Data retrieval and modification can still be rendered useless if the data in your database isn't sound. Day 14 covers data integrity. This chapter enables you to minimize the amount of bad data that can enter your database.

This looks like a long week, but hang in there. You are going to cover some of the most difficult material in a database system, but by the end you will be two-thirds of the way though your 21 days and have a solid understanding of the material presented. Be sure to do the exercises at the end of the lessons because everything in database development tends to build on what preceded it.

DAY 8

Restoring SQL Server Databases

In yesterday's lesson you examined backups in SQL Server. You looked at how to use fault tolerance (in the form of hardware fault tolerance and Windows NT software fault tolerance) to prevent needing your backups. You learned about the types of backups available in SQL Server 7.0, including full database backups, differential database backups, and transaction log backups. You saw how to implement these backups with Transact-SQL and the SQL Server Enterprise Manager.

Today you will finish what is perhaps the most important but least glamorous aspect of supporting a relational database: backup and recovery. No matter how much work you do to make your database secure and your data available, data protection is the most critical aspect of your job. If your server crashes and all your data is lost, it's likely you've lost something else as well—your job! Today you will examine the restore process and what types of restore scenarios SQL Server supports. To lead off your examination of restoration, you will look at the recovery mechanisms SQL Server 7.0 uses. These include automatic recovery and manual recovery. Most of today's lesson deals with manual recovery—restoring a database to a consistent point in time.

Restoring Databases

Backups are good but not terribly useful in and of themselves. They're really handy, however, when you have problems with your server. If a disk quits functioning or a database file becomes corrupted, you will need to restore any databases affected by the loss of the files.

Another reason to restore a database backup is to restore a database to a logically consistent point in time. For example, suppose your boss deleted all the day's sales at 5 p.m. You can recover data from the previous full database backup and then apply all your transaction log backups (or any differential backups plus the transaction log backups) until the point in time right before your boss ran the delete command. This will recover the data with a minimal loss of work.

 Caution | SQL Server 7.0 cannot restore backups made with any previous release of SQL Server. SQL Server 7.0 can read backups made with SQL Server 7.0 only.

Before you examine recovery, you must understand that SQL Server has two different types of recovery: automatic and manual.

Automatic Recovery

Automatic recovery is the process SQL Server goes through each time the MSSQLServer service is started. You cannot disable it and don't need to do anything special to make it occur (hence the name automatic).

Each time SQL Server restarts, it goes through a particular set of steps that roll forward any committed transactions found in the transaction log that have occurred since the last checkpoint. Rolling forward transactions means that any committed transactions for a database are reapplied to that database. SQL Server then rolls back any transactions in the transaction log that have not been committed. Rolling back means that any transactions that were partially completed, but not committed, are removed from the database. When the automatic recovery process finishes, each database is left in a logically consistent form, and a checkpoint is issued. You will examine transactions further on Day 16, "Programming with SQL Server 7.0."

The automatic recovery process guarantees that no matter how or why SQL Server was stopped, it will start in a logically consistent state. Even if your server crashes suddenly, you will be able to recover cleanly. All committed transactions have their log pages written to disk immediately (known as a synchronous write). Therefore, any permanent changes to the database will have been successfully copied to disk and will be used during this process.

Automatic recovery processes each database in a particular order. It does this by first locating the master database files (master.mdf and mastlog.ldf), seeking its location in the Windows NT registry. You can find this information in the registry key HKEY_LOCAL_MACHINE\Software\Microsoft\MSSQLServer\MSSQLServer\Paramet ers. Here you will find the location where SQL Server believes it will find your master database files. You can see a sample of my (Windows NT) registry key set in Figure 8.1. The registry location is the same for all Windows platforms.

FIGURE 8.1

The SQL Server registry keys for service startup.

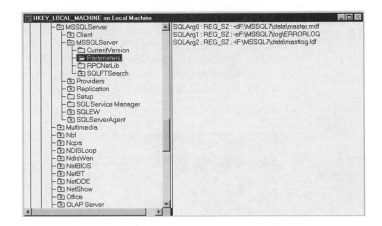

After SQL Server locates the master database files, it loads and recovers the master database. You must load and restore the master database first because it contains the references to the primary data file (the .mdf file) for the rest of the databases in the sysdatabases system table, in the filename column. After it has recovered the master database, SQL Server can begin the process of locating, opening, and recovering the rest of the databases. Each database keeps track of which files are associated with it by storing that information in the sysfiles and sysfilegroups system tables located in each database.

Before SQL Server can recover any other databases, it must recover the model database. The model database, remember, is the template database. You must recover the model database before you can continue because your next stop will be to create the tempdb database. You will need the tempdb database to perform a wide variety of queries or stored procedures in SQL Server. The tempdb database is re-created every time you start SQL Server. SQL Server creates the tempdb database by making a copy of the model database and then expanding the database to the appropriate size you had previously specified.

The msdb database is restored next, followed by the distribution database if it exists, the pubs and Northwind databases, and finally any user databases (the ones you care about).

You can examine this entire process by looking at the SQL Server Error Log:

1. Start SQL Server Enterprise Manager if it's not already open, connect to your server, expand the Management folder, and expand the SQL Server Logs option. You will see a list of the current error log and typically the last six error logs as well.

2. Highlight the error log you want to view, and it will appear in the right pane of the SQL Server Enterprise Manager (see Figure 8.2).

Note

Note that you can also view these files directly with an editor such as Notepad. You will find these files in the \mssql7\log directory, with the name errorlog.*, where * is the number of the backup. If it's the current error log, the filename is errorlog. (with no extension). The previous logs are named errorlog.1, errorlog.2, and so on.

FIGURE 8.2

The server error log view in Enterprise Manager.

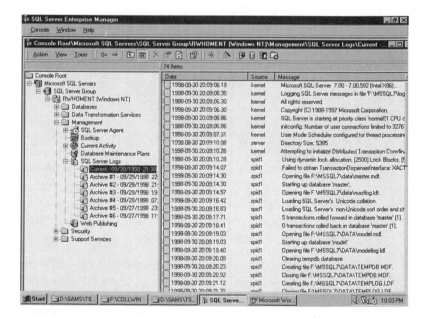

3. Start by finding the entry Opening File f:\MSSQL7\data\master.mdf.

This indicates that the master database is about to be opened and will be followed by the Starting Up Database 'master'. notation, which indicates that the master database primary data file is being opened and the master database is being examined. The next entry should be the opening of the mastlog.ldf file. You will see the Unicode and nonUnicode sort orders loaded for the current session with SQL Server.

8

You will then see the model database being recovered; then tempdb, msdb, and then your user-created databases (including pubs and northwind) are recovered. You will know that recovery was successful by the Recovery Complete entry in the error log.

Configuring Automatic Recovery

The most important thing you can do to configure automatic recovery is to configure the Recovery Interval option. This option specifies the maximum amount of time that SQL Server will take to perform automatic recovery on each database. The default value is 0, meaning that SQL Server will automatically configure how frequently it decides to issue a checkpoint.

This configuration parameter affects how often checkpoints occur. A checkpoint, remember, is the process that copies data pages and log records that have been modified in memory onto your disks. After a checkpoint is completed, transactions committed before the checkpoint no longer must be rolled forward (recovered).

You configure the recovery interval with the sp_configure system stored procedure. For example, to change the recovery to three minutes, run the following Transact-SQL code:

```
Exec sp_configure 'Recovery Interval',3
Go
Reconfigure with Override
Go
```

Unless you are experiencing performance degradation based on too many checkpoints, you should not change the recovery interval from the default automatic configuration.

Note

The recovery interval won't help you if you have a very long-running transaction. For example, suppose you have a system process that begins a transaction and then begins to run a series of updates that lasts hours, and at some point your server crashes. If you don't have enough memory to hold all the changes in memory, and some of these changes are written to disk, you will need to roll back these changes from your database. If you had previously configured your recovery interval to three minutes (as in the preceding code segment), it will probably still take more than three minutes to recover the database. To avoid this problem, keep the size of your transactions small so you can recovery quickly if there's a problem.

Manual Recovery

Manual recovery is the topic of the rest of today's lesson. Manual recovery is the process of recovering a database. This might include recovering from a full database backup, possibly recovering a differential database backup, and finally restoring one or more transaction log backups from your backup devices. The details of the recovery process will vary depending on the reasons for the recovery.

You can recover a database and then apply the transaction logs to fully restore a lost database or recover to a point in time to undo a change to your database. You can also use the differential database backups (if you've made them) to help you restore fewer transaction logs.

Restoring a database from a backup has the following restrictions:

- The database cannot be in use. A database is in use if anyone has issued the USE command and pointed to the database or if anyone is running any query against that database.

- You must have the proper permissions. Only members of the sysadmin serverwide role or the db_owner fixed database roles can recover a database. The right to do so can't be given away. Restoring a database is an extremely powerful right.

- You must restore the transaction logs in the sequence in which they were created. Each transaction log has a sequence number associated with it. You must restore the transaction log backups in the proper order or the recovery will fail. There are many considerations you will examine in today's lesson before you begin restoring your transaction log backups.

If the reason you're trying to recover is because you've lost a hard drive, you must first replace the disk that failed (including reestablishing mirroring or other redundant array of inexpensive disks [RAID] configurations) and then drop any affected databases. You can then re-create the databases or you can have the databases re-created as part of the restore operation.

If you perform a restore against a database that already exists, the default results in all the contents of the existing database being wiped out in favor of your backups (with some important considerations you will examine later).

Restoring from the Files (Reattaching a Database)

Before you examine the restore processes, you should consider one possible restore option. You can reattach a database if you have a copy of all the data files associated with it. SQL Server 7.0 has the capability to both detach and then reattach databases using Transact-SQL system stored procedures and the CREATE DATABASE option with the FOR_ATTACH option.

First, examine the CREATE DATABASE option. This code sample shows a create database that has two database files: test_data.mdf and test_log.ldf:

```
create database test
on (filename = 'F:\mssql7\data\test_data.mdf')
log on (filename = 'F:\mssql7\data\test_log.ldf')
FOR ATTACH
```

which should return

```
Successfully attached database 'test'.
```

Notice that all you must specify is the filename. When SQL Server has found the files, it can build all the other information it needs from the SQL Server system tables stored inside the database.

You can also use the sp_attach_db system stored procedure. Test this yourself by first creating a test database (like the one here), and then run the sp_detach_db system stored procedure as follows:

```
Exec sp_detach_db 'test'
Go
```

You should see something similar to the following:

```
Successfully detached database 'test'.
DBCC execution completed. If DBCC printed error messages,
contact your system administrator.
```

This will detach your test database from your server. You can then send your database files to anyone you want, and the recipient can run the following (or you can as well):

```
EXEC sp_attach_db @dbname = 'test',
@filename1 = 'F:\mssql7\data\test_data.mdf',
@filename2 = 'F:\mssql7\data\test_log.ldf'
```

Notice that the sp_attach_db system stored procedure is essentially issuing a CREATE DATABASE FOR ATTACH command. There is no functional difference in the two options (the create database or the sp_attach_db options).

Caution

> Note that this is not a good backup-and-restore policy. You should make full database backups, differential backups, and transaction log backups as described on Day 7, "Implementing Backups in SQL Server 7.0." As you will see later in today's lesson, you are severely restricting your recovery options by not using the built-in backup-and-restore capabilities of SQL Server.

Finding the Right Backup Set

Your first step is to find the correct backup set. There are two different ways you can proceed here: the hard way and the easy way. You should start (as always) with the hard way, because that's how you learn what's really going on. There are three Transact-SQL commands you can use to find out (to various degrees) what's on your backup devices:

- RESTORE LABELONLY supplies a single line of summary information about the entire backup set.

- RESTORE HEADERONLY supplies summary information about each item in the backup set.

- RESTORE FILELISTONLY supplies a list of the databases and logs backed up on a particular backup device.

Now look at each one of them in more detail.

RESTORE LABELONLY

When you run the RESTORE LABELONLY command, the media header of your backup device (you would typically use this command for tapes) is read and summed up as a single row. That row describes the name of the media you specified during your backup, the description you entered when you backed up the database, and the last date of a backup on the backup device. Other information is also returned, but unless you are working on an advanced backup strategy, you will not need to explore this information.

RESTORE LABELONLY FROM <backup_device>

where

- backup_device is the name of either a backup device or a variable placeholder for the backup device. You can also specify just the name of the file, tape, or named pipe you want to use for the restore. Again, you can also specify this as a variable.

RESTORE HEADERONLY

RESTORE HEADERONLY gets information about every backup on a backup device. The command returns one row for each backup that exists on a database backup. This is because, unlike the RESTORE LABELONLY command, RESTORE HEADERONLY reads information from each backup on a backup device, one at a time. This could be time consuming if you have several backups on a tape. For disk backup files, this command usually runs very quickly.

8

```
RESTORE HEADERONLY FROM <backup_device>
[WITH {NOUNLOAD ¦ UNLOAD}]
```

where

- *backup_device* is either the name of a backup device or a variable placeholder for the backup device. You can also specify just the name of the file, tape, or named pipe you want to use for the restore. Again, you can also specify this as a variable.

- NOUNLOAD/UNLOAD specifies that the tape is ejected (or not) when the RESTORE HEADERONLY command is complete.

▲

The results of this command include the names of the backups (as well as the descriptions) when the backups are set to expire. They include who created the backup, what server the backup came from, which database was backed up, how big the backup is, and when the backup began and was completed. Additionally, the results include the code page, sort order, database compatibility mode, and version of SQL Server used to make the backup. The information also includes internal information about log sequence numbers (which are beyond the scope of this book).

Whew! It's great to know that this much information is kept for each and every backup you've made!

RESTORE FILELISTONLY

The RESTORE FILELISTONLY command returns a list of the database and log files that were backed up on the specified backup device. You can get information about only one backup at a time, so if there are multiple backups on a backup device, you must specify which one you want to know about.

This information is particularly handy in disaster recovery situations. If you want to restore a database and don't know where the files were previously, you can find out by running RESTORE FILELISTONLY.

```
RESTORE FILELISTONLY FROM <backup_device>
[WITH [FILE = fileno] [[, ] {NOUNLOAD ¦ UNLOAD}]]
```

where

- *backup_device* is either the name of a backup device or a variable placeholder for the backup device. You can also specify just the name of the file, tape, or named pipe you want to use for the restore. Again, you can also specify this as a variable.

- fileno specifies which backup on the backup device you want to examine.

- NOUNLOAD/UNLOAD specifies that the tape is ejected (or not) when the RESTORE HEADERONLY command is complete.

▲

If you don't know the file number you want to examine, run the RESTORE HEADERONLY command to get a list of file numbers and which backup each applies to. If you do not specify the fileno parameter, it's assumed to be the first backup on the backup device.

Establishing That Your Backup Set Is Usable

Assume for a minute that you ran the appropriate DBCC checks on your database before you ran your backup. Also assume that you took advantage of the verify option available during backup. Does that mean your backup is ready to restore?

If you (like us) can't immediately say yes, you are not alone. Microsoft had this feeling as well because it provided the RESTORE VERIFYONLY command.

RESTORE VERIFYONLY

The RESTORE VERIFYONLY command simply checks that all your tapes or disk files are available for a restore, and that all the information needed can be read. This does not run the database DBCC checks on your backup—it simply checks that the tape/disk files can be read.

```
RESTORE VERIFYONLY FROM <backup_device> [,…n]
[WITH [FILE = fileno] [[,] {NOUNLOAD ¦ UNLOAD}]
[[,] LOADHISTORY]]
```

where

- *backup_device* is either the name of a backup device or a variable placeholder for the backup device. You can also specify just the name of the file, tape, or named pipe you want to use for the restore. Again, you can also specify this as a variable.

- fileno specifies which backup on the backup device you want to examine.

- NOUNLOAD/UNLOAD specifies that the tape is ejected (or not) when the RESTORE HEADERONLY command is complete.

- LOADHISTORY specifies that the information about the backup that you examine be added to the backup history tables in the msdb database. You will examine these tables shortly.

The MSDB Backup History Tables

A minor diversion is in order before you continue examining the actual restore commands. Every time you perform a SQL Server backup, the details of that backup are stored in the msdb database in the following system tables:

- Backupfile—Contains information about file backups.

- BackupMediaFamily—Contains information about media families. You got a brief introduction on media families in yesterday's lesson. Remember that they are typically used for parallel striped backups.

8

- BackupMediaSet—Contains information about media sets. Again, media sets are typically discussed when used with parallel striped backups, but every backup is part of a media set.
- Backupset—Contains information about each backup you make.
- Restorefile—Contains information about each restore of a file.
- Restorefilegroup—Contains information about each restore of a file group.
- Restorehistory—Contains information about every restore you run.

This is great news! Every time you create any kind of backup or perform a restore operation, it is recorded in these system tables as necessary. It doesn't matter whether the backup or restore is performed using Transact-SQL statements or using SQL Server Enterprise Manager. The implication here, however, is that you will need to back up your msdb database frequently to save this information in case you lose either the msdb or master database.

Okay, back to the meat and potatoes of your day—how to restore a database.

Performing a Full Database Restore

A full database restore takes a full database backup (you might think of it as a "normal" backup) and lays that backup down on your server. It uses the transaction log that was backed up with the database backup to recover the database, rolling forward any committed transactions and rolling back any uncommitted transactions, as of the time the database backup was complete. As with the backup commands, the Transact-SQL RESTORE command has more functionality than that of the SQL Server Enterprise Manager, and the SQL Server Enterprise Manager dialogs are much easier to understand when you see the commands running on SQL Server.

Several options are available when you restore a database. You can

- Move files around (from where they were when the database was backed up).
- Set the DBO USE ONLY database option during your restore (in case you're not finished yet or want to restrict access to your database).
- Choose to recover or not recover to a consistent point in time (depending on whether you want to apply transaction log backups).
- Create a standby file. You would create a standby file in case you wanted to continue applying transaction log backups but wanted to examine the state of a database in a "read-only" mode between restoring those backups. You learn about this situation shortly.
- Restart a restore that was interrupted at some point (for example, if a power failure occurred during your restore operation).

Now look at each option, and see how to perform a restore of your previous full database backup.

Caution	We cannot stress enough that you cannot restore a database using a backup made from any previous release of SQL Server.

Performing a Full Database Restore Using the Transact-SQL RESTORE Command

You use the RESTORE command to recover a database from a full database backup. First, look at the syntax of the command.

```
RESTORE DATABASE databasename FROM <backup_device> [, …n]
[WITH [DBO_ONLY] [[,] FILE = fileno]
[[,] MEDIANAME = {media_name ¦ @media_name_variable}]
[[,] MOVE 'logical_file_name' TO 'new_file_name'][,…p]
[[,] {NORECOVERY ¦ RECOVERY ¦ STANDBY = undo_file_name}]
[[,] {NOUNLOAD ¦ UNLOAD}] [[,] REPLACE] [[,] RESTART]
[[,] STATS [= percentage]]]
```

where

- *databasename* is the name of the database you want to restore.
- *backup_device* is the name of either a backup device or a variable placeholder for the backup device. You can also specify just the name of the file, tape, or named pipe you want to use for the restore. Again, you can also specify this as a variable.
- DBO_ONLY specifies that the database option DBO USE ONLY is set to true when the restore operation is complete.
- fileno specifies which backup on the backup device you want to restore.
- MEDIANAME specifies that the backup's stored media name is compared to the specified media name. If they don't match, the restore fails.
- MOVE specifies that for each logical filename you reference, the restore operation should find that logical file in the backup set and restore it to the alternative pathname and filename you indicate.
- RECOVERY indicates that the restore should roll back any uncommitted transactions and bring the database to a consistent state. After you have used the recovery option, you cannot restore any transaction log backups or differential backups to the database. The recovery option is the default if no other recovery option (NORECOVERY or STANDBY) is specified.

▼
- NORECOVERY indicates that the restore should not roll back any uncommitted transactions and that the restore will not bring the database to a consistent point. Use
  this option during the restore of your database when you want to apply transaction
  log backups or differential backups to the database after a full database restore.

- STANDBY specifies the pathname and filename of an undo file. The undo file keeps
  enough information to restart transactions rolled back during the recovery process.
  You use this option when you want to examine a database (in read-only fashion)
  between differential or transaction log restores. If the file you specify doesn't exist,
  SQL Server will create it for you.

- NOUNLOAD/UNLOAD specifies that the tape is ejected (or not) when the RESTORE
  HEADERONLY command is complete.

- REPLACE indicates that the restore should replace any database with the same name
  that currently exists on your server. A normal restore without this option specifies
  that if the database name is different than the name of the backed up database, or
  the set of files does not match from the backup to the existing database, the restore
  will fail. This is a safety check.

- RESTART restarts your backup from where it last left off. As indicated earlier in
  today's lesson, this option only applies when recovering from a multiple-tape backup, when you are on the second tape or later.

- STATS indicates that you would like a status report every specified percentage of
  the restore operation's progress. The default, just like in backups, is to let you
▲ know about the restore progress every 10% that completes.

An example is in order. To restore the pubs database, which was backed up onto the
pubs_backup backup device, accepting all defaults, you would run the following command:

```
RESTORE DATABASE PUBS FROM PUBS_BACKUP
```

If there were three backups stored on the pubs_backup backup device, and you wanted to
restore the third of these full database backups, you would run two sets of commands.
The first step is to verify that you really want file number three on the backup device,
while the second step actually performs the restore.

Step 1:

```
RESTORE HEADERONLY from pubs_backup
```

Step 2:

```
RESTORE DATABASE PUBS FROM PUBS_BACKUP WITH FILE = 3
```

To restore your pubs database but store the pubs.mdf file on the D drive of your computer after the restore, leave the database in a standby state, restore from file number 3, and provide notification of the restore's progress after every 25% of the restore is complete, you would run

```
RESTORE DATABASE PUBS FROM PUBS_BACKUP
WITH MOVE 'pubs' TO 'D:\pubs.mdf',
FILE = 3,
STANDBY = 'd:\standby.dat',
STATS = 25
```

and you should get output similar to this:

```
28 percent restored.
52 percent restored.
76 percent restored.
100 percent restored.
Processed 168 pages for database 'PUBS', file 'pubs' on file 3.
Processed 1 pages for database 'PUBS', file 'pubs_log' on file 3.
Backup or restore operation successfully processed
➥ 169 pages in 0.978 seconds (1.408 MB/sec).
```

At this point you would need to apply a transaction log or differential database backup to complete the recovery of your database, so you might run

```
restore database pubs from pubs_backup with file = 4, RECOVERY
```

where file number four was a differential backup that occurred after your full database backup, and you would get something like this from your command:

```
Processed 168 pages for database 'pubs', file 'pubs' on file 4.
Processed 1 pages for database 'pubs', file 'pubs_log' on file 4.
Backup or restore operation successfully processed
➥ 169 pages in 1.072 seconds (1.284 MB/sec).
```

Notice that SQL Server will not delete your standby file. Now that it is no longer needed, you will need to delete it.

The MOVE Option

The MOVE option enables you to perform easy migrations of data from one server to another. If your production server has drive letters H and I, for example, and these contain SQL Server data or log files, you can restore these backups to your development server. This is true even if that server only has drives C, D, and E. You simply specify the logical filenames from the old backup and provide the new location on the new server for each logical file.

8

> **Tip**
>
> Remember that you can find the list of files in a backup set with the RESTORE FILELISTONLY command.

This option also helps in a disaster recovery situation. It's possible, but not likely, that the server you end up with after a disaster won't have the same drive letters, so it's good to know how to use the MOVE option.

> **Caution**
>
> Just in case you think I'm emphasizing disasters a little too much, consider this recent (as of this writing) event on the Internet. I visited a Web site that apologized for its lack of content because its servers were stolen during a burglary. Still think it can't happen to you?

The REPLACE Option

The REPLACE option is useful because it tells you about some checks that are normally running during a restore. If the database name you backed up (for example, Accounting) is not the same as the one you are attempting to restore (for example, Sales), a normal restore operation is not allowed. This is meant to help prevent you from sounding like Homer Simpson and letting out a big "Doh!" after a restore (is that resume ready to go?).

It also helps you if the set of files doesn't match. If both the backed up database and the database you want to restore to are named Accounting, but the production (currently running) accounting database consists of 20 1GB files, and the backup is the wrong one (say, your test database of 20MB), SQL Server will notice and prevent the restore.

You can override this behavior in both instances by specifying the REPLACE option, which basically tells SQL Server to butt out—you know what you are doing.

> **Caution**
>
> Be very sure before you specify the REPLACE option. If you get a failure because of one of the conditions referenced here, it's usually time to step back, take a deep breath, and put a little thought into what you're doing. It's better to wait a minute than try to explain why you deliberately recovered the wrong database into production.

Restoring with Differential Backups

Restoring a differential backup works just like restoring a full database backup. There is no syntactical difference. Simply specify the correct file number from your backup devices.

You will be able to restore a differential backup only after you have restored a full database backup. You must also have specified either the STANDBY or NORECOVERY options during your full database restore to be able to apply your differential backups.

Your differential backups are cumulative, so if you have made three differential backups since your last full database backup, you must restore only the last of these differential backups.

Restoring from a Transaction Log

Restoring from a transaction log is relatively straightforward, as long as you keep the rules in mind. You can restore the transaction logs only in the sequence in which they were backed up. Unlike differential backups, transaction log backups are not cumulative, so you need all of them to be intact to be able to recover completely.

Unlike database or differential backup restores, which only let you recover to the point in time that the backup was taken, you can restore to a chosen point in time when recovering transaction log backups.

Using Transact-SQL to Restore Transaction Logs

You specify the RESTORE LOG command to recover a transaction log backup.

▲ SYNTAX

```
RESTORE LOG databasename FROM <backup_device> [, …n]
[WITH [DBO_ONLY] [[,] FILE = fileno]
[[,] MEDIANAME = {media_name ¦ @media_name_variable}]
[[,] {NORECOVERY ¦ RECOVERY ¦ STANDBY = undo_file_name}]
[[,] {NOUNLOAD ¦ UNLOAD}] [[,] RESTART]
[[,] STATS [= percentage]]
[[,] STOPAT = datetime]]
```

where

- *databasename* is the name of the database to restore.
- *backup_device* is the name of either a backup device or a variable placeholder for the backup device. You can also specify just the name of the file, tape, or named pipe you want to use for the restore. Again, you can also specify this as a variable.
- DBO_ONLY specifies that the database option DBO USE ONLY is set to true when the restore operation is complete.

▼

- fileno specifies which backup on the backup device you want to restore.

▼
- MEDIANAME specifies that the backup's stored media name is compared to the specified media name. If they don't match, the restore fails.
- RECOVERY indicates that the restore should roll back any uncommitted transactions and bring the database to a consistent state. After you have used the recovery option, you cannot restore any transaction log backups or differential backups to the database. The recovery option is the default if no other recovery option (NORECOVERY or STANDBY) is specified.
- NORECOVERY indicates that the restore should not roll back any uncommitted transactions, and the restore will not bring the database to a consistent point. Use this option on the restore of your database when you want to apply transaction log backups or differential backups to the database after a full database restore.
- STANDBY specifies the pathname and filename of an undo file. The undo file keeps enough information to restart transactions that are rolled back during the recovery process. You use this option when you want to examine a database (in read-only fashion) between differential or transaction log restores. If the file you specify doesn't exist, SQL Server will create it for you.
- NOUNLOAD/UNLOAD specifies that the tape is ejected (or not) when the RESTORE HEADERONLY command is complete.
- RESTART restarts your backup from where it last left off. As indicated earlier in today's lesson, this option only applies when recovering from a multiple tape backup, when you are on the second tape or later.
- STATS indicates that you would like a status report every specified percentage of the restore operation's progress. The default, just like in backups, is to let you know about the restore progress every 10% that completes.
- STOPAT indicates the date and time you want to choose as your point of consistency during the restore of the transaction log. Any transactions that were active (not committed) at this time will be rolled back.

▲

After you have recovered from your full database backup (and specified either the NORECOVERY or STANDBY options), you apply a transaction log like this (assuming the pubs_log_backup backup device exists and contains one or more transaction log backups):

```
RESTORE LOG pubs from pubs_log_backup
```

That's it. You've restored the log. The complete recovery of both the full backup and log backup looks like this:

```
RESTORE DATABASE pubs FROM pubs_backup WITH NORECOVERY
RESTORE LOG pubs from pubs_log_backup WITH RECOVERY
```

RECOVERY is the default option, so it's not necessary to provide it on the transaction log restore, but I included it here for clarity.

Now, for the sake of argument, assume you had made your database backup, then made three transaction log backups (file numbers 1, 2, and 3 on the pubs_log_backup backup device). You would run the following command sequence to restore the database and recover all your transaction log backups:

```
RESTORE DATABASE pubs FROM pubs_backup WITH NORECOVERY
RESTORE LOG pubs from pubs_log_backup WITH FILE = 1, NORECOVERY
RESTORE LOG pubs from pubs_log_backup WITH FILE = 2, NORECOVERY
RESTORE LOG pubs from pubs_log_backup WITH FILE = 3, RECOVERY
```

You will see results like this:

```
Processed 168 pages for database 'pubs', file 'pubs' on file 1.
Processed 1 pages for database 'pubs', file 'pubs_log' on file 1.
Backup or restore operation successfully processed 169 pages in 1.066
➥seconds (1.292 MB/sec).
Processed 1 pages for database 'pubs', file 'pubs_log' on file 1.
Backup or restore operation successfully processed 1 pages in 0.030
➥seconds (0.153 MB/sec).
Processed 1 pages for database 'pubs', file 'pubs_log' on file 2.
Backup or restore operation successfully processed 1 pages in 0.038
➥seconds (0.013 MB/sec).
Processed 1 pages for database 'pubs', file 'pubs_log' on file 3.
Backup or restore operation successfully processed 1 pages in 0.045
➥seconds (0.011 MB/sec).
```

Restoring to a Point in Time

To restore to a point in time, restore as you did previously, except for the transaction log within the time range you want to stop at. You can use the RESTORE HEADERONLY command to explore the time ranges covered by each transaction log backup. So, for the exact same commands you ran before, but stopping at a particular time during the third log restore, run the following:

```
RESTORE DATABASE pubs FROM pubs_backup WITH NORECOVERY
RESTORE LOG pubs from pubs_log_backup WITH FILE = 1, NORECOVERY
RESTORE LOG pubs from pubs_log_backup WITH FILE = 2, NORECOVERY
RESTORE LOG pubs from pubs_log_backup WITH FILE = 3, RECOVERY,
STOPAT = 'Aug 10, 1998 5:00 PM'
```

The restore will bring your database to what would have been a consistent state at exactly 5 p.m. on August 10, 1998.

Restoring Transaction Log and Differential Database Backups

Should you want to combine restoring differential database backups with transaction log backups, the only note you must remember is that you will need all the transaction logs that were active from the time of the differential backup forward.

For example, if in the previous example you had taken a differential database backup after the second transaction log backup, you could run the following set of code:

```
RESTORE DATABASE pubs FROM pubs_backup WITH FILE = 1, NORECOVERY
RESTORE DATABASE pubs FROM pubs_backup WITH FILE = 2, NORECOVERY
RESTORE LOG pubs from pubs_log_backup WITH FILE = 3, RECOVERY
```

You would see something like the following output:

```
Processed 176 pages for database 'pubs', file 'pubs' on file 1.
Processed 1 pages for database 'pubs', file 'pubs_log' on file 1.
Backup or restore operation successfully processed 177 pages in 1.091
➥seconds (1.322 MB/sec).
Processed 176 pages for database 'pubs', file 'pubs' on file 2.
Processed 1 pages for database 'pubs', file 'pubs_log' on file 2.
Backup or restore operation successfully processed 177 pages in 1.044
➥seconds (1.382 MB/sec).
Processed 1 pages for database 'pubs', file 'pubs_log' on file 3.
Backup or restore operation successfully processed 1 pages in 0.039
➥seconds (0.039 MB/sec).
```

Your database is now restored using the full database backup, then applying the differential backup, and finally applying the only transaction log backup made after the differential backup, transaction log backup number 3.

Restoring Files or File Groups

You can also restore individual files or a file group if you want. Just as you saw yesterday, today's lesson includes the syntax and an example here for completeness. Although file and file group backups and restores are very powerful features of SQL Server, they require sophisticated planning to ensure you can use them successfully, and they are beyond the scope of this book.

▼ SYNTAX

```
RESTORE DATABASE databasename <file_or_filegroup> [, …m]
[FROM <backup_device> [, …n]]
[WITH [DBO_ONLY] [[,] FILE = file_number]
[[,] MEDIANAME = {media_name ¦ @media_name_variable}]
[[,] NORECOVERY] [[,] {NOUNLOAD ¦ UNLOAD}]
[[,] REPLACE][[,] RESTART] [[,] STATS [= percentage]]]
<file_or_filegroup> :: =
{FILE = {logical_file_name ¦ @logical_file_name_var} ¦
FILEGROUP = {logical_filegroup_name ¦ @logical_filegroup_name_var}}
```

The only difference between this and the full database restore syntax is that you can specify either a file or file group name in the command.

If you had backed up the `test_data` file of a database named test to the backup device `test_file_backup`, you could restore it with the following commands:

```
RESTORE DATABASE test FILE = 'test_data'
FROM test_file_backup WITH NORECOVERY
RESTORE LOG test
FROM test_log_backup WITH RECOVERY
```

Note
You cannot restore a file or file group backup without next applying a transaction log restore to bring the database to a consistent state. This is just a hint at the complexity of a file or file group backup strategy.

Restoring with SQL Server Enterprise Manager

You made it! Now that you understand what's really going on behind the scenes, it's time to examine how easy it is to restore a database using the SQL Server Enterprise Manager.

Expand the Databases folder, right-click the database you want to recover, and select Task, Restore Database. Now a good question should pop into your head: What if the database you want to restore doesn't exist?

When you've connected to your server, click the Tools menu at the top of the screen and select Restore Database. You will end up in the same place in both cases—the Restore Database dialog (see Figure 8.3 for the pubs database on my system).

FIGURE 8.3

The Restore Database dialog.

As you can see in Figure 8.3, SQL Server Enterprise Manager makes restore a trivial affair. SQL Server, as you learned earlier today, remembers when backups have been made. It does this by storing information in system tables in the msdb system database. That information is what you see reflected in the Restore dialogs. For each box checked, SQL Server will restore that backup item. In Figure 8.3, you can see that a restore from a full database backup would have occurred, followed immediately by a restore of a transaction log. The full database restore happens with the NORECOVERY option because you apply a transaction log restore next. The transaction log restore occurs with the RECOVERY option, and your database will be available.

To perform a file or file group restore, simply click that option. To perform a point-in-time restore (assuming you are restoring one or more transaction logs), simply check the Point In Time Restore box.

If you click the Restore Backup Sets From Device(s) option, the dialog morphs into Figure 8.4.

FIGURE 8.4

The Restore Database dialog (using a device).

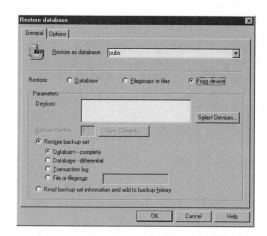

To choose a backup device, click the Select Devices button. You are presented with Figure 8.5.

FIGURE 8.5

The Choose Restore Devices dialog.

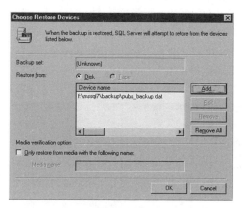

Click the Add button to select either a file containing a database or transaction log backup, or select a backup device.

8

After you have returned to the Restore database from device dialog, specify the kind of backup you'd like to restore. Then select the Backup Set number (the FILE parameter from the RESTORE command). Another nifty feature here is that you can click the View Contents button to be presented with the equivalent of the LOAD HEADERONLY command. However, here you can choose to restore the contents of the backup device, if multiple backups (for example, multiple transaction log backups) are contained on the device (see Figure 8.6).

FIGURE 8.6

The Select Backup dialog.

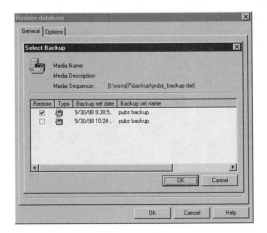

Finally, when you are back to the General tab of the Restore Database dialog, you will notice the option at the bottom of the dialog to allow you to update the backup history information in SQL Server's msdb database.

To change other restore options (as if you haven't examined enough yet), click the Options tab (see Figure 8.7).

FIGURE 8.7.

The Restore Database Options dialog.

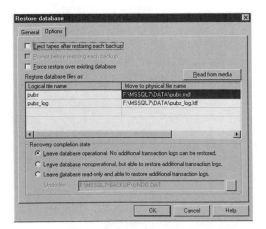

The following options are available on the Options tab:

- Eject Tapes After Restoring Each Backup—This option will do as indicated and eject your tapes when the restore is done.
- Prompt Before Restoring Each Backup—This option allows you to be notified between each restore you have selected on the General tab.
- Force Restore Over Existing Database—This issues the REPLACE option for the RESTORE DATABASE statement.
- Restore Database Files As—For each file in your backup set, you can rename it here. This is the MOVE option from the RESTORE DATABASE statement.
- Recovery Completion State—There are three options. The first, the default, is to leave your database operational (which is the same as specifying the RECOVERY option on the final restore).

  Use the middle option button when you want to continue applying differential or transaction log restores. This option specifies the NORECOVERY option on the final transaction log restore (or full database/differential restore if you choose not to apply any logs).

  The final option is the same as specifying the STANDBY option in a restore statement. As with the Transact-SQL RESTORE command, you must specify the location and filename of the undo file.

When you are ready to begin the restore operation, click OK. SQL Server Enterprise Manager will then submit the appropriate RESTORE or multiple RESTORE commands you have graphically specified.

Recovery Scenarios

Perhaps the most important thing you can do is look at how to apply the backup and restore techniques you have examined for the last two days' lessons.

Recovery After Losing a Disk

One of the most common recovery scenarios is to restore databases after a disk has been lost on the server. Perform the following steps in order to recover your database:

1. Verify that you have all the information you need to restore the devices and databases.
2. Capture the transaction log if it's still available.
3. Drop the affected databases.
4. Replace the failed disk.
5. Restore the databases and transaction logs as appropriate.

Now explore each of these steps in detail.

Verify That You Have All the Information You Need to Restore a Database

You should have the CREATE DATABASE statements to re-create any databases affected by the lost disk. The good news is that with SQL Server 7.0, as long as you can find your backups (or the backup tape), you can figure out what's on it with the commands you have examined in today's lesson (RESTORE HEADERONLY, RESTORE FILELISTONLY). All the information you need to recover your backups is contained in your backups now with SQL Server 7.0.

Capture the Transaction Log If It's Still Available

If your database files are damaged somehow, and the transaction log files are available (on another disk), you can run the BACKUP LOG command with the NO_TRUNCATE option. The idea here is that you will back up the transaction log entries that have occurred since your last backup, so you can recover those log entries when you are ready to restore your database.

Drop the Database

Because the database is suspect or partially lost, you can drop the database and then prepare for the restore. You run the DROP DATABASE command to drop the database and any files from your server. Note that the DROP DATABASE command works, even if the database is marked suspect.

Replace the Failed Disk

This step should be obvious. You will need, however, to reset any RAID configurations before restarting Windows NT. If you are using Windows NT RAID, you will need to configure the RAID setup in the Disk Administrator program before the next step. Refer to your Windows NT documentation if you are using Windows NT RAID or your hardware documentation otherwise.

Re-Create the Lost Databases (Optional)

If you want, you can re-create the database. This step is optional. The restore process can re-create the database for you.

Restore the Full Database Backup, Any Differential Backup, and Transaction Log Backups As Needed

After all you've learned in this week's lessons, this step should also be self-explanatory. Recover your full database backup and your last differential backup (if it exists), and then apply your transaction log (including the last log backup you made after the disk failed).

8

Run DBCC CHECKDB to Verify a Good Restore (Optional)

This step is optional, but a good idea. Run DBCC CHECKDB on every database you have recovered to verify that your backup and restore operation returned you to a good state. If it didn't for some reason, you will need to go to your previous backup and try the restore again.

That's it! You've successfully recovered your databases! As you can see, it's not rocket science, but it's sufficiently scary that you should practice recovery occasionally so that you are comfortable with each step when it's your production server with the problem instead of your test server.

Recovery After Losing the Master Database

The RESTORE procedure works fine as long as you did not lose your master database. What if you do? There are really two ways you can be affected by a lost master database. They relate to what you can do to repair the damage.

If you have the database or log file that has been corrupted or have logical problems (someone deleted all your logins, or something like that), but you can still get SQL Server running, you can simply restore the master database. However, and frankly the more likely scenario, is that when the master database fails, it will take your server with it. That's why it's such a good idea (as you will examine on Day 20, "Configuring and Monitoring SQL Server 7.0") to mirror the disks that hold your master database and transaction log files.

Restoring the Master Database

First, the easy scenario: To restore your master database from your full database backup, start SQL Server in single-user mode. The easiest way to do this is from a command prompt on the server running SQL Server 7.0. Open a command prompt and run the following sequence of commands:

```
NET STOP MSSQLSERVER
```

This will shut down the MSSQLServer Service.

Next, start SQL Server with the single-user mode switch (-m):

```
SQLSERVR.EXE -m
```

This starts SQL Server as an application running in the command window. Do not type in or close the command window; that's really SQL Server! When SQL Server quits spitting out text (that, not coincidentally, looks like the error logs you examined earlier in today's lesson), it is ready for you to use.

Next, start either your favorite query tool (or SQL Server Enterprise Manager), and restore your master database as you would any other full database backup. When the restore operation is complete, SQL Server will stop itself. Simply start the service to return to normal operations. You can use the following command to restart the service:

```
NET START MSSQLServer
```

Note

> You can restore the master database only when you are in single-user mode. If you aren't, SQL Server Enterprise Manager and the query tools will prevent you from doing so, and you will receive a message like this:
>
> ```
> Server: Msg 3112, Level 16, State 1
> Cannot restore any database other than master
> when the server is in single user mode.
> Server: Msg 3013, Level 16, State 1
> Backup or restore operation terminating abnormally.
> ```
>
> You must finish restoring the master database and restart SQL Server normally before you can restore any other databases.

Any changes you have made to your master database since your last full database backup will need to be manually applied—another fine reason to make frequent backups of your master database.

Rebuilding the Master Database

The other option is that your master database won't be available and functioning, and you'll basically have a dead server. As one of my favorite authors always says, "Don't Panic!" You can make it through this, and maybe even be a hero at the office.

When SQL Server won't start because your master database is dead, it usually means you have lost the disk (or disks) that held any of the master database files. The first step is to run the Rebuild Master utility (rebuildm.exe), found in your \mssql7\binn directory.

This utility assumes SQL Server is not running. When it starts, you will be presented with Figure 8.8, the Rebuild Master utility.

Click the Browse button to locate your \data directory from your CD (I have copied the necessary files to my hard drive in Figure 8.8). Click the Settings button to change the Sort Order, Character Set, or Unicode Collation settings (see Figure 8.9) if you did not accept the defaults when you installed SQL Server.

FIGURE 8.8

The Rebuild Master utility.

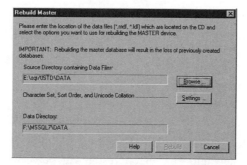

8

FIGURE 8.9

Selecting the appropriate rebuild options.

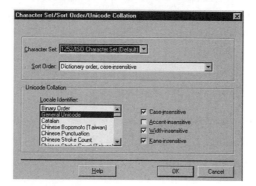

When you've set these options, click OK. Back in the Rebuild Master dialog, click the Rebuild option, and SQL Server will copy the original database files from your CD. This includes all the files for master, msdb, model, pubs, and northwind. It then starts SQL Server, which re-creates your tempdb database, and completes any conversions needed depending on your Sort Order and Character Set choices. When finished, it tells you that the rebuild is complete.

Restore Master and Then Other System Databases

After you have rebuilt your server, restore your master database backup as just described. Then you will need to restore your model database (if you have changed it), the msdb database, and your distribution database if this server is a distribution server used in replication.

Attach or Restore Databases If Necessary

Finally, restore any other databases that were affected. If you still have the database files, use the CREATE DATABASE FOR ATTACH command or sp_attach_db system stored procedure to reattach the databases to SQL Server.

DBCCs on the Entire Server

Finally, because you live in the land of the paranoid, after a crash like this, run DBCC CHECKDB on every database to verify that your server is back up and running without any corruption.

Summary

Backup and recovery is probably the most important part of maintaining your SQL Server system. As you saw in today's lesson, restore can be very straightforward using SQL Server Enterprise Manager, or it can get a bit complicated when rebuilding or restoring the master database. The only advice I can give you is to test backup and restore on a regular basis. It's the only way you will ever feel comfortable with this process.

Q&A

Q What is the command to restore a database from a backup?

A The RESTORE DATABASE command.

Q Which command would I use to restore a differential backup of the master database?

A You can't make one, so it's not an issue. You can only make full database backups of the master database.

Q What is the command to restore a transaction log but leave the database in an unrecovered state?

A The RESTORE LOG WITH NORECOVERY command.

Workshop

The Workshop provides quiz questions to help you solidify your understanding of the concepts presented in this chapter. In addition to the quiz questions, exercises are provided to let you practice what you have learned in this chapter. Try to understand the quiz and exercise answers before continuing to the next day's lesson. Answers are provided in Appendix A, "Answers."

Quiz

1. If you rebuild the master database, what other database must be recovered?
2. If you specify the `RESTORE FILELISTONLY` command, what will you get as a result?
3. Can you restore a backup made with multiple tapes onto a server with a single tape drive?
4. What configuration option is used to tune automatic recovery?
5. If your manager accidentally dropped the payroll table, how would you recover it?

Exercises

1. Create a test database, back it up, and then test restoring it. Try this for a full database backup, and then also test recovering transaction logs. Make changes to your database, such as creating a table, between each transaction log backup. When you restore, apply each transaction log and verify that only the appropriate changes are recovered with each restore.

2. Back up your database, make some changes, and then make a differential backup. Finally, make a transaction log backup after making additional changes. Restore from the backups using Transact-SQL commands only, and verify that the restores were successful.

3. Repeat number 2. However, stop after the full database backup using the `STANDBY` option after each restore, and examine the state of your database to see what's happening and verify that your changes really are being rolled forward and back. Of course, perform a `WITH RECOVERY` on the final transaction log restore.

DAY 9

Creating Tables

In yesterday's lesson, you learned how to restore your databases from backups. You looked at the different recovery mechanisms that SQL Server 7.0 uses. These include automatic recovery and manual recovery. You learned how to restore a single database, as well as how to apply transaction log backups to bring your database to point-in-time recovery. Now that you are finished being paranoid about your backups and restoration plans, you can learn how to create tables and add data to your database.

In today's lesson, you will learn how to add tables to your database. You first are presented with an overview of tables, and then look at the different data types used to create your tables. You then learn how to put all the information together to create and modify tables in your database using code. Then you'll see how Microsoft has simplified the code process for you by enabling you to create tables graphically with the SQL Server Enterprise Manager. As with other days' lessons, you are presented with some real-world questions and answers as well as a quiz and exercises.

Tables

Tables store all the data in your database and are organized into rows and columns (records and fields). Each column in your table can store a specific type of information or *data type*.

A single table represents an entity in your database. Each row in the table represents an occurrence of that entity. The columns in your table describe the attributes of that logical entity. For example, you might create a table of employees (where employees are a logical entity). A single row in your employees table represents a single instance of an employee. The columns that make up that table describe the employee. Some columns you might include are EmployeeID, FirstName, LastName, SSN (Social Security number), and others.

Now examine the concept of columns.

Columns

Each column (field) in your table must be assigned a name, a data type, optionally a length, and a nullability status. You can place columns in any order in your table definition. Each column must also have a unique name within the table and follow the rules for SQL Server identifiers.

A single database can have up to 2 billion tables in it, with each table holding up to 1,024 columns. The maximum length of any row is 8,092 bytes, less overhead inherent in the physical storage of rows in SQL Server. That overhead will vary depending on many factors beyond the scope of this book.

The maximum length for a single column is 8,000 bytes, and you can have up to 1,024 columns in a row; however, a row might not exceed a data page (8,192 bytes) for data and overhead. The exception to this is for the text and image data types, which allow up to 2GB of textual or binary information. These are not physically stored as part of a table row, so they do not count against the restriction that a data row fit in a single data page. You learn more about column lengths as well as table and row overhead later in this today's lesson.

SQL Server Identifiers

All SQL Server table names, as well as column names and any other object name, must follow the rules for SQL Server identifiers listed here:

- Identifiers can be from 1 to 128 Unicode characters in length including letters, symbols, and numbers.

- The first character must be a letter or the following symbols: @, #, or _ (underscore). @ and # have special meanings in SQL Server.

- You can use the following symbols after the first character: #, $, and _.

- Identifiers that begin with the @ symbol are used as local variables. Note that the @ symbol can appear only as the first character in an identifier.

- Identifiers that begin with the # symbol are used to signify that the object you are creating is a temporary object and can be referenced by the user during the session.

- Identifiers that begin with the ## symbol are used to signify that the object you are creating is a global temporary object and can be referenced by all users in the database.

- You can use embedded spaces in your identifiers, but to reference those objects you must encapsulate them in either double quotation marks or square brackets. For example, a table named Employee Pension would need to be referenced as "Employee Pension" or [Employee Pension] in the database. It is preferable (if you insist on using spaces in your identifier names) to use the square bracket syntax so as not to confuse constant strings with SQL Server identifiers.

Note Although using symbols and embedded spaces in identifiers is allowed in SQL Server, most developers avoid their use because they can lead to confusing SQL statements.

Table 9.1 shows some examples of valid and invalid identifiers.

TABLE 9.1 VALID AND INVALID IDENTIFIERS

Identifier	Comments
1001ArabianNights	Invalid identifier. Identifiers must begin with a letter.
@Addresses	This is only a valid identifier for creating a variable.
Table@Address	Invalid identifier. The @ symbol can only be the first character in an identifier.
#tblCities	This identifier is valid only if you are creating a temporary object that will be available to the user who created it.
##tblCities	This identifier is valid only if you are creating a temporary object that will be available to all users.

continues

TABLE 9.1 CONTINUED

Identifier	Comments
TblEmployee	Valid identifier. Although prefixing identifiers (tbl for table) is not necessary, it does make your SQL statements easier to read because the prefix denotes what the identifier represents. Other common identifiers are qry for query, tr for trigger, sp_ for system-stored procedures, and so on.
Titles	This is a valid identifier.
Author_Review	This is a valid identifier.
AuthorReview	This is a valid identifier.

Data Types

The data type specifies what kind of information (numeric, character, and so on) and how much space that information takes up in a particular column. Some data types have a variable length, while others have a fixed length. SQL Server data types can be broken down into the following groups: string, Unicode strings, binary, integer, approximate and exact numeric, special, date and time, money, autoincrementing, synonyms, user-defined, and computed column. Table 9.2 lists the different data types allowed in SQL Server 7.0.

TABLE 9.2 SQL SERVER 7.0 SUPPORTED DATA TYPES

Category	Data Type	Comments
String	char(n), varchar	Stores character strings.
Binary	binary(n), varbinary	Stores binary information in two-byte pairs.
Integer	int, smallint, tinyint	Stores integer values.
Approx. Numeric	float, real	Stores approximate numeric information.
Exact Numeric	decimal, numeric	Stores exact numeric information.
Special	bit, text, image	Stores a single bit, character information greater than 8,000 bytes, or image data.
Date and Time	datetime, smalldatetime	Stores dates and times.

Category	Data Type	Comments
Money	money, smallmoney	Stores currency values.
Auto-incrementing data types	timestamp	Stores values that are automatically incremented or set by the SQL Server.
Synonyms	(See Table 9.8)	Maps ANSI data types to SQL Server data types.
User-defined	(See Table 9.8)	You can create your own data types to store information.
Computed columns	(See Table 9.8)	Stores the expression used to compute the column. Note that it does not store the data, just the expressions used to create it.
Unicode data	Nchar, ntext, nvarchar	Stores data in a Unicode (double byte per stored character) format.

Nullability

The nullability of a column refers to whether an entry is required for that column. If you would like to allow a column to indicate that the value is unknown, specify NULL. If you would like to insist that each row must have an entry in that column, specify NOT NULL. If you do not specify NULL or NOT NULL, the default value for the database (or the SQL Server connection) will be used. When you first install SQL Server, the default in each database is that columns will be created with the NOT NULL option. As with most options in SQL Server, this default can be modified, even on a connection-by-connection basis. Therefore, it is an extremely good idea to always specify whether you want a column to have the NULL or NOT NULL attribute.

Now examine each data type that is available for your use in SQL Server 7.0.

Strings

Strings contain character data made up of letters, numbers, and symbols. You can store character data in either a fixed-length or a variable-length format using the char(n) or varchar(n) keywords. You can store a maximum of 8,000 characters in these data types.

When you create a fixed-length field, you are specifying that this field will always contain n bytes of information. If the data you entered in the field is less than n, it will be padded with spaces so that it always takes up *n* bytes. If you try to put more than *n* bytes of data in the field, your data will be truncated. Table 9.3 shows some examples of entering data into a field declared as Fname char(8). (The symbol * denotes a space in this example.)

TABLE 9.3 FIXED-LENGTH CHARACTER FIELDS

Data Entered	Fname *Contains*
Lawrence	Lawrence
Mark Anthony	Mark Ant
Denise	Denise**

When you use variable-length fields, you specify the maximum length that the field can be. But unlike fixed-length fields, the variable-length fields are not padded with spaces. This might make your database more efficient from a memory standpoint, but you will pay a price in performance. When a field has been declared as variable length, SQL Server will have to determine where the field stops and the next field begins. There is additional overhead associated with variable-length fields in the form of bytes added to the rows and the table. Varchar is useful when you are expecting a wide variation in data size, or you are going to allow null values in your field.

When you enter character data into SQL Server, you must enclose the data in single or double quotation marks. Single quotation marks are preferable so there is no confusion between string constants and SQL Server identifiers. To enter NULL into a field in SQL Server, use the NULL keyword without quotation marks.

Listing 9.1 shows an example of creating a table using the char and varchar keywords.

LISTING 9.1 USING CHAR AND VARCHAR

```
CREATE TABLE tblCustomers
(
CustID char(8) NOT NULL,
CustName varchar(30) NOT NULL,
Email varchar(50) NULL
)
```

Binary Data

The binary data type stores binary data. Binary data is stored as a series of 1s and 0s, which are represented on input and output as hexadecimal pairs. These hexadecimal pairs are made up of the characters 0 through 9 and A through F. For example, if you create a field like `SomeData binary(20)`, you are specifying that you are going to have 20 bytes of data.

As with the string data types, you can specify a maximum of 8,000 bytes for both the `binary(n)` and `varbinary(n)` data types. If you use the `binary(n)` data type, information you enter will be padded with spaces (`0x20`). The `varbinary` data type does not pad. If you attempt to enter data longer than the specified maximum length, the data will be truncated.

To enter data into a binary data type, you must precede the string with `0x`. For example, to enter the value `10` into a binary field, you would prefix it like this: `0x10`.

Here are some sample statements:

```
MyIcons varbinary(255)
```

```
MyCursors binary(200)
```

```
TinyWav varbinary(255)
```

Integers

There are three types of integer data types: `int`, `smallint`, and `tinyint`, which store exact, scalar values. The difference between the integer data types is the amount of storage space they require and the range of values they can store. Table 9.4 displays the integer data types and their ranges.

TABLE 9.4 INTEGER DATA TYPES

Data Type	Length	Range
Tinyint	1	0–255
Smallint	2	±32, 767
Int	4	±2, 147, 483, 647

Here are some sample declarations:

```
EmployeeAge tinyint NULL
```

```
EmployeeID smallint NOT NULL
```

```
CustomerID int NOT NULL
```

Tip

Integer data types perform better (in terms of storage, retrieval, and mathematical calculations) than any other data type. If you can use an Integer data type, it's the best way to go.

Approximate and Exact Numeric Data Types

SQL Server allows both approximate data types `float` and `real`, as well as exact numeric data types `decimal` and `numeric`. When you declare approximate data types, you specify a precision that is the maximum number of digits allowed on both sides of the decimal point. When you declare an exact data type, you must also specify a scale, which is the total number of digits allowed on the right side of the decimal point.

Table 9.5 lists the precision values allowed for both approximate and exact numeric data types and the number of storage bytes required.

TABLE 9.5   PRECISION AND STORAGE REQUIREMENTS

Precision	Storage
1–9	5
10–19	9
20–28	13
30–38	17

Note

SQL Server supports a default maximum precision of 28 digits. This is to ensure compatibility with the limits of front-end development tools like Microsoft Visual Basic and PowerBuilder. It is possible to modify this value. If you start SQL Server 7.0 with the /p option, a default precision of 38 will be used.

Approximate Numeric Data Types

The approximate numeric data types are `float(n)` and `real`. The numbers stored in these data types are made up of two parts: the mantissa and the exponent. The algorithm used to produce these two parts is not exactly precise. In other words, you might not get back exactly what you put in. This becomes a problem only when the precision of the number stored approaches the precision specified by the data type. For example, the precision allowed for floats is up to 38 digits. Floats and reals are useful for scientific and statistical data for which absolute accuracy is not necessary, but where your values range from extremely small to extremely large numbers.

Reals have a precision of seven digits and require 4 bytes of data storage. If you declare a float and specify a precision of less than 7, you are really creating a real data type. Floats can have a precision from 1 to 38. By default, a float has a 15-digit precision if no value is specified. You can perform all calculations on a float with the exception of modulo. (Modulo returns the integer remainder of integer division.)

For example, suppose you create the following data type:

```
SomeVal real
```

You can store the numbers 188,445.2 or 1,884.452, but not the values 188,445.27 or 1,884.4527 because they are longer than the default precision of seven digits. To hold these larger values, you should create a float variable with a precision large enough to hold all the digits. Because there are eight digits total, you declare your data type like this:

```
SomeVal float(8)
```

 Caution In general, you should avoid using float and real data types. If you can store the information you need in the decimal and numeric data types, you should do so. Calculations using float and real data types can lead to interesting and confusing results.

Exact Numeric Data Types

Exact numeric data types are `decimal` and `numeric`. Accuracy will be preserved to the least significant digit. When you declare an exact numeric data type, you should specify both a precision and a scale.

If you do not specify a precision and scale, SQL Server will use the default values of 18 and 0. Here is something interesting: If you specify a scale of 0, you are creating the equivalent of an integer data type because there can be 0 digits to the right of the decimal point. This is interesting because you can have very large, very precise numeric values that are bigger than ±2 billion.

If a column is declared as `decimal(7,2)`, it can hold the number 1000.55 and 11000.55, but not the numbers 11110000.55 or 1100.5678. If you attempt to place a number larger than is allowed by the precision and scale, the number will be truncated.

Listing 9.2 shows an example of using exact numeric data types.

LISTING 9.2   USING NUMERIC DATA TYPES

```
CREATE TABLE tblGold
(
AtomicWeight decimal(8,4),
MolesPerOunce numeric(12,6),
Density numeric(5,4)
)
```

Special Data Types

Several data types just don't fall well into any category. I have added them here in the
special data types section. You will learn about the `bit` data type and the two BLOB
(binary large object) data types, `text` and `image`, as well as the `RowGUID` data type (often
pronounced as "Row-Goo-id").

bit

The `bit` data type is a logical data type used to store Boolean information. Boolean data
types are used as flags to signify things like on/off, true/false, and yes/no. The values
stored here are either a 0 or a 1.

Bit columns can be NULL (unknown) and cannot be indexed. Bit data types require a single byte of storage space. If you have several bit columns defined in a table, SQL Server
will automatically group up to eight bit fields together into a single byte of storage space.
Here is an example of using the `bit` data type:

```
Gender bit NOT NULL
```

```
Paid bit NULL
```

```
Printed bit NOT NULL
```

Text and Image

`Text` and `image` data types are used when storage requirements exceed the 8,000-charac-
ter column limitations. These data types are often referred to as BLOBs. The text and
image data types can store up to 2GB of binary or text data per declaration.

When you declare a text or image data type, a 16-byte pointer will be added to the row.
This 16-byte pointer will point to a separate 8KB data page where additional information
about your data will be stored. If your data exceeds an 8KB data page, then pointers will
be constructed to point to the additional pages of your BLOB.

The storage and retrieval of text and image data can hamper your database performance because large amounts of data will be applied to your transaction logs during inserts, updates, and deletes. You can get around this problem by using the WRITETEXT command because this will apply changes to the data without making a corresponding entry to the transaction log.

> **Note**
>
> When you use nonlogged operations, you should back up your database immediately because the recoverability of your database is now at issue (as you examined on Day 7, "Implementing Backups in SQL Server 7.0").

An alternative to the large storage requirements of text and image data is to store these items as separate files and then store the path to those files in your database.

Here are some sample declarations of the text and image data types:

```
EmployeePhoto image
ScannedContracts image
Description text
Comments text
```

RowGUID

When you use merge replication, as discussed on Day 17, "Understanding Replication Design Methodologies" and Day 18, "Implementing Replication Methodologies," each column in your replicated tables must have a unique identifier. You accomplish this by creating a column in every replicated table as a uniqueidentifier data type. This uniqueidentifier data type has a property called ROWGUIDCOL. When the ROWGUIDCOL property is turned on, a globally unique identifier (GUID) can be assigned to the column. In this way, columns in one version of the replicated table will have the same GUID as in another version of the same table. If you make a change to a row in a replicated table with a ROWGUIDCOL, the ROWGUIDCOL will be modified by SQL Server. In this way, replicated rows from two databases can be tracked separately.

You can initialize GUIDs in two ways:

- Use the NEWID function.
- Convert a string constant into a hexadecimal digit in the form of (xxxxxxxx-xxxx-xxxx-xxxx-xxxxxxxxxxxx). Here is an example of a valid RowGUID: 8FE17A24-B1AA-23DA-C790-2749A3E09AA2.

You can use the following comparison operators with your `uniqueidentifier` data types:

- =
- <>
- IS NULL
- IS NOT NULL

Date and Time Data Types

Date and time data can be stored in either a `datetime` or a `smalldatetime` data type. It is interesting to note that date and time are always stored together in a single value.

Date and time data can take several different formats. You can specify the month using the full name or an abbreviation. The case is ignored and commas are optional.

Here are some examples using the alpha formats for April 15, 1996.

"Apr 15 1996"

"Apr 15 96"

"Apr 96 15"

"15 Apr 96"

"1996 April 15"

"1996 15 April"

 Note   If only the last two digits of the year are given, SQL Server will interpret values of less than 50 as 20yy, while numbers greater than or equal to 50 will be interpreted as 19yy. For example, April 15 03 would be interpreted as April 15, 2003.

You can also specify the ordinal value for the month. The ordinal value of an item is the positional value within a list of items. In the previous examples, April is the fourth month of the year, so you can use the number 4 as its designation.

Here are some examples using the ordinal value for April 15, 1996:

4/15/96 (mdy)

4-15-96 (mdy)

4.15.96(mdy)

4/96/15 (myd)

15/96/04 (dym)

96/15/04 (ymd)

There are several different time formats you can use also. Here are some examples:

16:30 (4 hrs, 30 mins)

16:30:20:999 (4 hrs, 30 mins, 22 seconds, 999 milliseconds)

4:30PM

Dates stored in the datetime data type are stored to the millisecond. A total of 8 bytes are used—4 for the number of days since January 1, 1900, and 4 for the number of seconds past midnight. (Dates prior to this are stored as negative numbers, making the range of dates 1/1/1753 to 12/31/9999.) The accuracy of your dates is within 3.33 milliseconds.

The smalldatetime data type uses a total of 4 bytes. Dates stored this way are accurate to the minute. Internally, one smallint (two bytes) is used for the number of days after January 1, 1900, and the other smallint is used for the number of seconds past midnight. The range for a smalldatetime are from 1/1/1900 to 6/6/2079.

Table 9.6 delineates the datetime data types.

TABLE 9.6 DATE TIME DATA TYPES

Data Type	Storage	Range
Datetime	8	1/1/1753–12/31/9999
Smalldatetime	4	1/1/1900–6/6/2079

Tip

Use smalldatetime for current dates in databases, especially those that are transitory in nature. These would be dates that you are not going to be using for more than a few years.

Do not use datetime to store partial dates like just the month, day, or year. If the only data you need is the year, a smallint or tinyint would be much more efficient. If you do not do this, then you will have to parse the date yourself every time you wish to insert, update, or otherwise work with the information.

Money

There are two money data types: money and smallmoney. Both have a scale of four, meaning they store four digits to the right of the decimal point. These data types can store information other than dollar values for international use, but there are no monetary conversion functions available in SQL Server. When you enter monetary data, you should precede it with a dollar sign. Table 9.7 shows you the money data types, their requirements, and their ranges.

TABLE 9.7 MONEY DATA TYPES

Data Type	Storage	Range
Money	8	±922,337,203,685,447.5808
Smallmoney	4	±214,748,3647

As you can see, smallmoney can hold up to 10 digits with a scale of four. The money data type is large enough to hold the U.S. national debt, with values in the hundreds of trillions.

Here are a couple sample declarations using the money data types:

```
AccountsReceivable money
```

```
AccountsPayable smallmoney
```

The Timestamp Data Type

Every time you add a new record to a table with a timestamp field, time values will automatically be added. timestamps go a bit further. If you make an update to a row, the timestamp will automatically update itself.

The timestamp data type creates a SQL Server-generated, unique, automatically updated value. Although the timestamp looks like a datetime data type, it is not. Timestamps are stored as binary(8) for NOT NULL columns or varbinary(8) if the column is marked as allowing null values. You can have no more than one timestamp column per row.

Note   The timestamp data type does not reflect the system time. It is simply a constantly increasing counter value.

You can use the timestamp data type to track the order in which items are added and modified in your table. Here are some examples using the timestamp data type:

```
LastModified timestamp NOT NULL
```

```
PhoneCall timestamp NOT NULL
```

Synonyms

To ensure that SQL Server data types map to American National Standards Institute (ANSI) data types, you can use the ANSI data types in place of the SQL Server data types. Table 9.8 lists the ANSI data types and their SQL Server equivalents.

TABLE 9.8 SQL SERVER SYNONYMS

ANSI Data Type	SQL Server Data Type
Character	Char
Character(n)	char(n)
char varying	Varchar
Character varying(n)	varchar(n)
binary varying	Varbinary
Dec	Decimal
double precision	Float
float(n) n = 1 - 7	Real
float(n) n = 8 - 15	Float
Integer	Int

9

Unicode Data

Unicode data uses the Unicode UCS-2 character set, which is a multibyte character set. When you use normal ANSI characters, one byte of data is required to store any given character. ANSI is sometimes referred to as "narrow" because of this. Unicode is known as a wide or multibyte character set. The UCS-2 Unicode character set uses 2 bytes to represent a single character. This is especially useful when you are dealing with databases that have different languages represented within them. For example, there are few enough letters in the English and Spanish languages that a single-byte character set can easily represent all letters in the alphabet. Now think of a language like Japanese. Even standard Japanese (Kana) has more than 1,000 characters in it. A standard 8-bit byte can represent only 256 characters, whereas a multibyte Unicode character can represent 65,536 characters.

You can use the nchar, nvarchar, and ntext data types to represent your Unicode information. nchar and nvarchar have a maximum limit of 8,000 bytes or 4,000 characters. For example, nchar(4000) is valid, but nchar(6000) represents 12,000 characters and will not fit on a single data page. Your nchar(6000) should either be broken into two separate nchar data types or a single ntext data type. The ntext data type can support up to 2.14GB of data.

Unicode data types are an extremely powerful new feature of SQL Server 7.0. If you have any plans for internationalization or using your SQL Server in countries that don't use U.S. English, storing your data with the Unicode data types is an excellent solution. Look for Unicode to become more of the standard storage mechanism as both Windows NT and SQL Server become better international solutions.

User-Defined Data Types

You can create user-defined data types for a specific database or to place in the model database. Remember, the model database is a template for creating new databases. In doing so, you can have your new user-defined data type available in all subsequent databases.

To create a user-defined data type, you must use the system-provided data types. For example, you can create a new data type called EmployeeID and define it as character or integer, but not as some nonexistent data type like column_id.

You must create the user-defined data type before you add it to a table. To create a user-defined data type, you can use the SQL Server Enterprise Manager or the sp_addtype system-stored procedure. You learn more about user-defined data types on Day 14, "Ensuring Data Integrity."

To create user-defined data types using SQL Server, use the sp_addtype system-stored procedure. For example, to add the same three user-defined data types to the pubs database, run the following SQL:

```
sp_addtype empid, 'char(9)', 'NULL'
sp_addtype id, 'varchar(11)', 'NULL'
sp_addtype tid, 'varchar(6)', 'NULL'
```

After you have declared a user-defined data type, you can use it as many times as you like in your database. For example, you can use the following CREATE TABLE statement:

```
CREATE TABLE tblEmployee
(
EmployeeId empid NOT NULL,
Fname char(15) NOT NULL,
Lname char(20) NOT NULL,
PensionPlan id NOT NULL
)
```

To add user-defined data types with the SQL Server Enterprise Manager, follow these steps:

1. Open the SQL Server Enterprise Manager.
2. Drill down to your pubs database.
3. Drill down to the User Defined Datatypes folder.
4. Right-click the folder and choose New User Defined Data Type from the context menu.
5. Fill in the Name, data type, length, and any rules or defaults it's bound to.
6. Click OK when you are finished.

To drop user-defined data types, you can use the SQL Server Enterprise Manager or the sp_droptype system-stored procedure.

In the SQL Server Enterprise Manager, follow these steps:

1. Expand your database and highlight the User Defined Data Types folder.
2. In the right panel, right-click the user-defined data type you want to drop and click Delete.

That's all there is to it. Using Transact-SQL, you can run the sp_droptype system-stored procedure like this:

```
sp_droptype empid
```

 Note

> A user-defined data type cannot be dropped if it is still in use in a table or has a rule or default bound to it. You examine what these terms mean on Day 14.

Computed Columns

A computed column is an exciting new feature in SQL Server 7.0. A computed column does not store computed data—rather, it stores the expression used to compute the data. For example, I might create a computed column on my table called Total with an expression of Total AS price * quantity.

The expressions you store can be created from a noncomputed column in the same table, constants, functions, variables, and even names. Your computed column will automatically compute the data when it is called in a SELECT, WHERE, and ORDER BY clauses of a query (which you examine on Day 11, "Retrieving Data with Queries"). They can also be used with regular expressions.

There are a few rules to follow when you are dealing with computed columns:

- Columns referenced in the computed-column expression must be in the same table.
- The computed-column expression cannot contain a subquery.
- Computed columns cannot be used as any part of keys or indexes; this includes Fkeys, Pkeys, and unique indexes.
- A computed column cannot have a DEFAULT constraint attached to it.
- Computed columns cannot receive INSERT or UPDATE statements.

Here are a couple of examples using computed columns:

```
CREATE TABLE tblOrder (
OrdID int NOT NULL,
Price money NOT NULL,
Qty smallint NOT NULL,
Total AS Price * Qty
)
```

This first table has a computed column called Total, which is made up of the price * qty fields.

```
CREATE TABLE tblPrintInvoice (
InvoiceID int NOT NULL,
InvDate datetime NOT NULL,
PrintDate AS DateAdd(day,30, InvDate)
)
```

In this example, you have a computed column called PrintDate that uses the DateAdd function to add 30 days to the InvDate column.

Create Tables

Now that you have seen all the data types available in SQL Server 7.0, it's time to put it all together with the CREATE TABLE statement. As with most things in SQL Server, there are two ways to create tables. You can use the SQL Server Enterprise Manager or you can use Transact-SQL scripts. You will first learn more about the CREATE TABLE statement.

CREATE TABLE

SYNTAX ▼

```
CREATE TABLE [database.[owner.]table_name
(
column_name datatype [identity¦constraint¦NULL¦NOT NULL]
[…]
)
```

▼ where

- *table_name* is the name of the new table following the rules for identifiers. It must also be unique within the database for its owner. This means that if two users have permission to create tables within a database, the tables themselves might have the same name, but they will still be considered unique because the owner's name forms part of the table name.

- *column_name* is the column name and must follow the rules for identifiers.

- *datatype* is the data type of the column.

▲ - The last piece is optional. You can specify the Identity property, field constraints, and nullability.

Listing 9.3 shows a sample CREATE TABLE statement.

LISTING 9.3 CREATING A TABLE

```
CREATE TABLE employees
(
emp_id tinyint IDENTITY NOT NULL,
Fname char(15),
Lname char(20) NOT NULL,
Address1 varchar(30),
Address2 varchar(30),
city varchar(30),
state char(2),
zipcode char(10),
start_date datetime
)
```

Caution

The previous CREATE TABLE statement is significantly simplified from what you would find in the SQL Server Books Online. Many of the additional options are specific to ANSI constraints, which you examine in great detail on Day 14.

Creating Tables with SQL Server Enterprise Manager

Using the SQL Server Enterprise Manager, you can visually create your tables. To create a table using SQL Server Enterprise Manager, follow these steps:

1. Connect to your SQL Server, expand your databases folder, and then expand the database you want to work with. Then highlight the Tables folder as shown in Figure 9.1.

FIGURE 9.1

Start in the Tables folder for the database where you want to add a table.

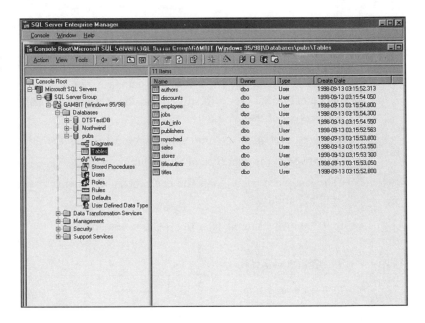

2. Right-click in the right pane and choose New Table from the context menu.

3. You will be asked to enter a table name, as shown in Figure 9.2. Add a name and click OK. In my example, I have used tblEmployees.

FIGURE 9.2

Enter the table name.

4. Now you can add information to Column Name, Datatype, Length, Precision, Scale, and Allow Nulls fields. If you want to create an Identity field, click the check box and then choose an identity seed and increment. You learn more about the `Default` and `IsRowGUID` on Day 14. As you can see in Figure 9.3, I have added several fields to my `tblEmployees` table.

5. When you are finished, click the Save icon to save your table, and then close the dialog box.

FIGURE 9.3

You can use the grid to specify the fields and properties instead of using code.

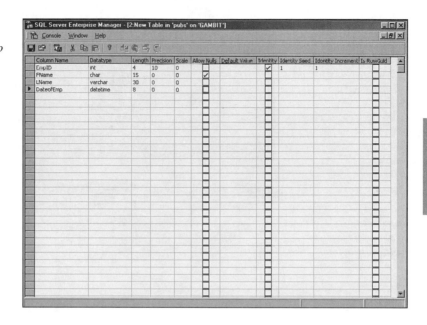

Dropping Tables

You can easily drop tables in SQL Server Enterprise Manager by right-clicking the table and selecting Delete from the context menu. To drop a table using Transact-SQL, run the DROP TABLE statement. For example, to drop the tblEmployees table, run

```
DROP TABLE tblEmployees
```

> **Note**
>
> System tables cannot be dropped.

To drop a table using the SQL Server Enterprise Manager, follow these steps:

1. Drill down to the Tables folder and right-click the table you want to drop. Choose Delete.
2. You will get a dialog similar to the one shown in Figure 9.4.
3. If you want to see any dependencies on this table, click the Show Dependencies button shown in Figure 9.4. Figure 9.5 shows the General tab, listing all the table's relational dependencies. When the table is no longer participating in any Primary Key/Foreign Key relationships, you can click the Drop All button shown in Figure 9.4 to remove the table. Again, these relationships are described in detail on Day 14.

FIGURE 9.4

You can drop the tables listed in this dialog or check for dependencies.

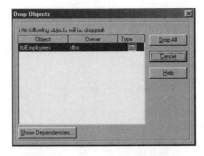

FIGURE 9.5

You should be aware of dependencies before dropping a table to ensure relational integrity.

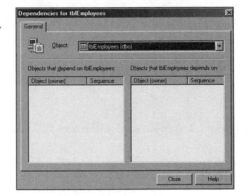

Summary

SQL Server has many native data types, which you can use to create columns within your tables. You must choose the data type for each column carefully because your choice can impact performance and the need for storage space. In addition, you cannot change the data type without dropping and re-creating the table.

SQL Server also enables you to create user-defined data types. You can use the sp_addtype system-stored procedure SQL Server Enterprise Manager to create them. They must be based on a native data type, and they must be defined before they are used in a table.

You can create tables with the SQL Server Enterprise Manager table editor or with the CREATE TABLE statement.

Q&A

Q Do you need to use user-defined data types?

A No. User-defined data types are not required, but they can make your columns and CREATE TABLE statements more readable. They also enable you to create a data type that can be reused in multiple locations.

Q What are some general rules when dealing with numeric values?

A Excellent question! Integer data types are the fastest data types in SQL Server and also require a small amount of storage space. If you can save your information in an int, tinyint, or smallint, do it. For larger number, or numbers that require a decimal point, you should use the exact numeric data types decimal and numeric rather than float and real. Floats and reals do not have the precision of the exact numeric data types.

Q What are some general rules when dealing with character data?

A This really depends on the type of character data you are dealing with. If you have columns that vary in length only a little (5 to 10 characters), then using a fixed-length column is probably a better choice than a variable-length field. Variable-length fields add about three bytes of overhead per row to your database and are slower to process than a fixed-length field. If your fixed-length fields vary greatly (20–100 characters), then a variable-length field might be a better choice. You really must weigh the speed of one type over another versus the amount of storage space lost on fixed-length data.

Q You said that I could have as many as 2 billion tables in my database. How many tables should I have?

A This really depends on the business scenario you are trying to model. If you have anything near 100,000 tables in your database, you might need to do some design work. A typical database of 5–10GB will have anywhere from 20 to 75 tables. Larger systems might have more.

Q Because text and image data types take up so much room in my database and are not logged when added, deleted, or modified, what are some other ways of handling these BLOBs?

A Many companies have found it useful to put their BLOBs in a separate directory on a fast file server somewhere on the network. They then store the path to the file in the SQL Server database as a varchar item. This approach has some advantages and disadvantages. The main disadvantage is consistency. If someone moves or deletes the file, how is SQL Server going to be notified of the update? On the upside, if you have thousands of documents or images, you are not using valuable storage space in your database.

9

Q What is the most important thing to remember about creating tables?

A The three rules of real estate are location, location, location. The three rules of database are design, design, design. Coming from a programming background, I always want to jump right in and start coding the project. I have found that in the long run this creates a lot of spaghetti code and tables in my database, and an exponentially increasing lack of efficiency. Spend the time designing your tables, relationships, user-defined data types, and constraints before you implement them. Keep printed documentation of your design somewhere as well. It is an invaluable tool for anyone who must prepare to maintain your SQL Server system.

Workshop

The Workshop provides quiz questions to help you solidify your understanding of the concepts presented in this chapter. In addition to the quiz questions, exercises are provided to let you practice what you have learned in this chapter. Try to understand the quiz and exercise answers before continuing to the next day's lesson. Answers are provided in Appendix A, "Answers."

Quiz

1. When should you choose the `char` data type over the `varchar` data type?
2. When should you choose the `varchar` data type over the `char` data type?
3. What are your alternatives to the `text` data type? When should you use each of them?
4. What would you specify are the best practices for using data types in SQL Server?
5. Which data type would you use for the following data (be sure to add any characteristics such as number of items in the string or the precision or scale)?
   a. Zip code
   b. Birth date
   c. Year of car manufacture
   d. Vehicle identification number
   e. Store ID where 95 percent of the stores require a 10-digit alphanumeric entry. The other 5 percent vary in size, but none require over 10 digits. The company owner is thinking of requiring all stores to have a 10-digit store number.
   f. Company name where the name varies in length from 10 to 50 characters.

    g. A date value in a short-term database. Dates will range over a period of 10 years.

    h. Money where you need to account for a scale of six.

6. You have created a table using the following CREATE TABLE statement:

```
CREATE TABLE table1
(
id char(10),
fname char(15) NULL,
lname char(15) NOT NULL,
comment varchar(255)
)
```

What is the maximum size of a row in this table?

7. Can the following CREATE TABLE statement be implemented? Why or why not?

```
CREATE TABLE phooey
(id char(10) NOT NULL,
fname char(15) NULL,
lname char(15) NOT NULL,
comment varchar(255),
notes text,
directions varchar(255),
house_picture image)
```

What is the maximum row size?

Exercises

First write down the answers to the following questions. When you are sure your answers are correct, create these objects in the database:

1. How would you create the following user-defined data types:

```
zip_code

phone_number

store_id

fax

email
```

2. What is the SQL required to create a table to hold information about stores. Data should include store identification, name, address, city, state, zip, owner, contact, fax, and email.

3. What is the SQL required to create a table to hold information about store sales. Data should include store identification, sales date, total sales, total returns, and deposit.

DAY 10

Using SQL Server 7.0 Data Transformation Services

In yesterday's lesson you learned how to create tables in SQL Server. You learned how to use data types, which describe the types of data to be stored in each column. You also learned how to create and use your own user-defined data types.

In today's lesson you will learn how to move and modify data from one data source to another. SQL Server 7.0 has three principal methods for moving data and one for both moving and transforming data.

You can use a backup-and-restore methodology to move all data and other objects, such as tables, from one location to another. This approach will not make changes to your data. You can use Bulk Copy Program (BCP) to transfer just data from one location to another. Although this utility will not make changes to your data, you can use it to gather certain columns and rows from one data source and transfer them to another. You will also take a look at the advantages of using a bulk insert to quickly move data from a file to your database.

The final element is the new Data Transformation Services (DTS) Manager in SQL Server 7.0. This utility at first glance is similar to the old Transfer Manager Interface found in SQL Server 6.x. DTS can be used to move data, schema, or both data and schema. DTS also includes the capability to transform (modify) your data. You can use DTS to change the format of your data from one data type to another, restructure and map your data to different tables, make your data consistent, and validate your data. You can include data logic to summarize, decode, convert, and decompose data.

In the past, much of this logic had to be handled through another utility or programming language such as Delphi or Visual Basic. SQL Server 7.0 includes this programmability with DTS through data transformation packages. Because these packages are complete modular units, you can incorporate them into your job scheduler for automated information transfer and modification.

Time to get to work. You'll first review using backup and restore to move data from one location to another. You will then take a closer look at the BCP program. You will finish today's lesson with a discussion of DTS. The DTS section is further broken down into the DTS packager and creating workflows.

Backup and Restore

You can use backup and restore to move your databases between servers, but it's probably not the optimal solution. When you back up the database, you also back up all the system tables, including the sysusers system table in the database. This can cause problems when you recover the database on another server. If the new server doesn't have all the same logins, the mappings for security might be compromised.

Microsoft now ships SQL Server 7.0 with a system stored procedure called sp_change_users_login. This stored procedure fixes the biggest problem with using the backup-and-restore technique: the invalid security mappings. After you've completed the restore, run this system stored procedure. But first you must verify that the logins are appropriately matched to users.

 Note

> Using backup and restore to move data from one SQL Server to another is not recommended for day-to-day movement of your data. You might run into database security issues if users from the originating server do not exist in the destination server. We do recommend using SQL Server Replication or DTS.
>
> Backup and restore is recommended in situations in which you are creating a "backup" or "standby" server.

```
sp_change_users_login {Auto_fix | Report | Update_One}
[, 'UserNamePattern' [, 'LoginName']]
```

The Auto_fix | Report | Update_One code indicates which action should be taken. Here's what each part does:

- Auto_fix tries to map usernames to login names. However, it assumes things that might not be true. You should be wary of using this option.

- Report lists all the broken named links. If you don't specify a parameter, a report is generated.

- Update_One fixes only one specific broken link, as specified by the next set of parameters.

- The UserNamePattern is a "like" comparison operator (such as % for all users, if you specify Auto_fix). The default is null for Report (report on all users). For Update_One, it reports on the username you specify here.

- The LoginName parameter is the name of a login from the sysxlogins table in the master database. If you are using Update_One, you specify the mapping you'd like corrected. Otherwise, it should be NULL.

▲

10

For example, after a recovery, you have a login of Ted on the new server. Ted has a particular SID or GUID (SIDs are used for NT-authenticated users; GUIDs are used for SQL Server-authenticated users). When you query the sysusers table in the newly recovered database you may find that a different GUID has been applied for Ted (SIDs are created and maintained by Windows NT and do not change). To return Ted's original GUID, you can run the following code:

```
Sp_change_users_login Update_One, 'Ted', 'Ted'
```

This changes the GUID field in the sysusers table in your recovered database to match the GUID for Ted in the sysxlogins table in the master database on this server.

BCP

Now that you have seen the potential issues involved with transferring data using backup and restore, it's time to take a look at using the bulk copy utility. You can use BCP to load data either into SQL Server from a file or from SQL Server to a file. You can use this utility when you must move data from SQL Server 7.0 to a previous version of SQL Server or to another database such as Oracle. You can also import data from another program, another database, or a legacy system. Keep in mind that this utility only transfers to or from a flat file, and it transfers only data. To transfer database schema, you must use backup and restore or DTS.

You can append data to an existing table, just as you can with any other program you can write that inserts data into a table. However, BCP usually runs faster than a program you can write to perform this kind of data load.

You can also export the data to a file. A new file is created if the file didn't previously exist; otherwise, the file's contents are replaced with the newly downloaded data.

There are some common naming conventions for files used with the BCP program. The following conventions are generally followed:

- .bcp—Native-mode data files
- .txt—ASCII text files
- .csv—Comma-separated files
- .fmt—Format files
- .err—Data-error files

Permissions

To copy data from SQL Server to a file, you must have SELECT permissions on the table or view from which you get data, as well as on the system catalog. Everyone can view the system tables by default if they have a database username, so this shouldn't be much of a concern. You also need operating system permissions to create or modify the file to which you want to write. Of course, file permissions are applicable only in the Windows NT environment because Windows 9x doesn't implement file system permissions. In an NT environment, this typically means the Change or Full Control permissions on the directory, as well as file permissions if you are creating a new file. File allocation table (FAT) and FAT32 partitions are not secured, so no special permissions are necessary at the file or directory level.

To import data into SQL Server from a file, you need READ permissions on the file (if on an NTFS partition). You also need INSERT permissions on the table you want to load in SQL Server.

▲ SYNTAX

Take a look at the BCP program's syntax.

```
Bcp [[databasename.]owner.]tablename ¦ view_name ¦ "Query"}
{in ¦ out ¦ queryout ¦ format } datafile
[/m maxerrors]
[/f formatfile]
[/e errfile]
[/F firstrow]
[/L lastrow]
[/b batchsize]
[/n] [/c] [/w] [/N]
```

▼

```
[/6] [/q]
[/C code_page]
[/t field_term]
[/r row_term]
[/i inputfile]
[/o output_file]
[/a packet_size]
[/S server_name]
/U login_id
[/P password]
[/T] [/v] [/k] [/E]
[/h "hint [,…n]"]
```

Take a look at the required parameters (those not in square brackets, or those contained within curly braces "{ and }"):

- *tablename*—The name of the table you want to export or import. This can be a global temporary table, a view, or a query. The database name will default to the default database of the user running the BCP command. The owner will default to the database username of the logged-in user. You might want to specify all the parameters here, such as pubs.dbo.authors for the authors table owned by user dbo (database owner) in the pubs database.

- *in/out/queryout/format*—Specifies whether data is being loaded into SQL Server or out of SQL Server into a file, or returned as a query.

- *datafile*—The name of the file you want to load data from or put data into when running your BCP program. You must specify the full path and filename of the file you want to use. As with any Windows NT program, it will default to the local directory from which you run the BCP program if you don't specify a path. Note that although the data file is required, you might not get an error message if you run BCP without a filename. You can use this to your advantage, however. If you want to create a format file (discussed shortly) but don't actually want to export data, you can leave this parameter off and just create the format file. Follow the previous naming standards when creating or referencing this file.

- /U—The login name you want to be validated with must be provided here.

Here are the optional parameters:

- /P—The password for the login name you provide with the /U parameter. If you do not specify a password, you will be prompted for one. Needless to say, you should provide a password when running batch BCP programs.

▼

- /S—The server name you'd like to connect to. If you do not specify a server name, BCP will attempt to connect to the local copy of SQL Server. If you do specify a server name, BCP will connect to your server over the network. From a performance perspective, it's best to load a data file onto the server without the /S parameter.

- /m *maxerrors*—The maximum number of errors you can get when importing data into SQL Server (such as poorly formatted rows) before the bulk copy is canceled. This is particularly useful for testing large data imports. If you type something wrong or have some other problem, you can cause the load to stop quickly rather than run for a long time and then find that the load failed. The default value if you do not provide this parameter is 10 errors.

- /f *formatfile*—The path and filename of the file used to determine how you format a file when extracting data from SQL Server or used to describe how SQL Server should interpret your file when loading data. If you don't provide this parameter on output, BCP will prompt you for formatting information. When finished, it will save the file as bcp.fmt by default.

- /e *errfile*—Specifies the path and filename of the file that BCP copies rows to when the rows fail during data loads into SQL Server. This way, you can examine each row that failed to load properly, correct problems, and then use the error file as your source file and run another BCP. If you don't specify an error file, none will be created, and problem rows will not be specifically identified. The naming conventions mentioned earlier suggest an extension of .err for this file.

- /F *firstrow*—A parameter that, if specified, can start you at a relative row number within your file during a data load. If you don't specify this parameter, your load will start with row number 1.

- /L *lastrow*—The last row to copy from your file during a data load. The default will be to load all rows until the end of the file.

- /b *batchsize*—Specifies the number of rows being inserted that will be treated as a batch. In this context, SQL Server treats each batch as a separate transaction. You'll learn more about this option shortly. If you don't specify this parameter, the entire load will be treated as a single batch.

- /n—Specifies that the data will be exported (or imported) using the native format for SQL Server data types. You should use this option only when moving data from one copy of SQL Server to another and only when moving data on the same platform (Intel, Alpha, and so on).

- /c—Specifies that data imports/exports will use character data types instead of SQL Server internal data types. It creates (or uses) a tab-delimited format between each column and a carriage return/line feed to indicate the end of a line.

▼

▼
- /w—Specifies that the data will be transferred using a Unicode format.
- /N—Specifies that the transfer will use Unicode characters for character data and native format for noncharacter data.
- /6—Specifies that the transfer uses SQL Server 6.x data types.
- /q—Specifies that quoted identifiers are being used. When this is the case, you must be sure that all references to quoted identifiers have double quotation marks around them.
- /C *code_page*—Allows you to specify a code page for the data file. This applies only to extended characters in the character set.
- /E—Specifies that identity columns should be loaded with values from your data file rather than using the identity property of the identity column on your table. You'll learn more about the identity property on Day 14, "Ensuring Data Integrity." Otherwise, identity values will be assigned as normal.
- /t *field_term*—Specifies the default field terminator.
- /r *row_term*—Specifies the value that BCP should use to determine when one row ends and another begins.
- /i *inputfile*—If you don't want to type all these parameters each time you run BCP, you can add all these parameters to an input file and then run BCP with the input file. When you specify the input file, you must use the full path and filename.
- /o *outputfile*—The name of the file that will receive messages and so on from BCP. You can capture output from running the program and then analyze the output later. This is particularly useful when running in batch mode.
- /a *packet_size*—The packet size that will be used on the network. The default value is 4,096 bytes (4KB) except on MS-DOS workstations, where it's 512 bytes. You can configure this option on the server as well.
- /T—Specifies that BCP will connect to SQL Server using a trusted connection.
- /v—Reports the current DB-Library version number.
- /k—Specifies that empty columns retain their NULL values rather than having a default applied to them.
- /h *"hint"*—Allows you to specify hints like sort orders on columns and check constraints. See the SQL Server Books Online for additional information on these hints.
▲

10

Native Mode Versus Character Mode

As you just learned, there are two ways to transfer data: native mode and character mode. Character mode specifies that data will be transferred into human-readable format. For example, numbers from an integer column will be human readable. The number 12,500 is readable just the way it is. In native mode, the data is kept in its internal format. The number 12,500 is stored in four bytes: 0x000030D4 (in hex).

Character mode is my preferred format because it's much more flexible. You can use native mode only when transferring data among SQL servers and preferably among servers on the same platform using the same character set. Character mode will allow the data to be transferred from or to just about any program. Also, if an error occurs in the file, character mode files are much easier to fix.

If you specify /c, you will not be prompted for additional information when running BCP. It will be assumed that your data will be formatted as plain ASCII text. If you specify /n, you also will not be prompted for additional information. Otherwise, you will be required to provide information about how you want your file to be formatted.

BCP was run to export a table with a single char(5) column in Figure 10.1.

FIGURE 10.1

A basic BCP export.

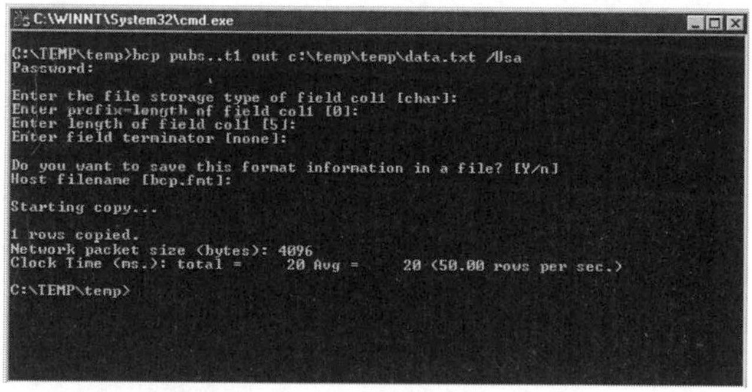

If you add the /c parameter, you will notice that it will no longer prompt you to format the output rows and build a format file (see Figure 10.2).

This leads you to the next item to examine: format files.

Format Files

Format files are used to specify the layout of data in your files or to document the layout for import. When you export data with BCP, you can build a format file if you choose not to use the /n or /c parameters. For import, you can build a format file yourself.

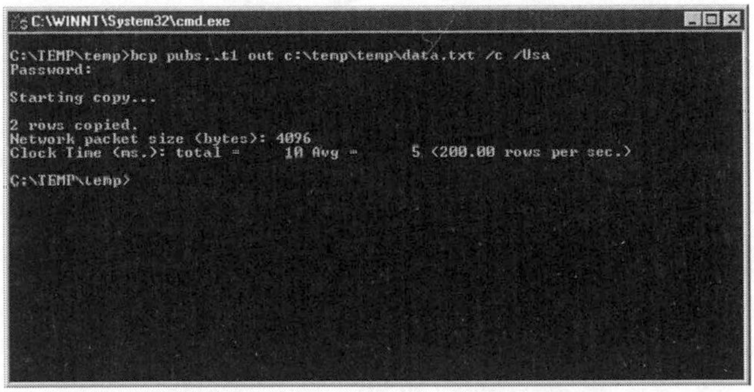

FIGURE 10.2

A basic BCP export.

For example, you can examine each option you are presented with when you specify that you want to create a format file during a BCP export. You will receive an additional request for a field length for character data, as represented in the following code. Otherwise, the requested information is consistent between data types.

```
Enter the file storage type of field COL1 [char]:
Enter prefix length of field COL1 [0]:
Enter length of field COL1 [5]:
Enter field terminator [none]:
```

The file storage type refers to how the data will be stored in the file. For character data, or to use a character-only data type, use the data type char. Otherwise, accept the default value from SQL Server. You can use any valid SQL Server data type.

The prefix length determines how much space is reserved to indicate how long this particular field is. For many types, this can be 0 bytes. For char or varchar data, this can be 1 byte long. For text or image data types, the default length is 4 bytes.

The field length specifies how long the data fields will be when being exported. You should probably accept the default values requested by SQL Server.

The last option is the field terminator. Just about any single character is a valid field terminator; however, it's best to specify a character that will not appear in your data. You can specify any value, including special characters. These include

- \t for a tab
- \n for a new line
- \r for a carriage return
- \\ for a backslash
- \0 for a "null terminator" (no visible terminator)

You can use these terminators for both field terminators (the previous /t option) or row terminators (/r).

The example produces a format file like this:

```
7.0
1
1       SQLCHAR         0       5       " "       1       COL1
```

The 7.0 on line 1 refers to the version with which this format file is associated. The next line references the number of columns in this format file. Then you will see one line for each column of data represented in the file.

The first number is the relative column number in the data file. The second entry on the line is the data type. BCP format files don't contain SQL Server data types; they contain special data types specific to these BCP files. Valid BCP format file data types include

BCP Data Type	Used for SQL Server Data Types
SQLBINARY	BINARY, IMAGE, TIMESTAMP, VARBINARY
SQLBIT	BIT
SQLCHAR	CHAR, SYSNAME, TEXT, VARCHAR
SQLDATETIME	DATETIME
SQLDECIMAL	DECIMAL
SQLFLT8	FLOAT
SQLMONEY	MONEY
SQLNUMERIC	NUMERIC
SQLFLT4	REAL
SQLDATETIM4	SMALLDATETIME
SQLMONEY4	SMALLMONEY
SQLTINYINT	TINYINT

The next field is the length of the prefix as described previously. Then the actual data length is listed. The next entry is the field terminator. Then the order of the column in the table data definition language (DDL) is necessary (also called the server column number), finally ending with the column name in the server.

Batch Sizes

When you load data into SQL Server with BCP, by default all data is copied in a single batch and a single transaction. This means that the entire load either completely succeeds or completely fails. Even if you are loading a million rows of data, the entire set of data is still copied in a single transaction. This can easily fill your transaction logs on a database. Therefore, it's probably appropriate to issue a "commit" periodically and begin a new batch. This will improve concurrency and allow you to do things like truncate the log on checkpoint. For more information on transactions see Day 16, "Programming SQL Server 7.0."

Fast BCP

BCP can operate in two modes, regular BCP and fast BCP. BCP at its lowest level is fundamentally running inserts. This means that each row is processed as an insert operation. It will be written to the transaction log, then the data will be modified, and then any indexes will be added. This is not the fastest way to add data to SQL Server.

If you drop all indexes on a table and set the Select into/bulkcopy option to true for a database, a fast BCP will execute. In this mode, the inserts will not be written to the transaction log. Because there are no indexes to be maintained and no transaction logging occurs, this operation runs very quickly. Data types and defaults will still be enforced—even during a fast data load. However, rules, constraints, and triggers will not be enforced.

 Caution   Be very careful performing nonlogged operations on a production server. Because the inserts are not logged, the database is unrecoverable until a backup occurs. See Day 8, "Restoring SQL Server Databases," for more information about the Select into/bulkcopy option and database recovery.

To get a fast data transfer to occur, follow these steps:

1. Drop all indexes on the affected tables.
2. Set the Select into/bulkcopy option.
3. Load your data with BCP.
4. Verify integrity that would otherwise be checked by rules, constraints, and triggers (for example, run queries).
5. Re-create your indexes.
6. Turn off the Select into/bulkcopy option.
7. Back up your database.

Now perform a couple of BCPs to see how you might use them in the real world. If you want to follow along, you will need to copy the data presented here into files on your system.

You are going to work with this table in both examples:

```
CREATE TABLE mytable
(cust_id  integer not null,
     cust_name char(30) null,
     city char(20) null ,
     state char(2) not null DEFAULT 'WA',
     zip  char(10) null)
```

This table represents customer data you will get from another system. The only required field is the cust_id and state fields. Additional data, such as the city, cust_name, and zip fields are optional (and hence, allow nulls). If a value is not supplied for state, it defaults to Washington ("WA").

In the first example, you are going to load a table from a data file that doesn't have as many columns of data as the table.

Your comma-delimited data file will look like this:

```
cust_id,city,state,zip_code
```

For example, two sample rows might look like the following:

```
1,Seattle,WA,98102
2,Bellevue,WA,98004
```

To load this properly, you will need to create a format file. In this case, here's the format file (which you should copy if you want to run this example):

```
7.0
5
1    SQLCHAR    0    9     ","    1     cust_id
2    SQLCHAR    0    0     ""     0     cust_name
3    SQLCHAR    0    20    ","    3     city
4    SQLCHAR    0    2     ","    4     state
5    SQLCHAR    0    10    "\r\n" 5     zip
```

Notice that you must change the server column number for cust_name to 0. This indicates to BCP that the data is not being passed in this file. You also must reset the field length of this column to 0 and specify no row terminator.

Now, when loading with BCP and with fewer columns in the data file than in the table, you will see something similar to Figure 10.3.

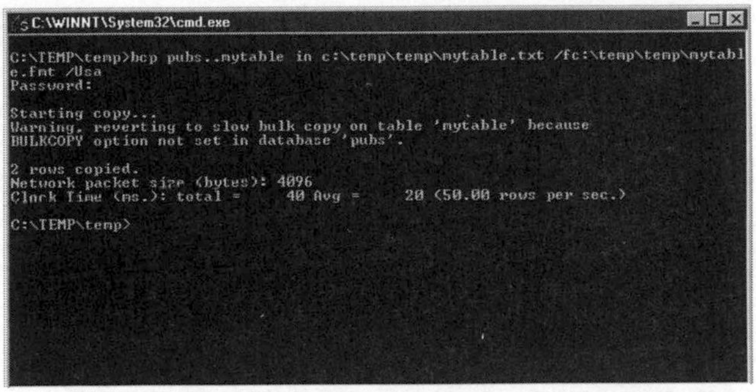

FIGURE 10.3

Loading with BCP.

Now perform the second example. This time your file has more data than you want to load. Your file should be in the following format, where the address is 30 characters long:

```
cust_id,cust_name,cust_addr,city,state,zip_code
```

Again, examine the two rows of sample data:

```
1,Joe Smith,1200 First Ave,Seattle,WA,98102
2,Marilyn Jones,123 116 Ave NE,Bellevue,WA,98004
```

This time a format file will reflect the column that exists in the data file but doesn't exist in SQL Server.

```
7.0
6
1    SQLCHAR    0    9     ","      1    cust_id
2    SQLCHAR    0    30    ","      2    cust_name
3    SQLCHAR    0    0     ","      0    cust_addr
4    SQLCHAR    0    20    ","      3    city
5    SQLCHAR    0    2     ","      4    state
6    SQLCHAR    0    10    "\r\n"   5    zip
```

In this example you added a field for cust_addr but indicated that it doesn't exist in the table by specifying its server column number as 0 and its data length as 0. Note that you still need the field terminator so BCP knows how much to skip over in your file.

As you can see, BCP is quite flexible, but working with format files can require some time to get right.

The real beauty of bulk copy and format files is that the bulk copy is a command-line utility that can be added to your batch scripts for automated processing. Now that you have looked at BCP and the issues surrounding a backup and restore, take a look at the hot new DTS tools.

10

Working with the BULK INSERT Command

▲ SYNTAX ▼

The BULK INSERT command is a new T-SQL statement found in SQL Server 7.0. BULK INSERT enables you to read a data file as if it were an OLE-DB recordset. This allows SQL Server to move the entire recordset into the table in one step, or in several steps, if you are using a predetermined batch size. Here is the syntax of the BULK INSERT command:

```
BULK INSERT [['database_name'.]['owner'].]{'table_name'
FROM data_file}[WITH
([ BATCHSIZE [= batch_size]]
[[,] CHECK_CONSTRAINTS]
[[,] CODEPAGE [= 'ACP' ¦ 'OEM' ¦ 'RAW' ¦ 'code_page']]
[[,] DATAFILETYPE [= {'char' ¦ 'native'¦ 'widechar' ¦ 'widenative'}]]
[[,] FIELDTERMINATOR [= 'field_terminator']]
[[,] FIRSTROW [= first_row]]
[[,] FORMATFILE [= 'format_file_path']]
[[,] KEEPIDENTITY]
[[,] KEEPNULLS]
[[,] KILOBYTES_PER_BATCH [= kilobytes_per_batch]]
[[,] LASTROW [= last_row]]
[[,] MAXERRORS [= max_errors]]
[[,] ORDER ({column [ASC ¦ DESC]} [,…n])]
[[,] ROWS_PER_BATCH [= rows_per_batch]]
[[,] ROWTERMINATOR [= 'row_terminator']]
[[,] TABLOCK])]
```

- *database_name*'—The name of the database in which the table you want to bulk insert data into is located.

- *data_file*—The full path and filename you want to import.

- CHECK_CONSTRAINTS—Specifies that table constraints are checked during the bulk insert operation.

- CODEPAGE—Specifies the codepage found in the data file. This option is necessary only when the data is of a character datatype and uses extended characters.

- DATAFILETYPE—Specifies what format the data in the file is stored as.

- FIELDTERMINATOR—Specifies what character is used as a field terminator. The default is a tab or \t character.

- FIRSTROW—Specifies which row you want to start the bulk insert process with. The default is the first row in the data file (that is, FIRSTROW = 1).

- FORMATFILE—Specifies a full path and filename of a format file to be used in conjunction with the bulk insert. This works in a similar fashion to the format file created for the BCP command.

- KEEPIDENTITY—Specifies that IDENTITY values being bulk inserted will keep their value rather than having a new IDENTITY value assigned to them as part of the insert process.

- KEEPNULLS—Specifies that NULL values retain their NULL values when bulk inserted.
- KILOBYTES_PER_BATCH—Specifies the number of bytes to transfer at a time. There is no default value because the BULK INSERT command seeks to move the entire data set in one chunk.
- LASTROW—Specifies the last row of data to move. By default, this is the last row in the data file.
- ORDER—Allows you to specify the sort order within the data file. If the data file is sorted and has a different sort order than the data in your table, specifying this option can greatly enhance performance.
- ROWS_PER_BATCH—Specifies how many rows to move in each batch. You can use this option when BATCHSIZE is not specified.
- ROWTERMINATOR—Specifies the end of a row of data. The default is the newline or \n character.
- TABLOCK—Specifies that a table lock will be used for the duration of this bulk insert. This can have performance benefits for the bulk insert operation.

For additional information on using the BULK INSERT please refer to the Microsoft SQL Server Books Online, or *SQL Server 7.0 Unleashed* by Sams Publishing.

Working with Data Transformation Services

Data in your organization might be stored in a large variety of formats and locations. With DTS you can import and export data between multiple heterogeneous data sources and data destinations. All this takes place through the use of OLE-DB providers. You can transfer data and schema; and if you are working with two Microsoft SQL Server 7.0 computers you can also transfer database objects like indexes, data types, constraints, and tables using the Object Transfer within the DTS component.

DTS exposes several different interfaces that allow you to do the following:

- Schedule DTS packages to automatically transfer and transform data.
- Create custom DTS packages that can be integrated into other third-party products through the Component Object Model (COM) interface.
- Transfer data to and from the following:
  - Microsoft Access
  - Microsoft Excel
  - SQL Server

10

- Open database connectivity (ODBC)-compliant databases such as Oracle, DB2, and Informix
- ASCII text files (both flat files and delimited files)

 A *data transformation* can be one of any operations applied to your data before it is stored in the destination. This can include the calculation of new values, the concatenation of values, breaking of values like a name field into a first name and last name field, as well any type of data cleaning you want to enforce.

DTS can be broken down into three major sections:

- Packages—A package encompasses all the steps and tasks needed to perform an import, export, or transformation.
- Import and Export Wizards—You can use these wizards to interactively create a DTS package. These utilities are also available from the command line as dtswiz and dtsrun. Using these utilities from the command line allows you to not only script them but to bypass many of the dialogs shown in the wizards.
- DTS Designer—The DTS Designer is a desktop environment complete with toolboxes and palettes, which experienced administrators can use to visually create complex tasks and packages. The DTS Designer is beyond the scope of this book. Please see *SQL Server 7.0 Unleashed*, published by Sams Publishing, or the SQL Server Books Online for additional information.

Note

> Because DTS is a COM-based set of components and servers, you can use any COM-compliant programming language like Visual Basic, PerlScript, or JScript to define your own customized transformations, packages, scripting objects, and data pump interfaces.

Data Transformation Packages

As stated earlier, a DTS package is a set of one or more tasks executed in a coordinated sequence. These packages can be created through the Import and Export Wizards, manually through the use of a scripting language, or visually through the DTS Designer. After you have created a DTS package, it is completely self contained and can be run from the Enterprise Manager, the Task Scheduler, or through the dtsrun command-line utility.

When you create a DTS package, you can store it in a variety of formats—each with its own distinct advantages.

SQL Server's msdb Database

You can store your DTS packages in the msdb database. When they are stored here, other SQL Server 7.0 servers can connect to the packages and use them. There is less storage overhead doing this than using the Microsoft Repository. This can help minimize the amount of space and time it takes to access and use the package.

Microsoft Repository

When you store a package in the Repository, you can make it available to other SQL Server 7.0 computers. The Repository has the advantage of making metadata available to other applications. The other major advantage of the Repository is its capability to track the lineage or history of transformations that the data has gone through. This includes data sources, destinations, and changes applied to the data.

COM-Based Structured Storage

The COM supplies a storage architecture made up of data objects and data streams. Data objects are analogous to directories in a file system, while stream objects are analogous to the files. One of the major advantages of the COM-based structured storage model is that the stream objects can easily be distributed through network file servers or email. Any COM-compliant program or programming language can then access the COM objects.

Package Security

All packages can have two types of security applied to them, the DTS owner and password and the DTS operator password. In addition to this, a DTS package stored in COM-based structured storage can also be encrypted. When a package is encrypted, all its components are encrypted except for the CreationDate, Description, ID, Name, and VersionID information.

A user or application with the DTS Owner password has complete access to all the package components. When a package is saved without an owner password, it is not encrypted. When you save a package with an owner password, it is encrypted by default.

A user or application with the DTS Operator password has the ability to execute the package, but it cannot access any package components directly.

Package Components

A DTS package is made up of several components that interact together to form the package and the workflows. These objects are the task objects, the step objects, the connection objects, and the data pump. Take a closer look at each of these individual components. You will then see how these components interact within the package architecture.

Task Objects

Packages are made up of one or more tasks. Each task defines a process or action that should be taken. Tasks are used to do the following work:

- Run a SQL command or batch
- Move data from one OLE-DB data source to an OLE-DB data destination
- Launch external programs, command executions, or batch files
- Gather results from another DTS package
- Execute another DTS package
- Execute a COM-based script (Visual Basic, JScript, PerlScript, and so on)

Step Objects

Step objects are used to coordinate the flow of tasks that make up your DTS package. Tasks that do not have an associated step object are never executed. Step objects are used to create your workflow.

Steps can be executed in several different methods. For example, you can design a step to fire only when the prior step completes, only when the prior step completes successfully, or only when the prior step fails. This type of relationship is based on precedence constraints. This means that the latter step has a precedence constraint on the prior step. After all the precedence constraints for a step are satisfied, the step can execute.

For example, say you have a two-step package you want to run. Step 1 is a CREATE TABLE statement. Step 2 is a CREATE INDEX statement. Step 2 will fire only after step 1 has finished successfully.

Because task objects are separate from step objects, you can associate one or more steps to a particular task object.

 Note

> Although a task can be associated with more than one step, that task can have only one instance of itself running at any one time. This means that if step 2 and step 4 are both associated with Task A, and step 2 is currently running, step 4 cannot begin until Task A in step 2 has completed.

Step objects can also be executed conditionally based on different runtime conditions. You can also execute multiple steps simultaneously to improve your performance. This is known as running steps in parallel. To accomplish this, create steps that don't have any precedence constraints assigned to them.

To assign precedence constraints, you can use the on success, on failure, and unconditional values from prior steps, or you can use return codes generated by a scripting language. Using the scripting languages allows you to implement if...then...else–style logic to your workflows. The following list describes how the precedence constraints operate:

- On success—Step 2 will wait until step 1 has completed successfully before beginning.
- On failure—Allows an alternative branch of steps to run when an error is encountered.
- Unconditional—Step 2 will not begin until step 1 has completed regardless of its success or failure.

DTS Connection Objects

DTS packages that connect to data sources have connection objects. There are two types of connection objects:

- Data source—Data source connections are used to specify the data source and destination servers, location, and format of the data and necessary passwords.
- Data file—Data file connections are used to specify the source and destination files including the location and format of the data.

A connection is made when a task object that needs it is invoked in a step. Otherwise the connection is dormant.

DTS Data Pump

The data pump is an OLE-DB service provider that handles the importing, exporting, and data transformation services. It loads as an in-process COM server in the SQL Server 7.0 process space. The data pump is used in conjunction with two or more connection objects. Because the data pump is COM based, you can extend its functionality with any COM-compliant programming language. Through these extensions, you can create your own complex procedural logic programs that you can implement and reuse. Figure 10.4 represents the flow of information through the data pump component.

DTS Object Transfer

The DTS object transfer is the upgrade to SQL Server 6.x's Transfer Manager Interface (TMI). With the DTS Object Transfer you can move data, schema, and objects from SQL Server to other SQL Server data sources. This is accomplished through the use of the Import and Export Wizards, which you will learn about later in today's lesson.

DTS Object Transfer uses the SQL-DMO rather than the OLE-DB functionality to make connections to data sources and data destinations.

10

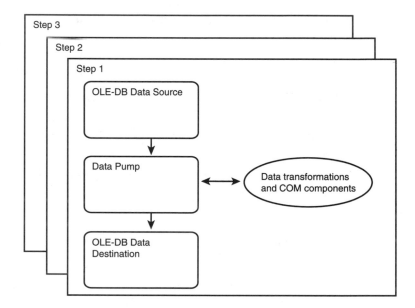

FIGURE 10.4

The DTS architecture.

DTS Import and Export Wizards

Through the use of the wizards, you can interactively create DTS packages for importing, exporting, and transforming your data. DTS is smart enough to check the destination objects for their existence. If the objects already exist, you can have the wizard include a step to drop and re-create the objects.

As a DTS user, you can do all of the following:

- Copy a table
- Copy the results of a query
- Create a query with the Query Builder inside the wizard
- Specify connection settings for data sources and destinations
- Transform data including column headings, data type, size, scale, precision, and nullability
- Run a COM-compliant script
- Save packages in the Repository, in the msdb, or to a COM-structured storage location
- Schedule a completed package for execution

All right—enough talking about it. It's time to work with the wizards!

Exporting Data Using the DTS Export Wizard

Follow these steps to export data:

1. Open the SQL Enterprise Manager and connect to your server.

2. From the Tools menu select Wizards.

3. In the Select Wizard screen, expand the Data Transformation Services node and then select the DTS Export Wizard, as shown in Figure 10.5.

FIGURE 10.5

Select the DTS Export Wizard.

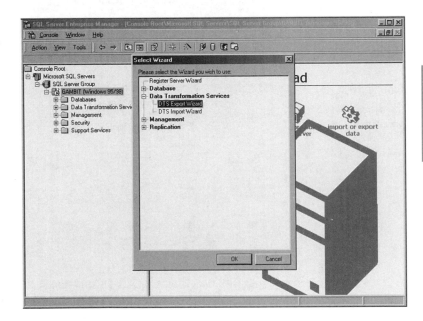

4. Click OK to continue.

5. You are now presented with the DTS Export Wizard screen. Click Next to continue.

6. You are presented with the Choose a Data Source screen, as shown in Figure 10.6. From here you can select an export server, login authentication credentials, and the export database. Please select the pubs database from your local SQL Server as the export database.

7. The Advanced button shows the advanced properties you can attach to this package (see Figure 10.7). Return to the Choose a Data Source screen, and click Next to continue.

10

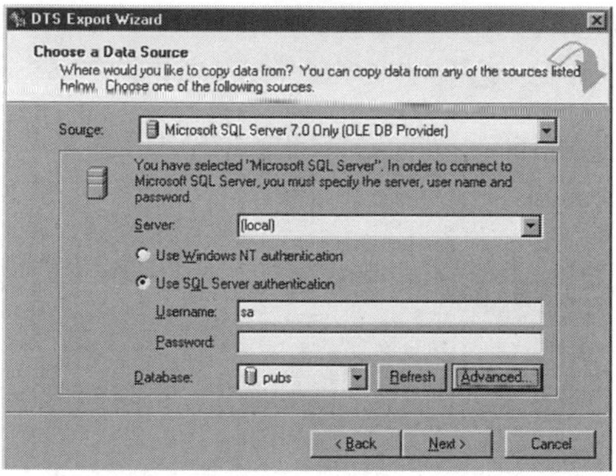

FIGURE 10.6

Choose a data source.

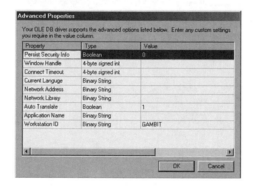

FIGURE 10.7

Advanced data source properties.

8. You are presented with the Choose a Data Destination screen. You can set the same types of properties, as shown in the Choose a Data Source screen. You are going to create a new database in your local server to export your data to. From the database combination box, select <new>. You are presented with a Create Database screen shown in Figure 10.8.

FIGURE 10.8

Create a database.

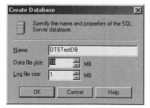

9. Fill in the Create Database information as shown here. The database name is DTSTestDB, the file size is 10MB, and the log size should be left at 1MB. When you are finished, click OK. You return to the Choose a Destination screen (see Figure 10.9). Click Next to continue.

FIGURE 10.9

Choose a destination.

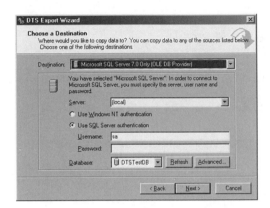

10. You are presented with the Specify Table Copy or Query screen (see Figure 10.10). From here you can choose to gather tables, run a query, or transfer database objects. Click Next to continue.

FIGURE 10.10

Specify a table copy or query.

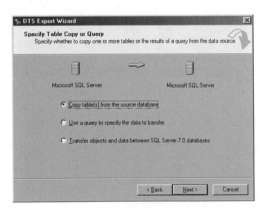

11. From the Select Source Tables screen (see Figure 10.11), select the authors, titles, and titleauthor tables. Leave the destination tables alone. You might have noticed that there is a transform button on each of the tables. If you click the ellipses, you will be given some advanced transformation options, as shown in Figures 10.12 and 10.13.

10

FIGURE 10.11

Select source tables.

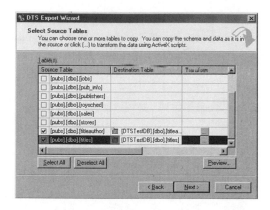

FIGURE 10.12

*The Transformations
and Column Mappings
tabs.*

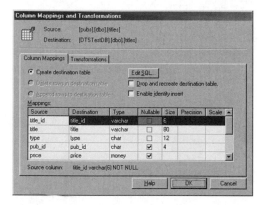

FIGURE 10.13

*The Transformations
scripting tab.*

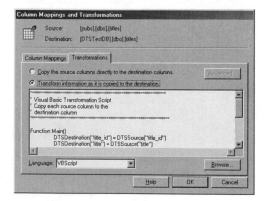

12. Click Next on the Select Table screen to continue. You are now presented with the Save, Schedule, and Replicate Package screen (see Figure 10.14). From this screen, specify that you want to run the package immediately and that you want to save the package in SQL Server.

FIGURE 10.14

Save, schedule, and replicate the package.

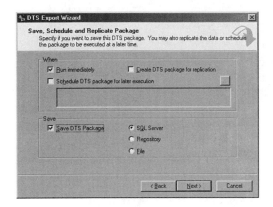

13. You are presented with the Save DTS Package screen. You should select a package name like TestExport. You should also specify the storage location, as shown in Figure 10.15.

FIGURE 10.15

Save a DTS package.

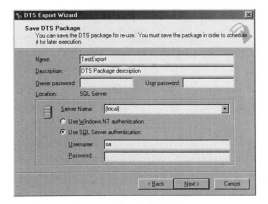

14. You are now presented with the Finish screen. Click Finish to complete the package creation and save.

15. Because you scheduled the package to run immediately, you will see the transfer take place and a summary grid to show the completed process as shown in Figure 10.16.

FIGURE 10.16

Transferring data.

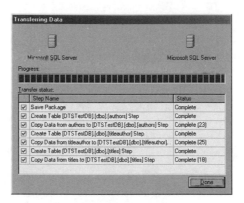

16. Click Done when you are finished. Take a look at your new database and the tables that were transferred.

Transferring Database Objects

You can use the DTS Object Transfer within the DTS screens to transfer database objects such as stored procedures and views from one SQL Server 7.0 computer to another. Note that this type of transfer can be done across different platforms and different sort orders.

To work with the Object Transfer follow steps 1 through 10 from the "Exporting Data Using the DTS Export Wizard" section. In step 10, you will need to specify the Transfer Objects and Databases Between SQL Server 7.0 Databases option, as shown in Figure 10.10. You then will be able to specify that you want to transfer all objects, or if you deselect that option, you can pick and choose individual objects to transfer, including tables, views, stored procedures, user-defined data types, and others.

Summary

In today's lesson you learned several different methods for moving data from one location to another. SQL Server 7.0 has three principal methods for moving data and one for both moving and transforming data.

You can use a backup-and-restore methodology to move all data and table schema from one location to another. This approach will not make changes to your data. You can use the Bulk Copy Program (BCP) to transfer just data from one location to another. Although this utility will not make changes to your data, you can use it to gather only certain columns and rows from one data source and transfer them to another. The final element is the new Data Transformation Services (DTS) Manager in SQL Server 7.0.

This utility at first glance is similar to the old Transfer Manager Interface found in SQL Server 6.x. DTS can be used to move data, schema, or both data and schema. DTS also includes the capability to transform (modify) your data. You can use DTS to change the format of your data from one data type to another, restructure and map your data to different locations, make your data consistent, and validate it. You can include data logic to summarize, decode, convert, and decompose data.

Q&A

Q Should I use DTS or replication to move data around?

A Normally when you want to make data available to other SQL servers, you will want to use replication because it runs on a regular basis and includes functionality to guarantee consistency.

Q The DTS looks interesting, but will I really use it?

A In our consulting practices, we have found that a large part of our job is data cleaning. Many companies have large mainframe databases that dump flat ASCII text files on a regular basis. These ASCII files must be imported into SQL Server. The DTS program allows you to not only import the data but also to make the necessary data type changes, split columns (like Name into First Name and Last Name), as well as many other transformations.

Q You talked briefly about the DTS Designer. Is it really that difficult to work with?

A That really depends on you. Administrators familiar with a visual interface for programming like Visual Basic or Delphi will find the DTS Designer fairly easy to use. For a beginner, it can be a daunting task because there is so much functionality exposed through the designer. I suggest you save your packages from the wizards and then look at them in the Designer. This will help ease you into its use.

Workshop

The Workshop provides quiz questions to help you solidify your understanding of the concepts presented in this chapter. In addition to the quiz questions, exercises are provided to let you practice what you have learned in this chapter. Try to understand the quiz and exercise answers before continuing to the next day's lesson. Answers are provided in Appendix A, "Answers."

10

Quiz

1. What permissions are required for you to use the BCP program?

2. What database objects does BCP enforce and ignore when you are transferring data into a table?

3. What is required to do a fast BCP?

4. When using DTS, what can you do to your data?

5. You want to upgrade a database from an Intel Pentium II 400MHz server running Windows NT 4.0 to a DEC Alpha running Windows NT 4.0. In addition, you are changing your sort order. How can this be accomplished?

Exercises

1. Use the DTS Import Wizard to do the following:

   - Create a new database called DTSNWind

   - Transfer all objects, but no data, from the Northwind database

2. Use the Export Wizard to move all data from the Northwind database to the newly created DTSNWind database.

DAY 11

Retrieving Data with Queries

When you have information in your database, it is time to learn how to extract just the data you want and to make modifications to that data. You are going to begin today's lesson with a simple statement and learn how to grab specific columns. You then expand on this simple SELECT with data manipulation and conversion techniques. You will then learn how to select information from specific rows in tables and eliminate duplicate information. You finish the lesson learning advanced query topics like subqueries, joins, and data correlation. Today is a long day but a very important one. Take your time with this chapter because SQL is a fundamental language used with nearly every relational database management system. In other words, most of the statements presented in this chapter can be used with little or no modification in any database. Let's start off with a simple SELECT statement.

Simple SELECT Statements

You can create queries to retrieve information from your database using the SQL Server Query Analyzer inside or outside the SQL Server Enterprise Manager as well as command-line utilities like osql. There are other utilities you can use also; these include the MSQuery program and the SQL Server English Query utility. Other tools and third-party utilities are available as well. You will concentrate on using the SQL Server Query Analyzer. In this section, you will look at using the SELECT statement to retrieve rows and columns from tables in your database.

SYNTAX

There are three basic components to the SELECT statement: SELECT, FROM, and WHERE. Here is the basic syntax:

```
SELECT <column_list>
FROM <table_list>
WHERE <search_criteria>
```

The SELECT portion of the statement specifies the columns you want to retrieve. The FROM clause specifies the tables from which the columns are to be retrieved. The WHERE clause limits the rows returned by your query.

▼ SYNTAX

The complete syntax for the SELECT statement is

```
SELECT [ ALL ¦ DISTINCT ][ TOP n [PERCENT] [ WITH TIES] ]
<select_list>
[ INTO new_table ]
[ FROM <table_sources> ]
[ WHERE <search_condition> ]
[ GROUP BY [ALL] group_by_expression [,…n]
[ WITH { CUBE ¦ ROLLUP } ]]
[ HAVING <search_condition> ]
[ ORDER BY { column_name [ ASC ¦ DESC ] } [,…n] ]
[ COMPUTE { { AVG ¦ COUNT ¦ MAX ¦ MIN ¦ SUM } (expression) }
➥[,…n] [ BY expression [,…n] ]
[ FOR BROWSE ] [ OPTION (<query_hint> [,…n) ]
```

▲

SELECT * FROM table_name is the most basic of all queries. When you use an asterisk (*) for the column_list it will retrieve all columns from the table. Inside SQL Server, the * is turned into a list of all the columns of the table.

In the pubs database, you can run this query to select all columns and rows from the employee table.

```
SELECT *
FROM employee

emp_id      fname       minit       lname       job_id      job_lvl
---------   -------------------     -----   --------------------------
PMA42628M Paolo                     M       Accorti
PSA89086M Pedro                     S       Afonso
VPA30890F Victoria                  P       Ashworth
H-B39728F Helen                             Bennett
L-B31947F Lesley                            Brown
F-C16315M Francisco                         Chang
. . .       . . .
GHT50241M Gary                      H       Thomas
DBT39435M Daniel                    B       Tonini

43 row(s) affected)
```

SYNTAX

To select specific columns, each column must be separated by a comma (,). You should not place a comma after the final column.

```
SELECT column_name [, column_name...]
FROM table_name
```

```
SELECT fname, lname, emp_id
FROM employee

fname       lname       emp_id
-------------------     ---------------------------------   ---------
Paolo       Accorti     PMA42628M
Pedro       Afonso      PSA89086M
Victoria        Ashworth        VPA30890F
Helen       Bennett     H-B39728F
Lesley      Brown       L-B31947F
Francisco       Chang       F-C16315M
. . .                   . . .
. . .       . . .
. . .       . . .
Gary        Thomas      GHT50241M
Daniel      Tonini      DBT39435M

43 row(s) affected)
```

11

ANALYSIS This query selected the first name, last name, and employee ID for each employee from the employee table.

When you execute a query with SELECT *, the column order will be the same as the column order specified in the CREATE TABLE statement. When you select columns from a table, the *column_list* order does not have to be the same as the table column order. You can rearrange the column order in your query output by rearranging the columns in the *column_list*.

You can take the previous query and rearrange the column order. The same information is returned, but it is displayed in a different column order.

```
SELECT emp_id, lname, fname
FROM employee

emp_id     lname       fname
---------  ----------------------                 ----------------
PMA42628M    Accorti      Paolo
PSA89086M    Afonso       Pedro
VPA30890F    Ashworth      Victoria
H-B39728F    Bennett       Helen
L-B31947F    Brown        Lesley
F-C16315M    Chang        Francisco
. . .                  . . .
. . .        . . .
. . .        . . .
GHT50241M    Thomas       Gary
DBT39435M    Tonini       Daniel

43 row(s) affected)
```

Changing Column Headings

When the results of a query are displayed, the column headings will be the names used in the *column_list*. Instead of using column headings, such as lname and fname, you can produce more readable column headings, such as FirstName and LastName, by aliasing the column headings. You can alias column headings using either SQL Server 7.0 syntax or American National Standards Institute Structured Query Language (ANSI SQL) syntax.

> **Note**   SQL Server 7.0 supports both the ANSI '92 SQL syntax standards and its own Microsoft SQL Server 7.0 flavor, which you've seen referred to throughout this book as Transact-SQL.

You can alias columns with SQL Server in two ways:

```
SELECT column_heading = column_name
FROM table_name
```

or

```
SELECT column_name   ' column_heading
FROM table_name
```

You can rewrite your query using the following SQL Server 7.0 syntax:

```
SELECT EmployeeID = emp_id, LastName = lname, FirstName = fname
FROM employee
```

You can also rewrite it using ANSI SQL syntax:

```
SELECT emp_id AS EmployeeID,  lname AS LastName,  fname AS FirstName
FROM employee
```

Both queries have the same results:

```
EmployeeID     LastName     FirstName
---------      -------------------     ----------------
PMA42628M      Accorti      Paolo
PSA89086M      Afonso       Pedro
VPA30890F      Ashworth      Victoria
H-B39728F      Bennett       Helen
L-B31947F      Brown        Lesley
F-C16315M      Chang        Francisco
. . .                       . . .
. . .          . . .
. . .          . . .
GHT50241M      Thomas       Gary
DBT39435M      Tonini       Daniel

43 row(s) affected)
```

Note

The AS keyword is not required. The following statement returns the same information shown in the preceding query:

```
SELECT empID EmployeeID, lname LastName, fname FirstName FROM
employee
```

Note

If the alias you used has spaces or is a SQL Server keyword, you must enclose the alias in single quotation marks or the SQL Server identifier delimiters [ ].

Here is an example using spaces and square brackets:

```
SELECT lname AS 'Last Name', fname AS [First Name]
FROM employee
```

Here is an example using an SQL keyword:

```
SELECT 'count' = Count(*)
FROM employee
```

11

> **Tip**
>
> Normally you will want to use the square brackets to encapsulate SQL Server identifiers rather than single or double quotation marks. The quotation marks might not work in certain instances because they depend on SQL Server settings. The square brackets, on the other hand, will always work.

Using Literals

You can also use literals to make output more readable. A literal is a string surrounded by single or double quotation marks included in the *column_list* and displayed as another column in the query result. The results will appear to have a label next to your column of information.

SYNTAX

The syntax for including a literal value is as follows:

```
SELECT 'literal'  [, 'literal'...]
```

INPUT/OUTPUT

```
SELECT fname, lname, 'Employee ID:', emp_id
FROM employee

fname      lname      emp_id
-------    -------    ----------------------------    ---------
Paolo      Accorti    Employee ID:    PMA42628M
Pedro      Afonso     Employee ID:    PSA89086M
Victoria   Ashworth   Employee ID:    VPA30890F
Helen      Bennett    Employee ID:    H-B39728F
. . .               . . .
. . .               . . .
. . .               . . .
Gary       Thomas     Employee ID:    GHT50241M
Daniel     Tonini     Employee ID:    DBT39435M

(43 row(s) affected)
```

ANALYSIS This query returns first name, last name, a column containing the literal string `Employee ID`, and the employee IDs for all employees from the employee table.

Manipulating Data

You can manipulate data in your query results to produce new columns that display computed values, new string values, converted dates, and more. You can manipulate your query results using arithmetic operators, mathematical functions, string functions, date-time functions, and system functions. You can also use the CONVERT function to convert from one data type to another for easier data manipulation.

Arithmetic Operators

You can use arithmetic operators on the following data types: `int`, `smallint`, `tinyint`, `numeric`, `decimal`, `float`, `real`, `money`, and `smallmoney`. Table 11.1 shows the arithmetic operators and the data types you can use with them.

TABLE 11.1 DATA TYPES AND ARITHMETIC OPERATIONS

Data Type	Addition	Subtraction	Division	Mult.	Modulo
	+	–	/	*	%
decimal	yes	yes	yes	yes	no
float	yes	yes	yes	yes	no
int	yes	yes	yes	yes	yes
money	yes	yes	yes	yes	no
numeric	yes	yes	yes	yes	no
real	yes	yes	yes	yes	no
smallint	yes	yes	yes	yes	yes
smallmoney	yes	yes	yes	yes	no
tinyint	yes	yes	yes	yes	yes

11

> **Note**
>
> Because modulo is the integer remainder from the division of two integers, it can be used only with the integer data types (`int`, `smallint`, `tinyint`).
>
> For example, 5 / 3 = 1 with a remainder of 2. Modulo (%) returns the value 2.

Operator Precedence

With arithmetic operations, two levels of precedence exist: data type precedence and operator precedence.

 Data type precedence is used when arithmetic operations are performed on different data types. When you use different data types, the smaller data type will be converted to the higher data type. For example, if you multiply a `smallint` by an `int`, the result will be an `int`. The only exception to this rule is when using the `money` data type, in which case the result will always be of data type `money`.

 Operator precedence is used when multiple operators are used. Operators follow the normal rules for operator precedence in which modulo is always evaluated first, followed by multiplication and division, followed by addition and subtraction—as read from left to right.

As with normal arithmetic operations, you can change the order of precedence by placing expressions within parentheses. The innermost expressions (most deeply nested expression) will be evaluated first. Parentheses can also be used to make the arithmetic operation more readable.

For example,

5 + 5 * 5 = 30 (The multiplication is done first.)

but

(5 + 5) * 5 = 50 (The nested expression is done first.)

In general it's a very good idea to enclose your arithmetic operations within parentheses to improve the readability and clarity of your Transact-SQL code.

Mathematical Functions

Mathematical functions enable you to perform commonly needed operations on mathematical data.

You can return mathematical data by using the following syntax:

```
SELECT function_name(parameters)
```

Table 11.2 lists the mathematical functions, their parameters, and their results. These examples include such operations as finding the absolute value, finding trigonometric function values, deriving square roots, and raising values to an exponential power. Table 11.3 shows some additional examples.

TABLE 11.2 MATHEMATICAL FUNCTIONS

Function	Results
ABS(*numeric_expr*)	Absolute value
ACOS, ASIN ATAN (*float_expr*)	Angle in radians whose cosine, sine, or tangent is a floating-point value
ATN2(*float_expr1, float_expr2*)	Returns the angle in radians whose tangent is between float1 and float2
COS, SIN COT, TAN(*float_expr*)	Cosine, sine, or tangent of the angle (in radians)
CEILING(*numeric_expr*)	Smallest integer greater than or equal to specified value
DEGREES(*numeric_expr*)	Conversion from radians to degrees

Function	Results
EXP(*float_expr*)	Exponential value of specified value
FLOOR(*numeric_expr*)	Largest integer less than or equal to specified value
LOG(*float_expr*)	Natural log
LOG10(*float_expr*)	Base-10 log
PI()	Constant 3.141592653589793
POWER(*numeric_expr,y*)	Value of *numeric_expr* to the power of *y*
RADIANS(*numeric_expr*)	Conversion from degrees to radians
RAND([*seed*])	Random float number between 0 and 1
ROUND(*numeric_expr,len*)	*Numeric_exp* rounded to the specified length, length in an integer value
SIGN(*numeric_expr*)	Positive, negative, or zero
SQUARE(*float_expr*)	Squares the specified value
SQRT(float_expr)	Square root of specified value

TABLE 11.3 MATHEMATICAL FUNCTIONS AND RESULTS

Statement	Result
SELECT SQRT(9)	3.0
SELECT ROUND(1234.56, 0)	1235
SELECT ROUND(1234.56, 1)	1234.60
SELECT ROUND($1234.56, 1)	1,234.60
SELECT POWER (2,8)	256.0
SELECT FLOOR(1332.39)	1332
SELECT ABS(-365)	365

Tip

When using mathematical functions with monetary data types, you should always precede the data type with a dollar sign ($). Otherwise the value is treated as a numeric with a scale of 4.

11

Caution

When using the float data type, you might get unexpected results from the SQL Server Query Analyzer and other tools. For example, if you run

SELECT ROUND(12.3456789E+5,2)

you will get back

1234567.8899999999

This is a function of open database connectivity (ODBC). SQL Server is still performing the rounding, but by definition float data types are imprecise and won't necessarily return what you expect. So, in general, you'll be better served by avoiding the float data type.

String Functions

When dealing with character information, you can use various string functions to manipulate the data (see Table 11.4). Most string functions manipulate only char, nchar, varchar, and nvarchar data types; therefore, other data types must first be converted. You can return character data by using the following syntax:

SELECT *function_name*(*parameters*)

TABLE 11.4 STRING FUNCTIONS

Function	Result
+*(expression, expression)*	Concatenates two or more character strings
ASCII*(char_expr)*	ASCII code value of left-most character
CHAR*(integer_expr)*	Character equivalent of ASCII code value
CHARINDEX*(pattern, expression)*	Returns starting position of specified patern
DIFFERENCE*(char_expr1, char_exr2)*	Compares two strings and evaluates their similarity; returns a value from 0 to 4, 4 being the best match
LEFT*(char_expr, integer_expr)*	Returns character string starting from the left and preceding *integer_expr* characters
LOWER*(char_expr)*	Converts to lowercase
LTRIM*(char_expr)*	Returns data without leading blanks
NCHAR*(integer_expr)*	Returns the Unicode character corresponding to the *integer_expr*
PATINDEX*('%pattern%', expression)*	Returns starting position of first occurrence in *Expression*
QUOTENAME*('string1', 'quote_char')*	Returns a Unicode string (nvarchar(129)) with valid SQL Server delimiters

Function	Result
REPLACE('string1', 'string2',	Replaces all occurrences of 'string3')string2 in string1 with string3
REPLICATE(char_expr, integer_expr)	Repeats char_expr integer_expr number of times
REVERSE(char_expr)	Returns reverse of char_expr
RIGHT(char_expr, integer_expr)	Returns character string starting integer_expr characters from right
RTRIM(char_expr)	Data without trailing blanks
SOUNDEX(char_expr)	Returns a four-digit (SOUNDEX) code to evaluate the similarity of two character strings
SPACE(integer_expr)	Returns a string of repeated spaces equal to integer_expr
STR(float_expr[,length	Returns character data [,decimal]]) converted from numeric data; length is the total length and decimal is the number of spaces to the right of the decimal
STUFF(char_expr1, start, length, char_expr2)	Deletes length characters from char expr1 at start and inserts char_expr2 at start
SUBSTRING(expression, start, length)	Returns part of a character or binary string
UNICODE('nchar_string')	Returns the Unicode integer value of the first character of 'nchar_string'
UPPER(char_expr)	Converts to uppercase

11

Take a look at the following examples.

You can submit the following to return a column called Name, which is a concatenation of last name, first initial, and employee ID:

```
SELECT lname + ', ' + SUBSTRING(fname,1,1) + '.'
AS Name, emp_id as EmployeeID
FROM employee
```

INPUT/
OUTPUT

```
Name    EmployeeID
------------------------------    ---------
Accorti, P.    PMA42628M
Afonso, P.    PSA89086M
Ashworth, V.    VPA30890F
Bennett, H.    H-B39728F
   .    .
```

```
    .    .
    .    .
Sommer, M.     MГC52317M
Thomas, G.     GHT50241M
Tonini, D.     DBT39435M

(43 row(s) affected)
```

Table 11.5 lists some more examples of string functions.

TABLE 11.5   MORE STRING FUNCTIONS

Statement	Result
SELECT ASCII('G')	71
SELECT LOWER('ABCDE')	abcde
SELECT PATINDEX('%BC%','ABCDE')	2
SELECT RIGHT('ABCDE',3)	CDE
SELECT REVERSE('ABCDE')	EDCBA

Date Functions

You can manipulate datetime values with date functions. Date functions can be used in the *column_list*, the WHERE clause, or wherever an expression can be used. Use the following syntax for date functions:

```
SELECT date_function (parmeters)
```

You must enclose datetime values passed as parameters between single quotation marks or double quotation marks. Some functions take a parameter known as a datepart. Table 11.6 lists the datepart values and their abbreviations.

TABLE 11.6   datepart VALUES

datepart	Abbreviation	Values
day	dd	1–31
day of year	dy	1–366
hour	hh	0–23
millisecond	ms	0–999
minute	mi	0–59
month	mm	1–12
quarter	qq	1–4

datepart	Abbreviation	Values
second	ss	0–59
week	wk	0–53
weekday	dw	1–7 (Sun–Sat)
year	yy	1753–9999

Table 11.7 lists the date functions, their parameters, and their results. Table 11.8 shows some date function examples.

TABLE 11.7 DATE FUNCTIONS

Function	Results
DATEADD(datepart, number, date)	Adds the number of dateparts to the date
DATEDIFF(datepart, date1, date2)	Number of dateparts between two dates
DATENAME(datepart, date)	Returns ASCII value for specified datepart for date listed
DATEPART(datepart, date)	Returns integer value for specified datepart for date listed
GETDATE()	Current date and time in internal format

TABLE 11.8 DATE FUNCTION EXAMPLES

Function	Results
SELECT DATEDIFF(mm, '1/1/97', '12/31/99')	35
SELECT GETDATE()	Apr 29, 1997 2:10AM
SELECT DATEADD(mm, 6, '1/1/97')	Jul 1, 1997 2:10AM
SELECT DATEADD(mm -5, '10/6/97')	May 6, 1997 2:10AM

Now look at a more complex query that involves many of the different pieces you have learned so far.

```
SELECT emp_id AS EmployeeID,  lname + ', ' + SUBSTRING(fname,1,1) +
➥'.' AS Name,
'Has been employed for ', DATEDIFF(year, hire_date, getdate()), '
➥years.'
FROM employee

EmployeeID    Name
---------    ----------------------------------    --------------------
```

```
PMA42628M    Accorti, P.    Has been employed for    5    years.
PSA89086M    Afonso, P.     Has been employed for    7    years.
VPA30890F    Ashworth, V.   Has been employed for    7    years.
H-B39728F    Bennett, H.    Has been employed for    8    years.
    .    .    .    .    .
    .    .    .    .    .
    .    .    .    .    .
MFS52347M    Sommer, M.     Has been employed for    7    years.
GHT50241M    Thomas, G.     Has been employed for    9    years.
DBT39435M    Tonini, D.     Has been employed for    7    years.

(43 row(s) affected)
```

System Functions

You can use several built-in system functions to get information from the system tables. You can return data by using the following syntax:

```
SELECT function_name(parameters)
```

You can use system functions in the *column_list*, WHERE clause, and anywhere else an expression can be used.

Table 11.9 lists some system functions, their parameters, and their results.

TABLE 11.9   THE SYSTEM FUNCTIONS

Function	Results
COALESCE(*expression1, expression2, ...expressionN*)	Returns first non-null expression
COL_NAME(*table_id, column_id*)	Returns column name
COL_LENGTH('*table_name*', '*column_name*')	Returns column length
DATALENGTH('*expression*')	Returns actual length of expression of any data type
DB_ID(['*database_name*'])	Returns database ID
DB_NAME([*database_id*])	Returns database name
GETANSINULL(['*database_name*'])	Returns default nullability of the database
HOST_ID()	Returns the host workstation ID
HOST_NAME()	Returns host computer name

Function	Results
IDENT_INCR('table_name')	Returns increment value specified during creation of identity column
IDENT_SEED('table_name')	Returns seed value specified during creation of identity column
INDEX_COL('table_name', index_id, key_id)	Returns indexed column name
ISDATE(variable ¦ column_name)	Checks for a valid date format. Returns 1 if valid, else returns 0
ISNULL(expression, value)	Returns specified value in place of null
ISNUMERIC(variable ¦ column_name)	Checks for a valid numeric format; returns 1 if valid, else returns 0
NULLIF(expression1, expression2)	Returns NULL if expression1 = expression2
OBJECT_ID('object_name')	Returns database object ID
OBJECT_NAME(object_id')	Returns database object name
STATS_DATE(table_id, index_id)	Returns the date that index statistics were last updated
SUSER_ID(['server_username'])	Returns server user's ID
SUSER_NAME([server_id])	Returns server user's name
USER_ID(['username'])	Returns database user's ID
USER_NAME([user_id])	Returns database user's name

This query uses two system functions to return the name of the second column of the employee table.

```
SELECT COL_NAME(OBJECT_ID('employee'),2)

fname
(1 row(s) affected)
```

Data Conversion

Because many functions require data in a certain format or data type, you might find it necessary to convert from one data type to another. You use the CONVERT or CAST function to modify your data types; you can use the CONVERT function anywhere expressions are allowed. The CONVERT statement has the following syntax:

```
CONVERT(datatype[(length)], expression [,style])
```

Table 11.10 lists the style parameter associated with its standard, and the format of the output.

TABLE 11.10 USING THE CONVERT FUNCTION FOR THE Datetime DATA TYPE

Style without Century yy	Style with Century yyyy	Standard	Date Format Output
—	0 or 100	Default	mon dd yyyy hh:mi AM (or PM)
1	101	USA	mm/dd/yy
2	102	ANSI	yy.mm.dd
3	103	British/French	dd/mm/yy
4	104	German	dd.mm.yy
5	105	Italian	dd-mm-yy
6	106	—	dd mon yy
7	107	—	mon dd, yy
8	108	—	hh:mi:ss
—	9 or 109	Default + milliseconds	mon dd, yyyy hh:mi:ss:ms AM (or PM)
10	110	USA	mm-dd-yy
11	111	Japan	yy/mm/dd
12	112	ISO	yymmdd
—	13 or 113	Europe default + milliseconds	dd mon yyyy hh:mi:ss:ms(24h)
14	114	—	hh:mi:ss:ms(24h)

You can submit the following query to convert the current date to a character string of eight and a date style of ANSI:

```
SELECT CONVERT(CHAR(8),GETDATE(),2)

--------
97.07.06

(1 row(s) affected)
```

```
SELECT emp_id AS EmployeeID,  lname + ', ' + SUBSTRING(fname,1,1) +
➥'.'
AS Name, 'Has been employed for ' + CONVERT(CHAR(2),
(DATEDIFF(year, hire_date, getdate()))) + ' years.'
FROM employee

EmployeeID    Name
----------    --------------------------------    ---------------
PMA42628M     Accorti, P.    Has been employed for 5   years.
PSA89086M     Afonso, P.     Has been employed for 7   years.
VPA30890F     Ashworth, V.    Has been employed for 7   years.
H-B39728F     Bennett, H.    Has been employed for 8   years.
   .     .     .
   .     .     .
   .     .     .
MFS52347M     Sommer, M.     Has been employed for 7   years.
GHT50241M     Thomas, G.     Has been employed for 9   years.
DBT39435M     Tonini, D.     Has been employed for 7   years.

(43 row(s)affected)
```

ANALYSIS This example is built on the query you ran in the "Date Functions" section earlier in today's lesson. In this example you combined the last three columns into one column by using the CONVERT function and string concatenation.

Choosing Rows

You have looked at various ways to retrieve, format, and manipulate the columns in the result set of a query. Now you will learn how to specify which rows to retrieve based on search conditions. You can do this by using the WHERE clause of your SELECT statement. Search conditions include comparison operators, ranges, lists, string matching, unknown values, combinations, and negations of these conditions.

The basic syntax for specifying which rows to retrieve follows:

SYNTAX

```
SELECT <column_list>
FROM <table_list>
WHERE <search_conditions>
```

Comparison Operators

You can implement search conditions by using comparison operators (see Table 11.11). You can select rows by comparing column values to a certain expression or value. Expressions can contain constants, column names, functions, or nested subqueries. If you are comparing two different character data types (such as char and varchar), or you are

11

comparing date data types (such as datetime and smalldatetime), these must be enclosed in single quotation marks. Double quotation marks are acceptable, but single quotation marks maintain ANSI compliance.

The syntax for the WHERE clause using comparison operators follows:

```
SELECT <column_list>
FROM <table_list>
WHERE <column_name> comparison_operator <expression>
```

TABLE 11.11   AVAILABLE COMPARISON OPERATORS

Operator	Description
=	Equal to
>	Greater than
<	Less than
>=	Greater than or equal to
<=	Less than or equal to
<>	Not equal to (preferred)
!=	Not equal to
!>	Not greater than
!<	Not less than
( )	Order of precedence

Here's an example:

```
SELECT emp_id, lname, fname
FROM employee
WHERE pub_id = '0877'

emp_id      lname      Fname
---------   --------------------------   --------------------
PMA42628M   Accorti    Paolo
VPA30890F   Ashworth   Victoria
H-B39728F   Bennett    Helen
 .    .    .
 .    .    .
 .    .    .
M-R38834F   Rance      Martine
DBT39435M   Tonini     Daniel

(10 row(s) affected)
```

ANALYSIS This query returned the employee ID, last name, and first name for all employees employed by the publisher with a pub_id of 0877.

Ranges

You can retrieve rows based on a range of values using the BETWEEN keyword. As with the comparison operator, if you are specifying ranges based on character data types (such as char and varchar) or date data types (such as datetime and smalldatetime), these must be enclosed in single quotation marks.

SYNTAX

The syntax for the WHERE clause using comparisons is as follows:

```
SELECT column_list
FROM table_list
WHERE column_name [NOT] BETWEEN expression AND expression
```

INPUT/ OUTPUT

```
SELECT lname, emp_id
FROM employee
WHERE hire_date BETWEEN '10/1/92' AND '12/31/92'

lname       emp_id
------------------------------    ---------
Josephs     KFJ64308F
Paolino     MAP77183M

(2 row(s) affected)
```

ANALYSIS This query returned the last name and employee ID for all employees hired between 10/1/92 and 12/31/92. The BETWEEN clause is inclusive. This means that both 10/1/92 and 12/31/92 are included as potential hire dates. Note that the smaller value must come first in the BETWEEN clause.

Lists

You can retrieve rows with values that match those in a list by using the IN keyword. If you are specifying ranges based on character data types (such as char and varchar), or date types (such as datetime and smalldatetime), you must enclose these types in single quotation marks.

SYNTAX

The syntax for the WHERE clause using comparisons is as follows:

```
SELECT <column_list>
FROM <table_list>
WHERE [NOT] column_name [NOT] IN (value_list)
```

If you want to find employees who work for publishers with a pub_id of 0877 or 9999, submit the following query:

```
INPUT/     SELECT emp_id, lname, fname
OUTPUT     FROM employee
           WHERE pub_id IN ('0877', '9999')

           emp_id     lname      fname
           ----------  -----------------------------     --------------------
           PMA42628M   Accorti    Paolo
           VPA30890F   Ashworth    Victoria
           H-B39728F   Bennett    Helen
           .    .    .
           .    .    .
           .    .    .
           A-R89858F   Roulet    Annette
           DBT39435M   Tonini    Daniel

           (17 row(s) affected)
```

You also can retrieve rows not in the list by using the NOT operator. If you want to find all
employees who do not work for publishers with a pub_id of 0877 or 9999 you can submit the following query:

```
INPUT/     SELECT emp_id, lname, fname
OUTPUT     FROM employee
           WHERE pub_id NOT IN ('0877', '9999')

           emp_id     lname                             fname
           ----------  ---------------------------------- --------------------
           PSA89086M Afonso                              Pedro
           F-C16315M Chang                               Francisco
           PTC11962M Cramer                              Philip
           A-C71970F Cruz                                Aria
           AMD15433F Devon                               Ann
           ......
           CGS88322F Schmitt                             Carine
           MAS70474F Smith                               Margaret
           HAS54740M Snyder                              Howard
           MFS52347M Sommer                              Martin
           GHT50241M Thomas                              Gary

           (26 row(s) affected)
```

> **Tip**
>
> Try using positive search conditions whenever possible. Avoid using NOT
> because the query optimizer does not always recognize negative search con-
> ditions. In other words, SQL Server must do a lot more work to return your
> result set when you use NOT. You can rewrite the preceding query using
> BETWEEN and AND statements.

Character Strings

You can retrieve rows based on portions of character strings, using the LIKE keyword. LIKE is used with char, varchar, nchar, nvarchar, text, datetime, and smalldatetime data. You can also use four wildcard characters in the form of *regular expressions*.

The syntax for the WHERE clause using the LIKE keyword follows:

```
SELECT <column_list>
FROM <table_list>
WHERE column_name  [NOT] LIKE 'string'
```

The available wildcards are

- %—String of zero or more characters
- _—Single character
- [ ]—Single character within the specified range
- [^]—Single character not within specified range

When you use the LIKE clause, make sure you enclose the wildcard characters in single quotation marks.

Take a look at the following examples.

You can submit the following query to return the title_id and title of all books with computer anywhere in the title from the titles table.

```
SELECT title_id, title
FROM titles
WHERE   title LIKE '%computer%'

title_id      title
--------      ---------------------------------------------------------
BU1111        Cooking with Computers: Surreptitious Balance Sheets
BU2075        You Can Combat Computer Stress!
BU7832        Straight Talk About Computers
MC3026        The Psychology of Computer Cooking
PS1372        Computer Phobic AND Non-Phobic Individuals:
              ➥Behavior Variations

(5 row(s) affected)
```

You can submit the following query to return the au_id, au_lname, and au_fname of all authors whose names begin with B or M from the authors table.

```
SELECT au_id, au_lname, au_fname
FROM authors
WHERE au_lname LIKE '[BM]%'
```

11

```
au_id            au_lname                                        au_fname
-----------      ---------------------------------------------   ----------
409-56-7008      Donnet                                          Abraham
648-92-1872      Blotchet-Halls                                  Reginald
724-80-9391      MacFeather                                      Stearns
893-72-1158      McBadden                                        Heather
```

(4 row(s) affected)

Unknown Values

NEW TERM   What is an unknown or null value? A *null* value is not the same as a blank char-
            acter string; nor is it the same as a 0 when dealing with numeric data. A NULL
occurs when a value is not assigned to a field. This is another way of saying that NULL is
equivalent to the value "unknown." In such cases, a NULL will fail all comparisons to
blanks, zeros, and other NULLs (when using the > or < comparison operators). So how do
you find rows based on NULL values? You can discriminate between rows in your tables
containing NULL values by using the IS NULL and IS NOT NULL keywords.

SYNTAX   The syntax for the WHERE clause using the IS NULL and IS NOT NULL operators is

```
SELECT column_list
FROM table_list
WHERE column_name IS [NOT] NULL
```

Examine the following examples.

You can submit this query to find all books that have no sales.

INPUT/
OUTPUT
```
SELECT title_id, title
FROM titles
WHERE ytd_sales IS NULL
```

or

```
SELECT title_id, title
FROM titles
WHERE ytd_sales = NULL
```

```
title_id    title
--------    -----------------------------------------------------------
MC3026      The Psychology of Computer Cooking
PC9999      Net Etiquette
```

(2 row(s) affected)

In contrast to the previous query, you can use the IS NOT NULL clause to find all books
that do have ytd_sales values by submitting the following query.

```
INPUT/       SELECT title_id, title
OUTPUT       FROM titles
             WHERE ytd_sales IS NOT NULL
```

or

```
SELECT title_id, title
FROM titles
WHERE ytd_sales <> NULL
```

```
title_id    title
--------    --------------------------------------------------------
BU1032      The Busy Executive's Database Guide
BU1111      Cooking with Computers: Surreptitious Balance Sheets
BU2075      You Can Combat Computer Stress!
BU7832      Straight Talk About Computers
   .    .
   .    .
   .    .
TC3218      Onions, Leeks, and Garlic: Cooking Secrets of
            ➥the Mediterranean
TC4203      Fifty Years in Buckingham Palace Kitchens
TC7777      Sushi, Anyone?
```

(16 row(s) affected)

Retrieving Rows Using Multiple Criteria

You have looked at selecting rows based on specific values, ranges, lists, string comparisons, and unknown values. You will now take a look at retrieving rows using multiple search criteria.

You can combine multiple search criteria using the logical operators AND, OR, and NOT. Using AND and OR operators allows you to join two or more expressions. The AND returns results when all conditions are true. The OR returns results when any of the conditions are true.

When more than one of the logical operators is used in the WHERE clause, the order of precedence can be significant. NOT is followed by AND and then OR.

Here is the syntax for a WHERE clause using multiple criteria:

```
SELECT column_list
FROM table_list
WHERE [NOT] expression {AND¦OR} [NOT] expression
```

SYNTAX

11

> **Note**   If you are using arithmetic operators joined by logical operators, arithmetic operators are processed first. Of course, you can always change the order of precedence using parentheses.

Take a look at some examples.

Query1

Consider the following: You want to retrieve the title ID, title, and price for all books that have a pub ID of 0877 or the word computer in the title, and for which the price is NOT NULL.

```
SELECT title_id, title, price, pub_id
FROM titles
WHERE title LIKE '%computer%' OR pub_id = '0877' AND price IS NOT
➥NULL

title_id    title    price    pub_id
--------    -------------------------------------------------------
BU1111    Cooking with Computers: Surreptitious Balance Sheets
➥11.95    1389
BU2075    You Can Combat Computer Stress!    2.99    736
BU7832    Straight Talk About Computers    19.99    1389
MC2222    Silicon Valley Gastronomic Treats    19.99    877
MC3021    The Gourmet Microwave    2.99    877
MC3026    The Psychology of Computer Cooking    (null)    877
PS1372    Computer Phobic AND Non-Phobic Individuals: Behavior
➥Variations    21.59    877
TC3218    Onions, Leeks, and Garlic: Cooking Secrets of the
➥Mediterranean    20.95    877
TC4203    Fifty Years in Buckingham Palace Kitchens    11.95    877
TC7777    Sushi, Anyone?    14.99    877

(10 row(s) affected)
```

Query2

Now run the query again and see whether you can get rid of that NULL value in your price field.

```
SELECT title_id, title, price, pub_id
FROM titles
WHERE (title LIKE '%computer%' OR pub_id = '0877')
➥AND price IS NOT NULL

title_id    title    price    pub_id
--------    -------------------------------------------------------
BU1111    Cooking with Computers: Surreptitious Balance Sheets
➥11.95    1389
```

```
BU2075    You Can Combat Computer Stress!    2.99    736
BU7832    Straight Talk About Computers    19.99    1389
MC2222    Silicon Valley Gastronomic Treats    19.99    877
MC3021    The Gourmet Microwave    2.99    877
PS1372    Computer Phobic AND Non-Phobic Individuals: Behavior
➥Variations    21.59    877
TC3218    Onions, Leeks, and Garlic: Cooking Secrets of the
➥Mediterranean    20.95    877
TC4203    Fifty Years in Buckingham Palace Kitchens    11.95    877
TC7777    Sushi, Anyone?    14.99    877
```

(9 row(s)affected)

ANALYSIS   Note that Query2 returns the desired results by changing the order of precedence.

Eliminating Duplicate Information

When selecting certain information from a table you might receive duplicate rows of information. You can eliminate duplicates by using the DISTINCT clause in the SELECT portion of the SELECT statement. If you do not specify the DISTINCT clause, all rows that meet the WHERE clause criteria will be returned.

SYNTAX

The syntax for the DISTINCT clause is

```
SELECT DISTINCT column_list
FROM table_name
WHERE search_conditions
```

Distinctness is determined by the combination of all the columns in the *column_list*. NULL values are treated as duplicates of each other; therefore, only one NULL will be returned.

Table 11.12 shows some SELECT statements with and without the DISTINCT clause. Query1 lists states in which authors live without listing duplicates. Query2 lists cities authors live in without listing duplicates. Query3 lists distinct combinations of cities and states.

TABLE 11.12   EACH QUERY SHOWS DISTINCT RESULTS

Query1	Query2	Query3
SELECT DISTINCT state FROM authors	SELECT DISTINCT city FROM authors	SELECT DISTINCT city, state FROM authors
State	*City*	*City and State*
CA	Ann Arbor	Ann Arbor, MI
IN	Berkeley	Berkeley, CA
KS	Corvallis	Corvallis, OR

continues

TABLE 11.12 CONTINUED

Query1	Query2	Query3
SELECT DISTINCT	SELECT DISTINCT	SELECT DISTINCT
state	city	city, state
FROM authors	FROM authors	FROM authors
State	*City*	*City and State*
MD	Covelo	Covelo, CA
MI	Gary	Gary, IN
OR	Lawrence	Lawrence, KS
TN	Menlo Park	Menlo Park, CA
UT	Nashville	Nashville, TN
	Oakland	Oakland, CA
	Palo Alto	Palo Alto, CA
	Rockville	Rockville, MD
	Salt Lake City	Salt Lake City, UT
	San Francisco	San Francisco, CA
	San Jose	San Jose, CA
	Vacaville	Vacaville, CA
	Walnut Creek	Walnut Creek, CA

If you just want to list the different cities where authors live, why not just use Query2 because it gives you the same cities Query3 does? To answer this, suppose two authors in your database live in Portland. If you run Query2 it would return Portland as one of the distinct values. However, one author lives in Portland, Oregon, the other in Portland, Maine. Obviously these are two distinct locations. So by submitting Query3 using the DISTINCT combination of city and state, it returns both Portland, Oregon, and Portland, Maine.

Notice that the results in all three queries are sorted. This might be by chance. Past versions of SQL Server sorted the values first, so the first value can be compared to the next value to make it easier to remove duplicate values. SQL Server 7.0 uses a more complex hashing algorithm to gather its information. This increases speed and efficiency, but you might lose the sorting. To guarantee that your data is sorted, you should include an ORDER BY clause in your queries.

Take a closer look at Query3.

```
SELECT DISTINCT city, state
FROM authors
```

The results returning Portland, OR, and Portland, ME, look like this:

```
city                      state
-------------------       ----
Portland      ME
Portland      OR

(2 row(s) affected)
```

Sorting Data Using the ORDER BY Clause

You can sort your query results by using the ORDER BY clause in your SELECT statement. The basic syntax for using the ORDER BY clause is as follows:

```
SELECT column_list
FROM table_list
[ORDER BY column_name | column_list_number [ASC|DESC]]
```

You can have any number of columns in your ORDER BY list as long as they are no wider than 900 bytes. You can also specify column names or use the ordinal number of the columns in the column_list.

These queries return the same ordered result sets.

Query1

```
SELECT title_id, au_id
FROM titleauthor
ORDER BY title_id, au_id
```

Query2

```
SELECT title_id, au_id
FROM titleauthor
ORDER BY 1, 2
```

You can use column names and ordinal numbers together in the ORDER BY clause. You can also specify whether you want the results sorted in ascending (ASC) or descending (DESC) order. If you do not specify ASC or DESC, ASC is used.

If you are sorting results based on a column that has NULL values, and ASC order is used, the rows containing NULLs will be displayed first.

When using the ORDER BY clause, the sort order of your SQL Server can make a difference in your result sets. The default sort order for SQL Server is dictionary order, case insensitive. If your SQL Server is using a sort order that is case sensitive, it can affect the ordering of your result sets. This is because a capital A is not considered the same as a lowercase a when you are using a case-sensitive sort order.

To find out what your server's current sort order is, you can execute the system-stored procedure sp_helpsort.

 Note

> You cannot use the ORDER BY clause on columns that are of text or image data types. This is true for text data types because they are stored in a different location in your database and can range from 0 to 2GB in length. SQL Server does not allow you to sort on a field this size. Image data types are also stored in their own separate 8KB data pages and are not sortable. A workaround is used to create a related table that has summary information about your image or text.

Midchapter Review

Now review what you have covered so far in this chapter.

So far you have built a foundation for data retrieval using the SELECT statement. You learned how to change your column headings and add string literals to your output using

SELECT *col_name* AS *new_col_name* to change a column heading

and

SELECT *string_literal*, *col_name* to add a string literal

You then expanded on your understanding of the SELECT statement using arithmetic operators, mathematical functions, string functions, and date and time functions. You then learned about system functions such as GetDate to further manipulate your data.

Many times the data you want to work with is not expressed in the format and data type you must use. You learned how to use the data conversion command CONVERT to alter your data from one data type to another.

You then continued expanding on the SELECT statement with a discussion and examples of choosing different rows of information by applying comparison operators, ranges of values, lists, and character strings.

You learned how to eliminate rows with NULL values. You also learned how to select distinct rows of information.

You finished up with this latest section on sorting your results using the ORDER BY clause.

Now that you've had a breather, continue with today's lesson learning how to work with some more advanced SELECT statements. You will now work with "advanced features" such as producing summary information with the GROUP BY and HAVING aggregate functions, as well as the COMPUTE and COMPUTE BY statements. You will also learn how to correlate data and perform subqueries. You will finish with a look at some other advanced queries that involve selecting data from more than one table. Just because these queries are advanced doesn't necessarily mean they are going to be too difficult for you. They are advanced because they tend to take a little more practice to master than the simple SELECT statements you have worked with already.

The second half of this chapter starts with aggregate functions.

Aggregate Functions

Aggregate functions can return summary values for an entire table or for groups of rows in a table. Aggregate functions are normally used in conjunction with the GROUP BY clause and are used in the HAVING clause or in the *column_list*. This might seem a little overwhelming at first, but bear with me. You will see each piece in its basic form, and then you will learn how to add additional pieces, one at a time. Table 11.13 lists the aggregate functions with their parameters and results.

TABLE 11.13 AGGREGATE FUNCTIONS

Function	Results
AVG([ALL ¦ DISTINCT] *column_name*)	Average of the values in the numeric expression, either all or distinct
COUNT(*)	Number of selected rows
COUNT([ALL ¦ DISTINCT] *column_name*)	Number of values in the expression, either all or distinct
MAX(*column_name*)	Highest value in the expression
MIN(*column_name*)	Lowest value in the expression
STDEV(*column_name*)	Returns the statistical standard deviation of all the values in the column name or expression
STDEVP(*column_name*)	Returns the statistical standard deviation for the population of all values in the given column name or expression
SUM([ALL ¦ DISTINCT] *column_name*)	Total of the values in the numeric expression, either all or distinct

continues

TABLE 11.13   CONTINUED

Function	Results
TOP *n* [PERCENT]	Returns the top *n* values or *n*% values in your result set
VAR(*column_name*)	Returns the statistical variance of values listed in the column name or expression
VARP(*column_name*)	Returns the statistical variance of a population of values listed in the column name or expression

Here are a few examples using the aggregate functions in the pubs database.

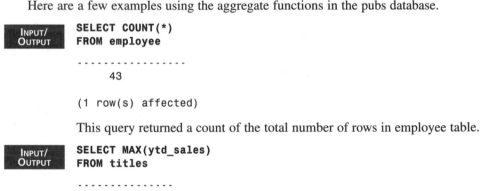

```
SELECT COUNT(*)
FROM employee
```

```
----------------
      43
```

```
(1 row(s) affected)
```

This query returned a count of the total number of rows in employee table.

```
SELECT MAX(ytd_sales)
FROM titles
```

```
--------------
22246
```

```
(1 row(s) affected)
```

This query selected the maximum value found in the ytd_sales column from the titles table.

```
SELECT SUM(qty)
FROM sales
```

```
--------------
493
```

This query selected all the values in the qty column of the sales table and added them up.

GROUP BY and HAVING

The GROUP BY clause groups summary data that meets the WHERE clause criteria to be returned as single rows. The HAVING clause sets the criteria to determine which rows will be returned by the GROUP BY clause. For example, you could find out which books have more than one author and then return the book title and the authors for each book.

Here is the syntax for the GROUP BY and HAVING clauses:

```
SELECT column_list
FROM table_list
WHERE search_criteria
[GROUP BY [ALL] non_aggregate_expression(s)
[HAVING] search_criteria]
```

The HAVING clause has the same effect on the GROUP BY clause as the WHERE clause has on the SELECT statement. Here are some examples of using the GROUP BY and HAVING clauses.

INPUT/
OUTPUT

```
SELECT title_id, count(title_id) AS Number_of_Authors
FROM titleauthor
GROUP BY title_id
HAVING count(title_id) > 1

title_id    Number_of_Authors
-------     ------------------
BU1032      2
BU1111      2
MC3021      2
PC8888      2
PS1372      2
PS2091      2
TC7777      3
```

11

ANALYSIS   This query found all books that have more than one author and returned the title_id and number of authors for each book.

The GROUP BY ALL clause will return all groupings, including those not meeting the WHERE clause criteria.

If you want to find all books with year-to-date sales of $4,000 or more and list all title IDs, you can submit the following query:

INPUT/
OUTPUT

```
SELECT title_id, ytd_sales
FROM titles
WHERE (ytd_sales>=4000)
GROUP BY ALL title_id, ytd_sales

title_id    ytd_sales
--------    ----------
BU1032      4095
BU1111      3876
BU2075      18722
BU7832      4095
MC2222      2032
MC3021      22246
MC3026      (null)
PC1035      8780
```

```
PC8888      4095
PC9999      (null)
PS1372      375
PS2091      2045
PS2106      111
PS3333      4072
PS7777      3336
TC3218      375
TC4203      15096
TC7777      4095
```

ANALYSIS   Notice that all books that don't meet the WHERE clause criteria are still listed.

Note   There are certain requirements that the GROUP BY and HAVING clauses must meet to comply with ANSI standards. One of these requirements is that the GROUP BY clause must contain all nonaggregate columns from the SELECT *column_list*. Another is that the HAVING clause criteria columns return only one value.

COMPUTE and COMPUTE BY

The COMPUTE and COMPUTE BY clauses are used to produce new rows of summary and detail data. They use the aggregate functions specified earlier. The COMPUTE clause returns detail rows and a grand total summary row. The COMPUTE BY clause returns new rows of summary data, much like the GROUP BY clause, but it returns the rows as sub-groups with summary values.

The syntax for the COMPUTE and COMPUTE BY clauses is

SYNTAX

```
SELECT column_list
FROM table_list
WHERE search_criteria
[COMPUTE] aggregate_expression(s)
[BY] column_list]
```

Here are a couple of examples. You are going to compare the COMPUTE BY clause with the GROUP BY clause.

GROUP BY Example:

```
SELECT type, SUM(ytd_sales)
FROM titles
GROUP BY type
```

```
type    ytd_sales
```

```
- - - - - - - - - - -     - - - - - - - -
business      30788
mod_cook      24278
popular_comp    12875
psychology     9939
trad_cook      15471
UNDECIDED      NULL
```

If you use the COMPUTE BY clause, you must also include the ORDER BY clause. Now, if your ORDER BY clause is

```
ORDER BY title_id, pub_id, au_id
```

then your COMPUTE BY clause can be one of the following:

```
COMPUTE aggregate_function (column_name)
BY title_id, pub_id, au_id
```

or

```
COMPUTE aggregate_function (column_name)
BY title_id, pub_id
```

or

```
COMPUTE aggregate_function (column_name)
BY title_id
```

As you can see, the columns listed in the COMPUTE BY clause must be the same as, or a subset of, the columns in the ORDER BY clause. The order of the columns in the COMPUTE BY clause must be the same as those in the ORDER BY clause, and you cannot skip columns. Enter the following and look at the results:

INPUT/
OUTPUT

```
SELECT type, ytd_sales
FROM titles
ORDER BY type
COMPUTE SUM(ytd_sales) BY type

type     ytd_sales
- - - - - - - - - - -     - - - - - - - - - -
business    4095
business    3876
business    18722
business    4095

    sum
    =========
    30788


type     ytd_sales
- - - - - - - - - - -     - - - - - - - - - -
mod_cook    2032
```

```
mod_cook     22246

     sum
     ========
     24278

type     ytd_sales
------------     ----------
popular_comp     8780
popular_comp     4095
popular_comp     (null)

     sum
     ========
     12875

type     ytd_sales
------------     ----------
psychology     375
psychology     2045
psychology     111
psychology     4072
psychology     3336

     sum
     ========
     9939

type     ytd_sales
------------     ----------
trad_cook     375
trad_cook     15096
trad_cook     4095

     sum
     ========
     19566

type     ytd_sales
------------     ----------
UNDECIDED     (null)

     sum
     ========
     (null)

(24 row(s) affected)
```

> **Note**
>
> The COMPUTE and COMPUTE BY clauses produce new rows of nonrelational data; therefore, they cannot be used with the SELECT INTO statement to create new tables. This also makes them nearly impossible to use programmatically.
>
> You cannot use COMPUTE and COMPUTE BY with text or image data types because these are nonsortable.

Super Aggregates (ROLLUP and CUBE)

To produce additional summary rows, referred to as super aggregates, you can use the ROLLUP and CUBE operators. You use the ROLLUP and CUBE operators in conjunction with the GROUP BY clause.

SYNTAX

The following is the syntax for the ROLLUP and CUBE operators:

```
SELECT column_list
FROM table_list
WHERE search_criteria
[GROUP BY [ALL] non_aggregate_expression(s)
[WITH {ROLLUP | CUBE}]]
```

The ROLLUP operator is typically used to produce running averages or running sums. You do this by applying the aggregate function in the SELECT *column_list* to each column in the GROUP BY clause moving from left to right. What does that mean? You'll understand this most easily with an example.

```
SELECT type, pub_id,
SUM(ytd_sales) AS ytd_sales
FROM titles
GROUP BY type, pub_id
WITH ROLLUP

type          pub_id    ytd_sales
-----------   ------    ----------
business      736       18722
business      1389      12066
business      (null)    30788
mod_cook      877       24278
mod_cook      (null)    24278
popular_comp  1389      12875
popular_comp  (null)    12875
psychology    736       9564
psychology    877       375
psychology    (null)    9939
trad_cook     877       19566
trad_cook     (null)    19566
```

11

```
UNDECIDED    877     (null)
UNDECIDED    (null)  (null)
(null)       (null)  97446
```

(15 row(s) affected)

ANALYSIS   The ROLLUP operator produced a row in your output for each row in the titles
table with a single type and pub_id. It then showed you the ytd_sales for each
item and produced an additional row for each type with summary information. In your
example, the rows with (null) in the pub_id field display the SUM of all of the
ytd_sales for that group of types.

Let me put this into English for you. In the titles table were two rows that had both a
business type and a unique pub_id (in the real table there are a total of four books of
type business, with one author (pub_id) writing three books and another author writing
the fourth). Each author who wrote business books had ytd_sales of 18,722 and 12,066,
respectively.

The ROLLUP operator then created a subtotal field that summed all of the business type
books (18,722 + 12,066) 30,788. The query then did the same thing for each group of
book types and authors in the table and then gave you a grand total (97,446) signified by
a (null) value in both the type and pub_id fields.

The CUBE operator will produce super-aggregate rows by using every possible combination of the columns in the GROUP BY clause. Like the ROLLUP operator, the CUBE operator
will produce the running averages and running sums but will also cross-reference
columns to return additional summary rows. Here is an example:

INPUT/ OUTPUT
```
SELECT type, pub_id,
SUM(ytd_sales) AS ytd_sales
FROM titles
GROUP BY type, pub_id
WITH CUBE

type       pub_id    ytd_sales
----------- ------ -----------
business      736    18722
business     1389    12066
business     (null)    30788
mod_cook      877    24278
mod_cook     (null)    24278
popular_comp  1389    12875
popular_comp (null)    12875
psychology    736     9564
psychology    877     375
psychology   (null)     9939
trad_cook     877    19566
trad_cook    (null)    19566
```

```
UNDECIDED    877     (null)
UNDECIDED    (null)    (null)
(null)     (null)    97446
(null)      736     28286
(null)      877     44219
(null)     1389     24941

(18 row(s) affected)
```

ANALYSIS The CUBE operator produced a row in your output for each row in the titles table with a single type and pub_id. It then showed you the ytd_sales for each item and produced an additional row for each type with summary information and another row for each pub_id. In this example, the rows with (null) in the pub_id field display the sum of all of the ytd_sales for that group of types, the rows with (null) in the type field display the sum of all the ytd_sales for that group of pub_ids.

When using ROLLUP or CUBE, some restrictions are placed on the GROUP BY clause. You can have a maximum of 10 columns in the GROUP BY clause and the sum of the sizes of those columns cannot exceed 900 bytes in size and you cannot use the GROUP BY ALL clause.

Note The ROLLUP and CUBE operators produce new rows of nonrelational data; therefore, you cannot use them with the SELECT INTO statement. Also, you cannot use ROLLUP and CUBE operators with text or image data types because these are nonsortable.

Data Correlation

In this section you will look at implementing joins to retrieve data from two or more tables. The results will appear as a single table with columns from all the tables specified in the SELECT column_list and meeting the search criteria. You will look at how to implement joins using both ANSI and SQL Server syntax, and then at the different types of joins: inner joins, cross joins, outer joins, and self joins.

Implementing Joins

To join tables, you must make a comparison of one or more columns from a table to one or more columns in one or more tables. The result of the comparison produces new rows by combining the columns in the SELECT column_list from the joined tables that meet the join conditions. When you join tables you can use either ANSI or SQL Server join syntax. The syntax for both ANSI and SQL Server syntax are as follows.

SYNTAX

ANSI Join Syntax

```
SELECT table_name.column_name, [...]
FROM {table_name [join_type] JOIN table_name
ON search_criteria}, [...]
WHERE search_criteria
```

The join statements for the ANSI syntax show up in the FROM clause of the SELECT statement. The WHERE clause selects rows from the joined rows to be returned. There are three types of ANSI join statements you can choose: INNER JOIN, OUTER JOIN, and CROSS JOIN.

SYNTAX

SQL Server Join Syntax

```
SELECT table_name.column_name, [...]
FROM table_list
WHERE table_name.column_name
join_operator table_name.column_name, [...]
```

In SQL Server syntax, the FROM clause lists the tables involved in the join. The WHERE clause includes the columns to be joined and can include additional search criteria that determine the rows to be returned. The join operators for SQL Server syntax are the following: =, >, <, >=, <=, <>, !>, and !<.

Inner Joins

Joins connect two tables based on a join condition producing results as a new table, with the rows that satisfy the join condition. Inner joins produce information when matching information is found in both tables. The most common types of inner joins are equijoins and natural joins.

NEW TERM In an *equijoin*, column values are compared for equality, and redundant columns are displayed as columns in the result set; whereas in a *natural join*, the redundant columns are not displayed twice.

Take a look at the following example to clarify what was just said.

INPUT/
OUTPUT

SQL Server Syntax

```
SELECT *
FROM publishers, pub_info
WHERE publishers.pub_id = pub_info.pub_id
```

ANSI Syntax

```
SELECT *
FROM publishers
INNER JOIN  pub_info ON publishers.pub_id = pub_info.pub_id
```

```
pub_id    pub_name    city    state    country    pub_id    logo
➥pr_info
```

```
----      --------     --------     ----    ----   ----   --------
736       New Moon Books    Boston     MA      USA    736    NEWMOON.BMP
➡New Moon Books…
877       Binnet & Hardley    Washington    DC      USA    877
➡BINNET.BMP     Binnet & Hardley…
1389      Algodata Infosystems    Berkeley    CA      USA    1389
➡ALGODATA.BMP Algodata Infosystem
1622      Five Lakes Publishing    Chicago    IL      USA    1622
➡5LAKES.BMP Five Lakes Publishing
1756      Ramona Publishers    Dallas    TX      USA    1756
➡RAMONA.BMP     Ramona Publishers
9901      GGG&G    M¸nchen    NULL    GER    9901    GGGG.BMP
➡GGG&G…
9952      Scootney Books    New York    NY      USA    9952
➡SCOOTNEY.BMP     Scootney Books…
9999      Lucerne Publishing    Paris    NULL    FRA    9999
➡LUCERNE.BMP     Lucerne Publishing…
```

```
(8 row(s) affected)
```

ANALYSIS   In this example, the SELECT statement selects all columns from both the publishers and pub_info tables when the pub_id columns for the joined tables are equal. Note the redundant pub_id column.

Natural Joins

In a natural join, column values are compared for equality, but redundant columns are eliminated from the columns in the result set.

Here is an example of a natural join.

SQL Server Syntax

```
SELECT publishers.*, pub_info.logo, pub_info.pr_info
FROM publishers, pub_info
WHERE publishers.pub_id = pub_info.pub_id
```

ANSI Syntax

```
SELECT publishers.*, pub_info.logo, pub_info.pr_info
FROM publishers
INNER JOIN pub_info ON publishers.pub_id = pub_info.pub_id
```

```
pub_id    pub_name     city     state     country    …
----      --------     --------     ----    ----    …
736       New Moon Books    Boston     MA      USA    …
877       Binnet & Hardley    Washington    DC      USA    …
```

11

```
1389    Algodata Infosystems    Berkeley    CA    USA    ...
1622    Five Lakes Publishing   Chicago     IL    USA    ...
1756    Ramona Publishers       Dallas      TX    USA    ...
9901    GGG&G     M nchen        NULL       GER   ...
9952    Scootney Books    New York    NY    USA    ...
9999    Lucerne Publishing      Paris    NULL    FRA    ...
```

```
(8 row(s) affected)
```

ANALYSIS In this example, the SELECT statement selects all columns from the publishers table and all columns except pub_id from the pub_info table.

Cross or Unrestricted Joins

Cross or unrestricted joins return a combination of all rows of all tables in the join as the result set. A cross or unrestricted join is created not by using the WHERE clause in the SQL Server join of two or more tables, but by using the CROSS JOIN keyword for the ANSI join.

NEW TERM Combining all rows from all tables involved in the join yields what is known as a *Cartesian product*. In most cases, this type of result set is unusable unless your intention is to find every possible combination, such as some type of statistical or mathematical analysis. To put it another way, if you look at each table as a matrix and then you multiply the matrices, you get a new matrix with all combinations, as shown in Figure 11.1. Each row from Table1 is added to each row in Table2. If you add the number of columns from both tables, you get the resulting number of columns. If you multiply the number of rows in Table1 by the number of rows in Table2, you get the total number of rows returned by your query.

FIGURE 11.1

Creating a Cartesian product.

Table1	3 columns 3 rows	
A1	B1	C1
A2	B2	C2
A3	B3	C3

Table2	4columns 2 rows		
W1	X1	Y1	Z1
W2	X2	Y2	Z2

Result Set: 7columns (3+4)
                       6 rows (3*2)

A1	B1	C1	W1	X1	Y1	Z1
A1	B1	C1	W2	X2	Y2	Z2
A2	B2	C2	W1	X1	Y1	Z1
A2	B2	C2	W2	X2	Y2	Z2
A3	B3	C3	W1	X1	Y1	Z1
A3	B3	C3	W2	X2	Y2	Z2

Note

> Tables cannot be joined on text or image columns. You can, however, compare the lengths of text columns from two tables with a WHERE clause, but you cannot compare actual data.

Here is an example of creating a Cartesian product using the CROSS JOIN or *unrestricted join*. Say you want to list all book titles and their authors' IDs, and you submit the following query:

INPUT/ OUTPUT

SQL Server Syntax

```
SELECT titles.title, titleauthor.au_id
FROM titles, titleauthor
```

ANSI Syntax

```
SELECT titles.title, titleauthor.au_id
FROM titles CROSS JOIN titleauthor

title     au_id
--------------    ----------
The Busy Executive's Database Guide     172-32-1176
The Busy Executive's Database Guide     213-46-8915
  .    .
  .    .
  .    .
Sushi, Anyone?    998-72-3567
Sushi, Anyone?    998-72-3567

(450 row(s) affected)
```

ANALYSIS The results of the query you submitted yielded 450 rows. There are 18 rows in the titles table and 25 rows in the titleauthor table. Because an unrestricted or cross join returns all possible combinations, you get 18×25 = 450 rows—not quite the desired result, right?

To avoid submitting an unrestricted join, you should take the number of tables you are joining and subtract 1. N – 1 will be the number of join clauses needed, where N is the number of tables involved in the join (that is, three tables, 3 – 1 = 2, two join clauses). The number of join clauses might be more if you are joining based on a composite key.

Outer Joins

You can restrict rows from one table while allowing all rows from another table as your result set by using outer joins. One of the most common uses for this type of join is to search for orphan records. The outer join operators and keywords are as follows:

11

Caution In prior releases of SQL Server, you could use the following SQL Server syntax:

*= includes all rows from the first table and only the matching rows in the second table (left outer join).

=* includes all rows from the second table and only the matching rows in the first table (right outer join).

Unfortunately, these operators are not always guaranteed to produce the correct results. Problems can occur when NULL values are present. Therefore, when using OUTER joins, you should always use the ANSI outer join syntax.

ANSI Syntax:

LEFT OUTER JOIN	Includes all rows from the first table and only the matching rows in the second table
RIGHT OUTER JOIN	Includes all rows from the second table and only the matching rows in the first table
FULL OUTER JOIN	Includes all nonmatching rows from both tables

You have a table of customers and a table with orders. These two tables are related by a CustomerID field. With an equijoin or a natural join, you only return records when the CustomerID field has a match in both tables. Outer joins can be handy to get a customer list, and if a customer happens to have an order, that order information will also show up. If the customer does not have an order, the information from the orders table will show up as (null).

If you do a left outer join on these tables and specify the customers table first, the desired results will be returned. If you specify a right outer join, your results show all orders; if an order happens to have a CustomerID that does not match a CustomerID in the customers table, the customer information will be (null). (If you follow the rules of referential integrity, you should never have an order without a valid CustomerID. If this is the case, then your right outer join will have the same results as an equijoin or a natural join—all orders and customers when there is a match on CustomerID.)

The left and right outer joins can return the same results depending on the table order. For example, these two joins return the same information:

```
Customers.CustomerID *= Orders.CustomerID
```

and

```
Orders.CustomerID =* Customers.CustomerID.
```

If you want to find all the titles, whether they happen to have sold any copies, and the number of copies sold, you can submit the following query.

INPUT/OUTPUT   **SQL Server Syntax**

```
SELECT titles.title_id, titles.title, sales.qty
FROM titles LEFT  OUTER JOIN sales
ON titles.title_id = sales.title_id

title_id    title                                    qty
--------    -------------------------------------
BU1032      The Busy Executive's D…      5
BU1032      The Busy Executive's D…      10
BU1111      Cooking with Computers…      25
BU2075      You Can Combat Compute…      35
BU7832      Straight Talk About Co…      15
MC2222      Silicon Valley Gastron…      10
MC3021      The Gourmet Microwave        25
MC3021      The Gourmet Microwave        15
MC3026      The Psychology of Comp…    (null)
PC1035      But Is It User Friendl…      30
PC8888      Secrets of Silicon Val…      50
PC9999      Net Etiquette        (null)
PS1372      Computer Phobic AND No…      20
PS2091      Is Anger the Enemy?       3
PS2091      Is Anger the Enemy?       75
PS2091      Is Anger the Enemy?       10
PS2091      Is Anger the Enemy?       20
PS2106      Life Without Fear            25
PS3333      Prolonged Data Deprivat…     15
PS7777      Emotional Security: A …      25
TC3218      Onions, Leeks, and Gar…      40
TC4203      Fifty Years in Bucking…      20
TC7777      Sushi, Anyone?          20

(23 row(s) affected)
```

Self Joins

As the name suggests, a self join correlates rows of a table with other rows in the same table. Comparison queries for the same information are used the most for self joins. For example, if you want to list all authors who live in the same city and zip code, you will compare city and zip by executing the following query.

SQL Server Syntax

```
SELECT au1.au_fname, au1.au_lname,
au2.au_fname, au2.au_lname,
au1.city, au1.zip
FROM authors au1, authors au2
WHERE au1.city = au2.city
AND au1.zip = au2.zip
AND au1.au_id < au2.au_id
ORDER BY au1.city, au1.zip
```

ANSI Syntax

```
SELECT au1.au_fname, au1.au_lname,
au2.au_fname, au2.au_lname,
au1.city, au1.zip
FROM authors au1
INNER JOIN authors au2 ON au1.city = au2.city
AND au1.zip = au2.zip
WHERE au1.au_id < au2.au_id
ORDER BY au1.city, au1.zip
```

```
au_fname    au_lname    au_fname    au_lname    city          zip
--------    --------    --------    --------    -----------   ---
Cheryl      Carson      Abraham     Bennet      Berkeley      94705
Dean        Straight    Dirk        Stringer    Oakland       94609
Dean        Straight    Livia       Karsen      Oakland       94609
Dirk        Stringer    Livia       Karsen      Oakland       94609
Ann         Dull        Sheryl      Hunter      Palo Alto     94301
Anne        Ringer      Albert      Ringer      Salt Lake City   84152

(6 row(s) affected)
```

Notice that when you perform a self join on a table, you create an alias for the table name. You do this so that one table is treated logically as two tables.

> **Tip**
>
> A table alias is useful any time you do a multitable join operation. It allows you to create a more readable and shorter query statement because you reference the table alias instead of the table name.

Subqueries

A SELECT statement nested inside another SELECT statement is commonly referred to as a subquery. Subqueries can produce the same results as a join operation. In this section you will look at how the subquery is used, the types of subqueries, subquery restrictions, and correlated subqueries.

How to Use the Subquery

A SELECT statement can be nested within another SELECT, INSERT, UPDATE, or DELETE statement. If the subquery returns a single value, such as an aggregate, it can be used anywhere a single value can be used. If the subquery returns a list, such as a single column of many values, it can be used only in the WHERE clause.

In many cases a join operation can be used instead of a subquery; however, some instances can be processed only as a subquery. In some cases a join operation can yield better performance than a subquery, but generally there is little performance difference.

The subquery is always enclosed within parentheses and, unless doing a correlated subquery, completes before the outer query is processed. A subquery can contain another subquery, and that subquery can contain a subquery, and so on. There is no practical limit to the number of subqueries that can be processed other than system resources.

SYNTAX

Here is the syntax for a nested SELECT statement:

```
(SELECT [ALL ¦ DISTINCT] subquery_column_list
[FROM table_list]
[WHERE clause]
[GROUP BY clause]
[HAVING clause])
```

Types of Subqueries

A subquery can return a single column or single value anywhere a single value expression can be used and can be compared against using the following operators: =, <, >, <=, >=, <>, !>, and !<. It can return single column/many values that can be used with the IN list comparison operator in the WHERE clause. A subquery can also return many rows that will be used for an existence check by using the EXISTS keyword in the WHERE clause.

To find all authors who live in the same state as the bookstore that sells their publishers' books, you can run either of the following queries:

INPUT/OUTPUT

```
SELECT DISTINCT au_fname, au_lname, state
FROM authors
WHERE state IN
(SELECT state FROM stores)
```

or

```
SELECT DISTINCT au_fname, au_lname, state
FROM authors
WHERE EXISTS
(SELECT * FROM stores
WHERE state = authors.state)
```

```
au_fname        au_lname      state
------------------     --------------------------  -----
Abraham                Bennet              CA
Akiko                  Yokomoto                CA
Ann                    Dull                        CA
Burt                   Gringlesby          CA
Charlene               Locksley            CA
Cheryl                 Carson                  CA
Dean                   Straight                CA
Dirk                   Stringer                CA
Heather                McBadden        CA
Johnson                White                   CA
Livia                  Karsen              CA
Marjorie               Green                       CA
Michael                O'Leary                     CA
Reginald               Blotchet-Halls      OR
Sheryl                 Hunter                      CA
Stearns                MacFeather          CA

(16 row(s) affected)
```

There are restrictions on what you can do with subqueries. This list provides the rules by which you can create and use a subquery:

- It must be in parentheses.
- If used when a single-value expression is used, it must return a single value.
- It cannot be used in the ORDER BY clause.
- It cannot contain an ORDER BY, COMPUTE, or SELECT INTO clause.
- It cannot have more than one column in the *column_list* if used with the IN clause.
- It must have SELECT * if used with the EXISTS clause.
- Text and image data types are not allowed in the select list (except for the use of *).
- It cannot include the GROUP BY and HAVING clauses if used with an unmodified comparison operator (one without an ANY or ALL keyword).

Correlated Subqueries

A correlated subquery references a table from the outer query and evaluates each row for the outer query. In this aspect, a correlated subquery differs from a normal subquery because the subquery depends on values from the outer query. A normal subquery is executed independently of the outer query.

In the following example, the join query is rewritten as a correlated subquery. The queries will return the same information. The queries answer the following instruction: Show me authors who live in the same city and zip code.

INPUT/
OUTPUT

SQL Server JOIN Syntax

```
SELECT au1.au_fname, au1.au_lname,
au2.au_fname, au2.au_lname,
au1.city, au1.zip
FROM authors au1, authors au2
WHERE au1.city = au2.city
AND au1.zip = au2.zip
AND au1.au_id < au2.au_id
ORDER BY au1.city, au1.zip
```

```
au_fname    au_lname     au_fname    au_lname    city        zip
-------     -------      -------     -------     ----------  ------
Cheryl      Carson       Abraham     Bennet      Berkeley      94705
Dean        Straight     Dirk        Stringer    Oakland       94609
Dean        Straight     Livia       Karsen      Oakland       94609
Dirk        Stringer     Livia       Karsen      Oakland       94609
Ann      Dull      Sheryl    Hunter     Palo Alto      94301
Anne        Ringer       Albert      Ringer      Salt Lake City    84152
```

(6 row(s) affected)

SQL Server Correlated Subquery Syntax

```
SELECT au1.au_fname, au1.au_lname, au1.city, au1.zip
FROM authors au1
WHERE zip IN
(SELECT zip
FROM authors au2
WHERE au1.city = au2.city
AND au1.au_id <> au2.au_id)
ORDER BY au1.city, au1.zip
```

```
au_fname    au_lname    city        zip
--------    -----------  --------------    ---------
Abraham     Bennet      Berkeley      94705
Cheryl      Carson      Berkeley      94705
Livia       Karsen      Oakland       94609
Dirk        Stringer    Oakland       94609
Dean        Straight    Oakland       94609
Sheryl      Hunter      Palo Alto      94301
Ann      Dull     Palo Alto      94301
Albert      Ringer      Salt Lake City     84152
Anne        Ringer      Salt Lake City     84152
```

(9 row(s) affected)

Notice that the same data is returned; it's just formatted differently and is more readable.

11

SELECT INTO

The SELECT INTO statement enables you to create a new table based on query results. The new table is based on the columns you specify in the select list, the tables you name in the FROM clause, and the rows you choose in the WHERE clause. There are two types of tables you can create with a SELECT INTO statement: permanent and temporary. The syntax for the SELECT INTO is as follows:

SYNTAX

```
SELECT column_list
INTO new_table_name
FROM table_list
WHERE search_criteria
```

When creating a permanent table, you must set the SELECT INTO/BULK COPY database option. The SELECT INTO statement lets you define a table and put data into it without going through the usual data definition process. The name of the new table must be unique within the database and must conform to the rules for SQL Server naming conventions.

If columns in the *column_list* of your SELECT statement have no titles, such as derived columns like aggregate functions, the columns in the new table will have no names. There are two problems with this:

- Column names within a table must be unique; therefore, if more than one column has no header, the SELECT INTO will fail.

- If there is a column with no header in the new table, the only way to retrieve that column is to use SELECT *.

For these reasons, it is good practice to create column aliases for derived columns. Also, because using SELECT INTO is a nonlogged operation, you should back up your database immediately following this operation. You can also use the SELECT INTO statement to create temporary tables.

NEW TERM There are two types of temporary tables: local and global. A *local temporary table* is available only during the current user session to SQL Server and is deallocated when the session is terminated. A local temporary table is created by preceding the new table name with the # symbol. A *global temporary table* is available to all user sessions to SQL Server and is deallocated when the last user session accessing the table is terminated. A global temporary table is created by preceding the new table name with two ## symbols. These temporary tables reside in the tempdb database.

INPUT/OUTPUT

```
SELECT title_id, title, price
INTO #tmpTitles
FROM titles
GO
```

```
SELECT * FROM #tmpTitles
GO

title_id    Title       price
--------    ---------------------------------    ---------
BU1032    The Busy Executive's Database Guide    19.99
BU1111    Cooking with Computers: Surreptitious …    11.95
BU2075    You Can Combat Computer Stress!    2.99
.    .    .
.    .    .
.    .    .
TC3218    Onions, Leeks, and Garlic: Cooking Secrets …  20.95
TC4203    Fifty Years in Buckingham Palace Kitchens    11.95
TC7777    Sushi, Anyone?    14.99

(18 row(s) affected)
```

> **Tip**
>
> The purpose of the SELECT INTO statement is to create a new table. If you want to add rows to a preexisting table, use the INSERT statement or INSERT INTO, both of which you will learn about in tomorrow's lesson.

11

UNION Operator

You can combine the results of two or more queries into a single result set by using the UNION operator. By default, duplicate rows are eliminated; however, using UNION with the ALL keyword returns all rows, including duplicates.

```
SELECT column_list [INTO clause]
[FROM clause]
[WHERE clause]
[GROUP BY clause]
[HAVING clause]
[UNION [ALL]
SELECT column_list
[FROM clause]
[WHERE clause]
[GROUP BY clause]
[HAVING clause]...]
[ORDER BY clause]
[COMPUTE clause]
```

Here are the rules for using the UNION operator:

- All *column_list*s must have the same number of columns, same column order, and similar data types.
- If you use an INTO clause in one of the queries, you must use it in the first query.
- You can use GROUP BY and HAVING clauses only within individual queries.

- ORDER BY and COMPUTE clauses are allowed only at the end of the UNION statement to define the order of the final results or to compute summary values.

- Column names come from the first SELECT column_list.

```
SELECT title, stor_name, ord_date, qty
FROM titles, sales, stores
WHERE titles.title_id = sales.title_id
AND stores.stor_id = sales.stor_id
UNION
SELECT title, 'No Sales', NULL, NULL
FROM titles
WHERE title_id NOT IN
(SELECT title_id FROM sales)
ORDER BY qty
```

```
title       stor_name      ord_date      qty
---------------  ---------------  --------------  ------
Net Etiquette    No Sales    (null)    (null)
The Psychology …    No Sales    (null)    (null)
Is Anger the Enemy?    Eric the Read Books    Sep 13 1994…    3
   .     .     .     .
   .     .     .     .
   .     .     .     .
Onions, Leeks, and Garlic: …    News & Brews    Jun 15 19…    40
Secrets of Silicon Valley    Barnum's    May 24 1993…    50
Is Anger the Enemy?    Barnum's    Sep 13 1994…    75

(23 row(s) affected)
```

Summary

Today you built a foundation for data retrieval using the SELECT statement. You then learned how to change your column headings and add string literals to your output. You expanded on your understanding of the SELECT statement using arithmetic operators, mathematical functions, string functions, and datetime functions. You also learned about system functions that can be used to further manipulate your data.

Often, the data you want to work with is not expressed in the format and data type you must use. You learned how to use data conversion to alter your data from one data type to another.

You expanded on your knowledge by learning how to pull certain rows of information out of your database by applying comparison operators, ranges, lists, and character strings. You also learned how to eliminate rows with null values. You then studied methods of removing duplicate information by using the DISTINCT keyword.

You then covered how to sort your results using the ORDER BY clause with your data. You took a short breather at that point and then continued learning about some of the advanced features you can apply in SQL Server. This included aggregate functions like SUM and AVG and how to use them in a SELECT statement.

Recall that the aggregate functions can return summary values for an entire table or for groups of rows in a table, and are normally used in conjunction with the GROUP BY or HAVING clauses or in the *column_list*.

GROUP BY clauses group summary data that meet the WHERE clause criteria to be returned as single rows. The HAVING clauses can also be used to set the criteria to be returned by the GROUP BY clause.

The ORDER BY clause is used to sort your results. Remember that SQL Server sometimes returns results in sorted order, but it's not guaranteed unless you specify the ORDER BY clause.

You also learned about the COMPUTE and COMPUTE BY clauses, which can be used to produce new rows of summary and detail data. The COMPUTE clause is useful because it returns detail rows and a grand total summary row. The COMPUTE BY clause returns rows as subgroups with summary values.

To produce additional summary rows that are often called super aggregates, you learned about the ROLLUP and CUBE operators, which are used in conjunction with the GROUP BY clause.

The ROLLUP operator is typically used to produce running averages or running sums. The CUBE operator produces super aggregate rows by using every possible combination of the columns in the GROUP BY clause.

You also learned how to join tables using both the ANSI syntax and the SQL Server syntax. The join statements for the ANSI syntax show up in the FROM clause of the SELECT statement, whereas the WHERE clause is used for the SQL Server syntax. There are three types of ANSI join statements: INNER JOIN, OUTER JOIN, and CROSS JOIN. Inner joins are either equijoins or natural joins and return information when values in two tables are identical. Outer joins can show you all the information from one table; if the associated table has values that match, they will be displayed as well. Cross or unrestricted joins return a combination of all rows of all tables in the join as the result set.

You also learned about creating subqueries. These occur when you nest a SELECT statement inside another SELECT statement. Subqueries can produce the same results as a join operation.

The SELECT INTO statement allows you to create a new table based on query results. You can create either permanent tables or temporary tables. When you create a permanent table, you must have the SELECT INTO/DULKCOPY option set to true for the database. To create temporary tables, you prefix the table name with a # for a local temporary table, or a ## for a global temporary table.

Finally, you learned how to combine the results of two or more queries into a single result set by using the UNION operator.

Q&A

Q It looks like your SELECT statements can get pretty long. Is there a limit to how big they can be?

A Yes, queries are limited to 64KB in length.

Q Where can you find SELECT statements?

A SELECT statements are often found in front-end applications like Visual Basic and PowerBuilder. You can also find SELECT statements embedded in stored procedures, triggers, events, alerts, and many other locations in your SQL Server.

Q When should you use ANSI syntax and when should you use SQL Server syntax?

A In general, you should try to use the ANSI syntax because this implementation is a standard, the code is much more portable, and there is little or no performance gain/loss.

Q What does the following statement do?

```
SELECT SUM(qty) FROM sales
```

A This will return the sum of the qty field in the sales table.

Q Is it a good idea to use COMPUTE and COMPUTE BY?

A It is OK to use these statements, but remember that the data they return is nonrelational.

Workshop

The Workshop provides quiz questions to help you solidify your understanding of the concepts presented in this chapter. In addition to the quiz questions, exercises are provided to let you practice what you have learned in this chapter. Try to understand the quiz and exercise answers before continuing to the next day's lesson. Answers are provided in Appendix A, "Answers."

Quiz

1. What do these queries return?

   a.
   ```
   SELECT * FROM authors
   WHERE au_lname LIKE 'M%'
   ```

   b.
   ```
   SELECT emp_id AS EmployeeID,
       lname AS LastName,
       fname AS FirstName
       FROM employee
   ```

   c.
   ```
   SELECT ROUND ($7725.53, 1)
   ```

   d.
   ```
   SELECT lname + ', ' + SUBSTRING(fname,1,1) + '.' AS Name,
   emp_id AS EmployeeID
   FROM employee
   ```

2. Can you run a subquery as a join and vice versa?

3. True or False: ROLLUP and CUBE do not supply summary information.

4. Can you use a SELECT INTO statement to build a temporary table that everyone has access to?

Exercises

1. You want to retrieve title_id, title, and price for all books that have a publisher ID of 0877 or the word computer in the title, and when the price is NOT NULL. What is the Transact-SQL you would use? (Hint: Use the titles table.)

2. Write a query to find all books in the titles table that have price values that are NOT NULL.

3. Write a query to list all book titles and prices in the titles table in descending order based on price.

4. Create a query that returns the average of the ytd_sales figures from the titles table in the pubs database.

5. Using the GROUP BY and HAVING clauses, create a query that will find all books with more than one author. (Hint: Use the titleauthor table.)

6. Using the COMPUTE BY clause, create a query that will report the stor_id and a running sum of the quantity of books ordered. Use the sales table to do this.

11

7. Create a query using joins (either a SQL Server join or an ANSI join) to show an author's first name, last name, and book titles. (Use the au_fname, au_lname, from the authors table and the title field from the titles table.) (Hint: You must do two joins—one from authors to titleauthor and one from titles to titleauthor.)

8. Create a subquery to find authors who live in the same states as any of the stores.

9. Create a temporary table containing all the information from the employee table. Test the existence of your new table by selecting data from it.

DAY 12

Data Modification with Queries

On Day 11, "Retrieving Data with Queries," you looked at retrieving data using the SELECT statement. You saw how you could retrieve only some columns in a table and use the WHERE clause to restrict the rows to be returned. You looked at manipulating the data with numeric, string, and date functions. You also learned how you could summarize the data returned by using the aggregates GROUP BY and COMPUTE. Finally, you looked at using the SELECT statement to retrieve data from more than one table using the JOIN operation or by writing subqueries.

Today's lesson focuses on modifying the data in your SQL Server tables using the INSERT, UPDATE, and SELECT statements. However, before you learn about the actual statements, you will look at the relationship between data modifications and transaction logging.

Transaction Logging

SQL Server keeps track of changes to a database by logging almost every change made to the database and placing it in the transaction log. You learned about placement and management of the transaction log on Day 4, "Creating Databases, Files, and Filegroups." As you are making modifications to your data, be aware that every change is being written to the transaction log. When you perform an INSERT, a copy of the entire new row is written to the transaction log; when you run a DELETE, a copy of the entire deleted row is written to the transaction log.

With the UPDATE operation, it is not so straightforward. For some UPDATE operations, SQL Server just logs the bytes being changed. For many other UPDATE operations, SQL Server must make two entries into the log: The entire old version of the row is written to the transaction log, and then the entire new version of the row is written to the transaction log. The rules for when SQL Server just logs the bytes being changed, rather than adding before and after entries to the transaction log, is beyond the scope of this book. The amount of data written to the transaction log is also affected by the number of indexes, as you learned on Day 13, "Enhancing Performance with Indexing."

There are some exceptions to the logging requirements just discussed. You have already seen the BCP (Bulk Copy) utility (Day 10, "Using SQL Server 7.0 Data Transformation Services"), which is equivalent to multiple INSERT commands. If the fast version of BCP is being run, the individual rows will not be written to the transaction log as they are being inserted into the table; for the slow version of BCP, every single new row is written to the transaction log. Note, however, that some logging to the transaction log will take place for the recording of the space being allocated during the BCP operation, regardless of whether it is a "fast" BCP. In Day 10's lesson, you learned about the SELECT INTO operation, which is also not logged (with the previously noted exception about space allocation). In today's lesson you will learn about TRUNCATE TABLE, which is equivalent to a DELETE without the logging of every deleted row.

Now that you have some familiarity with how the transaction logging process works, it is time to look more closely at the statements that force logging to occur. You will begin with an inspection of the INSERT statement.

Before going any further, take a minute to copy some of your data to backup tables so that later you can refresh the tables you are working with.

Run the following queries to create copies of your publishers and sales tables. Make sure that you turn on the Select Into/Bulk Copy database option before you attempt to run these statements.

```
USE pubs
GO
SELECT * INTO tmpPublishers
FROM publishers
GO
SELECT * INTO tmpStores
FROM stores
GO
SELECT * INTO tmpTitles
FROM titles
GO
SELECT * INTO tmpSales
FROM sales
GO
```

And now, on to inserting data!

Inserting

The basic INSERT statement adds one row at a time to a table. Variations of the basic INSERT statement allow you to add multiple rows by selecting data from another table or by executing a stored procedure. In any of these cases, you must know something about the structure of the table into which you are inserting. The following can be useful to know:

- The number of columns in the table
- The data type of each column
- The name of the columns for some INSERT statements
- Constraints and column properties like identity

You will learn about constraints and identity columns on Day 14, "Ensuring Data Integrity." The following is the syntax for the INSERT statement.

▼ SYNTAX

```
INSERT [INTO]
    {<table_or_view>}
    {{[(column_list)]
VALUES
    ({DEFAULT ¦
    constant_expression} [,...n]) ¦
    select_statement ¦
    execute_statement} ¦
    DEFAULT VALUES}

<table_or_view> :: =
{ table_name ¦ view_name
¦ rowset_function
▲ }[,...n]
```

12

The simplest method for finding out the number of columns, along with their names and data types, is using the Table Properties dialog in the Enterprise Manager (see Figure 12.1). Follow these steps to open the Table Properties dialog:

1. Select a database from the Databases folder.
2. Select a table from the Tables folder.
3. Double-click the table, or right-click and choose Properties.

FIGURE 12.1

The Table Properties dialog.

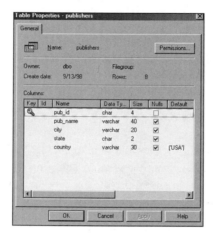

If you don't have SQL Server Enterprise Manager readily available, you can execute the sp_help system-stored procedure to get the same information. The following output shows only part of the information returned by sp_help.

  Examine the structure of the publishers table:

```
sp_help publishers
```

Part of the results will look like the following:

```
Column_name     Type        Length
- - - - - - - -   - - - - - -   - - - - - - - -
pub_id          char        4
pub_name        varchar     40
city            varchar     20
state           char        2
country         varchar     30
```

ANALYSIS The preceding output shows you the column name, the data type, and the position of each column. You will need this information when building your INSERT statements.

Using the INSERT VALUES Statement

The simplest form of the INSERT statement requires a value for every column of the table, in the order the columns were defined. This is the order as shown in the previous examples. To insert a single row into the tmpPublishers table, you can execute the following command:

```
INSERT INTO tmpPublishers
VALUES('9956', 'A New Publisher', 'Poulsbo', 'WA', 'USA')
```

If you have permission to INSERT into this table, and you are not violating any constraints, you should get the following message back from the SQL Server:

```
(1 row(s) affected)
```

 Note | Because the columns are all character data types, all values are enclosed in quotation marks. Numeric values are not enclosed in quotation marks.

The simplest form of the INSERT statement requires that you explicitly supply a value for each column, and each value must be in the correct sequence. If you want to supply the values in a different order, or if you do not want to supply an explicit value for a column, you can use another variant of the INSERT statement.

The following INSERT statement has a list of column names before the VALUES clause, and that list includes only a subset of the column names in the table; the values list then only needs to have values for the columns listed.

```
INSERT INTO tmpPublishers(state, pub_id)
VALUES('AK', '9932')
```

So what happens to the columns that aren't mentioned in the column list? If you inserted a new row, every column must have some value. If you don't supply a value, SQL Server must be able to determine one. For SQL Server to be able to determine a value, every column not mentioned in the list of columns must meet one of the following criteria:

- The column has a default value attached to it.
- The column is an identity column.
- The column allows nulls.
- The column is of type timestamp.

Defaults and identity columns are discussed on Day 14. You learned about nulls and timestamp columns on Day 9, "Creating Tables."

12

In the preceding INSERT statement, no value is supplied for the publisher name, the city, or the country. In the publishers table, the publisher name and city columns both allow nulls, and the country has a default value of USA. After executing the INSERT statement, you can run the following query to see the row you have just inserted:

```
SELECT * FROM tmpPublishers
WHERE pub_id = '9932'
```

Notice the null values and the default value for country:

```
Pub_id Pub_name            City            state   country
------ ------------------  ------------    ------  -------
9932   (null)              (null)          AK      USA
```

If you try to execute an INSERT statement, leaving out values for columns that did not meet one of the listed criteria, you get an error.

INPUT/ OUTPUT This INSERT does not supply a value for the pub_id column:

```
INSERT INTO tmpPublishers(pub_name, city, state)
VALUES('The Best Books', 'New Orleans', 'LA')

Server: Msg 515, Level 16, State 2
Cannot insert the value NULL into column 'pub_id',
➥table 'pubs.dbo.tmpPublishers';
column does not allow nulls. INSERT fails.
The statement has been aborted.
```

ANALYSIS Note that the error message is not entirely complete. The problem is not that the pub_id column doesn't allow nulls, but that it also does not have a default value and it isn't an identity column.

DEFAULT VALUES

There is one more variation of the simple, single-row INSERT statement, which you can use when you don't want to include a list of column names, but you do want SQL Server to use default values when they exist (this includes nulls and identity values also). You can use the keyword DEFAULT in the actual values list as a way of telling SQL Server that it should determine what value should be used. For example:

```
INSERT INTO tmpPublishers
VALUES('9950', DEFAULT, DEFAULT,'AK', DEFAULT)
```

If every column in a table has some kind of default value that SQL Server can determine, there is one more variation you can use. You can simply tell SQL Server to use all default values by using the keywords DEFAULT VALUES, as in the following INSERT statement:

```
INSERT INTO tmpPublishers DEFAULT VALUES
```

> When client applications like Microsoft Visual Basic or PowerBuilder connect to a database and add data, they are using the INSERT/VALUES statements you just looked at.
>
> You should also note that unbound grid-type controls used in the visual front-end tools do not automatically add data to the database. A developer would need to write some code to loop through all the values changed in the grid and then use INSERT/VALUES to place those rows into the database.

Inserting Data Using SELECT

All the preceding INSERT statements will insert a single row into a table. If you want to insert more than one row at a time, you must have a source where those rows already exist. That source is typically another table or a join between two or more other tables. In this form of the INSERT statement, you use a subquery to determine the rows of data to be inserted. You learned about subqueries on Day 11. The subquery's result set becomes the set of rows to be inserted. The number of columns in the subquery's result set must match the number of columns in the table, and the columns must have compatible data types. In this first example, you will create a table to keep track of addresses.

```
CREATE TABLE address_list
(name varchar(20) not null,
 address varchar(40) not null,
 city varchar(20) not null,
 state char(2)  )
```

```
This command did not return data,
and it did not return any rows
```

12

This table has four character fields, so any SELECT statement you use to populate it must return four character columns. Here is an example:

```
INSERT INTO address_list
    SELECT stor_name, stor_address, city, state
    FROM tmpStores
```

```
(6 row(s) affected)
```

> Unlike the subqueries you read about in yesterday's lesson, there are no parentheses around the subquery used with an INSERT statement.

The column names used in the subquery are ignored; the table already has column names associated with each field.

You can execute another INSERT statement to add more rows to your address_list table. Suppose you would like to add names and addresses from the authors table. Instead of just a single name, the authors table has a first name column (au_fname) and a last name column (au_lname). The address_list table is expecting just a single value for its name column, so you can concatenate the last and first names together. You can include a comma and space in the concatenated result.

```
INSERT INTO address_list
    SELECT au_lname + ', ' + au_fname, address, city, state
    FROM authors
```

(23 row(s) affected)

In this example, note that the concatenated last and first name fields is longer than the width of the name column in the new address_list table. SQL Server does not return an error message when you execute this statement. When trying to insert a character string of length L1 into a column defined with maximum length of L2, if L1 > L2, SQL Server will only insert the first L2 characters into the table. Take a look at the values in the address_list table:

```
SELECT * FROM address_list
```

name	address	city	state
White, Johnson	10932 Bigge Rd.	Menlo Park	CA
Green, Marjorie	309 63rd St. #411	Oakland	CA
Carson, Cheryl	589 Darwin Ln.	Berkeley	CA
O'Leary, Michael	22 Cleveland Av. #14	San Jose	CA
Straight, Dean	5420 College Av.	Oakland	CA
Smith, Meander	10 Mississippi Dr.	Lawrence	KS
Bennet, Abraham	6223 Bateman St	Berkeley	CA
Dull, Ann	3410 Blonde St	Palo Alto	CA
Gringlesby, Burt	PO Box 792	Covelo	CA
Locksley, Charlene	18 Broadway Av.	San Francisco	CA
Greene, Morningstar	22 Graybar House Rd	Nashville	TN
Blotchet-Halls, Regi	55 Hillsdale Bl	Corvallis	OR
Yokomoto, Akiko	3 Silver Ct	Walnut Creek	CA
del Castillo, Innes	2286 Cram Pl. #86	Ann Arbor	MI
DeFrance, Michel	3 Balding Pl	Gary	IN
Stringer, Dirk	5420 Telegraph Av	Oakland	CA
MacFeather, Stearns	44 Upland Hts	Oakland	CA
Karsen, Livia	5720 McAuley St	Oakland	CA
Panteley, Sylvia	1956 Arlington Pl	Rockville	MD
Hunter, Sheryl	3410 Blonde St	Palo Alto	CA
McBadden, Heather	301 Putnam	Vacaville	CA

```
Ringer, Anne          67 Seventh Av       Salt Lake City  UT
Ringer, Albert        67 Seventh Av       Salt Lake City  UT
Eric the Read Books   788 Catamaugus Ave  Seattle         WA
Barnum's              567 Pasadena Ave    Tustin          CA
News & Brews          577 First St        Los Gatos       CA
Doc-U-Mat: Quality L  24-A Avogadro Way   Remulade        WA
Fricative Bookshop    89 Madison St       Fremont         CA
Bookbeat              679 Carson St       Portland        OR

(29 row(s) affected)
```

In this last example, you will create a table to keep track of the names of all the publishers and the titles of all the books each publisher has published.

```
CREATE TABLE publisher_list
    (pub_name varchar(40) NULL,
     title varchar(80) NULL)
```

To populate this table you will need to join the tmpPublishers and tmpTitles tables. You should use an outer join so those publishers that do not currently have any books published are included.

```
INSERT INTO publisher_list
    SELECT pub_name, title
    FROM tmpPublishers LEFT OUTER JOIN tmpTitles
        ON tmpPublishers.pub_id = tmpTitles.pub_id
```

Inserting Data Using Stored Procedures

SQL Server has one more option for inserting rows into a table. If a stored procedure returns a single result set, and you know the number and type of columns that the result set contains, you can INSERT into a table using the results returned when calling that stored procedure.

You write your own stored procedures on Day 15, "Working with Views, Stored Procedures, and Triggers," but for now you can use a system-stored procedure. The sp_spaceused system-stored procedure returns information about the space usage of a single table. You can create a table to hold the results of running this procedure, and INSERT a row into this table at regular intervals. With the latter, you will be able to monitor the growth of the table over time.

Take a look at the output of the sp_spaceused system-stored procedure (Note: your results might vary slightly).

**INPUT/
OUTPUT**

```
EXEC sp_spaceused tmpPublishers

Name             Rows    Reserved    Data    index_size    unused
-------------    ----    --------    ----    -----         ---------
TmpPublishers    11      32 KB       2 KB    4 KB          26 KB
```

ANALYSIS This procedure returns six columns, all of which are character strings. Although it looks like the second column is numeric, it really isn't. The way you can determine the type is either to examine the code for the sp_spaceused system-stored procedure (you'll see how to do that on Day 15) or to try to create the table with an integer column. Notice the error message you get when you try to insert a row.

INPUT The following table should be able to hold the results:

```
CREATE TABLE space_usage
(table_name varchar(30) not null,
 rows varchar(9),
 reserved varchar(10),
 data varchar(10),
 index_size varchar(10),
 unused varchar(10)   )
```

To insert into this table you can execute the system-stored procedure sp_spaceused:

```
INSERT INTO space_usage
    EXEC sp_spaceused tmpPublishers
```

Caution

> You must make sure that if the system-stored procedure returns more than one result set, all the results must have the same number of columns and return the same type of data in the corresponding columns.

One very nice extension to this capability to insert rows from a system-stored procedure is the capability to insert rows from a remote stored procedure. If you have a procedure on a remote server that selects all rows from a table, you can execute that procedure to copy all the rows from the remote server to the local one. To run a remote procedure, you must specify the following in your remote procedure call:

- Server name
- Database name
- Procedure owner name
- Procedure name

For example, if you have a SQL Server named Wildlife with a database named Water and a procedure named Fish with an owner of dbo, you can run the following query:

```
INSERT INTO local_table
    EXEC Wildlife.Water.dbo.Fish
```

There are a few additional considerations when inserting data into a table with an identity column. These issues are covered on Day 14. Day 14 also covers restrictions that you might encounter when you attempt to insert values where there are check constraints or referential integrity constraints on the table.

Deleting

The second data modification statement allows you to remove one or more rows from a table.

DELETE

To remove rows from a SQL Server table, use the DELETE statement.

```
DELETE [FROM] {table_name ¦ view_name}
[WHERE clause]
```

> **Note** Note that the word FROM is optional, as is the WHERE clause.

The following DELETE statement will remove all rows from the tmpSales table.

```
DELETE tmpSales
```

```
(21 row(s) affected)
```

To remove only a subset of rows in a table, the WHERE clause allows you to qualify the rows to be removed. The WHERE conditions can include any of the conditions you learned about on Day 11, including relational operators (<, >, =) and the keywords IN, LIKE, BETWEEN, and so on.

The following DELETE statement will remove all books with a pub_name of "New Moon Books" from the publisher_list table:

```
DELETE publisher_list
WHERE pub_name = 'New Moon Books'
```

```
(5 row(s) affected)
```

DELETE Using a Lookup Table

A single DELETE statement can remove rows from a single table only. However, SQL Server enables you to include another table in your DELETE statement to be used as a lookup table. Usually, the lookup table will appear in a subquery. In this next example, you'll want to remove all titles published by New Moon Books. The tmpTitles table is the one to be modified, but it contains only the publisher ID, not the publisher name. You must look in the tmpPublishers table to find the publisher ID for New Moon Books, which will then determine the rows in the tmpTitles table to remove.

INPUT/ OUTPUT
```
DELETE publisher_list
WHERE pub_name =
    (SELECT pub_name FROM tmpPublishers
     WHERE pub_id = '9956')

(1 row(s) affected)
```

ANALYSIS The subquery accesses the tmpPublishers table and returns a single value for pub_name. That value is then used to determine which rows in publisher_list you are going to delete—that is, all rows with a pub_name equal to the returned value. Keep in mind that no more than one row will be returned because pub_id is the primary key of the publishers table. If more than one row could be returned by the subquery, you would have to use the IN keyword instead of the equals (=) symbol.

The next example uses a lookup table that returns more than one value. You'll want to remove all rows from the tmpSales table that indicate the sale of business books. The tmpSales table holds the title_id value of the book sold, but not its type. You must access the tmpTitles table to find which title_ids correspond to business books. Because you deleted the information in the tmpSales table earlier in today's lesson, you will need to repopulate the tmpSales table. Remember that when you started this chapter, you copied all the sales information to another table. You will now drop the tmpSales table and then re-create and repopulate it using a SELECT INTO statement. Run the following code.

INPUT/ OUTPUT
```
USE pubs
GO
DROP TABLE tmpSales
GO
SELECT * INTO tmpSales
FROM Sales
GO
```

Now remove all rows from the tmpSales table that are of type "business book."

INPUT/ OUTPUT
```
DELETE tmpSales
WHERE title_id IN
    (SELECT title_id FROM tmpTitles
     WHERE type = 'business')

(5 row(s) affected)
```

ANALYSIS The subquery accesses the tmpTitles table and returns a list of `title_id` values. Those values are then used to determine which rows in tmpSales you are going to delete, that is, all rows with a `title_id` equal to any of the returned values.

Transact-SQL has an extension that allows you to write `DELETE` statements using a `FROM` clause containing multiple tables. This makes the `DELETE` appear as a join operation, although only one table is having rows deleted. The functionality provided is the same as using subqueries. The second table is used only as a lookup table.

The following examples show how the `DELETE` statements use multiple tables in a `FROM` clause.

INPUT
```
DELETE publisher_list
WHERE pub_name =
    (SELECT pub_name FROM tmpPublishers
     WHERE pub_id = '0877')
```

This can be rewritten as

```
DELETE publisher_list
FROM publisher_list, tmpPublishers
WHERE publisher_list.pub_name = tmpPublishers.pub_name
AND pub_id = '0877'
```

```
(7 row(s) affected)
```

ANALYSIS The choice of whether to use the subquery method or the join method depends mainly on personal preference. I usually prefer the subquery method because there is no confusion as to which table is being modified and which table is only being used as a lookup table. You should also be aware that the join method is non-ANSI standard.

TRUNCATE TABLE

In the beginning of this section, you saw an example of a `DELETE` statement with no `WHERE` clause that would delete every row in the table. If you really want to remove all data from a table, while leaving the table structure intact, there is another alternative. This statement is `TRUNCATE TABLE`.

INPUT   `TRUNCATE TABLE tmpSales`

ANALYSIS Unlike the `DELETE` statement, this statement does not return a message about the number of rows affected. There are some other differences between `DELETE` with no `WHERE` clause and `TRUNCATE TABLE`:

- DELETE logs every row as it is deleted; TRUNCATE TABLE only writes the page and extent deallocations to the transaction log.
- DELETE maintains the indexes by removing pointers one at a time and logging each index adjustment; TRUNCATE TABLE shrinks the indexes in a single step and again only writes the page deallocations to the transaction log.
- TRUNCATE TABLE can only be executed by the table owner, a member of the db_owner database role, or the sysadmin server role; DELETE can be executed by any user who has been given appropriate permissions on the table.
- A DELETE trigger is not fired when a table is truncated but is fired when rows are deleted (see Day 15 for more information about triggers).
- TRUNCATE TABLE resets any identity value back to the seed; DELETE does not affect the next identity value to be used.

Updating

The third data modification statement you will look at is the UPDATE statement. The UPDATE statement allows you to change the value of columns within an existing row. Before going any further, now is a good time to make sure you have fresh data. Please run the following two queries to refresh the tmpSales, tmpPublishers, tmpStores, and tmpTitles tables.

```
USE pubs
GO
DROP TABLE tmpSales
GO
DROP TABLE tmpPublishers
GO
DROP TABLE tmpStores
GO
DROP TABLE tmpTitles
GO
SELECT * INTO tmpPublishers
FROM Publishers
GO
SELECT * INTO tmpSales
FROM Sales
GO
SELECT * INTO tmpStores
FROM sales
GO
SELECT * INTO tmpTitles
FROM titles
GO
```

UPDATE

The Syntax for the UPDATE Statement

```
UPDATE
    {table_name ¦ view_name}
SET
    column_name1 = {expression1 ¦ NULL ¦ (select_statement)}
    [, column_name2 = …]
[WHERE search_conditions]
```

The new part of the statement is the SET clause with which you specify the columns to be updated. As with the DELETE statement, the WHERE clause is optional.

The following UPDATE statement will change the ytd_sales (year-to-date sales) column in the tmpTitles table to 0 for every row. This is an example of what you might want to do at the beginning of every year.

INPUT/
OUTPUT
```
update tmpTitles
set ytd_sales = 0
```

```
(18 row(s) affected)
```

ANALYSIS
Without a WHERE clause, this statement will change the value of the ytd_sales column to be 0 in every row in the table.

The following example will update the city column for the publisher Algodata Infosystems.

INPUT/
OUTPUT
```
UPDATE tmpPublishers
SET city = 'El Cerrito'
WHERE pub_name = 'Algodata Infosystems'
```

```
(1 row(s) affected)
```

An UPDATE statement can make the new value in the column dependent on the original value. The following example changes the price of all psychology books to be 10 percent less than the current price:

INPUT/
OUTPUT
```
UPDATE tmpTitles
SET price = price * 0.90
WHERE type = 'psychology'
```

```
(5 row(s) affected)
```

An UPDATE statement can change more than one column. The word SET occurs only once, and the different columns to be changed are separated by commas. The following update statement increases the price of all popular computing books by 20 percent and will append the string (price increase) to the notes field of the same rows.

12

INPUT/
OUTPUT

```
UPDATE tmpTitles
SET price = price * 1.2, notes = notes + ' (price increase)'
WHERE type = 'popular_comp'
```

(3 row(s) affected)

UPDATE Using a Lookup Table

A single UPDATE statement can change rows from a single table only. However, SQL
Server does allow you to include another table in your UPDATE statement to be used as a
lookup table. Usually, the lookup table will appear in a subquery. The subquery can
appear in either the WHERE clause or the SET clause of the UPDATE statement. In this next
example, you want to change the publisher of all business books to be New Moon
Books.

INPUT/
OUTPUT

```
UPDATE tmpTitles
SET pub_id =
    (SELECT pub_id FROM tmpPublishers
     WHERE pub_name = 'New Moon Books')
WHERE type = 'business'
```

(4 row(s) affected)

ANALYSIS   The publisher name appears only in the tmpPublishers table, but the tmpTitles
table must be modified. The subquery accesses the tmpPublishers table and
returns the publisher ID for New Moon Books. This value is used as the new value in the
pub_id column of tmpTitles.

Just like for the DELETE statement, Transact-SQL has an extension that allows you to
write UPDATE statements using a FROM clause containing multiple tables. This makes the
UPDATE appear as a join operation, although only one table is having rows modified. The
functionality provided is the same as that used for subqueries; the second table is used
only as a lookup table.

The following examples show how the previous UPDATE statement can be rewritten using
multiple tables in a FROM clause:

```
UPDATE tmpTitles
SET pub_id = tmpPublishers.pub_id
FROM tmpTitles, tmpPublishers
WHERE type = 'business'
AND tmpPublishers.pub_name = 'New Moon Books'
```

The choice of whether to use the subquery method or the join method depends mainly on
personal preference. Just like in the DELETE statement, the subquery method seems much
clearer as to which table is modified, what the new value of pub_id is to be, and what
rows are changing. You should also remember that the join method is non-ANSI
standard.

There are also some UPDATE statements that are quite a bit more complicated to write using the join method. One such case is if the UPDATE statement uses subqueries for both the SET clause and the WHERE clause.

This next example changes the publisher of all psychology books published by New Moon Books to Binnet & Hardley.

INPUT/
OUTPUT

```
UPDATE tmpTitles
SET pub_id =
    (SELECT pub_id FROM tmpPublishers
      WHERE pub_name = 'Binnet & Hardley')
WHERE type = 'psychology' AND pub_id =
    (SELECT pub_id FROM tmpPublishers
      WHERE pub_name = 'New Moon Books')

(4 row(s) affected)
```

ANALYSIS
Again, the publisher name appears in the tmpPublishers table only, but it is the tmpTitles table that needs to be modified. The first subquery accesses the tmpPublishers table and returns the publisher ID for Binnet & Hardley. This pub_id value is used as the new value in the pub_id column of tmpTitles. The second subquery accesses the tmpPublishers table again to return the pub_id value for New Moon Books. This pub_id is used to determine which rows in the tmpTitles table need to be updated.

This UPDATE statement would be much more difficult to write using the join method because the tmpPublishers table would need to appear twice—once for determining the new value of pub_id and once for determining the pub_id of the rows to be changed. This is just another reason why I prefer the subquery method over the join method.

Summary

In today's lesson you learned the SQL statements used to modify data in your SQL Server tables. You can add new rows to a table with the INSERT statement. You can add them either one row at time or you can insert many rows that are coming from another table.

You can remove rows from a table with the DELETE statement, and you can change values in existing rows with the UPDATE statement.

Whenever you are doing data modifications, remember the logging that SQL Server does. Every new row is written to the transaction log, every deleted row is written to the transaction log, and with most updates, two versions of the row are written to the log: the row before the changes are made and the row after the changes are made. The only exceptions are the SELECT INTO operation, which doesn't log the new rows in a table,

12

and the TRUNCATE TABLE operation, which doesn't log the deleted rows. There is no magic switch to turn off logging for the server.

Q&A

Q How do you UNDO a DELETE or UPDATE operation after it is executed?

A By default, when a change is made to a table it is committed and permanent. There is no UNDO command in SQL Server. However, you can execute a DELETE or UPDATE within a transaction, and then the entire transaction can be rolled back. Transaction control is covered on Day 16, "Programming SQL Server 7.0."

Q What does the following statement do?

```
Insert Into Publishers default values?
```

A This will add a row to the publishers table and use the default values for each column if they are defined. If they are not defined, it will add null values.

Workshop

The Workshop provides quiz questions to help you solidify your understanding of the concepts presented in this chapter. In addition to the quiz questions, exercises are provided to let you practice what you have learned in this chapter. Try to understand the quiz and exercise answers before continuing to the next day's lesson. Answers are provided in Appendix A, "Answers."

Quiz

1. What happens if you execute a DELETE statement without a WHERE clause?

2. True or False: You must supply a value for every column in a row when inserting a new row.

3. What do joins in a DELETE or UPDATE statement allow you to do?

Exercises

The exercises assume your tmpTitles table in the pubs database is in its initial condition. If you have been modifying the table to practice the statements in this module, you will have to rebuild the pubs database. To do this, please run the INSTPUBS.SQL script in your \MSSQL7\Install folder. You should also re-create the tmpTitles table as

```
USE pubs
GO
SELECT * INTO tmpTitles
FROM titles
GO
```

1. Create a temporary table containing the title ID, title, publisher ID, and price of all modern cookbooks (`type = 'mod_cook'`). Use this table for the remaining exercises.

2. Insert the title ID, title, publisher ID, and price from all the traditional cookbooks (type = trad_cook) into the temp table.

3. Update the price of all books by 20 percent.

4. Decrease the price of all books published by Binnet & Hardley by 10 percent.

5. Delete all books with a price less than $10.

6. Delete all books with year-to-date sales greater than 10,000.

12

DAY **13**

Enhancing Performance with Indexing

On Day 12, "Data Modification with Queries," you looked at the INSERT, UPDATE, and DELETE statements, as well as the truncate table statement. Each of these statements enables you to modify or add data in your SQL Server databases. Without these commands, your database is either empty or read-only.

Today's lesson focuses on indexes. Indexes provide a set of logical pointers to your data, much like an index in the back of a book helps you find things you're looking for. Although all the queries you will examine later this week will work without indexes (select, insert, update, delete), they will usually run faster with indexes.

You'll be starting off by justifying why you would want indexes, and then examine some of the basics of B-tree indexes (the type of indexes that SQL Server implements). You will then look at the syntax of the CREATE INDEX statement. You will be introduced to several options and performance issues associated with indexes. You will finish this day's lesson with a discussion of some of the DBCC commands you can use in conjunction with indexes, as well as other maintenance issues. You also take a very brief look at the full-text indexing capabilities of SQL Server 7.0.

Why Use Indexes?

Why index? Well, there are many reasons. The most obvious reason is the one I just mentioned, which is speed. Without indexes, SQL Server accesses data by reading every page of data on each table you have specified in your SQL statement. This "table scan" (reading every page of the data) can be an excellent method of data retrieval. For example, if a table is small, or if you are accessing a large portion of the table, a table scan might very well be the best plan to access the data. However, quite frequently data access is much faster with an index. It can also speed up joins between tables.

Another reason to create an index is to enforce uniqueness. Having two identical rows in a table is not an error condition. However, that's probably not how most people want to store data. Imagine a system that keeps track of customers. If you can't tell your customers apart, you might have difficulty keeping customers when you bill them incorrectly. You have several options to uniquely identify your customers. You could give them numbers, use their names and birthdates together, use their credit card numbers, or use some other value or set of values. Regardless of the choice you've made, the way to tell SQL Server about your choice is with a *unique* index. There is a discussion of another way to enforce uniqueness, the unique constraint, on Day 14, "Ensuring Data Integrity," but even then SQL Server is still creating a unique index as its enforcement mechanism.

Index Structures

An index typically consists of a set of pages known as a B+ tree. A B+ tree looks something like Figure 13.1.

FIGURE 13.1

A B+ tree.

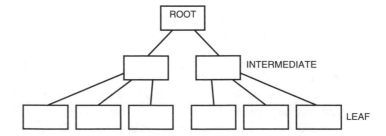

As mentioned previously, an index helps find data quickly. To find an individual row of data, you navigate the B+ tree to find that row and then move to the individual data row. You start with the root page. A pointer to the root page is found in the *sysindexes* table (oddly enough, in the column named root for *nonclustered* indexes). The root page contains index entries (the data for the column or columns you've indexed), as well as pointers to each page below the root page. Each index might have one or more intermediate levels. Again, each entry would have an index value and a pointer to the next page below.

NEW TERM On the leaf pages (the lowest level in the tree), what you find depends on whether a table has a *clustered index* or not. Logically speaking, you would find an entry for every row in the table being indexed, as well as a pointer to the data page and row number that has the actual data row. If the table also has a clustered index, any nonclustered indexes will contain the key values from the clustered index, rather than the data page and row number information. Clustered and nonclustered indexes are explained later, but for now think of a clustered index as a way to presort the actual data. Tables without a clustered index are called *heaps*, and nonclustered indexes are separate index structures that do not directly sort the data.

The data itself is stored on pages called *data pages* (there's no sense in making this hard). Each page is 8,192 bytes in size, with a header of 96 bytes. Hence, each page has 8,096 bytes available for storage. Each of these pages has the same basic structure.

Figure 13.2 shows an example of what an index might look like. This index is on a first-name column.

FIGURE 13.2

A sample B+ index.

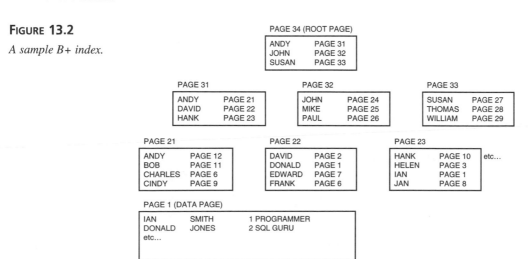

13

Each level of the index is a doubly linked list. Each page knows about the page before it and the page that is logically after it. On the root and intermediate levels of the index, each index value is the first value on the page of the next level below it. On the leaf level of the index, you will find one entry for each row in the table. Note that the index is sorted based on the column (or columns) you have chosen as your index key. This does not change the physical sort order of the data.

When you modify data in the table, every index on that table is also modified. SQL Server guarantees consistency between the data in your tables and their indexes. This is good, in the sense that you want to have excellent data integrity. However, it also means that INSERT, UPDATE, and DELETE operations that might have been rather quick before now could have quite a bit more work to do and might run a little bit slower. If you want to add a new row with the INSERT statement, it would normally take two input/outputs (I/Os)—one for the data and one for the log. If you have two indexes on the table, it will take at least two more, and perhaps more than that. You must balance your needs between data modifications and faster queries.

How do you use an index? Use Figure 13.2 to find a row of data. In the figure, imagine the index is on first name. To find the row with a first name of Donald, you would look on the root page. Because Donald is "less" than John, you would follow the entry for Andy to page 6. On page 6, you find that Donald is "higher" than David but "lower" than Hank, so you go to page 22. On page 22, you find that the entry for Donald points to page 1 (which is a data page because this is the leaf level of the index). In SQL Server, you would also find the row number of the row that contains Donald as the first name, but it was left off the figure for simplicity's sake. Now you read the row from page 1 and can access any information about Donald that is stored on the page. This is exactly how SQL Server uses an index to find data.

Index Options

Several options for indexes are available to you. You must specify these choices and understand them before you can create your indexes.

Clustered Indexes

NEW TERM There are two options for physical storage of your indexes. The first type is known as clustered. A *clustered* index physically re-sorts the data. Rather than having a completely separate index structure (such as the one described earlier), the leaf level of the index is the data. Accessing data using a clustered index is almost always faster than using a nonclustered index because the additional lookup of the data page/row from the leaf level of the index is not necessary.

Because the data is physically sorted in the order of the index key, you can have only one clustered index on a table (you wouldn't want to keep multiple copies of the data). Because only one clustered index is available, you must choose it carefully. Choosing a clustered index can be a fairly complex topic, but some basic guidelines are included here.

One major issue that comes up with clustered indexes is free space. To create a clustered index requires that at least 120 percent of the size of the table be available as temporary workspace. This free space must exist in the database where you are creating the index. To create the index, SQL Server copies the table, sorts the copy in the order of the index values (in ascending order), builds the index structures (the root page and any intermediate pages that are needed), and then drops the original table. When this operation is complete, the clustered index will take only about 5 percent more space than the table itself. The overhead (the nondata pages) of this type of index is relatively small, but it is dependent on the size of the values being indexed.

This might not sound too bad because you need the free space only during the index creation, but it can be difficult to justify. If you had a 500MB database, but one table in the database is 100MB, and you want to create a clustered index on that table, you would need at least 120MB of unused space in the database.

Another issue of critical importance in SQL Server 7.0 is that the key values (indexed columns) that you choose for your clustered index are "carried" along into the nonclustered indexes. Therefore, if you choose a wide clustered index—for example a Char(30)—not only will it take longer to search the clustered index itself, but all your nonclustered indexes will have to carry the Char(30) value of your clustered index key on every row in the nonclustered indexes. That's a significant amount of overhead, so you'll want to keep your clustered index keys as small as possible. You will also want to make sure that the clustered key you select is not updated frequently because all your nonclustered indexes would need to be updated when the clustered index values change.

The other issue to be aware of is the order in which you create your indexes. Because the clustered index key is part of the key values for each of the nonclustered indexes, each nonclustered index would need to be rebuilt. Therefore, always create your clustered indexes first.

Figure 13.3 is an example of a clustered index. Notice that the data is sorted in the order of the index key (our first name again), and the data on the leaf level of the index (the data page) is sorted by first name.

13

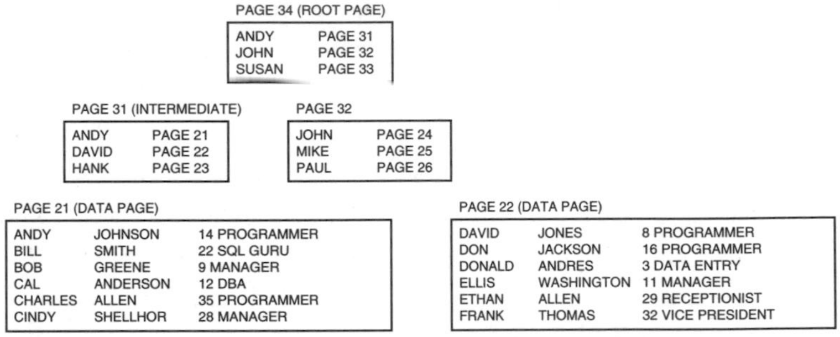

FIGURE 13.3

A clustered index example.

```
                                     PAGE 34 (ROOT PAGE)
                                     ┌──────────────────────┐
                                     │ ANDY      PAGE 31     │
                                     │ JOHN      PAGE 32     │
                                     │ SUSAN     PAGE 33     │
                                     └──────────────────────┘

              PAGE 31 (INTERMEDIATE)          PAGE 32
              ┌──────────────────────┐  ┌──────────────────────┐
              │ ANDY      PAGE 21     │  │ JOHN      PAGE 24     │
              │ DAVID     PAGE 22     │  │ MIKE      PAGE 25     │
              │ HANK      PAGE 23     │  │ PAUL      PAGE 26     │
              └──────────────────────┘  └──────────────────────┘
```

PAGE 21 (DATA PAGE)

ANDY	JOHNSON	14 PROGRAMMER
BILL	SMITH	22 SQL GURU
BOB	GREENE	9 MANAGER
CAL	ANDERSON	12 DBA
CHARLES	ALLEN	35 PROGRAMMER
CINDY	SHELLHOR	28 MANAGER

PAGE 22 (DATA PAGE)

DAVID	JONES	8 PROGRAMMER
DON	JACKSON	16 PROGRAMMER
DONALD	ANDRES	3 DATA ENTRY
ELLIS	WASHINGTON	11 MANAGER
ETHAN	ALLEN	29 RECEPTIONIST
FRANK	THOMAS	32 VICE PRESIDENT

Nonclustered Indexes

NEW TERM A *nonclustered index* is basically the same as a standard B+ tree index. Each index will have a root page, one or more levels of intermediate pages, and a leaf level, which will contain one row for each row in the table. Nonclustered indexes require more space overall than clustered indexes but take much less space during the creation process.

You can have up to 249 nonclustered indexes on a single table. The order in which you create them is not significant. When you create a nonclustered index, it does not change the order of the data, as does a clustered index. The rows in the leaf level of the index are sorted in the order of the columns chosen as part of the index. Each row contains a pointer to the page number/row number combination of the data in the table if no clustered index exists, or the value of the clustering index key if the table also has a clustered index. Refer to Figure 13.2 to see an example of a nonclustered index.

Unique/Nonunique Indexes

Uniqueness determines whether duplicate values are allowed in your index. For example, in the first name index you saw earlier, no two people would be allowed to have the same first name if the index were unique. The default for SQL Server indexes are nonunique, meaning that duplicate values are allowed.

If your data supports it, making an index unique can significantly improve performance when using that index. When the value you are searching for is found, no more searching of the index is necessary (because you know there will be only one entry, when you've found it you can stop looking for more).

Clustered indexes are particularly good candidates for unique indexes because SQL Server internally always forces clustered indexes to be unique. If you don't create a unique clustered index, SQL Server generates a hidden additional key value to force uniqueness of the index. So why make SQL Server do this if you have a good candidate key that's also unique?

Single-Column/Multicolumn Indexes

Many indexes will have only one column; however, it is easy to create a multicolumn index. Multicolumn indexes can be quite useful because you can reduce the number of indexes used by SQL Server and get faster performance. If you specify both columns together frequently during queries, the columns are an excellent candidate for what's known as a composite index (just another name for an index with multiple columns). Composite indexes can be clustered or nonclustered. Composite indexes can contain from 2 to 16 columns and can be up to 900 bytes wide.

The trade-off here is that if you make an index too wide, it will no longer be useful because it might take less time to scan the table instead of using the index. Indexing, unfortunately, involves a lot of trade-offs and rarely presents obvious choices for multiple applications.

SQL Server Indexes

SQL Server implements B+ trees to build its indexes. You use the CREATE INDEX statement to create the indexes you need.

Create Index Syntax

▲ SYNTAX

```
CREATE [UNIQUE] [CLUSTERED ¦ NONCLUSTERED] INDEX index_name
ON [owner.]table_name (column_name [, column_name ...n])
[WITH
    [PAD_INDEX][[,] FILLFACTOR = x]
    [[,] IGNORE_DUP_KEY]
    [[,] DROP_EXISTING]
    [[,] STATISTICS_NORECOMPUTE]]
[ON filegroup]
```

- UNIQUE—Specifies that no duplicates will be allowed for this index. The default is nonunique, and duplicate index entries will be allowed.
- CLUSTERED—Specifies that the data itself will be physically sorted and become the leaf level of the index. Clustered index values must be unique. If you create a UNIQUE clustered index, there's no problem. However, if you create a nonunique clustered index, a 4-byte "Uniquefier" will be added to each clustered index key to guarantee uniqueness.
- NONCLUSTERED—Specifies that a normal B+ index will be created as a completely separate object. This is the default type of index.
- *Index_name*—The SQL Server unique name for this object.

▼

- *table_name*—The name of the table that contains the columns you'd like to index.

13

▼ • *column_name*—The name of the column (or columns) to be indexed. You can create an index with up to 16 columns up to 900 bytes in width. The columns can't be of type text, image, bit, or ntext.

• *filegroup*—The name of the filegroup on which the index should be created. If not
▲ specified, the index is created on the default filegroup.

For example, the following lines of code create a table called myauthors in the PUBS database, and then copies all the data from the authors table. Then, the code creates an index on the au_id column of the myauthors table. The index is a clustered index and will enforce uniqueness.

```
USE PUBS
CREATE TABLE dbo.myauthors (
    au_id id NOT NULL ,
    au_lname varchar (40) NOT NULL ,
    au_fname varchar (20) NOT NULL ,
    phone char (12) NOT NULL ,
    address varchar (40) NULL ,
    city varchar (20) NULL ,
    state char (2) NULL ,
    zip char (5) NULL ,
    contract bit NOT NULL
)
INSERT myauthors select * from authors
Create unique clustered index myauind on myauthors (au_id)
```

The following code creates a nonunique, nonclustered index on the au_fname column of the same table:

```
Use pubs
Create index mynamindex on myauthors (au_fname)
```

Note that this Transact-SQL command is identical functionally and might be a little bit more obvious:

```
Use pubs
Create nonclustered index mynameindex on myauthors (au_fname)
```

The `fillfactor` and `pad_index` Options

The `fillfactor` option specifies how full each page in the leaf level of an index should be. The default fill factor is `0`. `fillfactor` is a configuration parameter, so be sure to check that it has not been changed. Remember that you can check this either from SQL Server Enterprise Manager or you can run `sp_configure` without any parameters. Your output will look something like this:

```
Exec sp_configure
go

name                       minimum  maximum      config_value run_value
------------------------   -------- -----------  ------------ ---------
allow updates              0        1            0            0
default language           0        9999         0            0
fill factor (%)            0        100          0            0
language in cache          3        100          3            3
max async IO               1        255          32           32
max text repl size (B)     0        2147483647   65536        65536
max worker threads         10       1024         255          255
nested triggers            0        1            1            1
network packet size (B)    4096     65535        4096         4096
recovery interval (min)    0        32767        0            0
remote access              0        1            1            1
remote proc trans          0        1            0            0
show advanced options      0        1            0            0
user options               0        4095         0            0
(14 row(s) affected) …
```

Look for the name "fill factor" in the output, and verify that the config_value and run_value columns both reflect a fillfactor setting of 0.

If you do not specify the fillfactor setting during the CREATE INDEX statement, the default value (typically 0) will be used. A value of 0 means that the leaf pages of your index will be almost full but that nonleaf pages (intermediate pages and the root page) will still have room for at least two more rows. If the fillfactor is 100, all the leaf pages will be 100 percent full, with no room for additional rows. Again, the root and intermediate pages will still have room for two additional rows. Any other value will be the percentage of each leaf page to fill with rows. SQL Server will round the percentage to the nearest row size, so you will rarely get exactly the percentage you ask for, but it will be as close as SQL Server can get it.

If you created a clustered index with a fillfactor of 50, each page would be 50 percent full. In Figure 13.4 you can see that the leaf page of the clustered index is only half full. The code might look like this:

```
CREATE INDEX aunameindex on authors (au_fname)
WITH FILLFACTOR = 50
GO
```

13

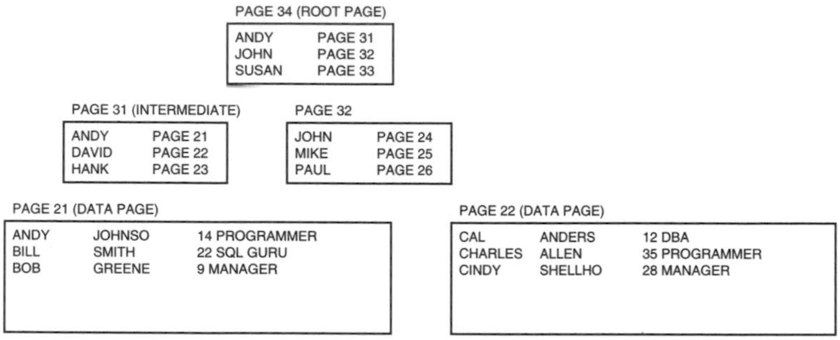

FIGURE **13.4**

A clustered index with `fillfactor` *equal to 50.*

> **Note**
>
> Note that `fillfactor` is not maintained on the index. If you create an index with a fill factor of 50 (meaning each page is half full), over time it is likely that some pages will fill up and others will get close to empty. If you would like to see your fill factor reestablished, you will have to do one of the following:
>
> - You could drop and re-create the index with the fill factor specified again.
> - You could use the DBCC DBREINDEX command.
>
> Each option will reinstate your fill factor. You will find the tool to help determine when you must reindex in DBCC SHOWCONTIG, also examined later in this lesson. However, SQL Server will automatically do quite a bit of this cleanup itself.

When you use the pad_index option with a fill factor, the option specifies that the non-leaf pages of the index will have the fill factor applied to them as well as to the leaf pages. The easiest way to understand the pad_index option is to look at an example.

If you create the same index as in Figure 13.4 but add the pad_index option, the nonleaf pages will now also have the fill factor applied. Notice that if your rows don't fit perfectly, SQL Server will get as close as possible to the fill factor you've requested. For example, the following code might create an index like the one in Figure 13.5:

```
CREATE INDEX aunameindex on authors (au_fname)
WITH FILLFACTOR = 50, PAD_INDEX
GO
```

So far, you have seen how fillfactor and pad_index work, but not why you would want to use them. There are many times when specifying a fill factor can be quite useful. To understand why this is the case, you should know a couple of terms. The first is a *page split*. When a SQL Server page is full and another row must be put on that page, a page split will occur. A new page will be assigned to the index or table, and 50 percent of the rows will be moved to the new page. Then the new row will be added in the appropriate location. As you might imagine, this can be an expensive operation if it happens frequently. If you use a fill factor when you create your index, you can allow new rows to be added without causing page splits. Setting the appropriate fill factor will likely improve performance. However, getting the proper fill factor will mostly come from experience.

Figure 13.5

A clustered index with pad_index.

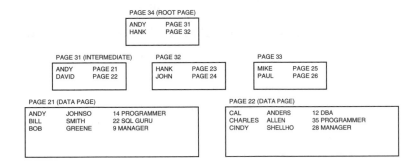

This can be particularly useful with clustered indexes because the leaf level of the index is made up of the actual data pages. Be aware, however, that applying a fill factor such as 50 to the clustered index will approximately double the size of the table. This can have a very dramatic impact on space usage and should be done with some caution.

Page splitting on heaps (tables without a clustered index) can be particularly expensive in terms of its impact because of the way nonclustered indexes are stored. Each row in the nonclustered index has a pointer to the data row's page-number/row-number combination. If a page split on the heap occurs, approximately half of the rows move. This means that half of the rows will have to modify each entry for each nonclustered index. All these modifications occur while you wait for your data insert or update to occur, resulting in slower response times. Therefore, you should probably have a clustered index on most tables. As you saw earlier, the nonclustered indexes don't point to the physical location of the rows if a clustered index exists, so page splits in the clustered index don't affect the nonclustered indexes.

When you add `pad_index`, you can avoid nonleaf page splits as well. This will increase space usage—but not nearly as much as the `fillfactor`.

The DROP_EXISTING Option

The `DROP_EXISTING` option specifies that an index should be dropped and re-created (essentially, this is a "reorganization" of the index). If you are dropping and re-creating the clustered index, you might think that nonclustered indexes would be affected.

However, SQL Server 7.0 is smart enough to simply drop and re-create the clustered index itself. Because the nonclustered indexes have the key value of the clustered index as their row identifier, and that value doesn't change during the CREATE INDEX with the DROP_EXISTING clause, there's no need to change the nonclustered indexes.

This option is most useful for clustered indexes, but it can also be used on non-clustered indexes. The DBCC DBREINDEX option later today has similar functionality, but the DROP_EXISTING option is probably a better long-term choice because Microsoft is slowly but surely moving away from DBCC commands.

The STATISTICS_NORECOMPUTE Option

SQL Server 7.0 automatically recomputes statistics on indexes as needed. You can disable this feature if you want by using the STATISTICS_NORECOMPUTE option. To reenable the automatic statistics gathering feature of SQL Server, run UPDATE STATISTICS without NORECOMPUTE. You'll learn more about UPDATE STATISTICS later in today's lesson. Turning off automatic gathering of statistics for your indexes generally is a bad idea. The SQL Server 7.0 optimizer is very dependent on accurate statistics to optimize your queries.

The IGNORE_DUP_KEY Option

The IGNORE_DUP_KEY option specifies that when running a multirow update against a table with a unique clustered index, duplicate rows from that insert are quietly discarded and the statement succeeds, but SQL Server will return a warning.

The following code sample shows how this works:

```
create table t1 (col1 int not null, col2 char(5) not null)
go
create unique clustered index myind on t1 (col1) with ignore_dup_key
go
create table t2 (col1 int not null, col2 char(5) not null)
go
insert t2 values (1, 'abcde')
insert t2 values (2, 'abcde')
insert t2 values (2, 'abcde')
insert t2 values (3, 'abcde')

insert t1 select * from t2
```

After running this code, you will get the following message:

```
Server: Msg 3604, Level 16, State 1
Duplicate key was ignored.
```

If you were to then select from table t1, you would see three rows, as expected.

Index Usage

You've examined index basics and how to create SQL Server indexes. However, you haven't seen which indexes to create or when they should be used.

When Will My Index Be Used?

You can start with the most obvious question: How do I know when an index will be used? When a query is submitted to SQL Server, the query is broken apart and analyzed. In terms of optimization for indexing, the most important part of the query is the WHERE clause. A statement in the WHERE clause of a query is the most likely way that SQL Server will know how to optimize your query to use an index. However, just because your query contains a WHERE clause doesn't mean that an index will be used. Take this query for example:

```
SELECT au_id, au_fname, au_lname
FROM pubs..authors
WHERE state = 'CA'
GO
```

If there's an index on the state column but most of the authors came from California, there's no point to using an index. A table scan (reading every data page in the table) will most likely be the most efficient plan to get the data. The term "the most efficient plan" means the most efficient in terms of minimizing the number of pages needed to be read by SQL Server. The other term for this is minimizing I/O and logical page reads.

Given a similar query that returns only one row, it will most likely make sense to use an index. For example, if there was a clustered index on the au_id column, this query would almost certainly use the index:

```
SELECT au_id, au_fname, au_lname
FROM pubs..authors
WHERE au_id = "341-22-1782"
```

How Do You Verify Index Usage?

The next question is how can you verify which index will be used by your query? SQL Server 7.0 includes many options to examine which indexes will be used to support your queries. You can use the Transact-SQL statements SET SHOWPLAN_ALL ON or SET SHOW-PLAN_TEXT ON. If you are using the SQL Server Query Analyzer to run the showplans, you can run either option. However, if you are using a command-line tool such as isql.exe or osql.exe, you should use the SHOWPLAN_TEXT statement option. To see the difference, run the script in Listing 13.1 to create a table and insert some data into the table. The script must insert some volume of data so that indexes have a chance to be used.

13

Note
Note that the SET options for showplan *must* be in a batch by themselves.
See Day 16, "Programming SQL Server 7.0," for more information about
batches.

INPUT   **LISTING 13.1**   MONITORING INDEXES

```
USE PUBS
CREATE TABLE PUBS..INDEXTAB
(col1 int not null,
 col2 varchar(250) not null,
 col3 varchar(250) not null,
 col4 varchar(250) not null,
 col5 varchar(250) not null)

insert indextab values (1,'adam','col3','col4','col5')
insert indextab values (2,'bob','col3','col4','col5')
insert indextab values (3,'charles','col3','col4','col5')
insert indextab values (4,'david','col3','col4','col5')
insert indextab values (5,'edward','col3','col4','col5')
insert indextab values (6,'frank','col3','col4','col5')
insert indextab values (7,'george','col3','col4','col5')
insert indextab values (8,'hank','col3','col4','col5')
insert indextab values (9,'ida','col3','col4','col5')
insert indextab values (10,'john','col3','col4','col5')
insert indextab values (11,'kim','col3','col4','col5')
insert indextab values (12,'loni','col3','col4','col5')
insert indextab values (13,'mike','col3','col4','col5')
insert indextab values (14,'nikki','col3','col4','col5')
insert indextab values (15,'oprah','col3','col4','col5')
insert indextab values (16,'paul','col3','col4','col5')
insert indextab values (17,'quan','col3','col4','col5')
insert indextab values (18,'richard','col3','col4','col5')
insert indextab values (19,'sam','col3','col4','col5')
insert indextab values (20,'tom','col3','col4','col5')
insert indextab values (21,'uma','col3','col4','col5')
insert indextab values (22,'vera','col3','col4','col5')
insert indextab values (23,'walter','col3','col4','col5')
insert indextab values (24,'xray','col3','col4','col5')
insert indextab values (25,'yuma','col3','col4','col5')
insert indextab values (26,'zane','col3','col4','col5')
insert indextab values (27,'ann','col3','col4','col5')
insert indextab values (28,'bill','col3','col4','col5')
insert indextab values (29,'cathy','col3','col4','col5')
insert indextab values (30,'dawn','col3','col4','col5')
insert indextab values (31,'ellen','col3','col4','col5')
insert indextab values (32,'fran','col3','col4','col5')
insert indextab values (33,'grant','col3','col4','col5')
```

```
insert indextab values (34,'helen','col3','col4','col5')
insert indextab values (35,'irwin','col3','col4','col5')
insert indextab values (36,'jack','col3','col4','col5')
insert indextab values (37,'kathy','col3','col4','col5')
insert indextab values (38,'lance','col3','col4','col5')
insert indextab values (39,'molly','col3','col4','col5')
insert indextab values (40,'nancy','col3','col4','col5')
CREATE CLUSTERED INDEX CL_MYINDEX on indextab (col1)
```

First run with the SHOWPLAN_TEXT option:

```
USE PUBS
GO
SET SHOWPLAN_TEXT ON
GO
select col1, col2 from indextab
where col2 = 'ann'
```

OUTPUT The output generated by these statements would look similar to this:

```
StmtText
-------------------------------------------------------
select col1, col2 from indextab
where col2 = 'ann'

(1 row(s) affected)

StmtText
-------------------------------------------------------
  ¦--Clustered Index
➥Scan(OBJECT:([pubs].[dbo].[INDEXTAB].[CL_MYINDEX]),
  ➥ WHERE:([INDEXTAB].[col2]=[@1]))

(1 row(s) affected)
```

As you can see from the output of the preceding showplan, SQL Server chose to use a clustered index scan to run this query. Next, examine the same query using the SHOW-PLAN_ALL option:

```
USE PUBS
GO
SET SHOWPLAN_ALL ON
GO
select col1, col2 from indextab
where col2 = 'ann'
```

and the output from these statements:

13

```
StmtText    StmtId      NodeId      Parent      PhysicalOp      LogicalOp
➥ Argument      DefinedValues      EstimateRows      EstimateIO
➥ EstimateCPU   AvgRowSize  TotalSubtreeCost        OutputList
➥ Warnings    Type      Parallel EstimateExecutions
-----------------------------------------------------------------------
-
-----------------------------------------------------------------------
-
----------------------------------- ----------------------- --------------
-
-------- ----------------- ----------------------- ---------------- --
-
------------------ ------------------ ----------------------- ----------
-
------------------ ----------------------------------------- ----------
-
------------- ----------------------------------------- -------- ----------
-
select col1, col2 from indextab
where col2 = 'ann'                  4    1    0    NULL      NULL    NULL
➥ NULL           NULL                          NULL
➥  NULL                        NULL        NULL                      NULL
➥                                   NULL                          ]
➥ SELECT                   0           NULL
  ¦--Clustered Index Scan(OBJECT:([pubs].[dbo].[INDEXTAB].[CL_MYINDEX]),
➥ WHERE:([INDEXTAB].[col2]=[@1]))  4          3               1
➥  Clustered Index Scan           Clustered Index Scan
➥  OBJECT:([pubs].[dbo].[INDEXTAB].[CL_MYINDEX]),
➥ WHERE:([INDEXTAB].[col2]=[@1])  [INDEXTAB].[col1], [INDEXTAB].[col2]
➥ 15.905415                3.7578501E-2           0.0001225
➥   140    0.037701      [INDEXTAB].[col1], [INDEXTAB].[col2]
➥ NO STATS:([INDEXTAB].[col2])  PLAN_ROW                0          1.0

(2 row(s) affected)
```

Note that this is the same information that was returned with the SHOWPLAN_TEXT option but with additional details. I recommend that you stick with using SHOWPLAN_TEXT unless you become an expert at tuning queries and understanding items such as the TotalSubtreeCost.

If you want to see which indexes are on a table, you can run the following sp_helpindex system stored procedure:

```
SET SHOWPLAN_ALL OFF -- or turn off any other showplan options first
GO
EXEC sp_helpindex indextab
GO

index_name        index_description                     index_keys
----------------  ------------------------------------  ----------
CL_MYINDEX        clustered located on PRIMARY           col1

(1 row(s) affected)
```

Now create a second index on the table so you can examine a plan on something other than a clustered index.

```
CREATE INDEX NONCL_MYINDEX on indextab (col2)
GO
SET SHOWPLAN_TEXT ON
GO
select col1, col2 from indextab
where col2 = 'ann'


StmtText
---------------------------------------------------------
select col1, col2 from indextab
where col2 = 'ann'

(1 row(s) affected)

StmtText
-----------------------------------------------------------------
  ¦--Index Seek(OBJECT:([pubs].[dbo].[INDEXTAB].[NONCL_MYINDEX]),
 SEEK:([INDEXTAB].[col2]=[@1]) ORDERED)

(1 row(s) affected)
```

Notice that SQL Server has now used an "index seek" on the index noncl_myindex. This simply means that the index is used to find all rows for ann.

You can also examine the plans using the SQL Server Query Analyzer's graphical showplan options. There are actually two plans you can see: the estimated plan (the tool button on the toolbar) or the actual showplan from running the query. The difference is that the actual showplan has exact numbers, whereas the estimated plan shows you what the SQL Server query optimizer thinks will happen. You run the same query as before, except you turn on the Show Execution Plan option (either from the Query menu or enable the option in the Execute Mode button). You will see something similar to Figure 13.6 when you click the Execution Plan tab at the bottom of your screen. If you move the mouse over any item in the graphical window, you are presented with detailed information about that particular query step. The output here is relatively simple, but for very large plans, the graphical plan can be a blessing compared to textual showplans.

All you've seen so far is what choice SQL Server made. The other part of the puzzle you must fill in is how SQL Server makes its decision. For the most part, the optimization is done based on how much work it will take to answer your question. SQL Server wants to answer your question as quickly as it can, doing the least amount of work. That usually translates into minimizing the amount of logical I/O that is done.

13

FIGURE **13.6**

The graphical show-plan in the SQL Server Query Analyzer.

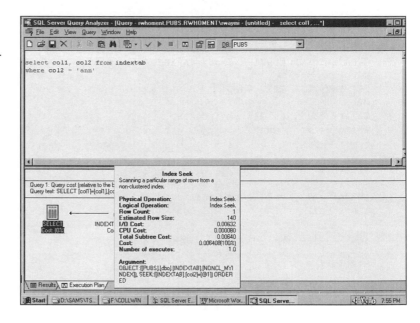

Logical I/O is data access by SQL Server. Each logical I/O means that SQL Server has read a single 8KB page. The total number of pages accessed will always equal the number of logical I/Os. SQL Server differentiates between logical and physical I/O. If a query takes 50 logical I/Os and only 20 physical I/Os, it means that 30 of the 50 pages it needed were already in memory. The other 20 pages had to be retrieved physically from the disks and brought into memory so that they could be read—hence the term *physical I/O*. SQL Server will attempt to minimize the amount of physical I/O access. You can see the amount of I/O a query will use by using the statement SET STATISTICS IO ON. Make sure you turn off the NOEXEC option before you use the statistics I/O command (if you've enabled it) because you must actually run a query to get statistics I/O information. Because SHOWPLAN options don't actually run a query, they are also incompatible with getting STATISTICS IO information.

```
SET STATISTICS IO ON
GO

SELECT col1,col2
FROM indextab
where col1 < 3
GO

STEP 1
col1        col2
----------- -----
```

```
1              adam
2              bob

(2 row(s) affected)

Table 'INDEXTAB'. Scan count 1, logical reads 2, physical reads 0,
↪read-ahead reads 0.
```

Note that it took two logical reads to answer this query: one read to get the root page of the clustered index and one to read the leaf page of the index. Remember that because it's a clustered index, the leaf page is the data page. SQL Server will normally favor using a clustered index.

In Figure 13.7 you can see how you can figure out these two logical reads. SQL Server must read the root page of the index and then the leaf level of the index to return the data. Note that this index has no intermediate pages (it's too small).

FIGURE 13.7

Your clustered index.

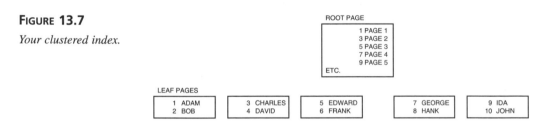

SQL Server also uses information about how much memory is available, how much central processing unit (CPU) time it will take to process each query option, and how busy the system is. Therefore, you might see SQL Server choose a plan that takes more I/O than another because it actually costs less when all factors are taken together. The SQL Server 7.0 optimizer is much more sophisticated than it was in previous versions, and will take more of this information in to make decisions about which indexes to use. If you examine the output from the SHOWPLAN_ALL report, you will see many of these numbers reported. How to use these numbers is beyond the scope of this book.

Now that you've seen how SQL Server wants to access your tables, what can you do about it? Also, what do you do if you've created indexes and you're sure that they should be used, yet SQL Server won't use them? You can override the optimizer.

Overriding the Optimizer

You can specify what's known as optimizer hints. The first thing to consider is that most of the time the SQL Server optimizer is correct. If you're still sure that you are right and that SQL Server is wrong, and you've updated your statistics and checked the SHOWPLAN

13

output, you can consider using optimizer hints. This section examines each of these options to provide the correct information to the SQL Server optimizer.

To select an index, specify either the index name or the index number as part of your select statement. You can find an index's number by querying the `sysindexes` system table in your database:

```
SELECT col1, col2
FROM indextab (index = noncl_myindex)
```

This query would normally have used a clustered index scan, but in this case you told it to use the nonclustered index that you created earlier.

 Caution

> SQL Server will always use the index you have selected, regardless of what the optimizer thinks is a proper choice. SQL Server will never reevaluate your selection, so remember to retest your choice periodically. This is especially true when you apply service packs or upgrade SQL Server. Therefore, it's rarely necessary, and sometimes downright dangerous, to use optimizer hints.

How would you force SQL Server to use a table scan? Well, it involves understanding a little bit about how indexes are numbered in the sysindexes table. Nonclustered indexes are numbered between 2 and 250. If a clustered index exists, it will have an index number of 1. If no clustered index exists, a row with index number 0 will be in the sysindexes table. It's possible to specify the index number in the optimizer hint rather than using the index name. Hence, the previous SQL statement might also look like this (assuming index number 2 was `noncl_myindex`):

```
SELECT col1, col2
FROM indextab (INDEX = 2)
```

To force a clustered index scan, you would write your query like this, and you can see that SQL Server does indeed do exactly as you've asked and uses a clustered index scan:

```
SET SHOWPLAN_TEXT ON
GO
SELECT col1, col2
FROM indextab (INDEX = 0)
WHERE col1 < 3


StmtText
--------------------------------------------------------------------
SELECT col1, col2
FROM indextab (INDEX = 0)
```

```
WHERE col1 < 3

(1 row(s) affected)

StmtText
-------------------------------------------------------------------------
  ¦--Clustered Index Scan(pubs..INDEXTAB.CL_MYINDEX,
WHERE:(indextab.col1<3))

(1 row(s) affected)
```

Just to see another use of this option, drop the clustered index on the table. This will
return the table to being a "heap." Then run the same query with the optimizer hint of
`INDEX=0`.

```
set showplan_text off
go
drop index indextab.cL_MYINDEX
GO
SET SHOWPLAN_TEXT ON
GO
SELECT col1, col2
FROM indextab (INDEX = 0)
WHERE col1 < 3
```

```
The clustered index has been dropped.
Index (ID = 2) is being rebuilt.
StmtText
------------------------------------------------------------
SELECT col1, col2
FROM indextab (INDEX = 0)
WHERE col1 < 3

(1 row(s) affected)

StmtText
------------------------------------------------------------
  ¦--Table Scan(pubs..INDEXTAB, WHERE:(indextab.col1<3))

(1 row(s) affected)
```

Notice that a table scan was used. This is because there was no clustered index on the
table. Remember, a table scan and a clustered index are essentially the same type of
operation. This is because the leaf level of a clustered index is the data, so a scan of that
level is the same as reading every single data page (a table scan).

13

Index Maintenance

Indexes must be maintained to remain efficient and useful over time. You must manually maintain these indexes (or set up automated plans to do so). Either way you will need an understanding of the basics of index maintenance.

Statistics

SQL Server knows statistical information about your data through a special object in the database (which I will refer to as the *statistics blob*). The statistics blob contains information about how data is distributed throughout the table and also calculates the average number of duplicates for the indexed columns. When you create an index, if there is already data in the table, a statistics blob will be created and populated with information about the columns that you have indexed. If you create an index on a table and then add the data, and have not turned off the automatic gathering of statistics, a statistics blob will be created for you. If you turn off the capability of SQL Server to automatically keep updated statistics about an index, this statistics blob will not be created. If this information doesn't exist, SQL Server must guess about how your data is distributed. When your query contains a clause, such as col1 < 3, SQL Server will consult the statistics blob to guess how many data rows will be returned. The more current your statistics blob, the better job SQL Server will do selecting the proper index (or deciding to use a table scan). Therefore, do not turn off the gathering of automatic statistics.

The truly paranoid (the authors of this book are members of this group) periodically will manually gather statistics as well. To update the statistics blob with current information, you run the UPDATE STATISTICS command.

SYNTAX

```
UPDATE STATISTICS {table}
[index
¦([index_or_column [, ...n])]
[WITH [ [FULLSCAN]
¦ SAMPLE number {PERCENT ¦ ROWS}] ]
[[,] [ALL ¦ COLUMNS ¦ INDEX]
[[,] NORECOMPUTE] ]
```

So, the following might be an example of how to update statistics on the authors table:

```
UPDATE STATISTICS authors
```

As long as automatic statistics gathering is enabled, there's no need to run this command frequently. On most of our servers, we run UPDATE STATISTICS once a week (mostly out of habit) on each table in the database. Microsoft has shipped a handy system stored procedure to do this for you: sp_statistics. To run this procedure, type exec sp_statistics in a query window. That's it; there are no parameters or anything to muck with, and it will automatically gather statistical information about each table's indexes in the database.

Turning Off Automatic Statistics

You can turn off automatic statistics (and then hopefully turn them back on again because they work so well) using the system-stored procedure sp_autostats.

```
sp_autostats 'tablename' [, 'statsflag'] [, 'indexname']
```

where

- *tablename* is the name of the table you want to change the autostats option on.
- *statsflag* is either on or off (turning on automatic statistics or turning them off if not specified).
- *indexname* is the name of the index you'd like to change. If you leave this parameter off, all indexes for a given table are affected by the change. If you leave off both the *statsflag* and the *indexname*, sp_autostats returns information about the current status of automatic statistics on the indexes of the table.

▲

So, to turn off automatic statistics on the authors table in the PUBS database, you would run

```
Use pubs
Exec sp_autostats 'authors','Off'
```

Column Statistics

An exciting feature of SQL Server 7.0 is the capability to track statistics on columns that are not indexed. This is known as keeping statistics on columns. You use the UPDATE STATISTICS command as you did before, except you specify the columns you'd like statistics on and use the WITH COLUMNS option. An example would look like this:

```
UPDATE STATISTICS authors (city) WITH COLUMNS
```

This command would update statistics on the city column of the authors table.

You might be asking yourself why this is useful. The answer is that the SQL Server Optimizer (the code that decides which index to use) can examine this statistical information to decide how best to read a table—much in the same way it can use indexed columns with statistics. So, if you specify a column in the WHERE clause of your select statements but don't want to index that column, it can still be used for optimization purposes with column statistics. When the Index Tuning Wizard is examined later, you will look at column statistics again.

13

When Were Statistics Last Gathered?

If you somehow end up taking over a new SQL Server (and promptly ran out and bought
this book—hooray for you on your excellent purchase), you might need to get a handle
on the current state of your SQL Server databases. One of the things you'll need to determine is how and when statistics are updated. Fortunately, you can find out when the last
time statistics were gathered with the STATS_DATE function:

```
SELECT STATS_DATE(table_id, index_id)
```

It's pretty straightforward, but it does require you to get the *table_id* and *index_id*. You
can get these by using the OBJECT_ID function

```
Use pubs
Go
Declare @tabid int
Declare @indid int
Select @tabid = object_id ('indextab')
Select @indid = 1 /* the clustered index */
SELECT STATS_DATE (@tabid, @indid)
```

and you would get output similar to this:

```
--------------------------
1998-08-01 17:11:05.860

(1 row(s) affected)
```

Tip

> If you don't get the preceding results, you might still have a showplan
> option turned on. Open a new query window and copy the code into your
> new window, or run
>
> ```
> SET SHOWPLAN_TEXT OFF
>
> GO
>
> SET SHOWPLAN_ALL OFF
>
> GO
> ```

The DBCC UPDATEUSAGE Command

DBCC UPDATEUSAGE corrects information in the SQL Server system table sysindexes. The
information in that table tells SQL Server things like how many pages are in the table
and how many pages are used by each index. That information is maintained automatically, but the possibility exists that the information in the system tables can become out of
date. To update the information, run DBCC UPDATEUSAGE.

▲ SYNTAX

```
DBCC UPDATEUSAGE ({0 ¦ database_name} [, table_name [, index_id]])
[ WITH [COUNT_ROWS] [, NO_INFOMSGS ]]
```

where

- *database_name* is the name of the database in which you want to work. If you specify just a database name, information in sysindexes will be updated for all heaps and indexes in the database.

- *table_name* is the name of a table for which you want to have information updated in the sysindexes system table.

- *index_id* is the index number of an index for a given table you want to have information updated for in the sysindexes system table. You can find the *index_id* for an index by running the sp_helpindex system stored procedure.

The DBCC SHOWCONTIG Command

Periodically your indexes will need to be reorganized. What this means is that over time indexes will not maintain their fill factor or will become fragmented and become less useful. To discover whether your indexes are fragmented and need to be reorganized, you can use the DBCC SHOWCONTIG command.

▲ SYNTAX

```
DBCC SHOWCONTIG (table_id, [index_id])
```

where

- *table_id* is the ID of the table you want to examine for fragmentation. You can get an object's ID by using the object_id('tablename') function.

- *index_id* is the internal number for the index you want to examine. Without this value, information is gathered for the clustered index (if it exists) or for the heap (a table without a clustered index).

Listing 13.2 is a script you can run to look at the results of DBCC SHOWCONTIG. Don't worry too much about the syntax. It'll all make sense by Day 21! Make sure you run this in a new query window (or turn off SHOWPLAN and any other options you might have enabled before).

13

LISTING 13.2   A SCRIPT TO SHOW YOU THE RESULTS OF DBCC SHOWCONTIG

```
USE PUBS
GO
DECLARE @tableid int
SELECT @tableid = object_id ('INDEXTAB')
DBCC SHOWCONTIG (@tableid)
GO
```

continues

LISTING **13.2**   CONTINUED

```
BCC SHOWCONTIG scanning 'INDEXTAB' table...
[SHOW_CONTIG - SCAN ANALYSIS]
---------------------------------------------------------------------
-
Table: 'INDEXTAB' (965578478)  Indid: 0  dbid:5
TABLE level scan performed.
- Pages Scanned................................: 1
- Extents Scanned..............................: 1
- Extent Switches..............................: 0
- Avg. Pages per Extent........................: 1.0
- Scan Density [Best Count:Actual Count].......: 100.00% [1:1]
- Extent Scan Fragmentation ...................: 0.00%
- Avg. Bytes free per page.....................: 6436.0
- Avg. Page density (full).....................: 20.48%

(10 row(s) affected)

DBCC execution completed. If DBCC printed error messages,
contact your system administrator.
```

ANALYSIS There's a significant amount of information here, but you'll need to focus on just two or three key items. First, you can see from the first line, where it indicates Indid: 0, that there is not a clustered index on the table. The next value to examine is the Scan Density. The higher the percentage, the better the shape your table is in. The other number to look at is the Avg. Page density (full). You want this number to be as close to your fill factor as possible.

When these numbers start to get somewhat low (there's no concrete number to use), it's probably a good time to reorganize your indexes. You could drop and then re-create your index. If it's a clustered index, you can use the DROP_EXISTING option to speed up that operation. This will put the index back into the original shape, including reapplying your fill factor options. It will also not affect your nonclustered indexes because the order and overall index structure of your clustered index is not affected when using the DROP_EXISTING option. If you drop and re-create the clustered index without this option, you will reorganize the data pages as well as the index structure.

DBCC SHOWCONTIG can be run by either members of the sysadmin fixed server role or the db_owner fixed database role.

The **DBCC DBREINDEX** Command

There's another option available that might be a better choice. This is the DBCC DBREINDEX command.

SYNTAX

```
DBCC DBREINDEX (['database.owner.table_name' [, index_name
[, fillfactor ]]])
[WITH NOINFOMSGS]
```

Many of the options are the same as in the `create index` statement, so you should refer to this statement for a review of the sorted data and fill factor options. However, if you specify a fill factor of 0, the original fill factor that was specified when the index was created will be used. Otherwise, it will be set to the fill factor value you specify. Do note, however, that if you want to specify an optional parameter, you must specify all the previous options. For example, to specify a fill factor, you must specify an index name, even if you provide a blank name. For example, use the following to rebuild the indexes on the authors table (all of them) with the original fill factor:

```
DBCC DBREINDEX ('authors','', 0)
```

If you specify a table, such as the following, every index on the table will be dropped and re-created, as shown in the previous output.

```
DBCC DBREINDEX ('indextab')
GO

Index (ID = 2) is being rebuilt.
DBCC execution completed. If DBCC printed error messages,
contact your system administrator.
```

You can also specify an individual index with which to work. In this example, you first create an additional nonclustered index on the authors table. Then issue the `DBREINDEX` command and specify the new index you just created.

```
CREATE INDEX noncl_col2_indextab on indextab (col4)
GO
DBCC DBREINDEX ('indextab','noncl_col2_indextab')

Index (ID = 3) is being rebuilt.
DBCC execution completed. If DBCC printed error messages,
contact your system administrator.
```

13

Caution

Be careful when specifying a fill factor with DBCC DBREINDEX. If you don't specify a particular index but use the fill factor setting, such as

```
DBCC DBREINDEX ('indextab', '', 50)
```

it will reset the fill factor on all indexes on the table (in this case to 50). This might or might not be what you've intended.

DBCC DBREINDEX has one big advantage over dropping and re-creating indexes. On Day 14, "Ensuring Data Integrity," you'll look at referential integrity and American National Standards Institute (ANSI) constraints. Some of these constraints create indexes behind the scenes. DBCC DBREINDEX can safely drop and re-create the indexes created with constraints, whereas the only way to do this otherwise is to drop and re-create the constraints. This can be extremely difficult, as you'll see on Day 14.

Members of the sysadmin server role, db_owner database role, or the owner of a table can run DBCC DBREINDEX.

 Tip

> A great alternative to having to use DBCC DBREINDEX in SQL Server 7.0 is to use the DROP_EXISTING option in the CREATE INDEX statement, which you looked at earlier today. Functionally, they are nearly equivalent, but you can rely on standard DDL instead of using a SQL Server internal function to accomplish the same task.

SQL Server Enterprise Manager

SQL Server Enterprise Manager can be used to manage indexes with the index properties dialog. The first thing you must know is that there are two different index control dialog boxes. You could expand the database with which you want to work (in the examples here it's the pubs database), highlight the Tables folder, and right-click on the table in the right pane that you want to work with. Select Design Table from the pop-up menu, and you will be at the Design Table dialog (what a shock). I selected authors, and if you do the same you will see something similar to Figure 13.8.

FIGURE 13.8

The Design Table dialog box.

Column Name	Datatype	Length	Precision	Scale	Allow Nulls	Default Value	Identity	Identity Seed	Id
au_id	id (varchar)	11	0	0					
au_lname	varchar	40	0	0					
au_fname	varchar	20	0	0					
phone	char	12	0	0		('UNKNOWN')			
address	varchar	40	0	0	✓				
city	varchar	20	0	0	✓				
state	char	2	0	0	✓				
zip	char	5	0	0	✓				
contract	bit	1	0	0					

As you can see in Figure 13.8, if you click the second button (Table and Index Properties), you will be presented with a properties dialog for the table. Notice that this is a different dialog from the general properties of a table. Click on the Indexes/Keys tab to be presented with Figure 13.9.

FIGURE 13.9

The Design Table dialog box properties.

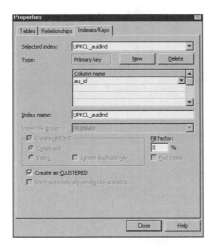

From this dialog you can use most of the indexing options that you've seen today. If you'd like to create, remove, or rename an index, you can do it here. You can choose to make an index unique, and if it is unique, decide whether it's a unique constraint (examined on Day 14) or a unique index. In practice, you'll find that you usually want a unique constraint rather than a unique index. If you choose to leave it as a unique index, you can set the Ignore Duplicate Key, which you examined earlier.

You can also specify that the index be clustered and turn off the automatic gathering of statistics. Note that automatic statistics are turned on unless you turn them off. Fill Factor and the Pad Index option are also available. The other option available here is for filegroups. If you are using filegroups (as described on Day 4, "Creating and Implementing Databases, Files, and Filegroups"), you can change the filegroup with which an index is associated.

However, there's what I consider a better index options dialog box available—it's shown in Figure 13.10. Here you can see in a much clearer fashion which indexes are available and which columns are indexed. You get to this dialog by right-clicking a table and selecting All Tasks, Manage Indexes.

13

Figure 13.10

The Manage Indexes dialog box.

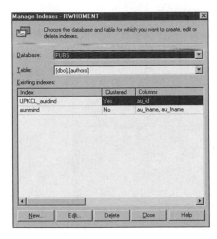

The real power of this option becomes apparent when you want to create a new index. Click the New button to see Figure 13.11. Notice that every option for SQL Server 7.0 is available for you to graphically specify.

Figure 13.11

The Create New Index dialog box.

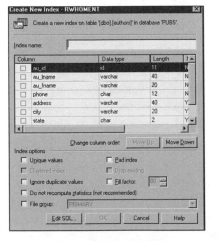

> **Note**
>
> So, why are there two completely different manage index dialog boxes? The one from the table properties is from a code component that is common to many Microsoft products (such as Microsoft Visual Studio). It is coded to support multiple databases, not just SQL Server 7.0. However, the Manage Indexes dialog box is purely for SQL Server 7.0, and thus all SQL Server-specific options can be made available.

Index Selection

Now that you've seen the options available to you and how you build indexes, your next logical question might be "Which columns should I index, and how should I index them?"

Good candidates for indexes include

- Primary key columns (discussed on Day 14)
- Foreign key columns (also discussed on Day 14)
- Columns on which you use the ORDER BY clause (discussed on Day 11, "Retrieving Data with Queries")
- Columns on which you use the GROUP BY clause (discussed on Day 11)
- Columns that you specify exactly in your WHERE clause (also discussed on Day 11)

In general, you should index columns that are included in your WHERE clause using conditions that don't include functions or calculations. In other words, the following probably indicates that a good candidate to index is the emp_id column:

```
WHERE emp_id = 5
```

However, the following probably won't be able to use an index, so there's no point in creating one for it (for this query, anyway):

```
WHERE SUBSTRING(emp_id,1,5) = 'Annet'
```

Statements like the first WHERE clause in the preceding paragraph are known as searchable arguments. Searchable arguments (also called SARGs) are the types of arguments that can be used by SQL Server. In addition to exact matches, you can sometimes use approximate matches on character columns. For example,

```
WHERE emp_lname LIKE 'w%'
```

would be searchable, but

```
WHERE emp_lname LIKE '%w%'
```

is not. Note that the % symbol specifies a wildcard. In the first example, the emp_lname column would be searched for values that begin with a w. The second example would search the emp_lname column for values that have a w anywhere in them. Imagine if you tried to do a search like this yourself on the telephone book. Could you easily find the second condition? SQL Server will have the same problem you would; as long as the first letter is specified, you've got somewhere to start.

13

One other point to consider is that not every column is a good candidate to index. You should not index the following:

- Columns using the text, image, or bit datatypes
- Columns that aren't very unique (such as male or female)
- Columns that are too wide to be useful indexes

The last option depends on your application and table, but it's a good bet that a char(200) is an unlikely candidate for an index.

You must be careful, however, because each index introduces maintenance, space usage, and performance issues. Generally, I recommend that you don't have more than three to four indexes on a table. For every rule there are quite a few exceptions, but this is a good guideline to follow. The next step after you've decided which columns to index is to figure out which type of index you need: clustered or nonclustered.

Clustered Index Choices

You get only one clustered index, so it's a good idea to choose this one first. Good candidates for clustered indexes include

- Very specific queries (where col1 = 5, for example).
- Queries with a range of data. Examples are WHERE col1 BETWEEN 5 AND 30 and WHERE col1 > 20.
- Queries on columns you ORDER BY or GROUP BY frequently.

A critical concern when selecting your clustered index in SQL Server 7.0 is that the key values (indexed columns) you choose for your clustered index are "carried" along into the nonclustered indexes. Therefore, if you choose a wide clustered index, such as a char(30), not only will it take longer to search the clustered index itself but all your nonclustered indexes will have to carry the char(30) value of your clustered index key on every row in the nonclustered indexes. That's a significant amount of overhead, so you'll want to keep your clustered index keys as small as possible. You will also want to make sure that the clustered key you select is not updated frequently because all your nonclustered indexes would need to be updated when the clustered index values change.

Another choice might be to index foreign key columns, which you examine on Day 14.

Nonclustered Index Choices

After you've selected your clustered index, the rest of the indexes you've decided to create must be nonclustered. Good candidates include

- Specific queries (yes, they're good for both types of indexes).
- Queries that can be answered entirely by using an index (called *covering index queries*). For example, if you had an index on the au_lname and au_fname columns of the authors table in the pubs database, the following query could be answered entirely from the index without accessing the data:

```
SELECT au_fname from pubs..authors where au_lname = "White"
```

- Columns you order by or group by.
- Columns on which you use functions (such as MIN, MAX, or COUNT).

The key issue here is that you only index columns that will be used in the WHERE clause of your queries and that you verify that the indexes you choose will be used by SQL Server using the SHOWPLAN options or the graphical showplan of the SQL Server Query Analyzer.

The SQL Server Index Tuning Wizard

You will examine the Index Tuning Wizard on Day 20, "Configuring and Monitoring SQL Server 7.0." It is mentioned here simply so you know that it wasn't missed, if you've seen it. However, you must understand more about the SQL Server Profiler utility before you can successfully use the wizard.

Full-Text Indexing

Full-text indexes enable you (for the first time in SQL Server) to create an index on a text column, as well as any other character column. This feature is not installed by default, but if you are on Windows NT Server and using the Standard or Enterprise Editions of SQL Server 7.0, you can install this feature during a custom setup. Full-text indexing is possible because of the merging of Microsoft Index Server technology into SQL Server 7.0. This feature requires that the Microsoft Search service be running (which it will be by default if you installed full-text indexing during setup). It also requires a unique index on each table you want to use for full-text indexing. Only the owner of a table can create a full-text index.

You can have only one full-text index per table, and the index is physically stored outside SQL Server (in your \mssql7\FTData directory). Unlike normal SQL Server indexes, full-text indexes are not self-maintaining. You will need to set up a periodic job to update the full-text indexes. You examine jobs in further detail on Day 19, "Using the SQL Server Agent." Setting up and using full-text indexing is unlike normal indexes, but the good news is that Microsoft has provided yet another wizard to assist you.

13

Highlight the table on which you want to create a full-text index in SQL Server
Enterprise Manager, and select Tools, Full-Text Indexing from the menu. The Full-Text
Indexing Wizard starts and walks you through creating your new index. The example
shown here is the pub_info table in the pubs database. I made this selection to show you
that you can index a column of datatype text, even though this wouldn't be possible with
normal SQL Server indexes. After the wizard starts, you will see an introduction screen.
After you have read the introduction, click Next to see Figure 13.12.

FIGURE 13.12

*Selecting a unique
index on your table.*

As just noted, a unique index is used for each full-text index you want to create (as a row
locator). Select the unique index to use (there's only one for pub_info), and click Next to
see Figure 13.13.

FIGURE 13.13

*Selecting eligible
columns from your
table.*

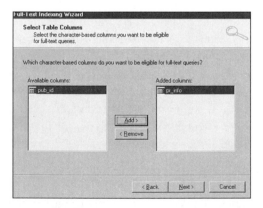

As you can see, I've selected the pr_info column, which is of data type text. Click Next
to see Figure 13.14, which enables you to select a catalog. To keep things simple, use a
new one (because there's probably not one on your system anyway), and name it
pub_info (as shown in Figure 13.14).

FIGURE 13.14

Selecting a catalog to store your full-text index.

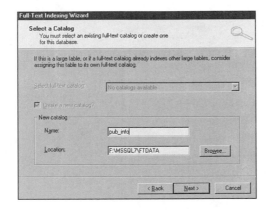

Click Next, and you will have the option of setting up a schedule to populate and update your full-text index. Rather than get into scheduling, skip this dialog box by clicking Next. You can still manually update the full-text index. Click Finish, and you are presented with Figure 13.15, showing that you have succeeded in configuring your full-text index. Notice that it reports that your full-text index has not been populated yet.

FIGURE 13.15

The finish dialog after completing the wizard.

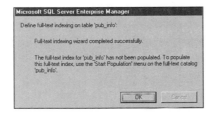

Click OK, and then expand your pubs database again, if it's not already done in SQL Server Enterprise Manager. Highlight Full-Text Catalogs, right-click the catalog you just created (named pub_info) in the right pane of Enterprise Manager, and select Start Population, Full Population from the pop-up menu (see Figure 13.16).

That's it! You've populated the index and can now query against it. That's when it gets hard, frankly. Querying full-text indexes isn't very easy in SQL Server 7.0. For example, run the following query in Query Analyzer and all the rows that contain the word sample are returned:

```
select pub_id, substring(pr_info,1,100) from pub_info
where CONTAINS (pr_info, 'sample')
```

Full-text queries can be somewhat complicated, so you should consult the SQL Server Books Online if you want to run much more sophisticated queries against full-text indexes.

13

FIGURE 13.16

Initializing the popula-
tion of your full-text
catalog.

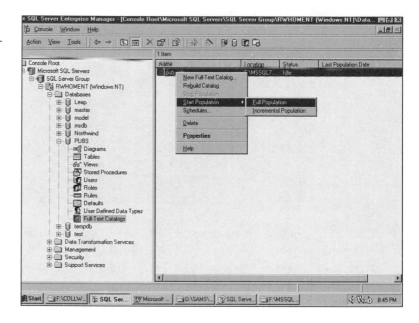

Summary

Indexes are not required but are extremely useful to speed up your queries. They are essentially the "go fast" option in SQL Server. A variety of options are available during the creation of your indexes, and several maintenance issues must be addressed. Your indexes will help you resolve queries faster and provide better overall performance as long as you maintain them properly.

Remember that you probably will not need to override the optimizer, but that option is available to you in the form of optimizer hints. It requires an understanding of the query, the data being queried, and the available indexes to make a good choice for optimization. If you are not comfortable with your knowledge level of all these things, you should let SQL Server pick the indexes for you. It's right almost every single time if you've performed your index maintenance properly.

You can manage indexes entirely in Transact-SQL, or you can use SQL Server Enterprise Manager. In the long run, it's good to know how to perform any operation either way, but you'll most likely use the Enterprise Manager dialogs. It's a lot easier than trying to remember the exact syntax of the Transact-SQL commands.

Q&A

Q What are some of the differences between clustered and nonclustered indexes?

A The number of indexes available (1 for clustered, 249 for nonclustered) and the contents of the leaf level of the index (data for the clustered index, rows pointing to the data for the nonclustered index).

Q How does SQL Server determine when to use an index?

A It analyzes the WHERE clause in your query as well as the statistics from the statistics blob and the information stored in the sysindexes system table.

Q When would you specify a fill factor setting on an index?

A When you want to leave free space in your indexes to allow for growth of the data and to reduce page splits.

Q How do you override SQL Server's choice of indexes?

A With optimizer hints such as SELECT ... FROM indextab (index = 1).

Workshop

The Workshop provides quiz questions to help you solidify your understanding of the concepts presented in this chapter. In addition to the quiz questions, exercises are provided to let you practice what you have learned in this chapter. Try to understand the quiz and exercise answers before continuing to the next day's lesson. Answers are provided in Appendix A, "Answers."

Quiz

1. How do you force SQL Server to choose a table scan?

2. How much free space do you need to create a clustered index?

3. What option do you turn on to verify the index selection of SQL Server?

Exercises

1. Write a query to select data from the sales table in the pubs database, where title_id = 'BU1032', and show SQL Server's index choice and how much I/O it will take.

2. Override the choice and use the clustered index.

3. Create a new table, along with a unique clustered index and two nonclustered indexes—each with a different fill factor. Then use DBCC DBREINDEX to reorganize the indexes, and reset the fill factor to 50.

4. Do the same thing from step 3, but accomplish the DBCC DBREINDEX and fill factor changes from within SQL Enterprise Manager.

13

DAY **14**

Ensuring Data Integrity

On Day 13, "Enhancing Performance with Indexing," you examined indexes and all the options available to you in SQL Server relating to indexes. Indexes can be a huge win for performance, but too many indexes can actually hurt performance. Selecting the proper indexing structure, including choosing which index will be your clustered index, is critical to enhancing the performance of your databases.

Today's lesson focuses on data integrity. You'll look at two kinds of mechanisms to enforce data integrity: procedural and declarative. Declarative integrity in SQL Server, combined with the IDENTITY property, is often referred to in the Microsoft documentation as declarative referential integrity (DRI). However, it encompasses more than what the name implies.

How to Enforce Data Integrity

When you examine data integrity, you are trying to ensure that the data in your database is correct—both from a literal standpoint (without errors) and from a business standpoint. As just stated, you can enforce integrity either procedurally or using declarative integrity.

NEW TERM | *Procedural integrity* means that you can use programmatic structures and separate objects to enforce data integrity. Frequently, this is done at the application program level. However, this means that if any data modifications occur outside that program, your integrity rules are not enforced. Therefore, it makes sense to put much of this integrity enforcement at the database level. You can perform that database integrity enforcement using objects such as triggers and stored procedures. You will learn about this in more detail on Day 15, "Working with Views, Stored Procedures, and Triggers." The rest of today's lesson covers defaults and rules as enforcement mechanisms, as well as user-defined data types in a bit more detail.

NEW TERM | The other approach is *declarative integrity*—in other words, the mechanisms to enforce integrity are declared as part of the definition of the objects (tables) in your database. They become an integral part of these objects. You will spend most of your time examining these objects because they provide critical functionality that would otherwise require significant amounts of programming to enforce.

Types of Integrity

Many components are used to enforce integrity in SQL Server 7.0. Some of these components are more obvious than others. There are three types of integrity: domain, referential, and entity.

Domain Integrity

NEW TERM | Data types help determine what values are valid for a particular column. This is known as *domain integrity*. The *domain* is simply the set of valid values for a particular column. Nullability is another option to determine which values are valid in the domain; in this case, whether the unknown value (null) is valid. You can put further restrictions on the domain of a column with user-defined data types, rules, and defaults if you want to use "traditional" SQL Server integrity objects. Otherwise, you can use American National Standards Institute (ANSI) constraints (default and check constraints) to enforce your domain integrity. Note that data types and nullability are always used, and the other components are optional.

Referential Integrity

NEW TERM | *Referential integrity* refers to the maintenance of relationships between data rows in multiple tables. You will enforce referential integrity with DRI, as mentioned earlier. You could, however, enforce integrity using triggers and programmatically control this functionality, but it takes quite a bit of work. SQL Server 7.0, however, only provides what's known as "delete restrict" enforcement. This means that if you try to delete a customer, and referential integrity is in place, you won't be able to delete the customer if there are still invoices outstanding for that customer. Another type of integrity enforcement is known as "delete cascade" integrity. With this type of referential integrity in place, you would be able to delete the customer, and all invoices would also be removed from your database. In order to accomplish delete cascade integrity, you would have to program it yourself (with triggers, stored procedures, or standard Transact-SQL statements).

Entity Integrity

 The last type of integrity you should be concerned with is *entity integrity*. This means that you can uniquely identify every row in a table. You can do this with a unique index (as mentioned on Day 13) or with declarative integrity (primary-key or unique constraints), which you'll learn today.

Traditional Methods of Integrity

Traditional (meaning backward-compatible) methods of ensuring integrity include user-defined data types, defaults, and rules. Now examine how these database items can help enforce database integrity.

> **Caution**
>
> Although you can use user-defined data types, defaults, and rules as integrity enforcement mechanisms, I discourage you from using them and recommend that you use ANSI integrity constraints whenever possible. ANSI integrity constraints are generally more flexible. Another benefit to ANSI constraints is that the SQL Server Query Optimizer, the component that helps select the physical execution plan of your queries, understands ANSI constraints and can use them to help make better decisions about access plans.

User-Defined Data Types

User-defined data types enable you to help ensure domain integrity. Normally when you create a table, you define each column with a system-supplied data type as well as whether the column allows nulls. You can also specify your own data types in SQL Server. Remember that the user-defined data types must be defined in terms of system-supplied data types. SQL Server 7.0 does not allow you to do things like create structures as new data types.

You would use these user-defined data types when you wanted to translate logical data types from your data model into physical data types in SQL Server. For example, if you modeled the use of postal codes in your data model on several tables, a user-defined data

14

type might be appropriate. If you made the decision to define the model as a char(10), you could create a data type called something like postal_code_datatype. The data type would be a char(10).

To create this data type, you could run an sp_addtype system-stored procedure, such as this:

```
Exec sp_addtype postal_code_datatype, 'char(10)'
```

```
sp_addtype typename, phystype [, nulltype]
```

where

- *typename* is the name of your user-defined data type. You would use this in place of the system data type in your CREATE TABLE statements.

- *phystype* is the system data type that you'd like to have used when you reference this user-defined data type. Quotes are optional in some cases, but it's safer to use them.

- *nulltype* is optional. If you specify it (in quotes), it will determine the nullability of a column if you don't specify it in a CREATE TABLE statement. If you don't specify this parameter, the data type will default to the system default for nullability (which is NULL in SQL Server 7.0 unless you change it).

▲ Types are stored in the systypes system table in each database.

> **Caution**
>
> For safety's sake, you should always specify nullability on your columns during your CREATE TABLE statements and not rely on this functionality.

For example, to create a state_code_type data type of char(2) that does not allow nulls by default, you could run

```
Exec sp_addtype state_code_type, 'char(2)', 'not null'
```

To use it, you would run

```
Create Table mytable2
(col1 state_code_type)
```

Col1 would not allow nulls because you've specified in the data type that you don't want to allow nulls. This is regardless of whether the database is set to allow nulls by default or not.

When you are finished with a user-defined data type (either because you never used it or because you've dropped all tables that use the data type), you can drop it with the sp_droptype system-stored procedure. If a user-defined data type is still in use anywhere, you will get an error if you try to drop it. You must first drop all tables that are using the data type before you can eliminate it.

SYNTAX

```
sp_droptype typename
```

where

- *typename* is the name of the user-defined data type you'd like to drop.

As you might expect, SQL Server Enterprise Manager provides an interface to support user-defined data types. Expand the database you'd like to work with (remember, data types are database specific), highlight User Defined Data Types, and view the data types you have created in this database. They will appear on the right side of the SQL Server Enterprise Manager console. To create a new user-defined data type, right-click the User Defined Data Types icon in the left pane and select New User Defined Data Type from the pop-up menu. You could also select Action, New User Defined Data Type from the menu when you have the User Defined Data Type folder highlighted, or click the New button of the Enterprise Manager toolbar (it looks like a yellow star). Either way, you see the User-Defined Data Type Properties dialog (see Figure 14.1).

FIGURE 14.1

The User-Defined Data Type Properties dialog.

To add a new user-defined data type, simply type the name you want it to have, select a system data type, fill in the length if necessary (it will dim out if not needed), and then check the Allow NULLs box if you want the data type to allow nulls by default. You will learn more about the defaults and rules when you explore those objects later in today's lesson. Click OK to add the user-defined data type.

To drop a user-defined data type, right-click on the data type (or data types) on the right panel of SQL Server Enterprise Manager, and select Delete from the pop-up menu. The Drop Objects dialog will appear. Click Drop All to drop the user-defined data types. Again, note that you cannot drop a user-defined data type that is in use. To find out

14

where your data type is being used (if at all), highlight it and click the Show
Dependencies button to view the list of objects using your user-defined data type. You
will be presented with a list of the tables and columns with which the data type is used.

> **Tip**
>
> If you would like to see this list of dependencies without dropping the user-
> defined data type, double-click the user-defined data type (or right-click and
> select Properties from the pop-up menu), and then click the Where Used
> button (see Figure 14.2). Optionally, right-click the user-defined data type
> and select All Tasks, Display Dependencies from the pop-up menu.

FIGURE 14.2

*The User-Defined
Data Type Properties
dialog: Seeing the list
of dependencies with-
out dropping the data
type.*

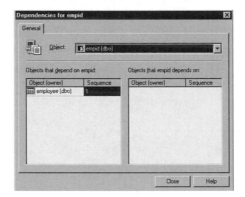

Defaults

Defaults are used to specify a value to add to a column when you don't want to directly
insert a value into that column. There are two kinds of defaults in SQL Server: ANSI
constraint defaults and standalone objects called defaults. In this section you will examine the standalone objects called defaults. ANSI defaults are examined later in today's
lesson. You must have been granted permission to run the CREATE DEFAULT statement (or
be a member of either the db_owner or db_ddladmin fixed database roles).

> **Tip**
>
> I recommend that you use ANSI default constraints rather than defaults cre-
> ated with the CREATE DEFAULT statements. ANSI constraints provide the
> same basic functionality while providing consistency with the other ANSI
> constraints.

Because defaults are separate objects in a database, they must have names that are
unique from all other objects in the database. When created, they are recorded in the

sysobjects system table in each database. The text of the CREATE DEFAULT statement is stored in the syscomments table. As with other objects in SQL Server 7.0, the definition of the object is stored in Unicode format.

As you might have guessed by now, you create defaults with the CREATE DEFAULT statement.

```
CREATE DEFAULT default_name
AS constant_expression
```

where

- The *default_name* must be unique in the database and must follow the rules for SQL Server identifiers.

- The *constant_expression* is a constant that is appropriate for the data type of any columns you'd like to use for this data type. For example, if you are referencing a char(2) data type, your constant should be either x or xx, where x is any valid character. If an integer, your constant should be an integer. If you are referencing binary data, it must start with an 0x character set (such as 0x13 for a binary value of 13). Money data types must begin with a dollar sign ($). Unicode data types begin with the letter N. You can also use system functions such as getdate() as long as they return the appropriate data for the data type.

As you learned on Day 11, "Retrieving Data with Queries," you can use defaults during an insert by either using the DEFAULT keyword or by simply not referencing the column in the column list.

There are a couple of concerns you must address when using defaults:

- The default must comply with any rules or ANSI check constraints you assign to the same columns or user-defined data types. If you have a rule on a column (such as a phone number column) that formatted the column as (xxx)xxx-xxxx, your default could not be Unknown. It would have to be something like (000)000-0000. You will examine the rules shortly.

- The default must not be incompatible with the data type of the column or user-defined data type it is assigned to. You cannot have a default of Unknown for a char(2) column. Likewise, a default of Unknown won't work for a numeric column. Note here that Unknown is the literal string—not the null value.

It's been implied so far that defaults apply to columns or user-defined data types. When you create a default, it is a standalone object in the database. It is not tied to any particular object. In order to actually use defaults, you must bind them to a column or user-defined data type. To bind a default, you use the sp_bindefault system-stored procedure.

14

▲ SYNTAX ▼

`sp_bindefault` *defname*, *objname* [, *futureonly*]

where

- *defname* is the name of the default you have already created.

- *objname* is the name of the object to which you want to bind your default and must be in quotes. You can bind to either a column or a user-defined data type. SQL Server knows you are binding to a column if your quoted text is in the format *tablename.columnname*. If there's no period (.) in the quoted text, you can assume that it's a user-defined data type name. You cannot bind a default to a system-supplied data type.

- *futureonly* applies only to user-defined data types. If specified, the default does not apply anywhere that the user-defined data type has already been used. Each time you use the user-defined data type in the future, the default will be bound. I recommend you don't use this option because it's a little confusing that sometimes the default applies and sometimes it doesn't, depending on when the `sp_bindefault` system-stored procedure was run.

When the binding is complete, any user-defined data type or column to which the default is bound will have the default applied during an insert, as appropriate.

To unbind the default, you would run the `sp_unbindefault` system-stored procedure.

▲ SYNTAX ▼

`sp_unbindefault` *objname* [, *futureonly*]

where

- *objname* is the same as in the `sp_bindefault` system-stored procedure, either a column on a table or a user-defined data type.

- *futureonly* applies only to user-defined data types. It unbinds the default from the user-defined data type, but the default still applies everywhere it was used before. Future uses of the user-defined data type will not have the default applied. For the same reasons as before, I recommend you don't use this option. You will not be able to drop the default until you explicitly unbind it from the columns it was used on before you ran `sp_unbindefault` with the *futureonly* option.

When you've unbound a default from a data type or default, it will no longer be used during an insert. You cannot drop a default until it has been unbound from all data types and columns.

```
DROP DEFAULT default_name [, default_name...]
```

This one is pretty straightforward. You can drop as many defaults as you want in a single statement. If you are the owner of the default, you inherently have the right to drop the default; otherwise, you must be a member of the db_owner or db_ddladmin fixed database roles or the sysadmin fixed server role.

Listing 14.1 shows some sample code for creating a table and user-defined data type and then apply some defaults.

INPUT **LISTING 14.1** CREATING A TABLE WITH A USER-DEFINED DATA TYPE

```
Use pubs
Go
Exec sp_addtype my_uddt_type, money
Go
CREATE DEFAULT intdefault as 0
Go
CREATE DEFAULT char5default as 'Hello'
Go
CREATE DEFAULT moneydefault as $10.00
Go
CREATE TABLE mytab
(intcol int not null,
 char5col char(5) not null,
 uddtcol my_uddt_type not null)
Go
```

Now bind the defaults to the data type and to the columns.

```
Exec sp_bindefault moneydefault, 'my_uddt_type'
Exec sp_bindefault intdefault, 'mytab.intcol'
Exec sp_bindefault char5default, 'mytab.char5col'
Go
```

Now insert a default row, and then select it.

```
INSERT mytab DEFAULT VALUES
Go
SELECT * FROM mytab
Go
```

You will see this return set, showing that the defaults were indeed used.

OUTPUT

```
(1 row(s) affected)

intcol      char5col uddtcol
----------- -------- --------------------
0           Hello    10.0000

(1 row(s) affected)
```

14

Take a look at this through the SQL Server Enterprise Manager. Start Enterprise Manager if it's not already open, and expand the Databases folder; then expand the pubs database. Highlight Defaults in the left pane to view defaults. Right-click the Defaults icon and select New Default; you will be presented with the Default Properties dialog (see Figure 14.3). You can also access this by selecting Action, New Default from the menu.

FIGURE 14.3

The Default Properties dialog.

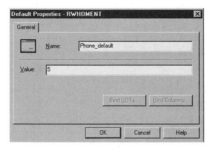

Type the name of the default you want to create. In the Value field, type the character string, numeric value, money value, or binary value you'd like the default to have. After you start typing in this window, the OK button becomes available. Click OK to add your default to the database.

After you create a default you can view it in the right pane of SQL Server Enterprise Manager. Right-click a default and select Properties (or double-click it) to change, view, or modify bindings for a default. Click the Bind Columns button if you want to bind the default to one or more columns in your database, as shown in Figure 14.4.

FIGURE 14.4

Binding a column with Enterprise Manager.

Select the table you want to get a column from for the binding in the Table list box; then highlight the column or columns you want to bind to and click the Add button to move them to the Bound Columns box. When you click Apply or OK, the binding will be attempted. You will receive an error message if the binding fails for some reason. To unbind a column, you simply find the appropriate table and then highlight the column in the Bound Columns box, and then click the Remove button.

To modify user-defined data types, click the Bind UDTs button to view the Bind Default to User-Defined Data Types dialog (see Figure 14.5). You will be presented with a list of all existing user-defined data types. Simply check the box in the Bind column to bind the default to the user-defined data type.

FIGURE 14.5

Binding a user-defined data type with Enterprise Manager.

To drop the default, right-click it and select Delete. Just as with user-defined data types, you can examine the dependencies the default has, and you must unbind the default from all user-defined data types and columns before you can drop the default object.

Rules

Rules further enforce domain integrity by providing more sophisticated checking of valid values. Rules are used to ensure that values

- Match a pattern (much like a *like* clause)
- Match a list of values (much like an *in* clause)
- Fall within a range of values (much like a *between* clause)

Rules, like defaults, are standalone objects that require special permission to create. You must be a member of the db_owner or sysadmin roles to create a rule. They are stored in

14

the same system tables as your defaults sysobjects and syscomments. Rules are checked for violations when inserts and updates are performed (whenever the column that the rule affects is referenced).

> **Tip**
>
> Not to sound like a broken record, but you are better off implementing ANSI constraints than using rules for most every instance of implementing this type of integrity. However, there are special cases, such as when you want the same integrity check on 100 tables, when it might be nice to create it once and then simply reference the rule 100 times. However, I still recommend ANSI constraints because the SQL Server Query Optimizer can use constraints during query optimization. This means that using constraints instead of rules could actually speed up your queries.

Rules are created using the `CREATE RULE` statement.

```
CREATE RULE rule_name
AS condition_expression
```

where

- *rule_name* is a valid and unique name in the database in which it's created.
- *condition_expression* is where all the excitement is. It is in the form `@variable_name <WHERE clause>`. The `<WHERE clause>` can be any valid `WHERE` clause, including arithmetic operators, `BETWEEN`, `IN`, `LIKE`, `AND`, `OR`, `NOT`, and other operators. However, a rule cannot refer to variable values or to other columns in the database. To do this you must use a check constraint or a trigger.

For example, to create a rule for a part number column, when the column must start with a p or a t, you could have a rule such as

```
CREATE RULE myrule AS @myvar like 'p%' OR @myvar like 't%'
```

> **Note**
>
> The `@myvar` is arbitrarily named. You could call it `@fredandethel` if you want. Most people create the variable name to be similar to the name of the columns or data type it's used with.

Rules, just like defaults, must also be bound to a data type or column. This is done with the `sp_bindrule` system-stored procedure.

```
sp_bindrule rulename, objname [, futureonly]
```

where

- *rulename* is the rule you'd like to bind to.
- *objname* is, as before, either a *tablename.columnname* combination or a user-defined data type.
- *futureonly* has the same meaning as before. The rule is not applied to existing columns declared with the user-defined data type you're binding the rule to. As before, I don't suggest you use the futureonly option because administration can become very confusing. Everything must be in quotes.

When the rules are bound, they are used just like defaults. When you perform an insert, the data you insert will be checked against the rule to make sure it's valid. If it's not, you will get a message similar to the following:

```
Server: Msg 513, Level 16, State 1
A column insert or update conflicts with a rule imposed by a previous
➥CREATE RULE statement. The statement was aborted. The conflict
➥occurred in database 'master', table 't9', column 'col1'.
The statement has been aborted.
```

If you want to unbind the rule, you would do that with the sp_unbindrule system-stored procedure.

```
sp_unbindrule objname [, futureonly]
```

where

- *objname* is the name of the user-defined data type or the *tablename.columnname* combination.
- *Futureonly* here means the same as sp_unbindefault. No column previously defined with a user-defined data type with this rule will lose its binding. You still will not be able to drop the rule until it is explicitly unbound from the columns that were referenced before the sp_unbindrule system-stored procedure was run for the user-defined data type.

To drop a rule, you run the DROP RULE statement.

```
DROP RULE rule_name [, rule_name...]
```

When you use the DROP RULE statement, you simply specify the rule names you want to drop. As with the DROP DEFAULT statement, you can drop as many rules as you want with a single command. The rules must not be bound to any columns or user-defined data types.

You can use the same table I used earlier to examine how rules work, as well as how they work in conjunction with defaults. Note that this depends on the script for the previously mentioned defaults having been run.

```
CREATE RULE char5rule AS @col LIKE 'h%'
Go
CREATE RULE intrule AS @intval < 100
Go
CREATE RULE moneyrule AS @moneyval BETWEEN $5.00 AND $10.00
Go
Exec sp_bindrule 'char5rule', 'mytab.char5col'
Exec sp_bindrule 'intrule', 'mytab.intcol'
Exec sp_bindrule 'moneyrule', 'my_uddt_type'
Go
```

Now insert a valid column (based on these rules).

```
INSERT mytab VALUES (90,'Howdy',$6.00)
Go
```

Test that your defaults comply with the rules.

```
INSERT mytab DEFAULT VALUES
Go
```

In each case, you will get (1 row(s) affected).

Now, insert an invalid set of values (based on the rules).

```
INSERT mytab VALUES (101,'Ralph',$20.00)
Go
```

SQL Server does not allow the invalid data to be entered. Now you can see how these two together greatly increase the way you can control the domain of valid values for a column.

Of course, SQL Server Enterprise Manager can again be used to perform all these operations. You can access the Rule Properties dialog by right-clicking on the Rules icon in your database and selecting New Rule from the context menu (see Figure 14.6). As before, you can also access this from the menu by selecting Action, New Rule.

FIGURE 14.6

The Rule Properties dialog.

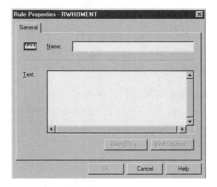

This dialog works exactly like the Default Properties dialog you looked at earlier.

ANSI Constraints and Declarative Integrity Mechanisms

You can use ANSI constraints and declarative integrity to ensure the accuracy of your data. These include the use of the IDENTITY property and the following constraints: default, check, primary key, foreign key, and unique.

The IDENTITY Property

The IDENTITY property was introduced in SQL Server 6.0. It enables you to use system-generated values in your tables. This is similar to the auto-number data type in Microsoft Access and Microsoft FoxPro databases. You are allowed a single column in each table with the IDENTITY property.

Typically, identity columns are used to generate what are known as system-assigned keys. To enforce entity integrity, you must have a way to uniquely identify every row in a table. If there is no natural column or set of columns that do this for you, you might want to create an identity column.

You can use the IDENTITY property only if the column to which it's being assigned is an integer or is compatible with an integer. Therefore, you can use the following data types:

- Tinyint
- Smallint
- Integer
- Numeric
- Decimal

14

You can use numeric and decimal only if they have a scale of 0 (such as numeric (12,0)). It must also not allow nulls. You might want to use these data types that scale a bit more because the IDENTITY property doesn't reuse values by default and won't wrap around. After it has been "filled up," no more inserts are allowed.

Each time you perform an insert into a table with the IDENTITY property enabled for a column, the next available value will be automatically inserted into that column.

IDENTITY [(*seed, increment*)]

where

- *seed* is the value identifying the starting value for the identity column. It is used for the first row inserted into the table.
- *increment* is the value that identifies the amount of change (expressed as an integer) that will occur between each value. This value can be positive or negative.

If you don't specify a seed or increment, they each default to 1. Hence, the first row would have a value of 1, the next 2, and so on.

The IDENTITY property is used during a CREATE TABLE or an ALTER TABLE statement, as discussed on Day 9, "Creating Tables." For example, the following would result in a value of 1 for col1 when the first row is added, then 101, then 201, and so on:

```
CREATE TABLE mytable5
(col1 int not null IDENTITY(1,100),
 col2 char(5) not null)
```

Because identity columns don't wrap, you can see that you might run out. Because you can't change data types in SQL Server after you've created a table, make sure you select a data type large enough to handle any conceivable values you might have for this column.

If you had used IDENTITY without the optional parameters, it would be set to (1,1).

You can refer to the column using the keyword IDENTITYCOL instead of the proper column name. Because there can be only one column in each table with the IDENTITY property set, SQL Server will always be able to figure out which column you're referring to. In the previous example, you could run SELECT IDENTITYCOL FROM mytable5 and SQL Server would return only the data for col1.

To get information about an identity column on a table, you can run the sp_help system-stored procedure, specifying the table name as a parameter. You can also use the system functions IDENT_INCR or IDENT_SEED.

SYNTAX

```
IDENT_SEED('tablename')
IDENT_INCR('tablename')
```

where

▲

- IDENT_SEED returns the seed parameter used during the create or alter table
- IDENT_INCR returns the increment parameter used during the create or alter table

From a programming perspective, an important question comes up right away. How would you know what value was last inserted? In comes the global value @@IDENTITY. Every time you insert a value into a table that has an identity column, the @@IDENTITY value is updated.

Try the code in Listing 14.2 to see how this works. You'll work with myidenttab, which was created earlier when you ran these commands as you learned about them.

INPUT **LISTING 14.2** USING @@IDENTITY

```
CREATE TABLE myidenttab
(col1 int not null IDENTITY(1,100),
 col2 char(5) not null)
Go
INSERT myidenttab (col2) VALUES ('howdy')
SELECT @@identity
```

Note: It should be 1.

```
INSERT myidenttab(col2) VALUES ('Movie')
SELECT @@identity
```

Note: Now it should be 101.

When you run the truncate table statement, it resets the identity value back to the initial seed. Ordinary deletes—even deletes of every row in the table—will not have this effect, however. Try it here:

```
DELETE myidenttab
Go
INSERT myidenttab (col2) VALUES ('Zebra')
SELECT @@identity
```

Note: It should be 201, even though it's the only row in the table.

```
TRUNCATE TABLE myidenttab
Go
INSERT myidenttab (col2) VALUES ('howdy')
SELECT @@identity
```

Note: It should be 1 again.

14

Identity values are kept as a pool in memory. It's not guaranteed that every one will be used because some transactions might be canceled, and sometimes server crashes occur. If you want your identity columns to be guaranteed to be unique, you must have a unique index on that column. Some people want to reuse identity values. By default, however, you cannot manually insert into identity columns. You can use the identity_insert option, however, to override that for a single table from within a single session.

```
SET identity_insert [database.[owner.]]tablename ON¦OFF
```

The preceding turns on the capability to directly insert into a table's identity column. You must be a member of the sysadmin role, the db_owner or db_ddladmin roles, or the table owner to turn this option on.

To use this on myidenttab, run this Transact-SQL code. You must run it all from within the same SQL Server Query Analyzer because of the session-specific set statement.

```
SET identity_insert myidenttab ON
Go
INSERT myidenttab (col1, col2) VALUES (2,'jolly')
Go
SET identity_insert myidenttab OFF
Go
SELECT * FROM myidenttab
```

This will insert the row you've requested into the table. You must specify the column list, even if you are specifying a value for every column in the table.

> **Note**
>
> Although it's not strictly a constraint or DRI option, another option you might consider in place of an identity (particularly for primary keys) is the UNIQUEIDENTIFER data type. If you define a column with the UNIQUEI- DENTIFIER data type—and set a default of the NEWID() function, which will automatically generate a new, globally unique value each time a row is added—you have a powerful mechanism to ensure uniqueness of your key values. Unlike using the IDENTITY property, UNIQUEIDENTIFIER values are unique in every table on every system. However, they are much larger than the typical identity column using the integer data type, so you should be cautious when using them too widely. Also, it's much harder to refer to a 16- byte binary number on a screen instead of a simple integer.

ANSI Constraints

ANSI constraints are functionally very similar to the traditional objects you looked at earlier. However, they are not separate objects; they are part of the definition of the tables in your database. They can be used to enforce domain integrity with default and check constraints, as with defaults and rules, or referential integrity, with primary keys and foreign keys. You can also enforce entity integrity with unique constraints or primary keys.

This can be a major improvement over defaults and rules. There's no need to keep a separate set of objects to be used with your tables and no need to keep track of bindings. Constraints are stored in the sysreferences, syscomments, and sysobjects system tables, and possibly the sysforeignkeys table, in each database.

Now examine the syntax of constraints as an extension to the CREATE TABLE and ALTER TABLE statements.

```
CREATE TABLE [database.[owner].]table_name

({col_name column_properties [constraint]

[[,] {next_col_name ¦ next_constraint}...])
[ON filegroup]
[TEXTIMAGE_ON filegroup]
```

This is the same code you worked with on Day 9, except now you will focus on where it says constraint. Constraints are of the form

```
[CONSTRAINT <name>] <Type of Constraint> [<Constraint Options>]
```

Here's the full syntax of the constraint option. (Don't worry—it's broken down in great detail later in today's lesson.)

```
<column_constraint> ::= [CONSTRAINT constraint_name]
{[ NULL ¦ NOT NULL ]¦ [ { PRIMARY KEY ¦ UNIQUE }
[CLUSTERED ¦ NONCLUSTERED]
[WITH [FILLFACTOR = fillfactor] ]
[ON {filegroup ¦ DEFAULT} ]]
]
¦ [ [FOREIGN KEY] REFERENCES ref_table [(ref_column) ]
[NOT FOR REPLICATION]
]
¦ CHECK [NOT FOR REPLICATION] (logical_expression)
}
 [ ...n]
<table_constraint> ::= [CONSTRAINT constraint_name]
{[ { PRIMARY KEY ¦ UNIQUE } [ CLUSTERED ¦ NONCLUSTERED]
{ ( column[,...n] ) }
[ WITH [FILLFACTOR = fillfactor] ]
[ON {filegroup ¦ DEFAULT} ]]
¦ FOREIGN KEY [(column[,...n])] REFERENCES ref_table [(ref_column[,...n])]
[NOT FOR REPLICATION] ¦ CHECK [NOT FOR REPLICATION] (search_conditions)
}
```

SYNTAX

14

▼ SYNTAX

```
ALTER TABLE table
{[WITH CHECK ¦ WITH NOCHECK]
{ [ALTER COLUMN column name
{[ new_data_type [ (precision[, scale] ) ] [ NULL ¦ NOT NULL ] ]
  ¦ [ {ADD ¦ DROP} ROWGUIDCOL ] }]
  ¦ ADD { [ <column_definition> ] ¦ column_name AS computed_column_expression
  [ <table_constraint> ] }[,…n]
  ¦ DROP { [CONSTRAINT] constraint_name ¦ COLUMN column }[,…n]
  ¦ {CHECK ¦ NOCHECK} CONSTRAINT {ALL ¦ constraint_name[,…n]}
  ¦ {ENABLE ¦ DISABLE} TRIGGER {ALL ¦ trigger_name[,…n]} } }
```

▲ Note that this is a simplified syntax.

There are two forms of constraints: column level and table level. Column-level constraints are applied at the column level of the create table, and table-level constraints are added as if they were additional columns. Examples are the easiest way to differentiate between them.

Column-Level Constraints

```
CREATE TABLE mytablea
(col1 int not null CONSTRAINT DF_a_col1 DEFAULT (0))
```

Table-Level Constraints

```
CREATE TABLE mytableb
(col1 int not null)

ALTER TABLE mytableb ADD
CONSTRAINT DF_b_col1 DEFAULT (0) FOR col1
```

Notice the FOR col1 option, specifying to which column the default applies. This is implied during a column-level constraint.

Default Constraints

Default constraints are very much like SQL Server defaults. However, default constraints only apply to columns—never to user-defined data types. You cannot apply default constraints to columns that are also identity columns. You also cannot use default constraints with columns defined with the timestamp data type. The difference here is that the default is "part" of the column, as opposed to having to be bound to the column. They are enforced during inserts only—just as SQL Server default objects are.

▼ SYNTAX

Column level:

```
[CONSTRAINT constraint_name] DEFAULT {constant_expression}
```

Table level:

```
[CONSTRAINT constraint_name] DEFAULT {constant_expression} FOR col_name
```

The CONSTRAINT constraint_name part of the syntax is optional. This is the part that identifies that you are adding a constraint explicitly (always a good idea from a documentation perspective), as well as giving the constraint a name. If you do not name a constraint, it ends up with a name like this:

```
DF__mytab__col1__117F9D94
```

Therefore, it's a good idea to name them because you'll see in a bit there are some operations you might want to run that require you to name the constraint you're working with.

The keyword DEFAULT is next, then either a constant appropriate for the data type, NULL, or a *niladic function*. Niladic functions include

- CURRENT_TIMESTAMP—Gets the current date and time; equivalent to SELECT getdate()
- SYSTEM_USER—Gets the current login name; equivalent to SELECT suser_sname()
- CURRENT_USER—Gets the current database username; equivalent to SELECT user_name()
- USER—The same as CURRENT_USER
- SESSION_USER—The same as CURRENT_USER

Functionally speaking, there is no difference here between table-level and column-level default constraints other than that default constraints must be specified as column level during a create table, and table- or column-level constraints during an alter table.

Here are a couple of examples to show default constraints:

```
CREATE TABLE defaulttab1
( intcol int NOT NULL CONSTRAINT df_intcol DEFAULT 0,
  char5col char(5) NOT NULL DEFAULT 'Hello',
  anumber numeric(10,0) NOT NULL
)
Go
```

Note that the first constraint is named, but the second one is not; therefore it will have a system-assigned name:

```
ALTER TABLE defaulttab1
```

14

```
ADD moneycol money NULL CONSTRAINT df_moneycol DEFAULT $2.00,
CONSTRAINT df_anumber DEFAULT 100 FOR anumber
Go
```

Run sp_help defaulttab1 to verify that the constraints are properly on the table, and you will see something like this in the constraint section of the report:

```
constraint_type            constraint_name                    constraint_keys
------------------------------------------------------------------------------
DEFAULT on column char5col DF__defaultta__char5__6F9499E4     ('Hello')
DEFAULT on column anumber  df_anumber                         (100)
DEFAULT on column intcol   df_intcol                          (0)
DEFAULT on column moneycol df_moneycol                        (2.00)
```

Notice the system-assigned name for the default constraint you didn't name.

Check Constraints

Check constraints function very much like rules. They provide a mechanism to enforce domain integrity for your columns. Unlike other ANSI constraints, you can have as many check constraints as you want on a single column. They have many of the same restrictions as default constraints, such as with columns' timestamp data type or the identity property. They are checked during inserts and updates, just as rules are.

However, check constraints can do something that rules cannot. Check constraints can refer to other columns as part of their enforcement of conditions. You can do this only with table-level constraints, however.

▼ SYNTAX

Column level:

```
[CONSTRAINT constraint_name]
CHECK [NOT FOR REPLICATION] (expression)
```

Table level:

```
[CONSTRAINT constraint_name]
CHECK [NOT FOR REPLICATION] (expression)
```

where

- CONSTRAINT constraint_name is optional, just as with default constraints.
- CHECK specifies that you are creating a check constraint. The expression can be any expression—just as with rules. However, now you can also reference other columns within the same table.
- NOT FOR REPLICATION prevents the check constraint from being enforced when the internal replication process inserts or updates the table.

As noted previously, only table-level constraints can have references to multiple

▲ columns.

Examples are probably the best way to see how they would work.

```
CREATE TABLE checktable
(col1 int not null CONSTRAINT ck_col1
     CHECK (col1 between 1 and 100),
 col2 char(5) null,
 zip_code char(5) null,
 col4 int not null,
 CONSTRAINT ck_col4 CHECK (col4 > col1),
 CONSTRAINT ck_zip_code CHECK
(zip_code like '[0-9][0-9][0-9][0-9][0-9]')
)

ALTER TABLE checktable
ADD CONSTRAINT ck_col2 CHECK (col2 like 'H%')
Go
```

Note that the rules will now be enforced. For example,

```
INSERT checktable VALUES (1,'Howdy','99901',2)
```

works, but

```
INSERT checktable VALUES (2,'Howdy','8834A',3)
```

will fail with the message

```
Server: Msg 547, Level 16, State 1
INSERT statement conflicted with COLUMN CHECK
constraint 'ck_zip_code'. The conflict occurred in database 'master',
table 'checktable', column 'zip_code'.
➥The statement has been aborted.
```

Primary-Key Constraints

Primary-key constraints are used for a combination of referential integrity and entity integrity. Every column used for a primary key must be defined with the NOT NULL attribute, and only one primary-key constraint can exist on a single table. The primary-key constraint might be referenced by foreign-key constraints. Some processes, such as replication or open database connectivity (ODBC) applications, might require declared ANSI primary keys.

Primary-key constraints are an implied creation of a unique index. By default, a unique clustered index is created.

14

Column level:

```
[CONSTRAINT constraint_name] [  PRIMARY KEY [ CLUSTERED ¦ NONCLUSTERED]
➥[ WITH [FILLFACTOR = fillfactor] ][ON {filogroup ¦ DFFAULT} ]
```

Table level:

```
[CONSTRAINT constraint_name] [  PRIMARY KEY [ CLUSTERED ¦ NONCLUSTERED]
➥{ ( column[,…n] ) } [ WITH [FILLFACTOR = fillfactor] ]
➥ [ON {filegroup ¦ DEFAULT} ]
```

where

- CONSTRAINT *constraint_name* is again optional.
- PRIMARY KEY creates the primary key (unique) index. Any index options are valid here, including changing the index to nonclustered, applying fill factors, and so on. By default, this option creates a clustered index.

▲ There is no functional difference here per se between column-level and table-level constraints. However, with a column-level constraint the *col_name* parameter is optional. If you don't specify it, it's assumed to be on the column you put the constraint with.

You can create a primary key on a single column or on up to 16 columns, as long as the total width of the columns doesn't exceed 900 bytes.

```
CREATE TABLE pktable
(col1 int not null CONSTRAINT pk_col1 PRIMARY KEY,
 col2 char(5) null
)
```

This creates a unique clustered index on col1 of table pktable.

```
CREATE TABLE pktable2
(col1 int not null CONSTRAINT pk2_col1
     PRIMARY KEY nonclustered (col1),
 col2 char(5) null
)
```

This creates a unique nonclustered index on col1 of table pktable2.

```
CREATE TABLE pktable3
(col1 int not null,
 col2 char(2) not null,
 col3 int null,
 CONSTRAINT pk3_col1col2 PRIMARY KEY (col1, col2)
)
```

This creates a unique clustered index on (col1, col2) of table pktable3.

In all instances, you will be able to view the index but won't be able to manipulate it directly. If you attempt to drop the index, for example, on the last table, you will get an error such as this:

```
Server: Msg 3723, Level 16, State 1
An explicit DROP INDEX is not allowed on index 'pktable3.pk3_col1col2'.
➥It is being used for PRIMARY KEY constraint enforcement.
```

Unique Constraints

Unique constraints enable you to create unique indexes, just as primary keys can, but with a bit more flexibility. You would typically create unique constraints if you have more than one column or set of columns that could be valid primary keys. This serves two purposes: it documents the potential key choices and allows foreign keys on other tables to reference the unique constraints (in addition to being allowed to reference primary-key constraints).

Unique constraints can also be created on columns that allow nulls. You can also have more than one unique constraint on a table.

Column level:

```
[CONSTRAINT constraint_name] [  UNIQUE [ CLUSTERED ¦ NONCLUSTERED]
➥[ WITH [FILLFACTOR = fillfactor] ] [ON {filegroup ¦ DEFAULT} ]
```

Table level:

```
[CONSTRAINT constraint_name] [  PRIMARY KEY [ CLUSTERED ¦ NONCLUSTERED]
➥{ ( column[,…n] ) } [ WITH [FILLFACTOR = fillfactor] ]
➥ [ON {filegroup ¦ DEFAULT} ]
```

Just as before, the name of the constraint is optional. Also, just as with primary-key constraints, at the column level you don't have to list any columns. It will assume just the column you create the constraint on otherwise.

Here's a quick example:

```
CREATE TABLE myuniquetable
(col1 int not null CONSTRAINT pk_myuniquetable PRIMARY KEY,
 col2 char(20) NOT NULL CONSTRAINT u_myuniquetable UNIQUE
)
```

This creates a primary key as well as a unique constraint. Both are unique indexes on table myuniquetable.

Foreign-Key Constraints

Foreign-key constraints protect referential integrity between tables. You create a foreign key on a table, which references another table's primary-key or unique constraint. This restricts data modifications against the table with the primary key as long as there are related rows in the tables with the foreign keys. It also prevents data from being added (or updated) on the table with the foreign-key constraint that would not contain valid data from the referenced tables.

14

Creating a foreign key does not create an index on the table; however, it's likely that this is a good candidate for an index. Therefore, you will typically need to follow your creation of tables with foreign keys with CREATE INDEX statements. You can refer to tables in the same database only when creating foreign-key constraints. You must have the appropriate permission (select or references) on the table you refer to, and any single table can have a maximum of 63 foreign keys pointing to it. There is no way to extend this limit.

Column level:

```
[CONSTRAINT constraint_name] [FOREIGN KEY] REFERENCES ref_table
➥    [ ( ref_column ) ] [NOT FOR REPLICATION]
➥        ¦ DEFAULT constant_expression ¦ CHECK [NOT FOR REPLICATION]
     (logical_expression)
```

Table level:

```
[CONSTRAINT constraint_name]  FOREIGN KEY [(column[,...n])]
➥    REFERENCES ref_table [(ref_column[,...n])]
➥    [NOT FOR REPLICATION]
     ¦ CHECK [NOT FOR REPLICATION] (search_conditions)
```

Again, the constraint name is optional. As with the other referential constraints, you don't have to have the column name referenced locally if it's a single-column constraint. Also, you don't have to name the column on the other table if the columns have the same name.

If you reference a multiple-column primary-key/unique constraint, you must be careful to reference it in the same order between your column list in the FOREIGN KEY list and the REFERENCES list. Self-references are supported, so you could reference the table to itself (with another column).

In Listing 14.3, you will create an employee table and an order table (which was entered by an employee). To verify that a valid employee entered the order, you could either program the functionality or declare it with foreign keys. Then, when someone tries to delete an employee, the individual wouldn't be allowed to do so as long as there are orders for that employee.

INPUT   **LISTING 14.3** SETTING CONSTRAINTS ON A NEW TABLE

```
CREATE TABLE emp
(emp_id int not null CONSTRAINT pk_emp PRIMARY KEY,
 emp_name char(30) not null)
Go
CREATE TABLE orders
(order_id int not null CONSTRAINT pk_order PRIMARY KEY,
```

```
  emp_id int not null CONSTRAINT fk_order
FOREIGN KEY (emp_id) REFERENCES emp (emp_id)
)
Go
INSERT emp VALUES (1,'Joe Smith')
INSERT emp VALUES (2,'Ann Jones')
INSERT orders VALUES (1,1)
INSERT orders VALUES (2,2)
  Go
```

All this works fine so far. Now try to insert an order for an employee that doesn't exist.

```
INSERT orders VALUES (3,3)
Go
```

```
Server: Msg 547, Level 16, State 1
INSERT statement conflicted with COLUMN FOREIGN KEY constraint
'fk_order'.
➥The conflict occurred in database 'pubs',
table 'emp', column 'emp_id'.
The statement has been aborted.
```

OK, now try to delete an employee that has an order.

```
DELETE emp WHERE emp_id = 1
Go
```

```
Server: Msg 547, Level 16, State 1
DELETE statement conflicted with COLUMN REFERENCE constraint
'fk_order'.
➥The conflict occurred in database 'pubs',
table 'orders', column 'emp_id'.
➥The statement has been aborted.
```

An example of the self-referencing behavior is something like this:

```
CREATE TABLE emp_manager
(emp_id int not null CONSTRAINT pk_emp_mgr PRIMARY KEY,
 mgr_id int not null CONSTRAINT fk_emp_mgr FOREIGN KEY
REFERENCES emp_manager (emp_id),
  emp_name char(30) not null)
```

This means that every manager must also be a valid employee.

```
INSERT emp_manager VALUES (1,1,'Ann Jones')
INSERT emp_manager VALUES (2,1,'Tom Smith')
```

This works fine, but now try to reference someone who doesn't exist yet

```
INSERT emp_manager VALUES (3,4,'Bob Newett')
```

and you get a similar message as before—that the foreign-key constraint was violated. This can be very useful in many real-world scenarios.

14

NEW TERM As you can see, foreign keys are quite powerful. However, they force you to use a database in a particular fashion—the *delete restrict functionality*. Delete restrict means that deletes of primary-key (or unique-constraint) rows are not allowed if any foreign keys point to them. You must first delete any rows on the tables with the foreign-key references before you can delete the primary-key rows.

NEW TERM Another way you might want to deal with data is with what is known as *delete-cascade* functionality. This functionality would imply that the previous DELETE from the emp table would have also deleted all related rows in the orders table. It's somewhat unlikely that you would use this functionality in most business environments, and far more likely that you'd do something like set an inactive status flag for the employee and not delete all orders taken by that employee when the individual leaves the company. SQL Server does not implement this functionality with declarative referential integrity; you must program it yourself.

Dropping Constraints

You can drop a constraint with the ALTER TABLE statement. For example, to drop the foreign-key constraint in our last example, run the following and the foreign-key constraint is dropped:

```
ALTER TABLE emp_manager DROP CONSTRAINT fk_emp_mgr
```

However, if you try to drop a primary-key constraint (or unique constraint) that still has foreign-key references, you will not be able to do so. For example, on your emp_manager table, if you try to drop the primary-key constraint with this code (without having dropped the foreign key):

```
ALTER TABLE emp_manager DROP CONSTRAINT pk_emp_mgr
```

you would get this error message:

```
Server: Msg 3725, Level 16, State 1
The constraint 'pk_emp_mgr' is being referenced by table 'emp_manager',
➥ foreign key constraint 'fk_emp_mgr'.
Could not drop constraint.
➥See previous errors.
```

SQL Server Enterprise Manager

All this functionality could be accomplished with SQL Server Enterprise Manager. To access this dialog, highlight the Tables icon inside your database, right-click on a table in the right pane, and select Design Table from the pop-up menu. You will be presented with the Design Table dialog, as shown in Figure 14.7.

FIGURE 14.7

The Design Table dialog.

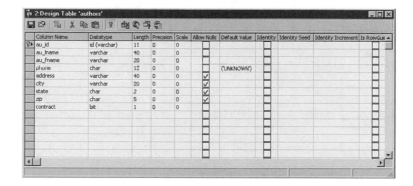

To set the primary key for a table, you simply highlight the column or columns you'd like to set as the primary key and then click the yellow key on the toolbar to set the primary key. After you do this and save it by clicking the floppy disk in the menu, your primary-key constraint will be created. Notice that the key icon is added to each column in your table that participates in the primary key.

To create a unique constraint for a table, click the table and Index Properties button on the toolbar (second button from the left), or right-click anywhere in the table and select Properties. Click the Indexes/Keys dialog, and fill in the appropriate information. This is the same dialog you were presented with on Day 13, "Enhancing Performance with Indexing." Remember to use the Constraint option after you've selected your columns and checked the Create UNIQUE check box.

To illustrate this dialog and to facilitate an examination of check constraints and foreign-key constraints, as well as primary-key and unique constraints, create a table named `ConstraintTab` in the pubs database. After you've created the table, add the following columns in the design view:

Column Name	Data type	Length	Nulls	Default
pkcol	int			
fkcol	int		check	
checkcol	char	10		
defcol	int			0
altpkcol	int			

Highlight the `pkcol` column, and click the yellow key to add a primary-key constraint. Also, make `pkcol` an identity (accept the default seed and increment values). When completed, the table should look like Figure 14.8.

14

FIGURE 14.8

The Design Table dialog for the `ConstraintTab` *table.*

Column Name	Datatype	Length	Precision	Scale	Allow Nulls	Default Value	Identity	Identity Seed	Identity Increment	Is Ro
pkcol	int	4	10	0			✓	1	1	
fkcol	int	4	10	0	✓					
checkcol	char	10	0	0						
defcol	int	4	10	0		(0)				
altpkcol	int	4	10	0						

At this point you've created a table with a default constraint on the `defaultcol` column, and a primary key on the `pkcol` column. Now create one more table, called `reltab` (for relationship table), with a single column, `pkcol` of data type int not null, and make it a primary key.

Now right-click the Diagrams folder and Select New Database Diagram. The Create Database Diagram Wizard pops up. Click Next, and then select the `ConstraintTab` and `reltab` tables (see Figure 14.9).

FIGURE 14.9

The Database Diagram Wizard select tables dialog.

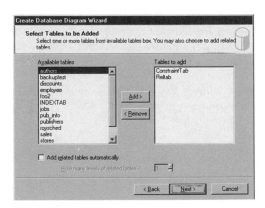

Click Next, then Finish. SQL Server Enterprise Manager will notify you that the tables you requested have been added to the database diagram. Click OK, and you will see your new database diagram (see Figure 14.10).

FIGURE **14.10**

The initial database diagram.

FIGURE **14.10**

The initial database diagram.

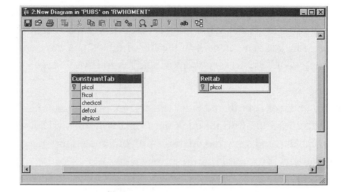

Click the `fkcol` column in the `ConstraintTab` table, and hold your mouse button down. Drag your mouse to the `reltab` table and release it. The dialog pictured in Figure 14.11 appears, showing you the primary key to foreign key relationship you are creating. Accept the defaults and click OK.

FIGURE **14.11**

Your newly created relationship.

Notice how the diagram has changed; your relationship is reflected by a line between the tables (see Figure 14.12). You can right-click the line to change the relationship properties or move the tables around any way you like to view these relationships.

FIGURE **14.12**

Your database diagram showing your newly created relationship.

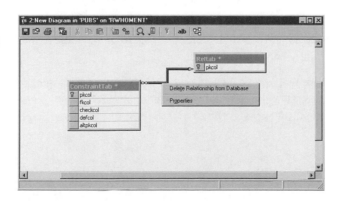

14

Click the floppy disk on the toolbar to save the diagram, and accept the default name (which should be DIAGRAM1 if it's the first one you have created). SQL Server Enterprise Manager then shows you the list of tables you have changed and asks you whether you would like to save them. Click Yes to save your referential integrity changes.

Go back to ConstraintTab and enter the design view (remember, right-click the table and select Design Table). Right-click the fkcol column, and select Properties. Click the Relationships tab, and view the relationship you created to your reltab table. The relationship dialog is shown in Figure 14.13.

FIGURE 14.13

The completed foreign-key constraint dialog.

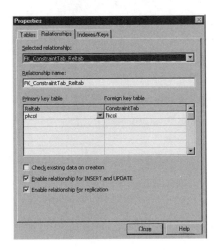

Now click the Tables tab, and in the CHECK constraints frame, click the New button to create a new check constraint. Complete the dialog as shown in Figure 14.14 to add a check constraint.

Finally, add a unique constraint as described previously by selecting a New index on the Indexes/Keys tab of the Table and Index Properties dialogs and completing the dialog as shown in Figure 14.15.

Now run the sp_help system-stored procedure on the table from the SQL Server Query Analyzer and view the constraints.

You'll notice that you've created one of each kind of constraint on this table as well as used the IDENTITY property. All the functionality relating to constraints and the IDENTITY property are fully exposed within SQL Server Enterprise Manager.

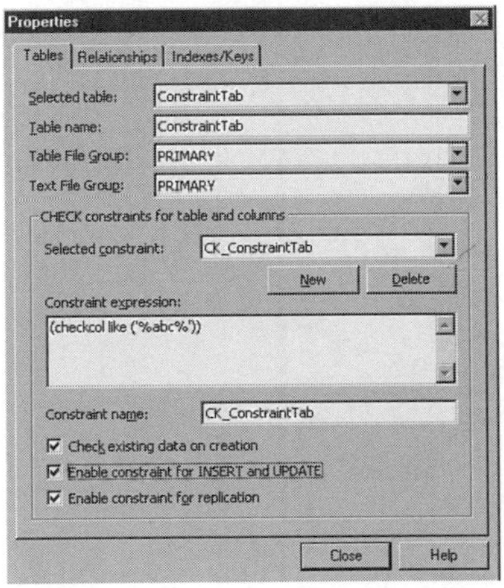

Figure 14.14

The completed check constraints dialog.

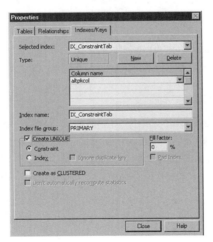

Figure 14.15

The completed unique constraint dialog.

Deferring Constraints

Foreign-key and check constraints can be deferred when they are created. Primary-key, unique, and default constraints cannot be deferred (because they create indexes in the case of primary-key and unique constraints, and defaults are never checked for previous data). When you alter a table and add one of these constraints, and specify the NOCHECK option, existing data is not validated. If you alter a table and add a check constraint, existing data is verified for validity. For example:

```
CREATE TABLE mytesttable
(col1 char(5) not null
)
```

14

```
Go
INSERT mytesttable VALUES ('Howdy')
INSERT mytesttable VALUES ('Grant')
```

Now try to create a constraint that would fail for some of the data:

```
ALTER TABLE mytesttable
ADD CONSTRAINT ck_mytest CHECK (col1 like 'h%')
```

And it fails:

```
Server: Msg 547, Level 16, State 1
ALTER TABLE statement conflicted with COLUMN CHECK constraint
 'ck_mytest'.
➡The conflict occurred in database 'pubs', table
 'mytesttable', column 'col1'.
```

However, if you create the same constraint with the NOCHECK option, it now works:

```
ALTER TABLE mytesttable
WITH NOCHECK
ADD CONSTRAINT ck_mytest CHECK (col1 like 'h%')
```

The same is true of foreign-key constraints. Be careful using this option because you are identifying that you might have invalid data in your database.

Disabling Constraints

You can also disable constraints temporarily so that you can add invalid data that violates your check constraints or data that would violate your foreign-key constraints. To do this, run the ALTER TABLE command with the WITH NOCHECK CONSTRAINT <constraintname> or with the WITH NOCHECK ALL option to disable all check and foreign-key constraints.

Continuing the previous example, the following would disable all constraint checking:

```
ALTER TABLE mytesttable
NOCHECK CONSTRAINT ALL
```

You could then add invalid data (data that violates the check constraint). You could reenable the constraint by running

```
ALTER TABLE mytesttable
CHECK CONSTRAINT ALL
```

Summary

You can choose to enforce data integrity in several ways. "Traditional" integrity enforcement options in SQL Server revolve around rules, defaults, and user-defined data types. You can also enforce data integrity and referential integrity using ANSI constraints. The proper choice is entirely up to your individual application needs. ANSI constraints and declarative referential integrity are typically preferred because they tend to perform better and are integrated into the definitions of objects. If you need some functionality, however, such as delete cascade referential integrity, you will not be able to use declarative referential integrity. You will need to use programming such as triggers or stored procedures.

You also learned about the IDENTITY property, which can help you create automatic key values when there is no natural primary key available for a table. Automatic key values are extremely useful in most database designs.

Q&A

Q What options could be used to enforce entity integrity?

A Unique indexes, primary-key, and unique constraints.

Q What does the identity property do to a column?

A It generates an automatic value for an integer column.

Q Can a rule refer to another column in a table?

A No. Only table-level check constraints can refer to another column.

Workshop

The Workshop provides quiz questions to help you solidify your understanding of the concepts presented in this chapter. In addition to the quiz questions, exercises are provided to let you practice what you have learned in this chapter. Try to understand the quiz and exercise answers before continuing to the next day's lesson. Answers are provided in Appendix A, "Answers."

Quiz

1. Is this a valid default definition?

   ```
   Create default mydefault as 'UNKNOWN'
   ```

2. Can you drop a rule while it's still bound to a column, even if there's no data in the table?

3. Is a numeric data type allowed for identity columns?

4. Can a foreign key refer to a table in a different database?

5. Can a unique constraint be deferred or disabled?

6. Can you drop the indexes created by some constraints?

14

Exercises

1. Create three tables, each with compatible data types. Create primary-key/foreign-key relationships between them using the database diagram features of SQL Server Enterprise Manager.

2. Create several tables using the IDENTITY property. Try different seed and increment values and add data to see whether they perform as you would expect. Also, run the truncate table statement to see the "resetting" of your identity options back to the initial seed value.

WEEK 2

In Review

Now take a quick refresher at what you covered during this second week.

On Day 8 you looked at restoring your databases and transaction logs. You also learned the importance of having an emergency plan in place. We can't stress enough that you must verify your backup and recovery process on a timely basis.

On Day 9 you learned how to work with the different data types available in SQL Server 7.0 to create your own table definitions.

On Day 10 you learned how to use the bcp program to import and export data between SQL Server and other storage locations. You also learned about the Data Transfer Services Wizard for moving data and database schema between any compatible components.

On Day 11 you developed a strong foundation for programming with the SELECT statement. You learned how to implement the use of arithmetic and mathematical operators. You learned how to use data conversion in your SELECT statements, and how to choose ranges and sort your selected data. You then extended your Transact-SQL development by learning how to do some database programming. This included the use of aggregates like AVG, COUNT, and the GROUP BY statements. You also learned how to take advantage of joins. You finished by correlating data using subqueries.

On Day 12 you learned how to insert, update, and delete data from your databases. This enables you to make modifications to data that already exists or to add and remove data.

Day 13 showed you how to speed up your queries through the use of proper indexing. You learned about the clustered and nonclustered indexes. You also learned about factors that can impact index performance, such as the fill factor. You finished the day with a quick look at the full-text indexing feature of SQL Server 7.0.

All these backups, modifications, and data selection are virtually useless if your database lacks integrity. To be sure of your data, you learned about the different types of data integrity, including entity, domain, and referential. You also learned the difference between procedural and declarative integrity and examined the IDENTITY value, defaults, rules, and constraints.

WEEK 3

At a Glance

During your third week, you are going to learn more about programming in SQL Server. Your lessons in Transact-SQL will cover views, stored procedures and triggers, programming basics, and more advanced programming techniques. You also learn how to streamline your administrative tasks using automation. You learn how to distribute your data over the enterprise using replication. You then take some time for performance tuning and optimization of SQL Server, and then finish up the week with a look at using SQL Server on the Internet.

Day 15 walks you through the use of views, stored procedures, and triggers. These can be implemented for both speed, ease of use, and database accuracy.

Day 16 gives you a foundation in the programming concepts used in Transact-SQL, as well as transactions and locking.

Day 17 examines the types of replication available with SQL Server 7.0 and introduces you to the terminology that's used for replication.

Day 18 implements the various types of replication you examined on Day 17.

Day 19 can be useful to you as a database administrator. You learn how to automate many mundane tasks involved with running and maintaining a database. You will even be able to have email sent to you when your automated tasks fail or succeed. This is all accomplished through the SQL Server Agent.

Optimizing your database for best performance and throughput is always a must. You begin to learn how to fine tune your database on Day 20.

15

16

17

18

19

20

21

Don't know what the Internet is? Been in a cave? Of course you do, and Day 21 introduces you to using your SQL Server on the Internet.

As always, do all the exercises presented to you at the end of each lesson. These not only build on what you have learned, they also give you a chance to test your understanding of the material presented.

DAY 15

Working with Views, Stored Procedures, and Triggers

Yesterday you learned about two different mechanisms that are used to enforce data integrity: procedural and declarative. Declarative integrity in SQL Server is often combined with the IDENTITY property and is referred to as declarative referential integrity (DRI). Essentially, you were trying to ensure that the data in your database was correct (without errors) and followed the rules of your business.

In today's lesson you will learn about views, stored procedures, and triggers. With these three database components, you will be able to hide much of the Transact-SQL complexities from the users of your databases. The first section discusses the creation and manipulation of views. Views enable you to specify exactly how a user will see data. You can think of them as stored queries. The second section covers stored procedures, which are precompiled SQL statements. Because stored procedures are precompiled, they run much more quickly than do queries.

You will finish Day 15 with a section on triggers. Triggers can be very complex, and they have several rules about how and when they should be created. Triggers enable you to ensure data integrity, domain integrity, and referential integrity within your database. You will also look at each of the three types of triggers: INSERT, UPDATE, and DELETE. As usual, some real-world questions and answers are provided at the end of this lesson, followed by quiz questions and, of course, some exercises to help strengthen your knowledge of what you've learned in today's lesson.

Creating and Manipulating Views

Views enable you to horizontally or vertically partition information from one or more tables in the database. In other words, with a view you can let the user see only selected fields and selected rows. Figure 15.1 shows a view that lets the user see only the author's last name and first name fields (vertical partition) and only authors with a last name that begins with the letter M (horizontal partition).

FIGURE 15.1

A view created from a horizontally and vertically partitioned table.

au_lname	au_fname	city	state	zip
Caloney	Sarah	Fresno	CA	90225
Deitrich	Johanna	Plano	TX	76503
Dominic	Anthony	Bend	OR	97922
Ferrous	Eric	Towns	ME	02566
MacFeather	Stearns	Bowie	UT	82331
McDonald	Stephanie	London	MO	55823
Oreland	Lars	Reno	NV	89509
Spinola	Michael	Moreno	NM	73220

au_lname	au_fname
MacFeather	Stearns
McDonald	Stephanie

Views can also be created to show derived information. For example, you can create a view that will show the author's last name, first name, and book title, and then a calculated or derived field showing the number of books sold multiplied by their royalty fee per book.

Views also have the following advantages:

- Control over what the user can see. This is useful for both security and ease of use. The user does not have to look at extra information that he or she doesn't require.

- Simplify the user interface by creating views of often-used queries. This will enable a user to run a view with a simple statement rather than supplying parameters every time the query is run.
- Security. Users can control only what you let them see. This might be a subset of rows or columns, statistical information, or a subset of information from another view.
- Because a view is a database object, you can assign user permissions on the view. This is much more efficient than placing the same permissions on individual columns in a table.
- Data can be exported from a view using the BCP utility.

Creating Views

In this section you will concentrate on how to create views, view restrictions, and the different types of views available such as joins, projections, and calculated information.

You can create views using the SQL Server Query Analyzer utility or through the SQL Server Enterprise Manager. Here are some examples using the SQL Server Query Analyzer utility.

The syntax for the view statement is

SYNTAX

```
CREATE VIEW [owner.]view_name [(column_name [, column_name…])]
[WITH ENCRYPTION]
AS select_statement
[WITH CHECK OPTION]
```

A simple create view statement looks like this:

```
CREATE VIEW all_authors
AS SELECT * FROM authors
```

You can use this view in a variety of different ways, as shown in the following examples:

```
SELECT * FROM all_authors

SELECT au_fname, au_lname
FROM all_authors

SELECT au_lname
FROM all_authors
WHERE au_lname like 'M%'
```

There are two options that you can specify in the CREATE VIEW statement: WITH CHECK OPTION and WITH ENCRYPTION. By default, data modifications made through a view are not checked to determine whether the rows affected will be within the definition of the view. In other words, inserts and updates can be made to the base table even if the view doesn't use them. For example, a view might horizontally partition a table and give you only records that have an author's last name beginning with the letter F. Without using the WITH CHECK OPTION, you could potentially add a new record with a last name of Meredith. The WITH CHECK OPTION forces all data modification statements applied through the view to use the criteria set within the SELECT statement that defines the view. The WITH ENCRYPTION option encrypts the CREATE VIEW statement in the syscomments system table. After a view definition has been encrypted, it cannot be seen by anyone. The only way to decrypt a view is to drop the view and then re-create it.

Here are a couple of sample views created with these two options enabled:

```
CREATE VIEW myCheck
AS select * from authors
WITH CHECK OPTION

CREATE VIEW myEncrypt
WITH ENCRYPTION
AS select * from authors
```

When you create views you should always test the SELECT statement before you make it into a view. This will allow you to avoid unexpected results. For example, you can create a view that returns all the rows in your table. For example, there might be only 500 rows in the table when you create your view. Two years from now that same table might return 10,000 rows of data. Is this still a good SELECT statement?

 Tip

When you create a view, you are creating a database object. You should try to avoid creating broken ownership chains. This can be accomplished by having only one developer create all the objects in your database. This is usually the dbo, or a developer aliased as the dbo. The dbo can then assign permissions to use the view to individual database users and database groups.

Here are some rules and restrictions you should be aware of when you are creating views:

- CREATE VIEW statements cannot be combined with other SQL statements in a batch.
- When you are creating a view, any database objects that are referenced by the view are verified at the time the view is created.

- When you are running a view, you must have SELECT permission on the objects referenced in the view definition unless the objects do not have an owner specified. This means that you could potentially create a view that you could not run. Permissions on views are checked each time the view is run—not when it is created.

- You cannot include the ORDER BY, COMPUTE, or COMPUTE BY clauses in your SELECT statement within a view.

- If you drop objects referenced within a view, the view still remains. You will receive an error message the next time you attempt to use that view. For example, if you create a view by joining information from two base tables and then drop one of the base tables, the view remains but won't run. To avoid this problem, you can use the sp_depends system-stored procedure to see what dependent objects the table has before it is dropped.

- Temporary tables cannot be referenced in a view. This also means that you cannot use a SELECT INTO clause in a view.

- If your view uses a SELECT * statement and the base table referenced in the SELECT statement has new columns added, the new columns will not show up in the view. The * is resolved at creation time into a fixed list of columns. You must alter the view to include the newly added columns.

- If you create a child view based on a parent view, you should be aware of what the parent view is doing. You could run into problems if the parent view is large and complex.

- Data in a view is not stored separately. This means that if you modify data in a view, you are modifying the data in the base tables.

- You cannot reference more than 1,024 columns in a view.

- You must specify names for all derived columns in your view.

- Triggers and indexes cannot be created on a view.

Gathering Information on Views

To get the text used in the CREATE VIEW statement, you can use the SQL Server Enterprise Manager or run the sp_helptext system-stored procedure and pass the view name as a parameter.

```
sp_helptext myCheck
```

```
CREATE VIEW myCheck AS
SELECT * FROM authors WITH CHECK OPTION
```

Note

> If a view was created with the ENCRYPTION option set, you cannot use
> sp_helptext (or the SQL Server Enterprise Manager) to view the text used to
> create the view. The view must be dropped and re-created before it can be
> read.

Tip

> You can also use the sp_depends system-stored procedure to get a report of
> the tables and views on which a view depends, as well as objects that
> depend on your view. You can run sp_depends on tables, views, stored pro-
> cedures, and triggers.

If you run sp_depends on the previous view, you must do the following:

```
exec sp_depends myCheck
```

In the current database, the specified object references the
following:

```
Name            Type          Updated      Selected       Column
------------------------------------------------------------------
Dbo.authors     user table    no           yes            au_id
Dbo.authors     user table    no           yes            au_lname
Dbo.authors     user table    no           yes            au_fname
Dbo.authors     user table    no           yes            phone
Dbo.authors     user table    no           yes            address
Dbo.authors     user table    no           yes            city
Dbo.authors     user table    no           yes            state
Dbo.authors     user table    no           yes            zip
Dbo.authors     user table    no           yes            contract
(9 row(s) affected)
```

You can also query the following system tables to gather information about a view:

- syscolumns: Returns columns defined within a view
- syscomments: Returns text of the CREATE VIEW statement
- sysdepends: Returns view dependencies
- sysobjects: Returns the view name

Types of Views

There are different types of views, each of which depends on the type of SELECT statement used to create the view. Now take a closer look at projections, joins, aggregates,
computed columns, and views based on other views.

Projection

 The simplest type of view is called a *projection*. A projection is simply a subset of columns in a table.

```
CREATE VIEW my_view
AS SELECT au_lname, au_fname
FROM authors
```

To run the newly created view

```
SELECT * FROM my_view
```

```
au_fname                 au_lname
------------------       -------------
Bennet                   Abraham
Blotchet-Halls           Reginald
Carson                   Cheryl
DeFrance                 Michel
del Castillo             Innes
Dull                     Ann
Green                    Marjorie
Greene                   Morningstar
Gringlesby               Burt
Hunter                   Sheryl
Karsen                   Livia
Locksley                 Charlene
MacFeather               Stearns
McBadden                 Heather
O'Leary                  Michael
Panteley                 Sylvia
Ringer                   Albert
Ringer                   Anne
Smith                    Meander
Straight                 Dean
Stringer                 Dirk
White                    Johnson
Yokomoto                 Akiko

(23 row(s) affected)
```

Joins

NEW TERM *Joins* link rows from two or more tables by comparing values in the specified columns. For example, you might like to give the user a list of authors from the `authors` table and the titles of the books they have written from the `titles` table. These two tables have a many-to-many relationship in the pubs database and therefore use the `titleauthor` table to create two one-to-many relationships as shown in Figure 15.2.

FIGURE 15.2

The authors *and* titles *tables are linked by the* title author *table.*

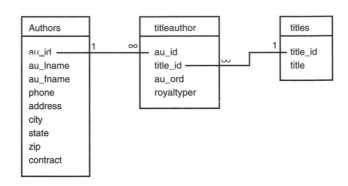

 INPUT/ OUTPUT

```
CREATE VIEW authors_titles
AS SELECT authors.au_lname, authors.au_fname, titles.title
FROM authors, titleauthor, titles
WHERE titleauthor.au_id = authors.au_id
AND titles.title_id = titleauthor.title_id
```

Then run

```
SELECT * FROM authors_titles
WHERE au_lname like 'M%'
```

```
au_lname        au_fname         Title
-----------     ----------       -------------------------
MacFeather      Stearns          Cooking with Computers:…
MacFeather      Stearns          Computer Phobic AND Non-Phobic…

(2 row(s) affected)
```

ANALYSIS This view resulted in a listing showing the last name, first name, and title of any books that all authors with a last name beginning with the letter M had written.

Other Types of Views

You can also create views using aggregate functions, computed columns, and views based on other views. Aggregates use aggregate functions like AVG, COUNT, and SUM. You can use computed columns to create summary data for your users. You can use a view from a view to further refine the original view. For example, your original view might give you information on all products with their corresponding prices and the quantity sold. You can create a new view from this view that computes the quantity by the number of units sold for a particular item number.

Here is a computed column view:

```
CREATE VIEW book_totals AS
SELECT title, (price * ytd_sales) 'Total'
FROM titles
```

You can now use this view:

```
Select * from book_totals
```

```
title                                      Total
-------------------------------------------  -------------
The Busy Executive's Database Guide        81,859.05
Cooking with Computers:  Surreptitious Balance…  46,318.20
You can combat computer Stress!            55,978.78
Straight Talk About Computers              81,859.05
Silicon Valley Gastronomic Treats          40,619.68
The Gourmet Microwave                      66,515.54
The Psychology of Computer Cooking         (null)
But Is It User Friendly?                   201,501.00
Secrets of Silicon Valley                  81,900.00
Net Etiquette                              (null)
Computer Phobic AND Non-Phobic Individuals…  8,096.25
Is Anger the Enemy?                        22,392.75
Life Without Fear                          777.00
Prolonged Data Deprivation: Four Case Studies  81,399.28
Emotional Security:  A New Algorithm       26,654.64
Onions, Leeks, and Garlic:  Cooking Secrets of …  7,856.25
Fifty Years in Buckingham Palace Kitchens  180,397.20
Sushi, Anyone?                             61,384.05
```

(18 row(s) affected)

 This view returned all the books in the `titles` table with a column called `Total`, which contains the price multiplied by the year-to-date sales figures.

Data Modification with Views

You can modify data in a view. Remember that when you modify data in a view, you are modifying data in the underlying tables themselves. Several rules apply when you are modifying data through a view:

- Modifications cannot affect more than one underlying table. If your view joins information from one or more tables, you can modify data in only one of the base tables.

- You can modify data only in a base table, so aggregates, computed columns, and columns with built-in functions cannot be altered.

- If you use the WITH CHECK option when you create or alter your views, all data to be inserted or modified through the view must conform to the restrictions in the SELECT statement used to create the view. For example, if your SELECT statement has a WHERE au_lname LIKE "M%", you can only add or modify rows that conform to that WHERE clause.

15

- `NOT NULL` columns defined in the base table, but not part of the view, must also have default values assigned to them for you to be able to insert a new row through the view.
- If the view contains a union, you can never use the view for an update.

Altering Views

With SQL Server 7.0, you can now alter a view using the `ALTER VIEW` statement. The `ALTER VIEW` syntax is the same as that used for the `CREATE VIEW` statement, except that you replace `CREATE` with `ALTER`.

The syntax for the `ALTER VIEW` statement is

```
ALTER VIEW [owner.]view_name [(column_name [, column_name…])]
[WITH ENCRYPTION]
AS select_statement
[WITH CHECK OPTION]
```

The advantage of using the `ALTER VIEW` statement is that all permissions already assigned to the view will be retained. If you were to drop and then re-create the view, this would not be true. Please note, however, that if your view accesses new objects that have an owner specified, those who have permission on your newly altered view must also have the appropriate permissions on those newly referenced objects.

Removing Views

You can remove views from your database by selecting the view in SQL Server Enterprise Manager and then right-clicking and choosing Delete from the context menu; or you can use a `DROP` statement.

To drop a view using code, use the following syntax:

```
DROP VIEW [owner.]view_name[,[owner.]view_name…]
```

To drop a view called `myCheck`, which is owned by the dbo, use this syntax:

```
DROP VIEW dbo.myCheck
```

```
This command did not return data, and it did not return any rows
```

Summary of Views

Views are very powerful and useful objects in your database design. You can give users access to certain columns and rows within your table, but a view is much easier to maintain than user permissions on individual columns and is therefore the preferred method of partitioning information. This is a performance consideration as well. When you place permissions on columns in a table, every time that table is referenced for any reason, the permissions must be checked on each referenced column.

Stored Procedures

NEW TERM *Stored procedures* are precompiled Transact-SQL statements stored in a SQL Server database. Because stored procedures are precompiled, they usually provide the best performance of any type of query. There are many system-stored procedures defined with an sp_ that gather information from system tables and are especially useful for administration. You can create your own user-defined stored procedures as well. In this section, you will look at how stored procedures are created and processed by the system. You will learn how to create stored procedures and gather information about them. You will also learn how to pass parameters to and from stored procedures. Finally, in this section you will learn how to create stored procedures that will execute automatically when SQL Server starts up.

Stored Procedures: The Sales Pitch

What makes stored procedures so great? What is so special about these SQL Server objects that they get their own section of this book? Stored procedures are fast-running sets of Transact-SQL commands stored in a SQL Server database. When you create a stored procedure, steps 1 through 4 in the following list are run. When you run a stored procedure for the first time, only step 5 must be run.

1. The procedure will be parsed into its component pieces.
2. The components that reference other objects in the database (tables, views, and so on) are checked for their existence. This is also known as resolving.
3. When resolving is complete, the name of the procedure will be stored in the sysobjects table and the code to create the stored procedure will be saved in syscomments.
4. Compilation continues, and during compilation a blueprint for how to run the query will be created. This blueprint is often called a normalized plan or a query tree. The query tree will be saved in the sysprocedures table.
5. When the stored procedure is first executed, the query plan will be read and fully optimized into a procedure plan and then run. This saves you the time of reparsing, resolving, and compiling a query tree every time you run the stored procedure.

Another benefit of using a stored procedure is that after being executed, the procedure plan will be stored in the procedure cache. This means that the next time you use that stored procedure in the same session, it will be read directly from the cache and run. This gives you a huge performance boost over running a standard SQL query again and again.

That sounds pretty good, but are there any more highlights? Yes there are! Additional stored procedure benefits are summarize here:

- You can use stored procedures to encapsulate business rules. After being encapsulated, multiple applications can use these rules, thus giving you a consistent data interface. This is also advantageous in that, if functionality must change, you must change it in only one place rather than once for each application.

- Performance is boosted for all stored procedures, but even more so for stored procedures that are run more than once as the query plan is saved in the procedure cache.

- With stored procedures, you can pass in arguments and get data returned, too.

- Stored procedures can be set up to run automatically when SQL Server starts up.

- Stored procedures can be used to extract data or modify data (not at the same time).

- Stored procedures are explicitly invoked. Unlike triggers, stored procedures must be called by your application, script, batch, or task.

Creating Stored Procedures

You use the CREATE PROCEDURE statement to create stored procedures. Stored procedures are created in the current database unless you are creating temporary stored procedures in tempdb. To create a stored procedure you must have the create procedure statement permission.

The following are rules for creating a stored procedure:

- The name must follow the rules for identifiers.

- Referenced objects must exist when your stored procedure runs. This is a new feature of SQL Server 7.0 called *delayed name resolution*. This enables you to reference objects that don't exist at compile time. You can have your stored procedure create temporary objects and then reference them later in the same stored procedure.

- You cannot create and then drop or re-create objects with the same name in a single stored procedure.

- You can have up to 1,024 parameters.

- You can reference temporary tables within your stored procedure. Local temporary tables will disappear when your procedure ends.

- Stored procedures cannot have the following Transact-SQL create statements in them: CREATE DEFAULT, CREATE PROCEDURE, CREATE RULE, CREATE TRIGGER, and CREATE VIEW.

- You can nest procedures within procedures (up to 32 levels deep).

- As with views, if you use a SELECT * in the stored procedure SELECT statement and the underlying table has new columns added to it, the new columns will not show up when the procedure is run. You must use the ALTER statement and recompile the stored procedure.

Here is the CREATE PROCEDURE syntax:

```
CREATE PROC[EDURE] procedure_name {;number}
 [{@parameter data_type} [VARYING] [= default] [OUTPUT]][,…n]
[WITH {RECOMPILE ¦ ENCRYPTION ¦ RECOMPILE, ENCRYPTION}]
[FOR REPLICATION]
AS sql_statement [...n]
```

Take a look at a couple of sample CREATE PROCEDURE statements and then you'll learn about the ;number, parameter, RECOMPILE, and ENCRYPTION components.

**INPUT/
OUTPUT**

```
CREATE PROCEDURE spAuthors
AS SELECT au_fname, au_lname
FROM authors
ORDER BY au_lname DESC
```

```
This command did not return data, and it did not return any rows
```

To use this procedure, you can execute it from the Query Analyzer window.

**INPUT/
OUTPUT**

```
EXEC spAuthors

Au_fname                         au_lname
-------------------              --------------
Yokomoto                         Akiko
White                            Johnson
Stringer                         Dirk
[. . .]                          [. . .]
Carson                           Cheryl
Blotchet-Halls                   Reginald
Bennet                           Abraham

(23 row(s) affected)
```

ANALYSIS The results are a two-column table with the last names and first names shown in descending order.

Gathering Information on Stored Procedures

To get the text used in the CREATE PROCEDURE statement, you can use the SQL Enterprise Manager or run the sp_helptext stored procedure and pass the view name as a parameter.

```
sp_helptext spAuthors

text
CREATE PROCEDURE spAuthors AS SELECT au_fname, au_lname
FROM authors ORDER BY au_lname DESC
```

> **Note**
>
> Like a view, if a stored procedure was created with the ENCRYPTION option set, you cannot use sp_helptext (or the Enterprise Manager) to view the text used to create the stored procedure. The procedure must be dropped and re-created before it can be read.

You can also use the sp_depends stored procedure to get a report of the objects on which a stored procedure depends. To apply sp_depends on the previous procedure, do the following:

```
sp_depends spAuthors

In the current database, the specified object references the
following:
```

Name	Type	Updated	Selected	Column
Dbo.authors	user table	no	yes	au_id
Dbo.authors	user table	no	yes	au_lname
Dbo.authors	user table	no	yes	au_fname
Dbo.authors	user table	no	yes	phone
Dbo.authors	user table	no	yes	address
Dbo.authors	user table	no	yes	city
Dbo.authors	user table	no	yes	state
Dbo.authors	user table	no	yes	zip
Dbo.authors	user table	no	yes	contract

```
(9 row(s) affected)
```

Creating a Group of Procedures

The first option you will look at is the ;number option. By specifying a semicolon and a number, you can create a group of stored procedures. Groups of stored procedures are often created for use in the same application. Maintenance is then easier because all procedures used by a particular application reference the same group. The following is an example of creating a group of procedures:

15

```
CREATE PROC group_sp;1
AS SELECT * FROM authors
GO
CREATE PROC group_sp;2
AS SELECT au_lname FROM authors
GO
CREATE PROC group_sp;3
AS SELECT DISTINCT city FROM authors
GO
```

ANALYSIS This batch of statements will create a single procedure called group_sp with three different procedures as part of it. To refer to individual procedures, execute them with their ;number as part of the name. For example, to get a listing of all the cities that authors live in, you do the following:

INPUT/ OUTPUT

EXEC group_sp;3

```
City
Ann Arbor
Berkeley
Corvallis
Covelo
Gary
Lawrence
Menlo Park
Nashville
Oakland
Palo Alto
Rockville
Salt Lake City
San Francisco
San Jose
Vacaville
Walnut Creek
(16 row(s) affected)
```

In SQL Server 7.0, you can now use the ALTER PROCEDURE statement. As with the ALTER VIEW statement, all permissions defined on the procedure are retained.

Note If you are working with a group of procedures, you cannot drop an individual procedure. You must drop the entire group and then re-create for a modification to be made.

Tip When you create stored procedures, test the SQL statements first and then create your stored procedure. This will let you avoid unexpected results.

When you drop grouped procedures, you need to drop only the procedure name. Any procedure that is part of that group will also be dropped.

```
DROP PROCEDURE dbo.group_sp
```

Using Parameters with Stored Procedures

Parameters enable you to create stored procedures that will behave a little differently every time they are called. For example, you can write a stored procedure that averages a series of test scores passed into it. You don't know what the scores are going to be when you create the procedure, but every time the procedure is run you get a new average. The syntax for the parameter portion of the CREATE PROCEDURE deserves a closer look.

Syntax

@parameter_name datatype [= default¦NULL] [VARYING] [OUTPUT]

The @parameter_name specifies the name of the parameter within the procedure. You can declare up to 1,024 parameters within a single stored procedure. The parameter data type can be any system-defined or user-defined data type, except for image. DEFAULT specifies a default value for the parameter. VARYING applies to the cursor (recordset) returned and is beyond the scope of this book. OUTPUT determines this as a return parameter.

The OUTPUT option allows you to pass information back out of the procedure to the calling procedure. I'll illustrate this point with some sample code. This stored procedure accepts five parameters, averages them, and then outputs the average:

**INPUT/
OUTPUT**

```
CREATE PROCEDURE scores
@score1 smallint,
@score2 smallint,
@score3 smallint,
@score4 smallint,
@score5 smallint,
@myAvg smallint OUTPUT
AS SELECT @myAvg =
(@score1 + @score2 + @score3 + @score4 + @score5) / 5
```

Note

Every parameter in a stored procedure must have a value for the procedure to run. If a parameter has a default value assigned to it, the user does not have to supply a value for that parameter unless he or she wants it to be other than the default. Finally, if you have a procedure that accepts four parameters and all of them have defaults assigned to them, you can call the procedure and only pass values for the first two parameters. You cannot call the procedure and pass a value for the first and third parameters and leave the second parameter blank if you are passing parameters in order. It is possible to pass parameters in SQL Server by reference—which means that you supply the parameter as name = parameter. This allows you to pass parameters out of order. When this is the case, you can specify any parameter in any order.

To extract the myAvg value from this procedure, you must first declare a variable and then run the procedure. Note that this example passes the parameters by position.

```
DECLARE @AvgScore smallint
EXEC scores 10, 9, 8, 8, 10, @AvgScore OUTPUT
SELECT 'The Average Score is:  ', @AvgScore
GO
```

```
----------------------    ---------
The average score is:    9
(1 row(s) affected)
```

ANALYSIS Let's review what you just did. You first created the procedure scores with myAvg declared as an OUTPUT variable. You then declared a temporary variable called AvgScore and passed the average score into your stored procedure call with the OUTPUT parameter. This placed the value of myAvg from the stored procedure into the AvgScore variable outside the procedure. You then used a SELECT statement to print out the value of AvgScore. Notice that when you passed your values into the stored procedure, you passed them in order by position. This is also known as passing by position. You can also pass by reference. You can do this by specifying the parameter name = value when you pass in your variables. When you pass by reference, you can pass your variables in any order. Here is some sample code:

```
DECLARE @AvgScore smallint
EXEC scores
@score1 = 10, @score3 = 9,
@score2 = 8, @score4 = 8,
@score5 = 10, @myAvg = @AvgScore OUTPUT
SELECT 'The average score is:  ', @AvgScore
GO
```

You will get the same results as before. Notice that you passed values out of order. Finally, if you start by passing by reference, you must pass by reference for the entire procedure call. You cannot switch between pass by position and pass by reference in the middle of a stored procedure call.

Another way to pass information back to the calling procedure is to use the RETURN keyword. This will pass a variable directly to the calling procedure without using the OUTPUT statements needed in both the stored procedure definition and the call to the procedure. Take a look at the code to use the RETURN keyword.

 **INPUT/
OUTPUT**
```
CREATE PROC MyReturn
@t1 smallint, @t2 smallint, @retval smallint
AS SELECT @retval = @t1 + @t2
RETURN @retval
```

After creating this procedure, enter the following to run it:

```
DECLARE @myReturnValue smallint
EXEC @myReturnValue = MyReturn 9, 9, 0
SELECT 'The return value is:  ', @myReturnValue
```

```
-----------------------     --------
The return value is:        18
(1 row(s) affected)
```

Using the WITH RECOMPILE Options

You can add the WITH RECOMPILE statements in either the CREATE PROCEDURE statements or in the EXEC PROCEDURE statements. Their location affects how the stored procedure is processed and run.

WITH RECOMPILE Used in the CREATE PROCEDURE Statement

When you use the WITH RECOMPILE statements in the CREATE PROCEDURE, the execution plan will not be saved in the procedure cache. The entire procedure will be recompiled every time it is run. This is similar to the way a standard query is handled. This can be useful in stored procedures with parameters that make the normal execution plan run poorly. By recompiling every time, the procedure can be optimized for the new parameters. Here is an example of a stored procedure with the WITH RECOMPILE option:

```
CREATE PROCEDURE MyRecompileProc
WITH RECOMPILE
AS SELECT * FROM authors
ORDER BY au_lname
```

WITH RECOMPILE Used in the EXEC PROCEDURE Statement

You can also use the WITH RECOMPILE statement in the EXEC PROCEDURE statement. This will compile the stored procedure for that single execution and then store the new plan in the procedure cache for subsequent EXEC PROCEDURE commands. Here is an example of using the WITH RECOMPILE option in an EXEC PROCEDURE statement:

```
EXEC spAuthors
WITH RECOMPILE
```

```
au_fname                      au_lname
------------------            --------------
Yokomoto                      Akiko
White                         Johnson
Stringer                      Dirk
[. . .]                       [. . .]
Carson                        Cheryl
Blotchet-Halls                Reginald
Bennet                        Abraham

(23 row(s) affected)
```

ANALYSIS The results are a two-column table with the last names and first names shown in descending order. The procedure was also recompiled and the new plan was stored in the procedure cache.

Forcing All Stored Procedures to Be Recompiled

You can force all stored procedures and triggers that reference a particular table to be recompiled at their next runtime by executing the sp_recompile stored procedure:

```
EXEC sp_recompile authors
```

Making Your Stored Procedures Run Automatically at SQL Startup

You can have stored procedures "autoexecute" at the startup of SQL Server. You can have as many autoexec stored procedures as you like, but each separate stored procedure will use up a user connection.

Tip

> You can have one stored procedure call other stored procedures and thus use only one user connection to the server.

The execution of these stored procedures will begin after the last database has been recovered at startup time.

To create these autoexec stored procedures, you use the sp_procoption stored procedures. Please see the Books Online or *Microsoft SQL Server 7.0 Unleashed* for more information.

Using the WITH ENCRYPTION Option

The WITH ENCRYPTION option encrypts the SQL statements used to create the procedure and stores the encrypted text in the syscomments table.

Here is an example of using the WITH ENCRYPTION option:

```
CREATE PROC encrypted_proc
WITH ENCRYPTION
AS SELECT * FROM authors
```

Of course this code does the same thing as when the WITH ENCRYPTION option is used with the CREATE VIEW statement. You cannot use sp_helptext or the SQL Enterprise Manager to view the text of the stored procedure.

Using Remote Stored Procedures

You can implement and run stored procedures on other SQL servers. This is called a remote stored procedure. To enable the use of remote stored procedures, follow these steps:

- The remote server must allow remote access. This is the default when SQL Server is installed, so unless you reconfigured your server without this option, you don't need to worry about turning it on.
- Both servers must have each other registered in their `sysservers` tables.
- Both servers must have your login ID in the `syslogins` table.

After you have set this up, you execute the stored procedures in a similar fashion as you have locally. The difference is that you must preface the stored procedure like this:

```
EXEC servername.dbname.owner.storedprocedure
```

For example, if you want to run the system-stored procedure `sp_addlogin` on the Accounting server, run the following code:

```
EXEC: Accounting.master.dbo.sp_addlogin Muriel
```

This adds the Muriel login ID to the Accounting SQL server.

Stored Procedure Summary

Stored procedures are a very powerful database component. System-stored procedures are useful for database administration and maintenance. User-defined stored procedures are useful for whatever you have designed them for. They have advantages over views and queries in that they are precompiled, and after their first execution, their execution plan is stored in the procedure cache that resides in random access memory (RAM). Another benefit of stored procedures is that you can assign permission to a user to run a stored procedure even if that user does not have permissions on the underlying tables. You can view some interesting stored procedure code by running the `sp_helptext` system-stored procedure on the stored procedures in the master database (for example, `sp_helptext sp_helpdevice`).

Working with Triggers

In this section you will learn about a special type of stored procedure called a trigger. Triggers are automatically invoked when you try to modify data that a trigger is designed to protect. Triggers help secure the integrity of your data by preventing unauthorized or inconsistent changes to be made. For example, suppose you have a customers table and an orders table. You can create a trigger that will ensure that when you create a new order, it will have a valid customer ID to be attached to. Likewise, you can create the trigger so that if you try to delete a customer from the customers table, the trigger will check to see whether you have any orders still attached to that customer, and if so, halt the delete process.

Triggers do not have parameters and cannot be explicitly invoked. This means that you must attempt a data modification to fire off a trigger. Triggers can also be nested up to 16 levels. Nested triggers work like this: A trigger on your orders table can add an entry to your accounts receivable table that will in turn fire a trigger to check to see whether the customer has any overdue accounts receivable and then notify you.

From a performance standpoint, triggers have a relatively low amount of overhead. Most of the time involved in running a trigger is used up by referencing other tables. The referencing can be fast if the other tables are in memory or a bit slower if they must be read from disk.

Triggers are always considered a part of the transaction. If the trigger or any other part of the transaction fails, it is rolled back.

In the past, triggers were the only means of enforcing referential integrity. In SQL Server 7.0 you now have the ability to use DRI, which makes most triggers unnecessary.

The Inserted and Deleted Tables

Triggers use the inserted and deleted tables. Both of these tables contain the same structure as the base table or the "trigger table" where the trigger has been created. The inserted and deleted tables reside in RAM because they are logical tables. If you add a new record to the base table, the record will be recorded in the base table itself, as well as in the inserted table. Having the values available in the inserted table enables you to access the information without having to create variables to hold the information. When you delete a record, the deleted record is stored in the deleted table. An update is much like a delete and then an insert. If you update a record, the original is stored in the deleted table and the modified record is stored in the base table, as well as in the inserted table.

Creating Triggers with the CREATE TRIGGER Statement

A table can have as many triggers as you want to create on any of the three trigger actions defined: INSERT, UPDATE, or DELETE. Each of these actions can be stored in a single trigger or multiple triggers. If stored in different triggers, each trigger name must be unique. For example, you can create a trigger called trInsUpdAuthors on the authors table with a trigger designed for INSERT and UPDATE actions. You can then create an additional trigger called trDelAuthors with the DELETE action defined. If you want to modify the `trInsUpdAuthors` trigger, you must drop the whole trigger and then re-create it or use the `ALTER TRIGGER` statement. You create triggers with the `CREATE TRIGGER` statement. Other rules apply to creating triggers as well:

- Triggers cannot be created on views or temporary tables. Triggers can, however, reference views and temporary tables.

- Triggers cannot return resultsets to the user. Therefore, you should be careful when you include `SELECT` statements. It is a common practice to use the `IF EXISTS` clause as part of a `SELECT` statement in your trigger code.

- Triggers should be used to maintain data integrity, to maintain referential integrity, and to encapsulate business rules.

- Triggers can be encrypted in the `syscomments` table if you specify the `WITH ENCRYPTION` option.

- `WRITETEXT` statements do not activate triggers. You use `WRITETEXT` to modify text or image data, and it is a non-logged transaction.

- The following SQL statements cannot be used in a trigger: all `CREATE` statements, all `DROP` statements, `ALTER TABLE` and `ALTER DATABASE`, `TRUNCATE TABLE`, `GRANT` and `REVOKE`, `RECONFIGURE`, `LOAD DATABASE` or `TRANSACTION`, `UPDATE STATISTICS`, `SELECT INTO`, and all `DISK` statements.

- Rollback transaction statements inside triggers can cause unexpected behavior in your calling programs.

Note If you modify a trigger with the `ALTER TRIGGER` statement, the old trigger will be completely replaced with the new trigger. If you drop a table with triggers on it, the triggers will automatically be dropped as well.

Now that all the rules are out of the way, take a look at the `CREATE TRIGGER` statement itself:

```
CREATE TRIGGER [owner.]trigger_name
ON [owner.]table_name
FOR {INSERT ¦ UPDATE ¦ DELETE}
WITH ENCRYPTION
AS sql_statements
```

Inserts and Updates

Take a look at a sample trigger for both inserts and updates to a table.

```
CREATE TRIGGER trAddAuthor
ON authors
```

```
FOR INSERT, UPDATE
AS raiserror ("'%d rows have been modified'", 0, 1, @@rowcount)
RETURN
```

This command did not return data, and it did not return any rows

ANALYSIS   You have just created a trigger that will fire off every time you try to add or update a record in the `authors` table. The trigger will send you a message about how many rows have been modified. Try inserting a new author and see what happens.

INPUT/OUTPUT
```
INSERT authors
(au_id, au_lname, au_fname, phone, address, city, state, zip,
contract)
VALUES
('555-66-7777', 'Leap', 'Frog',
 '800 444-5656', '123 Sesame Street',
 'West EastBrooke', 'CA', '90221', 0)
1 rows have been modified
(1 row(s) affected)
```

ANALYSIS   You successfully added your Leap Frog record to the `authors` table. The `1 rows have been modified` lets you know that your trigger did indeed fire off.

Deletes

When using the `DELETE` action, you should know that this trigger will not fire if a `TRUNCATE TABLE` statement has been executed. `TRUNCATE TABLE` deletes all rows from the table.

To test the `DELETE` action, first add another record to your table that is similar to the first record you created. You are going to change the primary-key field only for your Leap Frog record as follows:

INPUT/OUTPUT
```
INSERT authors
(au_id, au_lname, au_fname, phone, address, city, state, zip,
contract)
VALUES
('444-55-6666', 'Leap', 'Frog', '800 444-5656',
 '123 Sesame Street', 'West EastBrooke', 'CA',
 '90221', 0)
```

```
1 rows have been modified
(1 row(s) affected)
```

ANALYSIS   You successfully added a second Leap Frog record to the `authors` table. Note that you changed the `au_id` field to `444-55-6666`.

Now create a `DELETE` action trigger that will tell you how many rows are going to be deleted when you run this trigger.

```
CREATE TRIGGER trDelAuthors
ON authors
FOR DELETE AS raiserror
("%d rows are going to be deleted from this table!",
0, 1, @@rowcount)
```

This command did not return data, and it did not return any rows

Now delete all records with a first name of Leap.

```
DELETE FROM authors
WHERE au_fname = "Leap"
```

```
2 rows are going to be deleted from this table!
(2 row(s) affected)
```

Enforcing Data Integrity

You can use triggers to enforce data integrity within your database. In the past, referential integrity was enforced with triggers. With later versions of SQL Server, you can use referential integrity constraints. Triggers are still useful, however, to encapsulate business rules and force cascading changes in your database. A cascading change can be created with a trigger. For example, suppose a particular bookstore is no longer in business. You can create a cascading trigger that removes the store from the stores table and removes all sales associated with that store_id from the sales table. You can create this DELETE action cascading trigger.

First create a couple of dummy tables to work with.

```
sp_dboption pubs, 'Select Into', TRUE
go
SELECT * INTO tblStores from pubs..stores
SELECT * INTO tblSales from pubs..sales
```

```
CHECKPOINTing database that was changed.
(6 row(s) affected)
(21 row(s) affected)
```

Now run a quick SELECT statement to see what you have.

```
SELECT sa.stor_id, st.stor_name
FROM tblStores st, tblSales sa
WHERE st.stor_id = sa.stor_id
```

```
stor_id          stor_name
----------       -----------------------------------
6380             Eric the Read Books
6380             Eric the Read Books
7066             Barnum's
7066             Barnum's
7067             News & Brews
```

```
7067                    News & Brews
7067                    News & Brews
[. . .]                 [. . .]
7131                    Doc-U-Mat: Quality Laundry and Books
8042                    Bookbeat
```

```
(21 row(s) affected)
```

Remember the stor_id 7067; there are three of them, and that's what you will be deleting. Next, create the trigger on tblSales that will tell you how many sales will be deleted when the associated store from tblStores is deleted.

```
CREATE TRIGGER trDelSales
ON tblSales
FOR DELETE AS
raiserror('%d rows are going to be deleted from the sales table!'
, 0, 1, @@rowcount)
```

```
This command did not return data, and it did not return any rows
```

Now create the DELETE trigger on tblStores.

```
CREATE TRIGGER trDelStore
ON tblStores
FOR DELETE AS
DELETE tblSales FROM deleted where deleted.stor_id = tblSales.stor_id
```

```
This command did not return data, and it did not return any rows
```

Finally, go ahead and delete the stor_id 7067, which is the News & Brews store.

```
DELETE FROM tblStores
WHERE tblStores.stor_id = '7067'
```

```
4 rows are going to be deleted from the sales table!
(1 row(s) affected)
```

ANALYSIS The DELETE trigger on tblStores fired off and deleted all associated records in tblSales. The DELETE trigger in tblSales fired off to deliver the message that four rows are being deleted. If you rerun the previous SELECT statement, you will see that News & Brews is gone and that you no longer have 21 rows of data, but 17.

Encapsulating Business Rules

Encapsulating business rules are normally made with constraints, defaults, data types, and rules, but you can also use triggers. Triggers are especially useful when you must reference other tables because this action is not allowed in constraints, defaults, data types, and rules. To continue with your earlier examples, you can modify your trigger trDelSales on the tblSales table to run the business rule. Do not allow any store to be deleted if sales are greater than or equal to 20. Here is the code to implement this business rule.

You might need to drop this trigger before you can re-create it:

```
DROP TRIGGER trDelSales
GO
CREATE TRIGGER trDelSales
ON tblSales
FOR DELETE AS
IF (SELECT COUNT(*) FROM deleted
WHERE deleted.qty >= 20) > 0
BEGIN
PRINT 'You cannot delete any of these stores.'
PRINT 'Some stores have more than 20 sales!'
PRINT 'Rolling back your transaction!'
ROLLBACK TRANSACTION
END
```

```
This command did not return data, and it did not return any rows
```

Now test this new trigger.

```
DELETE FROM tblSales
WHERE stor_id = '7066'
```

```
You cannot delete any of these stores.
Some stores have more than 20 sales!
Rolling back your transaction!
(2 row(s) affected)
```

ANALYSIS There was at least one store with a stor_id of 7066 that had more than 20 sales. To verify, run this SELECT statement:

```
SELECT stor_id, qty FROM tblSales
stor_id          qty
----------       -------
6380             5
6380             3
7066             50
7066             75
7067             10
[. . .]          [. . .]
8042             10
8042             25
8042             30

(21 row(s) affected)
```

Now run the DELETE statement again using stor_id 6380. As you can see from the previous code, this should delete those stores because neither entry has a qty field of more than 20.

```
DELETE FROM tblSales
WHERE stor_id = '6380'
```

(2 rows(s) affected)

Rerun the SELECT statement and you will see that both stores with an ID of 6380 are gone, and you have 15 rows of data left rather than 17.

Enforcing Referential Integrity

Triggers also can be used to enforce referential integrity. This is their primary purpose in a database. They are especially useful in cascading updates and deletes. Triggers are tested last when data modifications occur. Constraints are checked first on the trigger table. If a constraint is violated, then the trigger will never fire.

Here is an example of a trigger that enforces referential integrity. This trigger will ensure that before a sale is added to the sales table, a valid store ID exists in the stores table.

INPUT

```
CREATE TRIGGER trInsUpdSales
ON tblSales
FOR INSERT, UPDATE AS
IF (SELECT COUNT(*) FROM tblStores, inserted
WHERE tblStores.stor_id = inserted.stor_id) = 0
BEGIN
PRINT 'The stor_id you have entered does not exist'
PRINT 'in the stores table!'
ROLLBACK TRANSACTION
END
```

ANALYSIS

This trigger will work on any single UPDATE or INSERT to tblSales. It makes sure that you have a valid stor_id in tblStore. If you run a SELECT INTO, though, this trigger might not fire properly. When you have multiple rows to deal with, you should check to make sure that the rowcount of stor_ids inserted equals the amount of sales you added. Here is how you code this trigger to handle multiple rows:

Again, you might have to drop this trigger before re-creating it here:

INPUT

```
DROP TRIGGER trInsUpdSales
GO
CREATE TRIGGER trInsUpdSales
ON tblSales
FOR INSERT, UPDATE AS
DECLARE @rc int
SELECT @rc = @@rowcount
```

```
IF (SELECT COUNT(*) FROM tblStores, inserted
WHERE tblStores.stor_id = inserted.stor_id) = 0
BEGIN
PRINT 'The stor_id you have entered does not exist'
PRINT 'in the stores table!'
ROLLBACK TRANSACTION
END
IF (SELECT COUNT(*) FROM tblSales, inserted
WHERE tblSales.stor_id = inserted.stor_id) <> @rc
BEGIN
PRINT 'Not all sales have a valid stor_id '
PRINT 'in the stores table!'
ROLLBACK TRANSACTION
END
```

Gathering Information on Triggers

As with the other components you have looked at in today's lesson, you can run the sp_helptext system-stored procedure to look at the text of a trigger statement. Of course, encrypted triggers will have no syscomments entries that you can look at. You should not encrypt any objects unless you absolutely have to. When you upgrade your database, those encrypted objects must be dropped and re-created. Unencrypted objects will be automatically upgraded to the newer version.

Trigger Summary

Triggers are a special type of stored procedure that are executed automatically when data is modified in the trigger table. Triggers help secure the integrity of your data by preventing unauthorized or inconsistent changes to be made. Triggers can be used to ensure data integrity, to ensure referential integrity, and to encapsulate business rules.

From a performance standpoint, triggers have a relatively low amount of overhead. Most of the time involved in running a trigger is used up by referencing other tables.

Summary

In today's lesson you learned about three powerful database objects: views, stored procedures, and triggers. Views enable you to give users access to certain columns and rows within your table. System-stored procedures are useful for database administration and maintenance. User-defined stored procedures are useful for whatever you have designed them for. Stored procedures have the advantage of being precompiled and therefore run much more quickly than views do. Triggers are a special type of stored procedure that are executed automatically when data is modified in the trigger table. Triggers help secure the integrity of your data by preventing unauthorized or inconsistent changes to be made.

Q&A

Q **Which is faster: triggers, views, or stored procedures?**

A Stored procedures and triggers are both faster than views. Stored procedures and triggers are both precompiled SQL statements and therefore run at the same speed and generally have the same amount of overhead. SQL Server's order of operations will run stored procedures and views before it will execute triggers. So for efficiency, if you can catch problems with a stored procedure, you won't get down to the trigger level just to have to roll back everything that's been done already.

Q **How can I get a list of all stored procedures in my server?**

A You can look at stored procedures database by database by running this query:

```
SELECT name
FROM sysobjects
WHERE type = 'P'
```

Q **How can I get a list of all triggers on my server?**

A You can look at triggers on a database-by-database basis if you run this query. It returns each table with its associated triggers.

```
SELECT name,
'INSERT' = object_name(instrig),
'UPDATE' = object_name(updtrig),
'DELETE' = object_name(deltrig)
FROM sysobjects
WHERE type = 'U'
AND (instrig <> 0 OR updtrig <> 0 OR deltrig <> 0)
```

Workshop

The Workshop provides quiz questions to help you solidify your understanding of the concepts presented in this chapter. In addition to the quiz questions, exercises are provided to let you practice what you have learned in this chapter. Try to understand the quiz and exercise answers before continuing to the next day's lesson. Answers are provided in Appendix A, "Answers."

Quiz

1. What do triggers enforce?

2. You can have _____ number of triggers per table.

3. Views can focus on only the data needed, provide security, and allow modifications to base tables, and they are faster than stored procedures. True or False.

4. You can update multiple base tables with a view. True or False?

5. You can use a stored procedure that returns information from base tables that you do not have permission on. True or False?

6. You can use a view that returns information from base tables that you do not have permission on. True or False?

7. Declared referential integrity (DRI), constraints, data types, defaults, and rules have eliminated the need for triggers. True or False?

8. When you drop a table, which of the following database objects are also dropped: views, stored procedures, or triggers?

Exercises

1. Create a view that shows which authors have written which books.

2. Create a trigger that will prevent you from adding a new book title without having a valid publisher.

3. Create a stored procedure that will show which books are selling in which stores. (Hint: You will need to join three tables to accomplish this.)

DAY 16

Programming SQL Server 7.0

On Day 15 you looked at views, triggers, and stored procedures. Using these database objects, you are able to use SQL to provide miniature programs. Although stored procedures and triggers are very powerful, you can make them even more powerful by combining standard SQL with the advanced programming features of Transact-SQL.

Today's lesson focuses on the programming features of the Transact-SQL language. You start off learning about batches and scripts. You then examine the different types of locking used in SQL Server for concurrency control. Finally, you finish this day's lesson with a discussion on implementing transactions.

Batches

NEW TERM A *batch* is a set of Transact-SQL statements that are interpreted together by SQL Server. The statements are submitted together, and the keyword GO marks the end of the batch. Here is an example of a batch run from the SQL Server Query Analyzer:

```
USE PUBS
SELECT au_id, au_lname FROM authors
SELECT pub_id, pub_name FROM publishers
INSERT publishers VALUES ('9998','SAMS Publishing', 'Seattle', 'WA','USA')
GO
```

Batches follow several rules. All the SQL statements are compiled together. If there is a syntax error anywhere in the batch, the entire batch is canceled. If you were to modify the previous set of SQL statements and introduce a syntax error, you would get an error message from SQL Server, and none of the statements would run. The following is an example:

INPUT/ OUTPUT

```
USE PUBS
SELECT au_id, au_lname FROM authors
SELECT pub_id, pub_name FROM publishers
INSERT publishers VALS ('9998','SAMS Publishing', 'Seattle',
'WA','USA')
GO
```

```
Server: Msg 170, Level 15, State 1
Line 4: Incorrect syntax near 'VALS'.
```

ANALYSIS The error message occurred from the INSERT statement. The VALUES keyword was replaced with the word VALS.

Some statements can be combined together in a batch, although other statements are restricted. The following CREATE statements can be bound together within a single batch:

- CREATE DATABASE
- CREATE TABLE
- CREATE INDEX

These CREATE statements cannot be combined with others:

- CREATE RULE
- CREATE TRIGGER
- CREATE PROCEDURE
- CREATE DEFAULT
- CREATE VIEW

If you try to combine them, you will receive error 111, which looks like this:

```
Server: Msg 111, Level 15, State 1
'CREATE VIEW' must be the first statement in a query batch.
```

> **Caution**
>
> Be careful when you use these statements. Although the CREATE RULE, CREATE DEFAULT, and CREATE VIEW statements return the error message listed in the previous code lines (111), CREATE PROC and CREATE TRIGGER merely append any SQL statements as part of the object until the keyword GO. For example, the following will return a syntax error:
>
> ```
> CREATE DEFAULT t1_default
> AS 'UNKNOWN'
> SELECT * FROM authors
> GO
> ```
>
> The following statement will create a single stored procedure without any further messages from SQL Server:
>
> ```
> CREATE PROC myproc
> AS
> SELECT * FROM authors
> RETURN
> SELECT * FROM publishers
> GO
> ```

16

Here are some additional rules for batches:

- You cannot alter a table and then use the new columns within the same batch.
- SET statements take effect immediately—except for the QUOTED_IDENTIFIER and ANSI_NULLS options.

Scripts

NEW TERM A *script* is a set of one or more batches. Scripts typically are executed as part of some unit of work that needs to be accomplished, such as a data load or database maintenance. Listing 16.1 shows you an example of a script.

INPUT **LISTING 16.1** AN EXAMPLE OF A SCRIPT

```
USE PUBS
SELECT au_id, au_lname FROM authors
SELECT pub_id, pub_name FROM publishers
INSERT publishers VALUES ('9997','SAMS Publishing', 'Seattle',
'WA','USA')
GO

SELECT * FROM stores
GO

DELETE publishers WHERE pub_id = '9997'
GO
```

Note that batches and scripts don't necessarily have anything to do with transactions, which you will learn about shortly. Microsoft ships a variety of scripts you can use as examples. They are located in the \INSTALL directory wherever you have SQL Server installed. You should look for files that end in .SQL. These scripts are excellent examples of how you should do your Transact-SQL scripting.

Transactions

NEW TERM   A *transaction* is a unit of work. Transactions are constantly being used, but you might not be aware of them. For example, what if a bank teller were to transfer $50 from a checking account to a savings account but forgot to put the money into savings? Most people would be pretty upset by that. They expect that if the money came out of checking it will go into savings. That's a transaction. The unit of work will complete all commands successfully, or it fails and undoes everything that it has done. We have come to expect transactions in our daily lives, but as a SQL Server developer you must manually program transactions for them to work properly. As an administrator, you will need to understand transactions because they can cause your transaction logs to fill up if they are used improperly.

Transactions are made up of the following four properties, which, when put together, are called the "ACID" properties.

- Atomic—A transaction is said to be *atomic* when it either completes in its entirety or aborts completely. If any one statement fails, all the statements that are part of the transaction fail.

- Consistent—A transaction is said to leave the database in a *consistent* state after it completes or fails. The changes made by a transaction will be consistent from one state to another.

- Isolated—A transaction is said to be *isolated* when it does not interact or conflict with any other transaction in the database.

- Durable—A transaction is said to be *durable* if the work is guaranteed to remain completed regardless of anything that happens to the database after the transaction has completed successfully. If the power fails and the database server crashes, the transaction is guaranteed to still be complete when the server restarts.

Transactions guarantee that the work being performed can succeed or fail completely, as described in the previous list. Locks provide part of that guarantee. During a transaction, no other transaction can modify data your transaction has changed until you have decided whether the change is permanent. While you are modifying the data, you hold an *exclusive lock* on it. Conversely, you cannot read another transaction's data if it's in the process of modifying that data. You are requesting a *shared lock* on the other data, but the other transaction is using an *exclusive lock* on its data that prevents you from reading it. You will examine locks in more detail later.

Transaction Types

There are three types of transactions: explicit, implicit, and automatic (referred to as "autocommit" in the Microsoft Books Online).

Explicit Transactions

Explicit transactions are transactions that you manually configure. Reserved words are used to indicate the beginning and end of explicit transactions. These reserved words include BEGIN TRANSACTION, COMMIT TRANSACTION, COMMIT WORK, ROLLBACK TRANSAC-TION, ROLLBACK WORK, and SAVE TRANSACTION.

To begin an explicit transaction, type the keywords BEGIN TRAN (or BEGIN TRANSACTION if you're in the mood to type more). To indicate to SQL Server that your transaction is complete and all work should be saved, you enter the COMMIT TRAN (or COMMIT WORK) statement. Hence, a typical transaction might look like this:

```
BEGIN TRAN

    UPDATE authors
    SET city = 'San Jose' WHERE au_lname = 'Smith'
    INSERT titles
    VALUES ('BU1122','Teach Yourself SQL Server 7.0 in 21 days',
     'business','9998',$35.00, $1000.00,10,4501, 'A great book!',
     ➥'8/1/1998')
    SELECT * from titleauthor

COMMIT TRAN
```

You will also need to cancel transactions. To do this you use the ROLLBACK TRAN (or ROLLBACK WORK) command. Here's an example of the ROLLBACK TRAN statement:

```
BEGIN TRAN
    Delete sales where title_id = 'BU1032'
    IF @@ERROR > 0
        ROLLBACK TRAN
    ELSE
        COMMIT TRAN
```

The ROLLBACK TRAN statement will cancel the transaction completely. Any work that was done in the transaction up to that point will be rolled back, or canceled. You also have the ability to create savepoints within a transaction and then selectively roll back to those points. Again, a code example illustrates this best:

```
BEGIN TRAN
    UPDATE table1 SET col1 = 5 WHERE col2 = 14
    SAVE TRAN savepoint1
    INSERT table2 values (3,16)
    IF @@error > 0
        ROLLBACK TRAN savepoint1
        DELETE table3 WHERE col1 > 2
    IF @@error > 0
        ROLLBACK TRAN
    ELSE
        COMMIT TRAN
```

Notice that the SAVE TRAN command has a name after it, known as the *savepoint* name. By including the savepoint name in the first rollback, you are expressing that instead of rolling back the entire transaction from the beginning, you would like to roll back to a particular named point—in this case savepoint1. The INSERT into table2 would be canceled if the first rollback was issued, but the transaction itself would continue. Essentially the INSERT would be "removed" from the transaction. Because there is no name given to roll back to in the later rollback, ROLLBACK TRAN will go all the way back to the BEGIN TRAN statement.

Now take a closer look at the TRANSACTION statements.

▼ SYNTAX

```
BEGIN TRANsaction [transaction_name]
COMMIT TRANsaction [transaction_name]
COMMIT [WORK]
```

transaction_name is an optional name you can assign to the transaction. You can substitute a variable wherever you see *transaction_name* as long as it resolves to a valid transaction name. It is not necessary to name a transaction; in fact it's better that you not name any transaction except the outermost BEGIN statement in your transaction. The *transaction_name* must be a valid SQL Server identifier. Note that with the following COMMIT WORK statement you are not allowed to specify a transaction name:

```
SAVE TRANsaction [savepoint_name]
```

savepoint_name is a placeholder used to indicate a safe point to abort some amount of work in a transaction, without canceling the entire transaction. The *savepoint_name* must be a valid SQL Server identifier.

```
ROLLBACK TRANsaction [transaction_name ¦ savepoint_name]
ROLLBACK [WORK]
```

Refer to the earlier discussion of BEGIN/COMMIT TRAN and SAVE TRAN statements for a description of the optional names. Note again that the ROLLBACK WORK statement does not allow you to specify either a transaction name or a savepoint name.

▲

As implied in the comments for BEGIN TRAN/COMMIT TRAN in the syntax box, transactions can be nested. However, this nesting is strictly syntactical in nature. Transactions cannot truly be nested. You might have multiple transactions appear to occur within a script, but in fact only one actual transaction is being used.

A global variable, @@trancount, applies directly to these transactions. When a BEGIN TRAN is issued, @@trancount is incremented by one. A SAVE TRAN has no effect on @@trancount. A ROLLBACK TRAN can have several effects, depending on whether a transaction name is specified. If no transaction name is specified, @@trancount is reset to 0 (all work is committed). If the last transaction name is specified, @@trancount is decremented by one. A ROLLBACK WORK statement always resets @@trancount to 0 (as well as canceling all work that was done from the first BEGIN TRAN). Examine this code to see how it works:

```
SELECT @@TRANCOUNT -- It should return 0.
BEGIN TRAN t1
SELECT @@TRANCOUNT -- It should return 1.
SAVE TRAN savepoint1
SELECT @@TRANCOUNT -- It still is set to 1.
ROLLBACK TRAN savepoint1
SELECT @@TRANCOUNT -- It still is set to 1.
BEGIN TRAN t2
SELECT @@TRANCOUNT -- It should return 2.
ROLLBACK TRAN
SELECT @@TRANCOUNT - It's back to 0.
```

Here are a few rules about explicit transactions. Some statements are not allowed as part of explicit transactions. These include the following:

- ALTER DATABASE
- DROP DATABASE
- RECONFIGURE
- BACKUP LOG
- RESTORE DATABASE
- CREATE DATABASE
- RESTORE LOG
- UPDATE STATISTICS

In addition, the following statements (included in SQL Server 7.0 for backward compatibility with SQL Server 6.x) are not allowed in transactions either:

- DISK INIT
- LOAD DATABASE
- LOAD TRANSACTION
- DUMP TRANSACTION

16

Other statements can appear together inside a transaction (although remember that this does not change any of the rules about which you learned earlier).

There is no published limit on the number of savepoints within a transaction. Once committed, there is no way to roll back a transaction.

You might have duplicate savepoint names within a single transaction; however, only the final instance of the savepoint name will actually be used if you roll back to that savepoint. For example,

```
BEGIN TRAN
    INSERT
    UPDATE
    SAVE TRAN transave1
    DELETE
    INSERT
    SELECT
    SAVE TRAN transave1
    INSERT
    DELETE
    IF @@ERROR <> 0
        ROLLBACK TRAN transave1
    ELSE
        COMMIT TRAN
```

In this example, the ROLLBACK TRAN transave1 statement will go back only as far as the second transave1 savepoint. The first savepoint is ignored after the name is reused.

 Caution When you issue a ROLLBACK TRAN statement within a trigger and no savepoint name is specified, the entire transaction is rolled back and the rest of the batch is not executed. However, processing might continue with the next batch. You will need to test for this in your code and verify that you handle this particular kind of rollback gracefully. It might be wise to simply return some kind of error in a trigger back to the calling routine and rely on the calling routine to properly deal with the state of a transaction. It's certainly much safer.

Calls to remote stored procedures are not normally considered part of a transaction.

```
BEGIN TRANSACTION
UPDATE table1 SET col1 = 5 WHERE col1 = 1
DELETE table1 WHERE col1 = 5
EXEC server2.pubs..usp_insertpublisher parm1 parm2 parm3
COMMIT TRAN
```

If the `pubs..usp_insertpublisher` stored procedure on server2 were to issue a `ROLLBACK TRAN` statement, it would not affect the local transaction.

However, there is a server configuration option called `REMOTE_PROC_TRANSACTIONS`. This configuration parameter, normally set to `0` (off), controls whether remote stored procedures are automatically enrolled (distributed). To enable automatic enrollment of remote stored procedures in transactions, run the following:

```
EXEC sp_configure "REMOTE_PROC_TRANSACTIONS", 1
RECONFIGURE WITH OVERRIDE
```

This affects all executions of remote stored procedures on the server, so enable it with caution. You learn about distributed transactions later in today's lesson, in the section "Distributed Transactions."

Automatic Transactions

Even when it doesn't appear that transactions are being used, they are lurking behind the scenes. Any execution of a data modification statement in SQL Server is an implied transaction.

In the following batch, each SQL statement is a separate transaction. Thus, this batch is actually three separate transactions. If any of the statements fail, it doesn't affect the others. Each statement will succeed or fail on its own, without regard to the other statements in the batch.

```
INSERT table1 VALUES (1,'abcde')
UPDATE table1 SET col1 = 5 WHERE col1 = 1
DELETE FROM table1 WHERE col1 = 5
GO
```

Transactions can also provide performance benefits. By not writing the transaction log entries to disk until the transaction is completed, SQL Server can provide more efficient utilization of the disk. Therefore, it's beneficial to group statements together. Take the previous statements and group them into a transaction and only five log entries are written, instead of nine.

```
BEGIN TRAN
INSERT table1 VALUES (1,'abcde')
UPDATE table1 SET col1 = 5 WHERE col1 = 1
DELETE FROM table1 WHERE col1 = 5
COMMIT TRAN
```

As you increase the grouping of statements, transactions can dramatically increase the efficiency of your data modification statements.

16

Implicit Transactions

Implicit transactions are provided for American National Standards Institute (ANSI) compliance. When implicit transactions are enabled, selected Transact-SQL statements automatically issue a BEGIN TRANSACTION. These statements must then be committed or rolled back explicitly.

Implicit transactions are enabled at the session level by issuing the following statement:

```
SET IMPLICIT_TRANSACTIONS ON
```

For the rest of that session, the following statements would need to be explicitly committed (or rolled back).

ALTER TABLE	GRANT	REVOKE
CREATE	DROP	DELETE
SELECT	INSERT	UPDATE
TRUNCATE TABLE	FETCH	OPEN

To turn off implicit transactions, you would run

```
SET IMPLICIT_TRANSACTIONS OFF
```

For example, the following two code snippets are identical (in terms of transactions). Note that you can verify this with the @@trancount variable.

```
CREATE TABLE table1 (col1 int not null)
BEGIN TRAN
INSERT table1 VALUES (1)
SELECT @@trancount
COMMIT TRAN
```

and

```
SET IMPLICIT_TRANSACTIONS ON
INSERT table1 values (2)
SELECT @@trancount
COMMIT TRAN
```

 Caution Enabling the IMPLICIT_TRANSACTIONS option requires that you must remember to commit or roll back every transaction. This is easy to forget—and if you do forget, you will tend to leave transactions open and hold locks (discussed later) far longer than you might want to. I recommend that you not enable this option unless you are very sure that you will remember to commit your transactions.

How Do Transactions Work?

Now that you've looked at explicit, implicit, and automatic transactions, consider a step-by-step description of what happens inside SQL Server during a transaction, using the set of SQL statements in Listing 16.2 as an example.

INPUT   **LISTING 16.2**   STEPPING THROUGH A SET OF TRANSACTIONS

16

```
BEGIN TRAN
    INSERT table1 values (1,'abcde')
    UPDATE table1 SET col1 = 5 WHERE col1 = 1
    DELETE FROM table1 WHERE col1 = 5
COMMIT TRAN
```

ANALYSIS   The following occurs in this listing:

1. When the BEGIN TRAN statement is sent to the database, the SQL Server parser detects the request to begin an explicit transaction. However, SQL Server 7.0 is smart enough that it won't allocate a log record in memory until any actual work has been done; so a transaction technically hasn't started yet.

2. Now the INSERT statement runs. SQL Server creates a log record in memory and allocates a transaction ID to associate with this new transaction. The new row is recorded in the transaction log, and then the data page for table1 is modified in memory (see Figure 16.1). If the needed page is not in memory, it is retrieved from disk.

FIGURE 16.1

Step 2 of the transaction process.

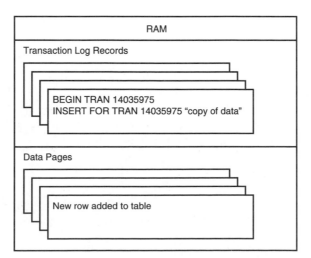

3. The next statement runs in a similar fashion. The UPDATE statement is recorded in the transaction log, and then the data page is modified in memory, as shown in Figure 16.2.

FIGURE 16.2

Step 3 of the transaction process.

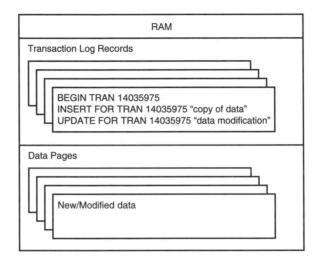

> **Note**
>
> In the previous example, a single row was listed in the log for the update. Most of the time it will probably be true that the log will actually show a delete followed by an insert, rather than a single modify record. It would require an "update in place" to get a single modify record to be written to the log. A variety of conditions are required to get an "update in place" to occur. These are enumerated on Day 12, "Data Modification with Queries."

4. When SQL Server receives the COMMIT TRAN, the log record is written to the transaction log file for the database (see Figure 16.3). This is your guarantee that the transaction can be recovered. Because the log changes are written to disk, it guarantees that the transaction is recoverable—even if power is lost or the database crashes before the data page is written to disk.

FIGURE 16.3

Step 4 of the transaction process.

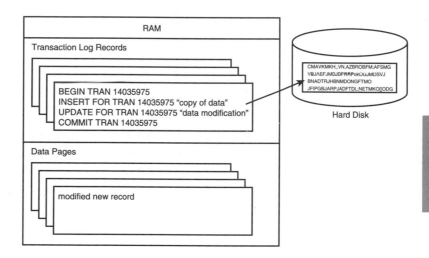

In SQL Server 7.0, log records are written in a separate file (or set of files) and are not accessible with Transact-SQL. Microsoft does not provide a utility to access the transaction log (other than the advanced DBCC LOG command, which is too advanced to cover in this book). Only SQL Server internal processes, such as backup and recovery, need to access the transaction log.

The CHECKPOINT Process

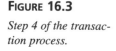 After the discussion of transactions, you might be wondering when the data pages get written to disk. The log records get written when the COMMIT TRAN statement is run. So when does the data get written to disk? The answer is in the CHECKPOINT process. The CHECKPOINT process is the internal process SQL Server uses to "flush" (or copy) the data pages from memory to disk.

The checkpoint helps assure that recovery of committed transactions won't take an excessive amount of time. After a checkpoint occurs, a log entry is written to indicate that all modified pages in memory have been written to disk. This gives the SQL Server recovery process a point in the transaction log where it is assured that no earlier committed transactions must be looked at to guarantee a complete recovery.

There are two kinds of checkpoints in SQL Server: automatic and manual.

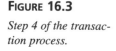 The *automatic checkpoint process* occurs based on internal SQL Server calculations. You configure how often the checkpoint process will occur with the RECOVERY INTERVAL configuration option. This option specifies, in minutes, the maximum amount of time it will take to recover each database in your system. If SQL Server thinks it would take that much time or longer to recover a database, it will issue the

automatic checkpoint. When this happens, all modified data pages (for this database) in memory will be written to disk, and all log records for this database will also be written to disk. The automatic checkpoint process wakes up every 60 seconds and cycles through each database, determining whether the database needs to be checkpointed. The default setting for the RECOVERY INTERVAL option is zero—meaning SQL Server will decide when a checkpoint is needed.

An automatic checkpoint will also occur in two other circumstances. The first is when you run the sp_dboption system-stored procedure to change a database option. SQL Server automatically issues a checkpoint for you. The second is when you shut down SQL Server. You can either issue the Transact-SQL command SHUTDOWN or shut down the MSSQLServer service.

Note
Note that for databases with the Truncate log on Checkpoint option set, the checkpoint process will truncate committed transactions from the log periodically (or when the transaction log fills up).

You can force a manual checkpoint at any time by typing the Transact-SQL command CHECKPOINT. Note that you must be a member of the db_owner role of a database to execute this command.

When a manual checkpoint is issued, all modified pages in memory are flushed to disk, in the same way as during the automatic checkpoint process. Note that a manual checkpoint has no effect on the transaction log (other than copying log records to disk), regardless of whether the Truncate log on Checkpoint database option is set.

Distributed Transactions

All the transactions you have considered so far have been on only one server. SQL Server 7.0 has the capability to support transactions that involve more that one server. This capability is supported with the Microsoft Distributed Transaction Coordinator (MSDTC) service.

There are three different ways to use distributed transactions:

- You could program distributed transactions with the DB-Lib, open database connectivity (ODBC), or object linking and embedding (OLE) DB Application Programming Interface (API). ActiveX Data Objects (ADO) also allows you to use distributed transactions. These options are beyond the scope of this book.
- You could use the Transact-SQL syntax BEGIN DISTRIBUTED TRANSACTION.

- You could use the SET REMOTE_PROC_TRANSACTIONS option to enable distributed transactions for a single session.

Now examine the last two methods more closely. To enlist the MSDTC service in your transaction and have it coordinate activity across multiple servers, all you must do is issue the BEGIN DISTRIBUTED TRANSACTION statement in exactly the same way you used the BEGIN TRAN statement. The earlier discussion about transactions mentioned that remote stored procedures operate outside the current transaction from which they are called. With distributed transactions, the remote stored procedures are now included within the transaction. If there is a failure on the remote server, it affects the calling server or servers as well. In the following code example, if there were a failure in the stored procedure called from server2, the transaction on your server would be affected as well:

```
BEGIN DISTRIBUTED TRANSACTION
UPDATE table1 SET col1 = 5 WHERE col1 = 1
DELETE table1 WHERE col1 = 5
EXEC server2.pubs..usp_insertpublisher parm1 parm2 parm3
COMMIT TRAN
```

SQL Server 7.0 includes the capability to query remote servers as part of any Transact-SQL statement. So the following code segment is also a valid distributed transaction in SQL Server 7.0:

```
BEGIN DISTRIBUTED TRANSACTION
INSERT remoteserver.pubs..remotetable (col1, col2) VALUES (1,2)
UPDATE localtab SET col2 = 5 WHERE col1 = 1
COMMIT TRAN
```

The third method is the SET REMOTE_PROC_TRANSACTIONS statement. When this option is set in a session, all remote stored procedures called during the statement are considered part of the transaction. You can also set the same configuration option with sp_configure, and the option will be set for all sessions from that time on. Before setting this as a server-wide configuration option, be sure you have tested the implications of this on any existing remote stored procedures.

Remote and Linked Servers

SQL Server 7.0 allows you to connect remotely with two types of remote databases: remote servers and linked servers. The remote server option is provided for backward compatibility and the linked server option is new to SQL Server 7.0.

Remote Servers

Remote servers enable you to execute stored procedures on remote SQL Server databases. These remote stored procedures might or might not be part of a transaction, depending on whether you've used the BEGIN DISTRIBUTED TRANSACTION or the SET

`REMOTE_PROC_TRANSACTIONS ON` Transact-SQL statements. To allow remote stored procedures to be run, you must set up the remote server using the following steps:

1. Add the name of the remote server to the sysservers system table on your SQL Server. Do this by running `exec sp_addserver <remoteserver>`.

2. On the remote SQL Server database, add your server to the sysservers table there. Again, run `exec sp_addserver <yourserver>`.

3. On your server, run the following Transact-SQL statements:
   ```
   EXEC sp_addremotelogin <remoteserver>, sa, sa
   EXEC sp_remoteoption <remoteserver>,sa, sa, trusted, true
   ```

4. On the remote server, run the code from Step 3, but reference your server.

You can now run remote stored procedures while logged in as sa. To set up other logins, you would need to run the previous stored procedures over again. To reference the remote stored procedure, use the four-part name—execute `servername.dbname.owner.procname`—with the execute statement. For example, if you were referencing the `byroyalty` stored procedure in the pubs database on server gizmo, you would run the following code:

```
Exec gizmo.pubs.dbo.byroyalty 10
```

This approach is very useful but isn't as flexible as using linked servers.

Linked Servers

Linked servers are new to SQL Server 7.0. Linked servers enable you to open what's known as an OLE DB rowset against a remote server. Unlike remote servers already mentioned, linked servers enable you to get data from non-SQL Server data sources. You can access any OLE DB data source in this fashion. Hence, you can access data from Oracle, Microsoft Access, Microsoft Excel, or any other OLE DB data source.

Perhaps an even more powerful use of linked servers is going well beyond what's allowed with remote servers. You can still execute remote stored procedures, but you can also join remote tables. To set up a linked server, you'd use the `sp_addlinkedserver` and `sp_addlinkedsrvlogin` system-stored procedures:

```
Exec sp_addlinkedserver 'remoteserver','SQL Server'
Exec sp_addlinkedsrvlogin 'remoteserver','TRUE'
```

Note   You must run the script instcat.sql from the SQL Server 7.0 install directory against any SQL Server 6.5 servers if you'd like to run distributed queries or remote stored procedures with the linked server options.

The previous code adds the remote server on your SQL Server and specifies that when you attempt to connect to the remote server, you should log in with whatever credentials you've used on the local server.

Now you can run queries like this:

```
Select t1.title, t2.pub_name
From pubs..titles t1 -- This is the local table
Inner Join remoteserver.pubs..publishers t2 -- This is the remote table
On t1.pub_id = t2.pub_id
```

This query joins the titles table from your local server with the publishers table from a remote server.

As you might have guessed, a lot of additional information might be needed to implement linked servers—particularly if you decide you need to join SQL Server tables with non-SQL Server data using the OLE DB heterogeneous data capabilities. Such topics are beyond the scope of this book, and I recommend that if you need further information about linked servers you reference Sams Publishing's *Microsoft SQL Server 7.0 Unleashed*.

Locking

Locking usually comes up in a negative context. Locking helps provide concurrency within the database. Often you'll hear someone talk about locking problems, but rarely will you hear about positive benefits; however, there are many. Without locking, SQL Server would have no mechanism to prevent multiple users from updating data at the same time.

In general, there are four types of locks in SQL Server:

- Shared—You can place a shared lock—also called a read lock—on data you are reading. A shared lock prevents other users from changing the data while you are looking at it. Shared locks are compatible with other shared locks.

- Exclusive—You can use an exclusive lock when you want to change data. It prevents other users from viewing or modifying the data you're working on until you release the lock. Exclusive locks are not compatible with other locks.

- Update—You use an update lock much like an exclusive lock. Update locks prevent others from modifying data while you are in the process of changing the data.

- Intent—An intent lock is used on a "higher" level object to indicate that a lock (one of the types of locks described) is being taken within that object. You will learn more about intent shortly.

> **Note**
>
> Update locks are necessary when a query goes through two phases to modify data: a search phase and a modify phase. It's possible that if SQL Server uses a shared lock during the search phase, another user could also acquire a shared lock on the same object. When the searching transaction goes to modify the data, it needs an exclusive lock. The other transaction might have already attempted to get an exclusive lock, and SQL Server won't give us an exclusive lock. Hence, a blocking or deadlock situation might occur. To prevent this, an update lock is used, which prevents another transaction from getting exclusive locks on the object that's been locked for update.

Lock Types

There are also different levels or types of objects that can be locked:

- RID—A RID is another term for a row-level lock. RID stands for Row Identifier. When a RID lock is taken, only one row at a time is locked.

- Key—This is a row-level lock that is taken within an index. The key lock will lock either a single key value or multiple key values (known as a key range lock). This lock type can help serialize transactions within an index.

- Page—A page is the standard 8KB unit in SQL Server. A page lock locks all the contents on a single page, which can be one or many rows.

- Extent—An extent lock is acquired when no more pages are available for a particular object and more data must be added. It indicates that a new set of eight pages (an extent) is being acquired for this object.

- Table—You can acquire a table lock either automatically via the escalation process (examined later), or you can request one explicitly. All pages in the table are locked as a unit.

- Intent—An intent lock is a way to indicate at the table level that there are page or row locks, or to a page that a row lock is in place. For example, if a single shared page lock is taken within a table, an intent shared lock will be taken at the table level.

In SQL Server 7.0, locking is completely dynamic. In prior releases of SQL Server, page-level locking was the default. However, SQL Server 7.0 decides which lock type to take when a query is optimized. For selects that access a very small amount of data, or small inserts, updates, or deletes, row-level locks (and/or key range locks) will likely be taken. For very large selects (such as `select * from largetable`), it might be more efficient to use page- or even table-level locking.

Row-level locking involves locking a single row at a time instead of a page or table. Row-level locking can be useful because a single page might contain many rows. Generally speaking, the smaller the unit of locking, the better the concurrency (the ability of multiple users to simultaneously access data). The trade-off, however, is that taking 5,000 row locks requires more resources, and hence more time, than does taking a single table lock. Because locking involves compromises, and it isn't always obvious which lock type you should take, it's best to leave the locking decisions up to SQL Server.

Controlling Locking

Normally you need not be concerned with controlling locking. For INSERT, UPDATE, and DELETE operations, SQL Server obtains an exclusive lock. However, SQL Server has the capability to configure locks on a query-by-query basis using locking hints for the SELECT statement. You specify them after the name of the table in your query. Occasionally, you will have to change the default locking behavior because of problems with transactions conflicting or blocking each other.

For example, to force an exclusive table lock on the authors table so that no one can modify the table while you examine it, you can run this query:

```
SELECT *
FROM authors (TABLOCKX)
```

There are different parameters you can use in place of TABLOCKX:

- NOLOCK—This requests that no locking be used. This is also referred to as a "dirty read." Using this optimizer hint allows a query to read data that has been locked for exclusive use. This introduces the possibility that data that has been changed, but not necessarily committed, could be read as part of the query. Although useful in some circumstances, this option should not be used unless you fully understand the ramifications.

- READUNCOMMITTED—This is the same as NOLOCK.

- READPAST—This option specifies that if some rows are locked, and you are reading several rows, including some that would normally stop you from continuing (you would be "blocked" until the locks were freed up), those rows will be skipped. Be very cautious in using this option because you could be missing data in your result set.

- REPEATABLEREAD—This option specifies that locking should comply with the REPEATABLE READ transaction isolation level. This generally means that when reading data, the locks you take won't be released until you finish your transaction—hence, no modifications of the data you've read can be modified until you're finished with it. Therefore, updates and deletes are prevented, but inserts are allowed.

- HOLDLOCK—This option requests that the lock you've taken be held for the duration of a transaction. Normally during a select statement, shared locks are acquired and released as soon as the next needed row or page is acquired. With this option, those shared locks are not released until the current transaction is either committed or rolled back. In addition, locks are taken in such a way that inserts are not allowed either. This is generally implemented with key range locks.
- SERIALIZABLE—This is the same as HOLDLOCK.
- UPDLOCK—This option requests an update lock rather than a shared lock. This is not an option that is normally used.
- ROWLOCK—This option forces the use of row-level locks.
- PAGLOCK—This option requests a shared page lock.
- TABLOCK—This option requests a table-level shared lock, rather than locking individual pages or rows.
- TABLOCKX—This option requests an exclusive table lock.

Lock Escalation

Lock escalation is the process of changing a lower-level lock (such as a row or page lock) to a higher-level lock (such as a table lock). SQL Server escalates locks when it determines the need to do so. You have no control over when this happens.

The LOCKS Option

One other configuration option is available for locks. That is, suprisingly enough, the LOCKS option. This is an advanced configuration option. The default value of zero means that SQL Server will adjust the number of locks as the needs of the system change. By default, SQL Server assigns 2 percent of the memory it uses to locks. You can set the number of locks manually if you want; however, if you run out of locks, SQL Server will put error messages in both the Windows NT Application Event Log and the SQL Server error log. All activities that require locks on the system will pause until more locks become available. Each lock requires a small amount of memory, so don't manually assign locks or set the parameter arbitrarily high without understanding the impact of this change.

Observing Locks

To see locks as they occur, you can run the sp_lock or sp_processinfo stored procedures. Here's an example of sp_lock on my system:

```
Exec sp_lock
Go
```

```
spid   dbid   ObjId          IndId   Type Resource         Mode    Status
------ ------ -------------- ------- ---- ---------------- ------- -------
1      1      0              0       DB                    S       GRANT
6      1      0              0       DB                    S       GRANT
7      1      0              0       DB                    S       GRANT
7      2      0              0       DB                    S       GRANT
7      5      0              0       DB                    S       GRANT
7      2      0              0       EXT  1:80             X       GRANT
7      1      117575457      0       TAB                   IS      GRANT
8      1      0              0       DB                    S       GRANT
```

(8 row(s) affected)

As you can see from the results of the sp_lock query, interpreting the results can be difficult. You will need to interpret the results by looking up the dbid (database IDs) from the sysdatabases table in the master database and the ObjID (object ID) from the sysobjects table in the appropriate database. You might need to look up the IndId (Index ID) from the sysindexes table in that database as well. The type column explains what kind of object is locked (database, table, extent, key, Page, Row [RID]). The resource indicates what is locked and depends on the type of lock:

- EXTENT (EXT)—Will be in the form fileno:Extent. For example, 1:35 means an extent lock is on file number 1 of the database, in extent 35.
- PAGE (PAG)—Will be in the form fileno:pageno. For example, 1:2401 would be a page lock on page number 2401 in file number 1 in the database.
- ROW (RID)—Will be in the form fileno:pageno:rowid. So 1:32:16 indicates file number 1, page 32, row 16 on that page is locked.
- KEY RANGE (KEY)—A key-range lock shows internal information from SQL Server that isn't interpretable by users.

Mode indicates the type of lock (S for shared, X for Exclusive, I for intent, and so on). *Status* is what you're most likely looking for. A GRANT status means the lock is currently being used. A WAIT status indicates the lock can't be taken because of another user holding an incompatible lock (lock compatibility is discussed next). CNVT shows that a lock is being converted to another lock (most likely, it's escalating). From a blocking perspective, you can treat it much like a WAIT status.

It might be easier to observe locks using the SQL Server Enterprise Manager's Current Activity dialogs to view locks. To see the Current Activity dialogs, expand your server name, expand the Management folder, and then expand the Current Activity option. Here you can view which processes (users) are running, what locks are held by process, and which locks are held by object. Figure 16.4 shows a sample of what that window might look like.

FIGURE 16.4

*The Locks/Process ID
Current Activity
dialog.*

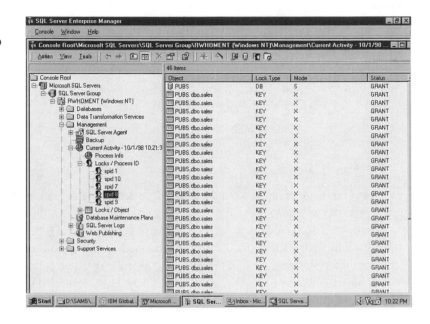

If you expand the Locks/Object option, you can observe the locks that are in place for
each object (see Figure 16.5).

FIGURE 16.5

*The Locks/Object
Current Activity
dialog.*

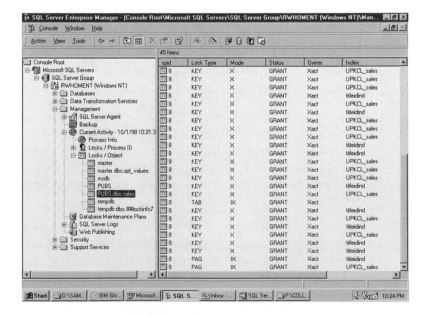

Lock Compatibility

Locks might or might not be compatible with other locks. Table 16.1 shows a compatibility matrix for locks:

TABLE 16.1   LOCK COMPATIBILITY

	IS	S	U	IX	SIX	X
INTENT SHARED (IS)	YES	YES	YES	YES	YES	NO
SHARED (S)	YES	YES	YES	NO	NO	NO
UPDATE (U)	YES	YES	NO	NO	NO	NO
INTENT EXCLUSIVE (IX)	YES	NO	NO	YES	NO	NO
SHARED WITH INTENT EXCLUSIVE (SIX)	YES	NO	NO	NO	NO	NO
EXCLUSIVE (X)	NO	NO	NO	NO	NO	NO

16

Notice that exclusive locks are incompatible with everything. If you think about this, it makes sense. When you are changing data, you don't want anyone else changing the exact same data. Shared locks, on the other hand, are reasonably flexible. When you're reading data, it's okay if other people are reading the same data.

Deadlocks

NEW TERM   A *deadlock* is a situation in which two transactions conflict with each other and the only resolution is to cancel one of the transactions. An example is the easiest way to understand deadlocks.

1. Create the two tables in Listing 16.3, and populate them with data:

INPUT   **LISTING 16.3**   SETTING UP A DEADLOCK

```
CREATE TABLE checking
(acct_num INT NOT NULL,
 last_name CHAR(30) NOT NULL,
 balance MONEY NOT NULL
 )
GO
CREATE TABLE savings
(acct_num INT NOT NULL,
 last_name CHAR(30) NOT NULL,
 balance MONEY NOT NULL
 )
GO
INSERT checking VALUES (1,'smith', $500.00)
```

continues

LISTING **16.3**   CONTINUED

```
INSERT checking VALUES (2,'Jones', $300.00)
INSERT savings VALUES (1,'Smith', $100.00)
INSERT savings VALUES (2,'Jones', $200.00)
GO
```

2. Now open two SQL Server Query Profiler windows. In the first window, run

```
BEGIN TRAN
    UPDATE checking
    SET balance = balance + $100.00
    WHERE acct_num = 1
```

You should get back

```
(1 row(s) affected)
```

3. In the second window, run

```
BEGIN TRAN
    UPDATE savings
    SET balance = balance - $100.00
    WHERE acct_num = 2
```

with the same results. So far, so good.

4. Now, in the first window, run

```
UPDATE savings
SET balance = balance - $100.00
WHERE acct_num = 1
```

Notice that the transaction is still running, while the other query window is blocking it. The results of running sp_lock are listed in the following table. Notice that for spid 9 it shows the word WAIT under status—indicating that the process is waiting to get a lock and can't run until spid 10 has released its lock on the required resource (in this case, RID 1:170:1).

spid	dbid	ObjId	IndId	Type	Resource	Mode	Status
9	5	0	0	DB		S	GRANT
9	5	1429580131	0	RID	1:170:0	X	GRANT
9	5	1429580131	0	RID	1:170:1	U	WAIT
9	5	1413580074	0	RID	1:167:0	X	GRANT
9	5	1429580131	0	PAG	1:170	IX	GRANT
9	5	1413580074	0	PAG	1:167	IX	GRANT
9	5	1413580074	0	TAB		IX	GRANT
9	5	1429580131	0	TAB		IX	GRANT
10	5	0	0	DB		S	GRANT
10	5	1429580131	0	RID	1:170:1	X	GRANT

```
10    5        1429580131  0      PAG  1:170              IX        GRANT
10    5        1429580131  0      TAB                     IX        GRANT
```

```
(12 row(s) affected)
```

5. In the second window, run

```
UPDATE checking
SET balance = balance + $100.00
WHERE acct_num = 2
```

and you should get a message like this:

```
Server: Msg 1205, Level 13, State 17
Your transaction (process ID #10) was deadlocked with another
process and has been chosen as the deadlock victim.
Rerun your transaction.
```

Notice that the original query has now completed. Run the following clean-up code in the first window:

```
COMMIT TRAN
GO
DROP TABLE checking
DROP TABLE savings
GO
```

Deadlock avoidance is important because time and resources are wasted when a deadlock occurs. One way to avoid deadlocks is to always access tables in the same order. In the previous example, if both transactions had started with the same table, the deadlock would not have occurred. One of the transactions would have waited for the other to complete before it began. When you do get a deadlock, it is generally a good idea to wait a second or two and then resubmit your transaction.

Note One common myth is that deadlocks won't occur when row-level locking is in effect. As you can see from the previous example, deadlocks don't have as much to do with row-level locking as they do with just needing the wrong locks at the wrong time. It's important to run thorough testing to eliminate as many deadlocks as you can from your applications.

Transaction Isolation Levels

Transaction isolation levels affect the default kinds and duration of locks that are taken during a SELECT statement. As you saw earlier, the types of locks taken can be overridden on a query-by-query basis. The isolation level performs similarly, but can be overridden on a session-level basis (meaning that all queries that run during a single session will have this setting take effect). To do this, use the SET TRANSACTION ISOLATION LEVEL statement.

SYNTAX

```
SET TRANSACTION ISOLATION LEVEL
    {READ COMMITTED ¦ READ UNCOMMITTED ¦ REPEATABLE READ ¦ SERIALIZABLE}
```

The default is READ COMMITTED, which means that a select query will only see data that the query can get a shared lock on (it will not do dirty reads). READ UNCOMMITTED is the same as the optimizer hint NOLOCK and will allow dirty reads on all queries during a particular session. Be careful with this option because you can view data that has not yet been committed in the database. REPEATABLE READ will not release shared locks until the transaction has been completed and is equivalent to the HOLDLOCK hint described earlier. It prevents updates and deletes of data you have read. Finally, SERIALIZABLE prevents not just updates and deletes of data you have read, it will also prevent inserts within the key range of any data you have read. Both REPEATABLE READ and SERIALIZABLE have dramatic effects on concurrency, and you should be very careful that you understand the consequences of using each of these before you implement them.

To view which isolation level is in force, use the DBCC USEROPTIONS command. Without having run the SET TRANSACTION ISOLATION LEVEL statement, you would see the following:

```
DBCC USEROPTIONS
GO

Set Option                      Value
-----------------------         ----------
textsize                        64512
language                        us_english
dateformat                      mdy
datefirst                       7
ansi_null_dflt_on               SET

(5 row(s) affected)

DBCC execution completed. If DBCC printed error messages,
 contact your system administrator.
```

Note the difference after turning on dirty reads with the READ UNCOMMITTED option:

INPUT/
OUTPUT

```
SET TRANSACTION ISOLATION LEVEL READ UNCOMMITTED
GO
DBCC USEROPTIONS
GO

Set Option                      Value
-----------------------         ----------
textsize                        64512
language                        us_english
dateformat                      mdy
datefirst                       7
```

```
ansi_null_dflt_on       SET
isolation level         read uncommitted

(6 row(s) affected)

DBCC execution completed. If DBCC printed error messages,
contact your system administrator.
```

16

Summary

In today's lesson you learned about transactions, distributed transactions, locks, batches, and scripts. You have seen how batches are used from the SQL Server Query Analyzer. You also examined scripts and saw that Microsoft provides several examples.

You have seen how to use transactions (and distributed transactions) to accomplish "units of work" with SQL Server. You have examined the ACID properties of a transaction to understand why they provide reliable and durable data consistency. You examined the three types of transactions: implicit, explicit, and automatic. Remember, implicit transactions can be dangerous if you're not prepared for them. The checkpoint process is used to periodically copy data from memory to disk. You can let SQL Server control the recovery interval, or you can adjust it yourself.

You also learned about locks, including the types of locks available in SQL Server 7.0, and examined the syntax for locks, how to override SQL Server's decision about when to use a particular kind of lock, and when the use of lock overrides is appropriate. Remember, the vast majority of the time SQL Server picks the correct choice, and you should be very conservative in overriding locks.

You have also learned how to observe locks using Transact-SQL and SQL Server Enterprise Manager. You have learned how to create a deadlock situation and how you can avoid them in the future.

Q&A

Q Is this a valid example of a batch?

```
BEGIN TRAN
    SELECT * FROM titles
    UPDATE titles set PRICE = $12.99 WHERE TITLE_ID = 'BU1032'
    ROLLBACK TRAN
    SELECT * FROM titles
COMMIT TRAN
```

A No. If you were to run the previous set of SQL statements, you would end up with the following error message:

```
Server: Msg 3902, Level 16, State 1
The COMMIT TRANSACTION request has no corresponding BEGIN
TRANSACTION.
```

This is because the transaction has been rolled back by the time the COMMIT TRAN is run.

Q **True or False? The COMMIT TRAN writes all modified pages in memory to disk.**

A False. The CHECKPOINT process writes modified pages from memory to database files in SQL Server (both data pages and log records). The COMMIT TRAN statement writes the modified LOG records for each transaction to the transaction log files for each database.

Q **What kind of locks are compatible with a shared lock?**

A Shared locks are compatible with shared locks and update locks. It doesn't matter whether they're row, page, or table locks. Extents and databases don't really get shared locks.

Q **What is it called when two transactions have an exclusive lock on a resource, and each of the other transactions needs to lock the resource the other transaction has locked?**

A A deadlock. Deadlocks can be avoided by accessing tables in the same sequence when you write separate processes—preferably in stored procedures.

Workshop

The Workshop provides quiz questions to help you solidify your understanding of the concepts presented in this chapter. In addition to the quiz questions, exercises are provided to let you practice what you have learned in this chapter. Try to understand the quiz and exercise answers before continuing to the next day's lesson. Answers are provided in Appendix A, "Answers."

Quiz

1. What CREATE statements are allowed within a single batch?
2. What locks will be held at the time of the COMMIT TRAN from the following batch?
3. How would I enable remote stored procedures to automatically be part of a distributed transaction at all times?
4. How would you cancel a transaction that you had begun with implicit transactions?

5. If you rolled back a transaction from within a trigger on table1 in the code listed here, would the SELECT * FROM AUTHORS be run?

```
BEGIN TRAN
INSERT table1 VALUES (3)
GO
SELECT * FROM AUTHORS
    COMMIT TRAN
```

Exercise

16

1. You have added a new book to your inventory (*How to Surf the Net in 3 Easy Steps*). Not only is the title new, but so is the publisher (waycool publishers) and the two authors (Ann Jackson and Bob Greene). Write a script to add all this information so it all completes or fails together.

DAY **17**

Understanding Replication Design and Methodologies

In yesterday's lesson you learned about the programming features of the Transact-SQL (T-SQL) language. You learned how to work with batches and scripts. You examined how locking is used in SQL Server for concurrency control. You also examined how to implement transactions in your SQL Server database.

In today's lesson you will learn about replication in SQL Server 7.0. You will learn what defines replication, why you might want to use replication, and what you might publish. You will also look at the different methods of data distribution and determine what best suits your needs. Replication uses a publisher/subscriber metaphor that is complete with articles and publications. You will learn about the different agents SQL Server uses to move your data from one location to another. You will then look at the different replication scenarios and examine the advantages of each. You will finish this day by taking a look at replicating data in heterogeneous environments.

Okay, that sounds like a lot; and you're right—it is a lot. You might also be asking your-self, "What about actually implementing a replication scenario?" Well, as to the first part, you must have a good foundation in what replication is, what it can accomplish, and what its uses are. As to the implementing, you'll learn about that in tomorrow's lesson. So now is a great time to get to work on replication.

What Is Replication?

Replication creates an environment that allows multiple copies of the same information to be distributed to multiple databases throughout your enterprise. Replication has the following benefits:

- Data is closer to the user.
- It removes the impact of read-intensive OLAP (online analytical processing) envi-ronments from the transaction-intensive OLTP (online transaction processing) envi-ronments.
- It reduces conflicts between multiple sites trying to work with the same informa-tion.
- Database sites can operate autonomously with the replicated data. This means that they can define their own rules, procedures, and views on their copy of the data.

There are two basic types of replication: replication and distributed transactions. Both types of replication allow you to keep the different copies of your data current. You can even use both strategies at the same time in your environment.

NEW TERM   *Replication* duplicates and distributes copies of your data to the different loca-tions in your environment. You can make these updates intermittently so you can keep those replicated sites more autonomous. The databases at each site don't have to be connected to the server publishing the data all the time. Replication can involve just moving transactions or moving an entire snapshot of the data.

Distributed Data Factors

There are many different factors to consider when you are trying to decide on a particu-lar method for distributing your data. These include site autonomy, transactional consis-tency, and latency.

NEW TERM   • Autonomy—Depends on the answers to the following questions: How much independence from the publishing database must your subscribing sites have? For how long is a version of the data at a subscription site good? How often do you need to connect to the publishing site and update your copy of the data?

- Transactional consistency—Refers to the transactions themselves. Do all the stored transactions need to be applied at the same time or not at all? If there is a delay in applying the transactions, but they are all processed in order, is this acceptable? Are the transactions being applied in a manner that docs not conflict with the consistency of your data?

- Latency—Refers to when the copies of the data are applied. Does your data need to be 100 percent in synch 100 percent of the time, or is it acceptable to have data update periodically? If you can have some latency, how big a lag is acceptable?

Before you get into the various distribution methodologies, keep some of the following in mind when you are trying to decide where and what to publish:

- What am I going to publish? Do the subscribers receive all the data or just subsets of my data? Should my data be partitioned by region values or zip codes? Should I allow subscribers of my data to send me updates? If I do allow updates, how should they be implemented?

- Who can have access to my data? Are these users online or offline? Are they across the country and connected with expensive phone lines?

- How often should I synchronize my data with the subscribers? How often do they get changes sent to them?

- What does the network look like? Is the network fast? Should I do more partitioning of data to minimize replication-bound traffic? Is the network reliable? Are all nodes in the network available at all times?

Now take a look at the different distribution methodologies that take these factors and put them into practice.

Distribution Methodologies

Keeping latency, transactional consistency, and site autonomy in mind, there are several different methods you can use to implement replication in SQL Server. In this section, you take a closer look at distribution methodologies and determine which methodology is most applicable in a given scenario.

Three basic types of replication can be combined to various degrees to create a total of six different methodologies. The replication types are transactional replication, snapshot replication, and merge replication. When you add in latency, transactional consistency, and site autonomy, you get the following methods of data distribution:

- Merge replication
- Snapshot replication
- Snapshot replication with updating subscribers
- Transactional replication
- Transactional replication with updating subscribers
- Distributed transactions

Take a closer look at each of these different methodologies and how you can determine which is best for you based on autonomy, latency, and transactional consistency.

Merge Replication

Merge replication has the highest amount of site autonomy. It can also afford the most latency, but it has the lowest amount of transactional consistency.

Merge replication allows each site to make changes to its local copy of the replicated data. At some point in time, the changes from the site are sent up to the publishing database, where they are merged with changes from other sites. Sooner or later, all sites will receive the updates from all the other sites. This is known as data convergence. The changes from all the sites will converge, and sooner or later all sites will have the same information, as shown in Figures 17.1 and 17.2.

FIGURE 17.1

Modified records converge at the publishing server.

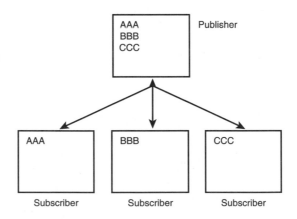

FIGURE 17.2

Converged records are sent back to all subscribers.

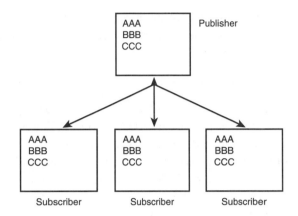

Transactional consistency is thrown out the window here because different sites might be updating data at different times. A particular site does not wait for its updates to be sent to every other site before continuing its work. In other words, every site is guaranteed to converge to the same resultsets but not necessarily at the same time.

It is possible with merge replication to generate conflicts. For example, Site A makes some changes to record number 27. Site B also makes changes to record number 27. They both send their versions of data back to the publishing server. The publishing server now sees that both of them made changes to record number 27. Which version of record 27 is the right one? Is it the version that was modified first? Is it the version that was modified last? What about other dependencies? For example, if changes in record 27 are based on data found in record 26, and record 26 is different on both machines, which one is correct? Determining the right answer can be a complex task. You will take a closer look at this a little later in this chapter.

Who should use merge replication? Good question. Because of the potential conflicts that can occur, merge replication is better suited to environments in which the chances of these conflicts are minimized. For example, sites that tend to make changes to their records only (indicated by a location ID in each record), but need the information from all the other locations, are good candidates for merge replication.

For example, you might create a database that tracks the criminal history of individuals. A large state like Alaska, where every little town might like to have a copy of this criminal history but can't afford to be in contact with the central database at all times, might be an excellent location to implement merge replication. Each town would be autonomous, and latency could be very high. The local police or sheriff could add new criminal information to the database and then send it back to headquarters to be merged with data from many other towns. There might still be conflicts if a criminal is moving

17

from town to town and causing problems, but these conflicts can be detected and the appropriate records can be updated—ahem, converged—and sent back to all the little towns.

Snapshot Replication

In snapshot replication, an entire copy of the items to be replicated is copied from the publishing server to the subscribing database, as shown in Figure 17.3. This type of replication is the easiest to set up and maintain. Snapshot replication has a high level of site autonomy. It also guarantees transactional consistency because all transactions are applied at the publication server only. The site autonomy can be very useful for locations that need read-only versions of the data and don't mind a higher amount of latency. When you are using snapshot replication, the subscription database should consider the replicated data as read-only. This is because any changes made to the data will not be sent back to the publication database. In addition, all changes that might have been made to the data will be wiped out when the next snapshot is downloaded.

FIGURE 17.3

Snapshots of the entire data set are sent to each subscriber. Changes to the data can take place only at the publishing server.

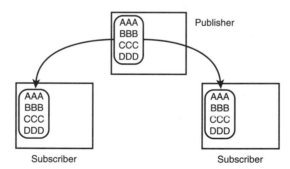

OLAP servers are excellent candidates for snapshot replication. The ad-hoc queries that management information systems (MIS) administrators apply to data are generally read-only, and data that is several hours or even several days old does not affect their queries. For example, a company MIS department might want to do some research on the demographics of items sold two months ago. Information from last week, or even today, won't make any difference in its queries. Furthermore, the department isn't planning to make changes to the data; it just needs the data warehouse. The site autonomy allows the MIS department to implement additional indexes on the data without affecting the OLTP publication database.

Snapshot Replication with Updating Subscribers

Snapshot replication with updating subscribers is an interesting animal. It combines snapshot replication, as described in the last section, with 2PC.

With this methodology, you have a certain amount of autonomy because the subscription database does not have to be in contact with the publishing database at all times. The only time the subscriber is working with the publisher is when a snapshot is being downloaded or the subscriber is using 2PC to update a transaction at both the local (subscription) location and the publishing database, as shown in Figure 17.4.

FIGURE 17.4

Snapshots are sent to each subscriber at regular intervals. For a subscriber to make a local change to replicated data, the same change must be successfully applied at the publisher or no change is allowed.

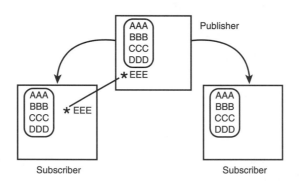

This also maintains a high degree of transactional consistency because transactions must be applied at both the subscription database and the publication database. The fact that other subscribers might have made changes to the publication database since your subscriber last downloaded a snapshot is irrelevant. The consistency is maintained by the fact that the transaction will fail on the publication server if the data being modified at both the publisher and subscriber are different. This works even with the latency-involved snapshot replication.

The subscription server can immediately begin working with the changed data because it knows that it has successfully updated the publication server. The publication server will converge the information, and in time all servers involved in the replication will receive the changes.

This methodology is useful in scenarios in which few but occasional modifications take place at the subscription servers. The longer the latency, the more likely that your 2PC will fail. This is because there is a better chance that the data at the publisher has been changed, but has not yet been replicated to the subscriber.

Transactional Replication

In transactional replication, the transactions are sent from the publisher to the subscribers. This type of replication is one way. The only way a subscriber can make changes to data is directly to the publishing database. The changes will then be replicated back down to the subscriber at the next synchronization, as shown in Figure 17.5.

FIGURE 17.5

In transactional replication, changes can be made only at the publisher. The changes (transactions) are then applied at each subscriber.

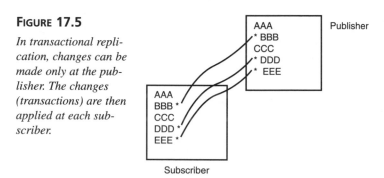

This type of replication allows for a medium amount of autonomy. The subscriber should treat the replicated data as read-only. This is important because changes made on the replicated data might not allow the future replicated transactions to be performed. There is generally a medium amount of latency involved in this type of replication as well. The subscriber does not have to be in touch with the publisher at all times, but regular synchronizations are useful, and the amount of data being moved is relatively small. Remember that snapshot replication must move all the published data from the publisher to the subscriber (whether or not it has been modified). In transactional replication, only the transactions that were performed are sent to the subscribers. This type of replication was used primarily in SQL Server 6.5. In SQL Server 6.5, you did not have the option of using any type of merge replication.

Transactional replication is most useful in scenarios in which the subscribers can treat their data as read-only, but they need changes to the data with a minimal amount of latency. An excellent example of transactional replication is found in an order-processing/distribution system. In this type of scenario, you might have several different publishing sites taking orders for goods. These orders are then replicated to a central distribution warehouse where pick tickets are created and the orders are filled and shipped. The warehouse can treat the data as read-only, and needs new information in a timely manner.

Transactional Replication with Updating Subscribers

With transactional replication with updating subscribers you lose even more autonomy at the subscription sites, but you minimize latency. With this methodology, you use the transactional replication described in the last section with 2PC.

When a subscription database attempts to make changes to data, the change is also written to the publishing database in a 2PC. This means that the change is written to both the subscriber and the publisher at the same time. Because of this, you have guaranteed transactional consistency. The change will then be converged with other updating subscribers and then sent back out to all the subscription databases.

This has less latency than using snapshot replication with updating subscribers because the transactions being replicated are much smaller (and quicker to move) than synchronizing an entire snapshot of your data.

Useful scenarios for this type of replication include low-volume reservation systems. In this type of system, a subscriber can look through a schedule of availability and then attempt to make a reservation. After the reservation has been scheduled, it can be replicated within a few minutes (or however long you determine) to all the other subscription databases. This updates all their schedules. You might be thinking to yourself, "Yeah that looks good, but what if I try to make a reservation that someone else already has booked, but that booking hasn't been replicated to this subscriber yet?" Remember that because this type of replication uses 2PC, you know that if your reservation is successfully committed, it was available and you didn't overwrite anyone else's reservations.

Distributed Transactions

Distributed transactions were available in SQL Server 6.5 and are still available in SQL Server 7.0. Distributed transactions, or 2PC, have almost no autonomy, no latency, and guaranteed transactional consistency.

As described earlier, changes are either all replicated simultaneously or not at all. This type of replication takes advantage of the MS DTC (Microsoft distributed transaction coordinator), which implements the 2PC protocol and applies transactions at all sites simultaneously.

Because every subscriber must be in contact with the publisher and each other at all times, this leaves little autonomy and no latency. This type of replication is useful in scenarios in which everyone must have real-time versions of the data.

High-volume reservation systems can take advantage of this type of replication. For example, an airline reservation system would find this type of replication very useful. Subscribers are off-site and reduce some of the workload on the publication server. The

17

guaranteed transactional consistency is displayed when a person in New York tries to get seat 2A on flight 2400 and another person in Idaho tries to get the same seat on the same flight. Only one of them will be able to book the seat, and the one who doesn't get the booking will know immediately.

The Publisher/Subscriber Metaphor

In case you haven't gathered already, replication in SQL Server 7.0 uses a publisher/subscriber metaphor. Just like a real publisher, several different pieces play a role in this metaphor. There are one or more publishers and subscribers, and a distributor.

A SQL server in your enterprise can play any or all of these roles simultaneously. The way in which you implement these roles gives you the different replication models, which you will learn about a little later.

NEW TERM   The *publisher* is the owner of the source database information. The publisher will make data available for replication and will send changes to the published data to the distributor.

NEW TERM   The *subscriber* database receives copies of the data (snapshot replication) or transactions held in the distribution database.

NEW TERM   The *distributor* receives all changes made to published data. It then stores the data and forwards it to subscribers at the appropriate time. A single distribution server can support multiple publishers and multiple subscribers at the same time.

To continue the publisher/subscriber metaphor, a publishing database creates articles. Articles are then bundled together to create a publication. Take a closer look at articles and publications.

Articles

An *article* is a single table or subset of data in a table. Articles are bundled together into publications. To publish a subset of data in an article, you must use some type of filtering to partition data in your table. You can use vertical partitions, horizontal partitions, or both, as shown in Figure 17.6. A vertical partition selects only certain columns from the table, whereas a horizontal partition selects only certain rows from the table. In addition to using SQL statements to create your articles, you can also use stored procedures.

Figure 17.6

Data partitioning.

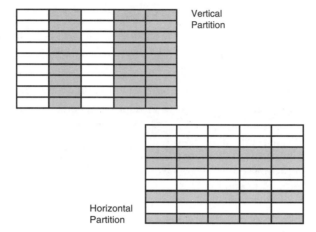

You can partition tables horizontally, vertically, or both. Each of these partitioned tables will become a single article that can then be subscribed to. You might find it more useful to actually change the physical implementation of your tables. For example, you might have a sales_info table that services three different regions. If you physically redesign your database, you can implement three separate sales_info tables (one for each region).

There are some data definition issues to consider when you are creating articles in your publications.

Data Definition Considerations

There are a few rules to keep in mind when you are creating your articles:

- IDENTITY columns are replicated, but the property is not. When an initial synchronization occurs, the values in the IDENTITY column are copied as integer values.

- Timestamp data types (which are different from date/time data types) are used to indicate the sequence of SQL Server activity on a row of data. They provide a history or lineage of changes made to that row. These values are replicated as binary data types.

- Uniqueidentifier creates GUIDs (globally unique identifiers). These are 128-bit IDs and are used with merge replication. These make it possible for each row to be uniquely identified even if you are converging rows from two separate tables. You can use the NEWID function to generate a GUID. The data type will be replicated, but the function will not.

- User-defined data types can be replicated only if they also exist in the subscription database.

Working with the IDENTITY Property

There are some special considerations when you are working with the IDENTITY property. Remember that C columns are changed to binary numbers on the subscribers. This occurs so that subscriber and publisher information matches. If you want to partition your tables at the subscription site, you'll want to add a new IDENTITY column. If you decide to do this, you'll have to use seed values and CHECK constraints to avoid any conflicts with transactions that are coming in. You can also use the uniqueidentifier data type with the NEWID function to guarantee unique keys.

When you get into scenarios in which you have multiple publishers and subscribers of the same information, you might want to allow subscribers to change data from their local region only but still view data from other regions. This is accomplished with the NOT FOR REPLICATION statement. You use the NOT FOR REPLICATION statements when you initially create an IDENTITY property, CHECK constraint, or trigger.

You can use NOT FOR REPLICATION statements when you add data at the subscriber. The CHECK constraint or trigger can fire off and make sure that the data you are modifying at the subscriber is owned by that particular subscriber. In this fashion, you can maintain referential integrity because a subscriber can add a local record with a valid IDENTITY column value. This IDENTITY column value will then be replicated as a binary number, as discussed earlier.

Publications

Publications are made up of one or more articles and are the basis for a subscription. When you create a subscription, you are subscribing to an entire publication. When you have subscribed to a publication, you can then "read" individual articles. You can maintain referential integrity with publications because all articles in a single publication are synchronized at the same time. You can create as many publications per database as you like.

When you work with publications and subscriptions, you can set up either push or pull subscriptions. The real difference between these two methods of data transfer is where the administration of the subscription is taking place.

Note

> You can publish to non-SQL servers and even implement replication on articles that have a different sort order and data type; however, this is not recommended.

There are some other publishing restrictions you should be aware of:

- Tables must have a primary key to ensure integrity. (The exception is when you are using snapshot replication.)
- You cannot replicate the following databases:
  - master
  - model
  - msdb
  - tempdb
  - distribution databases
- Publications might not span multiple databases. Each publication can contain articles from one database only.
- IMAGE, TEXT, and NTEXT data have limited support. Transactional and merge replication cannot detect changes in these values because they are stored separately from the tables and not logged when they are changed. The only type of replication that works with these data types is snapshot replication. You can schedule snapshots of your tables (including these fields) to occur on a regular schedule. This is often referred to as a scheduled table refresh.

Push Subscriptions

When you set up a subscription at the same time that you create your publications, you are essentially setting up for a push subscription. This helps to centralize subscription administration because the subscription is defined at the publisher along with the subscribers' synchronization schedule. All the administration of the subscription is handled from the publisher. The data is "pushed" to the subscriber when the publisher decides to send it.

 Note You can set up multiple subscribers at the same time when you are working with push subscriptions.

Push subscriptions are most useful when your subscribers need updates sent to them as soon as they occur. Push subscriptions also allow for a higher level of security as the publisher deems who is allowed to subscribe and when. Push subscriptions do take some additional overhead at the distribution database because it does the replication management.

Pull Subscriptions

A pull subscription is set up from each individual subscriber. The subscribers initiate the transfer of information on a timely basis. This is useful for applications that can allow for a lower level of security. The publisher can allow certain subscribers to pull information, or the publisher can allow anonymous subscriptions. Pull subscriptions are also useful in situations in which there might be a large number of subscribers. Internet-based solutions are good candidates for pull subscriptions.

 Note

> Only SQL Server subscribers can pull subscriptions. Other databases like Access, Oracle, and Sybase can use SQL Server 7.0 replication, but only in a push subscription scenario.

How Does Replication Work?

How does replication actually work? I'm glad you asked. Replication might seem very complex on the surface, but when you break it down into its component parts, it's not too bad. Essentially, replication is handled by four different agents. Each agent has its own specialized job to do. When you put all the agents together, you get replication. The following are the agents:

- Distribution agent—Moves information from the distribution database to the subscribers.
- Log reader agent—Monitors the transaction log of all published databases that are using it for replication. When it finds transactions that are part of a publication, it copies them to the distribution database where they can then be applied to the subscribers by the distribution agent.
- Merge agent—Merges modifications from multiple sites.
- Snapshot agent—Moves a snapshot of the data before replication can begin. This is required. If a snapshot of the data does not exist at the subscriber, you cannot apply transactions to the subscriber. It is also used for the various types of snapshot replication.

Now take a closer look at how each agent differs in its task when faced with the different replication methodologies covered earlier. Keep in mind that a replication methodology is applied at the individual publication level and that each subscriber can take advantage of different methodologies that have been applied to different publications.

How Does Merge Replication Work?

In merge replication, the merge agent can live on the distribution server or on each subscription server. In a push scenario, the merge agent lives on the distribution server. In pull scenarios, the agent lives on each subscriber. Figure 17.7 outlines the replication process presented in the following steps:

1. The snapshot agent (which lives on the distribution server) takes an initial snapshot of the data and moves it to the subscribers. Remember that the subscribers must first be synchronized with the publishers for replication to begin (with the exception of snapshot replication).

FIGURE 17.7

The merge replication process.

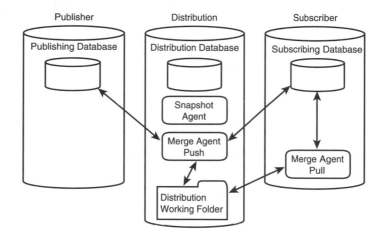

2. A distribution working folder is created on the distribution server to handle merges.

3. Replication now begins.

4. The merge agent takes modifications from the publishers and applies them to the subscribers.

5. The merge agent takes modifications from the subscribers and applies them to the publishers.

6. The merge agent receives any update conflicts and takes the appropriate action.

Note

Merge replication is best used when there are few chances for changes to be made to the same records by different locations.

Horizontally segmented tables are useful with merge replication. You can have separate publications created and subscribed to based on a region code or some other discriminatory mechanism.

For merge replication to work properly, some changes are made to the table schema as well as the distribution database. These changes are made to allow SQL Server to perform conflict resolution. Keep the following schema changes in mind when you decide to use merge replication:

- System tables are added to the distribution working folder. These are used to track changes for use during synchronization as well as for conflict resolution.
- SQL Server creates triggers on both the publishing servers and the subscription servers involved in merge replication. These triggers are fired when a data modification occurs in one of the tables involved in replication. Information about the change is stored in the system tables added to the distribution working folder. These saved changes allow you to track changes to each row or column of modified information.
- SQL Server creates a new `uniqueidentifier` column for each row in tables being replicated. A GUID or ROWGUID is then added to uniquely identify that row. In this fashion, when a record is updated at different sources, the different updates can be differentiated.

> **Note**
>
> Remember that you cannot vertically partition information when you are using merge replication.

When you allow updates to the same data to occur at multiple locations, you are going to run into conflicts. To resolve these conflicts, SQL Server does the following.

The system tables that are stored in the distribution working folder are used to track every change to a row. Each row's changes are listed and each entry has a ROWGUID. This history of modifications to a record is called the record's lineage.

NEW TERM   *Lineage* is a history of changes made to a row involved in merge replication. Changes are identified by a ROWGUID attached to the row and stored in the distribution working folder on the distribution server.

Using the lineage, the merge agent can evaluate both the current values and the arriving values and automatically resolve conflicts based on priorities you have assigned. You can customize these priorities, which are stored as triggers, to create your own conflict resolution process. You learn more about this in tomorrow's lesson, Day 18, "Implementing Replication Methodologies."

> **Tip**
>
> Remember that SQL Server 7.0 allows multiple triggers to be defined on a single table. Your conflict resolution scheme can be very complex.
>
> I suggest you pick a record to be the current record and then save both records in a separate table for a manual review. In this fashion you can test the quality of your resolution conflict process.

After you pick a record, the synchronization process continues and the whole cycle repeats itself.

Snapshot Replication Internals

Remember that snapshot replication copies the entire article or publication wholesale from the publisher to the subscriber. This includes snapshot replication with updating subscribers. The updates are done at both the subscriber and the publisher, but when a synchronization occurs the subscriber's data is completely overwritten by the incoming replicated article.

In snapshot replication there is no merge agent; however, the distribution agent is used. If you are using a pull subscription, the distribution agent is found on the subscription server. If you are using a push subscription, the distribution agent is located on the distribution server. Using a push or pull subscription in this type of scenario depends on many factors, not the least of which is how busy your distribution server is and how you want to manage subscriptions. Do you want to manage subscriptions centrally (push subscription), or do you want to manage subscriptions at each subscriber (pull subscriptions)?

Figure 17.8 outlines the snapshot replication process presented in the following steps:

1. The snapshot agent reads the published article and creates the table schema and data in the distribution working folder.

FIGURE 17.8

Snapshot replication process.

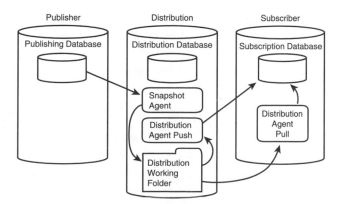

17

2. The distribution agent reads these schema and rebuilds the tables on the subscriber.

3. The distribution agent then moves the data into the newly created tables on the subscriber.

4. Indexes (if used) are then re-created on the newly synchronized subscription database.

Note

Snapshot replication occurs on demand. This means that the snapshot of the data is not stored in the distribution database, as occurs with the store-and-forward algorithm used in transaction-based replication.

Only status information about a snapshot is stored in the distribution database. The snapshot agent and the distribution agent do all the work at the time the synchronization is initiated.

Transaction Replication Internals

Remember that transaction-based replication copies just the transactions that occurred in the published databases to the distribution database. The updates are then applied to the subscription database generally as they occur. This reduces latency. The subscription database should be thought of as read-only because this type of replication is one-way. Changes to the data can be made only at the publisher.

Note

Although you should think of the subscription database as read-only, don't set the read-only database option to true. If you do, you will not be able to apply replicated transactions to it.

In transaction-based replication, there isn't a merge agent anymore; however, there is a log reader agent. Keep in mind that the snapshot agent is still around as well. You must have a basis for applying your transactions, and the snapshot agent accomplishes this for you. As in snapshot replication, the distribution agent is used. If you are using a pull subscription, the distribution agent is found on the subscription server. If you are using a push subscription, the distribution agent is located on the distribution server.

Figure 17.9 outlines the transaction replication process presented in the following steps:

1. The snapshot agent reads the published article and creates the table schema and data in the distribution working folder in the same manner as shown in Figure 17.8.

2. The distribution agent reads these schema and builds the tables on the subscriber.

FIGURE 17.9

Transaction replication process.

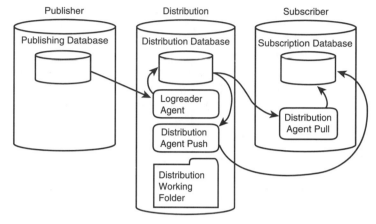

3. The distribution agent then moves the data into the newly created tables on the subscriber.

4. Indexes (if used) are then re-created on the newly synchronized subscription database.

5. Now normal transactional replication can begin.

6. The log reader agent watches the transaction logs of the publishing databases. When it finds a transaction, it moves the transaction to the distribution database, where it will be stored until the next synchronization process begins.

7. When the synchronization process is called (either by a push from the distributor or a pull from a subscriber), the transaction is read by the distribution agent and then applied to the subscription database.

Note

Transaction replication is commonly used when you want a minimal amount of latency and you can consider your subscription database as read-only. This type of scenario is useful when you want to remove the impact of OLAP services from your OLTP servers.

Replication Scenarios

Replication can be implemented in various scenarios. Each scenario has benefits for a given business situation. Take a look at the different scenarios and their associated benefits.

Central Publisher

In the central publisher scenario, shown in Figure 17.10, you can reduce the impact of OLAP services from the OLTP environment. In this scenario, the publishing server is also the distribution server. Keep in mind that the more subscribers you have, the larger the impact will be on the distribution server. This impact can be reduced somewhat by using a pull subscription in which the distribution agent resides on each subscriber.

FIGURE 17.10

Central publisher replication scenario.

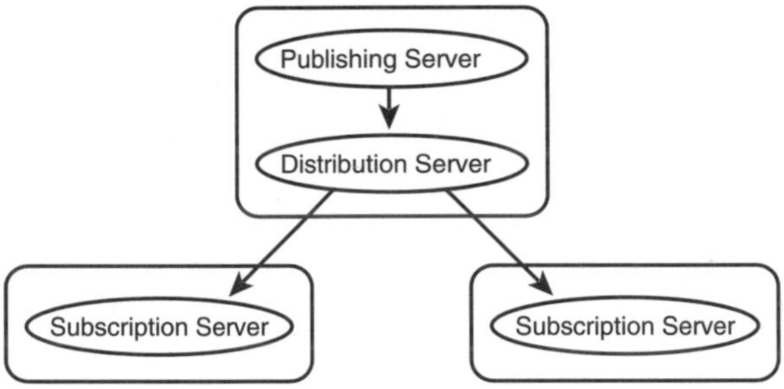

Although the distribution database lives on the publication server, it can support multiple publication servers and multiple subscription servers.

Central Publisher with a Remote Distributor

In the central publisher with a remote distributor scenario, you can further reduce the impact of the distribution database on your high-volume OLTP environment by moving it to its own server, as shown in Figure 17.11. As before, a single distribution server can support multiple publishers and multiple subscribers. This is the preferred scenario when you have situations with multiple publishers and subscribers.

FIGURE 17.11

Central publisher with a remote distributor scenario.

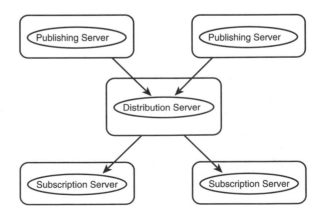

Publishing Subscriber

In the publishing subscriber scenario, your subscription server is also a publishing server. This can be very beneficial when you have a slow and expensive link (regular telephone lines) between the main publisher and a group of subscribers (see Figure 17.12). In this scenario, the subscriber also acts as a publisher for a series of subscription databases. In this manner, you can minimize the cost of your slow link by updating a single subscriber and then republishing the newly synchronized information to the rest of the subscription servers.

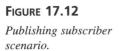

FIGURE 17.12

Publishing subscriber scenario.

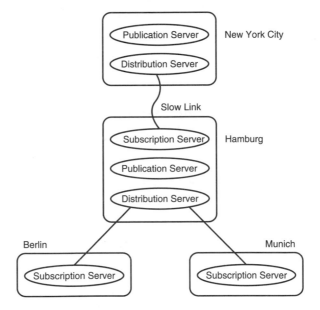

17

In Figure 17.12, your main publishing database is located in New York City. You can now synchronize on a schedule that minimizes your phone line costs to the main subscriber in Hamburg. Hamburg can then redistribute that data more locally to the Berlin and Munich locations.

Central Subscriber

In the central subscriber scenario, your subscription server is centrally located and one or more publishing servers sends it updates. This is useful for rollup reporting situations or central processing. For example, Figure 17.13 shows a central publisher scenario in which branch offices in Seattle, Los Angeles, and Detroit (the publishers) send orders to the Denver location. From the Denver location, these orders are then processed and the product is shipped.

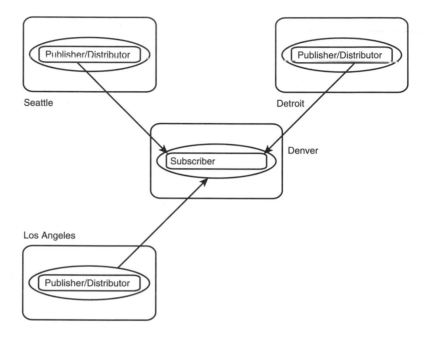

FIGURE 17.13

Central subscriber scenario.

To differentiate between orders coming from different locations, you should make some schema changes to your data as outlined here:

- Add a separate RegionCode column to your orders table.
- Make the new RegionCode column part of the primary key.

By creating a RegionCode column and making it part of your primary key, you can avoid conflicts. For example, what would happen if Los Angeles had an order number 2000 and Detroit also had an order number 2000? When they are both applied at the subscriber, there will be a conflict. By adding the region code, you now have a primary key that might look like 2 2000 for Los Angeles and 3 2000 for Detroit, as shown in Figure 17.14.

The central subscriber scenario lends itself well to a transaction-based replication. Each location that orders an item will have the item order replicated to the central location where it will be processed and shipped.

FIGURE 17.14

You should use some type of region code to differentiate rows of data coming from separate locations in the central subscriber scenario.

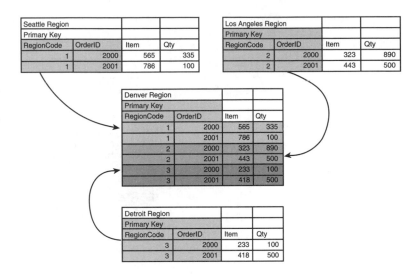

Multiple Publishers and Subscribers

Multiple publishers and subscribers are useful for reservation-type systems or any other system in which information about other regions must be available at each region. I like to look at an example of 800 call centers. When you dial an 800 number to order a particular product or to check on the status of an order, your call might be routed to any of the geographically dispersed call centers around the country. Figure 17.15 shows call centers in Bend, Boulder, and Atlanta. Each of these call centers must have information that might have been gathered at another call center. This is to support customers who want to check on the status of orders.

In a reservation-type system, you can implement this form of replication as well. I suggest you use distributed transactions to do this so that all locations have the same data at the same time. (You wouldn't want to double-book an airline reservation or hotel room, would you?)

17

FIGURE 17.15

Multiple publishers and subscribers sce nario.

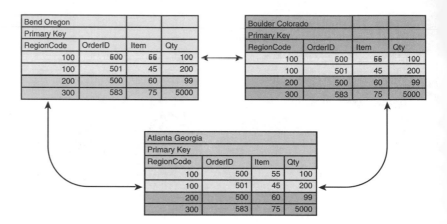

As shown in Figure 17.15, each location is both a publisher and a subscriber of information. Each shop subscribes to the other shops' published articles. Each shop should only publish articles it owns. In other words, use a `RegionCode` field to differentiate data owned by one or more shops. In this way, you avoid the conflicts discussed in the central subscriber section. For this to work properly, each shop should update data from its own location only. If you are going to use an updating subscriber type of scenario here, make sure you make your updates to all sites simultaneously to avoid conflicts.

Publishing SQL Server 7.0 Databases to the Internet

To enable publishing of your SQL Server database to the Internet, you must take care of some additional configuration changes. When you are working with both push and pull subscriptions, you must have the following configuration:

- Transmission Control Protocol/Internet Protocol (TCP/IP) must be enabled and installed on the computers running the distribution agent and the merge agent and any computers connected to the computers running these agents.

- Your publishing server and your distribution server should have a direct network connection other than through the Internet. This is not only for security but also to handle potential problems with latency.

- Your publishing server and your distribution server should be on the same side of the firewall (preferably the secure side of the firewall).

If you are going to allow pull subscriptions from the Internet, you must make the following additional configuration changes to your servers:

- IIS (Internet Information Server) must be installed on the same server as your distribution server.

- The merge agent and the distribution agent must be configured with the correct file transfer protocol (FTP) address. (The FTP address can be configured through the distribution agent utility or from a command prompt on the distribution server.)

- The FTP home folder on your IIS machine should be set to the distribution working folder (usually \\ComputerName\C$\MSSQL7\Repldata).

- The working folder must be available to your subscription servers.

Best Practices

To help ensure the best performance, keep the following items in mind when determining the type of replication you are going to use and the scenario you want to implement:

- Ensure network speed and availability.

- Immediately updating subscribers can be useful when there is sufficient network bandwidth.

- Publish partitioned data. There is no need to always send all the information all the time. Give the subscribers what they need and reduce network and distribution overhead.

- Pull subscriptions can take much of the workload off the distribution server. Remember that you will lose your centralized management of replication but gain some performance.

- Use a remote distributor in your scenarios. This can move the bulk of the workload involved in replication from your OLTP database. This is also a useful tool if you have a slow and expensive link between your distribution server and your subscription servers.

- Minimize updating conflicts by minimizing the chance for them to occur when you are using merge replication or updating subscribers.

- In merge replication or updating subscribers, make sure you include a region code as part of your primary key.

Replicating Issues in a Heterogeneous Environment

SQL Server 7.0 supports replication in a heterogeneous environment. This means you can use a SQL Server 7.0 publisher to send publications subscribers through open database connectivity (ODBC) and object linking and embedding database (OLE DB) drivers. In certain instances, you can even use SQL Server 7.0 as a subscriber to a non-SQL Server publisher.

Replication is supported on Windows 9x and Windows NT platforms. Replication to other platforms is supported through the use of the appropriate ODBC or OLE DB drivers and communications software. SQL Server 7.0 supports replication to Microsoft Access, Oracle, and any other database that complies with the SQL Server ODBC subscriber requirements. SQL Server ships with drivers for Oracle, Access, and IBM's Distributed Relational Database Architecture (DRDA) data protocol.

SQL Server 7.0 ODBC Subscriber Driver Requirements

The ODBC subscriber driver must

- Support ODBC Level 1 conformance
- Support T-SQL DDL (data definition language)
- Run in 32-bit mode
- Be thread-safe
- Allow updates

Publishing Data to Non-SQL Server 7.0 Databases

There are several things to keep in mind when you are trying to publish data to heterogeneous subscribers. Keep these points in mind when attempting to replicate to non-SQL Server 7.0 ODBC subscribers:

- SQL Server 7.0 does not support pull subscriptions. You must use push subscriptions from a SQL Server 7.0 publisher.
- Batched statements are not supported to ODBC subscribers.
- Data types are mapped to the closest data type available on the subscription database. For example, Microsoft Access has no concept of a text field. Access would receive a replicated text field as an Access memo data type.
- The ODBC DSN (data source name) must conform to SQL Server's naming rules for identifiers.

- When you are using snapshots, the data to be transferred will use the bulk copy program (BCP) character format. The BCP utility was discussed in detail on Day 10, "Using SQL Server 7.0 Data Transformation Services."

Non-SQL Server 7.0 Databases Publishing to SQL Server 7.0

It is possible for third-party databases to become publishers in the SQL Server 7.0 environment. To accomplish this, you must write a program that takes advantage of the SQL-DMO (SQL Database Management Objects). After you have created your programs to do this, you will be able to support all the various replication features found in SQL Server 7.0.

The SQL-DMO exposes the following COM (Component Object Model) objects for use in replication:

- Objects for replication administration
- Objects for replication monitoring
- Objects to take advantage of the distribution agent to forward transactions to subscription servers
- Objects to work with the distribution database for storage of replicated transactions
- SQL Server performance counters, several of which are grouped into the SQL Server performance objects and displayed in the SQL Performance Monitor
- Objects to expose your publisher to the SQL Enterprise Manager for graphical administration

17

Summary

In today's lesson you have learned about the replication methodologies in SQL Server 7.0. You covered information about what defines replication. You also learned about the three prime factors in determining what type of replication to use. These include autonomy for the subscribers, transactional consistency, and latency.

You then learned the distribution methodologies. These include merge replication, where both subscribers and publishers are able to update data. You then looked at snapshot replication. Snapshot replication is the easiest type of replication to install and maintain because the entire publication is transferred all at once. Remember that with snapshot replication, data at the subscriber is considered read-only.

You then looked at snapshot replication with updating subscribers. Remember that the updating subscribers do this through the use of 2PC (2-phase commit). You then learned about transactional replication, which is the most popular form of replication. Again, subscription information is considered read-only. Transactional replication with updating subscribers also takes advantage of the 2PC protocol to make updates at both the subscriber and publisher. Finally, you looked at distributed transactions. Distributed transactions work through the 2PC protocol and take advantage of the Microsoft Distributed Transaction Coordinator, which is part of the Microsoft Transaction Server. With distributed transactions, all sites are updated at the same time, or none of them are.

There are four types of replication agents that work in SQL Server. Each agent has its own set of tasks and responsibilities. The merge agent is responsible for handling conflict resolution and converging your records. The snapshot agent moves snapshots of your data from a publisher to a subscriber. The distribution agent moves transactions from the distribution database to the subscribers. The log reader agent handles transactional replication and monitors the transaction logs of replicated databases. When it finds transactions, it moves them to the distribution database where the distribution agent takes over. You also covered several different replication scenarios. SQL Server 7.0 supports replication in heterogeneous environments. This includes support for Access, Oracle, and any ODBC- or OLE DB-compliant database that also supports the SQL Server ODBC subscriber conformance issues.

All in all it was a long day. Congratulations on finishing it up. In tomorrow's lesson you will implement several different types of replication in SQL Server.

Q&A

Q Which is most important: transactional consistency, latency, or autonomy?

A Generally speaking, transactional consistency is of utmost importance. Latency and site autonomy are really up to you, but having the correct data should be the most important issue. Keep in mind that only merge replication has a chance to lose transactional consistency. All other types of replication support full transactional consistency.

Q Which type of replication do you see the most often?

A Currently, transactional replication is most common. This is because SQL Server 6.5 supported only transactional replication and distributed transactions. Transactional replication with updating subscribers will probably become the most popular form of replication because it supports transactional consistency, a reasonable level of site autonomy, and a low level of latency. It really is the best of all worlds.

Q How hard is it to modify the conflict resolution triggers?

A They are not too difficult. They are just triggers with code in them. When you feel good enough about programming in SQL Server, these triggers should be a snap. You can implement your triggers to move both the chosen version of a record as well as the unchosen version of the conflicting record to a separate table and evaluate how well your trigger code is working. Also keep in mind that because you are coding it, you can make the conflict resolution process as picky as you want it to be. The old magic 8-ball can help you decide which version of a conflicting record to update and which one to toss out (grin).

Q How does this ROWGUID thing work? What is it?

A A ROWGUID is a 128-bit unique identifier. It is alleged to be a globally unique number. SQL Server uses an algorithm that generates these numbers based on many factors. ROWGUIDs are commonly added to tables marked for merge replication. Using these ROWGUIDs, you can track the history or lineage of changes made to a particular record.

Q Can the distribution server support all the different types of replication at the same time?

A Yes. In fact, you can set up publications and subscriptions on the same servers that use different types of replication on a per-publication basis.

Workshop

The Workshop provides quiz questions to help you solidify your understanding of the concepts presented in this chapter. In addition to the quiz questions, exercises are provided to let you practice what you have learned in this chapter. Try to understand the quiz and exercise answers before continuing to the next day's lesson. Answers are provided in Appendix A, "Answers."

Quiz

1. Which agent reads the transaction log of published databases and then moves the data to the distribution database?

2. What does the distribution agent do?

3. What replication scenario is best suited to doing rollup reporting?

4. Where does the merge agent reside in a push subscription with merge replication?

Exercise

1. In this exercise, determine the best replication scenario to use given the following facts:

   - You have four sites in the United States that handle order processing. You have a central warehouse located in Wichita, Kansas, that must have pick tickets made up so that merchandise can be shipped.

   - You have three sites located in Great Britain that handle MIS duties and other types of administration. The British sites must have copies of all the records of shipped items and the orders placed for them.

   - The British locations do not want to have a dedicated line to the United States because it is deemed far too expensive.

DAY 18

Implementing Replication Methodologies

Yesterday's lesson was long, with many issues that readers new to SQL Server might have found confusing. Take a few minutes here to review what you covered.

You learned about the replication methodologies in SQL Server 7.0. You also learned about the three prime factors in determining what type of replication to use. The types included autonomy for the subscribers, transactional consistency, and latency. You then covered the distribution methodologies. These included merge replication where both subscribers and publishers are able to update data. You then looked at snapshot replication. Recall that snapshot replication is the easiest type of replication to install and maintain because the entire publication is transferred all at once. Remember that with snapshot replication, data at the subscriber level is considered read-only.

You then looked at snapshot replication with updating subscribers. Remember that the updating subscribers make updates at both the subscription database and the publishing database simultaneously, using 2PC (2 phase-commit).

You then looked at transactional replication, where subscription information is considered read-only. Transactional replication with updating subscribers also takes advantage of the 2PC protocol to make updates at both the subscriber and publisher levels simultaneously. Finally, you looked at distributed transactions. Distributed transactions work through the 2PC protocol and take advantage of the Microsoft Distributed Transaction Coordinator, which is part of the Microsoft Transaction Server. With distributed transactions, all sites are updated at the same time, or none of them are.

You then covered the four replication agents that work in SQL Server. The merge agent is responsible for handling conflict resolution and converging your records. The snapshot agent is used to move snapshots of your data from a publisher to a subscriber. The distribution agent is used to move transactions from the distribution database to the subscribers. The Logreader agent is used in transactional replication and monitors the transaction logs of replicated databases. When it finds transactions, it moves them to the distribution database where the distribution agent takes over.

You covered the different replication scenarios next. This included the central publisher, central publisher with a remote distributor, publishing subscriber, central subscriber, and multiple publishers and subscribers. You finished up with some information regarding replication in a heterogeneous environment. This includes support for Access, Oracle, and any ODBC- (open database connectivity) or OLE-DB- (object linking and embedding database) compliant database that also supports the SQL Server ODBC subscriber-conformance level.

Today you learn about the security issues involved with replication. You then learn how to set up publishing, distribution, and subscribing databases. Then you will focus on how to create a publication and learn about publication restrictions. You learn how to do your initial synchronization of your data and begin the replication process. You also look at how to implement both push and pull subscriptions and some of the considerations of each.

Replication management is covered next. You cover the issues involved with monitoring replication, creating replication scripts (used to make backups of your replication scenarios), NT's performance monitor as it applies to replication, distribution database backup issues, and replication agent histories. You finish up with a short section on troubleshooting the replication process.

> **Note**
>
> If you're like me, you spend a lot of time reading through technical information (such as this book) and would prefer to do it in a comfortable chair away from your computer. This chapter has many figures in it. I included many figures so that you can read the chapter while you are away from a computer and still get a good feel for what you would see and what is going on.
>
> This day's lesson is laid out with many step-by-step walkthroughs and their associated screen captures. I hope that you find the additional visual information useful.

Security Issues

To begin the replication process, you must first meet some basic replication requirements. These include the following:

- Each server involved in the replication process must be registered in Enterprise Manager.
- If you are working with SQL Servers from different domains, trust relationships between the domains must be established.
- Replication uses the same Windows NT Domain account that the SQL Server Agent uses. This account must have administrative privileges and should be a member of the Windows NT Administrators group.
- The account must have the log on as a service advanced user right.

18

> **Note**
>
> I strongly suggest that you create a single Windows NT Domain account that all SQL Server Agents will share. This way you can avoid any potential connectivity issues.
>
> If you decide to use alternative accounts, these accounts must be able to access the distribution server's working folder. You will have to add these accounts to the distribution server's Windows NT Administrators local group.
>
> You can also use SQL Server login accounts when you are using non-Windows NT computers.

Caution   Keep in mind that local system accounts *do not* have network access and therefore cannot participate in replication.

Now that the security issues are cleared up, it's time to start setting up your servers for replication.

Server Setup

In this section, you will prepare your servers using the Configure Publishing and Distribution Wizard in the SQL Enterprise Manager.

You must first install the distribution server before you can install any dependent publishing servers. You must have system administrator (sysadmin) rights to create the distributor. After you have installed the distribution service, you can view both local and remote distribution server properties. The distribution database is installed automatically when you set up your distributor. You can create additional distribution databases on both a local distributor or a remote distributor.

You must ensure the accessibility of the distribution working folder as well. By default, the distribution working folder is located in \\computer_name\C$\MSSQL7\Repldata. This folder is installed by default on Windows NT.

Note   If your distribution server is going to be on a Windows 9x system, the working folder must be explicitly shared as C$ for the defaults to work. Because the folder is shared with a dollar sign after it, only accounts that have administrative rights on the Windows 9x computer will be able to access it.

Finally, you must make sure that the distribution server has enough memory. By default, you must have at least 32MB on the server and 16MB allocated to SQL Server for the server to participate in replication as a distributor. If you are supporting many publishers or many subscribers, you might want to add additional memory.

You can uninstall a distribution server by using the Uninstall Publishing and Distribution Wizard in the Enterprise Manager. Keep in mind the following when you remove a distribution server:

- All publishers that use the distributor are disabled.
- All publications residing on those servers are deleted.

- All subscriptions to those publications are deleted.
- All distribution databases on the distribution server that is being uninstalled are deleted.

In the next sections, you will begin the process of installing and configuring your server for replication. You can use the same server for publishing, distribution, and subscribing. If you have multiple servers and want to try this, the steps are the same. As you go through each section, you will receive additional information as necessary. This is very similar to the format of Day 2, "Installing SQL Server 7.0."

Installing Replication

There are three distinct things you must do in order to install and enable replication:

- Install a distribution server.
- Create publications.
- Subscribe to these publications.

You will learn more about each of these steps as you do them. The first step is to install the distribution server.

Installing the Distribution Server

Follow these steps to install a distribution server:

1. Connect to your SQL Server through the SQL Enterprise Manager.
2. Highlight your server and select Tools, Replication, Configure Publishing and Subscribers from the menus, as shown in Figure 18.1. (This can also be accomplished by highlighting your server, selecting the Replicate Data option in the taskpad, and then selecting the Configure Replication option.)
3. You will see a welcome screen, as shown in Figure 18.2. Click Next to continue.
4. You now must choose a server to be the distribution server, as shown in Figure 18.3. By default, the computer you are connected to will be selected as the distributor. You can choose a different distribution server by clicking the No, Use Another Server option button and then selecting another registered server in your Enterprise. When you have made your selection, click Next to continue.

18

FIGURE 18.1

Installing replication on your SQL Server.

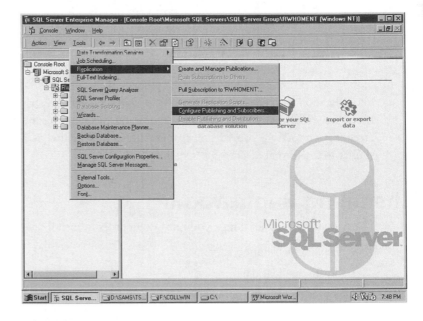

FIGURE 18.2

Configure Publishing and Distribution Wizard welcome screen.

FIGURE 18.3

Choose a distributor screen.

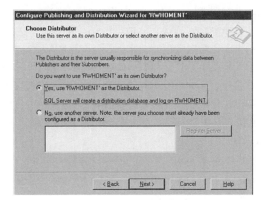

Keep in mind that by making the selected computer a distributor, additional disk space is going to be used to store snapshots and the distribution database. The various replication agents that will be running on that server will also need additional processor time.

5. Next choose whether to use a default configuration (see Figure 18.4) or to customize your settings. For this example, choose the Yes, Let Me Set the Distribution... option, and click Next to continue.

FIGURE 18.4

Use default configuration screen.

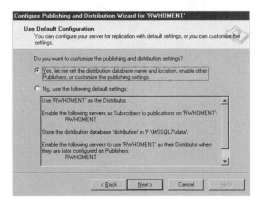

18

Notice that the default settings shown in Figure 18.4 specify that you will use RWHOMENTRWHOMENT as the distributor (RWHOMENTRWHOMENT is my computer name). RWHOMENT can subscribe to RWHOMENT, and RWHOME-NT can publish to RWHOMENT. The distribution database is also going to be stored in the \MSSQL7\Data folder. If you have other SQL Servers registered in Enterprise Manager, they will show up in this list as well. For example, if you had a SQL Server registered as Leap, you would be able to publish and subscribe with the Leap computer.

There are a few things to keep in mind when you install your distributor:

- Make sure you have enough disk space for the distribution working folder and the distribution database.

- The distribution database must be able to store all transactions between publishers and subscribers if you are using transactional replication.

- You must manage the distribution database's log file carefully for transactional replication because each transaction published to it and each subscription applied is logged.

> **Note**
>
> Snapshot and merge replication store data in the distribution working folder. The distribution database only tracks the status of your replication jobs in these replication methodologies.
>
> Remember that for transactional replication, all transactions are stored in the distribution database.

Now that you are a bit apprehensive about the size of your distribution database, here are some things to think about in terms of the size requirements for your distributor:

- The number of articles to be published.

- The size of the articles being published.

- Whether there are any text or image data types in the articles. If so, you must use either a scheduled table refresh or snapshot replication because these items are not replicated during transactional replication.

- How much latency between synchronizations can significantly increase the space requirements. Transactional information at the distribution will be retained until it is applied to the subscriber, which might be offline.

- If you are using transactional replication, how many INSERT and UPDATE statements there are. Remember that these statements contain actual data changes. If you insert 500 rows into a server, then 500 rows of data will need to be on the distribution server.

- If you are using transactional replication, how many transactions in a given time period are going to stack up. For example, how many transactions per half hour do you expect to be replicating?

6. From the Provide Distribution Database Information screen shown in Figure 18.5, you can specify the name of the distribution database, the folder in which to store the database file and the folder used to store the distribution log. Keep in mind that these files must reside on the distribution server (in this example, RWHOMENT). When you are finished making your selections, click Next to continue.

FIGURE 18.5

The Provide Distribution Database Information screen.

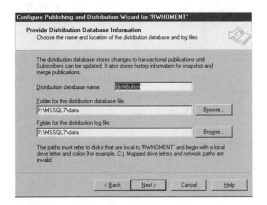

7. The Enable Publishers screen appears next. From here you can give permissions for other publishers to use this distributor. All you must do is select the registered server you want to give access to and then click the ellipses (...) button to set the security options. If you don't see your server listed, you can click the Register Server button to add one here. Make sure to place a check mark next to the name of your computer, and click Next to continue.

8. The Enable Publication Databases screen appears next (see Figure 18.6). From here you can specify whether to use transactional replication (including snapshot) or merge replication on your databases. You can specify replication types either by clicking in the check boxes next to the databases or by clicking the command buttons on the right. The command buttons affect all selected databases. In this example, select the Trans check box for the pubs database, and then Next.

There are a few rules to keep in mind when you are enabling a publication database:

- You must be a member of the sysadmin fixed server role.
- After you have enabled a database for publishing, members of the db_owner fixed database role can create publications.

FIGURE 18.6

*The Enable
Publication Databases
dialog.*

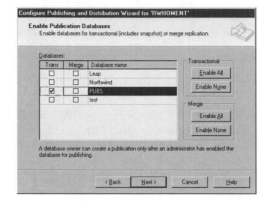

9. You will now see the Enable Subscribers dialog (see Figure 18.7). From here, all registered servers will be available for subscribing. You can also register additional servers by clicking the Register Server button. To enable a server, click the check box next to the server you want to have as a subscriber.

FIGURE 18.7

*The Enable
Subscribers dialog.*

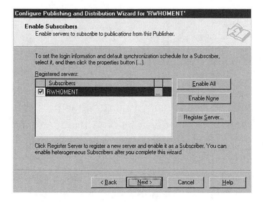

> **Note**
>
> The Register Server button shown in Figure 18.7 can be used to register Microsoft SQL Servers only. To add non-Microsoft SQL Servers, you can use Configure Publishing and Distribution from the Tools menu. You learn about this a little later in the "Creating a Publication" section of today's lesson.

10. You might have noticed the buttons with the ellipses (three periods) next to your servers. You use this button to bring up the login information used in replication as well as the default replication schedules you would like to implement. Click the ellipses next to your computer name. You should see something similar to Figure 18.8.

FIGURE 18.8

The General tab of the Subscription properties dialog.

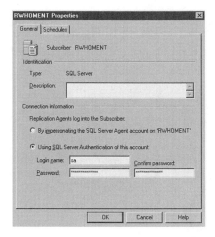

11. You can specify that you want to connect to the subscriber by impersonating the SQL Server Agent account on the subscriber's computer, or you can use the SQL Server authentication. If you use SQL Server authentication, you must specify a login name and a password.

12. The Schedules tab (see Figure 18.9) enables you to specify whether the distribution agent and the merge agent will be running continuously or whether they will be running at scheduled intervals. The default is to run the distribution agent continuously. If you click the Change button, you will be given options to schedule replication times. You will take a look at these later. Be sure that the Continuously option is selected and click OK to close the properties screen. You return to the Enable Subscribers screen (see Figure 18.7). Click Next to continue.

FIGURE 18.9

The Schedule tab of the Subscription Properties dialog.

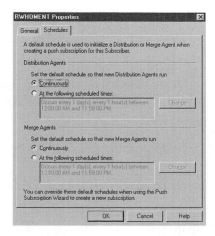

18

13. You will now be presented with the Completing the Configure Publishing and Distribution Wizard screen (see Figure 18.10). This screen provides a summary of what you are doing. Click Finish to complete this portion of the replication process.

FIGURE 18.10

Completing the Configure Publishing and Distribution Wizard.

After clicking Finish in the last step, you will see a progress screen detailing which portion of your selections are being implemented. A final screen then displays telling you that the Enterprise Manager has successfully enabled your computer as a distribution server for your computer. Click the Close button to close this dialog.

Note

> If your SQL Server Agent service has not been configured to start automatically, you may get a message to that effect. The message also has YES and NO buttons which enable to configure the agent start automatically.
>
> If this is the first time you are installing replication on this server, you may get another informational screen telling you that the Replication Monitor will be added to your console tree in the Enterprise Manager.

You might notice that the Replication Monitor icon now shows up in the console tree on the left side of your Enterprise Manager. This icon will not be available until replication has been configured on a particular server.

Congratulations, you have successfully installed a distribution server. Let's quickly review what you just did:

- You installed the distribution database on your server.
- You determined which servers can use this server (your distribution server) as a remote distribution server.

- You configured which servers can publish data.

- You enabled subscribers.

- You verified the distribution schedule for your subscribers using push replication with transactional replication methodology.

- You ensured that your publisher has enough memory and hard disk space. You might need additional hard disk space if your distribution server is unavailable.

Creating a Publication

In this section, you will create a publication, determine the replication type, determine snapshot requirements, specify whether anonymous or updating subscribers or pull subscriptions will be allowed, and define partitions on your data.

There are several different ways you can create publications. You can use the wizards, the console tree in Enterprise Manager, or menu options.

The Create Publication Wizard is used to create publications and specify the following options:

- Whether there are one or more articles

- Whether to schedule the snapshot agent

- Whether to maintain a snapshot at the distribution server

- The tables you want to publish

- The stored procedures you want to publish

- Publications that share agents

- Whether to allow anonymous updates from subscribers

- Whether to allow updates from subscribers

- Whether to allow pull subscriptions

Note   By default, each publication uses a separate Publishing agent.

In this example, you will create a publication that uses the authors table from the pubs database. You will install and use transactional replication to replicate this table to a new table called rplAuthors. You will then make changes to the original table and verify that the data was successfully replicated to the rplAuthors table. Here are the steps:

1. Connect to your server in the Enterprise Manager. Highlight your server and select Tools, Replication, Create and Manage Publications from the menu. This will start the Create and Manage Publications Wizard as shown in Figure 18.11. You should see the Northwind and pubs databases. Notice that the pubs database has a hand holding it. This indicates that you designated pubs as a publication database.

FIGURE 18.11

The Create and Manage Publications Wizard.

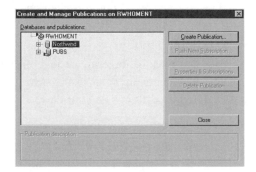

2. Select the pubs database and click the Create Publication button. You will first be given a welcome screen. Click Next to continue.

3. You will now need to specify what type of publication to use (see Figure 18.12): Snapshot, Transactional, or Merge. Select Transactional publication, and then click Next.

FIGURE 18.12

Choose a publication type.

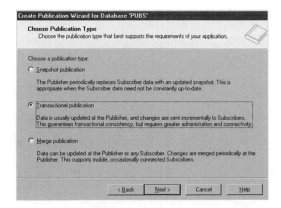

Note   If you are running the desktop edition of SQL Server, you will not be able to select a transactional publication because the desktop edition is only allowed to subscribe to publications.

4. You are now asked if you wish to allow immediate-updating subscriptions. Click No, Do Not Allow, and click Next to continue.

5. Next specify what type of subscriber you are going to support (see Figure 18.13). This includes SQL Server only, or both SQL Server and non-Microsoft SQL Servers. Leave the default of All Subscribers Will Be SQL Servers and click Next.

FIGURE 18.13

Specify a subscriber type.

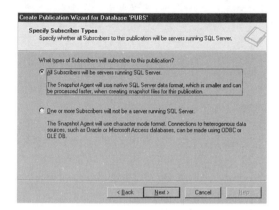

6. You may now specify articles as shown in Figure 18.14. You can have the list in the middle of the screen show both published and unpublished articles or just published articles. You can also publish all articles in a list or none of them by clicking the corresponding buttons. For this example, click the check box for dbo.authors. Click Next to continue.

18

FIGURE 18.14

Specify articles.

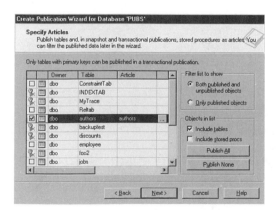

7. Specify the publication name and give it a description (see Figure 18.15). I'm going to change the publication name to Pubs_Authors. Click Next to continue.

FIGURE 18.15

Choosing a publication name and description.

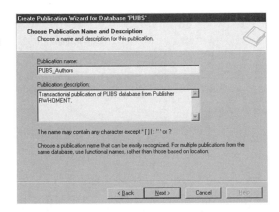

8. The Default Properties of the Publication dialog now appear, as shown in Figure 18.16. From here you can specify filters (partitions) for your data, or you can create the publication without filters and with the properties specified in the box. I will choose the Yes button and click Next to continue.

FIGURE 18.16

Use Default Properties of the Publication dialog.

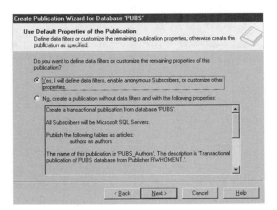

9. Next you are asked whether to filter data. Click No, and then click Next to continue.

As you might recall from yesterday, you filter or partition when you use your SELECT statements to gather only certain columns (vertical partition) or only certain rows (horizontal partition).

10. The next dialog enables you to specify whether you want to allow anonymous subscribers. Choose No and click Next to continue. Anonymous subscriptions are used in special pull subscription situations. Normally, the information about each subscriber is stored at the publisher, and subscriber performance information is stored at the distributor. This performance overhead can be avoided by specifying an anonymous subscription. Each subscriber keeps performance information in its local subscriber database. Anonymous subscriptions are useful when your publication has a large number of subscribers or the subscribers are coming in over the Internet.

11. Next you see the Set Snapshot Agent Schedule screen. The default schedule displays in the dialog and is scheduled for once every day at 11:30 p.m. If you click the Change button, you will be given a scheduling screen that you have worked with in other chapters. Click OK to return to the Set Snapshot Agent Schedule screen (see Figure 18.17). Because you want the replication to start quickly, click the checkbox for Create the first snapshot immediately; then click Next to continue.

FIGURE 18.17

Set Snapshot Agent Schedule.

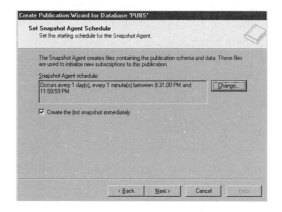

18

12. Click Next to continue from the Set Snapshot Agent Schedule screen. You are now given the Choose Publication Access List shown in Figure 18.18. This screen enables you to modify the list of users who have access to your publication. You can customize this list or choose to use the list the publisher has already created for you. Select the No, I Want To Use the Publisher's List button and click Next to continue.

FIGURE 18.18

Choose Publication Access List

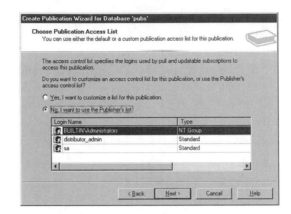

13. Next appears the completion screen for this wizard. Click the Finish button. You will see a list of tasks that the SQL Server is completing and then a successfully completed screen. Click Close when you are finished.

14. You will be back at the Create and Manage Publications dialog shown in Figure 18.11. Notice that your new Pubs_Authors publication is listed under the pubs database. From here you can create a new push subscription, create additional publications, look at the properties of the distributor and the subscriptions, or delete publications. You look at some of the items a little later in today's lesson. Click Close to close this dialog.

Creating a Subscription

Now you will create a subscription to gather the information you just published. When you configure subscribing you can make the following specifications:

- Select the publishers you want to subscribe to
- Specify the destination database that will receive the replicated data
- Verify that you have a valid account to access the distributor
- Specify a description of your subscriber
- Set a default schedule
- Specify the security mode

Follow these steps to enable your subscriber and complete the replication process:

1. You will be creating a pull subscription in this example, so connect to your server in Enterprise Manager. Highlight your server and choose Tools, Replication, Pull Subscriptions to <computername>. You should see a Pull Subscription screen similar to Figure 18.19.

FIGURE 18.19

The Pull Subscription screen.

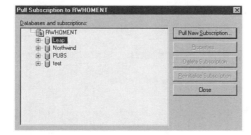

2. Click the Pull New Subscription button to continue. You will be shown the standard welcome screen. Click Next to continue.

3. You next see a Choose Publication dialog. You should see your server in the dialog box. Click the plus symbol (+) to expand the server and view the available publications as shown in Figure 18.20. Click the Pubs_Authors:pubs publication, and then click Next to continue.

FIGURE 18.20

The Choose Publication screen.

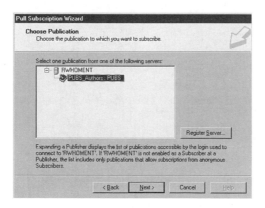

18

4. You may now be given a Synchronization Agent login screen. If you are, fill in the appropriate credentials and click Next to continue. If you don't see this screen, you will be given the Choose destination database dialog as shown in Figure 18.21. Because you are doing this all on a single server, you will create a new database. Click the New Database button. Give the new database the name of rplPubs. Click OK in the Database Properties screen to select the defaults for the rest of the Create Database process. In Figure 18.21, click rplPubs, and then click Next to continue.

FIGURE 18.21

Choose a destination database.

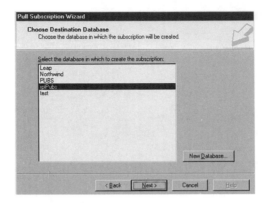

5. You next must specify how you will do your initial synchronization (see Figure 18.22). Be sure the Yes option is selected, and then click Next to continue.

FIGURE 18.22

Initialize subscription.

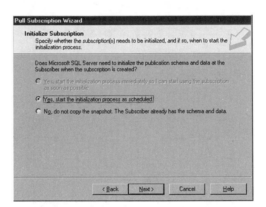

6. You can now specify the distribution agent schedule (see Figure 18.23). This is where you control how frequently the distribution agent updates the subscription you are creating. You can specify that it run continuously, run on a specific schedule, or that it have no schedule, in which you will perform a manual synchronization on demand. Select Continuously and click Next to continue.

*Set the distribution
agent schedule.*

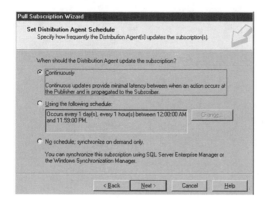

7. You next are presented with the Start Required Services screen (see Figure 18.24). If the service isn't started, clicking the check box next to the service will start it automatically after the subscription has been created. Be sure the check box next to your SQL Server Agent on your computer has been selected. Click Next to continue.

FIGURE **18.24**

*The Start Required
Services screen.*

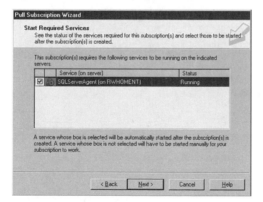

18

8. You should now see the completion screen. Click Finish to finish the installation. You will see a progress screen and then a final successful completion screen. Click Close to finish.

9. Your pull subscription screen should now appear. If you drill down, you will see that the pubs:Pubs_Authors subscription has changed. Now you can check the subscription properties. Click the Properties button shown in Figure 18.25.

FIGURE 18.25

*The Pull Subscription
dialog.*

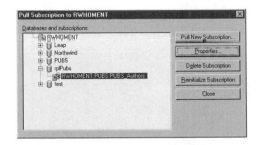

10. You will see the Pull Subscription property sheets. The General tab details the publisher, publisher database, description, and whether anonymous or updateable subscriptions are allowed. The security tab enables you to modify the SQL Server Agent login credentials. On the General tab, you can check the distribution agent properties by clicking that button. You will see a property page similar to the one shown in Figure 18.26.

FIGURE 18.26

*The Distribution Agent
Job Properties screens.*

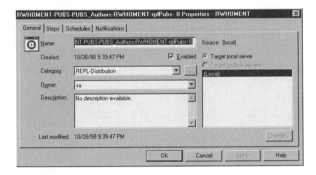

11. The General tab gives information regarding name, date created, category, owner, enabled/disabled, and target servers. If you click the Steps tab, you will see information regarding the scheduled steps that will be applied. The Schedules tab shows the current schedule for replication, and the Notifications tab enables you to specify how and whether you will be notified when a replication process occurs.

12. Click OK to close the Job properties windows. Click OK again to close the Pull Subscription property pages. Finally, click Close to close the Pull Subscription dialog. You should now be back at your Enterprise Manager.

Manual Synchronization

The snapshot agent will run when you specified it should. After this has occurred, the replication process will begin. You can force a synchronization to occur. Follow these steps to have the initial synchronization run by starting the snapshot agent:

1. In the Enterprise Manager, expand the Replication Monitor and expand Publishers and then your server; then click the Pubs_Authors:pubs item as shown in Figure 18.27. Depending on your current configuration, the first time you access the Replication Monitor you might be asked whether you want the Replication Monitor to automatically refresh itself. If you choose Yes, you will be able to set the refresh schedule.

FIGURE 18.27

The Snapshot Agent in the details pane.

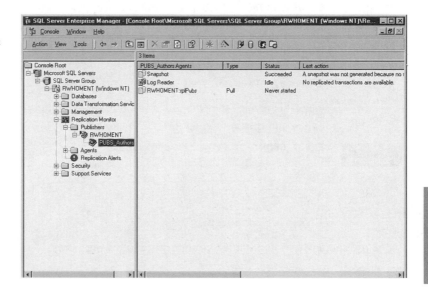

2. Right-click the snapshot item in the details pane and choose Start. The snapshot agent shows a status of running for a few seconds, and then the status changes to Succeeded.

3. If you right-click the snapshot agent after it has succeeded, you can see the agent history. Take a moment to review the Agent history.

Verifying the Initial Synchronization

You can verify that the snapshot agent has performed its duties appropriately and verify that the database schema and data were copied by using queries to view data in the new table.

To view the data, run the following query in the query analyzer:

```
USE rplPubs
GO
SELECT * FROM authors
GO
```

If you get data back, you know that the initial synchronization worked correctly.

Testing the Replication

Now you can test to see whether the replication will actually work. To do this, you will run several queries against both the pubs and rplpubs databases. Run the following queries.

The first one will determine how many rows are in the authors table. Run this query:

**INPUT/
OUTPUT**
```
SELECT COUNT(*) FROM pubs..authors
GO

- - - -
23

(1 row(s) affected)
```

Check this against the count in your other table by modifying your query slightly and then rerunning it.

**INPUT/
OUTPUT**
```
SELECT COUNT(*) FROM rplPubs..authors
GO

- - -
23

(1 rows(s) affected)
```

Now add a row to your table by running the following query:

**INPUT/
OUTPUT**
```
USE pubs
GO
INSERT INTO authors VALUES
('555-55-5555', 'Johnson', 'Susan', '555 555-5555',
'123 Anystreet', 'Fresno', 'CA', '90000', '1')
GO

- - -
(1 row(s) affected)
```

Rerun the SELECT COUNT query on both databases and verify that you now have 24 rows in your pubs..authors table and 24 rows in your rplPubs..authors table.

To double-check that the data was brought over, run the following query:

```
SELECT * FROM rplPubs..authors
WHERE au_lname = 'Johnson'
GO
```

You should get your row of data back. Let's delete this record from the publisher and verify that a deleted record will be replicated as well. Run the following query to delete the Susan Johnson record from the pubs..authors table.

```
DELETE FROM pubs..authors
WHERE au_lname = 'Johnson'
GO
```

```
(1 row(s) affected)
```

You can run your SELECT COUNT queries again to verify that there are now 23 rows in both the publisher (pubs) and the subscription (rplPubs) databases.

Close the query windows when you are finished.

Replication Considerations

There are several different things to remember when you are working with replication in SQL Server 7.0. These include some publishing restrictions and considerations when using updating subscribers. There are some performance considerations to keep in mind as well. In this section you will examine these topics more closely.

Publishing Issues

When you are using merge replication, you must ensure that every row of data that will be involved in the replication process has a unique identifier. This can be accomplished with the uniqueidentifier constraint and the ROWGUIDCOL property. When SQL Server finds a column with this constraint and property associated with it, SQL Server will automatically use that column as the row identifier for the replicated table. If that column is not found, it will automatically be created by SQL Server when you use the Merge Replication Wizard.

There are some restrictions to keep in mind as well, including the following:

- The system databases cannot be replicated. They include master, model, tempdb, msdb, and distribution.

- Each table or portion of a table involved in replication must have a primary key to ensure entity integrity. The only exception is snapshot replication, in which the entire contents are copied as a single unit.

- Publications cannot span multiple databases. When you create a publication, all the data must come from single database.

Keep these restrictions in mind when you are replicating with data that is used in non-logged operations. This includes text, ntext, and image data types. Here is a quick summary of the three main types of replication methodologies and how they are affected by these data types:

18

- Merge replication—Changes are not detected and data will not be replicated.

- Transactional replication—This uses the Logreader to detect changes. Because these are nonlogged operations, the Logreader will not detect them and will not replicate the data.

- Snapshot replication—Because this type of replication copies the entire contents of the article, these nonlogged values will be replicated.

Note   If you are planning to use the text, ntext, or image data types in your replication scenarios, you should either use snapshot replication or have the snapshot agent run on a regular basis to transfer these values to the subscribers.

Subscriber Issues

When you use the Immediate Updating subscriber option when you create a publication, you are specifying that the subscriber make updates to both the local copy of data and the publisher's copy of the data. After that change has been put into effect, data will be replicated to other subscribers at the next scheduled synchronization. (You cannot do this with merge replication.)

Use a timestamp column in your article to avoid potential conflicts. Remember that when changes are made to a record with a timestamp value, the timestamp automatically updates itself. In this fashion, you can always tell which record was modified first. Updating subscribers should be used in instances where there will be few updates from the subscribers.

Performance Issues

Here are some suggestions for optimizing the performance of your replication methodologies:

- Use pull subscriptions to offload work on your distributors. Although this option is not as convenient for administration, it can have a major impact on the distribution server's performance.

- Use a remote distributor. Recall that a remote distributor can support multiple publishers and multiple subscribers. By moving the distribution task to a different SQL Server, you can reduce the impact of distribution on your OLTP (online transaction processing) servers.

- Use updating subscribers. This option maintains transactional integrity and reduces the need for conflict resolution, which is associated with merge replication. If you decide to use updating subscribers, make sure you have a reliable network connection; otherwise transactions made at the subscriber will not be allowed.

- Replicate only the data you need. By taking advantage of partitioning (filtering) your data, you can replicate a minimum amount of information and thus reduce the overall impact of replication on your SQL Servers.

- Keep in mind that most types of replication increase network traffic. Make sure you have configured your network with the appropriate amount of bandwidth. For SQL Servers involved in heavy use of replication, you might want to place involved computers on a separate physical subnet.

- Use primary keys on all your tables involved in replication. This will ensure relational and entity integrity.

- Use the same domain user account (SQL Server Agent) for all your SQL servers involved in replication. Because all servers can be part of the domain or involved in a trust relationship with the domain, they can all take advantage of the same SQL Server Agent account. This takes much of the administrative headache out of maintaining SQL Server security.

Maintaining Replication

In this section, you will learn more about maintaining and monitoring replication. Through the use of the Replication Monitor you can administer your publishers, subscribers, and publications. You can look at agent profiles and modify their properties. You can also work with replication histories and set replication alerts.

As part of your replication maintenance, you will need to monitor the size of your distribution database as well as track the cleanup jobs to ensure that they are running at the appropriate times. You should also prepare for the possible failure of your replication servers. By maintaining good backups of your distribution database, you can ensure that recovery and resynchronization will flow smoothly.

You can administer many replication servers through the Enterprise Manager. You can create replication scripts to ease the task of replication configuration for multiple subscribers.

Replication Monitor

The replication monitor is available only on the SQL Server acting as the distributor. It is used to view status information about publishers, subscribers, and publications. You can also view scheduled replication agents and their historical data. This includes information about inserts, updates, transactions, and so on. The replication monitor also allows you to view and modify the agents' profiles and properties. In the next section, you take a closer look at the properties associated with replication agents.

Replication Agents

To gather information about the replication agents, follow these steps:

1. Open Enterprise Manager on the SQL Server designated as the distribution server (for the installation here, it's the same server as the publisher).

2. Connect to your server and drill down through the Replication Monitor to Agents. Click the snapshot agent in the console tree as shown in Figure 18.28.

FIGURE 18.28

The Agents folder of the Replication Monitor.

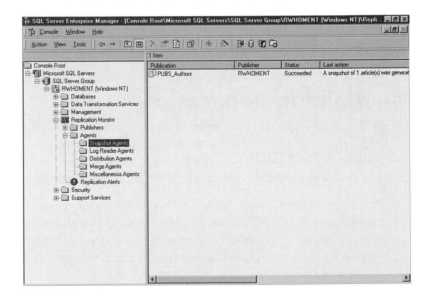

3. Right-click the Pubs_Authors item in the details pane and then choose Agent History. You will now see the Snapshot Agent History file. The list can be filtered to show the following sessions:

- All sessions

- Sessions in the last 24 hours

- Sessions in the last two days

- Sessions in the last seven days

- Sessions with errors

4. If you view the sessions in the last two days you should see a list of attempts, but there was no new subscription available. If you scroll to the bottom of the list, you will see at least one item that states Generated Snapshot with 1 Article(s). That was the initial synchronization taking effect, as shown in Figure 18.29.

FIGURE 18.29

The Snapshot agent history.

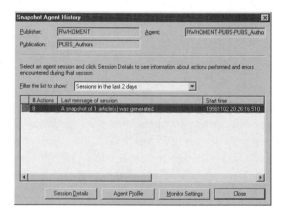

5. If you select that item in the list and click the Session Details button, you will be given additional information as to what exactly took place during the snapshot process (see Figure 18.30).

FIGURE 18.30

Session details.

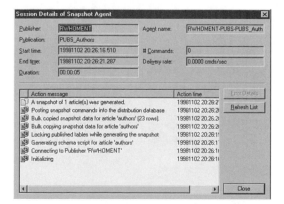

18

6. Click Close to close the Session Details screen. Click Close again to close the snapshot agent history screen.

7. Now that you are back at the console tree and details pane, right-click your Pubs_Authors agent again, and this time choose Agent Properties. This brings up the Job Properties pane for this particular agent, as shown in Figure 18.31. The Job Properties page shows general information about this replication agent.

FIGURE 18.31

Job Properties General tab.

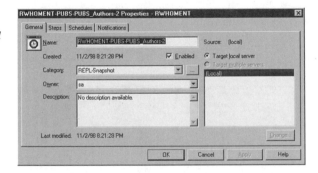

8. Click the Steps tab. You are now presented with the steps involved with running this particular job. As shown in Figure 18.32, the snapshot agent's job has three steps. These include log startup message, run replication agent, and detect non-logged shutdown. You are also shown whether each job was successful or failed. You can move these steps around, delete steps, or add additional steps.

FIGURE 18.32

The Job Properties Steps tab.

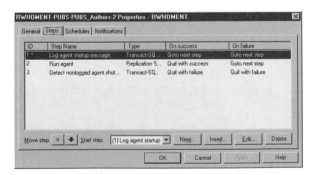

9. Click the Schedules tab. This shows the scheduling information for your replication agents (see Figure 18.33). You can edit, delete, and add new jobs here. You can also create a new alert here.

FIGURE **18.33**

*Job Properties
Schedules tab.*

FIGURE **18.33**

*Job Properties
Schedules tab.*

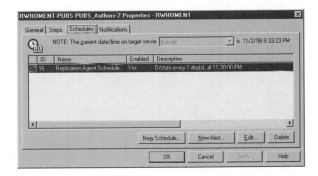

10. Click the Notifications tab. From here (see Figure 18.34) you can specify email
and page operators, as well as a net send operator to notify on success or failure of
this operation. You can also have it write to the Windows NT application log. A
final check box enables you to automatically delete the job after it has completed.
Click OK to close the Job Properties page.

FIGURE **18.34**

*Job Properties
Notifications tab.*

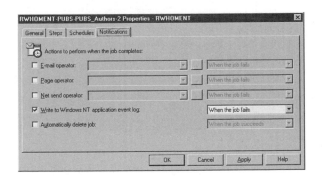

18

Distribution Server Management

Now it's time to look at some replication maintenance issues. You should develop a plan
for managing the size of your distribution database as well as develop distribution database backup strategies.

Monitor the size of the distribution database to ensure that there is enough space available for all your replication jobs. This can be done by determining the retention period
for your replication history and your replication transactions. You should also track your
cleanup jobs. A cleanup job occurs whenever an item in your replication history or replication transactions are removed. These options can be configured through the Distributor
Properties pages.

Note | There is at least one cleanup on each distribution server for each subscriber. If you have a distribution server with 10 subscribers, there will be at least 10 cleanup jobs on that distribution server.

Follow these steps to work with Distributor Properties:

1. Right-click the Replication Monitor icon in your console tree. From the Context menu, choose Distributor Properties. You should see something similar to Figure 18.35.

FIGURE 18.35

Publisher and Distributor Properties.

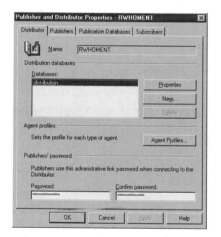

2. From this central location, you can look at all kinds of information. After you have installed replication, this will be the central location where you can monitor and manage all aspects of your replication scenario. Click the distribution database and then click Properties. You should now see something similar to Figure 18.36. You can specify that you want to store transaction records for at least some minimum length of time, but not more than some maximum length of time. The defaults are 0 and 24, respectively. You can also specify a minimum length of time to store your replication performance history.

FIGURE 18.36

Distribution Database Properties page.

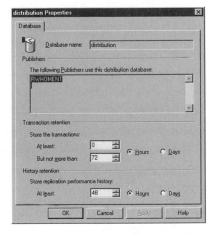

3. Click OK to return to the Publisher and Distributor Properties page.

4. This screen (refer to Figure 18.36) is available after you have installed your distribution database. The Publishers tab enables you to specify the available publishers. The Publication Databases tab allows you to modify databases available for publication. The Subscribers tab allows you to add and edit subscribers.

You can look in the SQL Server Agent\Jobs icon in the console view to check on your replication cleanup jobs. The following cleanup jobs should process on a normal schedule (see Figure 18.37).

18

FIGURE 18.37

Replication cleanup tasks.

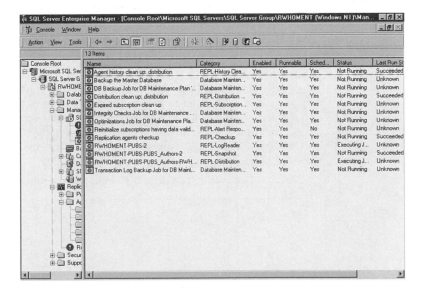

- Reinitialize subscriptions on data validation failure—This will reinitialize all subscriptions that failed because of a failure in data validation.

- Replication checkup—This will watch for replication agents that are not actively adding items to their history log.

- Replication distribution cleaned up: distribution—This cleanup job removes transactions from the distribution database after they have aged out.

- Replication history cleaned up: distribution—This cleanup job removes records from the replication agent history tables in the distribution database.

- Subscription cleanup—This job searches for inactive subscriptions from the published databases and removes them.

As you can imagine, with all the additions and deletions from these databases, as well as the regular logged transactions involved with replication, the distribution database and its transaction log can grow very quickly.

Even if you don't actually make a backup of your distribution database, you should at least truncate the transaction log on a regular basis. If you keep backups of the distribution database, and if the database fails for some reason, you will not have to go through the whole process of re-creating the distribution server, the publishers, and the subscribers again. You simply restore the database and resynchronize your data.

Note

As you might have guessed, I just wrote the buzzword "backup" and instantly got a bit paranoid. I would like to point out one excellent reason to make backups of your distribution database.

If the distribution database runs out of space, any transactions that are waiting to be published cannot be removed from the transaction log on the publisher.

At first that doesn't sound so bad, but think it through for a second. If the items cannot be removed from the transaction log of the publisher, the publisher cannot do standard transaction log dumps, which in turn means that sooner or later your publishing databases' transaction log will fill to capacity and you will no longer be able to make modifications at the publisher.

So make backups of your distribution database, or at least use the BACKUP TRANSACTION with TRUNCATE_ONLY statements to clear the logs.

Replication Scripts

Replication scripts contain the Transact-SQL statements necessary to create and configure a particular replication scenario. They have the following benefits:

- You can use a script to configure many servers in an identical fashion. This saves you the trouble of continually using the wizards.

- You can use the scripts to track different versions of your replication environment. As you make changes to your environment, you can create additional scripts.

- You can quickly and easily customize an existing replication environment.

- You can use the scripts as part of your recovery process. You can use the scripts to essentially reinstall any or all aspects of your replication environment.

When you are creating a script for multiple servers, you will have to make slight modifications. Mainly, you must make changes to the computer name referred to in the script. Although this might be time consuming, it is far quicker than walking through the wizards several times.

You can follow these steps to create a replication script:

1. Highlight your server in the console tree and choose Tools, Replication, Generate Replication Scripts. You are presented with the dialog box shown in Figure 18.38.

FIGURE 18.38

Generate SQL Scripts—General tab.

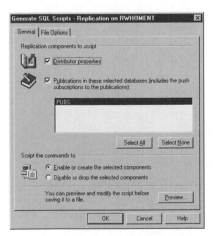

18

2. From the General tab, you can select which replication components you want to
have scripted. You can select the distributor properties and as many publications as
you want. You can also specify whether you want to have the script enable or create the selected components or disable or drop the selected component. The
Preview button enables you to look at the generated script. Click the Preview button now and look at the script that is generated (see Figure 18.39). From the preview pane, you can specify a filename and storage location for your script.

FIGURE 18.39

*Replication
Component Script
Preview.*

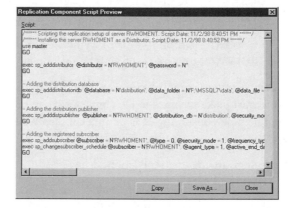

3. Click Close to close the Script Preview. Now click the File Options tab. The File
Options tab enables you to specify in what format the script will be saved (see
Figure 18.40). By default, the script will be saved in Unicode and will append to
an existing file (if you are saving it to an existing file).

FIGURE 18.40

*Generate SQL
Scripts—File Options
tab.*

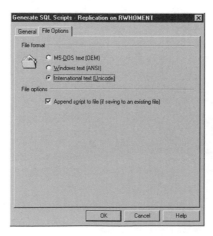

4. Click OK. You will be asked to specify a file location and filename for your new script file. The default location is the \MSSQL7\Install folder. This is an excellent location for it because this folder contains many other scripts used during the installation of your SQL Server. Enter the default filename of replication.sql and click Save.

To execute a replication script, you can use the Query Analyzer. Open the script file there and execute it as you would any other saved script.

Performance Monitor and Replication

SQL Server is tightly integrated with Windows NT. One integration is through the Windows NT Performance Monitor. SQL Server creates counters, several of which are combined into a performance object. For example, there is a Windows NT performance object called Processor. The Processor object has many counters, several of which are %Processor Time, %User Time, and Interrupts/sec.

Replication in SQL Server also exposes some performance objects and counters you can use to track the performance of the various aspects of replication. Table 18.1 lists some of the replication-related counters and their associated values.

TABLE 18.1 SQL SERVER PERFORMANCE OBJECTS

Perf. Object	Counters	Explanation
SQL Server Replication Agents	Running	Number of replication agents currently running, including Distribution, Logreader, Merge, and Snapshot
SQL Server Replication Dist. (same as the SQL Server Replication Logreader)	Dist:Delivered Cmds/sec	Logreader commands delivered per second in the last batch
	Dist:Delivered Trans/sec	Logreader transactions delivered per second in the last batch
	Delivered Latency	Logreader latency in seconds
SQL Server: Replication Logreader	LogReader:Delivered Cmds/sec	The number of commands per second delivered to the Distributor
	Logreader:Delivered Trans/sec	The number of transactions per second delivered to the distributor

continues

18

TABLE 18.1   CONTINUED

Perf. Object	Counters	Explanation
	Logreader:Delivery Latency	The current amount of time, in milliseconds, elapsed from when transactions are applied at the Publisher to when they are delivered to the Distributor
SQL Server Replication Merge	Conflicts/sec	Number of merge replication conflicts per second
	Downloaded Changes/sec	Number of download changes per second that are merged from the Publisher to the Subscriber
	Uploaded Changes/sec	The number of rows per second merged from the Subscriber to the Publisher
SQL Server Replication Snapshot	Snapshot:Delivered Cmds/sec	The number of commands per second delivered to the Distributor
	Snapshot:Delivered Trans/sec	The number of transactions per second delivered to the Distributor

Using Stored Procedures

All right, you knew it was coming. You saw how to do all the implementation through the Enterprise Manager. Of course, you can use stored procedures to build the same implementation of your replication scenarios. Probably the easiest method to accomplish this is to create everything you need in the Enterprise Manager and then generate your replication scripts. On the upside, creating your own replication scenario exclusively through scripts is beyond the scope of this book. However, there are some useful stored procedures you can use to gather additional information about the replication process in place on a given server. The following is a short list of the stored procedures used to manage SQL Server 7.0 replication. A double asterisk (**) marks stored procedures you will most likely use to gather information about your replication scenario.

```
sp_help_agent_default          sp_help_agent_parameter

sp_help_agent_profile          sp_help_publication_access
```

sp_helparticle	sp_helparticlecolumns
sp_helpdistpublisher	sp_helpdistributiondb
sp_helpdistributor**	sp_helpmergearticle
sp_helpmergearticleconflicts	sp_helpmergeconflictrows
sp_helpmergedeleteconflictrows	sp_helpmergefilter
sp_helpmergepublication	sp_helpmergepullsubscription
sp_helpmergesubscription	sp_helppublication**
sp_helppublication_snapshot	sp_helppullsubscription
sp_helpremotelogin	sp_helpreplicationdb
sp_helpreplicationdboption	sp_helpreplicationoption
sp_helpsubscriber**	sp_helpsubscriberinfo**
sp_helpsubscription**	sp_helpsubscription_properties
sp_link_publication	sp_linkedservers
sp_mergedummyupdate	sp_mergesubscription_cleanup
sp_publication_validation	sp_refreshsubscriptions
sp_reinitmergepullsubscription	sp_reinitmergesubscription
sp_reinitpullsubscription	sp_reinitsubscription
sp_removedbreplication	sp_replcmds**
sp_replcounters**	sp_repldone**
sp_replflush	sp_replication_agent_checkup
sp_replicationdboption	sp_replicationoption
sp_repltrans**	sp_resynch_targetserver
sp_revoke_publication_access	sp_subscription_cleanup

There are others, but this list is long enough as it is.

Administration Considerations

Managing replication can be a fairly administration-intensive task. It doesn't have to be. The following suggestions can help keep the replication management tasks more streamlined:

- Create and monitor replication alerts. With appropriate alerts set, you can proactively administer your replication enterprise. You can see potential problems coming and take corrective action before they have a chance to get out of hand.

- Ensure that replication jobs and agents are running properly. You can find this information by periodically checking the replication histories and error logs to verify whether replication is occurring as scheduled.

- Ensure that there is available disk space. The distribution database needs space to store transactional information as well as track the replication process itself. Make sure you make backups of the distribution database or at least monitor the distribution database's transaction log closely.

- Create a recovery and resynchronization plan. Create and store replication scripts. They are useful for recovery and version control as well as for duplicating multiple identical servers. Test the recovery and resynchronization plan once in a while and time how long it takes.

- Security issues are probably the largest troubleshooting problem you will encounter in SQL Server replication. If possible, have all servers involved in replication use the same SQL Server Agent account. In this manner, you avoid much of the potential security issues.

- Network connectivity is another troublesome issue. Ensure that you have enough bandwidth on your network to support your replication tasks.

- Remove the impact of the distribution database on your OLTP server by using some type of remote distribution.

- When you are building your replication scenarios, try to implement snapshot replication first. This is the simplest form of replication to implement and maintain. When you are satisfied that there are no connectivity and security issues, change the replication type to whatever you want.

Troubleshooting

Troubleshooting—now this is an art form. Troubleshooting takes a certain amount of technical know-how and a lot of practice. This section will help to make you technically adept at troubleshooting replication, and it will certainly give you some excellent suggestions for tracking down the source of the errors plaguing your system.

When you are dealing with replication, there are only several places where problems can occur:

- Security
- Log reader agent
- Distribution agent

Take a closer look at how errors here affect the system.

Initial Snapshot Jobs Are Not Applied at the Subscriber

Remember that before replication can begin, an initial snapshot of your data must be applied to the subscriber. When it is not applied, the most likely cause of the problem is with the snapshot agent itself. Check the snapshot agent histories and see what is happening. Has the snapshot even been scheduled? If it has been scheduled, was the attempt made to take a snapshot of your data? Do your snapshot agent and your subscriber have the right security enabled?

If the snapshot agent is not getting any data and therefore not trying to apply a snapshot to the subscriber, there might be a problem with the security between the snapshot agent and the publishing database.

If the snapshot agent is doing absolutely nothing, you can verify that it has been enabled and that the distribution server is online and available.

No Subscribers Are Receiving Replicated Information

If none of your subscribers are receiving replicated information, it is unlikely that the distribution agent is at fault, because none of the subscribers is getting data. It is more likely that the Logreader agent can no longer (or will no longer) read data from the published databases' transaction logs. To verify whether the Logreader agent or the distribution agent are failing, check the agent histories. Verify that jobs are being passed from one to the other.

If these tasks don't appear to be running, try changing their schedule a little bit and see what happens.

One Subscriber of Many Is Not Receiving Replicated Information

If only one (or several of many) is not getting replicated information, you know that the Logreader agent is working properly (otherwise, how would the other subscribers be getting their information?). You should check for the following problems:

- The distribution agent for the failing server is working properly. (Check the agent histories.)
- The subscribing database is unavailable. The database might have been marked for read-only, DBO-use only, and so on.
- The subscription server is unavailable. Has the server been shut down? Do you have network connectivity?
- The SQL Server Agent's security credentials have been modified.
- The distribution agent is waiting to perform a manual synchronization of your data.

Replication Recovery Issues

The manner in which SQL Server replication has been designed allows it to recover itself in most instances. There are some considerations you should keep in mind regarding your publishing server, distribution server, and subscribing servers.

Publishing Server Recovery

The Logreader agent uses pointers in every published database to keep track of where it left off reading transactions. This makes recovery a relatively simple process if the publishing server is offline for some reason. When the publishing database is back online or is again available, the Logreader agent will begin where it left off.

If, for some reason, the publishing databases are rebuilt and reloaded with data, the pointers will be off. You should resynchronize your publishers and subscribers to continue the process of replication.

Distribution Server Recovery

Distribution servers generally keep track of where they left off sending jobs (transactions) to the subscribers. When your distribution is offline and then comes back online, it will continue processing where it left off. Normally all will be well. If there is an extended period of downtime, you might need to restore your distribution server. You should have a coordinated backup scheme to guarantee that the distribution server is backed up along with the publishing servers. In this way, the Logreader agent is in synch with the publishing database, and automatic recovery will take place.

If they are out of synch and the Logreader agent's pointers are off, (you have conflicting restored databases between the publisher and distributor) you will have to resynchronize your publishers and subscribers. If this does not work, then unsubscribe and resubscribe to the databases.

Subscription Server Recovery

If a subscription server goes down, simply bring it back online. Replicated transactions are stored on the distribution server and will be applied when the subscriber is back online. If you are using snapshot replication, the entire snapshot will be sent down at the scheduled time. If you are using merge replication, the merged records will be converged back down to you at the synchronization. This is all true if your subscriber has been down for only a short while.

If your subscriber has been offline for an extended period of time, it is possible for transactions that are to be applied to the subscriber to have aged out of the distribution database. If you know a subscriber is going to be down for an extended period of time and you don't want to hassle with a resynchronization (you might have an extremely large database and don't want to snapshot it across the network again), you can edit the cleanup jobs associated with that snapshot agent. You can also modify the retention period for transactions associated with that subscriber, as discussed earlier in today's lesson.

Summary

You began today's lesson by studying how security is handled with respect to replication. You learned that replication uses the SQL Server Agent to interact with different servers (publishers, distributors, and subscribers). You then looked at the requirements necessary for your server to be involved in replication.

From there you went through an extensive step-by-step process to install and configure your distribution server. When the distribution server was installed, you could then create publications. You walked through another step-by-step process to create a publication. After you created the publication, you used the same machine to build yourself a subscriber. You ran the snapshot agent for the initial synchronization process, and you tested replication.

The next major section you examined was on replication considerations. This included information about issues concerning the publishing servers, subscription servers, and distribution servers and other replication issues.

You then looked at the process of maintaining your replication scenarios. You looked at the replication monitor item in the console tree of the Enterprise Manager. You then took a closer look at the replication agents (snapshot agent, distribution agent, Logreader agent, and merge agents) and at their histories and scheduled tasks.

You next looked into the management of your distribution server. This included information about managing the size of your transaction log as well as the replication history files. You also learned about replication scripts. Recall that replication scripts can be extremely useful as part of the recovery process, for use in creating multiple identical subscribers, and for replication scenario histories.

You then perused the counters and objects exposed by SQL Server to the Windows NT Performance Monitor. You saw many items that you can use to track the efficiency of your replication scenario. You then overviewed the stored procedures associated with replication. When you have some spare time, take a closer look at the stored procedures highlighted for you.

18

You finished today's lesson with a look at some administrative considerations. You learned how you "should" set up your SQL Server replication scenarios. You then looked at some methods for tracking down and alleviating errors in the replication process. Remember that very little can go wrong with replication. When something does, it is most likely a security issue, the Logreader agent, or the distribution agent. In most cases, the replication scenario will fix itself. In a few cases, a resynchronization is all that is necessary. In very few extreme cases, you will have to unsubscribe and resubscribe.

Q&A

Q Which type of replication is most common?

A Transactional replication is the most common form of replication. It guarantees transactional consistency and has a low to moderate amount of overhead.

Q What about merge replication? Do you expect it to become one of the most used types of replication?

A It is possible with the amount of remote users out there that this will be the case. You should try to minimize the impact of merge replication by taking advantage of region codes in your tables. In this manner, the same piece of data is less likely to be altered at two locations at the same time.

Q Should we use scripts to create and install replication?

A That depends. For the initial replication, publication, and subscription, use the Enterprise Manager and then, through the Replication Monitor, generate replication scripts. In this way, you have used the easy interface to create what you need and then had the interface create scripts for you that are excellent for use in a recovery scheme.

Q How important is replication recovery?

A That really depends on your business needs. Keep in mind that replication is pretty much self-sustaining. If a publisher goes down for a while, automatic recovery will work. If a distribution server goes down for a short period of time, it will simply pick up where it left off and catch up. If a subscriber goes down for a short period of time, it will be caught up when it comes back online. The only real problems you have to worry about with recovery is that transactions don't age out of the replication agents before they have a chance to be applied. The other point is to ensure that you are regularly managing the size of the distribution database's transaction log.

Workshop

The Workshop provides quiz questions to help you solidify your understanding of the concepts presented in this chapter. In addition to the quiz questions, exercises are provided to let you practice what you have learned in this chapter. Try to understand the quiz and exercise answers before continuing to the next day's lesson. Answers are provided in Appendix A, "Answers."

Quiz

This chapter was much more of a walkthrough than an exercise in study. There is no quiz for this chapter. Please take the time to try the exercise, however.

Exercise

Modify the publication and subscriptions you did today to reflect merge replication rather than transactional replication.

18

DAY **19**

Using the SQL Server Agent

In yesterday's lesson you examined advanced replication features, including merge replication and updating subscribers to transactional replication. These features can be extremely beneficial to extend your replication architecture. They are particularly useful for users on laptops who might be disconnected periodically or remote sites that must have immediate updates given to a central publisher.

In today's lesson you examine the automation features of SQL Server 7.0, including the SQL Server Agent service. This service provides many advanced features for SQL Server 7.0. This feature set includes the capability to run scheduled jobs, monitor SQL Server events, and set alerts that can launch a job or notify you via email, pager, or a net send command. In addition, replication is built entirely around SQL Server Agent scheduled jobs.

Why Automate SQL Server?

The first question you might ask is why you should automate SQL Server. As an administrator who's done my share of 2 a.m. support calls, I can tell you that it's not much fun to get up at that time of night, and anything you can do to enable a database to help you avoid those calls is something you should do! If SQL Server is configured properly, you can set the server up so that when problems happen, the most common errors can be intercepted and resolved without a call to wake you up. You can also automate routine database maintenance, such as data loading, integrity checking, and backups.

The SQL Server Agent service enables you to fully automate this maintenance using scheduled jobs. You can schedule job types, including database maintenance jobs, a full-text job, a Web assistant job, or a variety of replication jobs. There is also a generic job type to support running Transact-SQL commands, Windows NT command files, or Active Script (VBScript or JavaScript). Replication tasks are an advanced option, and are examined fully in *SQL Server 7.0 Unleashed* from Sams Publishing. You'll create Web assistant jobs on Day 21, "Integrating SQL Server and the World Wide Web." You can create jobs that do not necessarily run on a regular schedule but are preconfigured to run when you need them. This includes any type of job mentioned here. You can also have jobs that run only when you explicitly request them to run, rather than on a scheduled basis.

You can also configure alerts that can respond appropriately when a particular event occurs or a specific error message is generated. The response could be to generate an email, to page an operator, or to launch a job to correct a problem. The capability to use alerts is central to making SQL Server easier to administer and avoiding those 2 a.m. phone calls!

You can run everything yourself, and it is not necessary to use the SQL Server Agent service. However, even in an environment in which only one SQL Server is being used, you will find that several tasks are just easier to manage if you let the system perform them for you. If you take advantage of this built-in functionality, you can focus on designing your databases properly and on dealing only with true exceptions to normal processing.

Which Scheduling Tool Should You Use?

After you've decided to take advantage of automating SQL Server, your next question might be whether the proper tool to use is the SQL Server Agent service. The SQL Server Agent service is much more than a simple scheduling engine; it allows you to set up responses to error conditions and send you email (or even page you). However, if your background is in Windows NT, and you have scheduled other jobs (such as

Windows NT backups) using the Windows NT Scheduler service, you might consider using that scheduling engine to support SQL Server.

The Windows NT Schedule Service

As a pure scheduling engine, you might be inclined to consider using the Windows NT schedule service with the AT command. The AT command schedules commands and programs to run on a computer at a specified time and date. The Schedule service must be running to use the AT command.

If you ask for help on the AT command by typing

```
C:> AT /?
```

at the Windows NT command prompt, you get the following help:

```
AT [\\computername] [ [id] [/DELETE] ¦ /DELETE [/YES]]
AT [\\computername] time [/INTERACTIVE]
    [ /EVERY:date[,...] ¦ /NEXT:date[,...]] "command"
```

\\computername	Specifies a remote computer. Commands are scheduled on the local computer if this parameter is omitted.
id	Is an identification number assigned to a scheduled command.
/delete	Cancels a scheduled command. If id is omitted, all the scheduled commands on the computer are canceled.
/yes	Used with cancel all jobs command when no further confirmation is desired.
time	Specifies the time when command is to run.
/interactive	Allows the job to interact with the desktop of the user who is logged on at the time the job runs.
/every:date[,...]	Runs the command on each specified day(s) of the week or month. If date is omitted, the current day of the month is assumed.
/next:date[,...]	Runs the specified command on the next occurrence of the day (for example, next Thursday). If date is omitted, the current day of the month is assumed
"command"	Is the Windows NT command, or batch program to be run.

For example, to schedule an automated backup, you could type

```
C:> AT \\MYSERVER 12:00 /EVERY:M,T,W,TH,F c:\mssql7\backup.cmd
```

This would set up a call to the backup.cmd program in the mssql7 directory, which could contain calls to isql.exe or osql.exe to perform backups. This command would run every weekday at midnight.

This is certainly an option to allow you to schedule your backups. It is also a good option if you are already familiar with the AT command and scheduling tasks this way. You can also purchase the Windows NT 4 Resource Kit and use a graphical version of

19

the AT command. Both versions rely on the Windows NT schedule service to perform the scheduled tasks.

The SQL Server Agent Service

The SQL Server Agent service allows you to set up simple jobs or multisite, multistep jobs. You can graphically set up email integration so there is no need to write your own calls to the mail subsystem on your computer. The jobs can call Windows NT command files as the AT command does, take advantage of direct usage of Transact-SQL commands, or, even more interestingly, use Active Script language options. The interface is also much more intuitive than figuring out the AT command and writing batch files.

The SQL Server Agent service is made up of a set of components that work together to automate your SQL Server. These components include

- The scheduling engine—The scheduling engine performs the equivalent of the Windows NT schedule service. It starts scheduled jobs at the appropriate intervals based on the date and time of the Windows clock on the SQL Server computer.

- The alert engine—The alert engine monitors, receives events from the Event engine, and performs an action (such as launching a job or sending an email or pager notification). It can also monitor SQL Server performance counters that would normally be read by the Windows NT Performance Monitor utility.

- The event engine—The event engine monitors the Windows NT application event log and captures messages posted by SQL Server. It then passes those messages on to the alert engine.

- The job engine—The job engine runs jobs either on a predetermined schedule or when dynamically requested. It records whether a task runs successfully or fails, and it also can send out email or write a message to the Windows NT event log on success or failure. A job consists of one or more job steps, as you will see later in today's lesson.

Note
The SQL Server Agent service relies on entries in the Windows NT application event log when running on a computer with Windows NT. When running on a computer with the Windows 95 or Windows 98 operating system, a SQL Server Profiler trace begins because the event log does not exist in a non-Windows NT environment. However, the SQL Server Agent is still fully functional in a Windows 9x environment.

These engines work together to automate administrative control of your SQL Server environment. When an event occurs that is written to the Windows NT application event log, the event engine captures the message and passes it to the alert manager. The alert manager determines whether the alert is one it has been configured to watch for; if so, it might launch a job or send an email or page. The job might also then cause a message to be written to the Windows NT event log, and the cycle starts over again.

SQL Server Agent Configuration

When you first install SQL Server, you select a service account to run the SQL Server services, including the SQL Server Agent service. This is just one of the configuration options you might set to control the Agent service.

General   To begin configuring your Agent service, start up SQL Server Enterprise Manager (if it's not already running). Connect to your server and expand the Management folder. Right-click the SQL Server Agent service and select Start if the service is not running.

After you have started the service and the icon has the green play button, right-click the icon or the text and select Properties to see Figure 19.1.

FIGURE 19.1

The SQL Server Agent Properties dialog box.

Configuring the Service Account   The first option on this dialog box is to configure which Windows NT account is used to run the SQL Server Agent service (on Windows 9x platforms, this option is not available). I have the service running under the local server's context (shown as "." in the dialog box) as my account on my Windows NT server. If you are using a domain account (as is recommended in a real networked environment), you will see DOMAIN\Username fully qualified. If you have the System

Account option selected, you should probably change this option to use a nonsystem account. If you do not use a nonsystem account, you will be unable to take advantage of the email integration features of SQL Server 7.0. In addition, you will not be able to run any jobs that would otherwise run on multiple servers or need to access remote servers for resources (such as backing up to a remote file server).

Configuring the Mail Session Option for the SQL Server Agent   The next option after the service account is the Mail Session configuration option. Here you select the email profile you have set up. Setting up SQLMail to work properly requires several steps, so you will look at how to do so shortly. For now, leave the Mail Profile blank.

Configuring the Error Log for the SQL Server Agent   The last option on the General tab is to configure the error log for the SQL Server Agent. This is a completely separate error log from the SQL Server error log (the log for the MSSQLServer service). This error log is primarily used for difficulties with jobs. Figure 19.2 shows the error log for the SQL Server Agent on my system. You can view the one on yours by right-clicking the SQL Server Agent icon and selecting Display Error Log.

FIGURE 19.2

The SQL Server Agent error log.

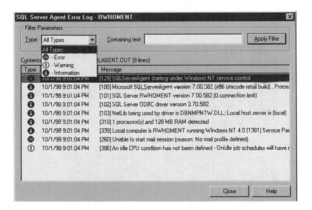

Notice that several filtering options are available, or you can simply view the entire error log (as Figure 19.2 shows).

Back on the General properties tab for the SQL Server Agent, the following configuration options are available for the error log:

- Include Execution Trace Messages—This option includes all details of events for the SQL Server Agent service. You would usually turn it on when troubleshooting problems with the SQL Server Agent.

- Write OEM File—The SQL Server Agent error log is written in Unicode format by default. This makes the log file usable anywhere in the world, but it doubles its size. If you want the log to be written in non-Unicode text, check this box.

- Error Message Pop-Up Recipient—Here you specify the Windows NT account name of an operator who should be notified when a pop-up error occurs. The user is notified via a "net send" command in Windows NT, and a message box appears on any computer into which the user is logged.

Advanced   After you have completed your general dialog box configuration changes, click the Advanced tab to see Figure 19.3. Here you can configure options to restart your SQL Server services in the event of a failure, to forward events to another SQL Server, and to set the CPU Idle configuration for your server.

FIGURE 19.3

The Advanced configuration of the SQL Server Agent.

Restart Services   You can set the option to automatically restart either the MSSQLServer service or the SQL Server Agent service in the event of an unexpected shutdown. As you see here, the option is already set for the MSSQLServer service by default. Simply check or uncheck the box next to the option to turn this feature on or off. It's just one more way to automate your SQL Server environment to require less manual intervention. If your SQL server crashes for some reason, you can avoid a call in the middle of the night to simply restart the services.

SQL Server Event Forwarding   Here you specify another SQL server to send your events to if you do not want to configure event handling on the local SQL server. The idea behind this option is that you can choose to forward events from your server to a central SQL server system. The central SQL server can be configured with alerts for multiple servers and can then be centrally controlled. This can offload a considerable amount of work to the central server; however, it will also potentially slow down the speed of response to events on your server because the events will need to be forwarded to the central server.

19

Configuring an event-forwarding server will also increase network traffic to the central server as more messages are sent to that server. Therefore, you don't want to specify an event-forwarding server that's already busy handling a production database.

The Forward Events for Errors with Severity of or Above option allows you to configure for only errors with a severity level of the level you specify (or higher) to be forwarded to the event forwarding server. Only unhandled events will be forwarded; this means that if you configure an alert locally to respond to an event, it will not be forwarded.

The following table explains the severity levels.

Severity 0–10	These messages are considered informational in nature.
Severity 11–16	These severity levels indicate that a user can fix the errors.
Severity 17	This severity level indicates insufficient resources, such as running out of locks.
Severity 18	This severity level indicates that an internal error has occurred in SQL Server. The error is nonfatal, and your connection to the server is not interrupted.
Severity 19	This severity level indicates that an internal nonconfigurable resource has been exceeded.
Severity 20	This severity level indicates that a fatal error has occurred with your connection.
Severity 21	This severity level indicates that a fatal error has occurred in your connection, which affects all connections to a database.
Severity 22	This severity level indicates that the table or index you are using has become corrupted.
Severity 23	This severity level indicates that the database you are using has been corrupted by a hardware or software problem.
Severity 24	This severity level indicates that some kind of hardware-level error has occurred.
Severity 25	This severity level indicates that an internal system error has occurred.

As you can see, errors with a severity level higher than 18 are really nasty errors. These errors often result in a call to Microsoft SQL Server product support.

Idle CPU Condition   One option for SQL Server Agent jobs is that they run when the central processing unit (CPU) is considered to be idle. When you check the box for The Computer Is Idle When:, you are allowed to edit the CPU percentage and the amount of time for that percentage to remain in effect. The default is that the CPU must be less than 10 percent busy for at least 10 minutes (600 seconds) before the server is considered to be idle. If you want to change the default values, simply enter different ones here. Again, think carefully before changing these defaults because you typically would only invoke processor- or disk-intensive tasks during idle conditions, and wouldn't want other users on the system when these jobs are run.

Connection   You will examine the Alert and Job System options later in today's lesson, when you examine each of those systems. Click the Connection tab to complete the initial configuration of your SQL Server Agent (see Figure 19.4).

FIGURE 19.4

The Connection configuration of the SQL Server Agent.

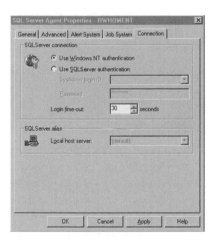

19

Unlike previous releases of SQL Server, you can use a SQL Server Authentication mode account for the SQL Server Agent service. The default on a Windows NT computer is to make a Windows NT authenticated connection to your SQL Server. If you want to use SQL Server authentication, or you are on the Windows 9x platform, simply click the Use SQL Server Authentication button and supply the appropriate credentials. The account used in either case should be a member of the sysadmin fixed server role.

Login Time-Out specifies how long the SQL Server Agent will wait after it requests a connection to SQL Server before it assumes that the MSSQLServer service is not running. The default is 30 seconds.

The other option on the Connection tab is to use an alternative name to connect to your SQL server. If you configured an alternative server name using the SQL Server Client Configuration utility (for example, forcing Transmission Control Protocol/Internet Protocol [TCP/IP] sockets to a nondefault socket number), you would specify that alternative name here. This is an advanced configuration option and should not be changed in most environments.

SQLMail Integration

As you have seen, there are several configuration tasks to complete before using the SQL Server Agent. Although you can use the default options, it is useful to look them over and verify the settings before you begin.

One feature you just learned about was the option to integrate email with SQL Server. This option has historically been called SQLMail. This feature enables you to configure a mail profile and then have the SQL Server services use this profile to send (and receive) email. It can be really useful to receive reports indicating whether your jobs have completed successfully. In addition, you can have SQL Server send a message to your pager if something serious goes wrong that you need to know about.

There are actually two different SQL Mail configurations to set up in SQL Server 7.0. The MSSQLServer service can use extended stored procedures to send and receive email. This mail configuration is the SQLMail option you see in the Support Services folder of SQL Server Enterprise Manager.

The other email configuration is for the use of the SQL Server Agent service. This is the email integration that would be used for the most exciting options of SQLMail—the capability for SQL Server itself to automatically notify you under the conditions examined earlier.

If your MSSQLServer and SQL Server Agent services are using the same Windows NT account configuration for their respective services, you can configure and use a single mail profile for both services. This is the recommended configuration and is assumed for this book.

If your SQL Server services are using the Local System account, you should change them to use a user account now. You just saw how to change the SQL Server Agent Service, and you examined how to change the service account for the MSSQLServer service on Day 2, "Installing SQL Server 7.0." If you have not set up the Windows NT account yet, refer to Day 2 to see how to set up and properly configure an account to run the SQL Server services.

Note For Window 9x users, your mail will always run in the context of whatever user is logged into Windows. The SQL Server services always run under the security context of whatever user is logged in on a Windows 9x platform. Therefore, the profile you select will be one of your mail profiles—not one for a service account as described here.

Configuring a Microsoft Outlook Messaging Profile

The first step when you have your service account selected is to log in to your Windows NT computer running SQL Server using the service account security credentials. If you accepted the setup configuration from Day 2, you will be logging in as SQLService with a password of password. The SQL Server services need you to specify the name of the mail profile they should use. Any mail profile you select will come from the profile of the user configured for the services. Therefore, you must log in using that account.

Right-click the inbox on your desktop or on the Microsoft Outlook icon if you have Outlook installed. This book references Outlook 98, the most recent mail client available from Microsoft as of the writing of this book. Select Properties, and you will see Figure 19.5.

FIGURE 19.5

The default Mail properties dialog box.

Note You might see something similar to Figure 19.6. You will see Figure 19.6 (or something similar) if a mail profile has already been configured for the user (which is likely if you are running on the Windows 9x platform because you are probably using email yourself). You have two choices: You can use a pre-configured profile or you can set up a new profile. To set up a new profile, click the Show Profiles button, and you should see Figure 19.5, except with one or more profiles already present. Simply follow along now to configure a profile for SQL Server.

19

FIGURE 19.6

The default Mail prop erties dialog box for a preconfigured user.

Now click Add, and you will receive the option to specify whether you want to add Internet Mail service or use Microsoft Exchange Server (see Figure 19.7). You must have installed these options when you installed Microsoft Outlook for them to appear in this dialog box.

FIGURE 19.7

Specifying the type of email server you have.

Microsoft Exchange Server

If you select Microsoft Exchange Server you are presented with Figure 19.8. Simply type the name of the Microsoft Exchange Server computer and specify either your full name or your email alias.

Click Next, and you see Figure 19.9. If you select Yes in response to the question, Do You Travel With This Computer? a copy of your mail will be kept on your computer. If you select No (the default), your mail will reside only on your Microsoft Exchange server.

FIGURE 19.8

Microsoft Exchange Server configuration.

FIGURE 19.9

Do you travel with this computer?

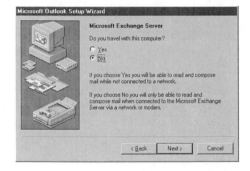

Click Next, and you are prompted for the location of your personal address book (see Figure 19.10). If you already have one, locate it here or complete the pathname and file-name. Otherwise, accept the default.

19

FIGURE 19.10

The Personal Address Book configuration dialog box.

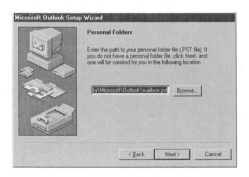

Click Next again, and the next screen appears, asking whether you want to have Outlook start each time you log into Windows. Accept the default (no), and click Next.

Figure 19.11 shows that you have successfully configured your Microsoft Exchange Server, as well as your personal address book. Outlook also adds the Outlook Address Book for you.

FIGURE 19.11

The configuration confirmation dialog box.

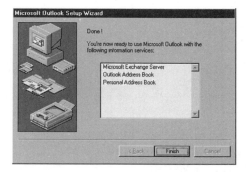

Click Finish, and your profile has been configured. Notice that the default name of the profile is MS Exchange Settings. This is kind of hard to type, so I recommend one final step. Highlight the MS Exchange Settings profile, and click the Copy button. Figure 19.12 appears. As in the figure, enter a simple name to type. I typically call it SQLMail. Click OK and close the mail dialog box. Now, when prompted for a mail profile name, you can type SQLMail (or whatever simple name you entered).

FIGURE 19.12

Copying the mail profile to a new name.

Internet Mail

Not everyone is using Microsoft Exchange Server yet as a mail server. Another popular option is to use an Internet mail provider. If you check the Internet E-mail option (from Figure 19.7) and click Next, Figure 19.13 appears.

FIGURE 19.13

Preparing to configure your Internet email account.

Click the Setup Mail Account button to see Figure 19.14.

FIGURE 19.14

Entering your email account information.

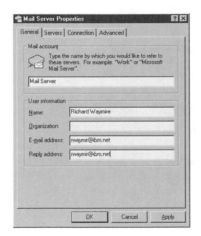

As you can see, I have entered my name and email address in the appropriate dialog box. I have chosen to use my personal email account for SQL Server. You must enter whatever account information you decide to use before you click the Servers tab. When you do click the Servers tab after entering the appropriate information here, you are presented with Figure 19.15.

Here, enter the name of your Simple Mail Transfer Protocol (SMTP) email server for outgoing mail, the POP3 (Post Office Protocol 3) server for incoming mail, and your login information. You should obtain this information from your Internet service provider (ISP). After you have configured this information, you can click the Connection tab (see Figure 19.16).

19

FIGURE **19.15**

Copying the mail profile to a new name.

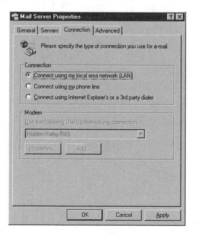

FIGURE **19.16**

Connection information for your Internet email profile.

If you are on a local area network (LAN), leave the default option checked. If this is a home computer, and you would like SQL Server to automatically dial your ISP when it is time to send any mail, click the Connect Using My Phone Line option. If you want SQL Server to connect only when you have manually dialed up to the Internet, leave the selection on the Connect Using My Local Area Network (LAN) default option. If you are not dialed into the Internet, SQL Server will log an error when attempting to connect to your mail server.

Click OK when you have selected the option you would like to use. You are then returned to the Personal Address Book screen (shown earlier in Figure 19.10) and again asked to configure your personal address book. Specify the filename here if it already exists, or accept the default to create a new address book.

Click Next again, and you are prompted to either select an existing set of personal folders or create a new set. Your Internet email will be delivered into the folder you specify on this configuration screen.

Click Next again, and you will see a screen asking whether you want to have Outlook start each time you log into Windows. Accept the default (no) and click Next.

You should then see the final screen that shows that you have successfully configured your Internet email server, as well as your personal address book and personal folders. Outlook also adds the Outlook Address Book for you.

Click Finish, and your profile has been configured. Notice that the default name of the profile is MS Exchange Settings. This is kind of hard to type, so as I recommended earlier, take one final step: Highlight the MS Exchange Settings profile, and click the Copy button. Enter a simple name to type like SQLMail. Click OK and close the mail dialog box. Now, when prompted for a mail profile name, you can type SQLMail.

Configuring SQLMail for SQL Server

Okay, now that you've successfully configured a mail profile, it's time to configure SQL Mail for SQL Server. First, configure SQL Mail to support the use of the mail-related extended stored procedures. Switch back to SQL Server Enterprise Manager, expand the Support Services folder for your server, and right-click SQL Mail. Select Properties, and complete the SQL Mail configuration dialog box (see Figure 19.17).

FIGURE 19.17

The completed SQL Mail Configuration dialog box.

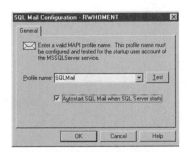

19

Enter the SQL Mail profile name as shown in Figure 19.17, and check the Autostart box to automatically start SQL Mail when you start the MSSQLServer service. You can test that everything works correctly by clicking the Test button. You then see Figure 19.18.

FIGURE 19.18

A successful test of your mail profile.

 Caution

If you are using a personal folder (also known as a PST) when using Internet email, you must not have a password on the folder if you are to successfully use SQL Server. You will get an error similar to Figure 19.19.

Simply turn off the password in the same way you turned it on, and then come back to this dialog box and try again.

FIGURE 19.19

Failure of the Mail profile because of a password-protected PST.

After you have completed the SQL Mail configuration dialog box and successfully tested your profile, click OK. To start SQL Mail immediately, right-click SQL Mail and select Start from the pop-up menu. You will get confirmation that SQL Mail started successfully, and the icon will turn green (indicating that the service is running).

Configuring SQL Mail for Use with the SQL Server Agent

To configure the same profile for the SQL Server Agent, right-click the agent (in the Management folder), and select Properties from the pop-up menu. Under Mail Session, select SQL Mail from the drop-down list, and click the Test button to confirm that everything works here as well. If you get any kind of error, verify that your SQL Server Agent service is using the same account as your MSSQLServer service. When you click OK, you will be prompted to restart the agent so that the changes you have made will take effect. Select Yes, and the agent will stop and restart. Now SQL Mail will be fully functional.

Sending Email from SQL Server

To send email from SQL Server via a Transact-SQL query, you use the extended stored procedure xp_sendmail.

▲ SYNTAX

```
xp_sendmail {[@recipients =] 'recipients [; recipientn]'}
    [, [@message =] 'message']
    [, [@query =] 'query']
    [, [@attachments =] attachments]
    [, [@copy_recipients =] 'recipient [; …recipientn]'
    [, [@blind_copy_recipients =] 'recipient [; …recipientn]'
    [, [@subject =] 'subject']
    [, [@type =] 'type']
    [, [@attach_results =] {'true' ¦ 'false' ¦ 'NULL'}]
    [, [@no_output =] {'true' ¦ 'false'}]
    [, [@no_header =] {'true' ¦ 'false'}]
    [, [@width =] width]
    [, [@separator] = separator]
    [, [@echo_error =] {'true' ¦ 'false'}]
    [, [@set_user =] 'user']
    [, [@dbuse =] 'dbname']
```

There are several options, but you will focus on only the most important ones here.

The following are the most common parameters:

```
@recipients= recipient
```

Specifies the name of the email recipient. If you want to specify multiple recipients, simply put semicolons between the names of the recipients.

```
@subject= subject
```

Specifies the subject of the message.

```
@message=message
```

Specifies the message that will be in the body of the message that is sent.

```
@query = query
```

Specifies a query to be run; the results will then be sent to the user specified in the `@recipients` parameter.

```
@attachments = attachments
```

Specifies the pathname and filename of an attachment to be sent with a message.

As with any stored procedure, you can pass parameters either by name or by position. For example, the following sends you an email with a subject of "test mail."

```
xp_sendmail @recipients = 'your email', @subject = 'test mail'
```

You can also send the message without specifying the parameters (by specifying them in order):

```
xp_sendmail 'your email', 'This is a message from SQL Server'
```

19

SQL Server can also receive email. You can send a query to SQL Server and run the sp_processmail stored procedure to process incoming messages. If the mail message is formatted properly, the body of the message will be interpreted as a query, and the query will be run and the results sent back to the user as a text file attachment.

```
sp_processmail [[@subject =] 'subject'] [,[@filetype =] 'filetype']
    [, [@separator =] 'separator'] [, [@set_user =] 'user']
    [, [@dbuse =] 'dbname']
```

>   @subject = subject

Specifies that SQL Server should process only email messages with the subject line you specify.

>   @filetype = filetype

Specifies the extension of the attachment that will be returned as part of the query. The default is to return a .txt file.

>   @separator = separator

Specifies the separator in the query output. The default is a tab.

>   @set_user = user

Specifies the security context of the query. The default user is Guest.

>   @dbuse = dbname

Specifies in which database the queries should be run. The default is the master database.

So if you were to send a message to SQL Server's mailbox, with a message body of

```
Select au_fname, au_lname from pubs..authors
```

then logged on to SQL Server as a member of the sysadmin fixed server role and ran this query:

```
exec sp_processmail
```

your message would be processed, the query would be run, and an email message would be returned to you with the results of the query as a text file attachment.

Jobs

As mentioned earlier today, jobs are the objects in SQL Server that you will configure to run tasks you need to complete. You usually create a job if you want one or more sets of commands to be run repeatedly.

Setting up a job occurs in four steps: You create the job, create your job steps, set the schedule for the job, and then set notification options for the job. Now switch to SQL Server Enterprise Manager and expand the Management folder; then expand the SQL Server Agent. You will see folders labeled Alerts, Operators, and Jobs. Highlight the Jobs folder, and in the right pane you will see any jobs that have already been created.

Creating the New Job

Right-click the Jobs icon, and select New Job from the pop-up menu. The New Job Properties dialog box appears (see Figure 19.20).

FIGURE 19.20

The New Job Properties dialog box.

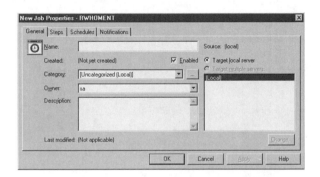

The first thing to do is to give the job a name. Because it's likely that you will want to have a job to create a backup for the master database anyway, name the job Backup the Master Database. Select the category of Database Maintenance because this is what you are doing here.

For the job owner, the default is that whoever you are logged in as will become the owner. Anyone can create a job in SQL Server 7.0. However, members of the sysadmin role can create jobs that are owned by other users. Leave this job owner at the default value.

In the Description field, enter a description for your job. The target server options will be examined shortly, but for now make sure you leave the option at the default of Target Local Server.

Job Steps

Click the Steps tab to prepare to create the steps of the job (see Figure 19.21). Each step is a separate command or set of commands to run.

19

FIGURE 19.21

The Job Steps dialog box.

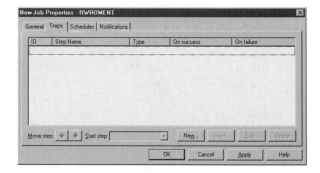

Click the New button to build the first job step. You are presented with the New Job Step dialog box (see Figure 19.22).

FIGURE 19.22

The New Job Step dialog box.

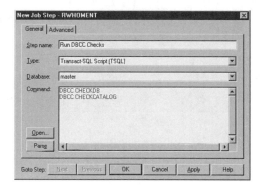

For this job, you should first run DBCC CHECKDB and DBCC CHECKCATALOG on your master database. Then, run the BACKUP DATABASE command to actually back up the master database. However, back up the master database only if the DBCC checks don't report any errors.

As you can see in Figure 19.22, I have already completed the dialog box for the DBCC step. Click the Parse button to verify that you have entered your Transact-SQL commands properly.

Click the Advanced tab to see Figure 19.23. Notice here that you have options that control the flow of execution, specify what to do in case of failure of this job step, and specify whether to keep the results of your Transact-SQL commands as an output file.

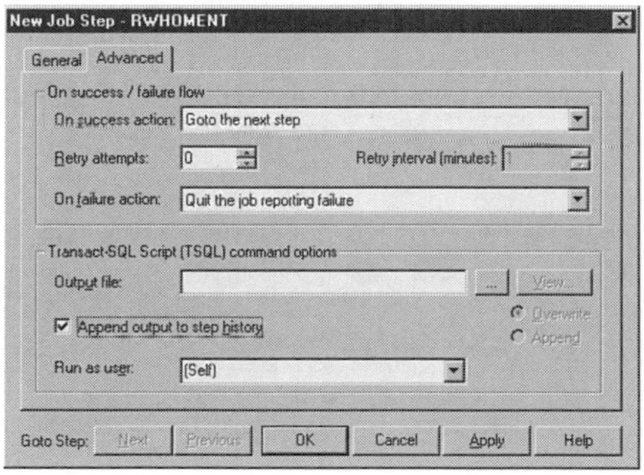

FIGURE 19.23

The Advanced tab of the New Job Step dialog box.

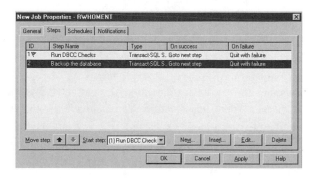

If you would rather keep the results of this job step in the history of the job as a whole, as opposed to keeping it in a separate file, check the Append Output to Step History check box. Accept all the other defaults, and click OK to finish this job step.

Now add another step to run the backup command. As a reminder, a valid command might be

```
BACKUP DATABASE master TO master_backup WITH INIT
```

Set the On Success Action option as Quit the Job Reporting Success. Make sure to append the output to step history. Figure 19.24 shows the completed Job Steps dialog box.

FIGURE 19.24

The configured Job Steps dialog box.

19

You should explore the dialog boxes for other job types as well. Specifically, look at the Active Script and Operating System Command (CMDExec) job types. These tend to be the three types of jobs you run most often. Notice how the dialog boxes change depending on the type of job you select.

Job Scheduling

Now you must define what the schedule will be for this job. Click the Schedules tab to configure the schedule for this job. When you do, Figure 19.25 appears.

FIGURE 19.25

The Job Schedules dialog box.

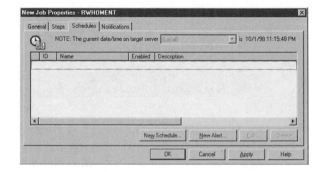

Click the New Schedule button, and set up the schedule for this job (see Figure 19.26).

FIGURE 19.26

The New Job Schedule dialog box.

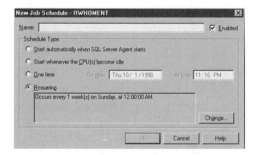

The options here are mostly self-explanatory. You can have this job automatically start when the SQL Server Agent service starts. You can have the job run when the CPU is idle (as you defined earlier in today's lesson), or you can schedule the job for a one-time run. Another option would be to not configure anything in this dialog box, which would make the job run only "on-demand"—when you explicitly request it to run.

The final option here (which is also the default) is to set a fixed schedule for the job. Notice that the default is to run the job once a week: on Sunday at midnight. Click the Change button to change this to a different schedule. You will then see Figure 19.27.

FIGURE 19.27

The Edit Recurring Job Schedule dialog box.

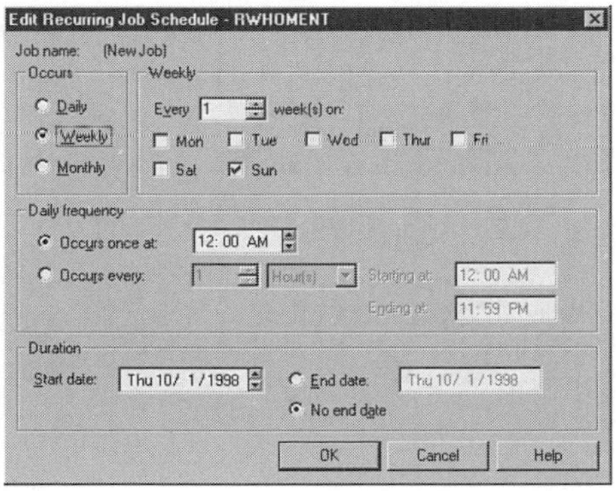

The Occurs frame specifies whether the job occurs daily, weekly, or monthly.

- Daily—When you specify Daily, the daily frame is displayed next to the Occurs frame. This option enables you to specify that the job occurs every x days (every day, every second day, and so on).

- Weekly—The Weekly option, when selected, displays the Weekly frame. This frame will display the option to run every x weeks (with the default being one). You can also specify which day of the week the job will run, and you can check as many days as you want. You can, for example, specify that a job occurs weekly, every one week, on Monday through Friday.

- Monthly—Selecting the Monthly option allows you to run a job on a specific day of the month (or every x number of months) or on the first, second, third, fourth, or last day, weekend day, or weekday of every x number of months. As you can see, this option is quite flexible.

The Daily frequency frame specifies at what time of day the job will run. You can also set up the Occurs Every option to run a scheduled job every x number of hours or minutes. You can specify a start time and end time for the job to run.

The Duration frame specifies a Start Date (which defaults to the current date) and an End Date (or the No End Date option). If you want to have a scheduled job that runs only for a specific duration and then stops running, you can set the End Date. When that date is reached, the job will not run again.

For this job, set the Occurs frame to Daily, and run the job at 6 a.m. Click OK to return to the New Job Schedule dialog box. Name the schedule (I chose Daily at 6 a.m.). Click OK and return to the Schedules tab, which should now look like Figure 19.28.

19

FIGURE 19.28

The completed Schedules tab.

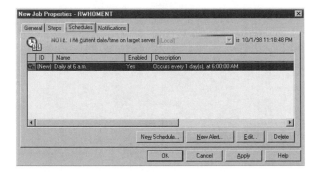

Job Notifications

Click the Notifications tab (see Figure 19.29). Here you can set options for an email to be sent, to have an operator paged, to use the Windows NT Net Send function to send a message (only on Windows NT), and to write to the Windows NT event log. For each option, you can specify whether the notification will happen when the job fails, when it succeeds, or whenever it completes (always).

FIGURE 19.29

The completed Notifications dialog box.

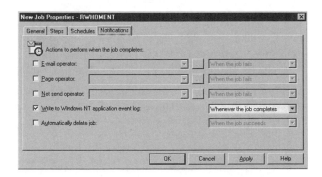

You can also request that the job be deleted if the job succeeds or fails as well. Configure the dialog box as shown in Figure 19.29. You will set email options for this job a bit later—after you have added an email operator. Click OK, and that's it! You have successfully created your first job. It only gets easier from here.

Job System Options

Some job options are universal across all jobs. Right-click your SQL Server Agent and select Properties. Click the Job System tab, and you will see Figure 19.30.

FIGURE 19.30

*The Job System config-
uration tab.*

You can choose to limit the size of the history kept for all scheduled jobs on your SQL Server installation. There are two options: to limit the maximum job history log size (1,000 rows is the default) or to limit the maximum job history rows per job (100 rows is the default).

If you disable this option, the history of your tasks will be kept forever. This task history is kept in the sysjobhistory table of the msdb database. Therefore, if you change these parameters or turn off the maximum size options, you will most likely need to increase the size of the msdb database. The job definitions are kept in the sysjobs, sysjobsched-ules, sysjobsteps, and sysjobservers system tables in the msdb database.

The Job Execution frame allows you to configure how long the SQL Server Agent will wait for any running jobs to complete after you have requested for the service to stop. The default is 15 seconds. The other option in this frame is specific to Multiserver opera-tions, examined shortly.

Finally, you will see that I have checked the last option, to allow only users who are members of the sysadmin fixed server role the right to run jobs of type ActiveScript or CmdExec. This is because these job types allow you full access to the server (or even the network) as if you were the account that is used to run SQL Server. This restriction pre-vents anyone who is not a SQL Server administrator from having that kind of access. You should always enable this option.

Click OK to set your Job System options.

19

Multiserver Jobs

You might have noticed several options throughout the last few pages that reference multiserver jobs. This is an advanced feature and generally isn't used unless you have at least three SQL Server machines on your network. If you want to understand multiserver jobs, please refer to the SQL Server documentation, or better yet, *Microsoft SQL Server 7.0 Unleashed* from Sams Publishing.

Alerts and Operators

Alerts allow you to specify events that SQL Server should watch out for. When these events occur, you can have the alert send you an email, send a page, send a `net send` command on Windows NT systems, or launch a job if needed. Some alerts are preconfigured when you install SQL Server and others you might want to add. As a first step, it's now time to create an operator to receive your email or pager notification.

Configuring Operators

To configure an operator, right-click the Operators option under the SQL Server Agent, and select New Operator from the pop-up menu. You will see Figure 19.31, the New Operator Properties dialog box.

FIGURE 19.31

The New Operator Properties dialog box.

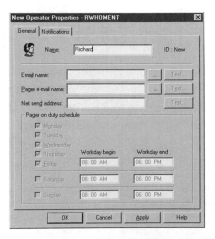

Name the operator (I've added my own name), and then click the three dots button next to the email name to add an email address for your operator. The same options apply for the Pager email name because it's based on the email capabilities of SQL Server 7.0. When you click the three dots button next to the email name space, you will see your personal address book. If there are no entries (because it's new, for example), click the New button to add a new operator. Select Internet Mail Address, and complete all the options you want. At a minimum, you must provide a name and email address (as I've done for myself in Figure 19.32).

FIGURE 19.32

Adding a new email address for a user.

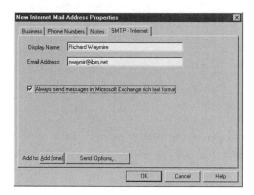

Click the Add(one) box to add the email address back to your operator to the New Operator Properties dialog box (as well as the personal address book of SQL Server).

Click OK, and you have successfully created an operator. If you do create a pager entry, you can also set the schedule for the operator to be paged. You won't click the Notifications tab yet because this will examine the alerts assigned to this operator, which you look at next. However, now is a good time to configure alerts.

Creating Alerts

Highlight the Alerts option under the SQL Server Agent. You will see that several alerts are preconfigured on your server. These alerts are preconfigured to cover the most severe errors that can occur in SQL Server (see Figure 19.33).

To create a new alert, right-click the Alerts option under the SQL Server Agent and select New Alert from the pop-up menu. You will see the New Alert Properties dialog box (see Figure 19.34).

19

FIGURE 19.33

The preconfigured alerts of SQL Server 7.0.

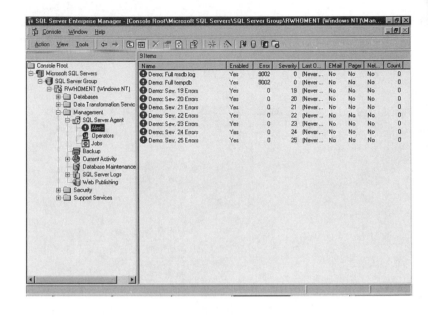

FIGURE 19.34

The configured New Alert Properties dialog box.

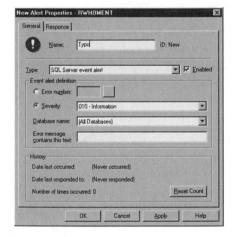

In Figure 19.34, I have begun creating an alert named Typo. Click the ellipse button next to the Error Number option to search for an error message that this alert should watch for. To make one that's easy to reproduce, configure error 208 (Object not found in a query). Type 208 in the Error Number field, and click Find. You will then see a dialog box with the error displayed. Click Edit to view Figure 19.35. You will need to change a default option for this error message.

FIGURE **19.35**

The Edit Message dialog box.

The SQL Server Agent can see messages only if they are posted to the Windows NT event log (or are configured to do so at a minimum on the Windows 9x platform). Click the Always Write to Windows NT Eventlog check box, as shown in Figure 19.35. Click OK and then OK again to complete the selection of this error. Change the database name to pubs so you are not overwhelmed with this if others are using your SQL Server. The fully configured alert should look like Figure 19.36.

FIGURE **19.36**

The fully configured alert.

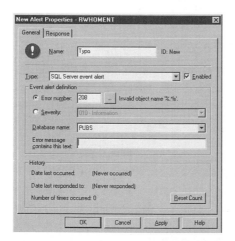

19

Click the Response tab to see Figure 19.37. Configure the options as shown—that Richard (or you on your server) will be notified when this alert occurs. Notice that you can also configure the alert to launch a job by checking the Execute Job check box and then select a job in the drop-down list. You can even launch the New Job Properties dialog box from here. Here I have configured the alert to back up my master database when this error occurs. Click OK when you have configured the response options.

FIGURE 19.37

The Response tab options for an alert.

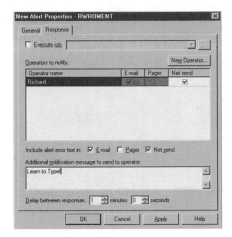

Testing Your Alert

Now is a great time to test this alert. Start the SQL Server Query Analyzer, switch to the pubs database, and run the following query:

```
Select * from nonexistanttable
```

You should get back

```
Server: Msg 208, Level 16, State 1
Invalid object name 'nonexistanttable'.
```

This will signal your alert and cause an email to be sent as well as your master database backup job to be launched. Switch to the Alerts entries for your server, and you should see that the Typo alert has a last-occurred value as well as a count of 1 (to show that the error has happened one time). You can also verify that you now have an email from SQL Server. Highlight your Jobs folder, and you can see that your job has run as well. If you don't see these changes reflected, right-click the Jobs or Alerts options in the left pane and select Refresh from the pop-up menu.

> **Tip**
>
> You might want to go back to your Error 208 and turn off the Always Write to Windows NT Eventlog. Otherwise, every typo you or anyone makes with this SQL server will be recorded in the event log.

Alerts are kept in the sysalerts system table in the msdb database.

Alert System Options

Now go back to the SQL Server Agent, right-click, and select Properties. Click the Alert System tab to view Figure 19.38.

FIGURE 19.38

The Alert System tab.

Most of these options are necessary only for pagers, such as adding a special prefix or suffix for pager emails. The documentation for your paging software will describe what must be entered here. You can also choose to have the body of your email in the notification page sent to the operator (if the operator has a text pager, that is).

The Fail-Safe Operator frame specifies the fail-safe operator to use, as well as whether to use email, a pager, or the Net Send option for that operator. If something should go wrong with an alert and none of the operators who should be paged are paged for some reason, you can designate an operator to receive a message about the notification failure. To do so, click the Operator drop-down list and select an operator. You can also create an operator here by selecting the New Fail-Safe Operator option, which will launch the New Operator dialog box. To not specify a fail-safe operator (the default), select (No Fail-Safe Operator).

Performance Monitor Integration

The Windows NT Performance Monitor utility has been fully integrated with SQL Server, via alerts in the SQL Server Agent. Go back to the New Alert Properties dialog box (right-click Alerts under the SQL Server Agent and select New Alert). Notice the Alert type drop-down list. If you click this drop-down list, you can select the SQL Server performance condition alert. This enables you to then pick any SQL Server performance counter and configure an alert—just as you did with SQL Server error messages.

19

Figure 19.39 shows a performance counter alert for the transaction log of the pubs database. When the transaction log is 80 percent full (or greater), this alert would be triggered.

FIGURE 19.39

*An alert using a
Performance Monitor
counter.*

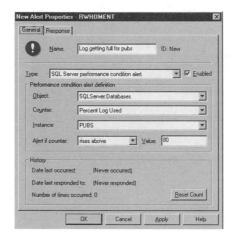

The Database Maintenance Plan Wizard

The Database Maintenance Plan Wizard will create a job (or multiple jobs) to automatically check the integrity of your database, reorganize your indexes, clean up unused space in your database, and create database and transaction log backups. You examined the program that actually runs behind the scenes, sqlmaint.exe, on Day 3, "Using the SQL Server 7.0 Tools and Utilities." It would be a good idea to use this wizard on your databases unless you want a highly customized maintenance plan for your databases.

To start the wizard, select Tools, Wizards from the menu bar in the SQL Server Enterprise Manager (after you've selected a server). Expand the Management entry, and select the Database Maintenance Plan Wizard. Click OK to launch the wizard, and you will be presented with the Welcome dialog box for the wizard. Click Next, and you will see Figure 19.40, requesting you to select one or more databases to perform regular maintenance on.

Select just the pubs database for now (see Figure 19.40) to keep things simple. Click Next, and you will see Figure 19.41. Here, specify whether you want indexes reorganized, statistics updated, and unused space removed from your database. Which options you select will depend on your database environment. Figure 19.41 has the option to reorganize your indexes selected, which will automatically re-create statistics for you. For pubs, there's no need to clean up unused space, but you could set the appropriate entries for your database.

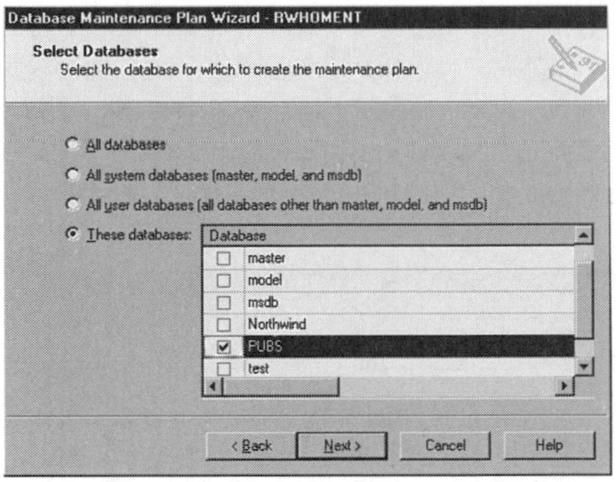

FIGURE 19.40

Select one or more databases for the Maintenance Plan Wizard.

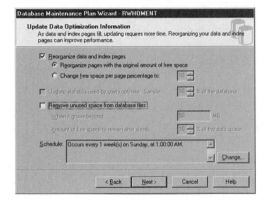

FIGURE 19.41

The Update Data Optimization Information dialog box using the Maintenance Plan Wizard.

19

Establish the schedule of the data optimizations by clicking the Change button next to the schedule, as you have done earlier in today's lesson. Click Next when you have completed the data optimizations and scheduling options, and you will see the Database Integrity Check dialog box (see Figure 19.42).

FIGURE 19.42

Data optimizations with the Database Maintenance Plan Wizard.

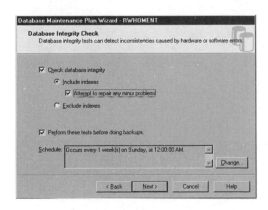

It's probably best to specify all options here, allowing full integrity checks to be run and directing that your backups be run only if no database corruption is found. Again, set the schedule for these integrity checks, and click Next. You will then see Figure 19.43, where you configure the backup options. These should be very familiar to you now, so select the options you want and set the schedule; then click Next.

FIGURE 19.43

Specifying your database backup plan.

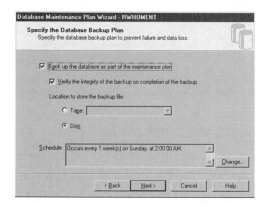

Indicate where you want your backups to be stored. If backing up to disk, specify a disk drive other than the one on which your data is stored. I recommend that you make a subdirectory for each database (it's easier to locate your backups that way) and also that you automatically have the backups deleted as they get old. These options are set in Figure 19.44.

FIGURE 19.44

Database backup options in the Maintenance Plan Wizard.

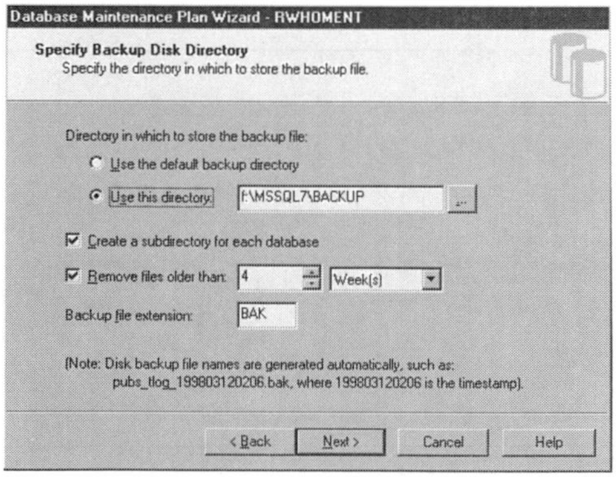

Click Next, and you will see the transaction log backup options (see Figure 19.45). Again, select the appropriate options for your log backups and click Next. You will see Figure 19.44 again—except now it's for your transaction logs. Complete the appropriate entries and click Next.

FIGURE 19.45

Transaction log back-ups in the Maintenance Plan Wizard.

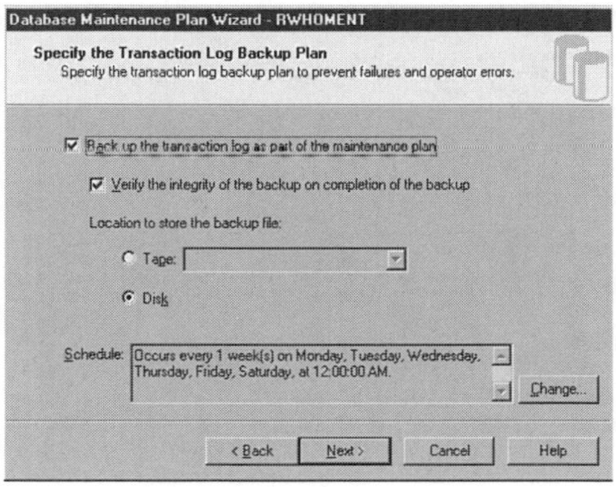

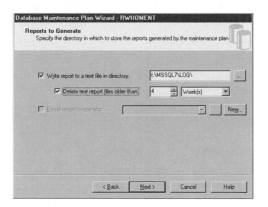

You will then have the option of having reports generated about the success or failure of your maintenance plans. As you would expect, you can also configure an email recipient for the maintenance plan (see Figure 19.46).

FIGURE 19.46

Specifying reporting options for the Maintenance Plan Wizard.

Finally, you have the option to keep historical information about your maintenance plans in the system tables of the msdb database, and you also have the ability to limit the number of rows of history kept (see Figure 19.47).

Click Next, and you'll see a report of the options you have chosen and a request to name the plan. After you complete this option, several scheduled jobs will be configured on your behalf. You can observe them in the Jobs window as described earlier in today's lesson. After you have done this, 90 percent of your database maintenance needs are taken care of for you.

19

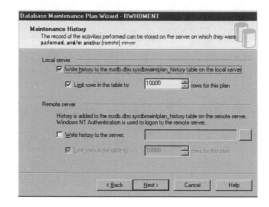

FIGURE 19.47

Capturing historical reporting information for the Maintenance Plan Wizard.

Summary

The SQL Server Agent service is not required when using SQL Server, but it can dramatically increase the functionality of your server. You can set up sophisticated jobs to automate functions such as backups and database integrity checks. You can set up alerts to react when events occur on your SQL Server databases, and you can even use the Windows NT performance counters for alerts. You've also seen the power of integrating email and paging features in with SQL Server to notify an administrator (or set of administrators) when an alert occurs or when a job is executed.

By taking advantage of SQL Server integration with these features and with a little bit of planning, you can dramatically improve the reliability and responsiveness of your server to problems. Planning ahead for the more common errors that can occur (and setting up tasks to respond to these errors) can dramatically reduce your server's unavailable times and make your users much happier with the job you're doing.

Q&A

Q Which service is responsible for managing scheduled tasks?

A The SQL Server Agent service.

Q Which system table contains the alerts you define on your SQL Server system?

A The sysalerts system table in the msdb database.

Q Which severity level indicates a severe problem with SQL Server itself?

A Severity 17 or higher.

Q **What must you do to take advantage of the Performance Monitor integration in SQL Server 7.0?**

A Set up an alert with the type set to SQL Server performance condition.

Workshop

The Workshop provides quiz questions to help you solidify your understanding of the concepts presented in this chapter. In addition to the quiz questions, exercises are provided to let you practice what you have learned in this chapter. Try to understand the quiz and exercise answers before continuing to the next day's lesson. Answers are provided in Appendix A, "Answers."

Quiz

1. What is the Windows NT alternative to the SQL Server Agent service to schedule tasks?

2. What profile is SQL Server referring to when it requests a mail profile name?

3. Which command would be used to receive a query via email and send the reply back to a user as a text file attachment?

4. How many scheduled tasks would you create if you wanted your transaction log to be backed up every three hours daily? The first backup should be `with init` (at 5 a.m.), and the rest of the log backups should be `with noinit`.

5. Which tool or wizard would you use to perform regular backups, database reorganizations, and integrity checks?

Exercises

1. If you didn't do so during the chapter, integrate email with SQL Server on your system.

2. Configure a performance monitor alert, and then cause the alert condition to fire. Verify that it works as expected.

3. Create a scheduled job to run a Windows NT command file. Experiment with the success and failure options of the job steps.

4. Configure the Database Maintenance Plan Wizard for each database on your system.

19

DAY 20

Configuring and Monitoring SQL Server 7.0

In yesterday's lesson, you examined the SQL Server Agent and how to take advantage of the features of the Agent. You can set up jobs to perform routine tasks so that you don't need constant interaction with your databases. You can set up alerts to monitor for exceptional conditions and have those alerts notify you via three different mechanisms: Net Send on Windows NT, email messages, or a pager notification integrated with an email server. You can even have an alert condition launch a job to perform corrective action. The jobs you create can be very complicated, have multiple steps, and include complex conditional logic. The jobs can be written in Transact-SQL, Windows NT command files, or even ActiveScript languages such as VBScript or JavaScript.

In today's lesson, you will examine how to configure and monitor SQL Server 7.0. This includes configuring your hardware, configuring Windows NT (there's not much you can do with Windows 9x), as well as configuring SQL Server itself. In terms of monitoring SQL Server, a variety of tools are available to monitor how SQL Server is performing. These tools include the Windows NT performance monitor, the SQL Server Profiler, and the Index Tuning Wizard.

One thing must be clear from the start. The best thing you can do to make your database perform is to implement a properly normalized physical database design. If you implement your database design poorly (or don't design your database), nothing you can do with hardware or software will ever make your database perform well.

Hardware Selection and Tuning

The first step to consider is the proper selection of hardware. People often ask what the most important component of a SQL Server system is. The answer is that a well-functioning machine requires components that work well together. However, if you had to pick one component, it would have to be memory. SQL Server rarely has too much random access memory (RAM). You should examine each component in detail.

Memory

SQL Server requires RAM to hold all data and index pages, as well as log records, in memory. It also holds compiled queries and stored procedures. SQL Server 7.0 has addressed one of the major areas of concern about memory by automatically using all available memory on your computer. You can tune this, and you will examine how to do so later in today's lesson. However, it is a separate question to ask how much RAM your computer should have. A good starting point on Windows NT systems being deployed with SQL Server is probably 128MB of RAM. If you can afford more, it's a good place to invest your money. For small implementations of SQL Server (and small is a hard term to describe), 64MB of RAM might be enough; but given today's inexpensive memory, you should start with the largest amount of RAM possible. On Windows 9x computers, the same recommendation applies. Although SQL Server will run with 32MB of RAM on your computer, this might not be enough to get the best performance possible out of SQL Server. SQL Server can take advantage of 2GB of RAM on Windows NT 4.0, and 3GB of RAM on Windows NT 4.0 Server Enterprise Edition. The limits are substantially higher for Windows NT Server 5.0 Enterprise Edition.

Processor

As with any system, it never hurts to have plenty of central processing unit (CPU) power. Although SQL Server is not necessarily the most CPU-intensive program, it certainly can use the CPU, depending on the workload being run. SQL Server and Windows NT can both take advantage of multiple processors. SQL Server 7.0 can take advantage of up to four processors. The Enterprise Edition of SQL Server 7.0 is capable of supporting eight processors by default and more depending on the hardware used. SQL Server is programmed to run a workload spread out over multiple CPUs and to provide thread parallelization (running SQL Server simultaneously on multiple CPUs, including parallelization within a single query).

Network

Although often overlooked, the network is critical to the success of your deployment of SQL Server. The first consideration is what kind of network card you should use in your server. You should use a 32-bit bus mastering network card. Not only will it have the best throughput in terms of raw amounts of data, but it also will tend to have the least impact on the CPU. Another consideration is the type of network card. Most networks are still 10MB Ethernet, although variations of 100MB networks, as well as ATM (Asynchronous Transfer Mode), FDDI (Fiber Distributed Data Interface), and so on, are becoming more popular. Remember that all your database activity will have to be sent through the network. If you have a 10MB Ethernet network card, you can expect throughput of about 1.2MB per second (Mbps). If you want more than that amount of data to be sent out of SQL Server, you will need to add a second or even a third network card.

Note

Make sure that you put each network card on a separate physical network. If you place multiple network cards on a single network, you will get duplicate name errors, and some or all of the network cards could be disabled. This is because your SQL Server machine would announce its presence on the network one network card at a time. When the second network card would announce its server name, the first card would announce that it already had this name. Because Network Basic Input/Output System (NetBIOS) has a flat name space, all names must be unique on the network. Therefore, the secondary network cards would return errors about name problems and not function properly. Again, simply place each network card on its own subnet to avoid this problem. When Windows NT 5.0 with the active directory is available, this consideration might not be as important.

Disks

20

Disks are a critical component of any server because that's where the data is. If you'd like to get access to your data, you typically must access it from your hard disk. The speed with which the data is written back to the disks is also important. There are also bandwidth considerations. Then there's...OK, I'll stop now. You first must examine what kind of disks you should use. More small disks are better than fewer large disks. Small computer system interface (SCSI) disks tend to perform better than integrated development environment (IDE) disks, but they cost a little bit more. However, it's worth the money. It is also worthwhile to use multiple SCSI cards in your computer, with disks distributed among them. A new specification called SCSI 3 might provide even further performance/speed enhancements. Some vendors are calling this Ultra SCSI. Make sure all components of the SCSI system are the same speed (all fast/wide, for example). Mismatches can cause devices to default to the slowest possible speed.

Another question that comes up frequently is the recommended layout of disks. The system files and the transaction log files should be duplexed. This means that they are mirrored, preferably on different SCSI controllers. The data files have two different options, either of which will work. The most expensive option is to have stripes of disks and then mirror the stripes. This can work by using hardware striping, and then use Windows NT mirroring of the stripes. This way, any disk in the system can be lost without causing any performance loss. You can also set up the disks using RAID-5 (redundant array of inexpensive disks). This is the less expensive option. However, your performance won't be as good using this option, and if you lose one of the disks you will see a significant loss of performance. Figures 20.1 and 20.2 show recommended intermediate and advanced configurations.

FIGURE 20.1

A high-fault–tolerant/moderate-performing server configuration.

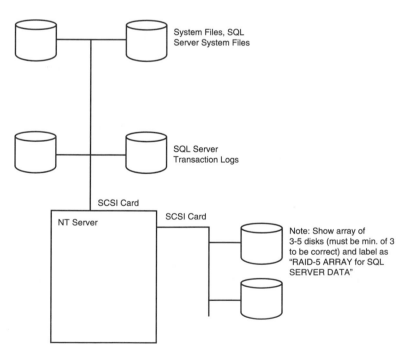

System Files, SQL
Server System Files

SQL Server
Transaction Logs

SCSI Card

NT Server

SCSI Card

Note: Show array of
3-5 disks (must be min. of 3
to be correct) and label as
"RAID-5 ARRAY for SQL
SERVER DATA"

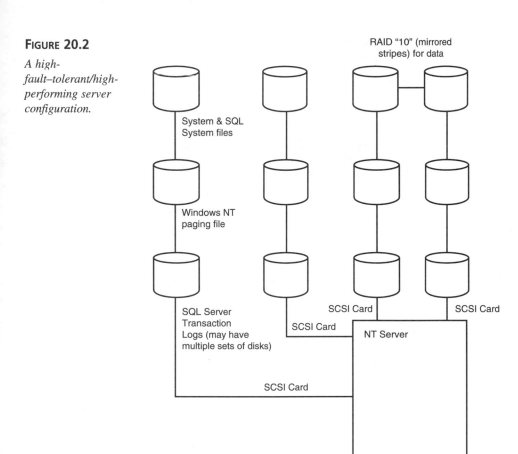

FIGURE 20.2

A high-fault–tolerant/high-performing server configuration.

There's a lot of information to consider about disks. Most well-known server vendors do an excellent job of putting together packages with all of this in mind. We have worked with servers from Compaq, HP, Data General, and IBM and had good luck with them. Most are superbly engineered, and the support staffs from the vendor companies understand how to tune and configure SQL Server and recommend systems that will support Windows NT and SQL Server well.

Windows NT Configuration Parameters

Most Windows NT configuration options that must be set are chosen by default by the setup program. The most important configuration option is to Maximize Throughput for Network Applications as the configuration value of the Server service in Control Panel, Network (see Figure 20.3). The SQL Server setup program sets this value correctly, and you should not change it.

20

FIGURE 20.3

*The Server tab of the
Network icon from the
Control Panel.*

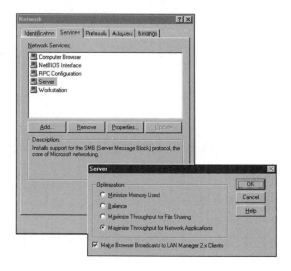

As mentioned on Day 2, "Installing SQL Server 7.0," SQL Server should be installed on a member server (or standalone server—they're really the same thing). SQL Server will function on a domain controller, but this is not a recommended implementation. Domain controllers have additional demands on their memory that can conflict with the memory needs of SQL Server.

This brings up the topic of additional services running on the SQL Server machine. Being a domain controller is mostly a function of another service running on the server. Other services such as Dynamic Host Configuration Protocol (DHCP) Server, Windows Internet Naming Service (WINS) server, domain name service (DNS) server, or other BackOffice applications will most likely interfere with the performance of SQL Server. You shouldn't run these services on the same machine as your database.

Another consideration is the Windows NT paging file. You should place the paging file on a disk not being used by SQL Server. Otherwise usage of the page file might interfere with SQL Server.

The earlier section titled "Disks" mentions using RAID to protect data. Using a hardware implementation of mirroring or RAID-5, rather than using Windows NT Server's RAID capabilities, is a good idea. Most hardware implementations will out-perform Windows NT server's built-in RAID capabilities.

Windows NT Performance Monitor Counters

This book does not attempt to provide a thorough discussion of Windows NT performance monitoring or performance counters. Windows NT Resource Kit provides a good discussion of Windows NT performance monitoring. However, a few counters are very important for SQL Server and deserve mention.

The objects and counters described here can be monitored with the Windows NT Performance Monitor tool. Now look at each of the four types of resources you already learned about in today's lesson.

Memory

One consideration for a machine dedicated to SQL Server is memory. In general, you will want to keep page faults to a minimum. Page faults occur when data is needed in memory but isn't found and must be fetched from disk. You can monitor this counter with the MEMORY object, Page Faults/Sec counter. Although the value will not be zero, it should not be a high value. What's a high value? Whatever is not normal for your server. In general, you would like to see this value be as close to zero as possible.

Another memory counter to consider is the MEMORY object, Available Bytes counter. This value should not fall below 4MB. If it does, Windows NT will attempt to reclaim memory from applications (including SQL Server) to free up some memory. If this value falls below 4MB frequently, you might have assigned too much memory to SQL Server. Note, however, that SQL Server 7.0 will automatically prevent paging unless you turn off automatic memory tuning.

Processor

The counter most commonly monitored is the PROCESSOR object, % Processor Time counter. This will tell you how busy the CPU is overall. Note that there is an instance number, starting at 0, for each CPU in the system.

Network

For network monitoring, you can use either the Performance Monitor tool or a network monitoring tool, such as Microsoft Network Monitor. There are literally too many network objects and counters to mention here. You can monitor objects based on each separate network protocol, such as NetBEUI, Transmission Control Protocol (TCP), User Datagram Protocol (UDP), Internet Protocol (IP), and so on. There are some SQL Server-specific counters you'll learn about later in today's lesson.

Disk

You can monitor disk usage only after you have turned on the Windows NT disk counters. You enable these with the command diskperf -y from a Windows NT command prompt and then restart the server. Otherwise all the disk counters will reflect a value of 0.

20

After you've enabled the disk counters, you can monitor the following counters: LogicalDisk object, Avg. Disk Quouc Length counter. If this value is consistently higher than the number you've configured for max asynch IO (which defaults to 8), you might want to increase this value. You might experience significant performance benefits on systems with multiple disks by increasing this counter.

You might also choose to monitor the PhysicalDisk object. The difference between this and the LogicalDisk object is that the PhysicalDisk counter monitors physical hard drives, whereas the LogicalDisk counter tells you about drive letters. Hence, if you have two logical disks on a single physical drive, you can use the PhysicalDisk counter to show how much activity is happening on the physical disk, as well as break it down on a logical disk by logical disk basis.

Configuring SQL Server

Configuring SQL Server 7.0 is relatively straightforward. There are still several options available to tune, but the good news is that you will almost never need to change these options. However, it's still useful to at least see what is available and know when you might need to change them.

> **Note**
>
> Only this section will deal with tuning for Windows NT–based SQL servers. For the Desktop version of SQL Server on Windows 9x, you would be wasting your time to put too much effort into tuning SQL Server for most implementations. The automatic tuning options will take care of the most important configuration options for you.

To begin examining these configuration options, you should turn on the Show Advanced Options configuration option to see all the configuration parameters available to you. Do this with the sp_configure system stored procedure.

```
Exec sp_configure 'Show Advanced Options',1
GO
RECONFIGURE with Override
GO
Exec sp_configure
```

You will see something like the following results:

name	minimum	maximum	config	_value run_value
affinity mask	0	2147483647	0	0
allow updates	0	1	0	0

cost threshold for parallelism	0	32767	5	5
cursor threshold	-1	2147483647	-1	-1
default language	0	9999	0	0
default sortorder id	0	255	52	52
extended memory size (MB)	0	2147483647	0	0
fill factor (%)	0	100	0	0
index create memory (KB)	704	1600000	0	0
language in cache	3	100	3	3
lightweight pooling	0	1	0	0
locks	5000	2147483647	0	0
max async IO	1	255	32	32
max degree of parallelism	0	32	0	0
max server memory (MB)	4	2147483647	2147483647	2147483647
max text repl size (B)	0	2147483647	65536	65536
max worker threads	10	1024	255	255
media retention	0	365	0	0
min memory per query (KB)	512	2147483647	1024	1024
min server memory (MB)	0	2147483647	0	0
nested triggers	0	1	1	1
network packet size (B)	512	65535	4096	4096
open objects	0	2147483647	0	0
priority boost	0	1	0	0
query governor cost limit	0	2147483647	0	0
query wait (s)	-1	2147483647	-1	-1
recovery interval (min)	0	32767	0	0
remote access	0	1	1	1
remote login timeout (s)	0	2147483647	30	30
remote proc trans	0	1	0	0
remote query timeout (s)	0	2147483647	0	0
resource timeout (s)	5	2147483647	10	10
scan for startup procs	0	1	0	0
set working set size	0	1	0	0
show advanced options	0	1	1	1
spin counter	1	2147483647	10000	0
time slice (ms)	50	1000	100	100
Unicode comparison style	0	2147483647	196609	196609
Unicode locale id	0	2147483647	1033	1033
user connections	0	32767	0	0
user options	0	4095	0	0

(41 row(s) affected)

Despite its huge increase in functionality, SQL Server 7.0 has fewer options than previous releases. As stated before, you will never need to tune the vast majority of these options. Most of them are set to 0 in the config_value and run_value options, meaning

20

that SQL Server will automatically tune the option for you. Unless you have a compelling reason to change these automatic settings, you should not do so.

From a performance and tuning perspective, there are a few configuration parameters you might want to change. Again, we can't say it too often: The odds are good that for all but the largest SQL Server implementations, you will not need to change these parameters. However, if you are managing a four-processor SQL server, you might need to consider these configuration options. In order to make the analysis of these options easier, today's lesson groups them into four categories: processor options, memory configuration options, input/output (I/O) options, and query/index options.

Processor Options

The first set of options to examine relates to SQL Server's use of the processors on your computer. You can configure the relative priority of the SQL Server process, which CPUs on your computer SQL Server will use, and the total number of operating system threads SQL Server can use on your computer. You can also set the maximum number of CPUs that can be used during parallel query operations. Each option is listed in a logical order to consider when making changes to your SQL Server configuration. In other words, it's probably better to consider changing the priority boost option (examined first) before considering changing the cost threshold for the parallelism option (examined last).

Priority Boost

The priority boost option determines whether the SQL Server threads on your computer run at normal priority (priority level 8 on Windows NT 4.0) or high priority (priority level 13 on Windows NT 4.0). When set to the value 0, you would be running at normal priority; when set to the value 1, you would be running at high priority. These settings are for a single-processor computer. On a multiprocessor computer, normal SQL Server priority is 15 and high priority is 24. When changing this option, you will need to restart the MSSQLServer service for the change to take effect. Monitor your computer carefully after setting this option because you could hurt any other process running on your SQL Server computer. However, on a dedicated SQL Server machine, you'll see improved performance by setting this option.

Affinity Mask

The affinity mask option is a bitmap representing which CPUs will be used for SQL Server (on a multi-CPU system). So to set processors 0, 1, and 3, you must set the bitmap pattern to 00001011 (because you set them from left to right, with position 1 equal to CPU 0, position 2 set to CPU 1, and so on). To make this simple, you enter the base-10 (normal number) equivalent to this, which is 11: $(8 \times 1) + (4 \times 0) + (2 \times 1) + (1 \times 1)$, starting from the first set bit. By default, SQL Server takes advantage of all the processors on your system—you change this option only when you want some processors to be reserved for Windows NT or another process running on your server. It's a good idea to let SQL Server use all available processors most of the time.

Max Worker Threads

The max worker threads option specifies how many operating system threads are available for use on your computer. The default is 255, which means SQL Server can launch up to 255 different simultaneous threads to the operating system. If more than 255 different threads are needed, queries and other system processes will share the available threads. This is called *thread pooling*.

Ironically, for smaller SQL Server systems (less than 100 users), you might improve performance by lowering this number. This configuration option is very hardware and environment specific, so you will simply need to tune the option down and verify any performance changes. A good starting point is 100 for smaller systems (again, less than 100 concurrent users).

Changes to this configuration parameter take effect immediately, without a restart of SQL Server.

Parallel Query Options

There are two parallel query options in SQL Server 7.0. Parallelism really takes two forms in SQL Server. The first form is SQL Server's capability to run some parts of a query in parallel and then recombine the processing to produce a single result. This kind of parallelism happens all the time in SQL Server.

The second kind of parallel query, and the one you configure, is SQL Server's capability to dedicate processors to a single query in parallel. This kind of parallel query is available only on multiprocessor systems, and typically runs only when you have more processors than users.

For example, it's Saturday night at 9 p.m. No users are on the system, and you start a job to run a huge report. If you have a four-processor system, SQL Server can choose to use all four processors to complete this report much more quickly than it would be able to otherwise. However, after the parallel query starts it will run until completing, using all the configured CPUs. If another user connects and tries to run another query, the new user's query performance will suffer because of this parallel query. For this reason, you should configure parallelism carefully if you have multiple processors.

Max Degree of Parallelism

This option specifies the number of threads available to use for parallel queries (between 1 and 32). A value of 0 indicates that all configured processors (from the affinity mask configuration) can be used, with one thread per processor. A value of 1 effectively turns off the parallel query. Any other value specifies the maximum number of CPUs used for a parallel query. Again, parallel queries will be considered only when your SQL server is relatively free of other activity.

On single-processor computers, this option is ignored. Changes to this configuration parameter take effect immediately, without restarting SQL Server.

Cost Threshold for Parallelism

This option specifies the number of seconds a query will take if executed without parallel query before a parallel execution plan is considered. The default value is 5 seconds, and the option can be set up to 32,767. In other words, if a query will take at least five seconds to run without parallel query, SQL Server will examine the option to use the parallel query facilities.

This option applies only to multiprocessor computers when the SQL Server affinity mask and max degrees of parallelism options are set to allow parallel queries to occur. Changes to this parameter take effect immediately, without restarting SQL Server.

SQL Server Enterprise Manager

Each of these configuration "groups" has a property page in the configuration of your server as part of the SQL Server Enterprise Manager utility. To access the processor properties of your server, right-click your server, select Properties, and click the Processor tab (see Figure 20.4).

The options in this dialog are self-explanatory now that you have examined them in detail.

FIGURE 20.4

The processor configuration options for your server.

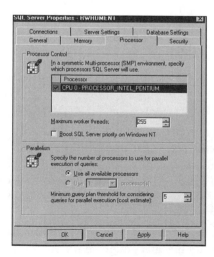

Memory Configuration Options

There are two memory configuration options you will examine. These are the min server memory and max server memory options. By default, SQL Server sets the min server memory to 0 and the max server memory to 2147483647MB (a really, really big number). This configuration means SQL Server will use automatic memory management. As SQL Server needs more memory, it will take more memory. However, to prevent paging, SQL Server's default keeps it from expanding so much that the total memory load on the server takes more than the amount of physical RAM—5MB. So on my 128MB system, SQL Server will never commit more RAM than 123MB (including Windows NT and any other running processes). However, you can set these options manually as well.

You would normally leave these settings unchanged; SQL Server 7.0 does an excellent job of dynamically allocating and deallocating memory as needed. However, if you are running another memory-intensive program, such as Microsoft Exchange Server, on the same computer, you might want to restrict how much RAM is assigned to SQL Server. Having a dedicated SQL Server machine is always a good idea.

Min Server Memory

If you set the min server memory, you are telling SQL Server to never use less than n megabytes of memory. For example, if you configure min server memory to 50 (megabytes), when you start SQL Server it will always request 50MB of memory to start.

If you also set the max server memory to 50MB, you're setting a "fixed" amount of memory that SQL Server will always use.

Max Server Memory

Setting the max server memory restricts the maximum amount of memory SQL Server can ever use. Again, the value is set in megabytes.

Min Memory Per Query

This option specifies the minimum amount of memory allocated for each user on your SQL Server for each query each server runs. The default value is 1,024KB, or 1MB. For most SQL Server computers, this default is enough memory. However, if you are using SQL Server 7.0 as a decision support or data warehousing database, you might want to increase this value. You can increase performance of queries doing large sorts or joins by allocating more memory before the queries actually need the memory (rather than finding the memory at runtime).

20

SQL Server Enterprise Manager

If you again select the properties of your server and click the Memory tab, you will see
Figure 20.5. You can leave the server set to dynamically allocate memory, set a fixed
memory size, or tune the minimum and maximum memory allocations. You can also set
the minimum memory allocation per query.

FIGURE 20.5

*The memory configu-
ration options for your
server.*

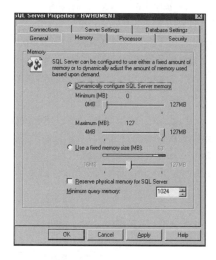

Tip

The option to Reserve Physical Memory for SQL Server sets the Set Working
Set Size configuration parameter. Setting this option never seems to make
any improvement in SQL Server (perhaps even hurts), so it's not examined
further here.

I/O Options

There is only one configuration parameter you should consider tuning on most SQL
Server configurations—the max async IO parameter. The best thing you can do for your
SQL Server disk and I/O performance is to spread your data across multiple disks and
multiple controllers, as you learned earlier in today's lesson.

The max async IO parameter is the number of outstanding writes that can be issued
simultaneously against your Windows NT I/O subsystem at any given time. The default
value is 32, which should perform well for most installations. If you are using multiple
hardware drive arrays, you might benefit from increasing the number of outstanding
writes that can be run. This is very dependent on the workload of your SQL Server, as

well as your hardware configuration, so you will be able to determine the optimal value only by changing this parameter and testing the performance in the new configuration.

There is no way to configure this option using SQL Server Enterprise Manager; you must run the `sp_configure` system stored procedure and restart SQL Server for any changes to the `max asynch IO` option to take effect.

Query/Index Options

Two options are available to tune or limit the running of queries or to tune indexes. These include the fill factor, which you already examined on Day 13, "Enhancing Performance with Indexing." The other option is the query governor cost limit.

Query Governor Cost Limit

SQL Server 7.0 has a query governor built into it. The default value for this option is `0`, meaning all queries are allowed to run. However, when you set this option to a nonzero number, you are telling SQL Server that any query predicted to run for longer than n number of seconds will be prevented from executing. Be careful when setting this option because you can easily prevent users from running queries that they need to run to perform their jobs. On the other hand, you can prevent those runaway one-hour queries from running as well. This option does not have a SQL Server Enterprise Manager interface.

Monitoring SQL Server Performance

Several utilities, as well as Transact-SQL commands are available to assist you in monitoring the performance of SQL Server. Among these are the performance monitor counters (which you saw briefly in yesterday's lesson when examining alerts), SQL Server Enterprise Manager's Current Activity windows, the SQL Server profiler, and some key system-stored procedures. You examine each of these in the following section.

SQL Server Performance Monitor Counters

The first stop on your monitoring tour will be with the Windows NT performance monitor again. This time, however, you will examine the performance monitor counters that SQL Server exposes. Notice that there is an option in the SQL Server 7.0 program group to start performance monitoring with some preconfigured SQL Server performance counters. As with the configuration options, today's lesson does not attempt to examine each counter (there are more than 100), just the big ones you should know about.

20

Memory

Consider the SQLServer.Buffer Manager object, Buffer Cache Hit Ratio counter to determine how efficiently memory is being used on your server. This value reflects how frequently data was found in memory when SQL Server went to find it. This value should be higher than 90 percent and preferably as close to 100 percent as possible. If you haven't done so, start the Performance Monitor (located in the Administrative Tools program group) and click the plus sign (+) on the toolbar. Scroll down to the SQLServer:Buffer Manager object, and you will see a dialog resembling Figure 20.6. This is the Buffer Cache Hit Ratio counter we are discussing. You can find other counters and objects by clicking on the appropriate drop-down menu items.

FIGURE 20.6

The Performance Monitor view for the SQL Server counters.

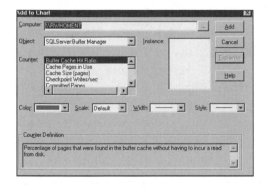

You might also want to monitor the SQLServer:Buffer Manager object, Cache Size (Pages) counter to view how much memory is being used to hold your data and indexes. This information is returned as pages, so you multiply the result by eight to return the approximate number of kilobytes of memory being used.

Processor

If you want to monitor how much of the CPU SQL Server is using, you can monitor the PROCESS object, % Processor Time counter, with an instance of SQLSERVR. You can monitor how much processor time the SQL Server Agent service is using by monitoring the instance of SQLAgent.

Network

There are no SQL Server-provided objects to monitor your network activity. Each network protocol can report its own statistics.

Tip

> If you are using Transmission Control Protocol/Internet Protocol (TCP/IP), you must install the Simple Network Management Protocol (SNMP) service for the TCP/IP-related performance counters to appear.

Disk

There are a significant number of IO counters to monitor for the SQLServer object. For example, in the SQLServer:Buffer Manager object, the Page Reads/sec counter will monitor read activity (from disk), and Page Writes/sec counter will monitor how much write activity is occurring on the server. Another counter you might want to monitor is in the SQLServer:Databases object, Log Flushes/sec. This counter indicates how many log records are written to disk each second and will give you an idea of how much work is being done. Related to this counter is the SQLServer:Databases object, Transactions/Sec, which indicates how many active transactions are in a database at any given time. Notice that these last two options are database specific, so you will need to select one or more databases from your Instance window to monitor the activity in that database.

System Stored Procedures for Monitoring Performance

There are a few system stored procedures you can use to monitor the performance of your SQL server. The most important two are sp_who and sp_monitor.

sp_who [[@login_name =] '*login*']

where

- *login* is the name of a login you would like to monitor. If you don't specify the login, information is returned for all logins. If you specify the keyword ACTIVE, only information on users who are currently running queries will be returned. System connections are always returned, even when you specify ACTIVE.

The output from sp_who will tell you who is connected, what computers the users are using, what databases they are using, and what command states they are in. For example, when I run

```
Exec sp_who
```

▼ SYNTAX

▲

20

I get

```
spid status       loginame        hostname   blk dbname cmd
---- ------------ --------------- ---------- --- ------ ----------------
1    sleeping     sa                         0   master SIGNAL HANDLER
2    background   sa                         0   pubs   LOCK MONITOR
3    background   sa                         0   pubs   LAZY WRITER
4    sleeping     sa                         0   pubs   LOG WRITER
5    sleeping     sa                         0   pubs   CHECKPOINT SLEEP
6    background   sa                         0   pubs   AWAITING COMMAND
7    sleeping     RWHOMENT\rwaymi RWHOMENT   0   master AWAITING COMMAND
8    runnable     RWHOMENT\rwaymi RWHOMENT   0   pubs   AWAITING COMMAND
(8 row(s) affected)
```

The other system-stored procedure is sp_monitor. sp_monitor returns the amount of system activity that has occurred since the system stored procedure was last run.

sp_monitor

There are no parameters to sp_monitor.

For example, on my system I ran sp_monitor, performed some activity, and then ran sp_monitor again. Here are the results:

```
last_run                   current_run                  seconds
-------------------------  -------------------------    -----------
1998-08-16 18:10:57.890    1998-08-16 18:11:59.327      62

(1 row(s) affected)

cpu_busy                   io_busy                      idle
-----------------------    -----------------------      ----------------------
4(0)-0%                    0(0)-0%                      3429(59)-95%

(1 row(s) affected)

packets_received           packets_sent                 packet_errors
-----------------------    -----------------------      -----------------------
374(20)                    194(10)                      0(0)

(1 row(s) affected)

total_read             total_write            total_errors          connections
-----------------      -----------------      -----------------     -------------
435(23)                80(2)                  0(0)                  18(0)

(1 row(s) affected)
```

As you can see, it reports quite a bit of useful information, including how busy the CPU was, how busy your disks were, how much network activity occurred, and how much disk activity occurred. Although this information is useful, it does require that you run the command before and after an activity you want to measure.

The Current Activity Window of SQL Server Enterprise Manager

An easier way to view SQL Server performance information is through the Current Activity window of SQL Server Enterprise Manager. To access this window, expand the Management folder for your SQL server, and then expand the Current Activity option (the globe). Then highlight the process info item in the left pane. You are presented with the dialog in Figure 20.7. If you see icons instead of Figure 20.7, select View, Detail from the menu.

FIGURE 20.7

The Current Activity window.

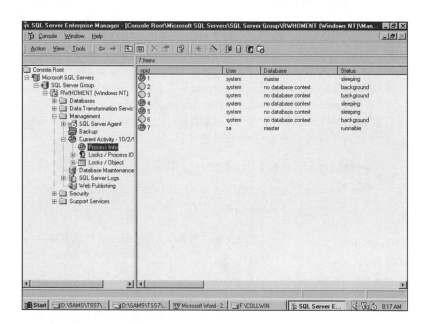

In this window you can see each connection in SQL Server. When you highlight a particular process and then right-click it, you can kill that process (if you are a member of the sysadmin or processadmin fixed server roles). You can also send the user a message (via the Windows operating system, not to the user's query tool), or select properties from the pop-up menu to see the last command the user has run (see Figure 20.8).

You can also examine the details of locking by selecting either Locks/Process ID or Locks/Object in the left pane to view locks by those groupings.

20

FIGURE 20.8

You can highlight an item and kill the process or send a message in the Process Details dialog.

Using the SQL Server Profiler

The SQL Server Profiler utility enables you to monitor all activity on your SQL server. There is an amazing array of events you can capture and record when using the SQL Server Profiler. The most useful part of using the SQL Server Profiler, however, is the simple ability to capture the Transact-SQL commands that are run on your server. You can use this as an audit trail or simply as a way to see what kind of work is being performed on your computer. You can also use a captured trace as input to the SQL Server Index Tuning Wizard. This wizard will help you select the proper indexes for a given set of queries. It's handy when you can simply run a trace for a typical business day, then hand the trace over to the Index Tuning Wizard. It runs for a while and then spits out the optimal set of indexes for you to use.

Setting Up and Starting a Trace

The first step in using this tool is to set up a trace. Start the SQL Server Profiler from your SQL Server 7.0 program group, and you are presented with the dialog in Figure 20.9.

FIGURE 20.9

The SQL Server Profiler lets you set up a trace.

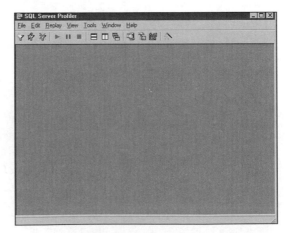

To begin one of the preconfigured traces, select File, Run Traces from the menu (or click the Play button on the toolbar). You are presented with a list of all the available traces you can run. SQL Server 7.0 ships with six preconfigured traces. Sample 1 is a good example of the kind of information you can see with a trace. Highlight Sample 1, and click OK to start the trace. Launch the SQL Server Query Analyzer (notice the icon on the toolbar for the Query Analyzer), and run the following query:

```
Use pubs
Select * from authors
```

Now switch back to the Profiler and look at the Transact-SQL statements (and other information) that were captured (see Figure 20.10). Although the queries you ran (the use command followed by the select command) were captured, several other commands were also captured. These commands are run every time the SQL Server Query Analyzer starts. They configure the environment before you begin to run queries. All commands that are run, even when you don't know they're being run, are captured here.

FIGURE 20.10

The SQL Server Profiler trace.

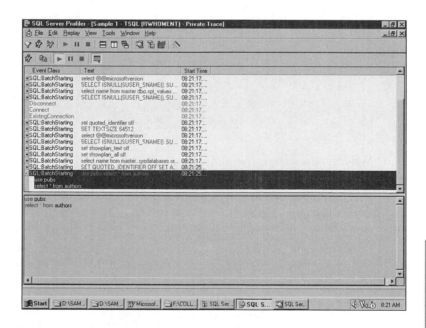

20

To stop the trace, simply click the stop button inside the query window. The trace will stop, and no more queries will be captured.

Now set up your own trace. Close the trace you were looking at, and click the New Trace button on the toolbar (the first one on the left). You are presented with the dialog in Figure 20.11 and can start entering the properties of your trace. You first must name the trace (I used My Trace, but you should probably use something more descriptive if you intend to keep your trace). You can set the trace to be shared with other users of your computer, or you can keep it private (only associated with your account on your computer).

FIGURE 20.11

Adding a new trace.

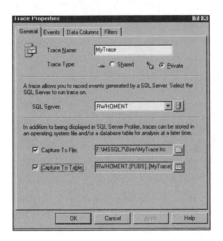

You can also capture your traces to a file or to a SQL Server table. If you select the Capture To File option you will be prompted for a location. The default location is in your \mssql7\binn directory, with a filename of *<tracename>*.trc. So for the trace I named My Trace, the filename would be My Trace.trc. You can also save your trace to a SQL Server table. If you check the Capture To Table option, you will be prompted for the server name, database name, owner name, and table name. Select a database on your SQL Server, and accept the default table name of [My Trace]. Notice that the table will have the same name as your trace, so it's a good idea to create your trace name with a valid SQL Server identifier. Figure 20.11 reflects all these selections.

If you click the Events tab (see Figure 20.12), you will have the option to select the information you want to capture in your trace. The default is to capture when users connect, when they disconnect, and what users are connected when the trace starts. You will also see any Remote Procedure Call (RPC) events or SQL Batch events when they complete. SQL Batch events are the calls into SQL Server that aren't RPC events.

FIGURE 20.12

*The Events tab of a
new trace.*

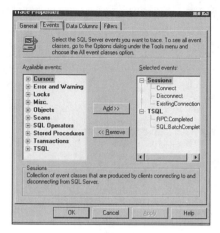

Notice that on the left side of the trace dialog is a significant number of additional events
you can capture. It takes time to explore these events, but when you master them you
will discover that there's not much you can't do with the Profiler.

Click the Data Columns tab to see which items will show up on your trace report (see
Figure 20.13). By default, you capture items such as what user was running a query,
what application the user was using, what SQL Server username the user was using, a
variety of performance information, and of course, the text of the command the user ran.
You will also see that you can group items of similar types. For example, if you want to
group events by SQL Server username, you can highlight the SQL User Name item and
then click the up button until SQL User Name appears under the Groups item. Your
report then groups its trace by SQL User Name, instead of listing events sequentially.
You can use grouping to make your reports more readable on the screen.

FIGURE 20.13

*The Data Columns tab
of a new trace.*

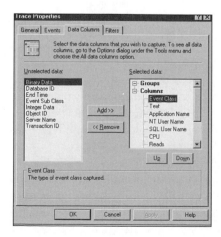

20

And last, but not least, you can filter your trace so you gather only the information you really want. Notice in Figure 20.14 that the Profiler excludes its Transact-SQL commands by default. To see that the Profiler utility is calling an extended stored procedure when it starts, remove this restriction by highlighting the words SQL Server Profiler% and then erasing them from the Exclude text box. This will remove the restriction that you won't see the work the Profiler itself performs.

FIGURE 20.14

The Filters tab of a new trace.

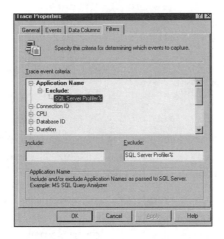

For each restriction you would like to place on your trace, highlight the option in the Trace Event Criteria window; then type the item you want to include or exclude in the appropriate text box. For each event criterion, the appropriate text box will appear.

Click OK, and your trace will start automatically. Notice in Figure 20.15 that the SQL Server profiler is calling the extended stored procedure `xp_trace_seteventclassre-quired`. It's a whole lot easier to use the graphical interface than to figure out which extended stored procedure to call, but if you want you can set up calls to this procedure yourself.

Again, this trace will simply capture all Transact-SQL statements and RPC events that occur on your SQL Server. If you leave it running, it will continue to do so. However, stop the trace now and verify that the trace file has been created by clicking File, Open, Trace File, and you should see My Trace.trc. Open this trace, and you will see that, indeed, all the commands you were viewing were captured and recorded in the trace file.

Setting Up an Audit Trail

As you can see, you have already set up an audit trail. All you must do is leave the trace running all the time on your server. It'll be a good idea to cycle the trace utility periodically simply to start a new trace file (so that the files are a manageable size).

You might also consider setting a Profiler trace to start automatically when SQL Server starts. You can do this with the xp_trace_setqueueautostart extended stored procedure.

FIGURE 20.15

A captured trace.

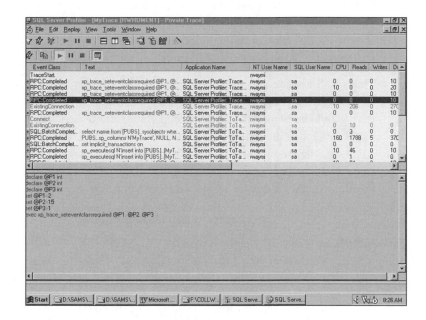

SYNTAX

```
xp_trace_setqueueautostart {'queue_name', autostart_value}
```

where

- *queue_name* is the name of the trace you want to have start automatically.
- *autostart_value* is 1 to indicate autostart, 0 to turn it off.

For example, if you configure a trace named myaudittrace with the Profiler utility, you can run

```
Exec xp_trace_setqueueautostart 'myaudittrace',1
```

And the next time SQL Server is started, the trace myaudittrace would start.

Using a Trace to Monitor Performance

The easiest way to use the Profiler to find your performance problems is—yes, you guessed it—by using a wizard. Start the Create Trace Wizard from the SQL Server Profiler by selecting Tools, Create Trace Wizard from the menu. You will see the Trace Wizard appear. Click Next after reading the introduction, and then notice that there are some preconfigured options here for you. For example, Find the Worst Performing

20

Queries is the top selection. Click Next, and select a database if you want. The default is to profile all databases. Select a minimum duration so you capture only queries worth investigating. Notice that the value is in milliseconds, so 1,000 is actually only a 1-second query. Click Next again, and you can select to trace all applications or select one or more applications if you know one that is causing a problem. Click Next one more time, and the Profiler has configured a trace for you. Click Finish to accept the default name for the trace (Worst Performing Queries).

That's it! The trace will start automatically, and you can view the selected traces. However, it's a good idea to stop the trace and edit it to set the file location to which the trace should be recorded. Click the Stop button and then the Properties button for the trace (furthest to the left in your trace window). Change the file option just as you did when creating a new trace. Figure 20.16 shows the changed trace. Now run the trace for some length of time (perhaps even 24 hours), and then stop it. This will allow the Profiler to gather a typical business day for your SQL Server.

FIGURE 20.16

The modified trace.

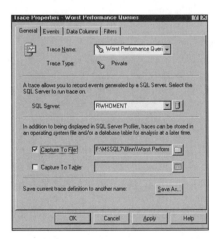

Index Tuning Wizard

The preceding discussion of traces leads rather nicely into a description of the Index Tuning Wizard. This wizard will review a saved trace file, and then recommend changes to your indexes on the server that would enhance the performance of the queries captured during the trace.

1. To start the Index Tuning Wizard, select Tools, Index Tuning Wizard from the menu in the SQL Server Profiler. Read the introductory screen, and then click Next to see the Select Server and Database dialog (see Figure 20.17).

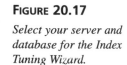

FIGURE 20.17

Select your server and database for the Index Tuning Wizard.

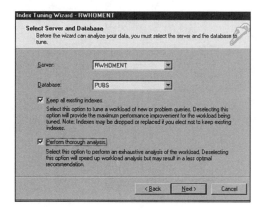

2. Select a server if you don't want to monitor your server. Then, select a database. The Index Tuning Wizard will recommend indexes for only one database at a time. The default is to not remove any indexes you already have and to perform a less thorough analysis. It's a good idea to leave this last option checked because you'd hate to have the wizard recommend indexes that aren't as good as they could have been.

3. Click Next, and you will be asked to identify the workload to be analyzed. If you already have a trace captured, you accept the default selection, I Have a Saved Workload File. Click Next again, and you will see the dialog in Figure 20.18. Specify a workload.

4. Select an existing trace file (such as My Trace.trc, as shown in Figure 20.18), or select the SQL Server table with your saved trace information. Click the Advanced Options button to view the dialog shown in Figure 20.19.

FIGURE 20.18

Specify Workload for the Index Tuning Wizard.

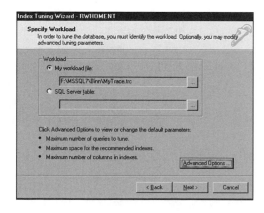

20

FIGURE 20.19

Advanced configuration options for the Index Tuning Wizard.

5. Click OK to accept any changes you make, and then click Next to view the Select Tables to Tune dialog (see Figure 20.20). By default, the wizard will attempt to optimize all tables in your database. Accept the default, and click Next.

FIGURE 20.20

The Select Tables to Tune dialog of the Index Tuning Wizard.

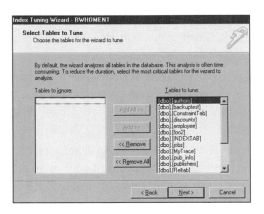

The Index Tuning Wizard will then perform an analysis of the workload you have given to it. This might take a while, depending on the size of your trace file. When completed, the recommended indexes will be shown in the Index Recommendations dialog (see Figure 20.21). Because the trace My Trace contained only two simple queries, the Index Tuning Wizard didn't recommend any changes. Notice that although it looks like three changes were recommended, the wizard shows that they already exist.

6. Click Next again, and you can select to run the wizard's recommended changes on a given SQL Server Agent Job Schedule or to save the changes as a Transact-SQL script and review or run them at your leisure (see Figure 20.22).

FIGURE 20.21

Index Recommendations of the Index Tuning Wizard.

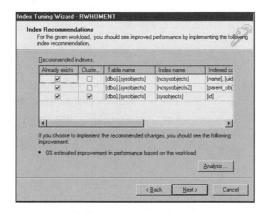

FIGURE 20.22

The Schedule Index Update Job dialog.

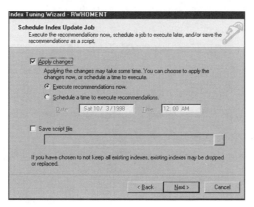

7. Because the wizard didn't recommend any changes in this case, don't select any options. Click Apply Changes (which won't actually make any changes), and then Next. Then click Finish on the final screen to exit the wizard.

That's it! The SQL Server team has turned a horribly complex job (selecting which indexes are needed on a server) into a few clicks of a wizard.

As you might have guessed, information about the Index Tuning Wizard and the SQL Server Profiler could be books themselves. So for additional information about them, please refer to *Microsoft SQL Server 7 Unleashed* from Sams publishing, which has much more detailed performance tuning information—including information about these utilities and wizards.

20

Summary

In today's lesson, you learned how to configure Windows NT and SQL Server for optimal performance. You also examined how to monitor SQL Server with the Windows NT performance monitor, as well as several built-in SQL Server tools. These include the SQL Server Profiler, the Index Tuning Wizard, and the Current Activity window of the SQL Server Enterprise Manager. Over time you will learn these tools in great detail, and they will become your closest friends when performance problems arise on your SQL Server.

Q&A

Q If you would like a quick snapshot of activity on SQL Server, where should you look?

A In the Current Activity window of SQL Server Enterprise Manager.

Q What kind of network card should you install in your server?

A A 32-bit bus mastering network card.

Q What kind of RAID array is best to use with your transaction logs?

A A mirrored, or even duplexed, set of disks is best.

Q Which tool would you use to select the proper indexes for your databases?

A The Index Tuning Wizard.

Workshop

The Workshop provides quiz questions to help you solidify your understanding of the concepts presented in this chapter. In addition to the quiz questions, exercises are provided to let you practice what you have learned in this chapter. Try to understand the quiz and exercise answers before continuing to the next day's lesson. Answers are provided in Appendix A, "Answers."

Quiz

1. In terms of overall performance impact, what component of the system deserves the most attention for performance tuning?

2. Why should the transaction logs be kept on different disks than the Windows NT paging file?

3. If you had manually configured SQL Server's memory, and you were concerned that you had over-allocated memory for SQL Server, what Windows NT counter would you monitor?

4. What parameter would you change in SQL Server to adjust the processors used by SQL Server?

5. Which SQL Server performance counter would you watch to determine how much work was being done by SQL Server?

Exercises

Performance tuning usually involves monitoring a system with many users. Because you might or might not have this available to you, you can do your best to simulate a multiple-user system.

1. Start the SQL Server Profiler and begin a trace. Make sure to save the trace information to a trace file. Then start up several SQL Server Query Analyzer sessions and run stored procedures and queries from each connection to SQL Server.

2. Start up SQL Enterprise Manager and monitor the activity with the current activity window. Observe what information can be seen and try each of the options, such as the Kill command, and observe the behavior of the client programs (the Query Analyzer in this case).

3. After you've captured a bunch of queries with a trace, stop the trace. Then, run the Index Tuning Wizard and see what kinds of changes the wizard can recommend for you. Script out the changes and see what the wizard can do for you.

20

DAY **21**

Integrating SQL Server and the World Wide Web

In yesterday's lesson you examined how to configure and monitor SQL Server and Windows NT. You saw that there are a significant number of parameters to configure for SQL Server, most of which you never need to touch for SQL Server 7.0. You also examined several performance monitor counters provided by SQL Server. You took a detailed look at the SQL Server Profiler and Index Tuning Wizard and looked at how they can help you monitor and tune your databases. You also looked at how to use the Profiler utility to provide an audit log for your server. For a more detailed examination of performance tuning and other advanced issues, please refer to *Microsoft SQL Server 7 Unleashed* from Sams Publishing.

Today's lesson examines how to integrate SQL Server 7.0 with the Internet, and more specifically with the World Wide Web (WWW). You have already seen how SQL Server can provide replication services over the Internet and allow subscribers over the Internet to make anonymous, scalable subscriptions to data on your servers. Everything you need to publish SQL Server data on the

Internet is built into either the database or Windows NT Server (with Windows NT's Internet server, called Internet Information Server).

SQL Server 7.0 includes the capability to create static WWW pages using a wizard known as the SQL Server Web Assistant. You can also create somewhat dynamic Web pages (by periodically regenerating your static Web pages) with SQL Server jobs. Other technologies, such as Active Server Pages (ASP) and ActiveX Data Objects (ADO), allow you to create Web pages that provide an interactive experience with SQL Server in the form of dynamic queries or data maintenance forms.

Terminology Used for the World Wide Web

In today's lesson you will gain a necessary understanding of the common WWW terms and technologies. Given the widespread use of the Internet, I hope most of these terms are review. However, just in case, here are the basics:

- Universal Data Access—This is the name Microsoft has given its set of data access technologies. Microsoft has built its data access around ODBC (Open Database Connectivity) and OLE DB. OLE DB is the future of data access, and technologies that you use today are all built on top of OLE DB (including ADO). You can get more information about Universal Data Access from Microsoft's Web site at http://www.microsoft.com/data.

- Web page—A Web page is a formatted text file written in a programming language known as Hypertext Markup Language (HTML). There are many versions of HTML, and the language is undergoing constant enhancements as the Internet grows and technology advances.

- Web server—A Web server is a server-based product that returns files to clients when requested. These files are typically returned in the form of Web pages to a client Internet browser. The Web server you will learn about in this book is (surprisingly enough) Microsoft's Internet Information Server (IIS). The code included here will work (or was tested, anyway) on IIS versions 3.0 and 4.0.

- Internet browser—An Internet browser is a client program that knows how to interpret HTML code and display information and graphics to a client. Some Internet browsers also have the capability to interpret and run programming languages at the client computer (such as Java or VBScript).

- Push Web page technologies—The first form of Internet access to SQL Server that today's lesson will examine is access to static Web pages. Static Web pages are pages that don't change based on a user's interaction. They are produced with a method known as *push technology*. Push Web page development consists of generating static Web pages and writing those pages to a directory on a WWW server. The Web server, such as Internet Information Server (IIS) then makes these pages available in the form of static Web sites. The majority of Internet sites have historically been developed using push technology with static Web pages. These static pages don't allow dynamic access to data. This type of Web page access is useful, but it is somewhat out of date because of the widespread use of "pull" technology.

- Pull Web page technologies—Pull technology allows Web pages to be built dynamically as a response to a query to SQL Server. This query can be in the form of a standard Transact-SQL statement, a set of options that build a query, or a form that updates data. This type of access is allowed through a variety of techniques:

  - Microsoft Internet Database Connector (IDC) files—IDC files are a simple and effective way to dynamically query SQL Server. This technology has been around for at least the last three releases of Internet Information Server (IIS).

  - Microsoft Active Server Pages (ASP) with ADO—ADO is currently Microsoft's recommended access method to query SQL Server data dynamically from the Internet. This happens in the form of server-side scripts written in VBScript or Java. VBScript is a subset of the Visual Basic programming language, and Java is a programming language originated by Sun Microsystems. Code is run by IIS, and Web pages are built and returned to the Internet client (typically a Web browser such as Internet Explorer).

  - Microsoft Remote Data Services (RDS)—RDS is a technology that allows scripts to be run at the client computer by the user's Web browser. Database access occurs over the Internet from the client. This technology is supported with ActiveX controls inside the client Web browser. Therefore, your Web browser must support ActiveX controls, which generally means you must use Internet Explorer. This method of data access allows more functionality but has security concerns that most likely will restrict the use of this technology to intranets. An intranet is a set of Web clients and at least one server that allows access inside an organization, rather than allowing access via the global Internet.

Push Updates to Web Pages Using the SQL Server Web Assistant

As just stated, the push method enables you to create static Web pages using SQL Server data. You can run a select statement with the SQL Server Query Analyzer, save the results, and then turn the results into an HTML document. To make this task easier, you can use an HTML editor such as Microsoft FrontPage or even Microsoft Word. However, SQL Server 7.0 includes the SQL Server Web Assistant to assist you in this task. You can also use the `sp_makewebtask` system-stored procedure.

Using the SQL Server Web Assistant Wizard

To start the SQL Server Web Assistant Wizard, you must first start SQL Server Enterprise Manager.

1. From the Tools menu, select Wizards. You are presented with the Select Wizard dialog (see Figure 21.1).

FIGURE 21.1

The Select Wizard dialog.

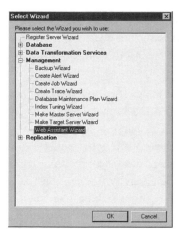

2. Expand the Management option, and select the Web Assistant Wizard. Click OK to launch the Wizard. You are presented with the Welcome dialog and a description of the wizard (see Figure 21.2).

FIGURE 21.2

The SQL Server Web Assistant Wizard welcome screen.

3. Click Next, and you are presented with the Select Database dialog (see Figure 21.3). Simply click the drop-down box and select the database you want to start with. This example deals with the pubs database.

FIGURE 21.3

The Select Database screen.

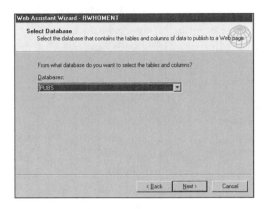

 Tip

As you know now, a query of your database can combine data from multiple databases and even multiple servers with SQL Server's heterogeneous query capabilities. Nothing about selecting a database here restricts you from querying multiple databases and multiple data sources later in the wizard.

4. You are then presented with the Start a New Web Assistant Job dialog (see Figure 21.4). Here is where you see that what you are really doing when you run this wizard is configuring a SQL Server job, just as you did on Day 19, "Using the SQL Server Agent." The question at the top of the screen is requesting a name for the job you are creating. Specify a name that will be unique across all jobs in your SQL server.

FIGURE 21.4

The Start a New Web Assistant Job dialog.

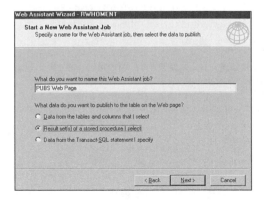

21

5. Below the job title, you have three options that will change the next several dialogs. Each option determines which query data will end up on your Web page. You can

   • Build your query with a graphical selection of the tables and columns you want to use. This option is intended for beginners to the Transact-SQL language or for a quick and dirty graphical selection of the data you need. It's smart to use this option for the simplest tasks and take advantage of the stored procedure or Transact-SQL query options to provide more powerful query capabilities.

   • Execute a stored procedure and display the results. This is the most powerful option available to you. As you saw on Day 15, "Working with Views, Stored Procedures, and Triggers," you have a wide variety of options available to you with stored procedures that simply aren't available when running a single query. If you plan to use the job that is created by this wizard on a scheduled basis, you are best served by writing a stored procedure and then using this option to execute that stored procedure.

   • Write your own Transact-SQL query and use the results. This option is the best when you want to return the results of a single query. The query you write can be very complicated and can return the results from one or more databases or even multiple servers. However, if you need any logic checking or control of flow-decision capabilities to determine the proper result set to display on your Web page, you should create a stored procedure and use the preceding Execute a Stored Procedure option.

   If you stick with the first option, you will be presented with the option to select a single table and then select one or more columns on that table. You can also specify a WHERE clause on the next dialog. After you've specified your WHERE clause using the graphical options in this dialog, you are sent to the scheduling dialog.

   If you select the third option, Data from the Transact-SQL Statement I Specify, you are presented with a blank text box where you simply type your query. After you have typed your query, click Next to move to the scheduling dialog.

   As mentioned earlier, this isn't the best option for an experienced SQL Server developer/administrator like you!

6. Create the following stored procedure using the SQL Server Query Analyzer (so you don't have to exit the wizard). Make sure you create the stored procedure in the pubs database.

```
Create proc fortheweb (@au_lname varchar(40) = 'Bennet')
As
SELECT a.au_lname as Author_LastName,
```

```
a.au_fname as Author_Firstname,
ta.royaltyper as Royalty_Percentage,
t.title as Book_Title
FROM authors a INNER JOIN titleauthor ta
ON a.au_id = ta.au_id
INNER JOIN titles t ON ta.title_id = t.title_id
WHERE a.au_lname = @au_lname
RETURN
```

7. Now, back to the Web Wizard. Select the Result Set(s) of a Stored Procedure I Select option, and click Next. You will then see Figure 21.5, the Select Stored Procedure dialog.

If you don't see your stored procedure on this page, you are experiencing a "feature" of SQL Server Enterprise Manager"—the need to refresh the list of stored procedures that the utility knows about. Cancel the wizard, expand the Pubs database folder, right-click the Stored Procedures folder, and select Refresh. You should see the fortheweb stored procedure in the right panel. Now restart the wizard and navigate back to the Select Stored Procedure dialog.

FIGURE 21.5

The Select Stored Procedure dialog.

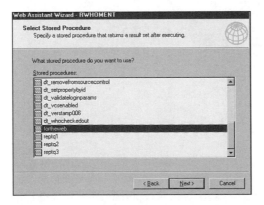

8. Highlight the fortheweb stored procedure, and click Next. The SQL Server Web Assistant Wizard is smart enough to know that your stored procedure takes a parameter; hence it presents you with the Set Stored Procedure Parameters dialog. Enter the value you want to pass to the Stored Procedure. Enter White, as shown in Figure 21.6.

21

FIGURE 21.6

The Set Stored Procedure Parameters dialog.

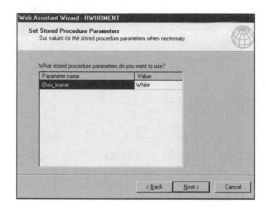

9. Click Next, and you are presented with Figure 21.7. This is the common scheduling dialog that each of the earlier options (graphically design a query, type in a query, or execute a stored procedure) all end up at.

FIGURE 21.7

The Schedule the Web Assistant Job dialog.

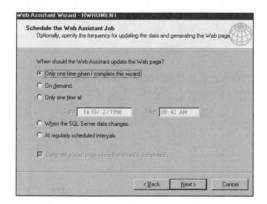

These scheduling options should look very familiar. You can choose any schedule you would like for the job generated by this wizard. However, the easiest option for the sake of today's lesson is to accept the default, Only One Time When I Complete This Wizard. You will still need to make sure the SQLServerAgent service is running on your server because a job is still run to generate the Web page.

10. Click Next, and you are asked to specify the path and filename for the Web page you are generating (see Figure 21.8). Change the location to c:\webpage1.htm so you can find the Web page easily when you are finished. It's a good idea to create your own Web page directory for the wizard or specify the appropriate location so your Web server can find the file if you plan to implement the file in production.

FIGURE 21.8

The Publish the Web Page dialog.

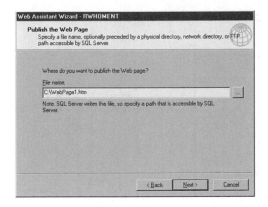

11. Click Next, and you are then presented with the option to format the Web page you are generating. You can use a template file if you have previously created one, or you can let the wizard help you format the HTML page. You also must specify in which language you want your Web page to appear.

Note
A template file is any HTML-formatted file that contains the `<%insert_data_here%>` entry to let the Web Assistant Wizard know where to insert data.

12. The next several dialogs help you format the Web page. You can specify a title for your Web page, the title of your query results, and some HTML sizing options for the page titles. You can also have a date or time entered on the page so users know when the page was last generated (this is the default). For today's lesson, simply accept all the defaults and click Next.

13. In the Format a Table dialog, accept all the defaults again. Here you would specify not to use the column headings from your query or to change the fonts and formatting of the text from your query results. Click Next again, and you can add hyperlinks to the page to jump users to another page (see Figure 21.9).

14. Modify the hyperlink options as you see in Figure 21.9. Click Next to view the dialog to Limit Rows (limiting the amount of output to your Web page). You also have the option of generating multiple pages of results that are linked together or making one long scrollable page of text (the default). Accept the defaults (as shown in Figure 21.10) and click Next.

21

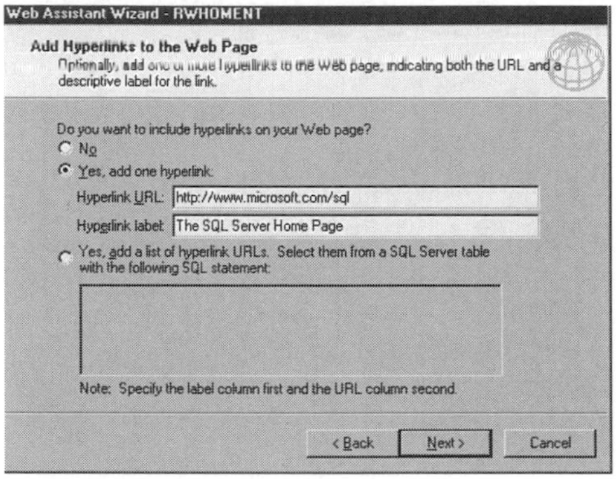

FIGURE 21.9

The Add Hyperlinks to the Web Page dialog.

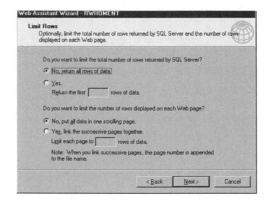

FIGURE 21.10

The Limit Rows dialog.

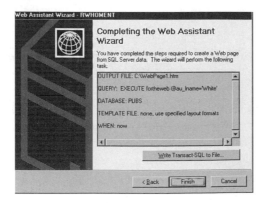

Whew! You made it! Click Finish to complete the wizard and begin the creation of the Web page (see Figure 21.11).

FIGURE 21.11

The completed Web Wizard dialog.

Now open Windows or Windows NT Explorer and browse the root of your C:\ drive. There you should find the file webpage.html. Double-click the file to bring up your default Web browser (Internet Explorer on some computers), and view the Web page you created (see Figure 21.12). Notice that the titles you requested are there, as well as the results of executing your stored procedure. Finally, the hotlink you requested to the SQL Server home page has been added. Click this link to prove that it's a real link (assuming you are on the Internet, this will take you to the SQL Server home page).

FIGURE 21.12

The completed Web page.

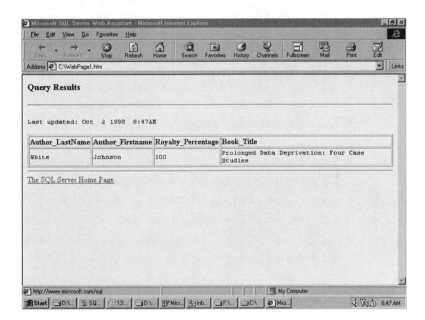

Using the `sp_makewebtask` System Stored Procedure

The Web Assistant Wizard provides a nice graphical interface, but you can perform the same functions using a call to the system-stored procedure sp_makewebtask.

```
sp_makewebtask [@outputfile =] 'outputfile', [@query =] 'query'
[, [@fixedfont =] fixedfont] [, [@bold =] bold]
[, [@italic =] italic] [, [@colheaders =] colheaders]
[, [@lastupdated =] lastupdated] [, [@HTMLHeader =] HTMLHeader]
[, [@username =] username] [, [@dbname =] dbname]
[, [@templatefile =] 'templatefile']
[, [@webpagetitle =] 'webpagetitle']
[, [@resultstitle =] 'resultstitle']
[
[, [@URL =] 'URL', [@reftext =] 'reftext']
| [, [@table_urls =] table_urls, [@url_query =] 'url_query']
]
```

SYNTAX ▼

21

```
▼   [, [@whentype =] whentype] [, [@targetdate =] targetdate]
    [, [@targettime =] targettime] [, [@dayflags =] dayflags]
    [, [@numunits =] numunits] [, [@unittype =] unittype]
    [, [@procname =] procname ] [, [@maketask =] maketask]
    [, [@rowcnt =] rowcnt] [, [@tabborder =] tabborder]
    [, [@singlerow =] singlerow] [, [@blobfmt =] blobfmt]
    [, [@nrowsperpage =] n] [, [@datachg =] table_column_list]
    [, [@charset =] characterset] [, [@codepage =] codepage]
```

where

- *outputfile* is the path and filename of the Web page generated by this stored procedure. This path can be a local drive specification or a UNC (universal naming convention) path to a remote computer.

- *query* is one or more queries you want to run to produce the query results for the Web page. This might also include calls to one or more stored procedures.

- *fixedfont* indicates whether the Web page uses a fixed (value = 0) or proportional (value = 1) font. If not specified, a fixed font is used.

- *bold* indicates whether the Web page uses bold text (value = 1) or not (value = 0). If not specified, normal (nonbold) text is used.

- *italic* indicates whether the Web page uses italic text (value = 1) or not (value = 0). If not specified, normal (non-italic) text is used.

- *colheaders* indicates whether the Web page uses column headers (value = 1) or not (value = 0). The default is to use column headers.

- *lastupdated* indicates whether a date/timestamp value is added to your Web page (value = 1) or not (value = 0). By default, a date/timestamp is added.

- *HTMLHeader* indicates the size of the HTML header. The value is 1, 2, 3, 4, 5, and 6, representing H1, H2, H3, H4, H5, and H6, respectively.

- *username* indicates the username to use when running the supporting query or queries for this Web page.

- *dbname* indicates which database to use when running your query or queries.

- *templatefile* is the path and filename of the HTML template file, as described earlier.

- *webpagetitle* is the title of the Web page. The default is SQL Server Web Assistant.

- *resultstitle* is the title shown over the results of your query or queries, with a default of Query Results.

- *URL* is a qualified reference to another Web page in the form http://www. somesite.com/page. If you specify the URL, you must also include the reftext parameter and cannot specify the table_urls or url_query parameters.

▼

▼
- *reftext* is the text the user will click to be taken to the URL provided in the URL parameter.

- *table_urls* is an option you want set to the value of 1 if your query returns URLs or set to the value of 2 if your query doesn't return any URLs.

- *url_query* is a select statement of the form Select URL, Description_of_URL from table. This returns the URLs for the table_urls parameter.

- *whentype* specifies when the Web page will be created:

  1. Create the Web page immediately. This Web job will be created, run, and then deleted.

  2. Create the Web job later, at the date and time specified with the targetdate and targettime parameters. If no time is specified, the job is run at midnight.

  3. Create the Web job every day specified by the dayflags parameter. You can also specify a time with the targettime parameter.

  4. Runs the job repeatedly, once every numunits unit of the unittype parameter units (minutes, hours, days, and so on). So if numunits = 5, unittype specifies minutes, the Web page job runs every five minutes and creates a new Web page.

  5. Creates the Web page only on request.

  6. Creates the Web page immediately, as well as saves the Web job to run again later (options 1 and 2).

  7. Creates the Web page immediately, as well as on particular days (options 1 and 3).

  8. Creates the Web page immediately and repeatedly (options 1 and 4).

  9. Creates the Web page immediately and on request (options 1 and 5).

  10. Creates the Web page immediately and when data changes (based on the datachg parameter).

- *targetdate* indicates the date the Web page should be built, in the form YYYYM-MDD (for example, 19981201 for December 1, 1998). Do not put quotes around this parameter.

- *targettime* indicates the time that the Web page should be built, in the form HHMMSS. It defaults to 000000 (midnight). Noon would be 120000. Do not put quotes around this parameter.

- *dayflags* is a hex value of the days to run the Web job. You would set the value
▼
  and then add them together to set multiple days. Here are the values:

21

▼   1 Sunday

           2 Monday

           3 Tuesday

           4 Wednesday

           5 Thursday

           6 Friday

           7 Saturday

To get Monday and Friday, you would add 2 + 32 = 34.

- *numunits* is the number of units as specified for the `unittype`.

- *unittype* specifies how often a Web page is updated. 1 is hours, 2 is days, 3 is minutes, and 4 is seconds. When combined with `numunits`, it states that the Web job runs every `numunits` of `unittype`. So if numunits = 2, and unittype = 1, then it specifies that the job should run every two hours.

- *procname* is the name of the stored procedure your job will run (given all the parameters in this stored procedure. If you don't name the stored procedure, it defaults to `Web_YYMMDDHHMMSS<spid>`. It's a good idea to name your procedures.

- *maketask* indicates whether a job is created to run the stored procedure and whether the stored procedure that is created is encrypted. There are three possible values:

     0 Create an unencrypted stored procedure but not a Web job.

     1 Create an encrypted stored procedure and also a Web job.

     2 Create an unencrypted stored procedure, and also a Web job.

- *rowcnt* is the maximum number of rows to be put on your Web page. The default is 0, indicating no limit.

- *tabborder* indicates whether the Web page should have a border around your results (value = 1) or not (value = 0). The default is to use a border.

- *singlerow* indicates whether each Web page should have only a single row on it (value = 1) or not (value = 0). The default is 0—to not have one row per page.

- *blobfmt* indicates that data of data type `text` or `image` should be included on your Web page (the default value = NULL) or created on separate pages and linked to your original page.

- *nrowsperpage* is the number of rows on each page of results that are generated.

- *datachg* is the list of tables or columns in which a trigger is created so that the Whenever Data Changes option can be used. You would specify them in the form

▼

▼ {TABLE=*name*[COLUMN=*name*]}[,...]. So if you wanted to specify the authors table and the Pub_id column of the publishers table, you would specify TABLE=authors,TABLE=publishers COLUMN=pub_id.

- *charset* specifies the Web browser character set. The default is N'utf-8'.
- *codepage* specifies the code page to use in the Web browser. The default is 65000,
▲ which is equal to N'utf-8' as a charset. Use the system-stored procedure sp_enumcodepages to find the values that are supported.

Wow! Aren't you glad you learned how to use the wizard? It's rare, but sometimes necessary, to use this stored procedure instead of the Web Assistant Wizard. I strongly recommend that you use the wizard whenever possible.

Pull Methodology for Dynamic Web Pages

As you have seen, the SQL Server Web Assistant Wizard is extremely handy to build static Web pages without much (or any) knowledge of HTML (or for that matter, Transact-SQL). However, the push methodology builds static pages—pages that do not change based on users or their needs. At best, these pages can be reset when data changes. The Internet has changed very rapidly and continues to change. Several other Microsoft technologies that relate to data access from the Internet have been upgraded as well. Each technique you examine here requires that Internet Information Server be installed and that you have administrative access to the service and the Web files.

Using the Internet Database Connector

The first method to access SQL Server from the Internet that you will examine is the Internet Database Connector (IDC). IDC access works with a technology known as Internet Services Application Programming Interface (ISAPI). ISAPI applies to Internet applications using Microsoft Internet Information Server. IDC access to databases is provided with open database connectivity (ODBC). ODBC is used to gain access to any relational database that has an ODBC driver.

IDC technology uses a combination of two files to produce your dynamic Web pages:

- IDC file—Contains your SQL statements and connection information (including the ODBC DSN [Data Source Name])
- HTX file—Contains a template HTML file that will be merged with the data queried with the IDC file and displayed via the client's Web browser

To understand how these files are used, you must step through a sample site and see them in action.

21

1. A user of a Web site fills out a form with parameters to help build a query for a database.

2. The user clicks a submit button, which collects the parameters and passes them in a call to the IDC file. The user might also simply click a hyperlink to call the IDC file, but no parameters will be passed.

3. The IDC file is used to build and run a query against your database.

4. The HTX file is used as a template, and the query results are merged into the HTX file.

5. The results are then sent back to the Web browser and displayed as a standard HTML file.

The Guest Book Sample Application

Microsoft's IIS 2.0 (or 3.0) includes a sample database application of an Internet guest book. You can use that built-in example to teach yourself how to use this set of technologies to provide dynamic Web pages. For the purpose of this discussion, you will need to have IIS version 3.0 installed on your system (it is included as part of Windows NT 4.0 service pack 4, which is required for SQL Server 7.0). Begin by opening your Web browser and typing http://yourcomputer.

The computer used in the Web site example is named SQLGUY, so you will use this computer name in all these examples (see Figure 21.13). The example shown here is viewed with Internet Explorer version 4.01 and IIS version 3.0.

Caution

Although the guest book is somewhat dated (coming from IIS versions 2.0 and 3.0), it is still useful. The sample application that comes with IIS version 4.0, which is itself part of the Windows NT 4.0 option pack, won't install on SQL Server 7.0 because some SQL Server 6.5-specific features were used as part of the setup. Therefore, I chose to use the IIS 3.0 functionality because it did work on SQL Server 7.0. You can follow the directions for the IIS 4.0 sample application and perhaps treat it as a SQL Server exercise to make it work with SQL Server 7.0. Hint: There's an invalid create index statement in one of the files.

Click the Database button on the upper right of your Web page to see the Internet Database Connector page (see Figure 21.14).

FIGURE 21.13

The Internet Information Server default Web page.

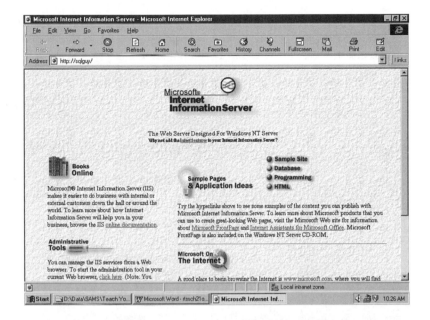

FIGURE 21.14

The Internet Information Server IDC Web page.

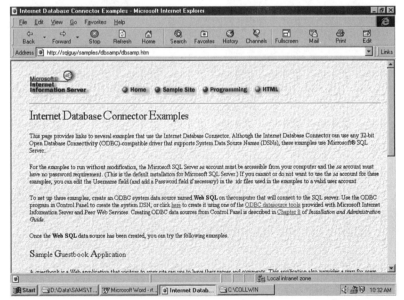

21

As you read through this page, you will see that you can set up a guest book rather quickly. First you must create an ODBC DSN. To do this, click Start, Settings, Control Panel; then select ODBC (32-bit). Add a System DSN (you might need to click the System DSN tab), choosing SQL Server as the type of driver to use. Name the DSN Web

SQL. Set the login ID as sa (or your login ID if you are not the system administrator [sa] of the database server), and the appropriate password. Set the default database to pubs, and complete the system DSN configuration.

When this step is complete, switch back to the IDC Web page in your Web browser, and scroll down to the section labeled Sample Guestbook Application. Click the highlighted text labeled "create a table," and you will see the following screen (see Figure 21.15).

FIGURE 21.15

Confirmation of successful table creation.

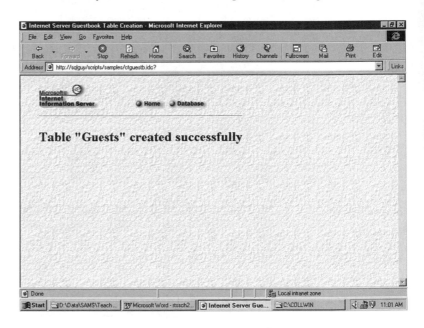

This indicates that you've had success in a couple of ways. First, it indicates that you set up your ODBC connection correctly. Second, you just used an IDC/HTX file combination to run a query. Notice that the address of the Web page you are viewing (http://SQLGUY/scripts/samples/ctguestb.idc?) references an IDC file. Examine that file (ctguestb.idc) by starting Windows NT Explorer and finding your InetPub\scripts\samples directory (see Figure 21.16).

Open the ctguestb.idc file and view it with Notepad. You will see the following text:

```
Datasource: Web SQL
Username: sa
Password:
Template: ctguestb.htx
SQLStatement:
+CREATE TABLE "Guests" (
+"FirstName" varchar(40),
+"LastName" varchar(40),
```

```
+"Email" varchar(40),
+"Homepage" varchar(80),
+"Comment" text,
+"WebUse" varchar(40)
+)
```

FIGURE 21.16

Windows NT Explorer and your scripts\samples directory.

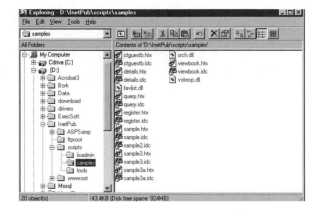

The file describes the ODBC DSN, username, password, template file, and SQL statement that will be run. The previous hyperlink you clicked calls this file. The query is run, and the template file (ctguestb.htx) is populated and displayed. View the HTX file to see the HTML template. This HTML file does not accept any parameters and simply displays a static HTML file.

```html
<HTML>
<HEAD><TITLE>Internet Server Guestbook Table Creation</TITLE></HEAD>
<BODY BACKGROUND="/samples/images/backgrnd.gif">
<BODY BGCOLOR="FFFFFF">
<TABLE>
<TR>
<TD><IMG SRC="/samples/images/SPACE.gif" ALIGN="top" ALT=" "></TD>
<TD><A HREF="/samples/IMAGES/db_mh.map">
<IMG SRC="/SAMPLES/images/db_mh.gif" ismap BORDER=0 ALIGN="top" ALT=" ">
</A></TD>
</TR>
<tr>
<TD></TD>
<TD>
<hr>
<CENTER>
<H1>Table "Guests" created successfully</H1>
</td>
</tr>
</TABLE>
</BODY>
</HTML>
```

21

Click the Database link to return to the main IDC Web page, and click the use the guootbook hyperlink. You are presented with the Guestbook Registry Web page (see Figure 21.17).

FIGURE 21.17

The Guestbook Registry Web page.

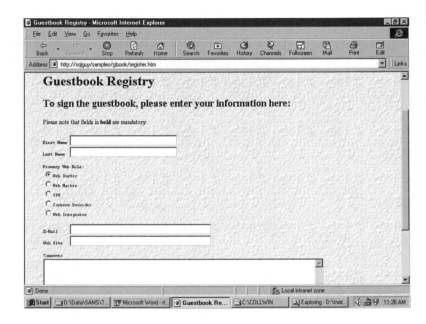

Complete the Web page, and click the Submit Entry button. This records the data in your SQL Server database. Again, examine the .IDC file referenced, the register.idc file:

```
Datasource: Web SQL
Username: sa
Template: register.htx
RequiredParameters: FirstName, LastName
SQLStatement:
+ if exists (
+    select * from Guests
+    where FirstName='%FirstName%' and LastName='%LastName%'
+    )
+      select result='duplicate'
+else
+   INSERT INTO Guests
+   (FirstName, LastName, Email, Homepage, Comment, WebUse)
+   VALUES('%FirstName%', '%LastName%', '%Email%', '%Homepage%',
+     '%Comment%', '%WebUse%');
```

Here you can see that a check is run for the existence of the user in the database, and if the user exists, the word duplicate is returned. Otherwise, an INSERT statement using parameters that came from the previous form is run. The results are then merged with the HTX file and displayed to you.

After you've added someone to your guestbook, you can find the guest by clicking the `Query Guestbook` hyperlink, and you will see the Query Guestbook form (see Figure 21.18).

FIGURE 21.18

The Query Guestbook Web page.

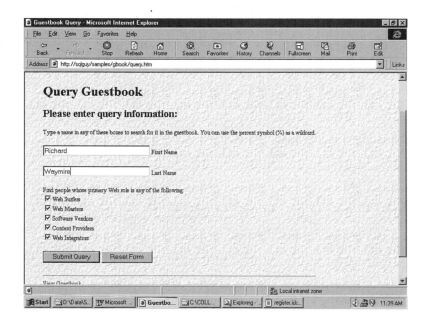

I've entered my name so I can find myself in the SQL Server Guests table. Click View, Source from your Web browser menu to see the HTML used by this Web page (query.htm). As you examine the HTML, you will see lines such as this:

```
<form action="/scripts/samples/query.idc" method=get>
<input type="text" name="FirstName" value="" size=30> First Name
<p>
<input type="text" name="LastName" value="" size=30> Last Name
<p>
```

The `input` lines are the text boxes you see on the Web page, and the `name` parameter is the name you will reference in your IDC file. Switch back now to your Web browser and click the Submit Query button. You are presented with a list of qualifying names in the database. This is called the query.idc file:

```
Datasource: Web SQL
Username: sa
Template: query.htx
```

21

```
SQLStatement:
+SELECT FirstName, LastName
+FROM Guests
+WHERE FirstName like '%FirstName%'
+and LastName like '%LastName%'
+and (WebUse like '%WebMaster%'
+   or WebUse like '%WebSurfer%'
+   or WebUse like '%ISV%'
+   or WebUse like '%ContentProvider%'
+   or WebUse like '%WebIntegrator%')
DefaultParameters:FirstName=%,LastName=%
```

What you see here is a query that uses parameters from the query.htm file you examined earlier. The name parameter from the form is used as the variable for your SQL query, wrapped in the % character. The results are then merged with the template file, query.htx.

```
<html>
<title>Guestbook Query Results</title>
<BODY BACKGROUND="/samples/images/backgrnd.gif">
<BODY BGCOLOR="FFFFFF">
<TABLE>
<TR>
<TD><IMG SRC="/samples/images/SPACE.gif" ALIGN="top" ALT=" "></TD>
<TD><A HREF="/samples/IMAGES/db_mh.map">
<IMG SRC="/SAMPLES/images/db_mh.gif" ismap BORDER=0 ALIGN="top" ALT=" ">
</A></TD>
</TR>
<tr>
<TD></TD>
<TD>
<hr>
<h1>Selected Guestbook Contents</h1>
<font size=2>
<%begindetail%>
<%if CurrentRecord EQ 0 %>
<h2>Here are the selected contents of the guestbook.
➥ Click a name to get details:</h2>
<p>
<%endif%>
Name: <a href="/scripts/samples/details.idc?FName=<%FirstName%>&
➥LName=<%LastName%>"><b><%FirstName%> <%LastName%></b></a>
<p>
<%enddetail%>
<%if CurrentRecord EQ 0 %>
<h2>Sorry, no entries match those criteria.</h2>
<%endif%>
<p>
<hr>
<a href="/scripts/samples/viewbook.idc?">View Guestbook</a>
<p>
```

```
<a href="/samples/gbook/query.htm">Query Guestbook</a>
<p>
<a href="/samples/gbook/register.htm">Add New Entries</a>
</font>
</td>
</tr>
</table>
</body>
</html>
```

The key to this file is the %begindetail% tag. From this point until the %enddetail% tag, you code how you want to return the results of the query. Again you will reference the % sign around your column names to show where the results of your query should go.

Coding Your Own IDC/HTX Files

Are you tired of looking at all this sample code yet? You can code your own data files and queries rather quickly. In this step, you will create the following three Web files to produce two Web pages:

- An HTML file that requests an author's last name
- An IDC file that queries the authors table and finds an author based on the last name you entered
- An HTX file to display the author you searched for

Here are the steps:

1. First, create the HTML file. If you have an HTML editor such as Microsoft FrontPage, you can build it there. However, you can also just type the following code with Notepad:

```
<html><head><title>Teach Yourself SQL Server 7 in 21 days
</title></head>
<body>
<p align="center"><strong>Our Sample Web Page</strong></p><P>
<form method="POST" ACTION="/scripts/samples/authors.idc">
<p>Enter the author's last name: <input type="text" size="20"
name="aulname"></p>
<p align="left"><input type="submit"
name="BtnSubmit" value="Submit"></p>
</form></body></html>
```

2. Next, create the authors.idc file just referenced in the scripts\samples directory on your Web server (the inetpub\scripts\samples directory by default). The file should look like this:

```
Datasource: Web SQL
Username: sa
Password:
```

21

```
Template: authors.htx
SQLStatement:
+SELECT AU_Fname, AU_Lname
+FROM Authors
+WHERE au_lname like '%aulname%'
```

3. And finally the authors.htx file:

```
<HTML><HEAD><TITLE>Our Web Results</TITLE></HEAD>
<BODY><TABLE>
<%begindetail%>
<TR><TD><%au_fname%></TD><TD><%au_lname%></TD></TR>
<%enddetail%>
<%if CurrentRecord EQ 0 %>
<h2>Sorry, no entries for that last name.</h2>
<%endif%>
</table></body></html>
```

4. When you have created these three files, open your Web browser and type the following to view your Web page (see Figure 21.19):

```
http://sqlguy/authors.htm
```

FIGURE 21.19

Your author's Web page.

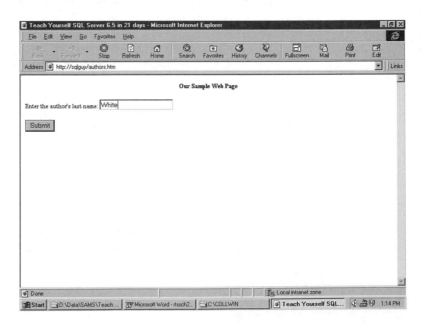

5. Enter an author's last name (White, for example), and click the Submit button. Your IDC file is called, your query is run against the authors table in the pubs database for this author, and the results shown in Figure 21.20 are displayed.

FIGURE 21.20

Your query results.

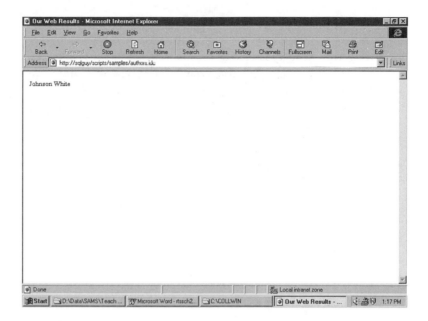

Congratulations! As you can see, it really isn't that hard. For serious Web developers you will want to add images, format your results, and so on, but you've seen the fundamentals and can proceed forward now.

Other Internet Access Methods for SQL Server

The most significant access technology from Microsoft's perspective at this time is ADO. ADO is a data access model to query OLE DB-compliant databases (those databases that have an OLE DB driver, including SQL Server). You write Active Server Pages (files with an .ASP extension) that are processed by IIS version 3.0 or later, and then the results are returned to a client's Web browser. The calls to ADO are written with server-side script, such as Microsoft's VBScript programming language. This means you can use virtually any Web client because only "normal" HTML code is returned to the client's Web browser.

ADO access to databases is much more powerful than IDC files, but it is also significantly more complex. You can either code ADO database access into your ASP files or create ActiveX controls (separate DLL files or executable programs) that call SQL Server. Those ActiveX controls can also be called as part of Microsoft Transaction Server. Understanding all these technologies and how they work together is a complex topic. For additional information about programming ADO and server-side scripting, see Sams.net Publishing's *Teach Yourself Active Server Pages in 14 Days*, ISBN 1-57521-330-3.

21

Finally, Microsoft also has a technology known as Remote Data Services (RDS). This technology was formally known as the Advanced Data Connector (ADC). This technology uses ADO to query databases but runs on your client Web browser using ActiveX controls. Therefore, your Web browser must support ActiveX controls. You can get more information about all these technologies by going to `http://www.microsoft.com/data` on the Internet. You can use Microsoft Visual InterDev to help you develop these Web pages and database access programs.

Summary

SQL Server is *the* database to use on the Internet. Microsoft has provided a great tool to build static Web pages: the SQL Server Web Assistant Wizard. You can build Web pages on a scheduled basis or even create triggers automatically to build Web pages. If you want to examine more advanced and interactive uses of SQL Server, you can use the IDC/HTX connectivity mechanisms. If you want to proceed even further, you can investigate using ADO as a programmatic interface to SQL Server, either on the server side or the client side using RDS.

Q&A

Q Can the SQL Server Web Assistant produce dynamic Web pages?

A No, it produces only static HTML pages.

Q Can you write IDC/HTX files to dynamically update data?

A Yes, see the sample guest book registration for an example of data modification in today's lesson.

Q If you already have a trigger on a table, can you also use the SQL Server Web Assistant to create triggers on the same table?

A Yes, SQL Server 7.0 allows the existence of multiple triggers of the same type on a table.

Workshop

The Workshop provides quiz questions to help you solidify your understanding of the concepts presented in this chapter. In addition to the quiz questions, exercises are provided to let you practice what you have learned in this chapter. Try to understand the quiz and exercise answers before continuing to the next day's lesson. Answers are provided in Appendix A, "Answers."

Quiz

1. Which Internet utility is appropriate to use when building static Web pages?

2. If you want to build a simple query interface to SQL Server on the Internet, which technology would you use?

3. For advanced query access and data maintenance, which technology would provide the most functionality?

4. If you receive a query syntax error, which file would you examine to find the error between these three: authors.htm, authors.idc, authors.htx?

Exercises

1. Run the SQL Server Web Assistant Wizard to build a static Web page for tables in the database. Try both a scheduled page and a page that changes when data changes (using triggers). Modify a table with a Web trigger, and verify that your Web page is updated.

2. If you didn't do so earlier, create an IDC/HTX file combination to allow queries against your SQL Server database.

3. As suggested earlier, if you have the Windows NT 4.0 Option Pack and IIS version 4.0, make the SQL Server scripts for the Exploration Air Web site install successfully. You will need to modify the SQL scripts found in the \iissamples\exair\source\sql directory under your INETPUB directory on your server.

21

WEEK 3

In Review

Let's look at what you covered this last week.

On Day 15 you looked at views and stored procedures and how to create and execute them. You also learned about creating triggers to enforce referential integrity as well as business rules. These included triggers on `INSERT`, `UPDATE`, and `DELETE`.

On Day 16 you learned the fundamentals of programming, including the creation and use of batch processing and transaction management. You learned the use of the `BEGIN TRAN`, `COMMIT TRAN`, and `ROLLBACK TRAN` statements. You also learned about the different locking mechanisms in SQL Server and how to implement control of flow statements such as `BEGIN` and `END`, `CASE`, `DELARE`, `IF`, and `ELSE` statements and `WHILE` loops. You finished Day 16 with a discussion on working with cursors.

On Day 17 you learned the terminology used with replication and the types of replication that are available.

On Day 18 you learned how to implement replication that you examined on Day 17.

On Day 19 you learned how to automate many of the day-to-day tasks involved with maintaining a SQL server. You learned how to implement tasks, alerts, and events, and then how to connect these components to your email system for notification purposes.

Day 20 focused on fine tuning your SQL Server. We could write an entire 21 days book on performance tuning and optimization. This lesson introduced you to enough of the major tuning functions to get your SQL Server to about a 90 percent efficiency. The other 10 percent is difficult to implement and is different for each environment and server. It requires many hours of studying the operation of the server and the use of its components. This lesson talked about hardware, NT and SQL Server parameters that could be set, and how to monitor SQL Server through the SQL Performance Monitor.

Day 21 taught you how to place SQL Server on the World Wide Web. You learned about push and pull updates and the ISAPI implementation. This lesson is a good starting place for developing Web-based SQL Server applications.

Congratulations on finishing this book! We hope that you have taken with you a new understanding of both the administration and implementation of a SQL Server database and can apply these new concepts to further your careers in this fast-paced, high-tech industry. Enjoy your newfound knowledge and may you live in interesting times.

APPENDIX A

Answers

Day 1, "Introduction to SQL Server 7.0 and Relational Databases"

Quiz Answers

1. The table.
2. Tables, columns, data types, stored procedures, triggers, rules, keys, constraints, defaults, and indexes.
3. Usually the SQL Server administrator.

Exercise Answer

Following is one way to look at creating objects and organizing them into tables and columns. Remember that Day 9 covers more details on different data types.

Normalizing Your Database Design

Normalizing the database consists of taking related objects and grouping them into tables.

For example, look at the used car dealership database as if it were a spreadsheet. The columns would be vehicle identification number (VIN), Make, Model, Color, Mileage, Photograph, Air Conditioning, Size of Engine, Transmission, Four-Wheel Drive, Power Locks, Other Features, Cost, List Price, Asking Price, Date Bought, Date Sold, Deposit, Deposit Date, Customer Name, Customer Address, Customer Phone, Salesperson Name, Salesperson Address, Salesperson Commission, and Salesperson ID.

You have a total of 25 columns to save for each car. Putting them in a spreadsheet would work for a small shop, but for large shops a spreadsheet would quickly become too cumbersome. You need a unique identifier to link these tables to each other. Vehicles have a natural unique ID in their VIN number. You can assign customers and salespeople unique numbers or use existing identifiers (like social security or last name plus address). In this case an assigned ID for the salespeople and the customer's Social Security number will work as identifiers.

You can see that information about vehicles, salespeople, cost and sales, and customers are related data. These variables can go into several tables, as appropriate:

- Vehicle—VIN, Make, Model, Color, Mileage, Photograph, Air Conditioning, Size of Engine, Transmission, Four-Wheel Drive, Power Locks, Other Features
- Salespeople—Salesperson Name, Salesperson Address, Salesperson Commission, Salesperson ID
- Sales Data—VIN, Cost, List Price, Asking Price, Date Bought, Date Sold, Deposit, Deposit Date, Customer ID, Salesperson ID
- Customer—Customer Name, Customer Address, Customer Phone, Customer ID, Comments

Finalizing the Database Design

To finalize the design, choose column names, choose the data type, and choose the length of each column (when appropriate). Also split names into first and last names because you might want to alphabetize them later.

The detailed design of a database is often referred to as the data dictionary because it defines the variables and tables in the database. Here is a breakdown of your data dictionary:

Vehicle: This table will contain vehicle information and have the following variables:

- VIN (Primary Key)—This is the vehicle identification number. This is a character field with a variable length of 30 characters (for nonstandard cars, and so on).

- Make—This is the make of the car. Valid responses are something like Ford, Nissan, and so on. This is a character field with a variable length of 30 characters.

- Model—This is the model of the car. Valid responses are something like Ranger, Altima, and so on. This is a character field with a variable length of 30 characters.

- Color—This is the color of the car. This is a character field with a variable length of 20 characters.

- Mileage—This is the mileage of the car. This is a numeric field with a length of 7 characters (max of 9,999,999—it will not track mileage to the tenth of a mile).

- Photo—This will be a photograph of the car, taken in 640×480×256 Joint Picture Experts Group (JPEG) format, so it can be published on the Internet easily. This will be an image field.

- AC—This is to indicate whether air conditioning is present. Valid responses are Y or N. This will be a character field set to a length of one.

- Size_of_Eng—This is to indicate how many cylinders the engine has. Valid responses are 3, 4, 6, 8, 10, and 12. This will be a `tinyint` (tiny integer—ranges from 0 to 255) field.

- Trans—This is the type of transmission, with valid responses being "standard" or "automatic." This will be a variable character field with a maximum length of nine.

- FWD—This is to indicate whether the vehicle is four-wheel drive. Valid responses are Y or N. This will be a character field set to a length of one.

- PL—This is to indicate whether the vehicle has power locks. Valid responses are Y or N. This will be a character field set to a length of one.

- Comment—This field will be used to hold comments about the vehicle and will be a text variable.

tblSalespeople: This table will contain information about the salespeople:

- Sales_ID (Primary Key)—This is the ID of the salesperson. All salespeople will be assigned an ID to help track sales, and so on. This will be a `smallint` (small integer—ranges from –32,768 to 32,767) field.

- Fname—This is the salesperson's first name. This will be a variable character field with a maximum of 30 characters.

- Lname—This is the salesperson's last name. This will be a variable character field with a maximum of 30 characters.
- Addr—This is the salesperson's address. This will be a variable character field with a maximum of 30 characters.
- City—This is the salesperson's city. This will be a variable character field with a maximum of 30 characters.
- State—This is the salesperson's state. This will be a character field with two characters.
- Zip—This is the salesperson's zip code. This will be a character field with nine characters.
- Commission—This is the salesperson's base percentage for his commission. This can later be used to calculate commissions based on profits on cars sold. This will be a `tinyint` variable.

tblSales: This table will track information about the purchase and sale of the vehicle.

- Invoice (Primary Key)—This will be the invoice number of the original purchase of the vehicle. This will be a varchar field with a maximum length of 20.
- VIN (Foreign Key)—This is the same as the field found in the vehicle table and will be used to create a key to that table.
- CustID (Foreign Key)—This variable also exists in the customer table. This field will be a key to the customer table.
- SalesID (Foreign Key)—This variable also exists in the sales table. This will be a key to the sales table.
- Cost—This is the actual cost of the vehicle. This will be a smallmoney field (it can handle up to $214,000).
- List—This is the list (blue book) price for the car. This will be a smallmoney field.
- Ask—This is the asking price. This might change because of a sale, advertisement, or incentive. This will be a smallmoney field.
- DateIn—This is the date that the vehicle was purchased by the dealer. This will be a smalldatetime field (keeps track of dates down to one-minute intervals).
- DateOut—This is when the vehicle was sold to a customer. This will be a smalldatetime field.
- Deposit—This is the amount of a deposit (if any) that the customer has put down on a vehicle. This will be a smallmoney field.
- Deposit Date—This is when the deposit was made. This will be a smalldatetime field.

tblCustomer: This table will keep track of the customers.

- CustID (Primary Key)—This will hold the social security number of the customer, which will also double as the ID number for the customer. It will be a nine-digit character field.

- Fname—This is the customer's first name. It will be a variable character field with a maximum of 30 characters.

- Lname—This is the customer's last name. It will be a variable character field with a maximum of 30 characters.

- Addr—This is the customer's address. It will be a variable character field with a maximum of 30 characters.

- City—This is the customer's city. It will be a variable character field with a maximum of 30 characters.

- State—This is the customer's state. It will be a character field with two characters.

- Zip—This is the customer's zip code. It will be a character field with nine characters.

- Phone—This is the phone number of the customer. It will be a 10-digit character field.

- Comments—This will be a text field where comments about the customer can be added.

Figure A.1 shows how your tables and their relationships might look.

FIGURE A.1

Relationships between tables.

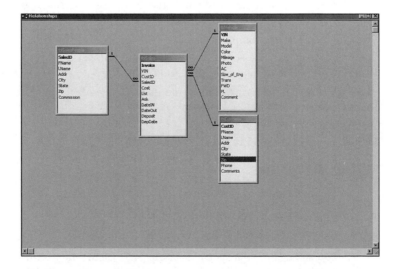

SQL Server ships with two default databases you can use to learn how to program SQL Server 7.0. Readers who have used SQL Server in the past will recognize the pubs database. The pubs database is an assortment of tables that track books, publishers, authors, stores, and sales. Figure A.2 is a sample view of the tables in the pubs database and their relationships.

FIGURE A.2

The pubs database.

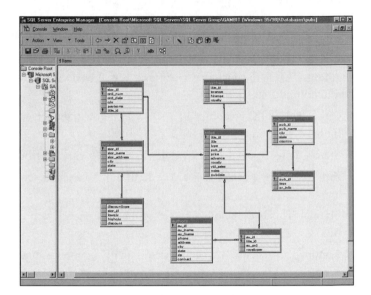

Readers familiar with the Northwinds database from Microsoft Access will also have an easy time transitioning into SQL Server 7.0 because a SQL Server version of the Northwinds Traders company database is included. Northwinds Traders is a fictitious company that buys and sells exotic foods from all over the world. The various tables and queries used to work with the data are in SQL Server 7.0. Figure A.3 shows a sample layout of the Northwinds database and its associated tables and fields.

Day 2, "Installing SQL Server 7.0"

Quiz Answers

1. The binary sort order would do this.

2. Only Unicode data columns in SQL Server 7.0.

3. The MDACs (Microsoft Data Access Components).

4. You should set up a special account that is a member of the administrator's group on the local computer.

A

5. You can use the SQL Service Manager or SQL Server Enterprise Manager, or you can run several Windows NT utilities. You can also run NET START MSSQLServer.

6. The NTFS file system—it has better security and reliability.

7. Select Full-text indexing under Server Components during a custom setup.

FIGURE A.3

The Northwinds database.

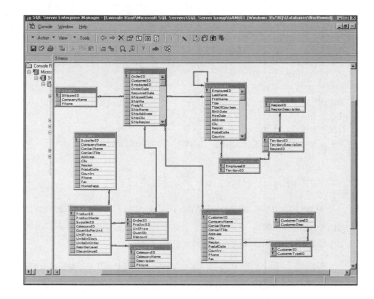

Day 3, "Using the SQL Server 7.0 Tools and Utilities"

Quiz Answers

1. Configure the registration information to not keep your login information by default, and require a separate login at every connection.

2. In the Client Network utility.

3. In the Server Network utility.

4. Performance Monitor, SQL Server Profiler, and SQL Server Query Analyzer.

5. SQLDiag.exe.

Day 4, "Creating Databases, Files, and Filegroups"

Quiz Answers

1.
```
CREATE DATABASE Accounting
ON
(NAME = Accounting_Data,
FILENAME = 'C:\mssql7\data\Accounting_Data.mdf',
SIZE = 20,
FILEGROWTH = 2,
MAXSIZE = 40)
LOG ON
(NAME = Accounting_Log,
FILENAME = 'C:\mssql7\data\Accounting_Log.ldf',
SIZE=5,
FILEGROWTH = 1,
MAXSIZE=10)
```

2. This adds a new data file called TestData2 with a filename of TestData2.ndf in the default directory. The initial size is 10MB. The default autogrowth of 10% is being used and the file has no maximum size.

3. Make sure that you are in the master database when you run this query:

```
DROP DATABASE Von, Ron, Don, Christina
```

Exercise Answers

1.
```
CREATE DATABASE Frog
ON
(NAME = FrogData1,
 FILENAME = 'c:\mssql7\data\FrogData1.mdf',
 SIZE = 3,
 FILEGROWTH = 2,
 MAXSIZE = 20),
(NAME = FrogData2,
 FILENAME = 'c:\mssql7\data\FrogData2.ndf',
 SIZE = 3,
 FILEGROWTH = 2,
 MAXSIZE = 20)
LOG ON
(NAME = FrogLog1,
 FILENAME = 'c:\mssql7\data\FrogLog1.ldf',
MAXSIZE = 5),
(NAME = FrogLog2,
 FILENAME = 'c:\mssql7\data\FrogLog2.ldf',
MAXSIZE = 5)
GO
```

A

```
2. ALTER DATABASE Frog
   ADD FILE
   (NAME = FrogData3,
    FILENAME = 'c:\mssql7\data\FrogData3.ndf')

   GO

3. DBCC SHRINKDATABASE (Frog, 80)
   GO

4. USE Frog
   GO
   DBCC SHRINKFILE (FrogLog2,EMPTYFILE)
   GO

5. ALTER DATABASE Frog
   REMOVE FILE FrogLog2
   GO

6. USE Master
   GO
   EXEC sp_dboption Frog, 'Single User', True
   GO
   EXEC sp_renamedb 'Frog', 'TreeFrog'
   GO
   EXEC sp_dboption TreeFrog, 'Single User', False
   GO

7. USE MASTER

   GO
   DROP DATABASE TreeFrog
   GO
```

Day 5, "Using SQL Server Login and User Security"

Quiz Answers

1. By deleting the BUILTIN\Administrators group in Enterprise Manager or by running the sp_revokelogin system stored procedure. This would revoke their rights to log in to SQL Server at all, however. You could also run the sp_dropsrvrole-member system stored procedure to remove them from membership in the sysadmin fixed server role.

2. You can add someone to the dbo user in the database, but a better solution is to add the individual to the database as a user and make his or her username a member of the db_owner fixed database role.

3. When the individual user needs specific permissions that are different from other members' of every single group he or she is a member of. This should be a rare situation.

Exercise Answers

1. This can be done with either `sp_addlogin` and `sp_adduser` or with SQL Server Enterprise Manager. The code would look like this:

```
Exec sp_addlogin 'george'
Exec sp_addlogin 'Henry'
Exec sp_addlogin 'Ida'
Exec sp_addlogin 'John'
Use pubs
Exec Sp_adduser 'George'
Exec sp_adduser 'Henry'
Exec sp_adduser 'Ida'
Exec sp_adduser 'John'
```

2. Remove John from the database user, and then run `sp_changedbowner` to make John the dbo.

```
Use pubs
Exec sp_changedbowner 'John','TRUE'
-- Oops ñ received an error
exec sp_dropuser 'John'
exec sp_changedbowner 'John','TRUE'
```

Day 6, "Working with Permissions"

Quiz Answers

1. `GRANT SELECT ON MyTable TO MARY`

2. Paul needs permission to `SELECT` on Joe.JoeView and `SELECT` on Mary.MaryTable.

3. Joe cannot `SELECT` from MYTABLE. `DENY` overrides all other permissions.

4. Joe can `SELECT` from MYTABLE.

5. Have all objects created by or with the owner of dbo.

6. `GRANT SELECT ON MYTABLE TO PUBLIC`

7. All statement permissions except `CREATE DATABASE`

Exercise Answers

1. This can be done with either `sp_addlogin` and `sp_adduser` or with SQL Server Enterprise Manager. The code looks like this:

```
Exec sp_addlogin 'george'
Exec sp_addlogin 'Henry'
Exec sp_addlogin 'Ida'
Exec sp_addlogin 'John'
Use pubs
Exec Sp_adduser 'George'
Exec sp_adduser 'Henry'
Exec sp_adduser 'Ida'
Exec sp_adduser 'John'
```

2. Remove John from the database user, and then run `sp_changedbowner` to make John the dbo.

```
Use pubs
Exec sp_changedbowner 'John','TRUE'
-- Oops ñ received an error
exec sp_dropuser 'John'
exec sp_changedbowner 'John','TRUE'
```

Day 7, "Implementing Backups in SQL Server 7.0"

Quiz Answers

1. RAID 1 will perform better (in general) than RAID 5 for writes; hence it is a better option for holding transaction logs.

2. Yes. Network locations are available for backup devices.

3. If the Truncate Log On Checkpoint database option is set or Select Into/Bulkcopy has been set and a full database backup has not been made, you can't make a transaction log backup.

4. In an off-site storage vault, if one is available.

5. No, a checkpoint is merely a copy of the data pages from memory to disk. It has no effect on your transaction log backups.

Exercise Answers

1. To create the backup devices, use SQL Server Enterprise Manager or run the following:

```
exec sp_addumpdevice 'disk', 'master_backup',
```

```
➥ 'c:\mssql7\backup\master_backup.dat'
exec sp_addumpdevice 'disk', 'msdb_backup',
➥'c:\mssql7\backup\msdb_backup.dat'
exec sp_addumpdevice 'disk', 'model_backup',
➥'c:\mssql7\backup\model_backup.dat'
exec sp_addumpdevice 'disk', 'pubs_backup',
➥'c:\mssql7\backup\pubs_backup.dat'
exec sp_addumpdevice 'disk', 'northwind_backup',
➥'c:\mssql7\backup\northwind_backup.dat'
```

To back up the databases, use SQL Server Enterprise Manager or run the following:

```
BACKUP DATABASE MASTER TO master_backup WITH INIT
BACKUP DATABASE MSDB TO msdb_backup WITH INIT
BACKUP DATABASE MODEL TO model_backup WITH INIT
BACKUP DATABASE PUBS TO pubs_backup WITH INIT
BACKUP DATABASE NORTHWIND TO northwind_backup WITH INIT
```

To view the database options, use SQL Server Enterprise Manager or run the following:

```
exec sp_helpdb
```

2. Note that NOINIT is just to prevent you from erasing your previous full database backups on the same backup devices. You could just as easily have created new backup devices.

```
BACKUP DATABASE PUBS TO pubs_backup WITH NOINIT, DIFFERENTIAL
BACKUP DATABASE NORTHWIND TO northwind_backup WITH NOINIT,
➥DIFFERENTIAL
```

3.
```
exec sp_addumpdevice 'disk', 'pubs_log_backup',
➥ 'c:\mssql7\backup\pubs_log_backup.dat'
use pubs
go

-- turn off the turncate log on checkpoint option
exec sp_dboption 'pubs', 'trunc. Log on chkpt.', FALSE
go
-- You must perform a full backup after turning off truncate Log
➥on checkpoint
BACKUP DATABASE PUBS TO pubs_backup WITH INIT
-- and finally, back up the log.
BACKUP LOG PUBS TO pubs_log_backup WITH INIT
```

Day 8, "Restoring SQL Server Databases"

Quiz Answers

1. All system databases other than master, as well as pubs and northwind, are reinitialized. You will need to recover or reattach all user databases.

2. A list of the files for each backup you examine on a backup file or tape.

3. Yes, a parallel striped backup can be restored using fewer tape drives than were used to make the backup.

4. The recovery interval option. It is set to automatic by default, and you should probably not change it.

5. Restore the last full database backup and then apply the transaction logs, specifying the STOPAT parameter to recover to a particular point in time.

Day 9, "Creating Tables"

Quiz Answers

1. When maximum speed is needed and storage space is not.

2. When storage space is the most important concern but speed is not.

3. Store the data in a file outside the database and store the filename in your table. You can also store your text and images in a separate table. You might also be able to break down a text data type into several smaller char fields.

4. Always specify NULL or NOT NULL. Use ROWGUID for global unique values, use the IDENTITY property for autoincrementing values and use Unicode for international databases.

5.   a. For a five-digit zip code: char(5), if it can hold 10 digits as in 40317-2291 then varchar(10).

    b. smalldatetime

    c. To store just the year value, tinyint; otherwise, use a smalldatatime

    d. VIN (assuming up to 20 chars) char(20)

    e. char(10)

    f. varchar(50)

    g. smalldatetime

    h. numeric(,6). If you said money, remember that the money data types support a scale of 4 only.

6. The maximum size is 10 + 15 + 15 + 255 + 3 (3 bytes of overhead for the varchar column) = 298 bytes per row.

7. Yes. Note that the fname field will be changed to a varchar field and the text and image columns will have a 16-byte pointer to the data pages where their data is stored. The maximum row size should be 582 bytes plus any associated overhead involved with the variable length fields.

Exercise Answers

1.
```
sp_addtype zip_code, 'char(5)', 'NOT NULL'
sp_addtype phone_number, 'char(14)'
sp_addtype store_id, 'int', 'NOT NULL'
sp_addtype fax, 'char(14)'
sp_addtype email, 'varchar(50)'
```

2.
```
CREATE TABLE stores(
id store_id,
name varchar(30),
addr1 varchar(50),
addr2 varchar(50),
city varchar(30),
state char(2) NOT NULL,
zip zip_code,
owner varchar(30),
contact varchar(30),
fax fax,
email email
)
```

3.
```
CREATE TABLE sales (
id store_id,
sales_date datetime,
tot_sales money,
tot_returns money,
deposit money
)
```

Day 10, "Using SQL Server 7.0 Data Transformation Services"

Quiz Answers

1. You must have SELECT permissions in the source database on both the data and the system tables. You must be the dbo in the destination database.

2. BCP will always enforce defaults and data types. BCP will always ignore rules, constraints, and triggers.

3. You must have the SELECT INTO/Bulk Copy database option enabled, and you must drop all indexes on the table.

4. You can transfer your data directly, transform it into other data types, summarize it, concatenate it, break it into component columns, and perform many other transformations.

5. You cannot use a backup-and-restore methodology here because the sort order changed and the processor architecture changed. I suggest you install SQL Server 7.0 on the new Alpha machine and then use the DTS Object Transfer Manager to move all objects, users, and permissions from the Intel machine to the Alpha machine.

Day 11, "Retrieving Data with Queries"

Quiz Answers

1a. This query returns all columns from the authors table, when the author's last name begins with the letter M.

1b. This query returns all rows from the employee table and the emp_id, fname, and lname columns. The column headings have been aliased as EmployeeID, LastName, and FirstName.

1c. This query rounds the dollar amount with a single digit to the right of the decimal point as 7725.5

1d. This query returns a column aliased as Name and the emp_id column aliased as EmployeeID from the employee table. The Name column is in the form of the last name, a comma (,), and the first initial of the first name.

2. Yes, in most cases, a subquery can be implemented as a join and vice versa.

3. False. ROLLUP and CUBE are designed to give you summary information.

4. Yes, to create this table make sure you prefix the table name with the ## symbol.

Exercise Answers

1.
```
SELECT title_id, title, price
FROM titles
WHERE (pub_id = '0877'
OR title LIKE '%computer%')
And price is not NULL
(Returns 14 rows)
```

2. SELECT * FROM titles

   WHERE price IS NOT NULL
   (Returns 16 rows)

3. SELECT title, price

   FROM titles
   ORDER BY price DESC
   (Returns 18 rows)

4. SELECT AVG(ytd_sales) FROM titles

5. SELECT title_id, count(title_id)

   FROM titleauthor
   GROUP BY title_id
   HAVING count(title_id) > 1

6. SELECT stor_id, qty

   FROM sales
   ORDER BY stor_id
   COMPUTE SUM(qty) BY stor_id

7. ANSI Syntax

   ```
   SELECT authors.au_fname, authors.au_lname, titles.title
   FROM authors
   INNER JOIN titleauthor ON authors.au_id = titleauthor.au_id
   INNER JOIN titles ON titleauthor.title_id = titles.title_id
   ORDER BY authors.au_lname
   ```

   SQL Server Syntax

   ```
   SELECT authors.au_fname, authors.au_lname, titles.title
   FROM authors, titles, titleauthor
   WHERE authors.au_id = titleauthor.au_id
   AND   titleauthor.title_id = titles.title_id
   ORDER BY authors.au_lname
   ```

8. SELECT * FROM authors

   WHERE authors.state IN
   (SELECT state from stores)

9. SELECT *

   ```
   INTO #tmpEmployees
   FROM employee
   GO
   SELECT * FROM #tmpEmployees
   GO
   ```

Day 12, "Data Modification with Queries"

Quiz Answers

1. A DELETE without a WHERE will remove every row from a table. It is more efficient to use the TRUNCATE TABLE command if you really want to remove all rows.

2. False. Identity values are never supplied. They are calculated by the SQL Server. For any column that has a default value or allows nulls, you do not need to supply a value, but you can supply one if you want.

3. Joins in a DELETE or UPDATE statement allow you to access values in another table to determine which rows to modify. The second table is used only as a lookup table and is not affected. Only one table at a time can be changed with any of the data modification operations.

Exercise Answers

1. Solution:
```
select title_id, title, pub_id, price
into #cook_books
from tmpTitles
where type = 'mod_cook'
```

2. Solution:
```
insert into #cook_books
    select title_id, title, pub_id, price
    from tmpTitles
    where type = 'trad_cook'
```

3. Solution:
```
update #cook_books
set price = price * 1.2
```

4. Solution:
```
update #cook_books
set price = price * 0.9
where pub_id =
    (select pub_id from publishers
     where pub_name = 'Binnet & Hardley' )
```

5. Solution:
```
delete #cook_books
where price < $10
```

6. Solution:

```
delete #cook_books
where title_id in
    (select title_id from tmpTitles
    where ytd_sales > 10000)
```

Day 13, "Enhancing Performance with Indexing"

Quiz Answers

1. By specifying an optimizer hint with an index number of 0.

2. At least 120% of the size of the table with which you're creating the index.

3. Set SHOWPLAN_TEXT to on or the graphical showplan of the SQL Server Query Analyzer.

Exercise Answers

1. ```
set showplan_text on
go
Select * from pubs..sales where title_id = 'BU1032'
Go
Set showplan_text off
Go
Set statistics io on
Go
Select * from pubs..sales where title_id = 'BU1032'
Go
```

(Remember, you can't run a query and see the showplan in a single step.)

2. ```
Select * from pubs..sales (index=1) where title_id = 'BU1032'
Go
```

3. Answers will vary; however, here is one potential answer:
```
Create table myindextab2
(col1 int not null,
 col2 char(5) not null,
 col3 varchar(50) null)
go
create unique clustered index myclindex on myindextab2 (col1)
➥with fillfactor = 100
go
create index mynonclindex1 on myindextab2 (col1,col2)
➥with fillfactor = 25
```

```
go
create index mynonclindex2 on myindextab2 (col3)
➥with fillfactor = 75
go
dbcc dbreindex ('myindextab2',' ',50)
go
```

4. Graphical answer: If you can do step 3, you can figure out step 4.

Day 14, "Ensuring Data Integrity"

Quiz Answers

1. Yes

2. No, it must be referenced elsewhere.

3. Yes, as long as the scale is 0.

4. No, foreign keys can only refer to tables in the same database.

5. No, it creates a unique index that cannot be disabled.

6. Not directly. You must manage them by controlling the constraints.

Day 15, "Working with Views, Stored Procedures, and Triggers"

Quiz Answers

1. Data integrity, referential integrity, and business rules.

2. As many as you like. There can be different triggers for INSERT, UPDATE, and DELETE statements.

3. False. Views are not faster than stored procedures. All the other criteria are true of views, however.

4. False. You can update only a single base table with a view.

5. True. This is one of the benefits of creating a stored procedure.

6. False. You must have permission on the base tables to run a view. It is interesting, however, that you can create a view on base tables that you do not have access to.

7. False. Although these things have made most triggers unnecessary, there are still many valid uses for triggers—for example, cascading updates and deletes.

8. Only triggers are dropped.

Exercise Answers

1. CREATE VIEW myView AS select au_lname, au_fname, t.title from

   ```
   authors inner join titleauthor ta on authors.au_id =
   ➡ta.au_id inner join titles t on ta.title_id = t.title_id
   ```

2. Create trigger mytrigger on titles for insert as

   ```
   if(select count(*) from inserted I inner join publishers p on
   ➡i.pub_id = p.pub_id) <> 1 raiserror(50001, 10, 1)
   ```

3. CREATE PROC myproc AS

   ```
   SELECT s.stor_name, t.title FROM
   stores s, titles t, sales sa
   WHERE t.title_id = sa.title_id
   AND s.stor_id = sa.stor_id
   ORDER BY s.stor_name
   ```

Day 16, "Programming SQL Server 7.0"

Quiz Answers

1. CREATE DATABASE, CREATE TABLE, CREATE INDEX

2. BEGIN TRAN

   ```
       UPDATE authors SET au_lname = 'Johnson' WHERE au_lname = 'Smith'
       INSERT publishers VALUES ('9991','SAMS','Indianapolis','IN','USA')
       SELECT * FROM publishers (HOLDLOCK)
   COMMIT TRAN
   ```

   The UPDATE statement will take two exclusive row locks on the authors table as
   well as two intent-exclusive page locks (the deleted and the inserted rows). The
   INSERT statement will take an exclusive row lock on a data page on the publishers
   table (page 99 in the following table). Finally, the SELECT statement will take several key-range locks on the publisher table (because of the HOLDLOCK option).
   Here are the results of sp_lock:

spid	dbid	ObjId	IndId	Type	Resource	Mode	Status
8	2	0	0	DB		S	GRANT
8	5	0	0	DB		S	GRANT
8	2	0	0	EXT	1:80	X	GRANT
8	5	117575457	1	PAG	1:87	IX	GRANT
8	5	117575457	2	PAG	1:122	IX	GRANT
8	5	197575742	1	PAG	1:99	IX	GRANT
8	5	117575457	0	TAB		IX	GRANT
8	5	197575742	1	KEY	(ffffffffffff)	IS-S	GRANT
8	5	117575457	2	KEY	(d59632855aa8)	X	GRANT
8	5	197575742	0	TAB		IX	GRANT

```
8    5    117575457    2    KEY    (39747cc5fc43)    X      GRANT
8    5    117575457    1    KEY    (02c094e89f8a)    X      GRANT
8    5    197575742    1    KEY    (030431363232)    IS-S   GRANT
8    5    197575742    1    KEY    (030130373336)    IS-S   GRANT
8    5    197575742    1    KEY    (040131373536)    IS-S   GRANT
8    5    197575742    1    KEY    (090a31333839)    IS-S   GRANT
8    5    197575742    1    KEY    (070f30383737)    IS-S   GRANT
8    5    197575742    1    KEY    (000039393939)    IS-S   GRANT
8    5    197575742    1    KEY    (000139393938)    IS-S   GRANT
8    5    197575742    1    KEY    (0c0b39393532)    IS-S   GRANT
8    5    197575742    1    KEY    (090839393031)    IS-S   GRANT
8    5    197575742    1    KEY    (000839393931)    X      GRANT

(22 row(s) affected)
```

3. By setting the REMOTE_PROC_TRANSACTIONS configuration item. You can set it either with the stored procedure sp_configure or the configuration screen in SQL Server Enterprise Manager. You would first have to set up either remote servers or linked servers for each server you'd like to connect with.

4. With either the ROLLBACK TRAN or ROLLBACK WORK statements.

5. Yes. The rollback tran inside the trigger would cancel the transaction as well as the batch. The SELECT * FROM AUTHORS is in the second batch and would therefore run. Note that the COMMIT TRAN would fail, however.

```
Server: Msg 3902, Level 16, State 1
The COMMIT TRANSACTION request has no corresponding BEGIN
TRANSACTION.
```

Exercise Answers

```
BEGIN TRAN
INSERT publishers VALUES ('9993','WAYCOOL PUBLISHERS',
 'Indianapolis', 'IN', 'USA')
INSERT authors VALUES ('111-11-1111','Jackson','Ann','425 999-9000',
'PO Box 1193','Snoqualmie','WA', '98065', 1)
INSERT authors VALUES ('111-22-1111','Greene','Bob','425 999-9000',
'1204 Sycamore Lane','Boulder City','NV', '89005', 1)
INSERT TITLES VALUES ('BU1403','How to Surf the Net in 3 Easy Steps',
 'business', '9993', $19.95, $3000.00, NULL, NULL, NULL,'8/1/1998')
INSERT TITLEAUTHOR VALUES ('111-11-1111','BU1403', 1, 50)
INSERT TITLEAUTHOR VALUES ('111-22-1111','BU1403', 1, 50)
COMMIT TRAN
```

This adds a new publisher, the two authors, and the new book title. It then adds the authors as having written the book (50/50 cut). Note that your answer might differ, but it should include the same set of tables within a single transaction.

Day 17, "Understanding Replication Design and Methodologies"

Quiz Answers

1. The log reader agent.
2. The distribution agent moves replicated transactions from the distribution database to the subscribers.
3. The central subscriber scenario.
4. The merge agent resides on the distribution server when you are using push replication. When you use pull subscriptions, the merge agent is on each subscriber.

Exercise Answer

There are several solutions you could implement, but given the facts in this scenario, I suggest a hybrid type of installation. One approach is to implement a central subscriber scenario at the warehouse in Wichita, Kansas. The other four sites throughout the United States would publish data to the central location.

The Wichita data could then be used in a publishing subscriber scenario with one of the British sites. The data coming into the Wichita database could be sent over the slow and expensive phone lines to a single database in the British Isles. That British database could then republish the data to the other administrative sites located in Great Britain.

Day 18, "Implementing Replication Methodologies"

No quiz or exercise answers.

Day 19, "Using the SQL Server Agent"

Quiz Answers

1. The AT command and the Windows NT Schedule service.
2. The name of the mail profile of the Windows NT user account that is being used to run the MSSQLServer or SQL Server Agent services.
3. Exec sp_processmail

4. Two scheduled tasks (one for the `with init` command and one without that runs every three hours).

5. The Database Maintenance Plan Wizard.

Day 20, "Configuring and Monitoring SQL Server 7.0"

Quiz Answers

1. The physical implementation of the logical database design. No amount of hardware or software tuning will make up for a poor design.

2. So that the disk activity of the log can have the highest priority and speed up overall throughput of SQL Server.

3. You would monitor the `MEMORY` object, `pages/sec` counter to look for a high level of swapping from memory to the paging file.

4. The affinity mask configuration with the `sp_configure` system stored procedure.

5. The `SQLServer:Databases` object, `Log Flushes/sec` counter would give you the best approximation of how many changes were being made on your SQL Server. CPU usage from the `PROCESS` object, `% Processor Time` counter, with an instance of `SQLSERVR` could also be used to measure activity. In fact, there is no one best counter. Monitoring is not as easy as a single counter.

Day 21, "Integrating SQL Server and the World Wide Web"

Quiz Answers

1. The SQL Server Web Assistant Wizard

2. The IDC/HTX access mechanisms

3. Microsoft ADO

4. The IDC file; it contains the SQL statement.

INDEX

Symbols

 # symbols
   global temporary table, 376
   identifiers, 277
% Processor Time counter, 663
%begindetail% tag, 711
%enddetail% tag, 711
@ symbol, identifiers, 277
@@IDENTITY value, 457
@@trancount variable, 517
   automatic transactions, 520
; number option, 494
**[ ] (identifier delimiters),
   aliases, 333**
10-digit CD Key, 32
1252/ISO Character Set, 39
2PC
   snapshot replication with
      updating subscribers, 547
   transactional replication with
      updating subscribers, 549

A

Accent insensitive, 40
access, denying, 145
access path (databases), 146
**Accessing and Changing Data
   book, 60**
account domains
   security options, 25
ACID properties, 514
ActiveX controls, 691
**Add New Network Library
   Configuration dialog box, 65**
**Add Users and Groups dialog
   box, 139**
**Administering SQL Server
   book, 59**
administration
   filegroups, 117
   replication, 609-610
   serveradmin server role per-
      mission, 169
Administrators group, 51
   Authentication Mode, pass-
      words, 132

**ADO (ActiveX Data Objects),
   713**
   code samples, 37
Advanced tab, 638-639
affinity mask option, 666
**Agent account, installing distri-
   bution servers, 581**
**Agent Properties dialog box,
   621**
Agent service, 618-621
   alerts, 645
      system options, 649
      testing, 648
   components of, 620
   configuration, 621-626
   Database Maintenance Plan
      Wizard, 650-653
   event handling, 623
   idle CPU, 625
   job steps, 637
   jobs
      creating, 637
      multiserver, 644
      notifications, 642
      scheduling, 640-641
      system options, 642-643
   operators, 644-645

SAMS
Teach Yourself
in 21 Days

Visual Basic 6

Greg Perry
ISBN: 0-672-31310-3
$29.99 US/$42.95 CAN

Sams Teach Yourself in 21 Days teaches you all the skills you need to master the basics and then moves to the more advanced features and concepts. This series is designed for the way you learn. Go chapter by chapter through the step-by-step lessons or just choose those lessons that interest you the most.

Other Sams Teach Yourself in 21 Days Titles

SQL
Bryan Morgan
ISBN: 0-672-31110-0
$39.99 US/$57.95 CAN

Microsoft Visual InterDev
Michael Van Hoozer
ISBN: 1-57521-093-2
$39.99 US/$57.95 CAN

Active Server Pages
Sanjaya Hettihewa
ISBN: 0-672-31333-2
$34.99

More Visual Basic 6
Lowell Mauer
ISBN: 0-672-31307-3
$35.00

Visual Basic 5 Complete Compiler Edition
Nathan Gurewich
ISBN: 0-672-31315-4
$79.99

Visual C++ 6 Complete Compiler Edition
Davis Chapman
ISBN: 0-672-31403-7
$49.99

Windows 98
Paul Cassel
ISBN: 0-672-31216-6
$29.99

Internet Programming with Visual Basic 6
Peter Aitken
ISBN: 0-672-31459-2
$29.99

Database Programming with Visual Basic 6

Curtis Smith

ISBN: 0-672-31308-1
$45.00 US/$64.95 CAN

Transact-SQL

David Solomon
ISBN: 0-672-31045-7
$35.00 US/$50.95 CAN

SAMS
www.samspublishing.com

All prices are subject to change.

Other Related Titles

Microsoft SQL Server Unleashed
Greg Mable, et. al.
ISBN: 0-672-31227-1
$49.99 US/$71.95 CAN

Sams Teach Yourself Windows NT Server 4 in 14 Days
Peter Davis
ISBN: 0-672-31019-8
$35.00 US/$50.95 CAN

Windows NT 4 Server Unleashed, 2E
Jason Garms
ISBN: 0-672-31249-2
$49.99 US/$71.95 CAN

Microsoft SQL Server 7.0 Programming Unleashed
John Papa, et al
ISBN: 0-672-31293-X
$49.99

Microsoft SQL Server 7 DBA Survival Guide
Mark Spenik
ISBN: 0-6722-31226-3
$49.99 US/$71.95 CAN

Building Enterprise Solutions with Visual Studio 6
G.A. Sullivan
ISBN: 0-672-31489-4
$49.99

Roger Jennings' Database Developer's Guide with Visual Basic 6
Roger Jennings
ISBN: 0-672-31063-5
$59.99

Microsoft Exchange Server 5 Unleashed
Greg Todd, et al
ISBN: 0-672-31034-1
$59.99

Windows NT Troubleshooting and Configuration
Robert Reinstein, et al
ISBN: 0-672-30941-6
$59.99

Special Edition Using Microsoft SQL Server 7.
Stephen Wynkoop
ISBN: 0-7897-1523-6
$39.99 US/$57.95 CAN

Roger Jennings Database Workshop: Microsoft Transaction Server 2.0
Steven Gray and Rick Lievano
ISBN: 0-672-31130-5
$39.99

SAMS
www.samspublishing.com

All prices are subject to change.